Law for Professionals

The *Law for Professionals* book series contains publications in all fields of the law aimed at professionals and practitioners. The book series is dedicated to publish high quality books that provide in-depth insights into the workings and the practical functioning of the law, international organizations or regional legal frameworks.

The authors contributing to the book series are experienced legal professionals and practitioners whose expertise combines theory and practice.

Professor Ademuni-Odeke

Insurance of International Sales' Contracts under Incoterms

Springer

Professor Ademuni-Odeke
Faculty of Law, Department of Maritime Law
Ankara University
Ankara, Türkiye

ISSN 2662-141X ISSN 2662-1428 (electronic)
Law for Professionals
ISBN 978-3-031-75135-6 ISBN 978-3-031-75136-3 (eBook)
https://doi.org/10.1007/978-3-031-75136-3

This Springer imprint is published by the registered company Springer Nature Switzerland AG
The registered company address is: Gewerbestrasse 11, 6330 Cham, Switzerland

To the grandchildren.
Jay
Gwen
And all their African sisters and brothers

Preface

Role of International Trade

Whatever its merits and demerits, international trade (in all its wider economic, financial, political, policy, physical goods and services' aspects) is important in enabling the sharing of geographical and technological advantages and benefits between nations, namely the industrialised North, which is unable to grow tropical fruits (except in glasshouses) and the less industrialised developing South, which has an abundance of good weather, minerals, and forest products to exchange. To most ordinary people, international trade is most manifest in the export and import of goods and services. This is because goods and services form the foundation and bulk of international trade transactions. Thus, the import and export of goods and services is essential for the global economy and, therefore, the human race. The Northerners often take for granted access to tropical fruits and vegetables grown in the South while the Southerners do likewise when enjoying luxury items manufactured in the North. As a benefit of economies of scale or comparative advantage, international trade evens out the benefits of these geographical "accidents" and their advantages and disadvantages.

To move goods and services across the globe, there are terms and conditions of international trade that have to be met. Most of us just want apples on our tables but few of us know how and under what terms and conditions they get to us. Exporting and importing professionals handle these issues. They are normally assisted by a body of other professionals such as international trade lawyers. The first port of call, in terms and conditions, is the sales contract between sellers and buyers. That means someone has to draw up these contracts and deal with all the terms and conditions of the exports and imports. Fortunately, because of the nature and complexity of issues involved, most are handled by lawyers. However, they are not that many international trade lawyers to handle all minor details of these issues. Besides, the few who are there can be expensive. We pay enormous sums for their time at law schools, rather than for the comparative services they offer.

The main part of the said terms and conditions are the transportation, delivery, insurance, and payments' logistics. These are all very complex issues that require other specialists such as freight-forwarders, shipping companies, insurers, bankers, etc. In addition to those problems, the export and import of goods and services can be exposed to unknown and untold risks. These are due mainly to the legal, time, logistical, economic, financial, political, cultural, and linguistic differences and physical barriers between importers and exporters' respective countries. Added to those barriers are risks of physical loss and/or damage to the goods as well as buyers' non-payments, parties' insolvencies, fraud, etc. involved in the export and import of goods and services. This is when the need for insurance originates and with it the role of institutions involved.

Role of the International Chamber of Commerce and Incoterms

This is when and where the ICC arises. For nearly 100 years since the 1920s, the ICC has tried to build logistical and other cultural bridges to overcome the above risks between exporters and importers. It did this by bringing together most businessmen and women to compare notes and experiences and to agree to ease their common problems. Accordingly, the ICC has achieved this through sharing common problems and preparing documents containing common positions in many aspects of export–import trade. In relation to the terms and conditions of export–import trade, the notable document is the International Commercial Terms (Incoterms)—latest being the 2020 version. Through its work in Incoterms, the ICC has eased the problems of both novices and experienced exporters and importers, who might not afford expensive lawyers, by providing a ready source of contractual template together with explanations and guidelines which they can adopt easily and use.

The two most important of the Incoterms trade terms are the Free on Board (FOB) and Cost, Insurance and Freight (CIF), accounting for nearly 80% of international trade transactions between them. This book covers international Incoterms' sales contracts generally and the above 2 principal ones in particular, including the American approach to them. Risks to which exporters and importers are exposed are underwritten by the institution of insurance. This is the main focus of the book and for those reasons, insurance dominates both the contents and presentation of the book. Hence, although the book is about most problems encountered by merchants, its main focus is the role played by insurance not just in Incoterms but also under common law and in other aspects of international trade transactions. Accordingly, most of the contractual terms and insurance requirements and obligations apply to all international sales *mutatis mutandis*.

Role of Insurance

Insurance is a positive aid to various business enterprises, importers, exporters, and persons engaged in international trade and commerce. No large or small-scale enterprise could possibly function had it not been possible to transfer many of its risks to insurers. Vast amount of capital is always at risk and without insurance businessmen would have to put aside some or large portion of their capital resources against the possibility of fortuitous losses. When there is insurance protection, the question of keeping aside a portion of capital to meet the unforeseen contingencies would not arise, as insurers would then come forward to indemnify the insured against these losses. Hence, not only is capital safeguarded by insurance, but it is also freed for further development of business and trade. Those who run businesses may have their own specialties to run their own business or trade, but may be handicapped by their lack of knowledge of risk management. Accordingly, insurance removes the anxiety thus arising by making available its expertise; business efficiency is thereby increased.

Furthermore, the knowledge that the business is protected from catastrophe losses will encourage enterprises and lead to the undertaking of ventures which might otherwise have been shelved as too risky for the individual concern to embark upon.

In the import–export sector dominated by maritime transport, marine insurance occupies important position in overseas trade and commerce. As it affords protection against fortuitous losses, it enables all those engaged in overseas trade to venture their capital freely than would otherwise be possible and in this way helps greatly to expand the scope of their operations. The study of the importance of marine insurance in international trade, particularly to exporters, will not possibly be complete unless its importance is emphasised. Central to marine insurance associated with all export and import, including those under Incoterms and common law, is cargo insurance. This wide and complex subject is treated in the book from both historic and current commercial function.

Reasons for the Book

The reasons for risking writing on such a complex topic are because of the author's experience of the subject from both academic (research and teaching), consultancy and industrial exposure. Above all, it was the author's realisation of the absence of any literature and texts that brings both together, under one roof, and explains in simple terms all the fabrics of the subject. The other reason being the enormous importance of insurance to international trade. The book handles the interface between insurance, international trade, and Incoterms as has never been attempted before. Every author thinks their work is unique and original, this one is no exception. For those reasons, the author's own considered view is that the book will contribute to knowledge and understanding of the subject. Although initially intended for students, teachers, and researchers, it is hoped that all those professionally and commercially involved in this vital and beautiful industry and practice will find the book useful and ease their export–import problems. The author further hopes the readers will enjoy reading the book as much as he enjoyed researching and writing it.

This book deals with insurance of international sales generally and Incoterms contracts in particular under and Anglo-American and other common law jurisdictions generally. It also covers tender of insurance documents under UCP 600 and compares it with similar insurances of the subject matter in selected civil law jurisdictions. This is because this area of the law and practice is global in its application.

In addition to his several clauses on the subject, the book is the first major outcome of the author's research on *Insurance of International Trade and Foreign Investments* finalised at Tulane and Southampton Universities Law Schools through the generous sponsorship of Lloyds of London Insurance and UK-US Fulbright Commission. It is anticipated that the book will form the first of two or three volumes on *Insurance of International Trade and Foreign Investments.*

As mentioned, the aim of the book is to fill a huge lacuna in the existing literature on the subject. Foremost, in the author's experience, even the most eminent common law scholars and jurists such as Sassoon (Sassoon, David, FOB and CIF Contracts, Sweet and Maxwell, 5th edn, 2012), Benjamin (Benjamin on Sales, 8th Edition, Sweet and Maxwell/ Thomson Reuters, 2010), Schmitthoff (Schmitthoff, Clive, The Law and Practice of International Trade, Twelfth Edition, Sweet and Maxwell, 2012), Chua (Chua, Jason, Law of International Trade: Cross Border Commercial Transactions, 5th Edition, Sweet and Maxwell, 2013) and the Encyclopaedias (e.g. John Birds, Jonathan Wright et al (General Editors), Encyclopaedia of Insurance Law, last release: May 2013; Lord Mackay of Clashfern, Halsbury's Laws of England, Vol. 60 (Lexis Nexis, 2011) and Vol. 91 (Lexis Nexis, 2012) treat the subject in existing literature only as a passing matter or as part of the general marine insurance. Even Crawford's book (Crockford, Neil (General Editor): Insuring Foreign Risks (Loose-leaf), Sweet and Maxwell (Reuters), London 2013) that comes closest relates only to regulatory rather than substantive aspects of the subject. During a literature review, the author was struck by the non-availability of any comprehensive materials and/or survey of the subject (both qualitatively and quantitatively) and in any meaningful manner.

The original remit of the book had been a modest examination of the subject and limited to only FOB-CIF under English Common Law. However, on consulting and comparing notes with colleagues in the Australia (John Dunt, International Cargo Insurance, Informa, 2012, ch. 7), Hong Kong (Dunt 2012, ch. 4), Singapore (Dunt 2012, ch. 5), South Africa (Dunt 2012, ch. 14), US (Dunt 2012, ch. 8), and other leading Common Law and Civil Law jurisdictions (such as Canada, India, New Zealand and Nigeria), it became apparent that the situation in those countries is not very different from that pertaining under English Common Law, hence the expanded title, aims, and objective of the book. It also transpired that common law and practice on the subject is international and that insurance of Incoterms law and practice has not only grown in importance, but is also universal.

Aims and Objectives of the Book

Against that backdrop, the general aim of the book is, therefore, to provide shorter and easily accessible book for practitioners and academia. The immediate objectives are:

(a) to challenge the traditional view, for instance, that insurance obligations in FOB and related contracts where the seller is not obliged to insure cargo are the preserve of the buyer and, therefore, that those contracts are harder to insure than, for example, the CIF and related contracts where sellers are obliged to insure. It also demonstrates that the orthodox view of the simplicity of the CIF-CIP and in which the seller is obliged to insure goods for the buyers' benefits is outmoded in the modern Incoterms 2020 and UCP 600 contexts;
(b) to demonstrate that the nature and the many variants of FOB, for instance, make it very difficult for parties to determine their respective insurance obligations with any certainty. This is in marked contrast to the CIF-CIP without comparative equivalent variants. Wider considerations of these contracts, undertaken in the book, reveal that the above old-fashioned views and assumptions are based on a narrower perspective and underrated appreciation of the complexity of the subject. Rather, those assumptions should be regarded as only a general rule, which are subject to exceptions;
(c) to provide an informed and wider picture of the tasks and considerations that confront parties when determining their Incoterms choices and, therefore, insurance obligations. The book demonstrates that there are more issues for a party to consider, when taking out insurance, in the Incoterms that exclude seller's obligations to insure goods than in those that do;
(d) to establish that, with perhaps a few quantitative exceptions, parties' insurance obligations in the former contract categories are not qualitatively or quantitatively different from those of the latter counterparts. The earlier assumptions are probably based on, especially the differences between the FOB and related contracts and the CIF and related contracts, as they developed in the twelfth and eighteenth centuries, respectively. The said erroneous assumptions seem to have totally ignored the influence of subsequent technological, transportation, finance, globalisation, and other related developments;
(e) to fill the gaping large lacunae on available literature on the subject;
(f) to make available to other scholars, researchers, and teachers of international trade law, materials that they can use and probably expand on. The author was struck by the non-availability of any comprehensive materials and/or survey of the subject (both qualitatively and quantitatively) in any meaningful literature, referred to above; and
(g) to provoke debate among, especially, academics and practitioners in the field and, therefore, bridge the gap in the approach to the subject between academia and legal practice, on the one hand, and between academia and commercial practice, on the other.

Under those circumstances, and for those reasons, it is the author's considered opinion that all those involved in the pursuit of trading, insuring, financing, researching and teaching export trade law and insurance of especially insurance of Incoterms will find the book of some use.

Schemes in the Book

In its approach, the book has V Parts of two and three chapters each, respectively.

Part I, consisting of 2 chapters, opens with the Role of the ICC and Insurance in International Trade. It opens by introducing the brief history and functions of the ICC as well as Incoterms in international sales (Chap. 1). This is followed by a similar treatment of the origin and important role of insurance, marine insurance, and cargo insurance in international trade including the relevant laws and principles governing cargo insurance (Chap. 2).

Part II, consisting of 3 chapters, is devoted to insurance of contracts, which exclude sellers' obligations to provide insurance for the buyer. The opening Chap. 3 deals with the nature and characteristics of contracts, which exclude sellers' obligations to provide insurance at common law. Chapter 4 repeats the same treatment of contracts, which include sellers' obligations to provide insurance for the benefit of buyers also at common law. Chapter 5 deals with the 9 out of 11 contracts, which exclude sellers' obligations to insure goods under Incoterms 2020.

Part III, consisting of 3 chapters, deals with insurance of contracts, which include sellers' obligations to provide insurance to the buyer. Chapter 6 concerns the nature and characteristics of the contracts generally. Chapter 7 examines the same contracts at Common Law. Chapter 8 treats the same contracts under Incoterms 2020.

Part IV, on Piracy, War Risks, and other insurance considerations, contains 3 chapters. Chapter 9 deals with insurance of War, Piracy, and Terrorism from the traditional commercial sources. Chapter 10 deals with Other Insurance Avenues and Considerations. Chapter 11 deals with Tender of Documents under Common Law, Incoterms and under the UCP 600 for contracts financed by letters of credit.

Part V deals with traditional Dispute Settlement, Claims, and Concluding Remarks and contains 3 chapters. Chapter 12 deals with Conflict of Laws. Chapter 13 deals with Claims and Settlement. Chapter 14 contains Concluding Remarks.

Innovativeness of the Book

To appreciate the place and role of insurance on the contracts, the book puts the matter into perspective and context by inclusion of wider, but related, discussions of the nature of, passage and transfer of property and risks in Incoterms contracts, as prerequisite background. However, coverage of the subject matter in the book is limited to sellers' and buyers' insurance and related obligations with only limited coverage of the routine mechanisms of effecting insurance itself.

The CIF and related contracts' contents of the book puts together and updates earlier treatment under Incoterms 1990 (see Ademuni-Odeke, Insurance Element in CIF and CIP INCOTERMS, 4(4) TIL&P, pp. 86–92), followed by similar examination of FOB and related contracts (Ademuni-Odeke, Insurance of FOB Contracts in Anglo-American and Common Law Jurisdictions Revisited, 31 (1) Tul.MLJ, pp. 425–462) insurance under common law. However, unlike those forerunners (Ademuni-Odeke, Elements of CIF and CIP Insurance, 4 (4) TIL&P 1995, pp. 17–25), the book focuses on Incoterms 2020 and changes introduced by it. It traces the origins of Incoterms rules and insurance obligations from the common law and concludes, for instance, that common law obligations may no longer necessarily tally with those under Incoterms 2020 or indeed under the UCP 600. An example of the point in question is the detailed analysis of the insurance requirements at common law and its influence on the equivalent treatment in Incoterms 2020 Clauses A5/B5 of CIP-CIP.

Apart from the general tables of contents, each chapter also opens with own subcontents making it easier for the reader to follow. In addition, the numberings of the paragraphs make it easier to cross-reference. Other innovations and attractions of the book include: additions of challenging "Further Food for Thoughts", comprehensive list of further readings and references used and sub-conclusions under each chapter. This approach is intended to provide useful materials for those who may wish to delve more into each aspect of the subject and book.

Furthermore, the book maintains that although in theory, the insurance provision in contracts without the seller's insurance obligations may be straightforward, this is not necessarily borne out by the practical reality. The book is, therefore, a bold attempt to expose those assumptions and to put under one-roof comprehensive insurance aspects of insurance of exports generally and under common law and Incoterms in particular. This is achieved in a manner and extent never attempted before in either a major or minor publication on the subject.

Consequently, the book firstly, details insurance requirements both at common law and under Incoterms in new approach and supported by case law by examining sellers' and buyers' own and additional insurance not provided by either the common law or Incoterms. These are: sellers' and buyers' contingency insurance; sellers' and buyers' pre-and post-shipment insurance; sellers' and buyers' own interest policy; export credit insurance; benefit of the carriers' liability insurance; state war, piracy and terrorism risks policies; and other practical aspects overlooked by both the common law and Incoterms. These additional avenues and considerations are covered in Chap. 9.

Secondly, it critically examines the differences between the various contracts thereby exposing factors which parties need to consider in determining the choice of the respective Incoterms contracts with a view to minimising their liability and, therefore, their insurance needs. This is necessary in order to sort out and make sense of the myriads of Incoterms Rules.

Thirdly, in adopting this method, the book reminds the reader of external insurance and shipping factors that sellers and buyers need to bear in mind while contracting. These are namely: state interventions in shipping arrangements; governmental controls of export insurance contracts; effects on embargoes and sanctions; exchange controls; and buyers' bankruptcy and other defaults on sales and insurance contracts. For those reasons the book: provides the reader (students, academics, insurers, carriers and practitioners) with invaluable materials and in a holistic and modern context that had never before existed under one roof; thereby filling the *lacunae* on available literature.

Finally, the book maintains that despite the few material differences with other means of contracting for international sales such as the CISG and Commodity Contracts, international sales practices between Incoterms and other contracts and between the common law and other jurisdictions are basically the same.

Equally, insurance principles and requirements are the same. For those reasons the book should be applicable to and useful to all involved in international sales contracts.

Southampton, UK
Ankara, Turkey
December 2024

Ademuni-Odeke

Acknowledgments

Like most aspects in life, a piece of work or achievement is normally attributed to the hard work or genius of a single individual. Indeed, this author is tempted to take all the honours for this book. But in reality, those kinds of attributes are normally selfish and inaccurate to say the least. As the English poet, John Donne, writing in the seventeenth century, famously wrote that "no man is an island". In 1624, John Donne wrote, "No man is an Island... any man's death diminishes me, because I am involved in mankind, and therefore never send to know for whom the bell tolls; it tolls for thee["]. We are at once alone and together in this difficult world and finding that equilibrium is our spiritual task". Consequently, behind every woman and man is family, relations, friends, and sometimes volunteers and sponsors or benefactors. Any achievement is, therefore, normally the product of generosities, goodwill, and sacrifices from some or most of these groups. This author is, therefore, no different. In that context, and in this book, his input is only part of a wider contribution.

The author is, accordingly, indebted to:

- Lloyd's of London Insurance for the generous Fellowship that enabled him to conduct the main research on Insurance of International Trade and Foreign Investments in the US;
- US-UK Fulbright Commission in London for supporting his application to Lloyds of London Insurance;
- The Admiralty Centre, Tulane University Law School, New Orleans, USA, for hosting him during the above research sabbatical and for their continued support ever since;
- The ICC, Paris, France for permission to reproduce Incoterms 2020 and UCP 600 materials in the Bibliography and Annexes;
- The ILU/IUA for permission to reproduce the Lloyds Marine Policy and Institute Cargo Clauses A-B, and C in the Annexes;
- The Grain and Feed Trade Association (GAFTA) for permission to reproduce the CIF Sample Sales Contract No. 81 and the FOB Insurance Terms Contract No 72. in the Annexes;
- The UK Government Stationery Office for permission to reproduce the Marine Insurance Act 1906 in the Annexes;

- The UK International Finance (UKEF) of the Export Credit Guarantee Department (ECGD) for permission to reproduce the UKEF Policy in the Annexes;
- Professors Martin Davies (Director) and Robert Force (Emeritus Director), Admiralty Law Institute, Tulane University Law School, New Orleans, USA and their staff for secretarial support, while in residence,
- Professor James Duggan, Director and his staff, Library Services, Tulane University Law School, for their enormous help with material's research and friendship;
- Professor Michael Simples (former Director), Institute of Maritime Law, Southampton University Law School, for hosting him, during further research and synthesising the materials;
- Michelle O'Donovan, formerly of the International Marine Underwriters (IMU), New York, USA;
- John Miklus, formerly of the American Institute of Marine Underwriters (AIMU), New York, USA;
- Mrs. Clare Old, Administrator, Institute of Maritime Law, Faculty of Law, The University of Southampton for her support during the synthesising stage of the Tulane Research;
- Mrs. Sara Le Bas, Librarian, Institute of Maritime Law, Faculty of Law, The University of Southampton for her library assistance during the synthesising stage of the Tulane Research;
- Megan Gold, Research Assistant at Tulane Law School, New Orleans, USA;
- Debo Awofase, Research Assistant at the Institute of Maritime Law, Southampton University;
- Faik Yetgin, Special Research Assistant, Department of Maritime Law, Faculty of Law, University of Ankara;
- All my other Research Assistants at the Department of Maritime Law, Faculty of Law, University of Ankara;
- John and Helen Spelman, Avalon Associates, Essex, for their invaluable secretarial and initial editorial support;
- My grandchildren Jay Devlin-Odeke and Gwen Fae Saunders-Odeke who constantly asked "where is granddad and when is he coming back?", during my long absences from home.
- My children Zinzile Anke Akon'go Ademuni-Odeke and Daniel Ateker Ademuni-Odeke, for missing their father for long periods; and
- And above all to my partner, Wilhelmina Mary Duyvesteijn, for the sacrifices she has made all these years in enduring my long absences while researching, consulting, teaching and presenting papers at conferences.

Contents

Part II Insurance of FOB and Related Contracts That Exclude Selle's Obligations to Provide Insurance to the Buyer at Common Law

Part VI Important Legal Documents

List of Abbreviations

AC	Appeal Cases
AC	Arrival Contracts
ADR	Alternative Dispute Resolution
AIMU	American Institute of Marine Underwriters
All ER	All England Law Reports
BOP	Business Owners' Policy
C&F	Cost and Freight (Common Law)
C.I. F and I	CIF and [Bankers'] Interest
C.I.F.	Cost Insurance and Freight
C.I.F.& F.O	CIF and Foreign Exchange
CA	Court of Appeal
CBRN	Chemical, Biological, Radiological and Nuclear Weapons
CCC	Care, Custody and Control of goods
CESCE	Compania Espanola de Seguros de Credito a la Exportacion, SA of Spain
CFR	Cost and Freight (Incoterms)
Ch.D	Chancery Division
CI.F. and E	CIF and Exchange [Rates]
CIF Out-Turn Contract	CIF contracts normally used in the bulk oil trade
CIF	Cost Insurance and Freight
CIF&C	CIF and Commission
CIF-DC	CIF Delivered Contracts
CII	Chartered Insurance Institute
CIM	Uniform Rules Concerning the Contract of International Carriage of Goods by Rail
CIP	Cost and Insurance Paid
CISG	The Convention on International Sale of Goods
CLC	Commercial Law Reports
CLR	Commonwealth Law Reports
CNF	Cost Net and Freight
COFACE	Compagne Françoise d'Assurance pour le Commerce Exterieur of France
COGSA	Carriage of Goods by Sea Act
COSEC	Companhia de Seguro de Creditos EP of Portugal

COTIF	The Convention concerning International Carriage by Rail
CPT	Carriage and Insurance Paid To
DCP	Delivery Cost Paid (Discontinued)
DDP	Delivery Duty Paid
DDU	Delivery Duty Unpaid
DEQ	Delivered ExQuay (Discontinued)
DTI	Department of Trade and Industry
ECGD	Export Credit Guarantee Department of the UK (forerunner of UKEF below)
ECIO	Export Credit Insurance Organisation of Greece
ECOSOC	Economic and Social Council of the United Nations
EDC	Export Development Corporation of Canada
EKN	Exportkreditnamnden (Swedish Export Credits Guarantee Board)
EKR	Eksportkrediradet (The Export Credit Council) of Denmark
ERG	Geschaftsstelle fur die Exportrisikogarantie (Office for the Export Risk Guarantee) of Switzerland
Ex-Finance	Export Finance, replacement of the ECGD
EXGO	Export Guarantee Office for New Zealand
EXIMBANK	Export–Import Bank
EXIMPORT	Export–Import
EXQ	Ex Quay (Discontinued)
EXW	Ex-Works
FAS	Free Alongside Ship
fc&s	free from capture and seizure
FCA	Financial Conduct Authority
FCA	Financial Conducts Authority
FCA	Free Carrier
FFO	Free Freight Out
FIOS	Free In, Out and Stowed
FLR	Federal Law Report (Australia)
FOBST	FOB and trimmed (for coal trade)
FOB	Free on Board
FOBA	FOB (Air) (Merged into Free Carrier (FCA) above)
FOR	FOB (Rail) (Merged into Free Carrier (FCA) above)
FOS	Financial Ombudsman Services
FOSFA	Federation of Oils, Seeds and Fats Associations
FOT	FOB (Truck)
FPA	Free of Particular Average
GA	General Average
GAFTA	Grain and Feed Trade Association
GIE	Garanti-Instituttet for Eksportkredit of Norway
HKA	Hermes Kreditverscherungs-Aktiengesellschaft (leading partner in the consortium) in Germany

HL	House of Lords (now the Supreme)
IATA	International Airline Passenger Association
ICA	International Court of Arbitration
ICC	Institute Cargo Clauses (Cargo Clauses)
ICC	International Chamber of Commerce
ICC	International Criminal Court
ICI	Insurance Corporation of Ireland PLC
ICLR	International and Comparative Law Quarterly
IFA	Incoterms for Americans
ILA	Institute of London Underwriters
ILU	Institute of London Underwriters
IMD	Insurance Mediation Directive
IMO	International Maritime Organisation
IMU	International Marine Underwriters
INCOTERMS	Rules for Interpretation of International Commercial Terms
IoE	Institute of Export
IUA	International Underwriters Association
IUMI	International Union of Marine Insurance
IUMI	International Union of Marine Underwriters
JBL	Journal of Business Law
JCL	Journal of Contract Law
JML&C	Journal of Maritime Law and Commerce
KB	Kings Bench
LIRMA	London International Insurance and Reinsurance Market Association (LIRMA)
LJKB	Law Journal Kings Bench
LLLR	Lloyds List Law Reports
Lloyds Rep	Lloyds Report
Lloyds	Lloyds of London Insurance
LM&CLQ	Lloyds Maritime and Commercial Law Quarterly
LMA	Lloyds Market Association
LMA	London Markets Association
LMG	London Market Group
LT	Law Times
LUA	International Underwriting Association
LUN	London Underwriters Union
MIA 1906	Marine Insurance Act 1906
MRC	Market Reform Contract
NCM	Nederlandsche Credietverzekering Maatschappij, N.V in the Netherlands
NSW	New South Wales (Australia)
NVOCC	Non-Vessel Operating Common Carrier
NYPE	New York Produce Exchange [Charterparty Form]
OdD	Office du Ducriore of Luxembourg OND

OECD	Organization for Economic Co-operation and Development
ONDD	Office National du Ducriore of Belgium
OJ	Official Journal of the European Union
P&I	Protection and Indemnity [Clubs]
PC	Privy Council (The)
POI	Proof of Insurance
PPI	Policy Proof of Insurance
QB	Queen's Bench
RTC	Reservation of Title Clause
RTC	Retention of Title Clause
SACE	Sezione Speciale l'Assicurazione del Credito all'Esportazione of Italy
SGA	Sale of Goods Act 1893/1979
SLS	Society of Legal Scholars
SOLA	Convention for Safety of Life at Sea 1974, as amended
SUA	Convention for the Suppression of Unlawful Acts Against the Safety of Maritime Navigation, Protocol for the Suppression of Unlawful Acts Against the Safety of Fixed Platforms Located on the Continental Shelf, 1988
TLR	Times Law Reports
TRIA	The Terrorism Risk Insurance Act (US)
UCC	Uniform Commercial Code of the United States of America
UCP	Uniform Custom and Practise for Documentary Credits 500 and 600
UCP	Uniform Customs and Practice for Documentary Credits
UKEF	UK Export Finance (Successor ECGD)
UKPC	United Kingdom Privy Council Cases
UKTI	UK Trade and Investment
UNCITRAL	United Nations Conference on International Trade Laws
UNCTAD	United Nations Conference on Trade and Development
UNDP	United Nations Development Programme
URC	Uniform Rules for Collections
USCIB	United States Council for International Business
FINNVERA	Finish Export Credit Agency
WA	With Average
WLR	Weekly Law Reports
WMD	Weapons of Mass Destruction
WTO	World Trade Organization
YAR	York Antwerp Rules

Part I

Insurance and International Trade

1 The Role and Importance of the International Chamber of Commerce and Incoterms in International Trade and Sales

Abstract

As the opening and introductory chapter of the book, and contained within Part I of the book, this chapter lays out the foundation of the book. It contains a summary of the history and key functions of the International Chamber of Commerce (ICC) and its International Commercial Terms (Incoterms) in international trading systems generally and international sales contracts under incoterms in particular. In so doing, it includes the development of Incoterms' insurance clause and its connections with delivery and carriage contracts, sales and general export trade risks, documentation, and passage of property/titles, inter alia. The chapter links these parties' contractual obligations with the need for their insurance coverage including under Incoterms for American Guidelines. The issues raised in this chapter form the basis of discourse and are expanded in subsequent chapters of the book. Like all the remaining chapters, the chapter contains materials on: "Further Food for Thoughts", Reference sources used, Further Readings, and "What readers and practitioners should watch out for", especially in Incoterms contracts' "**No Insurance Obligation**", clauses to guide the reader.

1.1 Introduction

This book deals with insurance of International Sales Contracts at Common Law and under Incoterms. Incoterms is one of the many ICC creations. The ICC has rules and practices governing both the Incoterms and their insurances thereof. To enable a better understanding of how all this gels in together in the book, this chapter provides a detailed background of the history and developments of the: ICC; Incoterms and insurance provisions; and its relationship with the UCP 600. Documentary aspects of insurance are covered in Chap. 11 (post) which deals with tender of insurance documents under the UCP 600. Also covered, in this chapter, are the

P. Ademuni-Odeke, *Insurance of International Sales' Contracts under Incoterms*, Law for Professionals, https://doi.org/10.1007/978-3-031-75136-3_1

relationship between export trade and the ICC Incoterms (the latest being Incoterms 2020), "Incoterms for Americans Guidelines 2020". The chapter clarifies the sometimes confusing, "**No Obligation to Insure**", and the "Requirement for Information and Notice" in the Incoterms insurance provisions and guidelines.

1.2 The ICC and International Commercial Transactions

To understand international trade terms, generally and Incoterms' insurance clauses in particular, one needs to appreciate the nature of the ICC. Incoterms and the UCP 600 are both ICC products. ICC is the largest and most representative business organization in the world. Its hundreds of thousands of member-companies found in over 130 countries have interests spanning every sector of private enterprise. It develops and updates rules and practices for world commerce. Its world network of national committees keeps the ICC's International Secretariat in Paris informed about national and regional business priorities and practices. More than 2000 experts drawn from ICC's member companies feed their vast knowledge and experience into crafting the ICC stance on specific business issues.[1]

The UN, the WTO, UNCITRAL, the OECD and many other intergovernmental bodies, both international and regional, are kept in touch with the views of international business through the ICC. The ICC has observer status at the UN and UN Specialised Agencies and was the first non-governmental organization to be granted general consultative status with the United Nation's ECOSOC. Although the idea of the ICC was conceived in 1890, it was formally founded in 1919[2] to serve world business by promoting trade and investment, open markets for goods and services, and the free flow of capital. Its International Court of Arbitration (ICA) was created in 1923 and its Institute of World Business Law has existed since 1979.

The ICC's most significant function is the preparation and promotion of its uniform rules of practice for international commercial transactions. Its aim is to provide a codification of international practice occasionally selecting the best practice after ample debate and consideration. Its rules of practice are designed by bankers, insurers and merchants with hands on and not by legislative bureaucrats with political and local considerations or national allegiance. The rules accordingly demonstrate the practical needs, customs and practices of business. Because the rules are incorporated voluntarily into contracts, they are flexible while providing a stable base for international review, including judicial scrutiny. Its flagship, the Incoterms Rules, are also updated regularly, normally every 10 years since Incoterms 1980, the latest being Incoterms 2020. International revision is thus facilitated, permitting the incorporation of the changing practices of the commercial parties.

The ICC is the nearest commercial equivalent body to the global, political and special United Nations. Celebrating the 1st Centenary in 2019, the ICC had as its

[1] For details of the ICC see http://www.iccwbo.org/.

[2] For ICC Brief History see: http://www.iccwbo.org/chamber-services/chamber-resources/history-of-chamber/.

primary objective facilitating the flow of international trade at a time when nationalism and protectionism threatened the easing of world trade. It is probably equally important today in the era of neo-nationalistic protectionism. It was in that spirit that the UCP (one of its two flag ships) were first introduced in 1923—to alleviate the confusion caused by individual countries' promoting their own national rules on letter of credit practice. Together with the UCP, the aim was to create a set of contractual rules that would establish uniformity in practice, so that there would be less need to cope with often conflicting national regulations.

The universal acceptance of the UCP by practitioners in countries with widely divergent economic and judicial systems is a testament to the rules' success. The latest UCP, (UCP 600), the subject of Chap. 9 of this book, contains detailed rules on the nature and types of insurance and transport documents acceptable for tender under letters of credit. The ICC's other flag ship, the Incoterms, is discussed immediately below and throughout the book. Although not the direct interest of this book, the ICC work covers transport, banking, education and arbitral wok as well their bearings on insurance contracts.

1.3 The Incoterms 1923–2020 and International Sales Contracts

From the foregone, the two most important ICC trade rules are Incoterms dealing with contractual terms including insurance and the UCP dealing with payment terms. Of the two, the Incoterms is the older having been around for over 80 years. Similar in aims and objectives to the UCP, they are a series of pre-defined commercial terms published by the ICC that are widely used in international commercial transactions or procurement processes. A series of three-letter trade terms related to common contractual sales practices, the rules are intended primarily to clearly communicate the tasks, costs, and risks associated with the transportation and delivery of goods. Although products of a non-governmental organisation, the rules are widely accepted by governments, legal authorities, and practitioners worldwide for the interpretation of most commonly used terms in international trade. Some jurisdictions such as Jordan and Iraq have even adopted them into national commercial codes. They are intended to reduce or remove altogether uncertainties arising from different customs and interpretation of the rules in different countries. As such, although non-mandatory, they are regularly incorporated into sales contracts worldwide. Being a product of a non-governmental organization, they are not binding either on states or individual parties unlike international conventions.

First conceived in 1929 and published in 1936,[3] Incoterms have been periodically updated, with the eighth version—Incoterms 2020, the latest—having been published in mid-September 2019 and entering into force on January 1, 2020. "Incoterms" is a registered trademark of the ICC. The eighth published set of Incoterms 2010 defined 11 rules, reducing from the 15 used in Incoterms 2000 by

[3] Ramberg (2000), pp. 8–10.

introducing two new rules:[4] In the prior version, the rules were divided into four categories, but the reduced 11 pre-defined terms of Incoterms 2020 are subdivided into two categories based only on method of delivery. The larger group of seven rules applies regardless of the method of transport, with the smaller group of four being applicable only to sales that solely involve transportation over water. Although voluntary, Incoterms are probably the most observed and used international instrument.

1.4 Origins, History and Purpose

1.4.1 General Introduction

Apart from using Common Law principles or a written contract, export-import parties may opt for the Incoterms' Model, the latest being 2020, or the ICC *Model International Sale Contract*[5] for their contract's formation. Before embarking on detailed discussions on insurance aspects of Incoterms, the rules need putting into context. Incoterms is a set of international rules promulgated by the ICC for the uniform interpretation of commonly used trade terms in foreign trade. They describe in detail the responsibilities of the sellers and buyers in international trade. The Incoterms rules have become an essential part of the daily language of trade. They have been incorporated in contracts for the sale of goods worldwide and provide rules and guidance to importers, exporters, lawyers, transporters, insurers and students of international trade.

Below are short descriptions of the 11 rules from Incoterms 2020 edition. Apart from the two (FOB and CIF) annexed to this book, these should be read in the context of the full official text of the rules which can be obtained from the ICC Store. These extracts can be reproduced provided that the source is cited and a link to the ICC Store is mentioned. Incoterms up to 2010 were classified into E, C, F and D classes, each class determined by the delivery means and transportation system and parties' insurance obligations and requirements. More information available on the dedicated page. Incoterms 2020 now classifies them into only two categories: those for all transport modes including multimodal[6] and those for maritime transport (sea and inland waterways).[7]

---

[4] Delivered at Terminal (DAT) and Delivered at Frontier (DAF) (both now discontinued); Delivered at Place (DAP) that replace four rules of the prior version (Delivered Ex Ship (DES) and Delivered Ex Quay (DEQ)); and Delivered Duty Unpaid (DDU).

[5] ICC *Model International Sale Contract*, 1997 Edition, ICC Doc. No. 738E.

[6] Namely: Ex Works (EXW), Free Carrier (FCA), Carriage Paid To (CPT), Carriage and Insurance Paid To (CIP), Delivered at Place (DAP), Delivered at Place Unloaded (DPU) and Delivery Duty Paid (DDP).

[7] Free Alongside Ship (FAS), Free On Board, Cost and Freight (CFR) and Cost Insurance and Freight.

1.4.2 Purpose of Incoterms

The ICC have published a series of predefined commercial terms which are used for, and which are aimed at, assisting transacting parties to unambiguously and efficiently communicate some of the terms applicable between the buyer and seller.

These commercial terms (referred to as "Incoterms" or "International Commercial Terms") are nothing more than a series of three letter acronyms. The letters in the acronyms signify and communicate concepts such as:

(a) Who is responsible for a task;
(b) Who carries the costs of the transportation and insurance (and to what extent); and
(c) Where the risk will pass.

Incoterms 2020 is the ninth set of Incoterms published by the ICC (with the first of them being published in 1936). Over the years, Incoterms have been added, deleted and updated culminating in the Incoterms 2020 as the most recent version. As mentioned above, Incoterms 2020 consists of 11 pre-defined terms, subdivided into two categories (based only on the method of delivery). Seven predefined terms may be used regardless of the method of transport (*Rules for Any Mode or Modes of Transport "General Terms"*) and the remaining four predefined terms are intended solely for use where the method of transportation is by water, specifically where the condition of goods can be verified at the point of loading on board a ship (so this would naturally exclude containerised freight) (*Rules for Sea and Inland Waterway Transport "Maritime Terms"*). The purpose of Incoterms is to provide a set of international rules for the interpretation of the most commonly used trade terms in export trade.

Thus, the uncertainties of different interpretations of such terms in different countries can be avoided or at least reduced to a considerable degree. Unless the parties expressly incorporate them in their contracts, the terms do not have automatic force of law in themselves; the parties have to provide so expressly in their contract, including which Incoterm they wish to adopt. Frequently parties to a contract are unaware of the different trading practices, especially in insurance, in their respective countries. This can give rise to misunderstandings, disputes, and litigation with all the waste of time that this entails. This can be costlier were goods to be lost or damaged and had not been insured by either party. In order to remedy these problems, the ICC first published in 1936 a set of international rules for the interpretation of trade terms. These rules were known as Incoterms 1936. Amendments and additions were later made in 1953, 1967, 1976, 1980, 1990, 2000, 2010 and currently 2020, in order to bring the rules in line with current international trade terms.

They are presented in a new format, which allows the parties to follow a systematic process to determine their respective obligations. The new layout has ten duties to each party, "A" for the seller and "B" for the buyer, e.g. Clauses A1–A10 and Clauses B1–B10. The Carriage duties are contained in Clauses A4/B4 and while insurance duties are in Clauses A5/B5 respectively. The rules provide guidelines as to insurance and other general terms of international (or even national in the US) sale of goods contracts. Other than that, the rules are self-explanatory. Incoterms rules are recognised by UNCITRAL as the global standard for the interpretation of the most common terms in foreign trade.

1.4.3 Systematic and Progressive Development of Incoterms and Incoterms Insurance Clause[8]

1.4.3.1 Pre-ICC Incoterms' Common Law Origins of Incoterms

The FOB (c. seventeenth century) and the CIF (c. eighteenth century) were among the common law contracts which preceded both the ICC and Incoterms. The term "free on board", or "f.o.b." was used historically by the Chief Justice of the Supreme Court of South Australia, Samuel James Way in relation to the transfer of risk from seller to buyer as goods are shipped in the Judicial Committee of the Privy Council, in *Colonial Insurance Company of New Zealand v The Adelaide Marine Insurance Company (South Australia)*.[9] In the case Justice Way, found as fact that in the particular contract considered in this case, "the letters 'f.o.b.' were used with the meaning that the [goods] were to be put at the buyer's risk immediately they were put on board [ship] and consequently that the buyers had an insurable interest". Those principles and the FOB risk elements were indorsed Lord Devline in the leading case of *Pyrene Co Ltd v Scindia Steam Navigation Co Ltd.*[10]

The term "cost, insurance, freight" or "c.i.f." also predates the introduction of Incoterms. The first reported English court case which referred to c.i.f. was *Tregelles v. Sewell* 1862,[11] where the court established that under c.i.f. terms, risk passes to the buyer on shipment. In the case of *E. Clemens Horst Co. v. Biddell Brothers*,[12] the UK House of Lords ruled in 1911 that "the sellers in a c.i.f. contract were entitled to payment of the price upon tender of the bill of lading and insurance policy." The purchasers' intent to wait for satisfactory delivery and inspection was overruled.[13] Shortly afterwards in 1915–1916, the case of *Arnhold Karberg & Co. v. Blythe, Green, Jourdain & Co.*[14] in the High Court and Court of Appeal showcased judicial debate about whether a c.i.f. bill of lading could evidence a sale of goods, Scrutton J ruling in the High Court that it did not, because a c.i.f. sale is "not a sale of goods, but a sale of documents relating to goods".[15] The Court of Appeal upheld his

---

[8] References Incoterms I–X, if any, are for purposes of this chapter and book only and are not the official ICC designations and numberings.

[9] Judicial Committee of the Privy Council, *Colonial Insurance Company of New Zealand v The Adelaide Marine Insurance Company (South Australia)*, UKPC 57, 18 December, 1886.

[10] *Pyrene Co Ltd v Scindia Steam Navigation Co Ltd* [1954] 2 QB 402.

[11] *Tregelles v. Sewell* 18627 H & N 574, 158 ER.

[12] *E. Clemens Horst Co. v. Biddell Brother*, UKHL 680, handed down 3 November 1911, on appeal.

[13] Ibid.

[14] *Arnhold Karberg & Co v Blythe, Green, Jourdain & Co.* (1915) 2 KB 379.

[15] *Arnhold Karberg Arnhold Karberg & Co v Blythe, Green, Jourdain & Co* [1916] 1 KB 495.

decision but Bankes LJ and Warrington LJ argued that "a c.i.f. contract is a contract for the sale of goods to be performed by the delivery of the documents".[16]

Thus, the older and leading Incoterms had roots in the common law while the drafting of the latter Incoterms too were heavily influenced by common law academics, practitioners and jurists. The ICC concept itself developed in the 1890s while Incoterms developed in the 1920s to accommodate growing technological and other developments in international trade following WWI as follows.

1.4.3.2 Incoterms 1923: ICC's First Sounding of Commercial Trade Terms

1.4.3.2.1 The Original Rules

The first Incoterms, Incoterms 1923, was first published in 1923 4 years following the ICC's creation in 1919, contained just six rules (FOB, FAS, C&F, EXSHIP, CIF and EX QUAY) of the commonly used terms in just 13 mainly European and Latin American countries. They were the first rudimentary soundings of global commercial trade terms. However, the C&F has ever-since become CFR and EX QUAY has disappeared altogether. Of these C&F became Free Carrier and Ex-Quay has been discontinued.

1.4.3.2.2 The Original Incoterms Insurance Clauses

Although Incoterms came into being much earlier, the insurance clauses did not start until Incoterms 1953. See Sect. 1.4.3.5.2 below. This does not mean trading on Incoterms was without insurance but that agreement on the right insurance format was not till Incoterm 1953.

1.4.3.3 Incoterms 1928: Clarity Improved

The second Incoterms, Incoterms 1928, improved on the rudimentary Incoterms I. It enhanced and expanded them from 6 to 13 rules, improved their interpretation and extended their use in from 13 to more than 30 countries, albeit still mainly European, Australasian and Latin American. However, they were not formally published. Further developments were hindered by the transportation limitation to predominantly maritime and road.

1.4.3.4 Incoterms 1936: Global Guidelines for Traders

1.4.3.4.1 Changes Introduced

The third Incoterms, Incoterms 1936, was the first official publication of the Rules. Following further studies, the third and first formal version of the Incoterms rules was officially published in 1936. However, for some reasons the official publication included only the original 6, namely: FAS, FOB, C&F, CIF, Ex Ship and Ex Quay contracts. The interruptions of WW II (1939–1945) suspended the use of Incoterms for obvious reasons.

---

[16] Todd, P., Arnhold Karberg, updated 16 April 1996, archived 3 May 2014, accessed 20 May 2022.

1.4.3.4.2 Developments in Insurance Clauses

For reasons given in Sect. 1.4.3.2.2 above, there were no insurance clauses in the first publication of Incoterms in 1936 and thereafter until the 1953 version. They were instead more focussed on establishing the trade rules themselves and were then interrupted by WWII, 1939–1945.

1.4.3.5 Incoterms 1953: Rise of Rail Transportation

1.4.3.5.1 Changes Introduced

The fourth Incoterms, Incoterms 1953, was the first resumption after WWII. However, following the damages and dislocation of WWII, the necessary changes meant that Incoterms was not resumed for 8 years until the 1953. Thereafter developments in rail transportation technology debuted three new trade terms for non-maritime transport in the fourth Incoterms. The new rules comprised of DCP (Delivered Costs Paid), FOR (Free on Rail) and FOT (Free on Truck) raising number of the rules from 6 to 9. Development of the rail system introduced newer risks to which the insurance clauses responded. These are now supplemented by the parties' insurance obligations in the *Convention Concerning International Carriage by Rail's* (COTIF) 1980, and its *Uniform Rules concerning the Contract of International Carriage of Goods by Rail* (CIM), forming Appendix B to the Convention. FOR and FOT have now been replaced by the modern Free Carrier (FCA).

1.4.3.5.2 Developments in Insurance Clauses

Incoterms 1953 marked the beginnings of concerted developments in insurance clauses. As indicated above, developments in rail road and transportation technology and the interruptions of WWII, suspended use of Incoterms until the 1950' (i.e., 1953 to be exact). Meanwhile rail and road transportation were on the rise and so three new Incoterms were introduced for non-maritime transport: Free on Rail (FOR), Free on Truck (FOT), Delivered Costs Paid (DCP which became CIP) and Ex-Works (EXW). The new rules between them introduced land (truck and rail) risks and therefore land transport insurance. Incoterms 1953 also continued the first concerted start of the progressive developments of insurance provisions. The CIF insurance clauses (Clause 5) was as developed then as was one 27 years later in Incoterms 1980 (see below) and included the provision of the policy in a transferable form.

1.4.3.6 Incoterms 1967 Revision: Misinterpretations Corrected

1.4.3.6.1 Changes Introduced

The fifth Incoterms, Incoterms 1967, did not introduce much improvements. The fifth Incoterms Revision in 1967 simply corrected the misinterpretations of the previous version and added two more trade terms to address delivery at frontier (DAF) and delivery at destination (DDP) raising the number from 9 to 11 rules. However, DAF has ever since disappeared. Equally the insurance provisions remain as those of Incoterms 1953.

1.4.3.6.2 Developments in Insurance Clauses

This topic is covered, under the respective headings, in each of the 10 Incoterms above and below. Against that backdrop, insurance clauses, developed in 1953, were updated and greatly improved in Incoterms 1990, 2000, 2010 and now 2020 to accommodate technological developments in transport, finance and communication.

Incoterms 2010:

Institute Cargo Clauses were incorporated into Incoterms 2000.Under Incoterms 2010, both CIP and CIF required insurance coverage equivalent to Institute Cargo Clauses (C).

Incoterms 2020:

In the 2020 Incoterms, the insurance clauses for CIP and and CIF have been updated, with CIP now requiring "All Risks" insurance (Institute Cargo Clauses A) while CIF retains the requirement for "specific risks" insurance (Institute Cargo Clauses C).

In CIP the seller is now obligated to obtain cargo insurance cover compliant with Institute Cargo Clauses (A), which provides a more comprehensive "all risks" coverage.

In CIF the seller's obligation to obtain insurance remains at the level of Institute Cargo Clauses (C), which covers specific risks.

Main Changes

The main change is the increased insurance obligations placed on the seller when using the CIP Incoterm, requiring a higher level of insurance coverage.

Other Incoterms:

In other areas, FCA do not obligate either party to insure the goods, but it is highly recommended.

1.4.3.7 Incoterms 1974 Revision: Advances in Air Travel

1.4.3.7.1 Changes Introduced

The sixth Incoterms, Incoterms 1974, increased use of air transportation gave cause for another version of the popular trade terms in 1974 adding the new term Free On-Board Airport (FOB Airport or FOBA), to allay confusion around the main term FOB by signifying the exact "vessel" used, thereby raising the number from 11 to 13 rules and introducing and extending the marine cargo policy to the concept of insurance of air cargo to cover air risks. Insurance of these Incoterms were supplemented by the air transport conventions-the *Warsaw Convention* 1929 as amended.

1.4.3.7.2 Progressive Developments in Insurance Clauses in Incoterms 1967–1976

Thus, both Incoterms 1967 and Incoterms 1976 added meaningful value to the progressive developments of both rules. However, the addition of FCA (from FOR and

FOT) during this period did not alter the parties' insurance obligations. Accordingly, despite the above developments, the first to the sixth Incoterms did not advance the progressive developments of the insurance clause that much. This was notwithstanding the fact that introduction of air cargo naturally added the risks in, and therefore, insurance of air-cargo. Notwithstanding that, it did not provide for its FOB (Airport) insurance, leaving it to the parties to sort out their own insurance problems. It will be recalled that the FOB (Airport) was introduced for air freight to avoid confusion with the FOB Incoterm. However, the basic insurance obligations remained unchanged. This is mainly because the very nature of the FOB family of contracts is that they excluded insurance obligations from the sellers' duties (see Part II, Chaps. 4–5 below).

1.4.3.8 Incoterms 1980: Proliferation of Container Traffic

1.4.3.8.1 Changes Introduced

Incoterms, Incoterms 1980, was the first time the ICC published the rules for the 10-year cycle revision. Responding to the proliferation of container traffic, it also marked the expansion of carriage of goods in containers and new documentation processes, led to the introduction of the new trade term FRC (Free Carrier...Named at Point), which provided for goods not actually received by the ship's side but at a reception point on shore, such as a container yard. It is doubtful whether FRC also replaced the C&F but the C&F became the CFR and the FCR became the FCA. However, containerisation reduced the risks to which goods were exposed although it did not involve newer insurance concepts.

1.4.3.8.2 Developments in Insurance Clauses

The seventh Incoterms marked the beginning of modernization Incoterm Rules due to the reduced transport risks resulting from the introduction of containers. These are now reflected in the FCA insurance clauses. By now the insurance clause had become a permanent feature of the rules by 1980 albeit still being restricted to CIF and CIP. This is important because the buyer in case of loss or damage to the goods, normally turns to the insurer. The extent of the cover for risks of loss of or damage to the goods varies under different terms of insurance. CIF and CIP insurances were based on the principle of minimum liability for the seller, who only had to procure insurance in the so-called FPA terms. This meant that the insurer is 'free' and did not have to pay in case of partial (particular) loss or damage.

Owing to this limitation in the insurance cover, the FPA insurer, in principle, only had to pay when the incident 'generally' affects ship and cargo (the 'marine adventure') such as stranding's, collisions and fire. Sometimes the shipper was called upon to pay contributions to the sea carrier for such costs or sacrifices which may have been incurred on account of extraordinary measures to save the ship and cargo from a common danger (e.g., costs for salvage or expenses in ports of rescue), so-called general average expenditure. In this case the FPA insurer would cover his liability and deliver 'general average bonds', that may be necessary to tender to the sea carrier in order to have the cargo released.

Another drawback for the insurance clause up to and in Incoterms 1980 was that the FPA insurance would cover only total (other than partial) loss or damage of the insured goods. The FPA insurance was really only sufficient for rough cargoes such as iron ore or coal. Fragile or valuable goods that were particularly liable to damage or theft required more expensive insurance cover. This is usually achieved through the so called 'All Risks' policy, a concept which was not popular then. The extent of the cover may vary but the policy covers in principle all risks of fortuitous loss or damage to insured cargo from the time the goods leave the sellers' warehouse until they reach the warehouse at the agreed destination. In view of the limited protection offered by the FPA terms, it was important that the CIF and CIP buyers, when the contract was made, requested the seller to get more expensive cover whenever necessary. This is customarily also done with respect to some special risks which are excluded in the ordinary insurance policy but which could be re-introduced by special clauses, such as war and strikes, riots and civil commotion clauses.

Finally, the insurance clause in the rules did, and still, excluded coverage for other than transport risks of the goods. Thus, although the war and other exceptions could now be covered by agreement between the parties, the wider commercial and political risks of the import-export trade nonetheless remain outside the scope of Incoterms.

1.4.3.9 Incoterms 1990: A Complete Revision and Consolidation

1.4.3.9.1 Changes Introduced

The eighth Incoterms, Incoterms 1990, was the second 10-year cycle revision of the rules. Incoterms 1990 also marked the beginning of modernization first thereby simplifying the Free Carrier term by deleting rules for specific modes of transport (i.e., FOR; Free on Rail, FOT; Free on Truck, and FOB Airport; FOB Airport), replacing them with the general term FCA (Free Carrier…at Named Point) instead. Secondly, other provisions accounted for increased use of electronic messages.

1.4.3.9.2 Developments in Insurance Clauses

Incoterm 1990 first, retained the restriction of insurance to only the CIF and CIP Rules. Secondly, the key development in insurance clause were twofold:

1. the consolidation of the minimum cover principle; and
2. the realisation of the inadequacy of the "minimum cover" for manufactured goods as outlined below.

Together with the "**No obligation**" provisions (see below), the "minimum cover" concept carried out from common law principles was to dominate the debate in insurance in all the Incoterms to-date insurance clauses were contained in Clause A3(b), with A3(a) being for transport.

1.4.3.10 Incoterms 2000: Amended Customs Clearance Obligations

1.4.3.10.1 Changes Introduced

The ninth Incoterms, Incoterms 2000, was the third 10-year cycle review of the rules. Incoterms 2000 also started the first modern updates of the terms leading to what it is now. Furthermore, certain customs and clearance and in exporter and importer of records requirements in parts of FAS and DEQ led to the amendments of the two terms.

1.4.3.10.2 Developments in Insurance Clauses

These were the same as for Incoterms 1990 above. Thus, there were no meaningful further progressive development in insurance clauses in the decade between 1990 and 2000. It also introduced the "**No Obligation**" concept and "Requirements for Notice and Information" for insurance purposes in contracts that exclude sellers' obligations to provide insurance to the buyer.

Insurance was in Clause A3(b) and B3(b) with A3(a) and B3(a) being retained for transport.

1.4.3.11 Incoterms 2010: Reflections on the Contemporary Trade Landscape

1.4.3.11.1 Changes Introduced

The tenth Incoterms, Incoterms 2010, was the fourth 10-year cycle review of the rules. Incoterms 2010 also introduced improved on Incoterms 1990 and Incoterms 2000 changes. These were mainly reflections on the contemporary trade landscape. By far the most widespread changes were introduced by Incoterm 2010 which consolidated the D-family of rules, removing DAF (Delivered at Frontier), DES (Delivered Ex Ship), DEQ (Delivered Ex Quay) and DDU (Delivered Duty Unpaid) and adding DAT (Delivered at Terminal) and DAP (Delivered at Place). Other modifications included an increased obligation for buyer and seller to cooperate on information sharing and changes to accommodate "string sales." It reduced the numbers from their maximum of 14 back to the previous, and current, 11 rules and introduced 2 new categories of *Rules for any mode of transport* with 7 rules and *Rules for sea and inland waterway transport* with 4 rules (see Sects. 1.5.2.1 and 1.5.2.2 below).

1.4.3.11.2 Developments in Insurance Clause

However, in comparison, by far the major changes to the insurance clauses had been made by Incoterms 2000. Consequently, apart from drafting changes, the creators of the *Institute Cargo Clauses* (Cargo Clauses) were acknowledged for the first time as the London Market Association (LMA) and the International Underwriters

Association (IUA).[17] Nevertheless, the seller was still required to obtain cargo insurance complying at least with the minimum cover provided by Cargo Clauses (C).

Furthermore, parties were made aware that this minimum level of insurance covers only major casualties, such as total loss of cargo. The buyer also had the option of the seller providing, at his (the buyer's) expense and where procurable, any additional cover, for example, cover provided by Cargo Clauses (A) or Cargo Clauses (B) or any similar clauses and/or cover complying with the War Clauses and/or Strikes Clauses or any similar set of clauses. This acted as a sort of insurance a bolt-on business deal or activity is one that you make or do in addition to your usual deals or activities "bolt-on", but the buyer was required to pay more for this. If the buyer wished for the seller to arrange for this "bolt-on" insurance, it was recommended that this is included in the sale contract. Other changes to the insurance clauses are indicated below.

1.4.3.12 Incoterms 2020: Looking Ahead

1.4.3.12.1 Resume of Changes Introduced

The eleventh and latest Incoterms, Incoterms 2020, was the fifth 10-year cycle revision of the rules. It was published in the second half 2019, entered into force on 1 January 2020 and has kept pace with the ever-evolving global trade landscape. It is the latest and the current rules. The rules greatly improved the layout and:

(a) retained the 11 Rules;
(b) removed the passage of property/title clause;
(c) further rearranged and improved the **No Obligation** concept;
(d) clarified the insurance clauses and requirements for notice and information to enable parties take up primary and additional insurance;
(e) introduced the requirement for security; and
(f) introduced the CIF notion of "buying and selling afloat" to other Incoterms.[18]

1.4.3.12.2 Development of the Insurance Clause

Accordingly, Incoterms 2020 has not altered the basic terms in which sellers' insurance obligation were compulsory in Incoterms 2000 and Incoterms 2010. The position remains that, with the exception of CIF and CIP rules, Incoterms place no obligation on the seller or buyer to provide insurance cover to each other in all its remaining 9 rules. However, depending upon the actual term used for each shipment, the seller or buyer bears responsibility for loss or damage to the goods at

---

[17] "The Incoterms 2010 rules are the first version of the Incoterms rules since the revision of the Institute Cargo Clauses and take account of the alterations made to those clauses. The Incoterm rules place information duties relating to insurance in Clause A3/B3 which deal with contracts of insurance. These provisions have been made from the more generic Clauses found Clause A10/B10 of the Incoterms 2000 rules. The language in Clause A3/B3 relating to insurance has also been altered with a view to clarifying the parties' obligations in this regard"—Introduction, Incoterms 2010, ICC Publication No. 715E, para 6 at p. 8.

[18] For IFA 2020, see chapter 2 pp. 5–6.

some point during transit. Prudence would, therefore, dictate that this exposure to financial loss be insured against. So, Incoterms' position is that in two rules (CIF and CIP) the seller must provide insurance and in the remaining 9 rules the seller does not have to. However, it does not mean parties on those 9 rules should make some insurance arrangements or for those in CIF and CIP to provide more cover. That notwithstanding, they cannot provide lesser cover unless otherwise agreed. The "Explanatory Note" for users draws attention to the possibility of restrictive practices at destination. This is covered in Chap. 9 of this book. That notwithstanding, there are still similarities and differences between Incoterms 2020 and its immediate predecessor.

One other editorial change was the reversal to Incoterms 1953 format of the Insurance Clause back to A5 for the seller and Clause B5 for the buyer, from the A3(b) for the seller and B3(b) for the buyer, that applied between Incoterms 1953 to Incoterms 2010.[19]

1.5 Classification of Incoterms

1.5.1 Pre-2020 Incoterms Classifications

1.5.1.1 General Comments

Up to Incoterms 2010, Incoterms were grouped into 4 categories: C, D, E and F classes. Each type was divided into four groups: E, F, C and D. These categories are determined by the delivery location and which party is responsible for covering the cost of each part of the journey. They are still relevant and used in contemporary literature. The groups are then split into sub-categories which refer to various scenarios, as itemised below.

1.5.1.2 The C-Group

Was used where the seller can arrange and pay for most of the freight charges up to the foreign country. It includes CFR (C&F), CIF, CIP and CPT -C terms (CFR, CIF, CPT, CIP). The seller has to contract for carriage, but does not assume the risk of loss or damage after the shipment. The only C-Group and the only 2 Incoterms (CIF and CIP) that requires sellers to provide insurance for the buyers' benefit are also from this category.[20]

1.5.1.3 The D-Group

This group first featured in Incoterms 2000, which had 14 Incoterms, but not in the Incoterms 2010 or the current Incoterms 2020 version. It is possible that they may be still in use in some jurisdictions hence their mention in this book. Furthermore, parties are still free to contract on those terms. However, care must be taken to ensure that both parties agree on their obligations in this case. The D Group is used

[19] See chapter 8 (post); for IFA 2020 provisions, see chapter 8, pp. 33–36.

[20] Ibid.

where the seller can pay for most of the delivery charges to the destination country. DAF, DES and DDQ in Incoterms 2000 were discontinued by Incoterms 2010. They have been replaced by DAP, DDP, and DPU in Incoterms 2020. The seller is not obliged to contract for insurance under this category.[21]

1.5.1.4 The E Group

Group E was used where the seller did not want to arrange transport. The only contract in this group was, and remains, the EXW or "Ex-Works" which means the seller's only responsibility is to make the goods available at or outside his/her workshop, factory or depot, without carriage, delivery, risks or insurance obligations. Under the EXW, the seller only makes the goods available to the buyer at the seller's own premises. It is the only contract in which the seller does the least while the buyer does the most. Accordingly, the EXW contract seller does not provide insurance.[22]

1.5.1.5 The F Group

The "F" Group was used where the seller can arrange some transport within his/her own country. The group now includes the FCA, FAS, FOB and American FOB. Under the "F"-terms the seller is called upon to deliver the goods to a carrier appointed by the buyer. The seller has no insurance obligations to the buyer under this group.[23] Further, classifications of Incoterms were introduced by Incoterms 2020.

1.5.2 Further Classifications in Incoterms 2020

1.5.2.1 Principal Incoterms 2020 Changes

Whereas Incoterms 2000 divided the rules into E, C and D classifications, Incoterms 2010 and Incoterms 2020 introduced two further categories based on transportation modes: 7 Rules that can be used for any mode or modes of transport; and 4 Rules for sea and inland waterway transport.[24] These new classifications cut across the previous ones, as itemised below.

1.5.2.2 Rules for Any Mode of Transport

Seven (EXW, FCA, CPT, CIP, DAP, DDP and DPU) of the 11 Incoterms rules can be used in and for any mode (air, rail, road and water) of transportation. They could be technically categorised as "multimodal" transport (also known as "combined transport")—the transportation of goods under a single contract, but performed with at least two different modes of transport; the carrier is liable (in a legal sense) for the entire carriage, even though it is performed by several different modes of transport.

---

[21] For insurance of Group D, see Chap. 5 (post).

[22] Ibid.

[23] Ibid.

[24] See also under Incoterms 2020 at pp. 12–17; Comparisons between Incoterms 2010 and Incoterms 2020 below.

But multi-modalism applies to the second category ("maritime" transport Incoterms) below as well. However, like the water transport (maritime) below, they can also be used unimodally. In both categories. classifications are based on the nature of performance requirements without and any bearings on the previous C, D, E and F letter groupings. The summary of the respective parties' detailed obligations under all the groups are covered below. The appreciation of parties' insurance duties is precondition of the understanding of their subsequent insurance obligations.

1.5.2.2.1 THE *EXWORK* (EXW)

Commercial Context Of

Under this Incoterm the seller makes the goods available at its premises, or at another named location. This term places the maximum obligation on the buyer and the minimum obligation on the seller. The term is often used while making an initial quotation for the sale of goods without any costs included. It means that a buyer incurs the risks for bringing the goods to the final destination. In this scenario, the seller could be responsible for loading the goods onto the collecting vehicles but does not clear them for export. In circumstances where the seller does load the goods, he does so at the buyer's risk and cost. It means that the seller delivers when it places the goods at the disposal of the buyer at the seller's premises or at another named place (i.e., works, factory, warehouse, etc.). The seller does not need to load the goods on any collecting vehicle, nor does it need to clear the goods for export, where such clearance is applicable.

Caution to *EXW* Contractual Parties

The parties are well advised to specify as clearly as possible the point within the named place of delivery, as the costs and risks to that point are for the account of the seller. The buyer bears all costs and risks involved in taking the goods from the agreed point, if any, at the named place of delivery. It means that the seller delivers when it places the goods at the disposal of the buyer at the seller's premises or at another named place (i.e., works, factory, warehouse, etc.). The seller does not need to load the goods on any collecting vehicle, nor does it need to clear the goods for export, where such clearance is applicable. The seller makes the goods available at their premises, or at another named place. This term places the maximum obligation on the buyer and minimum obligations on the seller. The term is often used while making an initial quotation for the sale of goods without any costs included.

EXW also means that a buyer incurs the risks for bringing the goods to their final destination. Either the seller does not load the goods on collecting vehicles and does not clear them for export, or if the seller does load the goods, he does so at buyer's risk and cost. If the parties agree that the seller should be responsible for the loading of the goods on departure and to bear the risk and all costs of such loading, this must be made clear by adding explicit wording to this effect in the contract of sale. There is no obligation for the seller to make a contract of carriage, but there is also no obligation for the buyer to arrange one either—the buyer may sell the goods on to their own customer for collection from the original seller's warehouse. However, in common practice the buyer arranges the collection of the freight from the designated location, and is responsible for clearing the goods through Customs. The buyer is also responsible for completing all the export documentation, although the seller does have an obligation to obtain information and documents at the buyer's request and cost. For insurance purposes parties should bear in mind that the term is used for all modes of transport.

EXW Documentary Requirements

These documentary requirements may result in two principal issues. Firstly, the stipulation for the buyer to complete the export declaration can be an issue in certain jurisdictions (not least the European Union) where the customs regulations require the declarant to be either an individual or corporation resident within the jurisdiction. If the buyer is based outside of the customs jurisdiction, they will be unable to clear the goods for export, meaning that the goods may be declared in the name of the seller by the buyer, even though the export formalities are the buyer's responsibility under the EXW term.

Secondly, most jurisdictions require companies to provide proof of export for tax purposes. In an EXW shipment, the buyer is under no obligation to provide such proof to the seller, or indeed to even export the goods. In a customs jurisdiction such as the European Union, this would leave the seller liable to a sales tax bill as if the goods were sold to a domestic customer. It is, therefore, of utmost importance that the seller discusses these matters with the buyer before the contract is agreed. It may well be that another Incoterm, such as FCA seller's premises, may be more suitable, since this puts the onus for declaring the goods for export onto the seller, which provides for more control over the export process, all of which have bearings on parties' insurance obligations.[25]

For insurance coverage of EXW, see Chap. 5.

1.5.2.2.2 The Free Carrier (FCA)

The seller delivers the goods, cleared for export, at a named place (possibly including the seller's own premises at the cost of the seller). The goods can be delivered to a carrier nominated by the buyer. In many respects this Incoterm has replaced FOB. It should also be noted that the chosen place of delivery affects the obligations of loading and unloading the goods at that place. If the delivery location is under the control of the seller, the seller is responsible for loading. Any other location will result in the obligation being deemed to be that of the buyer. FCA means that the seller delivers the goods to the carrier or another person nominated by the buyer at the seller's premises or another named place. The parties are well advised to specify as clearly as possible the point within the named place of delivery, as the risk passes to the buyer at that point. The seller delivers the goods, cleared for export, at a named place (possibly including the seller's own premises). The goods can be delivered to a carrier nominated by the buyer, or to another party nominated by the buyer. FCA is usable for any mode or modes of transport.

---

[25] See Sects. 1.5.4 and 5.5.7 below.

In many respects this Incoterm has replaced FOB in modern usage, although the critical point at which the risk passes move from loading aboard the vessel to the named place.

It should also be noted that the chosen place of delivery affects the obligations of loading and unloading the goods at that place. If delivery occurs at the seller's premises, or at any other location that is under the seller's control, the seller is responsible for loading the goods on to the buyer's carrier. However, if delivery occurs at any other place, the seller is deemed to have delivered the goods once their transport has arrived at the named place; the buyer is responsible for both unloading the goods and loading them onto their own carrier. Although not directly responsible for insurance aspects, the seller should be aware of covering himself for possible breach of the confusing myriads of duties; for which he would own insurance. Insurance aspects are covered in Chap. 8. The only variant is "FCA seller's premises". This Incoterm was officially added to the revised version of Incoterms 2000: it is the responsibility of the seller to load the merchandise.[26]

For insurance coverage, see Chaps. 5 and 8 (post).

1.5.2.2.3 Carriage Paid To (CPT)

CPT replaces the C&F (cost and freight) and CFR terms for all shipping modes outside of non-containerised sea freight. The CFR remains in use for containerised cargo. In this Incoterm, the seller pays for the carriage of the goods up to named place of destination. The goods are considered to be delivered when the goods have been handed over to the first or main carrier, so that the risk transfers to the buyer upon handing goods over to that carrier. CPT means that the seller delivers the goods to the carrier or another person nominated by the seller at an agreed place (if any such place is agreed between parties) and that the seller must contract for and pay the costs of carriage necessary to bring the goods to the named place of destination. The seller also contracts for insurance cover against the buyer's risk of loss of or damage to the goods during the carriage. The buyer should note that under CIF and CIP the seller is required to obtain insurance only on minimum cover. Should the buyer wish to have more insurance protection, it will need either to agree as much expressly with the seller or to make its own extra insurance arrangements. CPT is used for any mode or modes of transport. This is not a common law creature and so has no case precedence yet.[27]

For its insurance coverage under Incoterms see Chaps. 5 and 8 below.

1.5.2.2.4 Carriage and Insurance Paid To (CIP)

This term is broadly similar to the above CPT term, with the exception that the seller is required to obtain insurance for the goods while in transit. It is also equivalent to the CIF minus Freight. CIP requires the seller to insure the goods for 110% of the contract value under at least the minimum cover of the Cargo Clauses (A), or any similar set of clauses. The policy should be in the same currency as the contract, and

[26] See Sect. 5.5.7 below.

[27] See Sect. 5.8 post.

should allow the buyer, the seller, and anyone else with an insurable interest in the goods to be able to make a claim. CIP can be used for all modes of transport, whereas the Incoterm CIF should only be used for non-containerized sea-freight. Apart from the seller not being responsible for freight, this contract resembles the CIF above. Like FOB, FAS, CFR and IF, CIP falls in the category of Incoterms usable in sea and inland waterway transport. This too is not a common law creature.[28]

For its insurance coverage under Incoterms see Chaps. 5 and 8 below.

1.5.2.2.5 Delivered at Place (DAP)

This is another former D Incoterms category. It is a new in Incoterms 2020 rules under which the seller delivers goods to the buyer's facility or another named location (other than a terminal) in the destination country. The buyer is responsible for import clearance and any further in-country carriage. This Incoterms stipulates that the seller delivers the goods when they are placed at the disposal of the buyer on the arriving means of transport ready for unloading at the named placed of destination. Under DAP terms, the risk passes from the seller to the buyer from the point of destination mentioned in the contract of delivery. This term is one of two terms considered to be replacement terms for the DDU, which is eliminated from Incoterms 2010 rules.

It should be compared to, DDU and DDP. Buyer is responsible for import clearance and any further in-country carriage. It is one of the new Incoterms' 2020 terms that replaced the DAF, DES, DEQ and DDU from the Incoterms 2000 and 2010. The term may be used for any mode of transport including multimodal transport. What is the difference between DDP and CIF? As per Inco terms of shipping, DDP means Delivered Duty Paid (named destination mentioned). CIF means, Cost, Insurance and Freight (paid up to the destination mentioned).[29]

Although a D Incoterms category, its characteristics are akin to that of FOB and its insurance coverage is, therefore, discussed under FOB-related contracts in Chap. 5 as well as Chap. 8 for Incoterms (post).

1.5.2.2.6 Delivered at Place Unloaded (DPU)

This is another former D category. The seller bears all risks involved in bringing the goods to and unloading them at the named place of destination. In this Incoterms rule, therefore, the delivery and arrival at destination are the same. DPU is the only Incoterms rule that requires the seller to unload goods at destination. The seller should therefore ensure that it is in a position to organise unloading at the named place. Should the parties intend the seller not to bear the risk and cost of unloading, the DPU rule should be avoided and DAP should be used instead.[30]

For insurance coverage, see Chaps. 5 and 8.

---

[28] For Incoterms insurance purposes see Chap. 8 (post).

[29] Ibid.

[30] See Sects. 5.11 and 5.13 (post).

1.5.2.2.7 Delivered Duty Paid (DDP)

DDP means that the seller delivers the goods when the goods are placed at the disposal of the buyer, cleared for import on the arriving means of transport ready for unloading at the named place of destination. Here the seller is responsible for delivering the goods to the named place and country of the buyer, and pays all costs in bringing the goods to the destination including import duties and taxes. The seller is not responsible for unloading. This term places the maximum obligations on the seller and the minimum obligations on the buyer. No risk or responsibilities transfer to the buyer until delivery of the goods at the named place or destination. The seller bears all the costs and risks involved in bringing the goods to the place of destination and has an obligation to clear the goods not only for export but also for import, to pay any duty for both export and import and to carry out all customs formalities. In Incoterms DDP the seller delivers the goods, without unloading, at buyer's premises or a nearby place in the country of destination. The only difference between Incoterms DDP and DAP is that in DDP all costs and taxes of import clearance are paid by the seller while in DAP are paid by the buyer. DDP versus EXW. The term DDP is exactly the opposite of EXW.

For insurance coverage see Chaps. 5 and 8.

1.5.2.3 Rules for Sea and Inland Waterway Transport

1.5.2.3.1 Maritime Transport Incoterms

The remaining 4 Incoterms (FAS, FOB, CFR, and CIF) can only be used for maritime transport-also known as maritime transport Incoterms. Maritime in this context is used loosely to include deep sea (oceans and seas) as well as inland waters (canals, lakes and rivers). Other than CIF, in all these Incoterms, insurance obligations in this category have identical insurance obligations (Clause B5) to those of the 6 above. The buyers' insurance obligations are the same but without the requirement for information to the seller. Thus, the buyer has no obligation to the seller to make a contract of insurance. Although the minimum requirement is inapplicable both sellers and buyers should be aware of the need for additional and own contingency insurances.

The remainder of this clause examines the wider practical-related issues raised above.

1.5.2.3.2 Free Alongside Ship (FAS)

FAS means that the seller delivers when the goods are placed alongside the vessel (e.g., on a quay or a barge) nominated by the buyer at the named port of shipment. The risk of loss of or damage to the goods passes when the goods are alongside the ship, and the buyer bears all costs from that moment onwards. The seller delivers when the goods are placed alongside the buyer's vessel at the named port of shipment. This means that the buyer must bear all costs and risks of loss of or damage to the goods from that moment. The seller is required to clear the goods for export. FAS is usable for any mode or modes of transport.[31]

For insurance coverage see Chaps. 5 and 8.

1.5.2.3.3 Free on Board (FOB)

The most important former F Class and the oldest and second most important in export trade globally by volume of transactions after the CIF is the FOB. It is also the only Incoterms with many variations or classifications into standard, classic, simple and with additional duties (extended). Under FOB terms the seller bears all costs and risks up to the point that the goods are loaded on board the vessel. The seller must also arrange for export clearance.[32]

For common law coverage, see Chap. 3; common law insurance, Chap. 4; and incoterms insurance coverage see Chap. 5.

1.5.2.3.4 Cost and Freight (CFR)

CFR means that the seller delivers the goods on board the vessel or procures the goods already so delivered. The risk of loss of or damage to the goods passes when the goods are on board the vessel. the seller must contract for and pay the costs and freight necessary to bring the goods to the named port of destination. The seller pays for the carriage of the goods up to the named port of destination. Risk transfers to buyer when the goods have been loaded on board the ship in the country of Export. The Shipper is responsible for origin costs including export clearance and freight costs for carriage to named port. The shipper is not responsible for delivery to the final destination from the port (generally the buyer's facilities), or for buying insurance. If the buyer does require the seller to obtain insurance, the Incoterm CIF should be considered. CFR should only be used for non-containerized sea-freight and inland waterway transport; for all other modes of transport, it should be replaced with CPT.

The seller pays for the carriage of the goods up to the named port of destination. Risk transfers to buyer when the goods have been loaded on board the ship in the country of Export. The Shipper is responsible for origin costs including export clearance and freight costs for carriage to named port. The shipper is not responsible for delivery to the final destination from the port (generally the buyer's facilities), or for buying insurance. If the buyer does require the seller to obtain insurance, the Incoterm CIF should be considered. CFR should only be used for non-containerized sea-freight and inland waterway transport; for all other modes of transport, it should be replaced with CPT. This contract resembles the CIF below save for insurance obligations, which would make it attractive to the seller who, apart from his own additional insurance needs, has no insurance obligations to the buyer. The term is used for both sea and inland waterways transport.[33]

---

[31] See Sect. 5.10 (post).

[32] See Sects. 5.3 and 5.4 (post).

[33] See Sect. 5.6 (post).

For insurance coverage of (C&F) CFR at common law see Chap. 7 and under Incoterms see Chap. 8.

1.5.2.3.5 Cost Insurance and Freight (CIF)

CIF means that the seller delivers the goods on board the vessel or procures the goods already so delivered. The risk of loss of or damage to the goods passes when the goods are on board the vessel. The seller must contract for and pay the costs and freight necessary to bring the goods to the named port of destination. 'The seller also contracts for insurance cover against the buyer's risk of loss of or damage to the goods during the carriage. The buyer should note that under CIF the seller is required to obtain insurance only on minimum cover. Should the buyer wish to have more insurance protection, it will need either to agree as much expressly with the seller or to make its own extra insurance arrangements. This term is broadly similar to the above CFR term, with the exception that the seller is required to obtain insurance for the goods while in transit to the named port of destination. CIF requires the seller to insure the goods for 110% of their value under at least the minimum cover of the Cargo Clauses (C), or any similar set of clauses. The policy should be in the same currency as the contract. The seller must also turn over documents necessary, to obtain the goods from the carrier or to assert claim against an insurer to the buyer. The documents include (as a minimum) the invoice, the insurance policy, and the bill of lading.

These three documents represent the cost, insurance, and freight of CIF. The seller's obligation ends when the documents are handed over to the buyer. Then, the buyer has to pay at the agreed price. Another point to consider is that CIF should only be used for non-containerized sea-freight; for all other modes of transport, it should be replaced with CIP. This term is broadly similar to the above CFR term, with the exception that the seller is required to obtain insurance for the goods while in transit to the named port of destination. CIF requires the seller to insure the goods for 110% of their value under at least the minimum cover of the Institute Cargo Clauses of the Institute of London Underwriters (which would be Institute Cargo Clauses (C)), or any similar set of clauses. The policy should be in the same currency as the contract.

The seller must also turn over documents necessary, to obtain the goods from the carrier or to assert claim against an insurer to the buyer. The documents include (as a minimum) the invoice, the insurance policy, and the bill of lading. These three documents represent the cost, insurance, and freight of CIF. The seller's obligation ends when the documents are handed over to the buyer. Then, the buyer has to pay at the agreed price. Another point to consider is that CIF should only be used for non-containerized sea-freight; for all other modes of transport, it should be replaced with CIP. It will be apparent in Chaps. 7 and 8 ahead that together with the CIP (below) these are the only Incoterms requiring sellers to insure goods on behalf of the buyer. CIF is used for both sea and inland water transport but not for air transport.

This term is broadly similar to the CFR term, with the exception that the seller is required to obtained insurance for the goods while in transit to the named port of destination.

For insurance coverage of CIF at common law see Chap. 7 and under Incoterms see Chap. 8.[34]

1.5.2.4 Insurance Implications of the New Incoterms' Classifications

The CIP is among the 7 that fall into the new first category while CIF is in the latter 4. However, whatever the type of the divisions, they do not seem to affect the nature of the respective insurance duties. Apart from the CIP, sellers' insurance obligations in all the remaining 6 of the 7 rules (EXW, FCA, CPT, DAP, DDP, DPU) in this category have identical provisions under Clause A5, namely that: "The seller as no obligation to buyer to make a contract of insure. However, the seller must provide the buyer at the buyer's request, risk and cost with information in the possession of the seller that the buyer needs to obtain insurance".

Consequently, the only seller's insurance-related obligation in the category is provision of notice and/or information to enable the buyer obtain insurance under Clauses A10/B10. However, the seller should bear in mind the implications of '**No Obligations**' caution and to take care of own sellers' insurance interests. In this respect buyer's insurance obligations, (Clause B5), would be the reversal of the CIF and CIP sellers. Incoterms silence on this, being non-contractual, the implication as well as practicality and common sense is that the buyer is responsible to insure from delivery (Clause A2/B2), to destination (Clause A3/B3) points, respectively. Furthermore, the buyers are, where they wish, advised to take additional and own contingency insurance. However, the minimum requirement is inapplicable although "notice" and "information" are.

Generally, both parties should pay particular attention to issues arising from delivery and passage of property and risks. The above classifications were, however, changed by the current Incoterms 2020 into 2 categories of: 7 (EXW, FCA, CPT, CIP, DAP, DPU, and DDP) of general or multimodal transport; and 4 of maritime transports (FAS, FOB, CFR and CIF).

1.6 The Order of Responsibilities in Incoterms 2020

Incoterms 2020 has streamlined the functions, removed passage of property from the responsibilities, divided delivery of goods from delivery of transport/documents but retained the 10 categories' listing as follows:

A1/B1: General obligations
A2/B2: Delivery/Taking delivery
A3/B3: Transfer of risks
A4/B4: Carriage
A5/B5: Insurance
A6/B6: Delivery/transport document
A7/B7: Export/import clearance

[34] Sections 8.2–8.7.

A8/B8: Checking/packaging/marking
A9/B9: Allocation of costs
A10/B10: Notices.

Although all the functions are important in export trade, this book focuses on the most relevant: insurance (Clause A5/B5) and to a limited extent delivery (Clause A2/B2); passage of risks (Clause A3/B3); and provision of information and notices (Clause A10/B10).

1.7 Incoterms and the Insurance Contract

1.7.1 General Overview

With the exception of 2 terms (CIF and CIP), Incoterms place no obligation on the seller or buyer to provide insurance in all its remaining 9 terms. Indeed, with a few exceptions such as in third party motor and oil tanker insurance under the *International Convention on Civil Liability for Oil Pollution Damage*, 1969 (CLC), there is no compulsion for a business to take out. However, depending upon the actual term used for each shipment the seller or buyer bears responsibility for loss or damage to the goods at some point during transit. Prudence would dictate that this exposure to financial loss be insured against.

1.7.2 Incoterms 2020 at a Glance

Like all its predecessors, Incoterms 2020 rules are the official terms published by the ICC. They are a voluntary, authoritative, globally-accepted, and adhered-to text for determining the responsibilities of buyers and sellers for the delivery of goods under sales contracts for international trade. Also, like all its predecessors, Incoterms 2020 provides a set of international rules, published by the ICC effective 1 January 2020, for the interpretation of the most commonly used trade terms. It divides transaction costs and responsibilities between buyer and seller, reflects state of the art transportation practices and closely corresponds to the *U.N. Convention on Contracts for the International Sale of Goods* (CISG). Like its successor (Incoterms 2020), Incoterms 2010 dealt with the questions related to the delivery of the products from the seller to the buyer. This includes the carriage of products, export and import clearance responsibilities, who pays for what, and who has risk for the condition of the products at different locations within the transport process. It should be noted that all contracts made under Incoterms 2010 before 2020 remain valid. Moreover, although the use of Incoterms 2020 is recommended, parties to a contract for the sale of goods can agree to choose any version of the Incoterms rules after 2021. However, it is important to clearly specify the chosen version.

1.7.3 Comparisons Between Incoterms 2010 and 2020

There are many superficial differences between the 2010 and the 2020 version. Detailed outline of those changes and differences are beyond the scope of this section and chapter.[35] However, the principal ones were the reduction of the number of Incoterms from 13 to 11 by Incoterms 2010. In the 2010 version Four Incoterms (DAF, DES, DEQ, DDU) were replaced from the 2000 version by two new Incoterms (DAT and DAP). Reasons for the replaced Incoterms (DAF, DES and DEQ) being that they were not used much in day-to-day trading. Incoterms 2020 has retained the 11 Rules. The other principal differences between the 2010 and the current 2020 version are the incorporation of DAT into DAP. Parties should be aware of security-related clearances introduced by Incoterms 2010 and 2020.

1.7.4 Incoterms 2020 Insurance Cover and Security-Related Clearances

Like its 2010 predecessor, the Incoterms 2020 also more prominently feature insurance and security-related obligations of the seller and buyer in the various terms. The insurance obligations are now found in Clauses A3/B3 under each Incoterm. Security obligations; for example, the obligation to obtain security related clearances or chain-of-custody information, are set forth in Clause A2/B2, A10/B10, A4 and A7 A9/B9 of each Incoterm. The Contracts of Carriage/Insurance are contained in Clause A3 and Clause B3. The seller is required to obtain cargo insurance complying at least with the minimum cover provided by Clauses (C) of the Institute Cargo Clauses. Parties should, however, note that this is the minimum level of insurance and covers only major casualties, such as total loss of cargo. The buyer also has the option of the seller provides, at the buyer's expense and where procurable, any additional cover, for example, cover provided by Cargo Clauses (A) or (B) or any similar clauses and/or cover complying with the War Clauses and/or Strikes Clauses or any similar set of clauses. This acts as a sort insurance "bolt-on", but the buyer will be required to pay more for this. If the buyer wishes for the seller to arrange for this "bolt-on" insurance, it is recommended that this is included in the sale contract.[36]

1.7.5 Incoterms and Contracts that Exclude Sellers Insurance Obligations to the Buyer

1.7.5.1 Introduction

In addition to the two arrangements (multimodal and water transport) above, Incoterms are further divided into 2 further classifications: those in which the seller provides insurance to the buyer (CIF and CIP) and those in which the seller does

[35] For this see *Guide to Users,* Incoterms 2020 ICC Doc. No. 723E, Chapter IX, pp. 12–17.

[36] See Incoterms 2020 p. 16.

not. Of the 11 Incoterms 9 (CFR, CPT, DAP, DDP, DUP, EXWORKS, FAS, FCA and FOB), exclude parties' insurance obligations to each other. They contain information on but do not provide for either party's insurance obligations. That's why the common Clause A5 in these contracts provide that the seller has no obligation to the buyer to make a contract of insurance. However, the seller must provide the buyer, at the buyer's request, risk and cost with information in the possession of the seller that the buyer needs for obtaining insurance. While Clause B5 provides that the buyer has no obligation to the seller to make a contract of insurance, hence the contentious "**No Obligation**" issues below. Thus, the seller has no obligation to the buyer to make a contract of insurance and vice-versa. There are no other guidelines on the **No Obligation** concept due to lack of reported common law cases. In contrast, for instance, the type of FOB contract envisaged in the Incoterms 2020, and others before it, is the common law strict form, in which it is the buyer's duty to provide insurance, and yet the FOB has many other variations.

Incoterms is, therefore, of no use to common law classic FOB or common law extended FOB. Precautionary, and as a matter of practice, however, when selling FOB sellers can safeguard their interests by arranging adequate insurance whilst goods are still at their risk, bearing in mind that where the consignee affects insurance, the seller has no claim under such insurance for loss or damage up to FOB. This is dealt with in Chap. 9 of this book. This is also what Sassoon was alluding to, inter alia, his observation in the opening quotation to Chap. 4 of this book. Incoterms 2020 seems to be in agreement with this position, at least with regard to premature transfer of risks. "In some cases, the risk can be transferred from the seller to the buyer even before the seller has fulfilled his delivery obligation. This could happen because of

(a) the buyer's failure to do what is required of him to enable the seller to deliver the goods to him, or
(b) the buyer's failure to take delivery of the goods under Clause B5."

Therefore, the buyer must give such notice to the seller as the latter requires preparing the delivery (Clause B2), or the buyer must nominate the carrier under F-terms and accept the goods from the carrier as agreed. Moreover, a buyer having undertaken under DPU to clear the goods for import must fulfil his obligation to do this within the agreed time so the seller can proceed with the on-carriage of the goods to destination as intended. If the buyer fails to do this, he must bear all additional risks of loss of or damage to the goods resulting from his failure to do so.[37]

Other insurance and commercial considerations under Incoterms 2020 are where shipment duties are split between the buyer and the seller such as in strict or extended FOB or when parties use FCA instead of FOB. In this case, Notes to Incoterms 2010

[37] Cf. *ICC Guide to Incoterms 2000*, p. 61; see also Sect. 1.15 above on requirement of notice.

for instance cautions that, problems arise when the transportation risk is split between the seller and the buyer at some intermediate point. In this case, in this case the seller has no insurable interest after he has reached the pointed noted in Clause A4 of Incoterms, while the buyer has no insurable interest before that point. This means that an FOB buyer has no insurable interest before the goods have crossed the ship's rail, and that, accordingly, the FOB seller remains at risk until that point has been reached.[38]

> If the parties use FOB when FCA should have been used instead, the seller remains at risk even after the goods have been handed over to the carrier nominated by the carrier's terminal or at a place other than the ship itself. Normally, sellers have general insurance arrangements (so-called open cover) which protect them in such cases. However, a seller who fails to cover himself adequately in these situations will not normally benefit from the buyer's insurance, even if that insurance contains a so-called transit clause to the effect that the insurance protection last from warehouse to warehouse, thereby covering the period before the goods on board. There two reasons for this: first, the FOB-seller is not a contracting party to the FOB-buyer's insurance contract; and second, the FOB-buyer has no insurable interest before the goods have passed the ship's rail[39]

However, to guard against such eventuality, the parties would find it prudent to use the door-to-door insurance. This type of transit insurance also seems highly recommended by freight forwarders and other shipping agents. A party who is unsure of which insurance he needs should, therefore, contact these special brokers, or better still take out a contingency insurance. Detailed discussions on FOB insurance are the subject of Chaps. 4 and 5 above.

1.7.6 Incoterms and Contracts that Include Sellers' Insurance Obligations to the Buyer

The remaining 2 Incoterms (CIP and CIF) include sellers' obligations to make a contract of insurance on behalf of the buyer, but not vice-versa. Their nature and characteristics have been covered (ante) and will be covered further ahead. While these terms do not feature in the current version of Incoterms (Incoterms 2020), it is possible that they may be seen in sales order contracts. Care must be taken to ensure that both parties agree on their obligations in this case. Incoterms 2020 aligns different levels of insurance coverage in CIF and CIP. The nature of CIF and characteristics of CIF including its insurance aspects are dealt with in Chaps. 6–8 (post). The relevant Clause A5/B5 of both contracts are covered in Chap. 8 (post).

---

38 Cf., ICC Guide to Incoterms 2010, p. 26.

39 Ibid.

1.8 Limitations of Incoterms on Insurance

1.8.1 What Incoterms Is About

One of the reasons for the insurance shortfalls is Incoterms narrow focus. For the above reasons, parties to the Incoterms contract should beware of its limitations. There are restrictions on what it can do. Exhaustive as they may at first appear, Incoterms deal with only 3 broad aspects of the international sales contract, namely:

(a) contractual obligations in relations to the provision and delivery of goods:
   1. Contracting with carriers;
   2. Obtaining licences and certificates;
   3. Customs clearances;
   4. Taking out insurance; and
   5. Obtaining and delivery (tendering) of shipping and insurance documents;

(b) Time (but not the incidents) for the passage or transfer of risks from the seller to the buyer during delivery at both ends of the contractual performance; and

(c) Apportionment of costs between the parties, such as freight, premiums, packaging, loading and/or unloading, checking, documents and certificates including pre-shipment inspection when required.[40]

However, international sales contracts, it seeks to regulate, involves and requires more guidelines and regulations than is indicated here. The above narrow focus extends to the grave limitations Incoterms themselves.[41]

1.8.2 What Incoterms Is Not About

Equally parties to Incoterms contract should be cautioned on the number of aspects it cannot do. There are numerous aspects of the sales contract that both Incoterms generally and the Insurance Clauses in particular do not deal with at all or not in details, all of which have direct and indirect bearings on insurance considerations.[42] Insurance and other contractual problems encountered by Incoterms are due to variety of reasons.[43]

1.8.2.1 Incoterms Is Not in Itself the Sales Contract but Only a Model Term

Parties, therefore, have to look elsewhere for complement. This is because Incoterms is not a creation of international Convention or a product of intergovernmental

[40] For details of what the Incoterms rules do see, Introduction to Incoterms 2020, ICC Pub. No. 723E, par I, p. 2.

[41] See Incoterms 2020 p. 2; IFA (2020).

[42] See Incoterms 2020, pp. 2–3 (What Incoterms do not cover).

[43] Ibid; For Incoterms For Americans (IFA) 2020, See chapter 3 pp. 9–11.

organisation. It is instead an invention of a non-governmental organisation (the ICC) and as such does not have automatic application. Consequently, it only applies where and when parties expressly provide that it will provide the basic terms and conditions of their contract. This is with the exception of jurisdictions such Jordan, Iraq and others in the Arab Gulf have incorporated Incoterms into their commercial laws. Where they have been incorporated into domestic commercial law, their application becomes mandatory in those countries. Other than that, they remain instruments of a private business organisation—albeit being the most observed and widely applicable international commercial rule. Consequently, insurance and other contractual these terms are agreed upon separately between the two transacting parties and the items are defined by the express terms in the sales contract and by the governing law. For the UK, this is partly contained in ss.12–16 of the *Sale of Goods Act 1979* (*SGA* 1979), as amended.

1.8.2.2 Incoterms Is Only One of the International Sales Facilities Available to Export-Import Merchants

The other options being: bespoke contracts, the *Convention on International Sale of Goods* (CISG) and Commodity Trade Association Standard Term Contracts such those of the Grain and Feed Trade Association (GAFTA) and the Federation of Oils, Seeds and Fats Associations (FOSFA), domestic and regional trade rules, among others. GAFTA, FOSFA and other commodity form contracts include both sales forms and insurance terms. Examples and standard form sales and insurance contracts of GAFTA is used in several contexts in this book and Annexes therein. Other alternatives include Templates run by trade organizations ICC Guidelines using the ICC International Sales Contracts. All these have extensive insurance provisions. Incoterms, therefore, only part of the web of export trade practices that should be seen in context of the interface with other instruments such as the Cargo Clauses and the Commodity Trade Clauses, the banking and transport practices. For instance, in practice, the insurance documents should be tenderable under Clause 28 of UCP 600 where the CIF and CIP contract are financed by a letter of credit. Even the latest stage of the insurance clause in Incoterms 2020 has not altered those fundamentals. At least there is some liaison between Incoterms and UCC 600.

1.8.2.3 Incoterms 2020 Is Independent of Associated Contracts

Incoterms is a contract of sale; it is model or set of recommendations and/or guidelines for transacting international sales and associated contracts. Although associated with those contracts Incoterms is independent of them. Indeed, apart from those on the insurance requirements under CIP and CIP Clause A5/B6, Incoterms does not deal with and/or provide any details in relation to the terms and conditions of the carriage, delivery of, payments for, property (title) in and risks to the contact goods and services. In that respect, Incoterms almost follows the CIF's principles of the separation of goods from documents or the UCP 600's independence of the letter of credit from the underlying contract on which it may be based. It is for those reasons that Incoterms only comes into when parties expressly and voluntarily provide for its application. It is normal to find that Incoterms is normally found in a sentence or paragraph in several pages of a written international sales contract. It is for the same reasons that despite reference of Incoterms in a sales, carriage, insurance and delivery country the responsible party to individually and additionally contract for those categories in fulfilment or performance of the international sales contract.

1.8.2.4 Incoterms Does Not Deal with (Tile) or Ownership Issues

Incoterms 2020 does not deal with passage of property and has removed the corresponding Incoterms 2010 (Clause A3/B3). Yet passage of especially risks issues is at the very heart of insurance which underpins the transaction. This is principally because of its being creation of private non-governmental organisations rather than a public Convention by intergovernmental organizations. Its use is voluntary, not mandatory, and applies only when expressly provided by the parties. Hitherto passage of risk without transfer of title affects the guilty parties' liabilities insurance obligations. It may also be subject to the *Retention of Title Clause.* These too are covered by legal systems referred to immediately above.[44]

1.8.2.5 Incoterms Avoids Consequences of Breaches of Contract

Both Incoterms and its Insurance Clauses duck the consequences failure to provide insurance or insufficient insurance, breach of other terms of the contract, dispute resolutions and conflict of law of issues.[45] They also circumvent parties' liabilities for damages and for failure to perform insurance and other contractual obligations, remedies for contractual breach and conflict of laws issues. Instead, they only provide guidelines as to shipment, delivery, passage of property, passage of risks and insurance. Those too are governed by national laws, regional laws or the *UN Convention on International Sale of Goods* (CISG) or contractual customs of particular trades. Of the underlying sales contract or of the insurance contracts or the parties' failure to secure import and export licences, customs clearances.

Only deal with which party should provide the goods and perform the shipment, customs clearances, licenses, insurance, etc. It does not delve into the mechanics of doing so or damages and other consequences for failure to perform those tasks. For insurance purposes, it is concerned only with which party bears the risks and the CIF and CIP sellers' providing insurance for the buyers' benefits, in accordance with the underlying contract, but not necessarily those conforming to Incoterms. Neither does it delve into the practicalities, principles of and/or sources of the cargo policy. The Incoterms generally and the Insurance Clause in particular are, therefore, only a of guidelines.[46]

---

[44] See, Incoterms Retention of Title—A practical Guide to 19 national legislations, ICC Doc. No. 467.

[45] Incoterms and Conflict of Laws (Incoterms 2020), pp. 2–3; see also Chap. 13 (post).
See, Ademuni-Odeke (1996), pp. 7–14.

[46] Incoterms is only Guidelines, see Incoterms 2020 Incoterms pp. 1–17 (Introduction to Incoterms 2020).

1.8.2.6 Incoterms Is Not Concerned with External Factors Affecting Carriage and Insurance

And finally, Incoterms is not concerned with any internal or outside obstacles and other exterior factors that parties might encounter in the course of providing the necessary insurance cover. One of the major commercial risks is lack of knowledge about the international market. If an exporter who does not have proper knowledge about the area of sales where he markets his product, no doubt, he may fail in international business. These are namely: restrictive insurance and related shipping practices, embargoes, etc. This list is by no means exhaustive.[47] The above limitations encompass the Incoterms insurance clauses themselves (see Chap. 9 ahead).

1.8.3 Incoterms Does Not Deal with Jurisdictional Issues

The rest of this chapter and book deals with Incoterms 2020.

First, Incoterms is not a product of an international Convention—but rather of an invention of a non-inter-governmental organisation. It is a creation of a non-governmental organisation and as such does not have automatic application as does, for instance, the CISG. Instead, it only applies where and when parties expressly provide that it will provide the basic terms and conditions of their contract.[48]

Secondly, some jurisdictions such those in the Arab Gulf have incorporated Incoterms into their commercial laws. Other than that, it remains a private commercial organisation instrument—albeit the most observed and widely applicable.

Third, Incoterms do not cover, however, ownership or title transfer of the goods. These terms are agreed upon separately between the two transacting parties. It only provides guidelines as to shipment, delivery, passage of property, passage of risks and insurance.

Fourth, and, in some jurisdictions, Incoterms has been incorporated into domestic commercial law, which makes it mandatory in those countries.

Fifth, as alluded to above, Incoterms by themselves DO NOT

(a) constitute a contract;
(b) supersede the law governing the contract;
(c) define where title or property transfers; nor,
(d) address the:
    1. price payable;
    2. currency; and/or
    3. credit terms.

These items are defined by the express terms in the sales contract and by the governing law. Sixth, and finally, the duty costs of the goods may be calculated against a specific Incoterm: for example, in India, duty is calculated against the CIF value of

[47] See Introduction to Incoterms 2020, Pub. Doc. No. 723E, para II pp. 2–3.

[48] Incoterms deals with only what the parties provide.

the goods, and in South Africa the duty is calculated against the FOB value of the goods. Because of this it is common for contracts for exports to these countries to use these Incoterms, even when they are not suitable for the chosen mode of transport. If this is the case, then great care must be exercised to ensure that the points at which costs and risks pass are clarified with the customer.[49]

1.9 Incoterms and Contract Carriage Risks

The contract of carriage has a direct bearing on insurance. Indeed, together with the policy or insurance documents, the bill of lading or transport documents is one of the three principal documents required for tender. The other being the invoice. These are part of transit risks or transport risks—risks in goods transport which include: goods damaged in transit, loss and theft, fire, explosion, stranding, sinking, piracy and war risks. For Incoterms these are covered in in a limited way in Clause A4/B4 which, and except for certain FOB related Incoterms contracts, puts responsibilities on the seller. The manner of performance might affect either parties' insurance obligations. These carriage obligations are detailed under the respective contracts in following chapters. This function is included prior to insurance obligations in each Incoterm in Chaps. 5 and 8. However, the full treatment of carriage and transit risks are beyond the scope of this, section, chapter and book.[50]

1.10 Incoterms and Goods' Delivery Risks

Risks to the goods while in transit is the basis of insurance. Goods are the essence of the Incoterms contract. That's is why Clause A1/B1 (for the seller) provides that the seller must provide the goods and the commercial invoice in conformity with the contract of sale and any other evidence of conformity that may be required by the contract. Any document to be provided by the seller may be in paper or electronic form as agreed or, where there is no agreement, as is customary; and the corresponding Clause B1 (for the buyer) provides that the buyer must pay the price of the goods as provided in the contract of sale. Any document to be provided by the buyer may be in paper or electronic form as agreed or, where there is no agreement, as is customary. And Delivery and the contract of carriage normally go together. These are covered in Clause A2/B2 which, apart from certain FOB contracts, puts the responsibility on the seller. Once the manner of performance might impact on insurance liabilities. Discussions on this are included prior to those on insurance obligations in Chaps. 5, 8 and 10. This chapter does not represent full coverage of delivery risks in export/import trade.

---

[49] Incoterms 2020 pp. 4–6; Clause A3/B3 (Transfer of Risks) in all Incoterms.

[50] For details of carriage and transport risks, see Incoterms For Americans 2020 pp. 4–6/Incoterms Guide to Transport [Clause A/B on carriage].

1.11 Incoterms and Delivery of Contract Documents'

1.11.1 Transport Documents

One of the innovated changes of Incoterms 2020 is the formal acknowledgment and extension of the concept of the-hitherto "buying and selling afloat" to other Incoterms. For those reasons, equally the symbolic delivery of goods using documents (delivery of documents) is also crucial for the contract and therefore insurance. Presumably due to the heightened role of documents in international trade, Incoterms 2020 now has a separate provision of delivery of documents from the delivery of goods. This is to align it with current practice of importance of documents in export trade. This is now contained in Clause A6 Delivery/transport document for the seller and Clause B6 (Proof of delivery for the buyer). For Instance, Clause A6 of FCA provides that the seller must provide the buyer at the seller's cost with the usual proof that the goods have been delivered in accordance with Clause A2. The seller must provide assistance to the buyer, at the buyer's request, risk and cost, in obtaining a transport document. Where the buyer has instructed the carrier to issue to the seller a transport document under B6, the seller must provide any such document to the buyer.

While the corresponding Clause B6 provides that the buyer must accept the proof that the goods have been delivered in accordance with Clause A2. If the parties have so agreed, the buyer must instruct the carrier to issue to the seller, at the buyer's cost and risk, a transport document stating that the goods have been loaded (such as a bill of lading with an onboard notation). Where the Incoterm contract involves credit, the UCP 600 provides all the necessary procedural guidelines in Clauses 1–17 and 29–39.

1.11.2 Insurance Documents: Incoterms 2020/UCP 600

Insurance documents are contained in Clause 28 of UCP 600 while other documents are in Clauses 18–27. These are detailed are in Chap. 10 (post) on tender of insurance policy and other documents. This is detailed ahead under insurance obligations in Chaps. 5, 8 and 10 (post).

1.12 Incoterms and Transfer of Title and Property

As in risks, the timing on passage of properly is essential for insurance. It is the property or title to the goods that insurance preserves or protects. It is the party that has property that bears the risk of loss and therefore for who insurance is crucial. The literal meaning of passing of property is the transfer of the ownership on an agreed price. The ownership is transferred only when the proprietary of the property rights are transferred from the seller to the buyer. However, unlike its predecessors Incoterms 2020 does not include a clause directly on the subject but can discerned indirectly from Clause A2/B2 (Delivery), Clause A3/B3 (Transfer of Risks) and Clause A4/B4 (Carriage). It does not mean that Incoterms 2020 is not concerned with it or that it is less important; they decided to leave to national and international rules governing passage. However, Incoterms only provides guidelines on passage of property but does not deal with the law governing ownership of property which are subject to contractual provisions and/or the laws of the seller's or buyer's country. Otherwise, the passage of property has a direct bearing on the part incurring insurance responsibilities subject to the application of the *Reservation or Retention of Title Clauses*.[51] Transfer of Risks or Passage of Property are also covered by the SOGA 1979, CISG, Cargo Clauses and all the Commodity Standard Term Contracts, which apply to Incoterms Sales Contracts and insurance.

1.13 Incoterms and Passage of General Export Risks

1.13.1 Export/Import Risks

As alluded to above the passage of risks closely follows but might predate passage of property and the party having property (title) bears risk and is, therefore, advised to insure. This is particularly pivotal in export/import contracts where multiple jurisdictions may be involved. During a transaction, the passage of risk is a phase in which the risk of damage or loss passes from the seller of the product to the buyer. For different products/items, the passage of risk occurs at different phases in its transaction. Risk, however, passes to the buyer on conclusion of the contract of sale; in other words, one could contract to buy goods that are stolen or destroyed before he/she takes ownership, he/she could end up losing both the cargo and the purchase price. Exports/imports are also exposed to more than the passage of title and related immediate risks.

They include loss of or damage to goods in transit, non-payment for your goods or services, the cost of returning to your premises any goods that a buyer abroad refuses to accept, political or economic instability in the buyer's country, a new customer's credit worthiness, currency fluctuations, political risks, Exporters can face significant political risks when doing business in various countries, legal risks—laws and regulations vary around the world, Credit & Financial Risk, Quality Risk, Transportation and Logistics Risk, Language and Cultural Risk. Provisions on risks in the *SGA* 1979, CISG, Cargo Clauses and standard term commodity contracts also apply to Incoterms contracts.

[51] See, Incoterms Retention of Title—A practical Guide to 19 national legislations, ICC Doc. No. 467.

1.13.2 Sellers Additional Exporting Risks

In addition to all the above, sellers/exporters are additionally exposed to political and other risks.[52] Exporters can face significant political risks when doing business in various countries including but not limited to:

(a) currency exchange risk;
(b) legal risks such as varying laws and regulations vary around the world;
(c) credit & financial risks; quality of goods' risk;
(d) transportation and logistics risk; transit risks; and
(e) language and cultural differences' risks.

Furthermore, commercial risks peculiar to the seller in addition include:

(a) rejection or non-payment by the buyer;
(b) damages and/or loss by the carrier;
(c) damages from fraud, theft and piracy;
(d) loss of or damage to goods in transit;
(e) non-payment for your goods or services;
(f) the cost of returning to your premises any goods that a buyer abroad refuses to accept;
(g) political or economic instability in the buyer's country;
(h) a new customer's credit worthiness; currency fluctuations; and
(i) a fault that causes an end-customer to sue.

These are also listed in the MIA 1906, cargo clauses

1.13.3 Buyers Additional Importing Risks

In addition to the above general and common risks, buyers'/exporters are in addition are exposed to:

(a) buyers' failure or late delivery;
(b) wrong delivery; and
(c) sellers insolvency;

The above lists are not conclusive. These are covered, in a limited way, by Clause A3/B3 and repeated under each Incoterms insurance in Chaps. 5, 8 and 10.

---

[52] See Chap. 11 for details.

1.14 Incoterms and Requirement for Insurance Notice and Information

Although originally the preserve of especially common law FOB, Incoterms FOB has now embraced the need for notice and information particularly in relation to insurance purposes. This is now covered directly and indirectly by Clauses A2/B2 (Delivery/Taking Delivery), A3/B3 (Transfer of Risks), A4/B4 (Carriage), A5/B5 (Insurance), and A10/B10 (Notices). Although the common law requires FOB seller, but not the CIF seller, to give notice to the buyer, Incoterms is now moving in that general direction with the provision of notice featuring prominently in Clauses A5 and A10.[53]

1.15 "Incoterms for Americans Guidelines"

Incoterms for Americans Guidelines (IFA) 2020 Edition is not a rival publication to the official ICC Incoterms. Rather, it is a publication that explains the application of Incoterms and describes the 11 ICC Incoterms 2020, the C&F and 4 others [previous ones] in clear American business English for the US [and probably Canada], with proforma invoice illustrations. Fully revised to explain the ICC Incoterms 2020 Edition, it is written for U.S. exporters, importers, freight forwarders, customs brokers, foreign trade bankers and their overseas counterparts who wish to do business with them. It is a comparison of Incoterms with the UCC shipment and delivery terms facilitating their use in U.S. and probably Canadian domestic trade. Reasons for the publication are the lack of North American familiarity with the mainly Europhile and internationally oriented designed trade code which Americans claim:

(a) frequently confuse Incoterms rules and title transfer;
(b) frequently have serious risk blind spots;
(c) will sooner or later find their larger customers using Incoterms rules domestically;
(d) frequently misuse Incoterms rules to their disadvantage; and
(e) American increasing reliance on the official Incoterms and the corresponding unofficial phasing out of the trade terms in the UCC.

Written in clear American business English by a leading expert,[54] the completely updated Incoterms for Americans 2020, explains Incoterms 2020 rules in both international and domestic use. It was prepared for the United States Council for International Business (USCIB), the sole U.S. affiliate of the ICC whose membership includes some 300 leading U.S. companies, professional service firms and associations.

[53] See also Chaps. 2, 5 and 7 below.

[54] Frank Reynolds who was and still is the US representative to the ICC and the Incoterms Drafting Committee.

It presents the 11+ Incoterms 2020 from a U.S. and North American trading perspective by:

(a) prioritizing in order of usefulness to Americans;
(b) narrating through lifelike case study situations;
(c) detailing resulting documentary expectations;
(d) matching each with appropriate international payment term possibilities;
(e) describing U.S. regulatory ramifications;
(f) explaining risk and cargo insurance pitfalls; and
(g) illustrating each with typical proforma invoice quotations.

It is commendable that instead of creating a rival ICC, the world's largest trading nation so far has opted for unity by instead proving explanations and guidelines to Incoterms for its citizens and trading community. As pointed out by Schmitthoff,[55] there are clearly differences between say the British and Commonwealth concepts and the American practice as contained in the UCC. For those reasons this book will regularly make references to Incoterms for Americans for comparative purposes with the North American practice.

1.16 Incoterms 2020s Changes to Insurance Provisions

The latest version of Incoterms is Incoterms 2020. Although previous Incoterms had contained insurance provisions, Incoterms 2010 were the first Incoterms version since the revision of the Institute Cargo Clauses in 1982 and took account of alterations made to the clauses. The 2020 rules restored insurance clause designations back to Clause A5/B5 of each Incoterms 1953 rules. Clause A5/B5's insurance provisions have also been altered to clarify party's obligations.[56] It is also advisable to look at the general obligations in Clause A1/B1, the risk bearing Clause A3/B3 as well as the Requirements for Notice in Clauses A5/B5, A7/B7 and Clauses B10/B10. Risks and, therefore, allocation of insurance obligations may vary slightly due to nature of Incoterms or party's unwitting breaches thereof.

With the exception of CIF and CIP terms, Incoterms place no obligation on the seller or buyer to provide insurance. It leaves it to the parties to agree among themselves on insurance arrangements and other additional measures. Hence the expression "**No Obligation**" below under all other Incoterms except for CIF and CIP. However, depending upon the actual term used for each shipment, the seller or buyer bears responsibility for loss or damage to the goods at some point during transit. Prudence would dictate that this exposure to financial loss be insured against. The reason it leaves it open is because of lack of agreement from the customs and usages of many commercial cultures.

[55] Schmitthoff (2012), pp. 18–19.

[56] Incoterms 2010 pp. 8–9.

Insurance is crucial in export trade transactions. An insurance policy is the vehicle used to insure goods moving in international trade. Most cargo insurance policies are written on an open cover basis[57] or blanket policies[58] and floating policies[59] which will cover all future shipments of an assured when he is responsible for providing insurance or when he is responsible for loss or damage during the "main carriage phase" of transit; that is when he is responsible for loss or damage to the goods from a point in the country of origin until the goods are delivered to a point in the country of destination. Equally, most export policies do not automatically insure the seller or buyer when their responsibility for loss or damage is solely within either the country of origin or solely within the country of destination.

Coverage for these exposures, however, can usually be added to an export policy by endorsement, or they may be covered under the assured's domestic transit or property insurance policies. Parties who are unsure of their insurance obligations should refer to the Insurance Guidelines in CIF and CIP[60] and Other Insurance Considerations[61] later in this book.

Following below is a summary of commonly used terms of sale illustrating the point at which responsibility for loss or damage transfers from the seller to the buyer during international transit and when insurance obligations kick in. Also included are comments which should be taken into consideration when arranging insurance and a table representation of summaries for each Incoterm.

1.17 The Problem of 'No Obligation' in Incoterms' Insurance Clauses

With the exception of the CIF and CIP, due to its historical developments and advisory role, Incoterms uses **No Obligation** under parties' insurance duties. This can be misleading; therefore, parties have to be very careful about expressions 'No obligation' in Incoterms especially in relation to insurance, otherwise they might be left

[57] *Open covers* have almost same meaning and function as blanket policies below. When there are regular shipments of goods it is usual to arrange an open cover to avoid the necessity of separate policies for each sending. The two most common methods are the floating policy and the open cover. The following features are common to both; see also Blanket policies below.

[58] *Blanket* policies are policies which in a single sum insured, covers a number of separate items of property without subdivision of the amount. The approach is not unique to exports and indeed started in fire insurance and motor insurance for large risks and also in fidelity guarantee insurance to cover the whole staff without mention of the name or position, the premium being computed on the number of employees in specific categories insurance; see also open covers above.

[59] *Floating policies* in marine insurance are policies covering loss of or damage to specified goods irrespective of the ship in which they are consigned. They are provided for in s.29 of the MIA 1906. As to the practice of effecting floating policies see Arnould's paragraphs 241–246; *Dunlop Brothers v Townend* [1919]2KB 127 (omission to declare consignments covered by government insurance).

[60] Incoterms 2020 para. 4 at p. 52 (CIP) and para. 8 at p. 124 (CIF).

[61] Ibid.; and Chap. 10 on other insurance considerations.

exposed or under insured. For insurance purposes the expression may imply, but does not necessarily mean, that the party in question should not bother at all about insurance. All it means is that the party in question does not owe the other a duty to contract for insurance on their behalf and for their benefit. The responsible party should, however, ensure that they have adequate insurance cover for their own delivery obligations before property and risks pass to the other party. Even when they feel they have performed their obligations adequately; they should still also take out contingency insurance to cover any pre- and post-shipment eventualities such premature passage of risk.

The drafting of Incoterms' insurance provisions in their current form may be understood by seasoned merchants acquainted with Incoterms, export and insurance matters, but not to novices. For those reasons, perhaps there needs to a warning to all parties along the lines that that the parties may wish to or are strongly advised to take insurance to cover their risks and any possible breaches on their respective your parts. Instead, this is explained in accompanying documents to Incoterms.[62]

> As appears from the expressions "the seller must", and "the buyer must" Incoterms are only concerned with the obligations which the parties owe to each other. The words "no obligation" have therefore been inserted whenever one party does not owe an obligation to the other party. Thus, if for instance according to A3 of the respective term the seller has to arrange to pay for the contract of carriage we find the words "no obligation" under the heading "contract of carriage in B3 setting forth the buyer's position. Again, where neither party owes the other an obligation, the words "no obligation will appear with respect to both parties, for example, with respect to insurance.

> In either case, it is important to point out that even though even party may be under "no obligation towards the other to perform a certain task, this does not mean that it is not in his interest to perform that task. Thus, for example, just because a CFR buyer owes his seller no duty to make a contract of insurance under B4, it is clearly in his interest to make such a contract, the seller being under no such obligation to procure insurance under A4"[63]

Although Incoterms is widely used globally, it does not follow that it is equally widely and commonly understood. Hence the need, for instance, for "Incoterms for Americans", for a region whose understanding differs from those of the Common Law, European and other traditions.

1.18 Broader Contexts of Insurance in International Trade

In the broader context parties should be aware of Incoterms' limitations both in insurance and other aspects thus:

(a) External policy factors affecting the developments in Incoterms generally and the insurance clause in particular;

[62] For instance, paragraph 10 of Ramberg (2000): **'the expression "no obligation"'**, p. 184.

[63] Reproduced in Incoterms 2000, p. 19.

(b) Elaboration of the implications of the, "**No Obligation**";
(c) Further insights into "**what incoterms do and do not do**";
(d) Implication of the requirements for insurance Notice;
(e) Extent of requirement for information for both mandatory and additional insurance;
(f) Other Incoterms' limitations;
(g) Restrictive state practices in maritime transport and marine insurance market;
(h) Effects of sanctions, embargoes and force majeure on export trade; and
(i) Alternative sources of cargo insurance market.

These are not dealt with directly in Incoterms but are nevertheless significant factors that should concern anyone involved with export-import generally and export insurance in particular. They are contained in most export trade, Incoterms and cargo insurance Commentaries and Guidelines. As discussed above, the fact that only the sellers in CIF and CIP have contractual insurance obligations to the buyers does not mean the sellers in the remaining 9 Incoterm rules do not have insurance responsibilities to the buyers except to themselves. Neither does it mean that, despite the **No Obligation** notice under their respective insurance obligations to the sellers, buyers in all the 11 rules are free of all indirect insurance obligations to both sellers and themselves. In short, all parties in all the 11 rules owe some insurance duty to themselves: for additional covers and to provide notice and information to their contractual counterparts detailed above. Furthermore, all parties should be aware of internal and external factors affecting marine insurance and maritime transport. For those reasons Incoterms should, therefore, be treated only as guidelines and/or starting point. One particular aspect is the wider insurance outlook (see Chap. 9, New Clause).

1.19 Further Food for Thoughts

1.19.1 Multiplicity of Incoterms

A principal argument against Incoterms generally is their multiplicity.

First, although now reduced to 11 rules from their peak of 14 in Incoterms 1980, there are still a sheer number of them. The number could be reduced by combining a few. For instance, there is not much difference between say CIF and CIP and many others-so why not amalgamate them? Although Incoterms since 1990 have made great effort to clarify and reduce them, 11 are still too many. There are not much differences between most. These can be puzzling to especially novice merchants. Because they are legal terms, written from a legal perspective, incoterms can be confusing or easily misunderstood. And making the wrong choice might turn a shipment into an expensive nightmare.

It is for these reasons that Reynolds developed Incoterms for Americans to explain these differences. Furthermore, in the US and other common law jurisdictions, the C&F is still in use despite the new official Incoterms CFR.

It is assumed that the ICC carried out thorough investigations among merchants to determine the differences between the Incoterms and, therefore, the necessity to retain so many. But this is neither apparent nor discussed anywhere, let alone during the consultations for Incoterms 2020, Nor are there indications of the proportion of world trade is conducted under each Incoterm.

Secondly, the original categorisation of the rules into C–F made sense as they followed alphabetical order; the new categorisation by a mixture of multimodal and maritime transport does not have a coherence.

For those reasons, the rules would benefit from their review and reduction into the 6 most common (DDP, EXW, FAS, CIF, and FOB); and merging of CIF and CIP. That would avoid the confusions caused by the overlaps and duplications.

1.19.2 General Caution on Incoterms

For users of Incoterms, there should be a warning in red, as is the case with exclusion of liability in the law of contracts, so that parties make the appropriate choice and know where they stand. Parties should also be exposed to alternative export contract choices and, therefore, made aware that Incoterms is only one of the many contract systems on international trade transactions. Among the many alternatives are:

(a) the bespoke contracts with the assistance of legal firms or through "Dot It Yourself" (DIY) contracting;
(b) the ISIG system which also make reference to Incoterms;[64]
(c) use of standard form templates contracts; and
(d) the Commodity Trade systems such as FOSFA and GAFTA.

Furthermore, contracting parties should be made aware that the use of Incoterms is not mandatory, but only voluntary or advisory (being a product of non-governmental private business organisation rather that an intergovernmental governmental public convention). Additionally, parties should note that Incoterms only applies once they agree to use it. Debattista cautions that they (parties) should also be careful on attempting to change the terms and conditions of any Incoterms.[65]

From the above, contracting parties have to factor in Clauses in their contracts dealing with issues not the subject of Incoterms as it is generally agreed that it does not deal with consequences of passage of risks, property, governing law of the contact or any conflict of law issues.

---

[64] Especially Clause CISG; See also Schwenzer and Fountoulakis (2007), pp. 100–1003 where these, including the case of *BP Oil International and BP Exploration Oil Inc. v. Empressa Estatal Petroels de Ecuador* US Ct App (5th Cir), 11 June 2003 CISG online and is discussed.

[65] "**Cautions with variants of incoterm rules**" para 78, see p. 17, Incoterms 2020.

1.19.3 Other Disadvantages

In addition to the above, a further disadvantage is that many exporting and importing companies may not be able be to keep up with all the modifications that take place. This can leave some companies in an advantageous situation, and yet others at a disadvantage. That perhaps explains the apparent popularity of the CIF and FOB contracts. Put differently, why sellers often choose CIF because they have a better understanding of their shipments, while buyers often choose FOB for the same reasons.[66] These two types are the most used incoterms. This problem can be seen as an advantage or disadvantage depending on the perspective. Another disadvantage of incoterms is that many transport companies try to benefit from them. They often cite shipments using one method and purchases using another. The reason for this is to save money and gain more control over the merchandise.

1.19.4 Inflated Costs

The old Group C Incoterms generally expose the buyers to inflated costs, because the seller bears the responsibilities for paying freight and insurance costs. This is a disadvantage to the importer, especially if the exporter chooses to quote the final figure without itemizing the individual entries for freight, insurance and currency fluctuation costs. Moreover, a buyer accounting for an inventory of expensive shipments may experience delays as Incoterms do not cover the transfer of titles or ownership. This can be unsatisfactory, from a commercial viewpoint because an inventory of expensive goods can help a business push down expenses and report higher income. Another disadvantage of Incoterms is that many shipping companies try to benefit from them.[67] They will often quote shipments using one method and purchases using another. The reason for this is to save money and to gain more control over the goods.

1.19.5 Persistent Changes

The meanings of many Incoterms have changed over the years. And even with the entry into of a new Incoterms, contracts entered on the bases of a previous one will be honoured for a while. One disadvantage of such multiple changes is that many companies may not keep up with every modification that takes place. This can leave certain companies at an advantage, and yet others at a disadvantage.

---

[66] Source: El Insiginia—https://blog.elinsignia.com/.

[67] See: Cole-Ingait (2017).

1.19.6 Shipping Company and State Preferences

Another issue with Incoterms is that shipping companies and buyers both have different preferences regarding which terms to use. As mentioned above, sellers often choose CIF because it is rigid and predictable such that they hold a better grasp on their shipments; buyers often choose the more flexible and sometimes confusing FOB for the same reasons.[68] These two types are the most commonly used Incoterms. However, the differences between the two is often exploited by governments for commercial and sometimes political reasons. This issue can be viewed as an advantage or disadvantage depending on the perspective. Another issue with Incoterms is that shipping companies and buyers both have different preferences regarding which terms to use.

1.19.7 Incoterms Avoidance of Title Problems

It will be apparent throughout the book that Incoterms rules are silent on when title passes from seller to buyer; this now needs to be defined separately in each export sales contract. This is unsatisfactory as it leaves parties having to make assumptions about passing of title to the goods, based on the Incoterms rule in use; with the consequences that such miscalculations can be catastrophic.

1.19.8 Incoterms Avoidance of Breaches of Contract Issues

Incoterms does not deal with issues arising from breaches of contracts. See also under "Avoidance of Applicable Laws" and "Avoidance of Conflict Resolutions" below.

1.19.9 Incoterms Avoidance of Applicable Law Issues

Incoterms does not deal with issues arising from Applicable Laws; see also: "Avoidance of Breaches of Contracts" above; and "Avoidance of Conflict Resolution" and Chap. 13 below.

1.19.10 Incoterms Avoidance of Conflict Resolutions

Incoterms does not deal with issues arising from "Conflict Resolutions" or "Dispute Settlements"; see also under "Avoidance of Title Problems"; "Avoidance of Breaches of Contract Laws" and "Avoidance of Applicable Laws"; Sects. 1.19.7 to 1.19.10 above; and Chap. 13 below.

---

[68] See, VanBaren (n.d.).

1.20 What to Watch Out in Choice of Incoterms Contracts

1.20.1 Place of Delivery Should Be Specified Precisely

For instance, for CIF this should be e.g., "CIF Southampton" for goods from New York and not "CIF New York". The reverse should be the case for FOB and all "FREE" family and related contracts.[69]

1.20.2 Use of *EXW* Should Be Avoided Where Possible

One major disadvantage of EXW to buyers is related to customs clearance. According to the EXW terms, sellers are required to facilitate the paperwork for export clearance. If sellers' information is inaccurate, the buyers are still responsible for the additional cost and results of delays. Thus, although it is the contract with least sellers' duties and maximum buyers' duties respectively, EXW can be a very tricky contract to perform. Because of the different moments at which delivery takes place under EXW versus FCA, the risk that the goods are damaged during loading varies. According to EXW, such risk shifts to the buyer, whereas under FCA it remains with the seller. This is because of the:

(a) the uncertainty about the destination of the goods;
(b) non-existence of evidence of the exit of the goods from the country of origin;
(c) incidents in the loading of the goods; and
(d) difficulties in using the contract with letters of credit;[70]

1.20.3 FCA to be Used Only for Delivery in the Country of Origin

This is to do with complications in relation to delivery of Incoterms generally and the FCA in particular. So, while FCA is not incredibly different, the disadvantage of using it can be that sellers are not as familiar with the process. When exporting products from any country, the best Incoterm is frequently where both the buyer and seller have the most experience. In FCA this is to do with:

(a) different places of delivery;
(b) different types of cargo;
(c) adaptation to multimodal transport;
(d) documents justifying the export; and
(e) compatibility with letters of credit.[71]

---

[69] "INCOTERMS 2020-Obligations, Costs and Risks", ***Global Negotiator***, pp. 133–134.

[70] Ibid at pp. 134–135.

[71] Ibid, at pp. 135–136.

1.20.4 Container Cargo to be Used Only with Any Means of Transport

Container operations are limited by site constraints. Containers are a large consumer of terminal space (mostly for storage), implying that many intermodal terminals have been relocated to the urban periphery. It is a capital intensive operations which tends to hike up the costs. It is prone to thefts, loses and fraud due to its nature of operations. It is also prone to illicit trade especially in narcotics as the carrier cannot tell what is in a sealed container. This is in line with Incoterms 2020 advice that in such cargo, FCA, CPT or CIP should be preferred to FOB, CFR and CIF.[72] While there was a shortage of containers at the height of the Covid pandemic, the global economy is now facing the opposite problem: too many containers. On top of falling freight rates, data shows container depots — used to house containers after they are unloaded — are now filling up or full.

1.20.5 Sea Transport Incoterms to be Used Only for Goods Loaded on Board

This is partly because, among other things, Incoterms 2020 relegates sea transport in favour if multimodal transport.[73] In addition to the above, there are additional problems of Costs of Repositioning Empty Containers which affects incoterms trade and consequently increase in insurance risks and costs. The shipping industry suffers from inefficiencies, which means that empty container repositioning causes a serious problem of every 1 in 3 containers being globally carried empty. This costs the shipping industry up to $20 billion per year.

1.20.6 Exporting "C" and Importing "F" Needs Careful Monitoring

Reasons for these are problems of exporting C importing F discussed in Chaps. 8 and 10 (post). These reasons for this caution to the parties include:

(a) cost savings considerations;
(b) need to meet contractual deadlines;
(c) necessity of control of export/import documentation; and
(d) need to comply with letters of credit.[74]

[72] Ibid, at pp. 136–137.
[73] Ibid, at pp. 137–138.
[74] Ibid, at pp. 138–139.

1.20.7 "D" Incoterms Should Be Used Only for Low-Risk Countries

This is common sense, insurance companies set their premium levels depending on the risk levels of either parties' country. The assumption is that less developed countries have lower-level infrastructures making it difficult for parties to manage and control the inevitable logistics and supply chains. These countries are also prone to press the restrictive practices pedals because of the scarcity of foreign exchange reserves and earnings. It is for those reasons that parties sometimes attempt to change the particular terms of an incoterm by adding including extra duties. An example in point is the FOB contract where the buyer may require the seller to nominate the vessel (contract for shipping) where no such domestic capacity exists in his country, or take out insurance for the same reason. Hence the birth of and/or the distinctions between the FOB strict or FOB classic with FOB with additional duties or extended FOB.[75]

1.20.8 Maximum Coverage Insurance Should Be Provided for International Transport

Contrary to the provision of only the minimum covers in CIF and CIP insurances, parties might consider the need for maximum coverage. Although the only two Incoterms CIF and CIP that provide for insurance indicate covers under cargo clauses C and A respectively, these are only recommendations which does not preclude parties from proving higher cover, especially for manufactured goods which are subject to higher risks.[76]

1.20.9 Use of Incoterms 2020 Variants Should Be Avoided at All Costs

This is to avoid confusions and to clarify the respective parties' obligations. In particular the followings should be avoided:

(a) "EXW loaded"—instead the parties should specifically state this as an additional sellers' function in the contract;
(b) "CIF maximum cover"-instead the cover needed should be clearly enumerated e.g., an "All Risks" or "cargo clauses A+ War Risks+ Strikes Clauses" as above;
(c) "DDP VAT unpaid"; and
(d) "DDP VAT excluded".[77]

---

[75] Ibid, at p. 139.

[76] Ibid, at pp. 139–140.

[77] Ibid, at p. 141.

1.20.10 The Intended Version of Incoterms Should Be Precisely Indicated

Despite the coming into force of the latest Incoterms 2020, it does not follow that parties should not opt for an earlier Incoterms 2010 or even Incoterms 2000. However, to exercise such options parties should indicate precisely and expressly the version they intend to use rather than assuming or leaving it to the courts to intervene when the confusion had given rise to a dispute. For the same reason parties are reminded that, unlike Conventions, Incoterms have no automatic application and are, therefore, binding only parties have expressly provided that their contracts shall be so governed by it.[78]

1.20.11 Parties Should Be Aware of Countries Using CIF and FOB for Domestic Shipments

Because of their complimentary nature of these two oldest Incoterms, the US and Canada and some countries have taken the liberty to require that their exporters and importers, respectively, should alternate the contracts so as to maximise foreign exchange revenues with a view to promoting domestic shipping, insurance and related industries.[79]

1.20.12 Parties Should Acquaint Themselves with State Restrictive Trade Practices

For the same reasons as above, parties need to employ internal and external commercial intelligence to avoid falling into such loopholes.[80]

1.20.13 Parties Should Be Aware of Trade Sanctions and Embargoes in Operation

Although operated as countervailing actions by other countries and/or international organizations to punish national misdemeanours, trade sanctions and embargoes operate in the same way as restrictive trade practices. For those reasons, although some do so deliberately to maximise earnings, parties should ensure they do not breach such orders, breaches of which can be costly.[81]

---

[78] Ibid.

[79] See Chap. 9.

[80] Ibid.

[81] See Sects. 10.29 and 10.30 (post).

1.20.14 Remember What Incoterms Does Not (Incoterms 2020)

- address all the conditions of a sale;
- identify the goods being sold nor list the contract price;
- reference the method nor timing of payment negotiated between the seller or buyer;
- when title, or ownership of the goods, passes from the seller to the buyer;
- specify which documents must be provided by the seller to the buyer to facilitate the customs clearance process at the buyer's country; and
- address liability for the failure to provide the goods in conformity with the contract of sale, delayed delivery, nor dispute resolution mechanisms.

1.21 Concluding Remarks

The ICC and its main creation, Incoterms, are important in international trade. Through its various commissions, ICC works in areas spanning arbitration, banking, competition, e-business, customs and trade facilitation, financial services and insurance, taxation, trade policy, and transport and logistics. The core mandate of the ICC is to act as a court of last resort with the capacity to prosecute individuals for genocide, crimes against humanity and war crimes 3 when national jurisdictions for any reason are unable or unwilling to do so.

The use of Incoterms, on the other hand, eliminates inconsistencies in language by giving all parties the same definition of specific terms within a trade agreement. As a result, the risk of problems during shipment is reduced since all parties clearly understand their responsibilities in performing trade under the given contract. Although there are 11 different incoterms, sellers and buyers regularly underestimate the importance of them and their impact on international trade. Many traders believe that the clear and plain language used in the contract will be enough to ensure that all parties keep their trading obligations. Traders very often cannot see that incoterms eliminate discrepancies in contract language by giving the same definition of specific trade agreement to all parties and reducing the risk of problems that may occur during the shipment.

Incoterms are only relevant for a sales contract, however the agreement between parties to use certain Incoterms has also an effect on other contracts. For example, a seller who has agreed on FOB incoterm, is bound to choose sea transportation as he has to present a bill of lading to the seller. Therefore, other transportation methods are completely inadequate. Failure to understand the correct definition of each Incoterm used will lead to problems throughout the supply chain and may affect payment of goods, delivery schedules and even cause conflict between seller's and buyer's responsibilities, including who completes the customs declarations and makes duty payments.

The Incoterms rules have become an essential part of the daily language of trade and it is extremely important that the terms of sale are discussed upfront, which will help you to reduce the risk in a transaction. By specifying the seller's and buyer's obligations, there is no confusion with regards to rules of transportation from one country to the other. However, it is worth remembering that Incoterms do not cover ownership or title transfer of the goods. These terms have to be agreed upon separately between the two transacting parties. In the last decades, for many companies, a strategic necessity results within the scope of globalization to use broader access to new markets and to take part in international business. Most pursued goals are market protection, cost minimization, capacity utilization and maximization of profit. Hence, world trade gains importance, and those goods are traded in larger numbers and diversities on international markets.

In addition, International Trade language is one of the most important and complex instruments. Even a small variation in wording can have a major impact on aspects of a business agreement, as in any business that is complex and sophisticated. From industry-to-industry word definitions often vary, especially concerning global trade. Such essential expressions as "delivery" can have a far different meaning in business than in the rest of the world. For business terms, to be efficient, expressions must mean the same thing. Often the contracting parties are not aware of different commercial customs in their respective countries. Misunderstandings, conflicts as well as litigations and the involved effort of time and costs are resulting from that. Therefore, the ICC published the Incoterms.

1.22 Further Readings

Books

- Guillermo Jimenez, ICC Export-Import Basics, ICC Document No. 543.
- Jones, UCP 600-Eight Years on, 10(3) S. & T.I May (2015) pp. 4–7.
- Ramberg, Synchronization of Contracts of Sale, Carriage, Insurance and Financing in International Trade, in Sarcevic (ed.) International Contracts and Conflicts of Laws (A Collection of Essays) (1990) 86 at 87.
- Debattista, The new UCP 600 - changes to the tender of the Sellers's shipping documents under letters of credit, J.B.L. 2007, June, pp. 329–354.
- Ellinger, Documentary Credits and fraudulent documents, in Kee and Chan (eds), Current Problems of International Trading Finance, 2nd edn, NUS.
- Gao, The Fraud Rule in Letters of Credit: A comparative Study 2002 Kluwer.
- ICC, Incoterms 1980, ICC Document No. 353.
- ICC, Guide to Incoterms 1980, ICC Document No. 354.
- ICC, Incoterms 1990, ICC Document No. 461.
- ICC, Guide to Incoterms 1990, ICC Document No. 560.
- ICC, Incoterms 2000, ICC Document No. 560.
- ICC, Guide to Incoterms 2000, ICC Document No. 620.
- ICC, Incoterms 2010, ICC Document No. 715E.
- ICC, Guide to Incoterms 2010, ICC Document No. 720E.
- ICC, Incoterms 2020, ICC Document No. 724E.
- ICC, UCP 500, ICC Document No. 500.
- ICC, UCP 600, ICC Document No. 600.

- ICC, Guide to Export/Import, ICC Document No. 790E 5th Edn 2018.
- ICC, Model International Sale Contract, ICC Document No. 738E 2013.
- Mastering the Business of Global Trade: Negotiating Competitive Advantage Contractual Best Practices, Incoterms, and Leveraging Supply Chain Options.

Clauses

- Arora, The dilemma of the issuing bank: to accept or reject documents under a letter of credit, [1984] LMCLQ 81.
- Bennett, Documentary credits: a reasonable time for what?, [1997] *LMCLQ* 169.
- Bennett, Strict compliance under UCP 500, [1997] *LMCLQ* 7.
- Bennett, Original sins under the UCP, [2001] *LMCLQ* 88.
- Buckley, Potential pitfalls with letters of credit, [1996] 70 *ALJ* 217.
- Chatterjee, Letters of credit transactions and discrepant documents: an analysis of the judicial guidelines developed by English courts, [1996] JIBL 510.
- Dolan, Strict Compliance with letters of credit: striking a balance, [1985] *Banking LJ* 18.
- ICC, The merchants of peace, http://www.iccwbo.org/about-icc/history/.
- ICC, International Chamber of Commerce (ICC), http://www.iaaca.org/AntiCorruptionAuthorities/ByInternationalOrganizations/InterGovernmentalOrganization/201202/t20120215_805467.shtml
- Johnson, Analysis of Incoterms as Usage under Article 9 of the CISG, 35 *U. Pa. J. Int'l L.* 379 (2013–2014).
- Kozolochyk, Strict Compliance the reasonable document checker, [1990] 56 *Brooklyn LR* 48.
- Malfliet, Incoterms 2010 and the mode of transport: how to choose the right term, Ghent University, Belgium, pp. 163–179, https://biblio.ugent.be/publication/1212622/file/1212631
- Oduntan, Gbenga, *C.I.F. Gatwick' and Other Such Nonsense Upon Stilts: Incoterms and the Law, Jargon and Practice of International Business Transactions, International Company and Commercial Law Review,* 21(6) (2010), pp. 214–223.
- Olegario Llamazares, Practical Guide to Incoterms, https://www.globalnegotiator.com/en/practical-guide-incoterms
- Ramberg, CISG and Incoterms 2000 in Connection with International Commercial Transactions, 2008.
- Ramberg, Incoterms 2010, 13 *Eur. J.L. Reform* 380 (2011), pp. 3–4.
- Ramberg, To what extent Do Incoterms 2000 vary Articles 67(2), 68 and 69?, *Journal of Law and Commerce*, Vol. 25, pp. 219–222.
- Suraraska, Amchang and Sawatwong, Decision-Making on Incoterms 2020 of Automotive Parts Manufacturers in Thailand, *Journal of Asian Finance, Economics and Business* Vol 7 No 10 (2020), pp. 461–470.
- Ulph, UCP 600: Documentary Credits in the Twenty-first Century, *J.B.L.* 2007, June, pp. 355–377.

Reports

- UNDP Shipping and Incoterms, 2001, http://www.undp.org/content/dam/undp/documents/procurement/documents/UNDP-Shipping-Guide.pdf.
- US Department of Commerce, International Trade Administration, Know Your Incoterms, https://www.trade.gov/know-your-incoterms.
- World Bank, World Bank Logistics Performance Index, Incoterms Explained.
- World Bank, Evaluating the Shift in Incoterms for Indonesian Export Products (issued 01/12/2016, modified 25/05/2021), https://openknowledge.worldbank.org/handle/10986/30951?show=full&locale-attribute=es.

Websites Sources

- Constantin Căruntu, Mihaela Loredana Lăpăduşi: "Complex Issues regarding the Role and Importance of Internationally Codified Rules and Incoterms" Petroleum-Gas University of Ploiesti BULLETIN Vol. LXII No. 1/2010 98 - 110 Economic Sciences Series, https://citeseerx.ist.psu.edu/viewdoc/download?doi=10.1.1.1043.3472&rep=rep1&type=pdf
- Incoterms Explained.Com: Incoterms 2020 – some responses from the industry, https://www.incotermsexplained.com/incoterms-2020-some-responses-from-the-industry/
- Incoterms Explained. Com: Freight Insurance and the rules, https://www.incotermsexplained.com/freight-insurance/
- Incoterms Explained.Com: Pitfalls of CPT, https://www.incotermsexplained.com/pitfalls-of-cpt/
- Incoterms 2020 security-related costs, https://www.incotermsexplained.com/incoterms-2020-security-related-costs/

References

Ademuni-Odeke (1996) The EC conflicts of laws' regime for insurance contracts. Tolley's Professional Negligence 12(1):7–14

Cole-Ingait P (2017) Advantages & disadvantages of Incoterms. https://bizfluent.com/info-8660596-advantages-disadvantages-incoterms.html

Ramberg J (2000) ICC guide to Incoterms 2000: understanding and practical use

Ramberg J (2011) ICC guide to Incoterms 2010, ICC Publ. Nr. 720E

Schmitthoff (2012) The law and practice of international trade, 12th edn. Sweet and Maxwell

Schwenzer I, Fountoulakis C (2007) International sales law. Routledge-Cavendish/Taylor Francis

VanBaren J (n.d.) Advantages & disadvantages of Incoterms. https://www.ehow.co.uk/info_8660596_advantages-disadvantages-incoterms.html

The Role and Importance of Insurance in Incoterms and International Sales' Contract

2

Abstract

Continuing the introductory function within PART I of the book, this chapter focuses on the principal subject of the book-Insurance of International Sales Contracts. It does so by providing a summary insurance generally and the applicable marine insurance in particular. It questions whether insurance is a luxury or a necessity in commercial transactions generally and international trade in particular. It also explains the origin and nature of parties' varying insurance obligations. The chapter then discusses: the role of insurance in the allocation of risks; the assumption of its ease in FOB and complexity in CIF contracts respectively; progressive development of Incoterms' insurance clauses; insurance principles applicable to Incoterms contracts; limitations of Incoterms insurance clauses; the "minimum" insurance requirement problems; parties' policies and loss reliefs; air and aviation export policies; export credit insurance; other state supported policies; and principal, hybrid, alternative and subsidiary policy documentation. Like the above and all the remaining chapters, the chapter contains materials on "Further Food for Thoughts", reference sources used, further readings, and "What readers and practitioners should watch out for", especially in Incoterms contracts' "**No Insurance Obligation**", clauses to guide the reader.

2.1 Introduction

Besides the Incoterms themselves, the other central subject of this book is their insurance. For those reasons the role of insurance in Incoterms was briefly introduced in the last chapter. This chapter charts out the importance, background to insurance of international trade generally and, of the two most important Incoterms contracts, CIF and FOB in particular. It also introduces:

P. Ademuni-Odeke, *Insurance of International Sales' Contracts under Incoterms*, Law for Professionals, https://doi.org/10.1007/978-3-031-75136-3_2

(a) the contracts, notably the FOB and CIF contracts;
(b) the aims and objectives of the book;
(c) insurance principles and doctrines applicable to Incoterms as part of export trade;
(d) Incoterms and common law; types of the policies; and
(e) sources of export policies.

Insurance against perils is an important aspect of both domestic and international commercial transactions. Indeed, the concept of insurance is one of the most innovative mechanisms ever invented by merchants and business. The idea that for as little as two hundredth of the venture value cover can be obtained for millions, if not, billions of its losses. How does insurance help international trade? In international trade, insurance enables businesses to reduce risk by protecting them from bankruptcy and instability. These reasons may take place in foreign trade. Explore more—characteristics of foreign trade. There are several types of insurance that can protect export and import (EXIMPORT) companies from specific issues. Why marine insurance is important in foreign trade? Marine cargo insurance is necessary to meet the contractual obligations of exports. To align with agreements such as cost insurance and freight (CIF) or carriage and insurance paid (CIP), the exporter needs to take marine insurance to protect the buyer's or their bank's interest and honour the contractual obligation.

It provides that in the event of loss or damage to business or cargo due to hazards during voyage, an insured party will be able to recover losses from the insurer. The type of export insurance required depends on the circumstances of the contract and mode of transport agreed between parties to transport the cargo. Such insurance forms might include marine, aviation and land (rail and road). Likewise, the type of insurance contract depends on the Incoterm adopted, where applicable, by the parties in a sales contract. For instance, the CIF and CIP sales contracts requires the seller to obtain insurance cover for the voyage. While the FOB and the remaining 8 of the 11 Incoterms contracts, however, place no obligation on the buyer or seller to obtain insurance, although it is prudent for the buyer to protect against potential losses. Furthermore, it is not uncommon for the buyer in an FOB contract, for instance, to request the seller to arrange insurance on an understanding that they will reimburse the insurance costs incurred.

Is insurance contract important in exportation? Therefore, before business begins exporting, it is recommended that it asses assess the different risks that it may face and consider whether it needs to insure against them. As well as physical loss or damage to goods, and faulty goods or services, the seller you also need to consider non-payment by your customers. Insurance obtained must cover only those goods that are being sold and stipulated in shipping documents. The insurance must also cover the entire voyage of the sale contract. Where it covers only part of the transit, the buyer will be able to reject the documents upon tender. The basic policy excludes war and other contractual exclusions, for which the parties will need additional cover. The insurance required is part of the marine policy. Marine insurance contracts may be divided into hull insurance or cargo insurance.

There is no uniform law or convention for international marine insurance. However, commercial customs, usage and practices in international marine insurance have played a significant role in regulating marine insurance internationally. Thus, the marine insurance contract is subject to both general principles of contract law and relevant domestic marine insurance law. Institute Cargo Clauses (Cargo Clauses) have become part and parcel of the terms and conditions of export policies. Channels for obtaining cover are no longer restricted to direct approach to insurers, insurance agents and brokers. They now include carriers, banks and financial institutions, freight forwarders and other methods now include online facilities. These are some of the issues covered in this chapter and book.

2.2 Brief History of Marine Insurance and International Trade

2.2.1 The Origin of Marine Insurance

The history of international trade and, therefore, cargo insurance is tied up with the history of insurance and banking generally and marine insurance in particular. Maritime insurance was the earliest well-developed kind of insurance dating back to 600-400BC. Its history started as mutual associations and later extended to loans to merchants. Its exact and early origins are unclear but is attributed to the Chinese who traded in the South China Sea and the Indian Ocean. Later origins associated with the Codes of Hammurabi[1] and spread eventually as maritime merchants' loans, to the Babylonians,[2] Persians[3], Hellenic Greeks[4] and Eastern Roman Empire[5]

[1] See generally, *A Brief History of Insurance*, https://omnius.com/blog/a-brief-history-of-insurance-from-hammurabis-code-to-cognitive-computing/Hammurabi and Insurance; see also Halsbury's Laws of England, Vol. 8, pp. 274–283.

[2] Insurance in some form is as old as historical society. So-called bottomry contracts were known to merchants of Babylon as early as 4000–3000 bce. Marine insurance became highly developed in the 15th century. In Rome there were also burial societies that paid funeral costs of their members out of monthly dues. Insurance begins in Babylon in 1750 BC. Babylonians also practiced insurance in the form of a system, called the Code of Hammurabi, c. 1750 BC. It was practiced by the early Mediterranean sailing merchants.

[3] See generally, Hashempoor (2013), pp. 1217–1230.

[4] See generally, Whit Thompson: How Insurance Began: 3000 Years of History, https://www.wsrinsurance.com/how-insurance-began-3000-years-of-history/; http://wsrinsurance.com/how-insurance-began-3000-years-of-history/; for the influence of Greek and Roman Law, Halsbury's Laws of England, Vol. 8 pp. 275, 276.

[5] The history of insurance traces the development of the modern business of insurance against … I (527–565) of the Eastern Roman Empire, the Digesta seu Pandectae (533).

civilisations. It was then spread by the Phoenicians[6] in the East Mediterranean to the Western Roman Empire (Italy)[7] and the Western Mediterranean.

2.2.2 The Age of Roman Refinement

The system was refined by the Western Romans when Hammurabi's *bottomry* bond[8] concept was further refined and the polity[9] (policy) *subrogazione*[10] (stepping in ones' shoes) and other further marine insurance concepts and contracts both developed in Rome, Florence, Genoa, Lombardy and other Italian cities in the fourteenth century.

As to when the first modern policy was issued is still doubtful. The original policy was issued as a loan against a ship in order to bypass Pope Gregory's strict antiusury laws.[11] It was thought the first marine policy was issued in Florence in 1350. This was pushed 3 years back to a marine policy crafted in Genoa, Italy on October 23, 1347; nevertheless, Professor Federigo discovered that the first written insurance contracts were actually dated a further 4 years back to February 13, 1343, in Pisa.

2.2.3 The Central European Landbridge to the *Hensiantic* League

The role played by the Central European Traders and the Hensiatic League group in the development of insurance is sketchy. Although not much is written about this group, along with international trade, its insurance practise spread to northern

[6] Gregory DL Morris, attributes origin to the Phoencians1200-600 BC although he thinks the first formal marine insurance policy was not created until around 1350, *A Brief History of Marine Insurance:* https://riskandinsurance.com/brief-history-marine-insurance/; History of Insurance-this matter.com https://thismatter.com/money/insurance/insurance-history.htm.

[7] However, the modern origins are probably from the Romans (modern Italians), hence the origins of insurance terms such *respondentia, polizia* (policy) and *subrogazione* (subrogation)-See Historical Development of Insurance https://www.britannica.com/topic/insurance/Historical-development-of-insurance.

[8] Bottomry bonds- the same mechanism as above but this time loans against the ship itself, not the goods; see https://en.wikipedia.org/wiki/Bottomry now s.10 of the MIA 1906; see also Halsbury's Laws of England, Vol. 8 pp. 263, 277; Vol. 11, p. 448.

[9] Polity-Cementing the link between modern insurance and Italy; see Swiss Re, A History of Insurance, https://www.swissre.com/dam/jcr:638f00a0-71b9-4d8e-a960-dddaf9ba57cb/150_history_of_insurance.pdf, p. 8.

[10] Ibid; now contained in ss 79-81 of MIA; Parks Insurance, Vol. 12, p. 541.

[11] For this and the effect of other Usury laws on insurance see Halsbury Laws of England, Vol. 8 pp. 101, 106, 277 and 278; Marshall's Treaties on the Law of Insurance, Vol. 13 p. 484; for the policy in England see Sir William Holdsworth, A History of English Law, Vol. 8 pp. 175, 277, 279, 280, 284; Vol. 11, p 448; Vol. 13, p. 331.

European through the land bridge to Central European Trade Fairs,[12] the Northern European *Hensiatic* League.[13] This is contrary to logic that its journey to Northern Europe should have been through Spain, Portugal and the Iberian Peninsula and then via the sea route from Genoa. However, there is no written evidence to back this theory.

On the contrary, the popular consensus attributes its northerly movements to the Lombard Merchants[14] with a jump from there straight to Lombard Street in London.[15] It is, however, generally agreed that the policy itself comes from the Italian just as the doctrine of subrogation originated from Italian and the concept of *respondentia*[16] came from there and the refinement of Hammurabi's bottomry bond also took place there. The development of the policy and its principles were an accidental invention to avoid Papal prohibition of issuing loans.

The origins and payment of premiums varied with intuitive estimates of the variable risk from seasons and pirates. It can be said that the concept of a person or persons underwriting the ventures of another person or persons is not new.

2.2.4 The "Monarchic" State Insurance

From that viewpoint, from its new base in London and North Western Europe, modern marine insurance is credited with the European discoveries of the new world as European monarchs underwrote the voyages of discoveries:

---

[12] No trade or legal historians have credited the development of insurance to the ancient trade fairs. A Medieval fair was a huge open air gathering held each year, mostly on a holiday or on a religious anniversary. It was the greatest event in the economic life of a medieval town. During this time merchants from all over Europe gathered in the town to buy or sell products. Merchant fairs were large and sold goods from all over Europe and the east. They attracted merchants from many countries. https://www.encyclopedia.com/science/encyclopedias-almanacs-transcripts-and-maps/medieval-trade-fairs-and-commercial-revolution.

[13] Likewise, no trade or legal historians attribute the development of insurance to the League. The Hanseatic League, also called Hansa, German Hanse, organization founded by north German towns and German merchant communities abroad to protect their mutual trading interests. The league dominated commercial activity in northern Europe from the 13th to the 15th century. https://www.britannica.com/topic/Hanseatic-League.

[14] The Lombard Merchants were thought responsible for pushing insurance, banking and shipping from the Hanseatic League to London.

[15] Ibid; they are assumed to have settled in Lombard Street.

[16] Respondentia-method developed by Roman merchants to avoid the Papal (Pope Gregory IX condemned the practice as usury in his *decretal Naviganti* of 1236 (de Roover, Florence Edler (November 1945). "Early Examples of Marine Insurance". *The Journal of Economic History*. 5 (2): 172–200, at p.175); See also Kingston, Christopher (March 2011). "Marine Insurance in Philadelphia During the Quasi-War with France, 1795–1801". *The Journal of Economic History*. 71 (1): 162–184-anti-usury laws by instead issuing loans against goods on board the vessel; now s.10 of MIA 1906.

(a) Elizabeth I of England[17] underwrote the voyages of Sir Francis Drake and Sir Walter Raleigh among others;
(b) Isabella of Spain[18] underwrote Christopher Columbus after his failure to obtain similar cover from the Ligurians of Genoa;
(c) King Charles I of Spain[19] underwrote the Portuguese Magellan and Vasco Da Gama's Eastern ventures; and
(d) Prince Henry the Navigator[20] underwrote voyages of discovery for João de Santarém, Pedro Escobar, Lopo Gonçalves, Fernão do Pó, and Pedro de Sintra

Although no premiums were paid upfront for these royal patronages and state underwritings for these adventurers, the insured voyagers in turn undertook to deliver looted gold, silver, and other riches to the monarchs and ultimately the respective states claimed the discovered territories to the sovereign monarchs.

2.2.5 The Influence of the *Lex Mercatoria*

In continental Europe, modern marine insurance law originated in the Lex Mercatoria (law merchant).[21] Further refinement was achieved by the common law in London and England through customs and usages of merchants. For instance, in 1601, a specialized chamber of assurance, separate from the other Courts, was established in England. By the end of the seventeenth century, London's growing importance as a centre for trade was increasing demand for marine insurance.[22]

---

[17] These practices of monarchs [states or governments] such as Elizabeth I (1533–1603) underwriting the voyages of discoveries of navigators such as Sir Francis Drake and Sir Walter Raleigh, in return for riches and territories discovered by the expeditions gave rise to commercial insurance of risks later by insurance companies. For the role of this era in the UK see "Exploration and Trade", Chap. 4 in the History of Lloyds List pp. 56–64.

[18] Isabella I of Spain also known as Isabella of Castile 1451–1504 was, together with her husband Ferdinand II of Aragon, became famous for supporting and financing Christopher Columbus's 1492 voyages that led to the opening of the New World and to the establishment of Spain as the first global power which dominated Latin America.

[19] In doing this King Charles I of Spain was following the footsteps of his parents' (Isabella I and Ferdinand II above).

[20] Prince Henry the Navigator 1394–1460- also known as Dom Henrique of Portugal, Duke of Viseu, better known as Prince Henry the Navigator, was a central figure in the early days of the Portuguese Empire and in the 15th-century European maritime discoveries and maritime expansion.

[21] For the effect of the Italian Merchant on the development of insurance see Halsbury's Laws of England, Vol. 5, pp. 75,85 and 101.

[22] For introduction of insurance into England, Sir William Holdsworth, A History of English Law, Vol.8 pp. 275 and 276.

2.2.6 Edward Lloyds' London Coffee House

It is at this stage that one the two most influential individuals entered the scene. In the late 1680s, Edward Lloyd[23] opened a coffee house on Tower Street in London. It soon became a popular haunt for ship owners, merchants, and ships' captains and underwriters and thereby a reliable source of the latest shipping news. Lloyd's Coffee House[24] was the de facto first marine insurance market. It became the meeting place for parties in the shipping industry wishing to insure cargoes and ships, and those willing to underwrite such ventures. These informal beginnings led to the establishment of the insurance market Lloyd's of London,[25] and other offshoots: Lloyds List,[26] Lloyds of London Press,[27] the Stock Exchange, the Baltic Exchange, probably Lloyds Bank and several related shipping and insurance and financial institutions most of which still exist today

The participating members of the insurance arrangement eventually formed a committee and moved to the Royal Exchange which became the modern Stock Exchange on Cornhill as did the Society of Lloyd's the forerunner of the modern Lloyds of London Insurance. The establishment of insurance companies,[28] a developing infrastructure of specialists (such as shipbrokers, admiralty lawyers, bankers, surveyors, loss adjusters, general average adjusters, et al.), and the growth of the British Empire gave English law a prominence in this area which it largely maintains and forms the basis of almost all modern practice.

[23] Edward Lloyd's (c. 1648–15 February 1713) Coffee House was a significant meeting place in London in the 17th and 18th centuries See, Palmer, Sarah (October 2007). "Lloyd, Edward (c.1648–1713)". Oxford Dictionary of National Biography. Oxford University Press. doi:10.1093/ref:odnb/16829. Archived from the original on 15 July 2011. Retrieved 16 February 2011. Jump up to: a b c Marcus, G. J. Heart of Oak: A Survey of British Sea Power in the Georgian Era. Oxford University Press. p. 192. ISBN 0192158120.

[24] .Lloyds Coffee House became a famous source of British and global shipping tradition; see "Lloyds List-from Coffee House to the Computer", chapter 1 in Alan Cameron and Roy Farndon's (Edt) LLOYD'S LIST 1734–1984 ,250th Anniversary Special Supplement, Lloyds od London Press, April 1984 pp. 5–32; Halsbury's Laws of Wngland, Vol. 8, p. 293; Vol 13 pp. 331–332 and 484.

[25] Lloyds of London Insurance, see "Taking the Risk: Growth of the London Insurance Market", chapter 9, in Lloyds List 250th Anniversary Special Supplement, pp. 100–113.

[26] Lloyds List, the only current International Shipping Daily developed from the notes that Edward Lloyds posted on his notice board of the Coffee House, see chapters 1 and 25 of The History of Lloyds List details, supra.

[27] The Lloyds Empire (Lloyds Bank, Lloyds of London Insurance, Lloyds List) included Lloyds of London Press, which has ever-since been taken over by Informa.

[28] See the Creation of Statutory Corporations for insurance in Sir William Holdsworth, A History of English Law, Vol. 11, pp. 447–448.

2.2.7 The Age of English Codifications

The other influential individual was Lord Mansfield,[29] Lord Chief Justice who in the mid-eighteenth century began the merging of law merchant and common law principles. The growth of the London insurance market led to the standardization of policies and judicial precedent further developed marine insurance law. The era of codification followed the *South Sea Bubbles*[30] in the eighteenth and nineteenth centuries with legislations of the:

(a) the Marine Insurance Act 1745,
(b) Life Assurance Act 1774,
(c) the Marine Insurance Act 1788,
(d) the Gaming Act 1845,
(e) Policies of Marine Insurance Act 1868, and
(f) the Lloyds Act 1871.

Mention should also be made of the following related legislations:

(a) Merchant Shipping Act 1854;
(b) Bills of Lading Act 1954;
(c) Merchant Shipping Act 1894; and
(d) the Maritime Conventions Act 1911.

2.2.8 "The Finished Product"-The *Marine Insurance Act,* 1906

The *Marine Insurance Acts* of 1845, 1788 and 1868 were superseded by what was to become the universal marine insurance codification in 1906. The *Marine Insurance Act* (MIA 1906)[31] codified the previous common law; it is both an extremely thorough and concise piece of work. Although the title of the Act refers to marine insurance, the general principles have been applied to all non-life insurance.[32] To curb gambling tendencies which developed after MIA 1906, the *Marine Insurance (Gambling Policies) Act* 1909 was passed. This was later supplemented by the *Third Parties (Rights against Insurers) Act* 1930 and the *Marine and Aviation*

[29] William Murray, 1st Earl of Mansfield, (1705–1793 was a British Barrister, politician and judge noted for his reform of English law and credited with the drafting and codifications of several British insurance and commercial legislations.

[30] For this and the effect of the *Bubble Act*, see Sir William Holdswoth, A History of English Law, Vol. 13 p. 491.

[31] *Marine Insurance Act 1906*, Cap. 41 (Regnal. 6_Edw_7), probably the world's only comprehensive codification of marine insurance principles of the modern era: https://www.legislation.gov.uk/ukpga/Edw7/6/41/contents.

[32] For this and the beginnings of the Law of Insurance in England see A History of English Law, Vol.4 p. 361; Vol. 8 pp. 281–283; Vol.11, pp. 447 and 448.

Insurance (War Risks) Act 1952 to cater for later developments. The policy itself was embodied in the *Ships and Goods Policy* (SG Policy) 1400.

2.2.9 The Institute Rules

In the nineteenth century, Lloyd's of London Insurance and the Institute of London Underwriters[33] (a grouping of London company insurers) developed between them standardized clauses for the use of marine insurance under the SG Policy, and these have been maintained since subject to modifications in the twentieth and twenty-first centuries by the Lloyds Marine Insurance Policy (Lloyds Mar. Policy) and the Insurance Companies Marine Policy (the Companies' Policy) for the non-Lloyds market; both introduced in 1982.The introduction of the two policies were the London markets response to UNCTAD threats to internationalise the marine insurance market.

The new institute clauses for the new policies are now part of the International Union of Marine Insurance Underwriters (IUMI). These are known as the Institute Cla*uses* because the Institute covered the cost of their publication. Out of marine insurance, grew non-marine insurance and reinsurance industry and corresponding legislation. Marine insurance traditionally formed the majority of business underwritten at Lloyd's. Currently, Marine insurance is often grouped with Aviation and Transit (cargo) risks, and in this form is known by the acronym Marine, Aviation and Transport 'MAT' especially in British and American (notably in Delaware and Oregon) insurance market.

2.2.10 Parallel Continental Developments

Parallel marine insurance developments took place in the European continental Civil Law countries culminating into for instance the Napoleonic Codifications,[34] the *Ordonnance de la marine* of 1681[35] and *Ordonnance de la commerce* of France of 1673[36] and similar codifications in Germany, Italy, Portugal, the Nordic Plans in Scandinavian countries and Spain.[37] Consequently, like the British, the Germans, French, Portuguese and Spanish spread the systems into their own colonies world-

[33] The Institute of London Underwriters (ILU) was an association made up of marine, aviation, and transportation insurance companies. Established in 1884, it was meant to address problems concerning the risks they were underwriting. In 1998, the members of the association joined the London International Insurance and Reinsurance Market Association to form the International Underwriting Association of London (IUA) and is part of the International Union of Marine Underwriters(IUM) they are responsible for drafting Institute Clauses: see https://www.insuranceopedia.com/definition/2382/institute-of-london-underwriters-ilu.

[34] Napoleonic Codifications-in the form of 36 statutes passed between 1801 and 1803.

[35] *Ordonnance de la marine* of 1681.

[36] *Ordonnance de la commerce of France* of 1673.

[37] See, for instance, the *Barcelona Marine Code*, Sir Williams Holdsworth, Vol.8 pp. 281–283.

wide. The FOB, CIF, related contracts and other Incoterms, themselves developments from the UK colonial international trade, have benefited from this history that put insurance role at the heart of international trade.

2.2.11 Export of Insurance to the Colonies

With the corresponding spread of international trade practices, marine insurance was introduced by Britain to Australia, Canada, India, New Zealand, South Africa, the US and other English colonies through colonisation.[38] That history was also a continuation of the history of international trade, following the separation of insurance and banking from shipping and the formation of incorporated banks, shipping companies and insurance companies away from hitherto family run trading businesses that had had all the 3 sectors under one roof. That separation including developments in finance, transportation and communication was also central in developing the CIF contract away from the FOB, discussed below.

2.3 Insurance: Luxury or International Trade Necessity?

The concept on indemnity and insurance has not only protected international trade but were the back born of voyages of explorations and the voyages of discovery since the Spanish, Portuguese and English monarchs underwrote Christopher Columbus, Magellan, Vasco da Gama, Sir Francis Drake and Sir Walter Raleigh voyages. These concepts Monarchical underwriting (indemnities), but without reciprocal premiums, were developed into commercial transactions and later codified. Since then, insurance has become the backbone of both domestic and international trade.

There is no compulsion under English and/or other Common Law jurisdictions for a seller (exporter) or buyer (importer) to insure goods in transit. However, commercial considerations often compel arrangement of insurance. Only an uninformed merchant would proceed without insurance. Apart from this, it would appear common prudence for the merchant to insure goods whilst in transit. It is more so where credit to finance the venture is involved. Furthermore, without insurance, it would be necessary for merchants to set aside a large sum of money to cover possible losses, which money would be better employed in the merchant's other business. It would be pointless to hold large sums in reserve against possible losses when, for a relatively small outlay (premium), protection would be available through insurance.

Therefore, a scheme where payment of a tiny fraction of the shipment value makes full compensation in the event of a loss or damage is unparalleled. Equally, carriers, in order to protect their interests against liability to cargo-owners, would advise the merchant to insure their merchandise while in transit. Many events can

[38] For the role of the Common Law Jurisdictions on the development and export of insurance to the colonies see Sir William Holdsworth, A History of English Law,6 p. 635; Vol.8 pp. 291–293.

occur during transit that could lose you money if you're uninsured. For example, your haulier may be involved in an accident whereby your goods are destroyed, or your goods might be stolen. The result can be loss of profits, productivity and buyer goodwill. You can minimise the impact of such incidents on your business by being properly insured.

Insurance is, therefore, an essential element not only of domestic commerce but more so of international trade transactions, where the risks involved are higher and larger. As demonstrated above, operating on credits systems, export merchants would find it almost impossible to obtain finance for their ventures without insurance. Indeed, no one in their right mind would trade without insurance, for without it the alternative would be financial ruin and commercial suicide. For those reasons the insurance policy has been, and remains, an essential part of any export trade process.

2.4 Origin and Nature of Differences in Insurance Obligations Between Contracts

It is necessary to resort to history to appreciate the different insurance approaches in Incoterms generally, the FOB and CIF-CIP and Incoterms including and excluding insurance obligations. As discussed above, of the two, the merchant's insurance obligations are quite explicit and detailed in CIF-CIP, where insurance features prominently in the short designation of the contract (CIF-and CIP), compared to those in FOB and those excluding insurance obligations. Thus, there has been a tendency for those involved with the export process to assume that of the two, the fulfilment of the parties' insurance obligations is easier in FOB than in CIF contracts instance. This common law assumption can lead to unfortunate consequences. Reasons for this assumption are partly historic. First, at the FOB inception, the shipowner was also the carrier, importer, exporter, insurer and financier of the import/export transaction—"all three in one".[39] For those reasons, insurance considerations were not so prominent in the contract then, as the seller had no such obligation. Secondly, and as a later development, the FOB (unlike the CIF) was used predominantly for bulk cargoes only, that is, cargoes that are packaged but is loaded onto overseas vessel in loose form (e.g., coal, grain, oil, etc.). This development no doubt had effect on the nature and origins of risk allocations in both contracts.

Under those circumstances, the seller was responsible for losses only up to the time goods were loaded onto the overseas vessel provided by the buyer. Once cargo was loaded, it became the buyer's responsibility to arrange transportation and insurance to destination. Thirdly, also at its inception, documentary credit system did not operate in FOB sales in the same way that it did right from the beginning for the CIF sales. This is mainly because an FOB seller did not want payment for goods to depend on their safe arrival at destination; payment for them (goods) related to evidence that they had been loaded, so that title passed to the buyer at that point. That

[39] Sassoon (1967), pp. 32–37.

assumption has led to the general view that the seller's most important FOB function was the physical delivery of goods on board a vessel, whereas in CIF it is the symbolical delivery, i.e., delivery of documents relating to the goods rather than the goods themselves.[40] Insurance was, therefore, more pronounced in the latter, where there were more risks and less in the former for the reverse reason.

2.5 Insurance and Allocation of Export Sales' Risks

Accordingly, the common view is, and has remained, that unless the contract provides otherwise it is the duty of the FOB buyer (not the seller) to provide insurance and that the seller's only duty is to give such notice to the buyer as may enable him to insure goods during their (sea) transit. However, on closer examination, comparative duties between CIF and FOB may not be as clear-cut as they first appear, for, with modern developments in finance and especially transport technology, those differences between CIF and FOB performances have either narrowed or disappeared altogether. This is reflected in Incoterms 2010 which counsels caution.[41] It, therefore, follows that continued assumptions regarding parties' corresponding insurance duties can no longer be taken for granted and, therefore, need challenging and, may be, restating. This chapter argues that the hitherto common interpretation should be viewed with caution and only as a general rule subject to exceptions. With technological and other developments, these differences are soon disappearing and the manner of performances of both contracts converging.

Consequently, although on its face value insurance requirement does not seem to feature prominently in FOB, compared to CIF or CIP contracts, the nature and extent of the risks involved in both contracts are, and have always been almost the same, and are of equal importance. Equally, all factors considered, merchant's insurance responsibilities in both CIF and FOB contracts would on the surface appear to be the same. However, upon closer analysis, the exact nature of the parties' general and insurance obligations may be even more complicated, and more demanding, in common law FOB, considering that the contract is further divided into three categories.[42] That intricacy is summarised by Sassoon.[43] Those common law predicaments affects the insurance misconceptions between the 9 Incoterms in which insurance obligations are omitted and the 2 that have the reverse approach.

---

[40] Hence a further assumption that the CIF is a sale of documents goods rather than a sale of goods: see also, Ademuni-Odeke, "Nature of CIF Contracts", (edit).

[41] Ramberg, J *Guide to Incoterms* 2010, pp. 34–35 (The Incoterms Rules and Insurance) at 35 (when insurance is excluded).

[42] See Davis "The Various Types of FOB Contracts" Chapter XXX; Schimitthoff, The *Law and Practice of International Trade*, Chapter 2 at pp. 19-22 (edit).

[43] Sassoon, CIF *and FOB Contracts*, 5th Edn, 2012, pp.12-19 where he discusses passage of risks and property in both contracts.

2.6 Assumptions About the Ease of Insurance Where "No Obligations" Exist

For those reasons, the common view is, and has remained, that unless the contract provides otherwise it is the duty of the FOB buyer (not the seller) to provide insurance and that the seller's only duty is to give such notice to the buyer as may enable him to insure goods during their (sea) transit. However, on closer examination, comparative duties (between CIF and FOB) may not be as clear-cut as they first appear, for, with modern developments in finance and transport technology, those differences between CIF and FOB performances have either narrowed or disappeared altogether. Accordingly, such assumptions regarding parties' corresponding insurance duties can no longer be taken for granted and, therefore, need challenging and, may be, restating. This chapter argues that the hitherto common view should be viewed with caution and only as a general rule subject to exceptions.

Thus, although on its face value insurance requirement does not seem to feature prominently in FOB, compared to CIF/CIP contracts, the nature and extent of the risks involved in both contracts are, and have always been almost the same, and are of equal importance. Equally, all factors considered, merchant's insurance responsibilities in both CIF and FOB contracts would on the surface appear to be the same. However, upon closer analysis, the exact nature of the parties' general and insurance obligations may be even more complicated, and more demanding, in common law FOB, considering that in the contract is further divided into three categories as discussed ahead. That intricacy is summarised by Sassoon in the opening statement quoted at length above.

2.7 Assumptions About the Complexity Where "No Obligations" Exist

Insurance is an essential aspect of the contract. This is discussed exhaustively in Chap. 6 of the book below. There is not much to choose between the common law and incoterms on the CIF insurance. Both Chaps. 6 (CIF Common Law) and 9 (CIF Incoterms) that the seller must obtain at its own expense cargo insurance as agreed in the contract, such that the buyer, or any other person having an insurable interest in the goods, shall be entitled to claim directly from the insurer and provide the buyer with the insurance policy or other evidence of insurance cover.

The insurance shall be contracted with underwriters or an insurance company of good repute and, failing express agreement to the contrary, be in accordance with minimum cover of the Institute Cargo Clauses or any similar set of clauses. In the case of Incoterms, the duration of insurance cover shall be in accordance with Clause A5 and B5 of Incoterms latest being 2020. Unless provided the seller provides only minimal cover. However, when required by the buyer, the seller shall provide at the buyer's expense war, strikes, riots and civil commotion risk insurances if procurable. The minimum insurance shall cover the price provided in the contract plus ten per cent (i.e. 110%) and shall be provided in the currency of the contract. These issues are further elaborated in the two chapters.

2.8 Progressive Developments of Incoterms' Insurance Clauses

The evolution and progressive developments of Incoterms Insurance Clauses has closely followed technological developments in trade, communications and transportation.[44]

2.9 Limitations of Incoterms' Insurance Clauses

Equally Incoterms Insurance Clauses seem to leave out more that it seeks to regulate. Accordingly, parties to Incoterms contrasts are advised of the consequences to their insurance obligations resulting from the above limitations. Thus, with regard to the latter, although Clause A5 of CIF and CIP on insurance appears exhaustive, it too leaves out a lot on the essential aspects of the parties' adequate insurance requirements,[45] for the following reasons:

Clause A5 of CIF and CIP
(a) it emphasises the seller's insurance duty to the buyer but not to himself. It does the same for the buyer. In doing so it assumes that, once they have fulfilled the contractual obligations, the parties do not need any other insurance. However, that is not necessarily the case;

(b) for the buyer the corresponding Clause B5 provides simply that he has "no obligation" to provide insurance. As indicated below, that phrase can be misleading;

(c) it does not link [interface] risks and parties' breach of contractual obligations in the remaining 9 rules and the need for their insurance cover;

(d) it only attempts to bridge this gap in the oversights by requiring that the parties should liaise and provide notice and information affecting the duty to take out the policy, but without any adequate guidelines as to the nature and extent of the notice and information;

(e) other than that, specifying "insurance company of good repute", it does not deal with either the mechanism of procuring the policy or other alternative sources of insurance;

[44] For details see paragraph 1.4.3 above.

[45] See Ademuni-Odeke (2021), pp. 672–700.

(f) it does provide for only the minimum rather than full cover (see "Minimum Insurance" Cover immediately below); and finally

(g) it avoids the following fundament facets of the sales contract:

(i) effect of sanctions;

(ii) the imposition of tariffs;

(iii) export or import prohibitions;

(iv) force majeure or hardships;

(v) intellectual property rights; and

(vi) sanitary and phytosanitary matters.

Those public aspects of international trade, that also affects international commercial contracts, are the preserve of the WTO rules. Yet it covers only half of the parties' overall insurance needs. Detailed coverage of what Incoterms do not do and the public aspects of international commercial contracts are beyond the remit of this clause. In the author's considered opinion, Incoterms provides for about 10% coverage of international sales' insurance requirements. The other 90% are discussed in this clause.

2.10 The *"Minimum" Insurance Cover"* Problems

One of Incoterms' limitations is the provision for only the minimum insurance in the CIF and CIP contracts, leading to the need to search for additional cover elsewhere. Thus, unless otherwise provided, Incoterms provides for the provision of only the minimum insurance cover, leaving the parties to haggle for additional cover for the buyer and to cater for own insurance needs with which the rules do not seem concerned. It is the author's educated estimation that what it Incoterms provides is probably only 10% of the practical insurance requirements, the other 90% being sourced from elsewhere, namely: additional contractual, parties own needs and alternative sources such as state- sponsored insurances, export credit insurances, war risks insurance, Cargo Clauses exceptions and the minimum insurance under Cargo Clauses. There are explanations, backgrounds and developments to this state of affairs. Since their inception in 1953, Incoterms Insurance Clauses have provided for only minimum cover and based on the old Institute Cargo Clauses (Cargo Clauses) (1946) FPA. However, by Incoterms 1980 the Cargo Clauses' (1946) FPA terms were replaced by the new Cargo Clauses C's exceptions (Clauses 4–7 therein).

The Cargo Clauses A, B and C are now the principal governing terms of conditions for Incoterms, Commodity Trade and all other contracts. In the UK jurisdiction, this also coincided with the introduction of the new Lloyds Marine Form and the Insurance Companies' Policy Form replacing the old Ships and Goods (SG) Policy that had existed for nearly 400 years. Furthermore, particular average, war risks, and risks peculiar to the cargo or party's individual requirements have always been and remain excepted. Any higher cover has always been additional. For those reasons, neither the Incoterms nor the insurance clauses (minimum insurance requirements) therein consider the wider and practical requirements such as additional insurance, state restrictions and governmental interventions in shipping and cargo insurance for which the parties have to be very cautious. Consequently, parties, their insurers and lenders normally maintain intelligence for the benefit of their clients on these global insurance developments.

However, as only a flexible guide it would be daunting to expect provisions for detailed and other covers. As a flexible the CIF/CIP guide Clause A5 leaves room for parties to extend their obligations where applicable depending on parties' circumstances. It is evident from the above that, although it has some advantages, Incoterms are not perfect. (See also Chaps. 5, 8 and 10 (post))

2.11 Insurance Principles Applicable to Cargo Policies

2.11.1 Incoterms Insurance Contracts Are Contracts of Marine Insurance

2.11.1.1 Nature of the Contract

Incoterms contracts are contracts of insurance generally and marine insurance contracts in particular within sections 1 through to 3 of the MIA 1906. As such they are governed by the MIA 1906. Although not all insurance contracts are contracts of indemnity (e.g. life policies), Incoterms' policies, as marine insurance policies, are contracts of indemnity governed by that that doctrine and its corollaries. This is now covered in s.1 of the MIA, namely that: "A contract of marine insurance is a contract whereby the insurer undertakes to indemnify the assured, in a manner and to the extent thereby agreed, against marine losses, that is to say, the losses incident to marine adventure".[46] It will be apparent below that marine losses are interpreted broadly to include land and aviation risks to which Incoterms' risks are normally exposed, which also demonstrates the historical dominance of marine insurance in export trade.

2.11.1.2 Necessity of Exposure to Marine Risks

As predominantly marine activities Incoterms' shipments are exposed to marine risks and require marine cover. A number of comments are necessary here. First, although primarily intended for marine risks s.2 (1) of MIA 1906 anticipates that the policy may be extended thus: "A contract of marine insurance may, by is express terms, or by usage of trade, be extended so as to protect the assured against losses

[46] See also s.67 for definition and measure of indemnity.

on inland waters or on any land risk which may be incidental to any sea voyage". In international trade the extension is probably by trade usage. The contract would therefore cover, rail, road and multimodal transport. And although it does not provide so explicitly, it would also cover air cargo. Secondly, s.2 (2) of MIA 1906 extends its application to "any other contract other than a contract of marine insurance", which would include export and indeed all other insurance categories.

2.11.1.3 Necessity of Exposure to Maritime Adventures and Perils

The types of marine adventures and maritime perils anticipated in the act would include a number of risks to which Incoterms' shipments would be exposed. This is provided for in s 3 of MIA 1906, namely:

> **3. Marine adventure and marine perils defined**
> (1) Subject to the provisions of this Act, every lawful marine adventure may be the subject of a contract of marine insurance.
>
> (2) In particular there is a marine adventure where-
>
> (a) Any ship goods or other moveable are exposed to maritime perils. Such property is in this Act referred to as 'intangible property';
>
> (b) The earning or acquisition of any freight, passage money, commission, profit, or other pecuniary benefit, or the security of for any advances, loan, or disbursement, is endangered by the exposure of insurable property to marine perils;
>
> (c) Any liability to a third party may be incurred by the owner of, or other person interested in or responsible for, insurable property, by reason of maritime perils".
>
> "Maritime perils" means the perils consequent on, or incidental to, the navigation of the sea, that is to say, perils of the seas, fire, war perils, pirates, rovers, thieves, captures, seizures, restraints, and detainments of princes and peoples, jettisons, barratry, and any other perils, either of the like kind or which may be designated by the policy.

The section lists some, but not all, risks to which Incoterms' shipment would be exposed. These are now also contained in the ICC (post). Only elected export trade risks are covered in this chapter. War risks are in Chap. 10 (post). Although the above risks would normally refer specifically to marine risks relating to the shipowner, nevertheless those risks are shared by a modern merchant while exporting and importing cargo on Incoterms' contracts.

2.11.2 Indemnity Principles and Incoterms' Policies

Indemnity means security or compensation against loss or damage. It is a fundamental principle applicable to all insurance branches. It was introduced to discourage parties from gambling or defrauding insurance business. Hence the introduction of the *Insurance Contract (Gambling Policies) Act* 1909. The principle of indemnity is such principle of insurance stating that an insured may not be compensated by the insurance company in an amount exceeding the insured's economic loss. In type of insurance, the insured would be compensation with the amount equivalent to the actual loss and not the amount exceeding the loss. Although it has slightly different applications to life insurance, it is essential to export and hence Incoterms insurance. These are covered in ss.1 and 67 through 78 of MIA 1906

2.11.3 Coverage of Goods and Legitimate Risks:

2.11.3.1 Incoterms Policies Are to Cover Goods[47]

Although he may have to borrow (and therefore owe a bank), the Incoterm merchants' primary function is the trade in goods. Goods are defined in Rule 17 of the *Rules of Construction of the Policy* annexed to MIA 1906 as "--goods in the nature of merchandise, and does not include personal effects or provisions and stores for use on board. In the absence of any usage to the contrary, deck cargo and living animals must be insured specifically and not under the general denomination of goods".

Accordingly, in line with the definition of goods in the:

(a) *International Convention for the Unification of Certain Rules of Law relating to Bills of Lading* (Hague Rules),[48]

---

[47] Goods are defined in Rule 17 of the *Rules of Construction of the Policy* annexed to MIA 1906 as follows:

"17 The term "goods" means goods in the nature of merchandise, and does not include personal effects or provisions and stores for use on board.

In the absence of any usage to the contrary, deck cargo and living animals must be insured specifically and not under the general denomination of goods".

[48] Commonly known as the "Hague Rules", signed in Brussels, 25 August 1924 defines goods in Clause 1(c).

"Goods" includes goods, wares, merchandise and clauses of every kind whatsoever except live animals and cargo which by the contract of carriage in stated as being carried on deck and is so carried"; for insurance coverage and claims see paragraph 13.2.4 (post).

(b) The Hague-Visby Rules - The Hague Rules as Amended by the Brussels Protocol (Hague Visby Rules)1968,[49]
(c) *The United Nations Convention on the Carriage of Goods by Sea* (Hamburg Rules)[50]; and
(d) *The United Nations Convention on Contracts for the International Carriage of Goods Wholly or Partly by Sea* (Rotterdam Rules),[51]
live animals are not classified as goods. The followings are silent on carriage of live animals:
(e) *The United Nations Convention on Multimodal Transport* (MTO)[52];
(f) *The Convention on Carriage of Goods by Rail*[53];
(g) *The Convention on Carriage of Goods by Road*[54]; and
(h) *The Convention on Carriage of Goods by Air* (Warsaw Convention 1929 amended)[55]

Hence the requirement under Rule 17 of The *Rules for Interpretation of the Policy* of ensuring these risks separately and not necessarily as goods.

2.11.3.2 Incoterms Policies Should Not Be Wagering Contracts

Incoterms' merchant must take out the policy as result of engagement in legitimate business of trading in goods rather than a wager (bet), for under s.4 of MIA 1906:

[49] Commonly known as the "Hague-Visby Rules" definition of goods; for insurance coverage and claims see paragraph 13.5 (post).

'Goods' includes goods, wares, merchandise, and clauses of every kind whatsoever except live animals and cargo which by the contract of carriage is stated as being carried on deck and is so carried.

[50] Commonly known as the "Hamburg Rules" adopted in Hamburg on 31 March 1978, defines goods Clause 1(5), thus:

"Goods" includes live animals; where the goods are consolidated in a container, pallet or similar Clause of transport or where they are packed, "goods" includes such Clause of transport or packaging if supplied by the shipper". for insurance coverage and claims, see paragraph 13.2 (post).

[51] Commonly known as the "Rotterdam Rules" adopted by the UN General Assembly on 11 December 2008 defines goods in Clauses 1(24) thus: for insurance coverage and claims see paragraph 13.8 (post).

"Goods" means the wares, merchandise, and clauses of every kind whatsoever that a carrier undertakes to carry under a contract of carriage and includes the packing and any equipment and container not supplied by or on behalf of the carrier".

[52] For insurance coverage and claims see paragraph 13.2 (post).

[53] Ibid, paragraph, 13.3 (post).

[54] Ibid, paragraph, 13.4 (post).

[55] Ibid, paragraph, 13.5 (post).

4. Avoidance of wagering or gaming contracts

(1) Every contract of marine insurance by way of gaming or wagering is void.

(2) A contract of marine insurance is deemed a gaming or wagering contract

(a) Where the assured has not an insurable interest as defined by this Act, and the contract is entered into with no expectation of acquiring such an interest; or

(b) Where the policy is made "interest or no interest," or "without further proof of interest than the policy itself," or "without benefit of salvage to the insurer," or subject to any other like term:

Provided that, where there is no possibility of salvage, a policy may be effected without benefit of salvage to the insurer.

The injection of the principle of indemnity supplements anti-wagering objectives by ensuring that FOB, CIF and any other merchant is not engaged in wagering. The MIA 1906 is supplemented on this point by the *Insurance (Gambling Policies) Act* 1909

2.11.3.3 Incoterms' Policies Are Contracts of Indemnity

Indemnity is considered to be the exact compensation required to restore the insured to the financial position they enjoyed immediately before a loss occurred. Indemnity settlements can be reduced where it can be proved that there is under-insurance,[56] and therefore the insurers are only receiving a premium for a proportion of the entire value at risk. If this is the case, any claims payment will be reduced in direct proportion to the under-insurance.[57] S.67 of MIA 1906 defines as the sum which the assured can recover in respect of a loss on a policy by which he is insured, in the case of an unvalued policy to the full extent of the insurable value, or, in the case of a valued policy to the full extent of the value fixed by the policy is called the measure of indemnity. However, where there is a loss recoverable under the policy, the insurer, or each insurer if there be more than one, is liable for such proportion of the measure of indemnity as the amount of his subscription bears to the value fixed by the policy in the case of a valued policy, or to the insurable value in the case of an unvalued policy.[58]

This is a regulatory principal. This principle is observed more strictly in property insurance which includes Incoterms exports than in life insurances. The purpose of this principle is to set back the insured to the same financial position that existed before the loss or damage occurred. In marine, which includes Incoterms, the insured need not have interest at the beginning but must have at the time of life. The

[56] For Under Insurance See para 2.11.6.7.3.(post).

[57] See under Loss and Claims Chap. 12 below.

[58] See also ss79-81 which further limits the amount of indemnity which the insured can recover through subrogation and contribution.

leading insurable interest of case of *Dalby v The Indian and London Life Assurance Co*,[59] suggests that in non-marine such as life policy, the insured must have interest at the beginning but not at the time of loss [source judge and cite where possible]. Equally, the measure of indemnity in ss.67–78 of MIA 1906 governs the rules for claims. Entitlement to surplus is an exception to the indemnity [say more].

2.11.4 Incoterms Policies Should Disclosure and Not Misrepresent Material Facts

2.11.4.1 Contract of *Uberrime Fidei*

Under this insurance contract doctrine, both the parties should have faith over each other. As a client it is the duty of the Incoterms' insureds to disclose all the facts to the insurance company.[60] Although not common in export policies, any fraud or misrepresentation of facts can result into cancellation of the contract. This is covered in s.17 of MIA 1906 which provides that: "a contract of marine insurance is a contract based upon the utmost good faith and, if the utmost good faith be not observed by either party, the contract may be avoided by the other party". In essence, the principle "forbids either party by concealing what he privately knows, to draw the other into a bargain".

The principle is also part of the general contract regime. Most commercial contracts are subject to the principle of caveat emptor (let the buyer beware). Under these contracts, there is no need to disclose information that is not asked for. Insurance contracts are different in that they are based on facts which are within the knowledge of the insured, but of which insurers will not generally be aware. This is more export policies where parties may be geographically far apart. As the insurer is at a disadvantage, the law imposes a duty of *uberrima fides* or 'utmost good faith'. The principle of utmost good faith requires anyone seeking insurance to disclose all relevant facts. These are facts that would influence the judgement of a prudent underwriter in fixing the premium or determining whether they will take on the risk. Where material non-disclosure can be proved, a contract can be voided. In a new development, duties of disclosure will no longer apply to personal policies from 6 April 2013 after the coming into force of the Insurance Act 2015, which made amendments thereto.

2.11.4.2 Disclosure

Parties to insurance of international trade are bound by the requirement of disclosure. In *Berger v Pollock*[61] Justice Kerr suggested that disclosure is part of the principle of utmost good faith.[62] The principle of disclosure applies to all insurance

[59] *Dalby v The Indian and London Life Assurance Co* (1845) 15 CB 365.

[60] See generally, "*Uberrime Fides*", 32 *MLR* 615.

[61] *Berger v Pollock* [1973] 2 Lloyds 442.

[62] For an overvaluation amounting to non-disclosure see *Berger v Pollock* [1973] 2 Lloyds 442 Kerr J.

contracts including FOB and CIF contracts. This was the subject of US Court of Appeal decision in *The Papoos*.[63] It is covered in ss.17-21 of MIA 1906. The claimant insured might lose if he did not disclose when taking out cover. This duty has now been amended by the *Insurance Act* 2015. [See also Chap. 13 on Claims]

2.11.4.3 Representation

Representation is also part of the wider principle of utmost good faith[64] discussed above. The principle of representation applies to all insurance contracts including Incoterms insurance contract and the wider international trade. It is also covered in ss.17-21of MIA 1906. Section 20 provides that:

> **20 Representations pending negotiation of contract**
> (1) Every material representation made by the assured or his agent to the insurer during the negotiations for the contract, and before the contract is concluded, must be true. If it be untrue the insurer may avoid the contract.
>
> (2) A representation is material which would influence the judgment of a prudent insurer in fixing the premium, or determining whether he will take the risk.
>
> (3) A representation may be either a representation as to a matter of fact or as to a matter of expectation or belief.
>
> (4) A representation as to a matter of fact is true, if it be substantially correct, that is to say, if the difference between what is represented and what is actually correct would not be considered material by a prudent insurer.
>
> (5) A representation as to a matter of expectation or belief is true if it be made in good faith.
>
> (6) A representation may be withdrawn or corrected before the contract is concluded.
>
> (7) Whether a particular representation be material or not is, in each case, a question of fact.
>
> (8) This section does not apply in relation to a contract of marine insurance if it is a consumer insurance contract within the meaning of the Consumer Insurance (Disclosure and Representations) Act 2012.[65]

---

[63] *The Papoos* [1970] 1 Lloyds Rep 178, US Court of Appeal.

[64] See "Mistakes and Misrepresentation", 119 NLJ 1111.

[65] 20(8) was added (6.4.2013) by *Consumer Insurance (Disclosure and Representations) Act 2012* (c. 6), ss. 11(2) (c), 12(2) (with s. 12(4) (5)); S.I. 2013/450, art. 2.

2.11.5 Warranties & Conditions in Incoterms Policies[66]

2.11.5.1 Warranties

Parties should be aware of the peculiarity of insurance generally and marine insurance law use of the terms 'condition' and 'warranty'. In English law, a condition typically describes a part of the contract that is fundamental to the performance of that contract, and, if breached, the non-breaching party is entitled not only to claim damages but to terminate the contract on the basis that it has been repudiated by the party in breach. By contrast, a warranty is not fundamental to the performance of the contract and breach of a warranty, while giving rise to a claim for damages, does not entitle the non-breaching party to terminate the contract. The meaning of these terms is reversed in insurance law. Indeed, a warranty if not strictly complied with will automatically discharge the insurer from further liability under the contract of insurance.

The assured has no defence to his breach, unless he can prove that the insurer, by his conduct, has waived his right to invoke the breach, possibility provided in s.34(3) of MIA 1906. Furthermore, in the absence of express warranties MIA 1906 will imply them, notably a warranty to provide a seaworthy vessel at the commencement of the voyage in a voyage policy (s.39(1)) and a warranty of legality of the insured voyage (s.41)]. Thus insurance, a warranty is that by which the assured undertakes that some particular thing shall or shall not be done, or that some conditions shall be fulfilled or whereby he affirms or negatives the existence of a particular state of facts. Warranties are the statement according to which insured person promises to do or not to do a particular thing or to fulfil or not to fulfil a certain condition.

2.11.5.2 Express and Implied Warranties

Warranties are of two types. Express warranties are those warranties, which are expressly included or incorporated in the policy by reference. These are not mentioned in the policy at all but are tacitly understood by the parties to the contract and are as fully binding as express warranties. Warranties can also be classified as:

2.11.5.2.1 Affirmative Warranty

Affirmative warranty is the promise, which insured gives to exist or not to exist certain facts

2.11.5.2.2 Promissory Warranties

Promissory warranty in terms of the law of insurance is a warranty that facts will continue to be as stated all through the policy period. Such a warranty assures that a fact or condition is and will remain to be true. Promissory warranty is the promise in which insured promises that he will do or not do a certain thing up to the period of policy. They are different from conditions (below). A condition must be performed prior to the completion of another action. A warranty, by contrast, is essentially a promise that the facts a buyer gives a seller are genuine. It's not possible for

[66] See John Birds, "Warranties in Insurance Proposal Forms", [1977] JBL 231.

a contract of sale to be fulfilled unless the conditions are fulfilled. In marine insurance, implied warranties are very important. Warranties and conditions are covered in ss.33–41 of MIA 1906.

2.11.5.3 Conditions

The insurance policy does lump conditions and warranties together without distinguishing. That can be misleading, if not properly explained. Warranty and condition in insurance has a different meaning from those in ordinary contracts. In insurance a warranty is not merely a condition but statement of fact. Warranties are more vigorously insisted upon than the conditions because the contract comes to an end if a warranty is broken whether the warranty was material or not. A condition is different. In *W and J. Lane v Sprat*[67] Justice Roskil held: "By 'condition', I mean a contractual term of the policy, any breach of which by the assured will in the event of loss otherwise payable under the policy afford underwriters a defence to any claim irrespective of whether there is any causal connection between the breach of the contractual term and the loss"[68] Thus, a condition is a term of the policy the fulfilment of which the validity of the policy or the liability of the insurers depends. However, in case of condition or representation the contract comes to end only when these were material or important.

2.11.6 Insurable Interest and Insurable Value in Incoterms Policies

2.11.6.1 Insurable Interest

The Incoterms insured must have an insurable interest in the subject matter. At a point of insuring or claiming the claimant party must have an insurable insurance in the subject matter of the policy. The requirement supports the principle of indemnity to which export policy is subject. It is another fundamental principle of all insurance contracts including the Incoterms' insurance contracts. Therefore, the Incoterms merchant should use insurance solely for protection of export/import trade rather than for gambling which are prohibited by s.4 of the MIA 1906. To benefit the merchant must fulfil the conditions of s.5 of the MIA 1906 by standing to lose or gain from the export process. The section provides that subject to the provisions of the Act, every person has an insurable interest who is interested in a marine adventure. In particular, a person is interested in a marine adventure where he stands in any legal or equitable relation to the adventure or to any insurable property at risk therein, in consequence of which he may benefit by the safety or due arrival of insurable property, or may be prejudiced by its loss, or by damage thereto, or by the detention thereof, or may incur liability in respect thereof.

Section 6(1) must have been drafted with the interests of the shipper of goods such as the FOB and CIF seller in mind as his interests might attach at various times

[67] *W and J. Lane v Sprat* [1969]2 Lloyds Rep 229.

[68] Ibid at 236.

before contract, during manufacture or shipment or purchasing goods afloat. The section provides thus:

2.11.6.2 When Interest Attaches!

Unlike other types of insurance policies, it is not easy to determine when interest attaches in export policies. Otherwise, the guideline is contained in s6 of the MIA 1906 that the assured must be interested in the subject-matter insured at the time of the loss though he need not be interested when the insurance is effected. However, this is provided that where the subject-matter is insured 'lost or not lost', the assured may recover although he may not have acquired his interest until after the loss, unless at the time effecting the contract of insurance the assured was aware of the loss, and the insurer was not

Thus, under this principle of insurance, the insured exporter/importer must have interest in the subject matter of the insurance. Absence of insurance makes the contract null and void. If there is no insurable interest, an insurance company will not issue a policy. An insurable interest must exist at the time of the purchase of the insurance. For example, a creditor has an insurable interest in the life of a debtor, a person is considered to have an unlimited interest in the life of their spouse etc.

2.11.6.3 Insurable Interest Clause!

In relation to recovery after loss, cargo clause A reinforces the insurable interest requirement of s.6 of MIA 1906, thus:

> **11. Insurable Interest Clause**
> 11.1. In order to recover under this insurance the Assured must have an insurable interest in the subject-matter insured at the time of the loss.
>
> 11.2. Subject to 11.1 above, the Assured shall be entitled to recover for insured loss occurring during the period covered by this insurance, notwithstanding that the loss occurred before the contract of insurance was concluded, unless the Assured were aware of the loss and the Underwriters were not.

The rest of the guidelines on insurable interest are covered in ss. ss 3 and 4 through 16 of MIA 1906.

2.11.6.4 Extent of Cargo Insurable Interests

2.11.6.4.1 Insurable Interest Defined. [s5]

Insurable interest is now codified in s. 5 of MIA 1906 as follows.

> **5 Insurable interests defined.**
> (1) Subject to the provisions of this Act, every person has an insurable interest who is interested in a marine adventure.
>
> (2) In particular a person is interested in a marine adventure where he stands in any legal or equitable relation to the adventure or to any insurable property at

risk therein, in consequence of which he may benefit by the safety or due arrival of insurable property, or may be prejudiced by its loss, or by damage thereto, or by the detention thereof, or may incur liability in respect thereof.

2.11.6.4.2 Possession Not Necessary

It was noticed that the party that has property or title bears the risk. However, for that party to be liable, physical possession of the insured cargo is not necessary; it is the ownership or title to the goods that gives rise to insurable interest and entitlement to indemnity. Physical possession may give rise to liability but not an indemnity insurance as in bailor/bailee obligations of the carrier.

2.11.6.4.3 Partial Interest [s.8]

Full interest in the subject matter is not a prerequisite to entitlement to insurable interest. In a partial-interest property, ownership is broken down into fractional interests from a single, unified ownership. These fractions are expressed as percentage interests. Oftentimes, an owner will split a property among multiple inheritors, commonly family members, creating a partial-interest property. Equally, full ownership of the insured cargo or property is not necessary, partial ownership is all that matters. Thus, an insured can cover the whole exposure or just the proportion of the whole. This principle is now enshrined in s.8 of MIA1906 on partial interest, which confirms that a partial interest of any nature is insurable

2.11.6.4.4 Defeasible Interest [s7]

To give rise to insurable interest, contemporary existence of the subject is not necessary; it relates to future goods and/or interest too. In insurance a defeasible interest is insurable, is also known as a contingent interest (see immediately below). In particular, where the buyer of goods has insured them, he has an insurable interest, notwithstanding that he might, at his election, have rejected the goods, or have treated them as at the seller's risk, by reason of the latter's delay in making delivery or otherwise. For the same reason as above a defeasible. This is now covered in s.7 of MIA 1906, thus:

> **7 Defeasible or contingent interest.**
> (1) A defeasible interest is insurable, as also is a contingent interest.
>
> (2) In particular, where the buyer of goods has insured them, he has an insurable interest, notwithstanding that he might, at his election, have rejected the goods, or have treated them as at the seller's risk, by reason of the latter's delay in making delivery or otherwise.
>
> Defeasible interest is also sometimes referred to as contingent interest.

2.11.6.4.5 Contingent Interest [s7]

Defeasible interest is an interest is one that exists at the commencement but ceases during the period covered by the insurance. Aspects of defeasible interest fall under contingent interest. A contingency refers to a chance occurrence or uncertain outcome, the basis of insurance generally and export insurance in particular due to especially external risks in the latter. It is an interest that does not take effect until a condition (contingency) has been met in the context of insurance, contingency insurance supplements a primary policy or covers remote risks the primary one would be slow to cover. Future interests (contingent) are, therefore, covered together with defeasible interest (see immediately above) in the same provision (in s.7) of MIA 1906 above and further discussed in details in Chap. 9 (post). In marine cargo insurance, where the buyer has a defeasible interest, the seller has a corresponding contingent interest, because, unless the buyer exercises the option to reject the goods, that is to say, unless that "contingency" occurs, the seller's interest does not arise.

2.11.6.4.6 Interests in Profits

A person has an insurable interest in property whenever he would profit by or gain some advantage by its continued existence and suffer some loss or disadvantage by its destruction. This would include Incoterms and other export merchants. If they would sustain such loss, it is immaterial that exporters and importers are in the business to make a profit and, therefore, living and not just for the love of it. Accordingly, as commercial men and women Incoterms merchants are in it to recoup their expenses and include decent profits.

Profit is therefore a recognisable insurable interest. Profits are one of the insurable risks under the MIA. Furthermore, in the US, Section 1885 (Insurable Interests in profits) of the *California Insurance Code* provides that:

> **Section 1885 - Insurable interest in profits**
> In marine insurance, a person who has an interest in the thing from which profits are expected to proceed, has an insurable interest in the profits.[69]

2.11.6.4.7 Interests in Advance Freights[s12]

Also known as "pre-paid freight", advance freights payable in advance is at the risks of the cargo owner who includes it in the value of the goods insured under a cargo policy. But freight payable only, on the delivery of the goods at the destination, is at the risk of the ship-owner who has the insurable interest in it and therefore can insure it. An advance freight is an insurable interest. So, a party (normally the seller) whose duty includes contracting for and paying advance freight such as in the CIF and CIP has an insurable insurance for which they can take out a policy. This is now the subject of s.12 of MIA 1906. Thus, in the case advance freight, the person advancing the freight has an insurable interest, in so far as such freight is not repayable in case of loss.

[69] Ca. Ins. Code § 1885--Current through the 2021 Legislative Session--Enacted by Stats. 1935, Ch. 145.

2.11.6.4.8 When Interest Must Exist

Decided cases have established that the interest only has to exist at the inception of the contract and not at the time of loss. Once the policy has been properly created, the policyholder does not need to continue to hold an insurable interest in the life insured. This is covered by Clause 8 (Transit Clause) of cargo clauses A, B and C. Following on from the provision of s.7 of MIA 1906 above, it is clear that there is no need for interest at the commencement of the of the manufacture, purchase or shipment of the insured subject matter. However, there must be interest at the loss or damage and in order to claim. In practice an insured can have interest in goods prior to the sales contract. Further guidelines on this are from the cargo clauses.

2.11.6.4.9 Insurable Interests in Reinsurance Contracts

Insurance is purchased to provide protection from covered losses; reinsurance guards the insurance company from too many losses. They both contractually transfer the cost of the loss to the company issuing the policy. They both have deductibles. For insurable interest purposes, reinsurance contracts are treated the same way as the ordinary insurance contracts. An insurer can reinsure but the original insured has no interest in the reinsurance. This is now the subject of s.9 (Re-insurance) of MIA 1906, providing that

(1) The insurer under a contract of marine insurance has an insurable interest in his risk, and may re-insure in respect of it.
(2) Unless the policy otherwise provides, the original assured has no right or interest in respect of such reinsurance.

2.11.6.5 Characteristics of Insurable Risks

In insurable interest is an economic stake in an event for which a person or entity purchases an insurance policy to mitigate the risk of loss Insurable interest is nearly a legal right to insure. It is the legal financial interest of a man on a property, the interest being such that by the safety of the subject-matter he is benefited, by the loss, damage or destruction thereof he is prejudiced. A risk that conforms to the norms and specifications of the insurance policy in such a way that the criterion for insurance. However, not all risks are insurable. Insurable risks have certain characteristics:

(i) they must be capable of financial measurement;
(ii) there must be a large enough number of similar risks;
(iii) they must not be against public policy;
(iv) the premium needs to be reasonable; and
(v) there must be an 'insurable interest' for the person insuring.

Insurable interest is where you have a valid reason to insure and stand to suffer a direct financial loss if the event insured against occurs. Insurable interest exists when an insured derives a financial or other benefit from the continuous existence of an insured object. For example, a person has an insurable interest in their own car—but not in their neighbour's car. To demonstrate insurable interest, there must be something tangible that can be insured—such as property, life or rights imposed by law. Apart from ss4-15 of the MIA 1906, they are also a requirement in clause 11 of all the cargo clauses and in all commodity trade sales and insurance contracts.

2.11.6.6 Insurable Value

A problem might arise with regards the legislative provisions in section 16(2), 16(3) and 16(4) of MIA 1906 as to insurable value if they do not tally with Clause A5 of the CIF and CIP for instance regarding the 110% value. Most export policies allow for valuation to include expected profits. However, the CIF and CIP contracts enshrine that valuable in the contracts in the Incoterms which valuation has now become part of the common law. This is covered in s.16 of MIA 1906 providing that:

> **16 Measure of insurable value.**
> Subject to any express provision or valuation in the policy, the insurable value of the subject-matter insured must be ascertained as follows:
>
> (1) In insurance on ship, the insurable value is the value, at the commencement of the risk, of the ship, including her outfit, provisions and stores for the officers and crew, money advanced for seamen's wages, and other disbursements (if any) incurred to make the ship fit for the voyage or adventure contemplated by the policy, plus the charges of insurance upon the whole: The insurable value, in the case of a steamship, includes also the machinery, boilers, and coals and engine stores if owned by the assured, and, in the case of a ship engaged in a special trade, the ordinary fittings requisite for that trade:
>
> (2) In insurance on freight, whether paid in advance or otherwise, the insurable value is the gross amount of the freight at the risk of the assured, plus the charges of insurance:
>
> (3) In insurance on goods or merchandise, the insurable value is the prime cost of the property insured, plus the expenses of and incidental to shipping and the charges of insurance upon the whole:
>
> (4) In insurance on any other subject-matter, the insurable value is the amount at the risk of the assured when the policy attaches, plus the charges of insurance.

The value should be enough to cover all charges, expenses and reasonable profits but not too much to constitute misrepresentation. The insurable value of common law FOB will be covered in Chap. 4 while those of CIF will be the subject of Chap. 7. The Incoterms insurance value of especially CIF and CIP are subject to cargo clauses and the "minimum insurance" and 110% requirements of Clause A5 of CIF and CIP expounded in Chap. 8 (post). Otherwise, the doctrine of indemnity is based on the insurable value, whereas the marine insurance is mostly based on insured value. As in valued and unvalued policies below, the purpose of the valuation is to predetermine the worth of insured. The issue of the measurement of insurance value is also relevant for claims purposes [See Claims, Chap. 13 ahead].

2.11.6.7 Rights of Insurer on Payment

2.11.6.7.1 Subrogation

Subrogation has is not a preserve of insurance although in the latter I has a specific meaning. The insurance principle of subrogation, which applies to Incoterms insurance contracts, enables the insured to claim the amount from the third party responsible for the loss. It allows the insurer to pursue legal methods to recover the amount of loss. Taking an example from motor insurance, if an insured driver gets injured in a road accident, due to reckless driving of a third party, the driver's insurance company will compensate him/her for the loss and will also sue the third party to recover the money paid as claim. Thus, under the principle, if a policyholder has a claim paid by their insurer, they may also have a right to pursue funds from another source, such as a third-party who caused the incident. The principle of subrogation allows the insurer to pursue any rights or remedies which the policyholder may possess, always in the name of the insured.

This also ensures that the insured only receives the indemnity settlement entitled to and therefore they will not profit from the incident. However, it must be noted that in certain policies such as *Yorkshire Insurance Co Ltd v Nesbit Shipping Co Ltd*[70] including export policies such as *Lucas v Export Credit Guarantee Department*[71] especially those involving export credit guarantees[72] where the amount received by the insured exceeds insurable value, then the principle of subrogation might be "suspended". In those instances, the insured has been allowed to retain the surplus. The principle is linked to indemnity (above), double or over insurance, under insurance and contributions (below). The principle is now contained in s. 79 of the MIA 1906. Its full effect will be further dealt with under Losses and Claims Chapter including Air Cargo (War)and Air Cargo (Strikes) in Chap. 12 below/ cargo clauses.

2.11.6.7.2 Double Insurance

A principle applicable to Incoterms insurance contracts, double or over insurance is contained in s.32 the MIA 1906. Double insurance denotes insurance of same subject matter with two different companies or with the same company under two different policies. Insurance is possible in case of indemnity contract like fire, marine and property insurance.[73] Double insurance policy is adopted where the financial position of the insurer is doubtful. The insured cannot recover more than the actual loss and cannot claim the whole amount from both the insurers. Double insurance occurs when a business has insurance cover in respect of the same risk and subject matter from more than one insurer. Double insurance is not of itself a problem, but

---

[70] *Yorkshire Insurance Co Ltd v Nisbet Shipping Co Ltd* [1962 2 QBD 330.

[71] *Lucas v Export Credit Guarantee Department* [1974] 1WLR 909.

[72] Ibid.

[73] For apportionment of claims in the event of double insurance see 21 SG 652.

it can lead to insurers arguing about whether they need to pay out at all causing unwanted delay in the processing of claims [See also under Chap. 13 post)

2.11.6.7.3 Under Insurance

Underinsurance refers to an insufficient insurance policy. Whether it's a home damaged by a hurricane or fire, or an insured person experiencing a serious disease or accident, insurance should ideally cover enough of the expense that the policyholder can manage the difference. An Incoterms' party might wish to be self-insured for part of the risk and only insure the other part. Alternatively, the insured might wish to declare a lower insurable for the cargo than a true higher value. That is what under insurance is about. There are many reasons why an insured might wish to pursue this action. However, intention to defraud the insurer should not be one of them. *Fifth Liverpool Star Bowkett Building Society v Travellers' Accidents Insurance Co*[74] decided that unless there is an average clause in the policy, the assured is entitled to recover the whole amount of his loss up to the sum insured. A subset of subrogation, the principle applies to Incoterms insurance contracts. It supports subrogation and indemnity principles (above) and is contained in s.81 of MIA 1906.The effect of under insurance is covered in details under Loss and Claims, Chap. 13 below

2.11.6.7.4 Contribution

Discussed in *Commercial Union Assurance v Hayden*,[75] this principle deals with the effect of double or over insurance and under insurance and is applicable to Incoterms insurance contracts. Under the principle, an insured party may have policies with two or more insurers covering the same risk, although no necessarily with equal degrees of liability. Therefore, in the event of a claim, all of the insurers should pay an equitable proportion of the claim payment. Contribution is the right of an insurer to call upon the other insurers to share the costs of such a claim payment. The fundamental point is that, if an insurer has paid a claim in full, it can recoup a proportion of the costs from the other insurers of the risk. The principle is contained in s.80 of the MIA 1906 and it too is covered in details under Loss and Claims-Chapter 13 (post).

2.11.6.8 Loss, Damage and Claims

2.11.6.8.1 Proximate Cause

In the complex and wide-ranging industry in which he operates the Incoterms insured should also be aware of the doctrine of proximate cause. Although dealt with in details in the Loss and Claims Chapter of the book below, suffice to note here that proximate cause literally means the 'nearest cause' or 'direct cause'. This principle is applicable when the loss is the result of two or more causes, a common

[74] *Fifth Liverpool Star –Bowkett Building Society v Travellers' Accidents Insurance Co* (1893) 5 TLR 221.

[75] See *Commercial Union Assurance v Hayden* [1977] 1 All ER 441 CA.

feature of export and transportation insurance. The proximate cause means; the most dominant and most effective cause of loss is considered. This principle is applicable when there are series of causes of damage or loss.

That said the Incoterms policy will define the perils or insured events that cover is provided for. For example, a building insurance policy will provide various covers as standard—such as fire, lightning strikes and earthquakes—and cover for additional risks, such as escape of water, storm or accidental damage, can be requested. All contracts are subject to terms and conditions that will exclude certain causes of loss. Therefore, in the event of a claim, it is important to ascertain the cause of the loss in order to determine if that cause is insured or excluded. There may be multiple elements involved in a claim, so it is the 'proximate cause' that is taken into account. The proximate cause is the dominant cause that sets in play a chain of events. For example, if lightning damaged a building and weakened a wall, following which the weakened wall was blown down by high winds, lightning would be considered the proximate cause. See also Chap. 13 (post)

2.11.6.8.2 Constructive Total Loss

A constructive total loss is an insurance term where the cost of a repair for an item (e.g., house, boat or car) is more than the current value of that item. It can also refer to an insurance claim that is settled for the entire amount of a property on the basis that the cost to repair or recover the damaged property exceeds replacement cost or market value. A constructive total loss is when the cost for repair of an item (e.g., house, boat, or car) is more than the current value of that item. It also refers to the insurance claim that is settled for the full value of the associated coverage. Under section 60 of the MIA1906, an assured shipowner can claim for a constructive total loss (CTL) if the costs of repairing the damage (inclusive of salvage charges and other expenses) would be more than the value of the ship when repaired [Chap. 13!!]

2.11.6.8.3 Actual Total Loss

Actual total loss is a loss that occurs when an insured property is destroyed or damaged to such an extent that it can be neither recovered nor repaired for further use. Often, an actual total loss triggers the maximum settlement possible according to the terms of the insurance policy. A loss that occurs when the insured property is totally destroyed or is damaged in such a way that it can be neither recovered nor repaired for further use, or the insured is irretrievably deprived of it. Usually, this indicates the maximum settlement possible according to the terms of the policy. See Chap. 13 below.

2.11.6.9 Abandonment

2.11.6.9.1 What It Is

Abandonment is not defined in the Act. However, the nearest definition is that of the Abandonment Clause. A clause in a property insurance contract that, under certain circumstances, permits the property owner to abandon lost or damaged property and still claim a full settlement amount. A clause in a property insurance contract that, under certain circumstances, permits the property owner to abandon lost or damaged property and still claim a full settlement amount. If the insured party's property cannot be recovered, or the cost to recover or repair it is more than its total value, it can be abandoned and the insured party is entitled to a full settlement amount. Abandonment and all its requirements are now covered in ss. 62 of the MIA 1906 and discussed in details in Chap. 13 on claims [Chap. 13]

2.11.6.9.2 As a Prerequisite for Claim

One of the most important principles an Incoterms or any other insured needs to know is abandonment. The doctrine means different things in varying disciplines. However, in insurance, it only applies to or had its origins in marine insurance. In marine insurance it means the right of the owner of an insured property to abandon it in two scenarios, first where its loss cannot be avoided (called actual total loss or ATL), or secondly, where the cost of repairing the damage exceeds its value (called constructive total loss or CTL). The insured party can still claim full settlement from the insurer (who becomes the owner of the abandoned cargo), after serving the notice of abandonment subject to the conditions of the insurance policy. Most non-marine insurance policies (such as homeowners insurance policy), however, specifically prohibit abandonment of the insured property under any circumstance. It is covered generally in ss.55-66 of the MIA 1906. It is not defined by the Act. These are dealt with in details in the Loss and Claims Chap. 12 of the book below.

2.11.6.9.3 Notice of Abandonment

For claims purposes, an Incoterms insured is subject to the requirement for abandonment. It has several variations. In law, abandonment is the relinquishment, giving up or renunciation of an interest, claim, civil proceedings, appeal, privilege, possession, or right, especially with the intent of never again resuming or reasserting it. In marine insurance, the notice of abandonment is essentially given to die insurer to claim the loss as a constructive total loss. If he fails to do so, the loss can only be treated as a partial loss. It is normally included in a policy by an abandonment clause. An abandonment clause in a property insurance contract, under certain circumstances, permits the property owner to abandon lost or damaged property and still claim a full settlement amount.

The notice can be given orally or in writing. In practice it is a formal notice of relinquishment or unconditional surrender of all rights to a property, cargo, or ship by its insured owner to the insurer in the event of a constructive total loss. By this notice the insured party declares its intention to treat the loss as actual total loss. The notice must be given with reasonable diligence otherwise (or in the absence of a notice) the loss may be considered partial. In the UK, s. 62 of the MIA 1906 provides for requirement of the notice of abandonment. The Act forms the basis of all common law jurisdiction on the subject. See Chap. 13 below on Claims and Settlement

2.11.6.9.4 Effect of Abandonment

Rules for abandonment are complex. Insurers do not normally accept the notice for reasons of not prejudicing themselves and to give themselves time to minimise the potential loss, which can put the insurer in a limbo. However, barring any fraudulent intentions or other breach the situation is normally resolved. The legal effects of abandonment are now contained in s. 63 of the MIA 1906.

2.11.6.9.5 Assignment of Contract and Policy

Finally, but not least our insureds should be aware of the operation of assignment. This is more important in export policies such as Incoterms contracts where seller's/ consignors' shipments are intended for the benefit of the buyers/consignees. Assignment is a complex subject, but we will summarise here. As marine policy Incoterms' contracts are is assignable unless they contain terms expressly prohibiting assignment. They may be assigned either before or after loss. As marine policies they may be assigned by endorsement thereon or on other customary manner. A marine policy which governs Incoterms insurance is freely assignable unless assignment is express prohibited. As marine policies they are not incidents of sale. So, if there is intention to assign a policy when interest passes, e.g., through tender of the documents,[76] there must be an agreement to this effect.

2.12 Obtaining Insurances Contracts

2.12.1 General Introduction

There are a number of possible options when deciding where Incoterms or anyone else can go for a cargo insurance policy. However, parties should note that enterprises with specialist knowledge of this type of insurance are likely to have more claims experience and value-added services, although this may be reflected in any premium (price) they charge. Ait is also advisable that the merchant, where possible gets quotations from a number of suppliers before they make a decision. But first, they will also need to decide the form their policy should take. This will generally depend on their circumstances, history and trade patterns. Be that as it may it is common to get policies advice and/or policies from the following establishments:

2.12.2 Sources of Cargo Insurance

(a) Insurance Companies;
(b) Freight forwarders;
(c) Banks and Finance Institutions;
(d) Insurance Brokers;
(e) A general insurance business;

[76] See Chap. 11 on Tender of Insurance Documents.

(f) Carriers;
(g) Local Chambers of Commerce; and
(h) Online.

2.12.3 Placement of the Policy

(a) Submission of application form with the following details;
(b) Name of the shipper or consignor (the insured);
(c) Full description of nature of goods to be insured;
(d) Method and type of packing;
(e) Voyage (Point of commencement & Destination);
(f) Mode of Transit e.g., Sea, Air, Rail, Road;
(g) Risk Cover required;
(h) Quotation from the Insurance Company;
(i) Payment of Premium; and
(j) Issue of Cover Note/Policy Document

A Cover Note is a document granting cover provisionally pending the issue of a regular policy.

2.12.4 Who Can Contract For Insurance in Export Trade?

Insurance is often compulsory in many export trades contracts. It can be the obligation of the exporter or the importer to pay the insurance cost on the shipment, depending on the terms of the contract. However, the need for insurance goes beyond contractual obligations, and there are several valid arguments for buying it before dispatching the export cargo.

Goods should only be insured for transit by one of the following three parties:

(a) The Forwarding Agent on behalf of exporter or importer;
(b) The Exporter (shipper, consignor, seller), eventually transferring the policy to importer or his assignees; and
(c) The Importer (shipper, consignee, buyer), transferring it to subsequent buyers or assignees.

2.13 Policies and Loss Reliefs Available to Incoterms' Contractual Parties

2.13.1 Parties' Benefits of Other Policies

In addition to his own policy, including seller/buyer's interest policies, the insured might benefit from other policies taken by, especially carriers, to cover the same subject matter for the same risks or under carriers' liabilities. Additional policies might include of freight-forwarders, tortfeasors and buyers (in case of sellers) or sellers (in case of buyers).

2.13.2 Cargo Owner's Cargo Policy

2.13.2.1 Shipper's Cargo Policies

A cargo policy of insurance is the vehicle used to insure most goods moving in international trade. Most cargo policies do not automatically insure the seller or buyer when their responsibility for loss or damage is solely within either the country of origin or solely within the country of destination. Coverage for these exposures, however, can usually be added to a cargo policy by endorsement, or they may be covered under the assured's domestic transit or property insurance policies. However, the cargo owner can also benefit from the carrier's policy or charterer's policy below, where the loss has been occasioned by the carrier or charterers' negligence.

2.13.2.2 Consignor's [Other than Seller] Policy

Some, but not all, shippers are consignors. If the Incoterms' seller ships the goods, he is the consignor. The consignor, in a contract of carriage, is the person sending a shipment to be delivered whether by land, sea or air. Ordinary FOB and related consignors are not shippers but those of FOB with additional duties are. All CIF/CIP and related Incoterms' shippers, except those purchasing afloat are consignor. Some carriers, such as national postal entities, use the term "sender" or "shipper" but in the event of a legal dispute the proper and technical term "consignor" will generally be used. The consignor is the sender of a consignment while the consignee is the receiver of the consignment. The consignee may be a buyer or just an agent who acts on behalf of the consignor. The ownership of the goods or the consignment remains with the consignor until the goods have been paid for in full by the consignee

2.13.2.3 Consignee's Policy

In most contracts, including Incoterms ones, the buyer is the consignee. In a contract of carriage, the consignee is the entity who is financially responsible (the buyer) for the receipt of a shipment. Generally, but not always, the consignee is the same as the receiver. However, a consignee who has resold goods ceases to be one in favour of the second consignee (assignee). If sender sends a widget to receiver via a delivery service, sender is the consignor and receiver is the consignee. The difference between a shipper and a consignee is that the consignee is the receiver of the shipment and is usually the owner of the goods. This may be an individual or an exporting/importing company

2.13.2.4 Seller's Policy

Incoterms sellers are exporters and their policies are sellers' policies. This insurance protects exporters against non-payment of receivables by foreign importers. Key factors to be considered when purchasing export credit insurance include: The risks covered by the insurer (political, commercial) A seller can be, but may not necessarily be a shipper or consignor. A CIF seller who ships the goods himself is a shipper and consignor but one who buys and sells afloat. An Incoterms CIF/CIP seller is the policy holder of the insurance which transfers to the buyer who becomes the policy holder. But the Incoterms party who takes own his own additional policy (see Chaps. 5, 8 and 10) to cover contingencies or sellers' interests retains and remains the owner of that policy

2.13.3 Sailing [Statutory] Policies

2.13.3.1 Voyage Policies

Seven of the eleven Incoterms are subject to maritime transport and therefore subject to voyage policies. The policy is issued to cover a particular voyage from one port to another and from one place to another. The policy mentions the port of departure and the port of destination, between which the risks are generally underwritten. This policy is not suitable for hull insurance as a ship usually does not operate over a particular route only. However, this policy may include time factor also as from Bombay to London for one year. In this case the risk may be covered from one place to another covering a period of one year. The policy is used mostly in case of cargo insurance. The goods remain covered even when the ship halts at intermediate ports. The risks at the port of departure and at the port of destination may be covered by incorporating suitable, clauses in the policy. The liability of the insurer continues during landing and re-shipping of the goods. Voyage policies are defined in s.25 of the MIA 1906 as follows that

2.13.3.2 Time Policies

The seven Incoterms are eligible to time policies. Under this policy, the subject-matter is insured for a definite period of time, e.g., from 6 a.m. of 1st January, 1976 to 6 a.m. of 1st January, 1977. The policy is generally taken for one year although it may be for less than one year. This policy is commonly more used for hull insurance than for the cargo insurance. The policy may cover, while navigating the vessel or while under construction. Risks covered under construction are for more than 12 months. This was the subject of *Elcock v Thomson*.[77] There are standard clauses in relation to freight, premium, interests, etc., which are added to this policy. The time policy may be taken in case of goods and other movable vessels. See under voyage policies above. It may a short, medium or long-term time policies and governed by time charterparties. Modern practice is to have longest times known as bareboat charters and done under bareboat charterparties. Hence the text in the last two paragraphs of s.25 (1) above that: "and where the contract is to insure the subject-matter for a definite period of time the policy is called a "time policy.".

[77] See Campania Maritima Spa Brasilio SA Oceanus Mutual Underwriting Association (Bermuda) [1976] 3 All ER 243 CA.

2.13.3.3 Mixed Policies

The policy is issued to avoid the complication of the principle of insurable interest. These are called 'Policy Proof of Interest' and are honoured by the insurer even in absence of insurable interest. This policy is based on mutual understanding, so, it is called honoured policies. This is also called wagering policies because insurable interest is not required; consequently, it cannot be legally enforceable. This policy is a combination of time and voyage policies. It covers the risks during a period of time within which several voyages could be completed. A mixed policy means a policy that covers the aspects of both a voyage policy and a time policy. Like inflation targeting, a mixed policy approach is usually in practice in U.S. Unemployment and market bubbles are the primary goals of a mixed policy. A mixed charterparty is simply a combination of voyage and time where the hirer takes advantage of better turn arounds without losing out on time. Such policies may include two months with a minimum number of voyages and to cover the last voyage in the event of lapse of time. Hence the expression in section 25 that: "A contract for both voyage and time may be included in the same policy"

2.13.3.4 Valued Policies

Incoterm merchants can opt for a valued or unvalued policies. Under the former policy the value of loss to be compensated is fixed and remains constant throughout the risk except where there is fraud and excessive over-valuation. The value of the subject-matter is agreed between the insurer and the assured at the time of taking the insurance. It is also called insured value or agreed value. This was the subject of *Compania Maritima Spa Brasilio SA Oceanus Mutual Underwriting Association (Bermuda).*[78] It forms the measure of indemnity at the time of loss. The insured value is not necessarily the actual value. It may be total of invoice, e.g., cost of goods, freight; shipping charges, insurance and a certain percentage of margin (generally 10 per cent) to cover anticipated profits. Pursuant to s.27 of MIA 1906:

s.27 of MIA 1906

(a) a policy may be either valued or unvalued;

(b) a valued policy is a policy which specifies the agreed value of the subject-matter insured;

(c) Subject to the provisions of the MIA 1906, and in the absence of fraud, the value fixed by the policy is, as between the insurer and assured, conclusive of the insurable value of the subject intended to be insured, whether the loss be total or partial; and

(d) unless the policy otherwise provides, the value fixed by the policy is not conclusive for the purpose of determining whether there has been a constructive total loss. Unless overvalued, valued policies are acceptable under Incoterms and all insurance contracts.

---

[78] *Elcock v Thomson* [1949] 2 All ER 381 Morris J.

2.13.3.5 Unvalued Policies

Depending on the market and nature of the trade it is open to Incoterms' merchant to choose an unvalued policy. When the value of policy is not determined at the time of commencement of risk but is left to be valued when the loss takes place. The value thus left to be decided later on is called the insurable value or unvalued or valuable policy. In deciding the value, the invoice cost, freight, shipping and insurance charges are included and no margin for anticipated profit is added. Usually, unvalued policies are not common in marine insurance because evaluation of loss at the time of damage poses a difficult problem. It is extremely difficult when consignment goes nearer the port of destination. In hull insurance, the insurable value is determined taking into account the value of the ship at the commencement of risk including provision and, stores for officers and crew plus the charges of insurance. In insurance on freight whether paid in advance or otherwise, the insurable value is the gross amount of freight plus the charges of insurance.

Similarly, in cargo insurance it would be the cost of goods plus expenses and insurance charges. A limitation of insurable value is desirable not only to fix the measure of indemnity under an unvalued policy, but also to provide an approximate basis for the calculation of value in a valued policy. An unvalued policy is defined in s. 27 of MIA 1906 as a policy which does not specify the value of the subject-matter insured, but subject to the limit of the sum insured, leaves the insurable value to be subsequently ascertained, in the manner herein-before specified. Chief Justice Cockburn in *Chapman v Pole*[79] warned that: "You must not run away with the notion that a policy of insurance entitles a man to recover according to the amount represented as insured by the premiums paid. He can only recover the real and actual value of his goods".[80]

While Justice Pennefather elaborated even more in *Vance v Foster*[81] that a policy of insurance is a contract of indemnity, and that while the insured may name any sum he likes as the sum for which he will pay a premium, he does not by so proposing that sum, nor does the company by accepting by accepting the risk, conclude themselves as to the amount which the plaintiff is to recover in consequence of the loss, because although the plaintiff cannot recover beyond the sum insured upon each particular item, he cannot recover even that sum unless he proves that he has sustained damage, and then he will recover a sum commensurate with the loss he has sustained.[82]

2.13.4 Incoterms Beneficial (Carriers and Charterers') Cargo Policies

In addition to their own policies, Incoterms merchants do also benefit from a variety of other policies depending on whether the insured goods are subject to carriage in

[79] *Chapman v Pole* (1870) 22LT 306.

[80] Ibid at 307.

[81] *Vance v Foster* (1841) Ir Cir Rep 47.

[82] Ibid at 50.

a general or chartered-vessels. This coverage typically addresses liability exposures such as hull damage, safe berth, loading, unloading and stowage of cargo, damage to berthing facilities and other vessels and loss of life or bodily injury to third parties resulting from acts of the charterer. The policies involved would, therefore, include, but not be limited to each other's [buyers' and sellers'] policies, carriers' policies, freight forwarders policies, carriers and charterers policies and other third-party policies as appropriate, whether or not they are named herein. These are discussed below.

2.13.4.1 General Carriers' Cargo Liability

The above types of cargo policies apply to both cargo and ships' hull policies. However, in addition to his hull policy the carriers also liability to his customers for the cargo he carries. Motor carrier cargo legal liability insurance covers loss or damage to freight or cargo in transit. Common carriers offer their services to the general public and are liable for the cargo under terms of the bill of lading. Although carriers primarily insure their vessels through hull policies, they nevertheless insure liability to those whose cargo they carry. Thus, where the merchant is unable to recover from his cargo policy, he may recover from the carrier's policy in cases of negligence of and other damages attributed to the carrier. Alternatively, a cargo owner who has been paid is duty bound to assist his insurer claim subrogation from the carrier's insurer.

2.13.4.2 Carriers' Policies Other Than Charterers' Policies

Shipowner's liability to the cargo owner (endorser or indorse). This is envisaged in s. 3(1) (c) of MIA 1906 providing that: "Any liability to a third party may be incurred by the owner by the owner of, or other person interested in or responsible for, insurable property, by reason of maritime perils". In the modern contexts, carriers now include shipowners, ship operators, ship management companies, sub-contractors, and their agents. This is more in the context of multimodal transport

2.13.4.3 Charterer's Policies

2.13.4.3.1 Charterers General Liabilities

Charterers insurance obligations are covered by the Charterers Legal Liability Coverage—a type of marine insurance designed to provide coverage for the liabilities including those of care, custody, and control (CCC) assumed by a party chartering a vessel when the vessel's operation remains in the control of the vessel's owner. Although included in the generic modern terms of carriers, charterers have specific obligations imposed on them by the standard charterparty contracts. Their liability will depend on whether they are short term contractors such voyage,[83] time[84] or

[83] Clause 34 of the NYPE Voyage Charterparty Contract deals with insurance, https://www.irmi.com/term/insurance-definitions/charterers-legal-liability-coverage.

[84] Clause 39 of the Shell Time Charterparty, https://shippingforum.files.wordpress.com/2012/08/shelltime-4-as-revised-20031.pdf.

mixed[85] charterparty carriers. That liability differs significantly where they medium to long term charterers such as bareboat[86] charterers. In the latter they are regarded for all intents and purposes as shipowners responsible for the insurance of the vessel and all its liabilities to third parties such as cargo owners. According to the Incoterms merchant may instead sue the charterer instead or in addition.

In respect of liabilities for loss of or damage to cargo, charterers may, depending on the contract terms and the applicable laws, be considered as the legal "carrier" of the cargo. In such cases the charterer may in the first instance be responsible for risks and liabilities for cargo loss or damage, even though they may have rights of recourse against the shipowner or other third parties. However, full recovery in respect of these rights of recourse cannot be guaranteed. In many jurisdictions, the so called "identity of carrier clauses" in bills of lading which seek to identity the shipowner as the carrier are held to be ineffective and the charterer may be found liable.

2.13.4.3.2 Liability for Loss of or Damage to Cargo

This is a charterer's single most important area of risk. The charterer faces liability in two distinct ways. First, he may be found directly liable to the cargo owner because he issued his own bill of lading, or because under the relevant law (which will depend on where the accident occurred, or where the vessel trades, or the bill of lading terms), he may be determined by the courts to be the "carrier" under the Bill of Lading. Secondly, the charterer may be liable for damage to cargo because he has to indemnify the shipowner or disponent owner or his sub charterer under either a charter contract or a booking note or both.

Time charterers typically may have to indemnify owners under the charter for cargo damage caused by bad stowage or defective lashing or securing carried out by the charterer's stevedores. Voyage charterers bear a similar risk when they charter on FIOS terms. Under the Inter Club Agreement, whether or not incorporated into the NYPE charter, the charterer can be obliged to bear either 50% or 100% of cargo loss in certain circumstances. Even if a charterer has a complete right of indemnity in respect of cargo damage, either against the shipowner or disponent owner or sub charterer, he remains exposed if he cannot make a recovery because of insolvency of the other party, or inability to enforce his claim.

2.13.4.3.3 Charterer Named Under Owners Insurance Policy

It is sometimes thought that charterers can shelter themselves from charterer's risks and liabilities by agreeing with shipowners to take the benefit of the shipowner's own insurance cover. Clauses to the effect that the charterers shall have the benefit of the shipowner's insurance cover are still sometimes found in time, voyage, space or slot charters. However, charterers should be warned that they cannot rely on these clauses alone, as agreements of this type in the charter party are unenforceable as

---

[85] Clause 34 of the NYPE Mixed Charterparty.

[86] Clause 27 of the Barecon 89 Charterparty, https://www.fff-legal.com/wp-content/uploads/2017/02/Sample_Copy_BARECON_89.pdf.

between the charterer and the owner's insurer, as the insurer is not a party to the charter party. Therefore, such a clause in the charter party will in itself not provide the charterer with cover. Furthermore, even if the charterer is named under the owner's P&I policy, the charterer is often only covered for those liabilities which would fall on the owner and may not provide cover for the charterer's own liabilities.

The charterer is, therefore, better protected if he obtains his own insurance. Indeed, no International Group P&I Clubs will agree to name a third-party charterer under an owner's P&I policy. The only exceptions are when naming bareboat charters or where naming the charterer for "misdirected arrow" cover only (as, for example, seen in *Supplytime* 89 and 2005 charter parties). However, in these situations, at the very least the charterer should obtain copies of the current insurance policies to ensure he is named under the owner's P&I policy. In the case of Hull and Machinery insurance, it is not unusual for long term charterers to be named and waived under the ship owner's Hull and Machinery policy. This is often found where the vessels have high values, such as LNG vessels, and where the period of the charter parties may be exceptionally long, typically fifteen or twenty years.

2.13.4.3.4 Charterer Named Under Cargo Insurance

Another special situation where a charterer may be named under another insurance policy is in the case of traders who own the cargo whilst it is carried on board the chartered vessel. To save insurance costs, the charterer can arrange with his cargo insurers to be named and waived under the "all risks" cargo insurance in his capacity as charterer (as well as cargo owner). This will allow the charterer to exclude liability to cargo risks under his charterer's liability P&I cover.

2.13.4.3.5 Freight Forwarders' Policies

Freight forwarders are part of the sources of export insurance. However, insured consignors and consignees should be careful about these sources. First, although sometimes regarded as agents of the carrier or cargo owner, modern law requires them to take full liability for their actions. In some quite complex. Secondly, where they agents for the carrier, they undertake the agent's rights and liabilities. Third and finally, where they are the cargo owner's agents, they could still incur agency liabilities for negligence. For those reasons Freight Forwarders tend to take out policies to cover themselves as if they were carriers.

The UK Government Website[87] provides that:

> Many traders use freight forwarding companies. As well as transporting goods to and from specified locations, freight-forwarding includes booking the movement of goods, storage and customs clearance activity.
>
> Freight forwarders, by applying their STC, usually have limited liability for any claim for loss or damage to goods while in their care. When other parties (such as shipping lines, airlines or truck operators) are entrusted to complete all or part of the transportation movement and where a combined transport waybill or bill of lading is used, the exporter agrees

[87] https://www.gov.uk/government/organisations/uk-export-finance[checkand.

in turn to accept these operators' STC, which override those set by the freight forwarder. So, it is important that you read the STC of both the freight forwarder and the transport operator. Once you have chosen a freight forwarder, you should receive or ask for a copy of the British International Freight Association (BIFA) STC as soon as possible.

It's often difficult to prove that liability for a mishap lies with a freight forwarder (it could be the responsibility of any party across the supply chain) and, even if it does, the forwarder's liability will be limited. It is therefore advisable to arrange separate cargo insurance. Many forwarders will offer to act as a broker in obtaining this. They can be instructed to make insurance arrangements at any time, but preferably prior to booking the shipment.

2.14 Air and Aviation Cargo Policies

Insurance of Incoterms conveyed by any mode of transportation, especially the FCA (which replaced the FOB(A)) among other contracts, are best insured as air cargo. As indicated in Chap. 1 and this chapter, marine-based air cargo insurance is the most common method used to protect the value of air cargo from physical damage, theft, or general average. However, cargo insurance is not always automatically included for all air cargo shipped goods—this often varies by region. There are two types of air cargo—general and special cargo, each subject to differing insurable risks. General cargo includes high value goods, such as electronics, jewellery and pharmaceuticals. The air cargo system is vulnerable to several security threats including potential plots to place explosives aboard aircraft; illegal shipments of hazardous materials; criminal activities such as smuggling and theft; and potential hijackings and sabotage by persons with access to aircraft.

Air cargo constitutes about 5% of world freight, although that share seems to rise following Covid-19 disruption of world trade when urgent covid vaccines and personal protection equipment have had to be airlifted. However, who is responsible for insurance of air cargo? The sales contract will clarify in the terms of sale which party has the responsibility to insure and the consignment note will stipulate the responsible party. Usually, the party responsible for delivering the freight is responsible, whether they are the buyer or the seller. In many cases goods will be insured when they are delivered by truck, but only at a marginal per pound rate.

Air cargo is more appropriate for Incoterm rules for any mode of transportation (EXW, FCA, CPT, CIP, DAP, DDP and DPU). They would therefore be unsuitable for Incoterms rules for sea and inland waterway transport (FAS, FOB, CFR and CIF). Accordingly, the first category Incoterms' merchants who ship air cargo have aviation policies available to them, as goods transported by air are covered by air cargo policies. Air cargo could also benefit from the wider Aviation Insurance, of which it is a part. Aviation insurance may be further divided into hull insurance; cargo insurance; airport owners and operators' liability; hovercraft insurance; spacecraft insurance; and commercial aircraft insurance. International Conventions applying to the carriage of goods by air include the:

(a) Warsaw Convention,[88]
(b) Rome Convention,[89]
(c) Hague Protocol[90] and
(d) Montreal Protocol.[91]

These conventions together provide guidance to domestic air insurance law. The UK the principal terms and conditions for air cargo is Institute Air Cargo Clauses (All Risks); or the ICargo Clauses (A–C) and supplemented by the:

(a) Institute Air Cargo Clauses (Air);
(b) Institute War Clauses (Air Cargo);
(c) Institute Strikes Clauses (air cargo);
(d) Institute Cargo Clauses(air) (excluding sendings by post); and
(e) Etc

2.15 State Export Credit Policies

As will be apparent in Chap. 9[other insurance avenues and considerations] export credit policies would be available to Incoterms exporters and importers who qualify for them. Most seasoned, but not all, exporters/importers would be aware of export credit insurance facilities as sources of export policies and finance. Export credit insurance, sometimes known as trade credit insurance, business credit insurance, or just credit insurance is an insurance policy and a risk management product offered by private insurance companies and governmental export credit agencies to business entities wishing to protect their accounts receivable from loss due to credit risks such as protracted default, insolvency or bankruptcy. This insurance product is a type of property & casualty insurance, and should not be confused with such products as credit life or credit disability insurance, which individuals obtain to protect against the risk of loss of income needed to pay debts. Trade credit insurance can include a component of political risk insurance which is offered by the same insurers to insure the risk of non-payment by foreign buyers due to currency issues, political unrest, expropriation etc. See under War (Chap. 10) and Other Considerations (Chap. 11)

[88] The Convention for the Unification of certain rules relating to international carriage by air, signed in Warsaw, Poland, in 1929.

[89] (1) The Convention for the Unification of Certain Rules Relating to Damage Caused by Foreign Aircraft to Third Parties on the Surface; and (2) The Convention for the Unification of Certain Rules Relating to the Precautionary Arrest of Aircraft. Both conventions were signed in Rome, Italy, on 29 May 1933.

[90] Protocol to Amend the Convention for the Unification of Certain Rules Relating to International Carriage by Air, signed at the H.

[91] The Montreal Convention (formally, the Convention for the Unification of Certain Rules for International Carriage by Air) signed in Montreal, Canada, in 1999.

2.16 Other Publically Supported Policies

In addition to the above a myriad of other policies and schemes are available to Incoterms contracting parties. Under this category, in the UK, US and other major trading nations, governments provide state related policies and/or support. A number of developing countries too have started offering these facilities. See under War (Chap. 10) and Other Considerations (Chap. 11)

2.17 Principal Policy Documents

2.17.1 The Marine Policy

2.17.1.1 The Former SG Policy

The policy is the principal insurance document. It is covered in ss.22–32 and 50–51, 53–54 of the MIA 1906. The nature and characteristics of the policy are further covered in FOB (Chap. 4), CIF (Chap. 7) and tender of documents (Chap. 11). The original UK policy was the Ships and Goods policy (known as the SG Policy whose form is still annexed to the MIA 1906 Schedule 2). The SG policy was ended by the 1982 reforms and replaced by the Lloyds MAR Policy and the Companies MAR Policy. Despite these changes the SG Form is still retained in Schedule to the MIA 1906 for historic and sentimental reasons

2.17.1.2 The New Lloyds of London MAR Policy[92]

For the UK and other parties with access to the Lloyds insurance market the Lloyds Marine Insurance Policy (Lloyds MAR. Policy 1991) is the common. The Lloyds MAR Policy has now been replaced by the Market Reform Contract [MRC] Policy of the London Market Group. The same policy is used for hull and goods. Surprisingly, the Annex to the MIA 1906, still contains the SG Policy Form, not the new Lloyds MAR Policy or the new Companies Marine Policy Forms (See Para 15.10).

2.17.1.3 The New Insurance Companies Marine Policy

As noted above, the Lloyd's MAR policy was introduced by the 1982 insurance market reforms which also included the introduction of the new Institute Cargo Clauses (ICC). The Companies MAR Policy was introduced at the same time as the Lloyd's Mar Policy. Like the Lloyds Mar policy, the Insurance Companies MAR policy is also dual usage for hull and goods. The two policies are identical in content, coverage and format save that they serve the sides of the market, the Lloyds and the non-Lloyd's. Either policy can be used by the Incoterms parties. (See Para 15.10)

---

[92] http://www.lloydslistintelligence.com/llint/print-article.htm;jsessionid=8A18A2246A9E4295 0A747651EFD8C77B?documentId=130847&articleType=book.

2.17.1.4 The Slip Policy

Although the Incoterms insurance contract will normally be contained in policy, there are instances when it be in in a slip policy. A slip is a document submitted by a broker to underwriters containing particulars of a risk proposed for insurance. The underwriter signifies his acceptance by initialling the slip and indicating on it the share of the insurance he will take. A placing slip is a document created by a broker that contains a summary of the terms of a proposed insurance or reinsurance contract which is then presented by the broker to selected underwriters for their consideration. Currently rarely in use slip policy was derived from slip which is signed and sealed by the relevant signing office in order to become the policy. The slip is used in this way for both marine hull and cargo risks. In the latter instance the certificate of insurance is issued and, in all cases, a formal policy was issued on request. A new slip has been introduced under the MRC.

2.17.1.5 The Market Reform Contract [MRC]

2.17.1.5.1 The Market Reform Policy

The Market Reform Group has published an implementation guide to the new Market Reform Contract (MRC). The new version incorporates the changes to contract checking and documentation that take effect from 1 July 2007. As a result of these changes, the placing document will often form the final contract documentation. The Lloyds MAR Policy and the Companies MAR Policy [have both] been replaced by the Market Reform Contract [MRC] introduced by the London Market Group [LMG]. The original 2006 MRC has been amended from time to time. A similar scheme has been introduced in the US and other leading insurance markets. This represents a further reform a mere 24 years after the replacement of the SG policy that had lasted nearly 400 years. The MRC represents a modern and more efficient way of doing business

2.17.1.5.2 Is There a Future for These After the MRC?

The introduction of a placing standard—initially LMP and now MRC—has delivered value to the London Market by providing a standard form of submissions. It offers a clear structure and means that brokers present contracts in a consistent manner. The answer to this question is in the affirmative. From 31 March 2008 the MRCE must be used for all Open Market London Market risks, until then firms may choose whether or not to use it. So far, the indications are that none has opted out. So, there is a future for these in the MRC

2.17.1.6 Equivalent Foreign Policies

Although the London marine policy is the most universally well-known, other jurisdictions issue own policies with their own institute clauses which are acceptable as tender in the UK so long as they contain all the essential terms and conditions acceptable under the MIA. Whether these policies are valid in the UK and vice-versa in Incoterms is the subject of Chap. 11 post

2.18 Hybrid Export Policies

2.18.1 Open Policies

A type of insurance policy intended to cover and indefinite number of future individual requirement. Under the open policy, individual successive shipments are periodically reported or declared to the insurer and automatically covered on or after the inception date. Although popular in export trade, this is not actually a policy as there is no such document issued, but a mere scheme under which cover is provided. The MIA 1906 does not define an open policy but it seems to treat it as floating policies above. This is covered extensively both in the Incoterms and other tenders in Chap. 11 below. See also floating policy above. This mechanism has its origin in marine insurance. Most cargo policies are written on an open basis which will cover all future shipments of an assured when he is responsible for providing insurance or when he is responsible for loss or damage during the "main carriage phase" of transit; that is when he is responsible for loss or damage to the goods from a point in the country of origin until the goods are delivered to a point in the country of destination. They are acceptable evidence in CIF and CIP Incoterms and tender under Clause 28 of UCP 600. These might come under threat from the MRC See also Chap. 9 (post).

2.18.2 Open Covers

Although largely similar, there is nevertheless a difference between open policies and open covers. The open policy is a stamped document and is, therefore, legally enforceable in itself, whereas an open cover is unstamped and has no legal validity unless backed by a stamped policy/certificate of insurance. Like open policies and for the same reasons, open covers are not policy. Otherwise, open covers and open policies are the same. Open covers are different from "Open Cargo" or "Shipper's Interest" Insurance. Open covers are a mechanism of an annual or other type of policy.[93] Whereas the latter is a policy may be purchased by a carrier, freight broker, or shipper, as coverage for the shipper's goods. In the event of loss or damage, this type of insurance will pay for the true value of the shipment, rather than only the legal amount that the carrier is liable for. They are also covered extensively below. See also floating policy and open policies above. Open covers qualify both as evidence of insurance under Clause A5 of the CIF and CIP contracts and fit for tender under Clause 28 of the UCP 600.These might come under threat from the MRC.

[93] See under Open Policy below.

2.18.3 Blanket Policies

A blanket policy is a form of property insurance that covers more than one type of property at one location, or the same type at various locations, or multiple types at multiples locations. It allows the policyholder to extend the coverage of a basic homeowner's policy. Like open policies and open covers this policy too is not a policy document in the strict sense. The policy is taken to cover losses within the particular time and place. The policy is taken for a certain amount and premium is paid on the whole of it in the beginning of the policy and is re-adjusted at the end of the policy according to the actual amount at risk. If the actual coverage of risk is less than the total amount of insurance, the premium related to the excess amount is returned to the insured.

On the other hand, if the amounts of shipments are greater than the insured sum, additional premium is charged over the excess protection. Blanket policies seem to a generic name for open policies and/or open covers, themselves part of the floating policy. This is a policy which in a single sum insured, covers a number of separate items of property without subdivision on the amount. This policy has its roots in fire and fidelity insurance. The approach is used in fire insurance for large risks and also in fidelity guarantee insurance to cover the whole staff without mention of name or position, the premium being computed on a number of employees in specific categories (e.g. officials, non- accounting officials). They would be evidence in CIF and CIP Incoterms and proper tender under Clause 28 of UCP 600. Will these come under threat from the MRC (see Chap. 9].

2.18.4 Floating Policies

This policy describes the general terms and leaves the amount of each shipment and other particulars to be declared later on. The declaration is made in order of dispatch of shipment. The policy is taken for a round large sum which is specified at each declaration and is attached to each shipment. With each declaration the amount will be reduced till it is exhausted when the insured sum is said to be 'closed' and the policy is 'fully declared' or, 'run off'. The most popular form of contract is 'Open Cover'. It is an agreement between the insured and the insurer by which the assured on his part agrees to declare, and the insurer on his part agrees to accept all the shipments falling within the scope of the 'open cover' which is merely an 'original ship'. It is not a legal contract of marine insurance and suffers from the same legal disability as the 'original 'ship".

However, the insured and the insurers are honour bound. To give 'Open Cover' a legal form, a policy is issued for the purpose. Separate policies are not issued in case of each shipment but only one policy is issued at the time of entering into contract. All declarations are written on the back of the" policy. A classification clause is usually inserted in 'open cover' to provide the agreed rates of premium. Similarly, valuation clauses are also inserted to provide the basis for valuation in the event of loss taking place. This policy is suitable for a cargo-owner who makes regular shipments of cargoes. All his shipments are automatically covered as soon as the declarations are made. The floating policies are mostly used in the age of gigantic trade. Floating policies are contained in s.29 of MIA 1906 as follows:

> (1) A floating policy is a policy which describes the insurance in general terms, and leaves the name of the ship or ships and other particulars to be defined by subsequent declaration.
> (2) The subsequent declaration or declarations may be made by indorsement on the policy, or in other customary manner.
> (3) Unless the policy otherwise provides, the declarations must be made in the order of dispatch or shipment. They must, in the case of goods, comprise all consignments within the terms of the policy, and the value of the goods or other property must be honestly stated, but an omission or erroneous declaration may be rectified even after loss or arrival, provided the omission or declaration was made in good faith.
> (4) Unless the policy otherwise provides, where a declaration of value is not made until after notice of loss or arrival, the policy must be treated as an unvalued policy as regards the subject-matter of that declaration

They are probably evidence of insurance in Clause A5 of the CIF and CIP contracts but doubtful whether they would be acceptable tender under Clause 28 of the UCP 600.

2.19 Subsidiary and Alternative Documents

2.19.1 Insurance Slips (Policies)

A placing slip is a document created by a broker that contains a summary of the prospective risks and the terms of a proposed insurance or reinsurance contract which is then presented by the broker to selected underwriters for their consideration. It is a piece of paper containing all the pertinent information regarding the risk and the insurance terms and conditions that the broker submits to the underwriter at Lloyd's of London See under the slip policy above [Covered elsewhere!] The document, known as "The slip," contain information such as the name of the ship, the date of voyage, the description of the risk, the sum insured and the rate of premium. "The Slip" is in practice a complete and final contract. The document is given to underwriters, who then decide what fraction of the risk they are willing to insure. Their status is covered in Chaps. 4 and 6 post and the status of their tender is covered in Chap. 11. They are probably evidence of insurance in Clause A5 of CIF and CIP but not acceptable tender under Clause 28 of UCP 600.Will the slip be replaced by the MRC?

2.19.2 Insurer's Cover Note

A cover note is a temporary document issued by an insurance company that provides proof of insurance coverage until a final insurance policy can be issued.

During this time, the insurer may continue to evaluate the risks associated with insuring the holder of the cover note. A cover note is a temporary certificate of insurance issued by the Insurer before the issuance of a policy after the Insured has given a duly filled in proposal form and has paid the premium in full. This is a document normally issued by the insurer (hence insurers' covernote) pending preparation of the policy. It may be issued as evidence of a more permanent cover or it may be an acknowledgement of a temporary cover pending the insurers' final decision whether or not to accept the risk. However, if the loss occurs in the duration of the covernote then the insurer will be liable as if a full policy was available.[94] Covernotes are both valid evidence of insurance under Clause A5 of CIF and CIP contracts and acceptable tender under Clause 28 of the UCP 600. See also Chaps. 4 and 6 for coverage and 11 for tender. The futures of these after the MRC are uncertain.

2.19.3 Brokers' Cover Note

This is a note or document issued by an insurance broker confirming that insurance has been effected in certain terms. e.g. by adding language along the lines "A Broker Insurance Document is provided by (name broker) as evidence of cover for this insurance contract solely in their capacity as agent of the insured and it is not an insurer approved document It amounts to a warranty to his client that his instructions have been carried out and does not impose liability on the insurer who has not actually entered into any agreement and so if the covernote is issued in anticipation of making such an agreement which is not forthcoming the broker will be liable for breach of warranty. What is an insurance broker? An insurance broker is a professional who represents consumers in their search for the best insurance policy for their needs. They work closely with their clients to research coverage, terms, conditions, and price and then recommend the insurance policy that best fits the bill. As such it was decided in *Briot v S Cohen & Son (NSW) Ltd*[95] (1926) that such a document is not binding on the insurer as its issue does not make the broker an insurer. Brokers covernotes might be valid evidence under Clause A5 of the CIF and CIP contracts but are specifically forbidden as acceptable tender under Clause 28 of the UCP 600. See also Chaps. 4 and 6 for coverage and 11 for tender. The future of brokers' covernotes after the MRC is uncertain.

2.19.4 Certificate of Insurance

A marine insurance certificate is a document that an insured gives to the shipper responsible for their cargo or any other shipping-related activity. It certifies that the cargo is insured while in transit and is supported by a copy of an insurance policy. A certificate of insurance is a document used to provide information on specific

[94] See also Broker's cover note below.

[95] Briot v S Cohen & Son (NSW) Ltd (1926).

insurance coverage. The certificate provides verification of the insurance and usually contains information on types and limits of coverage, insurance company, policy number, named insured, and the policies' effective periods. This is a document which is issued to provide evidence of the existence of insurance. Certificates are required in law as evidence of the following classes of insurance:

(i) employer's liability insurance;
(ii) occupiers' liability insurance;
(iii) motor insurance (Road Traffic Cover only, which is compulsory); and
(iv) Oil cargo carrying vessels with regard to pollution.

In all other instances other oil cargo carriers, they may be required only by the contract of commercial custom, such as for tender for payment or under UCP for letters of credit in FOB and CIF contracts. Certificates are not only the alternatives to the policy but are also valid evidence for insurance under Clause A5 of the CIF and CI contracts and are specifically listed as valid tender Clause 28 of the UCP 600. See also Chaps. 4 and 6 for coverage and 11 for tender. Its future is not affected by the MRC.

2.19.5 Declarations Under Open Covers, Blanket Policies and Floating Policies

The nature and characteristics of Open Covers, Blanket Policies and Floating Policies have been covered above. Prospects of Blanket Policies as evidence of insurance under Clause A5 of the CIF and CIP contracts are similar to those of the actual policies and certificates. Floating Policies are statutory documents under s.29 of the MIA1906. Declarations under Open Covers are specifically named as an acceptable tender under Clause 28 of the UCP 600

2.19.6 Letters of Insurance

A letter of insurance is a document mentioned often in export trade literature but without clue of its appearances. This is a letter issued by the insurer to an insured consignor for the benefit of the beneficiary consignee to certify that the shipper has insurance in place for the shipment. Sometimes known as marine insurance certificate, it is a document that an insurer gives to the shipper responsible for their cargo or any other shipping-related activity. It certifies that the cargo is insured while in transit and is supported by a copy of an insurance policy. They are common practice in open policies, open covers and blanket policies.[96] However, contrary to public perception they are not letters of guarantees (LOGs) although the functions are

[96] See Chap. 12 for judicial interpretations.

almost similar. When used in medical insurance LOG is a guarantee of payment between a hospital and an insurance company.

It is pre-authorisation of the insurance company and allows you to benefit from "direct billing". It allows you not having to advance the expenses in case of an admission at the hospital. Otherwise, the LOGs also acts as a bond backed by an insurer or other secure financial institution. It gives investors a guarantee that principal and interest payments will be made. Many insurance companies specialize in financial guarantees and similar products used by debt issuers as a way of attracting investors. However, neither the letter of insurance nor the insurance letter of guarantee is a letter of credit. Letters of insurance good evidence of insurance under Clause A5 of CIF and CIP contracts and probably acceptable tender under Clause 28 of Incoterms. See also Chaps. 4 and 6 for coverage and Chap. 11 for tender. Its future is not affected by the MRC.

2.19.7 Declarations Under Insurance ("Declaration Insurance")

This is another instrument often heard of but rarely seen by the majority of the population. Both the letter of insurance and the insurance LOG are different from the declaration under insurance (insurance declaration) A marine or cargo declaration of insurance is a document provided by your insurance company that summarizes the coverage provided by the insurance company's cargo insurance policy. It contains all the most pertinent information regarding your home insurance. Although not synonymous with, but declarations have resemblances to letters of credit with which they perform the same function.

Schemes like letters of insurance, declarations under insurance as well as floating policies, open covers and blanket policies were introduced to reduce the amount of paperwork and thereby increase efficiency and profit margins. This was followed by online rather than hardcopy policies. Declarations under insurance are in the same category as Declarations under Open Cover and Declarations under Blanket Policies. See also Chaps. 4 and 6 for coverage and 11 for insurance documents acceptable for tender under UCP 600. Their future after the MRC is unclear.

2.20 Further Food for Thoughts

2.20.1 General Issues with Insurance

(a) Is insurance absolutely necessary for international trade?;
(b) If not, what are the alternatives?
(c) Are insurance principles clear?
(d) If not why do parties some times over or double insure?;
(e) Other than self-insurance and deliberate under-insurance, can't one trade internationally without insurance; is it really suicidal to do so?;

(f) Can't alternative means to insurance of guaranteeing loss coverage be developed?
(g) Are less seasoned parties aware of all the private and public sources of export insurance?;
(h) Isn't the existence of so many sources confusing?;
(i) Is the doctrine of subrogation and other insurance principles intended to fortify the indemnity principle that water-tight?;
(j) If so, how come there have been instances of windfalls, as discussed later on this book; and
(k) See also under Food Thought in Chap. 1 above and the ensuing Chapters of this book below

2.20.2 Perceived Disadvantages of Insurance

2.20.2.1 Can Be Expensive

A major fear of insurance buyers (insureds or assureds) is the price they have to pay. Sometimes, depending on the policy and certain factors that affect the cost, such as credit score and other potential risks to the insurance company, buying insurance can be expensive. But if bought at a right time, with the right reason and right amount of coverage, you might actually get the right price.

2.20.2.2 Rising Premiums

Most types of insurances have varying rates of premiums, and you should be very careful about it. Before buying a policy, make sure you know from the beginning if you have a guaranteed premium throughout the policy, or if it changes from time to time in relation to inflation. You should weigh out if you prefer a fixed premium or you'd like to take the risk, and more importantly, determine the amount you can afford to spare on the contract.

2.20.2.3 Not All Claims Might Be Paid Out

Sometimes, this issue also becomes a public misconception which drives insurance buyers away. While it's true that there are cases of denied claims, there's a ground for this to happen and thus shouldn't scare you away. For one, you might have presented wrong information during the underlying process. Or you weren't able to satisfy some requirements, or performed certain actions that could lead to nullification of your contract. To avoid this from happening, you need to be honest from the very beginning with your provider, and clarify any limitations or exclusions that could lead to denied claims.[97]

[97] See also: http://www.incomeprotectionadviser.co.uk/advantages-and-disadvantages-of-insurance/.

2.20.2.4 Tricky Terms and Conditions

While taking an insurance policy, some of the terms and conditions could be tricky that you may not get compensation for all the losses. It is important to read through the conditions before buying it. For those reasons Many businesses, particularly smaller ones, that trade internationally do not follow either of these approaches because they lack the legal resources to implement and follow through with them. They are still able to trade without them although they should not feel comfortable if they don't understand what framework that applies.

2.20.2.5 Lengthy Legal Formalities

Though you may have opted for a good plan, claiming the insurance money could take a long time due to its lengthy legal procedures to be carried out by the company.

Potential crime incidents: Life insurance policies could lead to potential crime incidents as the beneficiaries of the policy might get tempted to resort to wrong ways to get obtain the insured amount.

2.20.3 Problems of the Floating and Open Policy

Unlike ordinary cargo policies, floating, open and blanket policies are policies where only the amount of claim is specified and all other details are omitted till the time the ship embarks on its journey. This can have its advantages but can also have disadvantages where if the ship fails to embark on its journey or where the problems occur before such embarkation and the insured does not produce the necessary details or where the declarations on open covers has not been issued.

2.20.4 Other Considerations for CIP and CIF

Once the goods have been taken in charge by the carrier (or loaded on board the ship), the buyer is "on risk", and so must deal with the insurance company in order to make a claim. This has implications for the insurance document that the seller provides—it may need to be appropriately endorsed.

Some sellers have global freight insurance policies covering all their consignments. This often creates problems for the use of e.g. CIP. (For a single consignment, how can the insurance be costed, and how can arrangements be made allowing a buyer to make a claim?)

Some sellers find the requirement for the buyer to claim under the insurance policy unsatisfactory from a customer service perspective. In such cases, the seller may agree to take care of claims. A letter of subrogation can be supplied (seller takes over right to claim under the policy)

Even the highest of the Institute Cargo Clauses A excludes risks that the buyer may think are important for example War and Strikes (for which a standard Institute clause exists)"[98]

2.20.5 Mini Conclusion

While every financial instrument will have both advantages and disadvantages, it is recommended to choose wise based on your need and purpose. You can benefit from an insurance policy provided if the goals are clearly realised.[99]

All freight insurance usually excludes consequential loss, e.g. the knock-on effects of buyer missing a contract deadline or a sales season. This risk can sometimes be included by agreement with the insurer.

So, the risks to be covered should be discussed and then incorporated into the commercial agreement.

2.21 Concluding Remarks

It is hoped this second opening chapter has set the tone of the contents of the book. The topics discussed herein will be elaborated in the subsequent chapters. The chapter is intended to demonstrate the importance of insurance to international trade; highlight the interlinked history of marine insurance and international trade; introduce the various principles of insurance and marine insurance that apply to international trade and consequently the FOB and CIF insurance contracts; enumerate the sources of cargo insurance market and other insurance avenues; and outline the types of principal policy and related documents that would be available to the FOB and CIF merchants. The chapter also briefly introduces the tender principles and recent reform of the market practice through the MRC. Regarding the said reforms, the chapter concludes by questioning the future of the policy and related documents as well as the market practice following the MRC reform.

Insurance is a financial product that reduces or eliminates the cost of loss or effect of loss caused by different types of risk. Insurance is crucial or key to international trade. Importance of insurance is underlined by the fact that the world we live in is full of uncertainties and risks. Individuals, families, businesses, properties and assets are exposed to different types and levels of risks. International trade is exposed to wider and larger risks than any other type of business. This is true of common law and incoterms and FOB, CIF and related contracts. The role of insurance in international trade. Therefore, it is important that we reasonably avoid the risk of foreign trade, so as to effectively promote foreign trade. Insurance is a means of economic compensation. It plays an important role in international trade.

[98] https://www.incotermsexplained.com/freight-insurance/.

[99] See also, https://www.creditmantri.com/article-advantages-and-disadvantages-of-insurance-policies/.

Insurance: Importance, Types and Benefits. The life and property of an individual are surrounded by the risk of death, disability or destruction. These risks may result in financial losses. Insurance is a prudent way to transfer such risks to an insurance company.

2.22 Further Readings

Books

- Sassoon, C.I.F and F.O.B Contracts, 5th edn. 2012, Sweet & Maxwell/Thomson Reuters,
- Whitehead, Elements of Export Law (Elements of Overseas Trade Series), 1983, Woodhead-Faulkner, Cambridge
- Badger, Elements of Cargo Insurance (Elements of Overseas Trade Series), 19XX
- Whitehead, Elements of International Trade and Payments (Elements of Overseas Trade Series), 1983, Woodhead-Faulkner, Cambridge
- Stapleton, Elements of Export Marketing (Elements of Overseas Trade Series).
- Bugg, etl, Elements of Transportation and Documentation (Elements of Overseas Trade Series), 1984 Woodhead-Faulkner, Cambridge
- Branch, The Elements of Export Practice, Chapman & Hall, 1979, London & New York
- Branch, Elements of Shipping, Economics of Shipping Practice and Management, Chapman and Hall**,** New York and London
- Branch, A Dictionary of Shipping, International Trade Terms and Abbreviations, Chapman and Hall, New York and London.
- Huybrechts, Marc (edt) Van Hooydonk, Eric & Dieryck, Christian (edts) (The European Institute of Marine and Transport Law, Antwerp University Department of Law, Marine Insurance at the turn of the Millennium, Vol. 1, 2000, Intersentia, Antwerpen-Groningen-Oxford
- Huybrechts, Marc (ed) Van Hooydonk, Eric & Dieryck, Christian (co-ed) (The European Institute of Marine and Transport Law, Antwerp University Department of Law), Marine Insurance at the turn of the Millennium, Vol.2, 2000, Intersentia, Antwerpen-Groningen-Oxford
- White, Australian Maritime Law, 3rd edn 2014, The Federal Press (chapter 5 Marine Insurance by Associate Professor Damien Cremean at pp102-120)
- Fernandes, Marine Insurance Law of Canada, 1987, Butterworths, Toronto & Vancouver
- Ivamy, Chalmers' Marine Insurance Act, *1906*, 10th edn, 1993, Butterworths, London, Dublin & Edinburgh
- Buglass, Marine Insurance and General Average in the United States (An Average Adjuster's Viewpoint*)*, 3rd edn, 1991, Cornell Maritime Press, Centreville, Maryland
- Van Houtte, The Law of International Trade, 2nd edn, Sweet & Maxwell, 2002 (chapter 4 International Sales)

- Walker; Export Practice and Documentation, 3rd edn 1987, Butterworths (Chapter 3 Export Sales Quotation & Chapter 11 Cargo Insurance)
- Wilson, International Business Transactions-In a Nutshell, *2nd edn 1984,* West Publishing Co, St. Paul Minn (Chapter 12 Insuring Against Risk of Loss: The Overseas Private Investment Corporation (OPIC)
- Hoyle, The Law of International Trade, 2nd edn, 1984, Tax and Business Law Publishers, Bicester (Chapter 2 International Sale of Goods, Chapter 5, Marine Insurance)
- Tiplady, Introduction to the Law of International Trade, 1989, BSP Professional Books, (Chapter1 Sales of Goods under English Law, Chapter 2 CIF and FOB Contracts, Chapter 5 Marine Insurance)
- Day, etl The Law of International Trade, 2nd edn 1993, Butterworths, London (Chapter 1 The Outline of the Transaction,
- Singleton, Case Studies for Exporters, Croner's Reference Book for Exporters, 1998 Croner Publications Ltd
- Reynolds, The A to Z of International Trade, 2002 ICC Publication No 623, ICC Publishing House (Focus on Insurance, pp249-260)
- Ademuni-Odeke, The Law of International Trade, Blackstone Press Limited, 1999
- Twells, Exporters' Checklist, A step-by-step guide to Successful Exporting, 2nd edn, 1995, Lloyds of London Press.
- Folson, etl, A: International Business Transactions, 8th edn 2009, West/Thomson Reuters.
- Watson, Finance of International Trade, 4th edn, 1990, The Chartered Institute of Bankers
- Bradget, etl; Commercial Law, 1997, Blackstone Press Limited
- Inns of Court School of Law, Law of International Trade, Blackstone Press, 1998
- Inns of Court School of Law, Commercial Law, 1997, Blackstone Press, (Chapter 21 Insurance, Chapter 17 International Sales)
- Branch, Import/Export Documentation, 1990, Chapman & Hall
- Hudson, etl Marine Insurance Clauses, 4th edn 2005 Lloyds of London Press
- Cloughton, David, Riley on Business Interruption Insurance, 7th edn, 1991, Sweet & Maxwell
- Lloyds, Market-Insight from the World of Lloyds, 2013, Lloyds of London Insurance.
- Lloyds, Lloyds Cover to Cover, 2012, Lloyds of London Insurance
- Lloyds, *Cargo Claims and Recoveries*, Module 3, 2013, Lloyds of London Insurance
- --- Marine Insurance.Vol.1-Principles and Basic Practice, 5th edn, 1986, Witherbey & Co Ltd
- --- etl, Marine Insurance, Vol.2-Cargo Practice, 4th edn, 1985, Witherbey & Co Ltd
- Marine Insurance, Vol.3-Hull Practice, Witherbey & Co Ltd
- Analysis of Marine Insurance Clauses, Book 1, Witherbey & Co Ltd
- Analysis of Marine Insurance Clauses, Book 2, 19XX, Witherbey & Co Ltd.
- Schwenzer, et al (eds): International Sales Law, 2006, Routledge. Cavendish
- Morris, Importing for the Small Business, 1985, Kogan Page

- Birds, Birds' Modern Insurance Law. Sweet & Maxwell, 2014.
- Donaldson, et al (Editor), *Lowndes and Rudolf:* Law of General Average and the York-Antwerp Rules. Sweet & Maxwell, 1990.)
- Wilson, (1997). *Lowndes and Rudolf:* General Average and the York-Antwerp Rules. British Shipping Law Library: Sweet & Maxwell.
- Locker: Informed Insurance Choice? [The Insurer's Pre-Contractual Information Duties in General Consumer Insurance] Edward Elgar Publishing, Cheltenham, 2015
- Boland: Reinsurance: London Market Practice, Lloyds of London Press, 1996
- Mangone: Marine Policy for America, 2nd edn, Taylor & Francis, New York, 1988.
- Frederick Martin: The History of Lloyd's and of Marine Insurance in Great Britain: With an Appendix Containing Statistics Relating to Marine Insurance, Paperback English
- Unknown Author: The history of marine trades insurance, Published on Sep 22, 2014
- Dickson, P. G. M. (1960). The Sun Insurance Office, 1710–1960: The History of Two and a Half Centuries of British Insurance. Oxford University Press.
- Kingston, Christopher (June 2007). "Marine Insurance in Britain and America, 1720–1844: A Comparative Institutional Analysis". *The Journal of Economic History*. 67 (2). Cambridge University Press. pp. 379–409. JSTOR 4501157.
- Levy, Jonathan (2012). Freaks of Fortune: The Emerging World of Capitalism and Risk in America. Harvard University Press.
- Pearson, Robin, ed. (2010). The Development of International Insurance. Pickering & Chatto Publishers.
- Raynes, Harold E. (1948). A History of British Insurance. Pitman Publishing. ISBN 9780273416418.
- Palmer, Sarah (October 2007). "Lloyd, Edward (c.1648–1713)". Oxford Dictionary of National Biography. 1 (online ed.). Oxford University Press. doi:10.1093/ref:odnb/16829.
- Aubert, Jean-Jacques (2008). "Dealing with the Abyss: The Nature and Purpose of the Rhodian Sea-Law on Jettison (Lex Rhodia De Iactu , D 14.2) and the Making of Justinian's Digest". *Beyond Dogmatics: Law and Society in the Roman World. 8: 157–172.*
- Parks Insurance
- Marshall's Treaties on the Law of Insurance
- Birds, J. Birds' Modern Insurance Law. Sweet & Maxwell, 2004. (ISBN 0-421-87800-2)
- Donaldson, Ellis, Wilson (Editor), Cooke (Editor), Lowndes and Rudolf: Law of General Average and the York-Antwerp Rules. Sweet & Maxwell, 1990. (ISBN 0-420-46930-3)
- John, A. H. "The London Assurance Company and the Marine Insurance Market of the Eighteenth Century," Economica New Series, Vol. 25, No. 98 (May 1958), pp. 126–141 in JSTOR

- Roover, Florence Edler de. "Early Examples of Marine Insurance," Journal of Economic History Vol. 5, No. 2 (Nov., 1945), pp. 172–200 in JSTOR
- Wilson, DJ, Donaldson (1997). Lowndes and Rudolf: General Average and the York-Antwerp Rules. British Shipping Law Library: Sweet & Maxwell. ISBN 0-421-56450-4.

Selected Reports

- The Geneva Association: The Essential Role of Insurance Services for Trade Growth and Development, A Primer from The Geneva Association's Programme on Regulation and Supervision (PROGRES), 1st December 2011
- UNCTAD: Insurance in developing countries: an assessment and review of developments (1989-1993)
- UNCTAD/SDD/INS/2/Rev.1 - 05 Apr 1994 English
- UNCTAD: Insurance in developing countries: an assessment and review of developments (1989-1992)-UNCTAD/SDD/INS/2 - 21 Jan 1993 English
- UNCTAD: Establishment of the work programme of the standing committee on developing services sectors: fostering competitive services sectors in developing countries: insurance- TD/B/CN.4/15 - 09 Dec 1992
- UNCTAD: The Place of General Average in Marine Insurance Today- UNCTAD/SDD/LEG/1 - 08 Mar 1994 English
- UNCTAD: Model Clauses on Marine Hull and Cargo Insurance TD/B/C.4/ISL/50/Rev.1 - 01 Jan 1989 English
- UNCTAD: Cargo loss prevention: Suggestions for a domestic policy in developing countries TD/B/C.3/162/Supp.1 - 08 Mar 1982 English
- UNCTAD: Legal and documentary aspects of Latin American marine insurance legal régimes TD/B/C.4/ISL/51 - 03 Nov 1980 English UNCTAD
- UNCTAD: Legal and documentary aspects of the marine insurance contract. Report by UNCTAD. Secretariat TD/B/C.4/ISL/27/Rev.1, Geneva, UN, 1982.
- UNCTAD: Legal and Documentary Aspects of International Trade, Report by UNCTAD Secretariat, UNCTAD/SDTE/BFB/2, UN New York/Geneva 1999.

Clauses

- Fletcher: "The General Common Law and Section 34 of the Judiciary Act of 1789: The Example of Marine Insurance" *Harvard Law Review* Vol. 97, No. 7 (May, 1984), pp. 1513–1515
- John. "The London Assurance Company and the Marine Insurance Market of the Eighteenth Century," *Economica* New Series, Vol. 25, No. 98 (May 1958), pp. 126–141
- Roover, "Early Examples of Marine Insurance,"*Journal of Economic History* Vol. 5, No. 2 (Nov., 1945), pp. 172–200 Tuesday 15 February 2005 (accessed 23/02/2021)

Internet Materials

- Morris, G D LA Brief History of Marine Insurance, https://riskandinsurance.com/brief-history-marine-insurance/
- Memorial Publications of the Prudential Insurance Company of America (1915). The Documentary History of Insurance, 1000 B.C. - 1875 A.D. Newark, New Jersey: Prudential Press. https://archive.org/details/cu31924030231736.
- Mohammad Sadegh Nazmi Afsha, "Insurance in Ancient Iran" Gardeshgary, Quarterly Magazine, Vol. 4, No. 12, Spring 2002, Page 14–16

References

Ademuni-Odeke (2021) Incoterms 2020 sellers and buyers beware! What the new rules do not tell you about overall insurance obligation. J Bus Law 8:672–700

Hashempoor S (2013) Department of Economy, Academy of Sciences, Baku, Azerbaijan, "Insurance and History of Its Origin, and Its Surrounding Issues in Iran". J Basic Appl Sci Res 3(2):1217–1230

Sassoon DM (1967) The origin of F. O. B. and C. I. F. terms and the factors influencing their choice. J Bus Law pp 32–37

Part II

Insurance of FOB and Related Contracts That Exclude Selle's Obligations to Provide Insurance to the Buyer at Common Law

3 Nature and Characteristics of Contracts That Exclude Seller's Obligations to Provide Insurance for the Buyer at Common Law

Abstract

This chapter deals with the nature and characteristics of the above titled contracts. Although essential, unless otherwise provided, their insurance contractual obligations are normally performed by the buyer. Although these contracts are silent on these obligations, the buyer is responsible for insurance although the seller should take care of pre-shipment, seller's own additional and contingency insurances. Foremost of these contracts is the FOB and its variations such as Standard FOB, Classic FOB, and FOB with additional duties (Extended FOB). The others being Ex-ships contracts such as Ex-works, C&F, FAS and FCA. The chapter traces the development and nature of these contracts, factors determining their choice and other considerations other than the said factors. Also included, in the chapters are other variations such as FOB airport (FOBA), FOB "freight allowed", FOB "freight prepaid" FOB "named inland carrier", FOB Air (FOBA) FOB rail (FOR), FOB truck (FOT); Free out (FFO), FOB and trimmed (for coal trade); and FOB "named inland port of origin". Other issues include the North American FOB and the FOB under the American UCC. Initial references are made to the leading authorities on the subject such as *Pyrene v Scindia* (1949), *Wimble v Rosenberg* (19), and the *El Amira and El Minia* (1999).

3.1 Introduction

This chapter covers common law contracts in which contractual parties do not have to provide insurance cover to each other. Also known as the "Free" contracts, they include the previous C, E and F Incoterms classifications and are based on the FOB principals and characteristics. Despite ample coverage of the FOB in existing literature, it is still necessary to do so in this opening chapter to set the bases for discussions on insurance in latter chapters. Although the FOB is the dominant contract

P. Ademuni-Odeke, *Insurance of International Sales' Contracts under Incoterms*, Law for Professionals, https://doi.org/10.1007/978-3-031-75136-3_3

under this class of Incoterms, this chapter deals also with other related Incoterms such as C&F, FAS, FCA, FOR/FOT (still applicable in few jurisdictions) and Ex-Ship which have also been subject of common law interpretation.

Despite its common law origin, FOB is now also an Incoterm describing a term of sale that details the responsibilities of the buyer and seller for the international trade transaction. Under this term, the seller fulfils his obligation to deliver when the goods have passed over the ship's rail at the named port of shipment. This means that the buyer has to bear all costs and risks of loss of or damage to the goods from that point. The seller must clear the goods for export. FOB is a form of sale of goods used in overseas trade in all regions except North America where it is also domestic trade contract. This chapter focuses on the FOB contract, its origin and nature, factors determining its insurance and its other duties at common law, the US UCC, and Incoterms. The chapter does not cover all aspects of the contract but focuses only those that directly affect its insurance.

3.2 Nature of the Contracts

3.2.1 FOB Origin

The CIF and FOB, the most important and most frequently used trade terms are 2 of the 11 Incoterms and between them account for over 80% of world trade transactions. When using CIF, the responsibilities of the seller include transporting the goods to the nearest port, loading them on a vessel and paying for the insurance and freight. The goods are considered delivered once they reach the port of destination, where they then become the responsibility of the buyer. Unlike the CIF the FOB is a little more problematic regarding insurance because of its numerous and sometimes confusing classifications/variants.

3.3 The Contract Variants

3.3.1 The Standard FOB

FOB means that the seller delivers the goods on board the vessel nominated by the buyer at the named port of shipment or procures the goods already so delivered. The risk of loss of or damage to the goods passes when the goods are on board the vessel, and the buyer bears all costs from that moment onwards. Under FOB terms the seller bears all costs and risks up to the point the goods are loaded on board the vessel. The seller's responsibility does not end at that point unless the goods are "appropriated to the contract" that is, they are "clearly set aside or otherwise identified as the contract goods. Therefore, FOB contract requires a seller to deliver goods on board a vessel that is to be designated by the buyer in a manner customary at the particular port.

In this case, the seller must also arrange for export clearance. On the other hand, the buyer pays cost of marine freight transportation, bill of lading fees, insurance, unloading and transportation cost from the arrival port to destination. Since Incoterms 1980 introduced the Incoterm FCA, FOB should only be used for non-containerized sea freight and inland waterway transport. However, FOB is commonly used incorrectly for all modes of transport despite the contractual risks that this can introduce. In some common law countries such as the United States of America, FOB is not only connected with the carriage of goods by sea but also used for inland carriage aboard any "vessel, car or other vehicle."

In addition to classifications, FOB also has Variants, namely the "Arranged FOB" and "FOB Stowed" also known as "FOB Stowed and Trimmed".

3.3.2 The "ARRANGING FOB"

A related but separate FOB term "FOB CAP" ("customer-arranged pickup") is used to denote that the buyer will arrange a carrier of their choice to pick the goods up It is the term used by the freight brokers to indicate that the operations that take place prior to placing the merchandise aboard have been done and accomplished, as well as the export customs clearance operations, if needed. All these operations represent an extra cost, to be paid by the seller, which is sometimes called "fee of placing into FOB".

3.3.3 The "FOB STOWED and TRIMMED"

In the "FOB STOWED and TRIMMED", variation, the seller is responsible for the total charges incurred by the merchandise at the loading port, the loading aboard a nominated ship and paying for the loading charges including the stowage fee. The stowage fee is paid for the placement and arrangement of the goods on board. However, it has to be stipulated in the contract at which point the transfer of risks takes place. The seller must, should the case arise, provide for the buyer, at the right time, all the assistance needed to obtain all the documents and information regarding the security requirements for the export and/or import of the merchandise and/or for its transportation to its final destination. The cost of the documents furnished and/or the assistance given are costs and risks paid by the buyer.

3.3.3.1 FOB/Point of Departure

The buyer pays for everything.

The manufacturer pays for the charges up to the border without clearing the merchandise through customs.

3.3.3.2 FOB/Point of Sale

The merchandise arrives to a designated American city. It is then, the supplier, who pays for customs clearance. The chosen free port must always be marked, in general, the city.

3.3.3.3 FOB/Destination Customs Clearance

The American FOB (Freight on Board) Destination is an FOB shipping term which means that the seller retains the legal title to the goods until they reach the location of the buyer. It is normally applicable for purposes of the UK equivalent of the *Retention of Title Clause* (RTC) below. In this case, the seller pays for the transportation of the freight and takes care of additional freight charges until the goods reach the buyer. In this case, the manufacturer takes care of everything, without the cooperation of the buyer. It is also called DDP/Delivery duty paid. Most of the sales into the US are done on this basis.

3.4 Judicial Approach to the Contract Variants

3.4.1 The Variants

It names the port or ports of loading. There are many variants but a common feature is that it is for the seller to bear charges and expenses up to loading the goods on board an effective ship to be nominated by the buyer. 'Effective' means that the ship must be capable of taking the cargo within the contract time. Finally, expenses of carriage and insurance are for the buyer. In the principal FOB case of *Pyrene v Scindia*,[1] Justice Devlin distinguished three types of FOB. In the first 'classic' type *Wimble v Rosenberg*[2] Justice Devlin determined that the seller should procure a bill of lading in terms usual in the trade, the seller is directly a party to the contract of carriage at least until he takes out the bill of lading in the buyer's name. He thought, correctly so, that the first type, the classic, is probably based on the assumption that the ship nominated will be willing to load any goods brought down to the berth or at least those of which she is notified.[3] In the second, FOB strict, the seller is asked to make arrangements for shipping and perhaps to take the bill of lading in his own name, obtaining payment when he transfers it to the buyer as in CIF contracts.

In the third, "seller contracting with carrier", the shipping arrangements are made by the buyer or his forwarding agent and the seller, on the goods being loaded, obtains a mate's receipt which he hands to the buyer or his agent for them to obtain the bill of lading.

---

[1] *Pyrene v Scindia* [1954] 2 QB 402 at 424.

[2] *Wimble v Rosenberg* [1913] 3 KB 743).

[3] *Pyrene v Scindia* at p. 424.

3.4.2 The Distinctions between the Variants

The distinction between the first and second is that in the latter the seller, as an additional duty arranges for shipping. Distinctions between the first and third are that in the first the seller does and in the third he does not make a contract with the carrier and in the first but not in the third he holds, and may be bound to procure, a bill of lading. The third type, the extended or with additional duties, may now be the foremost often used. Additional duties in relation to carriage insurance may be placed on the seller so that the contract may resemble a CIF contract but the ultimate cost of these in the FOB contract falls on the buyer whereas it is the converse in a CIF contract. Variation in these charges is for the benefit or loss of buyer in the FOB contract and for the seller in CIF. On those bases, Justice Pearson in *Carlos Federspiel v Twigg*[4] decided that the FOB form is so flexible that a contract may be FOB although it does not mention FOB and refers the calculations on a CIF basis:

> It follows, therefore, that if and so far as this contract was in its true nature an FOB. contract, the natural time at which the property would pass would be on shipment. Undoubtedly this contract also contained some CIF features, and there is an express reference to what is called "approximate CIF. charges" in the pro forma invoice. If and in so far as it was a CIF. contract, the effect of the authorities is that the property would pass not earlier than shipment, perhaps later than shipment. But for the purpose of the present case there is no need to consider whether it would be on shipment or at some later time.[5]

While Lord Parker of Waddington, delivering the judgment of their Lordships, reinforced that position in *The Parchim*[6] that the sum included for freight in the price is a mere matter of calculation and would be payable separately by the buyer and deducted from the price, the price is really for cost only, in which case the contract had far more of the characteristics of a contract "FOB Taltal" than it had of a contract of "CIF European port". Although the right to cancel was provided for, he thought that there was very little probability of its becoming exercisable and that it was clear that what was really contemplated by the parties, although they provided for another somewhat remote contingency, was the shipment on *The Parchim* of a sufficient part of the nitrate which the sellers had ready, and the effect of the contract was to provide that on shipment, or at all events on notification of the shipment, the cargo was to be at the risk of the buyers. Consequently, if the ship was lost during the loading, the contract was to be cancelled only as regards the part of the cargo not loaded.[7] Thus, under an FOB contract seller must actually ship goods or cause them to be shipped; he as in a CIF contract, tenders documents covering goods already or appropriate to the contract a cargo which was not initially loaded fulfilment of the contract.

---

[4] *Carlos Federspiel v Twigg* [1957] 1 Rep 240.

[5] Ibid, at pp. 248–249.

[6] *The Parchim* [1918] AC 157.

[7] Ibid at 164.

It is unclear whether there is a fourth type, the simple. There is also a difference between the *variations* (above) and the classifications. It is the only contract with both characteristics.

3.5 Passage of Property and Title

Passage of property has a direct effect on the parties' liabilities and therefore indirect effect on insurance obligations. We have noted that under FOB contract, at common law, the seller undertakes to arrange the carriage, and possibly insurance. Since the general rule in s.20 of the *SGA* 1979 applies to FOB contracts, risk prima facie passes with property so that risk normally passes to the buyer when the goods are put across the ship's rail. Risk and property normally pass on shipment when the goods cross the ship's rail. Thus, whereas property under a CIF contract passes at the time the buyer pays and takes up the documents, the goods are deemed to be at the buyer's risk from the time of shipment. Loss/deterioration after the buyer has paid the price is clearly for the buyer's account. The goods are the buyer's property and at his risk. Under Incoterms, FOB means that the seller fulfils his obligation to deliver when the goods have passed over the ship's rail at the named port of shipment. This means that the buyer has to bear all costs and risks of loss of or damage to the goods from that point.

The new Incoterms has no provision on passage of property.

3.6 Passage of Risks

As in passage of property above, passage of risks has a direct effect on the parties' liabilities and consequently an indirect effect on their insurance obligations. At common law risk will pass on shipment even though property does not then pass, e.g. because the right of disposal has been reserved. It may be that in strictness risk passes when the seller's duties are completed and so if the contract were on 'FOB. and stowed' term—where the seller is also responsible for stowage, risk would pass when stowing is completed. Risk may be on the buyer before shipment when that has been delayed by his fault. This is when the need for his own insurance kicks in. Risk may however remain on the seller after shipment:

(a) when he fails to make a reasonable contract of carriage in accordance with the *SGA* 1979,[8]
(b) if it is his duty to arrange carriage, or
(c) if he fails to give notice to enable the buyer to insure under s. 33 (3), *SGA* 1979 or
(d) if he fails to load goods fit to endure the voyage.

[8] Sale of Goods Act 1979, s. 32 (2).

Under Incoterms 2020, FOB means that the seller fulfils his obligation to deliver when the goods have passed over the ship's rail at the named port of shipment. This means that the buyer has to bear all costs and risks of loss of or damage to the goods from that point.

3.7 Commercial Incident of the Contracts

The term FOB may be merely a basis for calculating export values for customs purposes and not refer to delivery. In American usage,[9] 'FOB named place of shipment' corresponds to the English and Commonwealth usage whilst 'FOB named place of destination' corresponds to ex ship or arrival contracts. In carriage by air the term FOB Airport, analogous to the shipping contract was amalgamated to the new FCA Incoterm.

3.8 Factors Determining Choice of Contracts

To put matters into context, the determination of the parties' insurance responsibilities in FOB contracts has much to do with the origin and development of the trade term.[10] Under English law the term FOB represents free on board and is normally followed by the name of the port of departure, e.g. "FOB London",[11] where goods are shipped from London. Chief Justice Bacon in *Exp. Rosevear China Clay Co. Re Cook*[12] further reinforced the idea that in commercial terms, FOB is, first and foremost, a price term though it often also relates to the party's delivery obligations. Decided as early as 1879, Rose ear *China Clay Co. Re Cook*, a case concerning possession by a carrier nominated and hired by the buyer in which Bacon CJ decided that: "Delivery 'free on board' only means 'the price shall be that which we stipulate for, and you shall not have to pay for the wagons or carts necessary to carry the clay from the place where it is dug; we will bear all those charges and put it free on board the ship, the name which you are to furnish'".[13]

With regard to insurance, it is important to note that in this context free has to be considered from the seller's viewpoint and means free from his/her freight and insurance obligations, which would for this purpose make the FOB similar to the

[9] UCC 2-319 (1).

[10] See, Sassoon, "The Origin of FOB and CIF Terms and the Factors Influencing their Choice", [1967], *JBL*, 32. (hereinafter, "Sassoon: The Origin of FOB and CIF Contracts").

[11] For details see Lord Mackay, *Halsbury's Laws of England*, 4th edition, Vol.41 para.348.

[12] Exp. *Rosevear China Clay Co. Re Cook* (1879) 11 Ch. D 560.

[13] Ibid at p. 565 per Bacon CJ.

CFR,[14] FAS,[15] EXW,[16] and related trade terms which exclude the sellers' obligations to insure. This is in marked contrast to CIF and CIP, the only two that include in their contractual terms the seller's duties to insure goods to the port of destination. As already noted above, this does not mean that risks in FOB contracts are any less important than those in CIF and CIP contracts.[17] This apparent difference in insurance emphasis is due to the separate developments of the two (CIF and FOB) as outlined above and ably elsewhere by Sassoon.[18]

3.9 The Essence of the Contracts

Otherwise, the essence of the FOB contract was summarised by Justice Devlin in the landmark case of *Pyrene Co Ltd v Scindia Navigation Co Ltd*[19] that the price paid to the seller includes all costs up to the loading of the goods and on to an overseas vessel nominated by the buyer, property and risk normally pass to the buyer at this point and all subsequent expenses are to the buyer's account.[20]

As to the classifications of the contract, *Pyrene Co Ltd v Schindia Navigation Co Ltd*, Justice Devlin said:

> In the first, or classic type, the buyer nominates the ship and the seller puts the goods on board for account of the buyer, procuring a bill of lading. The seller is then a party to the contract of carriage and if he has taken the bill of lading to his order, the only contract of carriage to which the buyer can become a party is that contained in or evidence by the bill of lading which is endorsed to him by the seller. The second is a variant of the first, in that the seller arranges for the ship to come on the berth, but the legal incidents are the same. The third is where the seller puts the goods on board, takes a mate's receipt and gives this to the buyer or his agent who then takes a bill of lading. In this latter type the buyer is a party to the contract of carriage ab initio.[21]

It is evident from Justice Devlin's statement on the essence of the FOB contract that FOB insurance does not feature prominently. Hence this book's argument that the

---

[14] Cost and Freight (CFR), where the seller delivers goods, cleared for export, to buyer is named carrier with no obligation for insurance or other charges thereafter.

[15] Free Alongside Ship (FAS), where the seller delivers goods alongside the vessel on the quay or in lighters at a named port of shipment, without insurance or any other obligations.

[16] Ex Works (EXW), where the seller only makes the goods available at his premises (i.e., works, factory, warehouse, etc) to the buyer. The seller is not responsible for insurance as the buyer bears all costs and risks from the seller's facility.

[17] For details of the role of insurance in CIF, contracts see generally, Ademun-Odeke, "The Insurance Elements Incoterms CIF and CIP Contracts", opct.

[18] See Note 10 supra.

[19] *Pyrene Co Ltd v Scindia Navigation Co Ltd.* [1954] 2QB 402 (case concerning export of fire-tenders FOB London to India, which has ever-since become the principal authority on passage of property on board vessels for overseas transmission). This statement has been referred to with approval by Donaldson LJ in *The El Amria* and *The El Minia* [1982] 2Lloyd's Rep.28 at 32.

[20] Ibid. at p. 424, per Devlin LJ.

[21] Ibid at p. 32.

statement should be viewed with caution. Justice Devlin's landmark decision was referred to with approval by Donaldson LJ in *The El Amria and The El Minia*[22] and by Lord Longmore in *Erg Raffinerie Mediterranean Spa v Chevron USA Inc*[23] and Lord Mance in *Scottish and New Caste International Ltd v Othon Ghallanos Ltd*,[24] both of which followed Justice Devlin in *Pyrene Co Ltd v Scindia Navigation Co Ltd*[25] and Lord Donaldson in The *El Amria and El Minia*[26] on the nature and types of FOB contracts. On appeal,[27] Donaldson in *The El Amria and El Minia* said:

> In *Pyrene & Co v Scindia Navigation Co.*, [1954] 1 Lloyds Rep321; [1954] 2QB 402 at 332 and 424 Mr. Justice Devlin instanced three types of FOB contract. In the first, or classic type, the buyer nominates the ship and the seller puts the goods on board for account of the buyer, procuring a bill of lading. The seller is then party to the contract of carriage and if he has taken the bill of lading to his order, the only contract of carriage to which the buyer can be party is that contained in or evidenced by the bill of lading which is endorsed to him by the seller. The second is s variant of the first, in that the seller arranges for the ship to come to the berth, but the legal incidents are the same. The third is where the seller puts the goods on board, takes a mate's receipt and gives this to the buyer or his agent who then takes the bill of lading. In this latter type he is party to the contract of carriage.[28]

Lord Mance in *Scottish and New Caste International Ltd v Othon Ghallanos Ltd,* said: "There is a considerable flexibility both within and between categorisations such as FOB, CFR (or C&F), CIF and ex-ship";[29] The editor of Benjamin's Sale of Goods,[30] quoting Devlin J in *Pyrene v Scindia Navigation Co Ltd.*[31] said that the fob contract has become a "flexible instrument", so much so that no really satisfactory definition of such a contract is possible".

[22] *The El Amria and The El Minia* [1982] 2Lloyd's Rep.28 at 32.

[23] *Erg Raffinerie Mediterranee Spa v Chevron USA Inc* [2007] EWCA Civ. 49; Sir Martin Nourse and Lord Buxton concurring; [2007] 2 All ER (Comm) 548; [2007] 2 Lloyds Rep 542.

[24] *Scottish and New Caste International Ltd v Othon Ghallanos Ltd* [2008] 1 Lloyds Rep 462 [2008] 2 All ER 768 at 778. "The editors of Benjamin's Sale of Goods (7th edn, 2006) observe at p 1653 (para 20-001) - quoting Devlin J in *Pyrene v Scindia Navigation Co Ltd* [1954] 2 All ER 158 at 167, [1954] 2 QB 402 at 424 - that the FOB contract has become '"a flexible instrument", so much so that no really satisfactory definition of such a contract is possible'. It embraces: (a) cases where the buyer arranges and nominates the ship, but the seller ships and takes the bill of lading in his own name as consignor, (b) cases where the seller arranges shipment and takes the bill in his own name as consignor and (c) cases where the buyer arranges and nominates the ship, and the seller ships but the buyer is named in the bill as consignor: Benjamin pp 1654–5 (para 20-003)."

[25] *Pyrene Co Ltd v Scindia Navigation Co Ltd* [1954]2 QB 402 at 424.

[26] *The El Amria and El Minia* [1982]2 Lloyds 28 at 32.

[27] *The El Amria* and *El Minia* [1981] 2 Lloyds Rep 119.

[28] *The El Amria and El Minia* [1982] 2 Lloyd's Rep.28 at 32.

[29] see *The Parchim* [1918] AC 157 and The Gabbiano [1940] P166 at 174-4.

[30] (7th edn, 2006) observe at p1653 (para. 20-001).

[31] *Pyrene v Scindia* Navigation Co Ltd [1954] 2 All ER 158 at 167, [1954] 2 QB 402 at 424.

3.10 Legal Incidence of the Contracts

It embraces:

(a) cases where the buyer arranges and nominates the ship, but the seller ships and takes the bill of lading in his own name as a consignor;
(b) cases where the seller arranges shipment and takes the bill of lading in his own name as consignor; and
(c) cases where the buyer arranges and nominates the ship, and the seller ships but the buyer is named in the bill of lading as consignor[32]:

Furthermore, in cases (a) and (b), the seller may be either the only party to the bill of lading or acting as agent for the buyer as more or less undisclosed) principal[33]: In either cases (a) and (b) the seller may of course pre-pay the freight and recoup himself by invoicing the buyer.

In *Erg Raffinerie Mediterranee Spa v Chevron USA Inc, on* appeal from Justice Langley's judgment[34] which required the court to decide whether an FOB contract which provides for a delivery period to be narrowed to a laycan period (viz a period before which laydays will not start and after which a seller may cancel the contract if the ship which is due to take the cargo has not served a notice of readiness to load) is a traditional FOB contract in which the buyer can terminate the contract if the goods are not shipped within the period originally designated for delivery, Lord Longmore observed that: "In a traditional FOB contract, time of shipment is of the essence of the contract.[35] This means that the goods must have been placed on board the ship by the end of the shipment period. This in turn means that the buyer needs to get the vessel to the loading port in sufficient time for such loading to occur.[36]

3.11 Distinction from Related Contracts

FOB resembles FAS and FCA. It is also suggested that it resembles the old C&F and/or the new CFR. However, in the *Scottish v Othon* case, Lord Mance disagreed with this assumption: He thought, there are three general differences between the FOB and C&F contracts:

(a) First, an FOB contract specifies a port or range of ports for shipment of the goods. A C&F contract specifies a port or ports to which the goods are consigned;

[32] Benjamin's Sale of Goods pp.1654-5(para 20-003).

[33] see Benjamin's Sale of Goods pp.1658-9(para20-008) and *East West Corp. v DKB* 1912 A/S, *Utaniko Ltd v P. & O Nedlloyd BV* [2003] EWCA Civ 83 at 84, [2003] 2 All ER 700 at [34], [2003] QB 1509.

[34] *Erg Raffinerie Mediterranee Spa v Chevron USA Inc* [2006] 2 Lloyd's Rep. 543.

[35] See Benjamin's Sale of Goods, 7th edn, 2006, paras 20-029 to 20-033.

[36] Ibid at p. 543.

(b) Secondly, an FOB contract requires shipment (whether by or on behalf of the seller or the buyer) of the goods at the port (or a port within the range) so specified; i.e. the seller cannot buy afloat[37]: In contract, under a C&F contract responsibility for shipment rests on the seller, and this can be fulfilled by the seller either shipping goods or acquiring goods already afloat after shipment, and moreover shipment can be at any port (unless the contract otherwise provides); and
(c) Thirdly, and as a result, a C&F contract involves (subject to any special terms) an all quote by the seller, who carries the risk of any increases (and has the benefit of any reduction) in the cost of carriage. In contrast, under an FOB contract, although the seller may contract for and pay the freight, the buyer carries the risk (and has the benefit) of any such fluctuation"[38]

Despite ruling out an FOB seller himself buying afloat at common law, Incoterms 2010 now makes it possible for him to do. Although insurance costs do not feature in theory in FOB as it does in CIF, in practice it does. Sellers do effect and charge buyers for it as there is nothing to stop those (sellers) from passing on pre-shipment insurance costs to the buyer:

(a) either in the cost and delivery expenses; or
(b) as agency and/or miscellaneous expenses in the invoice; or
(c) with prior agreement between the parties. As is further argued below, pre-shipment and other insurance costs, although borne initially by the seller, are in practice transferred to the buyer, the same way as in CIF.

Furthermore, the original FOB concept, where the buyer was also the carrier and self-insured, has continued in modern practice by trader-ship-owners, oil companies, commodity traders and charterers, who have continued the original FOB practice of assuming carriage and insurance responsibilities. Hence, Justice Devlin's comments, in *Pyrene and Scindia*, of the flexibility of the FOB contract.[39] Otherwise, for insurance purposes, the modern FOB is not that different from its younger-CIF kin with the exception that in the latter the insurance cost is itemised clearly in the invoice. For that reason, the notion that the CIF is three contracts in one (sale, insurance and affreightment) is no longer the preserve of CIF.

FOB related contracts are discussed in details at the end of this chapter.

---

[37] see Benjamin's Sale of Goods p.1660 (para. 20-009).

[38] *Scottish and New Caste International Ltd v Othon Ghallanos Ltd*, at p. 778.

[39] On the three types of FOB contracts, see also "Sale Contracts. Three types of FOB contract", http://www.lawandsea.net/COG/COG_SaleContracts_Types_of_FOB.html

3.12 American and Other Designations

3.12.1 The North American FOB

The North American (Canada and US) FOB is slightly different. In Canada and the US, the Incoterm FOB (Free on Board) does not refer to a shipment in a boat or to a port but to a North American destination, at the border. In the United States there could be, mainly, four types of FOB:

Because of their historical and legal tradition, the position of the FOB contract in most Common Law jurisdictions listed above are the same as those under the English ("motherland") practice. Although some Common Law jurisdictions have ever since made changes, these have not been major enough to make significant departure from the English either law or FOB contracts. The notable difference being that in the US the seller pays transportation and insurance, including the cost of loading cargo at the named point. For the US Customs' Service, the preferred term of sale is FOB for import valuations. In contrast, CIF is preferred in English and the other Common Law jurisdictions.

The US and Canadian experiences, which refer to "FOB vessels"[40] differ slightly from those of the English and the rest. In the US, the FOB contract has developed into a general delivery term, which denotes "free delivery" at a given point named at the end of the abbreviation FOB. For that reason, in the US experience the "FOB named place of shipment",[41] corresponds to the English and other Common Law usage of "FOB", whilst FOB named place of destination", which does not exist under English law corresponds to Ex Ship or Arrival Contracts.[42] Unlike the English and other largely precedence-based Common Law traditions, the US experience is based partly on precedence and partly on the codified UCC, which is the nearest equivalent to the ICC meaning of a codified system.[43] Another difference is that the English law meaning of "FOB" is the nearest equivalent to the US "FOB vessel".

---

[40] The seller arranges shipment, prepares documentation, and pays all costs, including the cost of loading cargo on board the vessel. More importantly, the seller also pays insurance but only to the loading port. Costs (including insurance costs) pass to the buyer once goods once goods have been loaded.

[41] The actual name is "FOB named port of exportation", where the seller arranges to deliver cargo to a named exportation port. The buyer pays all freight charges. Outside of the US, these quotes are often confused with FOB vessel above.

[42] See the American -Canadian case of *Northlands Airlines Ltd. Dennis Ferranti Meters Ltd.* (1970) 114 S.J.845 (discussed in Chap. 4 below),), *The Times*, October 23, 1970 (CA), in which a Canadian company used the term; in this case the Canadian legal position on the subject being almost similar to that of the US.

[43] See, the US *Uniform Commercial Code (*UCC), 2000 Edition, para 2-319 which provided that:

> Unless otherwise agreed, the term fob (which means "free on board" at a named place, even though used only in connection with the stated price, is a delivery term under which:

(a) when the term is FOB the place of shipment, the seller must at that place ship the goods ...and bear the expense and risk of putting them into the possession of the carrier; or

3.12.2 Other Designations

Other FOB related contracts discontinued in Incoterms but still in use in the US, Canada and other countries are:

- **FOB airport (FOBA);**
- **FOB "freight allowed";**
- **FOB "freight prepaid";**
- **FOB "named inland carrier";**
- **FOB Air (FOBA);**
- **FOB rail (FOR) (see para 3,21.1 post);**
- **FOB truck (FOT) (see para 3.21.2 post);**
- **Free out (FFO);**
- **FOB and trimmed (for coal trade); and**
- **FOB "named inland port of origin"**.

However, these latter categories have no insurance implications to the seller either pre- or post-shipment and are, therefore, not covered in this book. Other than that, with regard to insurance, the US position of FOB is similar to that under English law and the rest of the Common Law jurisdictions. With those exceptions the FOB has the same meaning as in the US, the English and other Common Law countries: namely, that the seller will deliver subject matter contracted for, on a certain conveyance, without expenses to the buyer.[44] Likewise, in price quotation, the term is also similar to that under the English and other Common Law jurisdictions and means that the seller assumes all responsibilities and costs up to the point of delivery under the old paragraphs 2-319 of the UCC.[45] In that context, although the issue of precedence did not seem to arise, the position of US courts in that respect is similar to that

(b) when the term is FOB. the place of destination, the seller must at his own expense and risk transport the goods to that place and there tender delivery of them…;
(c) where under either (a) or (b) the term is also FOB vessel, car or other vehicle, the seller must in addition at his own expense and risk load the goods on board. If the term is FOB. Vessel, the buyer must name the vessel and in the appropriate case the seller must comply with the provisions on this clause on the form of bill of lading.

Note, however, that this provision is deleted from the 2004 Edition of the UCC where the only entry on insurance is in Clause 2-501 relating to insurable interest in goods: the manner and identification of goods. For the discussion, see *Uniform Commercial Code. 2004 Edition*, pp. 153–154: the deleted 2003 Amendments to Clause 2 is retained in an to the 2004 Edition, pp. 1957–2031 with 2-319 at pp. 1988–1989.

[44] See the case of *Tyson v Seaport Grain Inc.*, Tex.Civ. App,338 S.W.2d 731 at 734.

[45] Note, however, that the 2004 Edition of the UCC omits most references to such divisions of the FOB by amending the provision, see footnote 16 above. Sections 2-319 through 2-324 have been eliminated apparently "because they are inconsistent with commercial practice". This may be so in the US but the rest of the world trading community still uses them. For an exhaustive treatment of passage of property, see Benjamin, paras 20-070 through 20-086 (pp. 1434–1448).

taken by Justice Kerr in the English case of *David T Boyd & Co. Ltd. V Luis Lonca.*[46] This position is also the same in the other major systems notably Australia,[47] Canada[48] and New Zealand[49] that have adhered to the Common Law tradition.

3.13 Effect of Passage of Property and Title on Insurable Obligations

In sales transactions, the party that has property [not necessarily possession] bears the risk and should insure. The party that has the property (and sometimes possession) also acquires insurable interests in the consignment. With a few exceptions discussed below, it is also at the critical point of passage of property that the respective parties lose and/or acquire insurable interests. A party with insurable interest in a venture is the one exposed to risks and who should insurance. When the insured does not have an insurable interest in the subject matter the policy is void and is unenforceable against the insurer. Equally, a successful claim in the event of loss will depend on proof of insurable interests at the time of such loss or damage.

However, contrary to popular view, that critical point at which insurable interest arises may not be as clear-cut to determine as it first appears. This is more so in FOB contracts despite the earlier positions adopted in *Pyrene v Scindia and The El Minia* and *The El Amria.* In *The Ciudad De Pasto and Ciudad De Neiva,*[50] for instance, Lord Justice Staughton clarified the question of passing of property, risk and other duties in the FOB contract that the expression FOB determines how the goods shall be delivered, how much of the expense shall be borne by the sellers, and when the risk of the loss shall pass to the buyers. It does not necessarily decide when property is to pass.[51]

When property, and insurable interest, attaches and/or pass may further depend on the parties' intentions and the surrounding circumstances of the contract. Nevertheless, if goods are ascertained parties are quite likely to have intended that property pass after shipment. However, unless sold in bulk, under certain conditions, property in unascertained goods does not pass on contract or shipment. The rider here being that the predominant characteristic of goods traded in FOB

---

[46] *David T Boyd & Co. Ltd, v Luis Lonca* [1973] Lloyds Rep 209, at 212 and 213 (a decision concerning, inter alia, seller's failure to nominate port of shipment but held on the relevant point that the fob contract could be void for uncertainty although complemented by the words "stowed good Danish port").

[47] In particular, see the Australia see the authority cited in Note 29 below; and generally, see "Developments in Australia" in *Insurance Law Monthly*, Vol. 17 No.1 January 2005, pp. 1–9 at 3 for differences between jurisdictions; see also *Insurance Law Monthly* Vol.7 No.4 April 2004.

[48] For Canadian case law see- Note 58 and the text thereunder.

[49] For New Zealand case law see- Note 72–75 below and the text thereunder.

[50] *The Ciudad De Pasto and The Ciudad De Neiva*: [*Mitsui & Co v Flota Mercante Grancolombiana,* SA, [1988] 2 Lloyds 208 (a case primarily regarding rights to title by buyer who had part paid, under section 19 of the *SGA* 1979).

[51] *Ibid,* at p. 210.

contracts fall in both categories, making it doubly difficult to ascertain when property passes.

Another complicating factor that merchants should be aware of, in FOB, is that sellers tend to reserve the right of disposal[52] until payments and other conditions are met. Furthermore, where the seller obtains a bill of lading in his own name, such as in the classic or extended FOB, passage of title is postponed until the seller makes the bill of lading available to the buyer or his agent or until some other condition is satisfied. Once again, contrary to popular view, FOB sellers sometimes take out the bill of lading in their own name, thereby further complicating their insurance obligations. This causes further twists. Additionally, s.19 of the *SGA* 1979,[53] on reservation of title, does not affect passage of risks and, therefore, the acquisition of insurable interest by a buyer who might at this stage have neither the property nor their possession.

3.14 Effect of *Reservation of Title Clauses* on Insurance Obligations

It is due to such unique and intricate FOB situations that merchants have to be alert against complacency. For those reasons, generalisations that it is always the FOB buyer who takes out insurance or whose task is easier are over-simplifications and only serves to complicate matters further. Facts and circumstance of each particular case need considering. Effects of retention of title clause and taking out the bill of lading in the seller's name, on passage of property and risks, being cases in point. However, how do the two factors relate to passages of property and risks and therefore affect the parties' respective insurance obligations? *The Parchim*,[54] *Freebold v Circle Products Ltd*[55] and earlier decisions,[56] support the proposition that when the

[52] For the Reservation of Title Clause and its effects on contracts on international trade, see, generally Section 19 of the UK *Sale of Goods Act*, 1979; See also Note 59 infra.

[53] (Cap.54 of 1979). The Act repeals and replaces the *Sale of Goods Act 1893,* which it reproduces. The Act should be read as amended by the *Sale of Goods Amendment Act* 1995 (1995 Cap.28), ss. 20A and 20B (not to mistaken with *The Sale of Goods Amendment Act* 1994 (1994 Cap.32) which abolished the rule of law relating to the sale of goods in market overt, or the *Sale and Supply of Goods Act 1994* (1994 Cap.35) which amended the *Supply of Goods and Services Act 1982* in relation to implied terms).

[54] *The Parchim* [1918] AC 157 (intention and presumption of passage of property on shipment is not defeated by withheld and ambiguous bill of lading).

[55] *Freebold v Circle Products* Ltd. (1970) 114 S.J.262, *sub nom. Freebold and Sturznickel (Trading as Panda O.H.G) Circle Products* [1970] 1 Lloyds Rep 499, CA (bill of lading taken to seller's order alters neither the nature of the fob contract nor the rules relating to passage of property under it).

[56] Such as *Mirabita v Imperial Ottoman Bank* (1878) 3 Ex. D 164 (suspension of passage of property- section 18 rule 5 and section 19(1) and (3) of the 1893 and the 1979 Acts were founded on the judgment of Cotton LJ in this case); *Wait v Baker* (1848) 2 Ex.1(passage in appropriation); and *Turner v Liverpool Docks* (Trustees of) (1851), 6 Ex. 543 (passage of property may be suspended although goods have been delivered on board buyer's ship).

bill of lading is taken to seller's order, there is presumption of intention to retain property, otherwise property passes on shipment. However, it should be remembered that the retention of title in FOB does not affect passage of property and is no defence to the buyer's failure to ensure that the seller has exercised the right.

On this point, the rest of the Common Law jurisdictions seem to follow English law authorities.[57] A notable exception is the US-Canadian case of *George Smith Trucking Co Ltd v Golden Seven Enterprise Inc.*,[58] where a co-defendant's reservation of title, by holding on to some export documents, was rendered ineffective by both the trial and appellate courts. We shall delve on the case at length. The facts of the case are that the first defendant (a wholesale food broker) purchased frozen meat from the second defendant for resale to Japanese buyers. The defendant then engaged the plaintiff (a trucking company) to transport the meat from the co-defendant's packing plant to Vancouver for shipment to Japan. There was no specific agreement between the two defendants as to when the property in the meat products passed and although the contract was FOB the second defendant's packing plant the second defendant did not assume risk. The straight bill of lading showed the first defendant as the consignee and in the usual course of the parties' dealings Canadian export and Japanese import documents would be delivered to first defendant's bank only upon payment in full. The first defendant placed three orders from the second defendant in January 1985. On February 4, the second defendant discovered that the first defendant had filed for bankruptcy in the US on February 1.

In the meantime, however, the plaintiff had already transported two of the orders to Vancouver. The plaintiff obtained an injunction to restraining export, and the meat was subsequently sold and the proceeds paid into court. On a stated case, the trial judge held that property in the meat passed to the first defendant when each order was loaded on the plaintiff's trucks, and the plaintiff was accordingly entitled to execute against the proceeds. The second defendant appealed arguing that it retained title to the meat until all the documents necessary for export had been delivered to the first defendant. The appeal was dismissed by Seaton JA (Macfarlane, JA concurring and Hutcheon JA dissenting) on the basis that the goods had clearly been appropriated to the contract. The majority decision was that the second defendant had not reserved a right of disposal by withholding some of the documents; it had merely dealt with the documents in a manner designed to secure payment and the documents it withheld were not title documents. Furthermore, the facts that the contract was FOB, that the first defendant assumed the risk and was named as a consignee very clearly pointed to title passing unconditionally when the meat was loaded on the trucks.

Although decided solely on the issue of passage of property, rather than FOB insurance obligations, the decision was rather an unusual with serious implications

---

[57] But see *New South Wales Leather Co Pty v Vanguard Insurance Co Ltd* (unreported Australian case) included as a Case Comment Clause Journal in *Lloyds Maritime and Law Newsletter* No.274, 1990, pp. 1–2.

[58] [1989] 3 WWR 544 (CAN), an fob on the determination of passage of property on loading goods on a truck and which involved Canadian, American and Japanese parties.

on passage of risk and, therefore, insurance obligations of the parties. The older and leading US authorities[59] decided under the old UCC Section 2-509 seem to agree on this point[60] Readers may also find the ICC's publication-*Reservation of Title Clause* useful.[61]

3.15 Effect of Passage of Risks on Insurance Obligations

The anomaly that risk can pass to a buyer who has neither property nor possession is not unique to FOB contracts.[62] In most contracts, unless contrary intention is shown, risk follows property, the FOB being no exception.[63] Indeed s.20 of the *SGA* 1979 provides that risk prima facie pass with property.[64] In many commercial contracts, the question of risk is dealt with by specific terms. There may be uncertainty or silence in which case the section will apply. Many traders (and consumers) are unaware of the significance of this aspect of the transfer of property and the effect that receipt of goods may have upon insurance. A seller retaining title may wish to make certain that the buyer insures the goods; while he may wish to stipulate in the contract of sale, default in obtaining adequate cover may mean that the seller is unprotected by insurance. It is, therefore, better in such a case for the seller to insure and add premium to the price.

In FOB contracts risk of damage or loss to the goods will pass on shipment of the goods and there may be a term in the contract of sale to that effect. *Pyrene v Scindia* decided that goods are shipped when they pass the ship's rail. However, risk may remain with seller if he does not comply with the requirements of s.32 (3).[65] If the seller fails to give notice under s.32 (3), goods are deemed to be at his risk during sea transit. As will be apparent shortly,[66] s.32 (3) (like s.32 (2)) negates in the particular case the ordinary presumption that risk attaches to property. If parties fail to expressly provide for risk to pass on shipment, i.e., when the goods cross the ship's

[59] Such as: *Silver v Wycombe, Meyer & Co., Inc* (124 Misc.2d 717, 477 N.Y.S.2d 288) (Civil Court of the City of New York 1984); *Jason Foods, Inc. v Peter Eckrich & Sons, Inc. 772 F.2d 214* (United States Court of Appeals, Seventh Circuit, 1985); and *Raylo Lumber Company v Oregon Pacific Lumber Company*, 222 Or.257, 352 P.2d 749 (Supreme Court of Oregon, 1960). For the general treatment of the subject, see *Benjamin*, paras 20-086 through 20-091 at pp. 1448–1452.

[60] For discussions of these cases and related issues see Speidel and Summers, Commercial Law, 4th Edition, West Publishing Co, pp. 646–671.

[61] ICC Retention of Title-A Practical guide to 19 national legislations, ICC Doc. No.467.

[62] See, generally, *Halsbury's Laws of England,* Vol.41 para. 348 and the case of Ingles v Stock (1885) 10 App. Cas 263 (HL). *sub nom Stock v Inglis* (1884) 12 QBD 564 (CA) (Scottish decision that risk passed to buyer, who had insurable interest, on fob contract on floating policy).

[63] Ibid; see also, generally, the case of *Cowas-Jee v Thompson* (1845) 5 Moo PCC 165 (the general rule on passage of risk based on the presumption that the buyer is the shipper and therefore bears the risk).

[64] (Take to main text) Which is same as at common law and Incoterms.

[65] Discussed in details in Notes 81-84 below and the texts thereunder.

[66] Ibid.

rail, what is the position where goods are damaged in the course of or during loading?

As already indicated, there appears to be two views on this. The first is that risk passes when goods pass the ship's rail and it is irrelevant whether they reach the ship safely on completion of the loading operation. This is the classic case of *Pyrene v Scindia.* The second is that risk passes only when the seller has fulfilled his obligations and only when goods are safely deposited in the vessel and the loading process is complete. This is in accordance with Justice Devlin's remarks in *Pyrene v Scindia* that until then the loading operation is incomplete and remains a continuing process. Once more, although this argument concerning the ship's rail may, at first, appear academic but in FOB contracts, it determines who bears the risk and consequently who is responsible for insurance. That notwithstanding, it would be a pity if such an important issue were left to be decided by the swinging of a sling in what amounts to a ping-pong game during the loading process. Indeed, Justice Devlin in *Pyrene v Scindia* envisaged this scenario by indicating the division of the loading into two parts was outdated when he said:

> … the division of loading into two parts is suited to more antiquated methods of loading than are now generally adopted and the ship's rail has lost most of its nineteenth-century significance. *Only the most enthusiastic lawyer could watch with satisfaction the spectacle of liabilities shifting uneasily as the cargo sways at the end of a derrick across a notional perpendicular projecting from the ship's rail …*[67] (*Emphasis added*).

Nevertheless, it is at this notional point that the seller relinquishes, and the buyer acquires, property and may be also insurable interest in the FOB cargo. This is so, regardless of the type of the FOB, both at Common Law and under Incoterms 2000, subject only to the premature passage of risk in the latter[68] In contrast, it will be apparent shortly that the rule in s.32 (2) and 32(3) does not, however, apply to CIF, EX-SHIP, and probably CIP contracts nor does it impose any new obligations on the seller to give notice to the buyer so as to enable him to insure for instance against war risks if, after the date of the contract, war becomes imminent.[69] This is in marked contrast to the position in the CIF, which dispenses with the requirement for notice, as insurance is inbuilt into the seller's contractual obligations.

[67] *Pyrene v Scindia*, opct, at p. 419.

[68] For the older position regarding risk of loss in American FOB cases see, James White and Robert Summers, Uniform Commercial Code, 2nd Edition, West Publishing Co, 1980, Chapter 5 at pp. 179–183.

[69] On this point see, generally, the case of *Law and Bonar Ltd. V British American Tobacco Co.Ltd.* [1916] 2 KB 605 (the issue in this case was whether the buyer was entitled to notice to enable him insure unusual risks). See also Benjamin's view at note 71 below and the texts there under infra.

3.16 Insurance Implications of Passage of Risks in Partial Deliveries

The effect of passage of property and risks and on insurance is less clear where the seller has made only partial delivery. The introduction of the seller's exercise of a reservation of title clause to protect himself against non-payment due to eventualities such as the buyer's default or insolvency and government intervention, only serves to complicate an already mudded issue. Although these issues are already eluded, there are added complications with regard to partial shipment. Benjamin discusses several scenarios that may lead to the seller's inability to provide full contractual shipment[70] and the insurance implications of such actions[71] with particularly reference to insurable interests in the consignment. There is no English or North American authority on this subject. However, it was the subject of court action in a case, involving Australian and New Zealand parties in *Colonial Insurance Co of New Zealand v. Adelaide Marine Insurance Co*,[72] but which came to London via the Privy Council appeal. Briefly, the seller delivered part of a cargo of wheat on board a ship chartered by the buyers, which was subsequently lost.

On the issue as to whether the loss fell on the buyers or sellers the court had to determine, preliminarily, whether property had passed and consequently whether the buyers had insurable interest in the partial shipment of wheat. Delivering the judgment on behalf of their Lordship, Sir Barnes Peacock, held that: "Their Lordships are of the opinion that the delivery of the wheat from time to time was delivery to the purchasers that it vested in them the right of possession as well as the right of property, and that at the time of the loss it was at their risk. The right which they had to return the wheat which had been delivered, in the event of the sellers neglecting, without lawful excuse, to complete the supply, did not prevent them from having an insurable interest. The interest in this was defeasible, not by the vendors, but at the option of the vendees in the event of the vendors not completing the contract".[73] The contract turned on the fact that the purchasers, as shippers, chartered the vessel and that delivery to such a vessel was delivery to the buyers. An earlier decision of *Anderson v. Morice*[74] was distinguished and *Oxendale v.*

---

[70] Benjamin, paragraph 20-074 (Shipment of part).

[71] Ibid., at p. 1414.

[72] *Colonial Insurance Co of New Zealand v. Adelaide Marine Insurance Co.* (1886) 12 App.Cas.128 (dealing with insurable interest in the buyer and passage of property).

[73] Ibid. at p. 140. (Note that although the case was heard on 26 and 30 November and decided on 18 December 1886, the case is in fact reported in (1887) 12 App.Cas 128 and not (1886) App.Cas 128 as reported in most publications. Cf. Sharp v. Sphere Drake Insurance (*The Moonacre) [1992] 2 Lloyds Rep 501 at 511-512 and Glengate Properties Ltd. Norwich Union Fire Insurance Society* [1996] 2 All ER 487 at 498 (cited by Benjamin at p. 14140) where the Exchequer Chamber held that the buyers had no insurable interest until the loading was completed as the risk was not intended to pass, and the buyers had no sufficient interest in the preservation of the goods until then.

[74] (1876) 1 *App.Cas* 713 (also dealing with insurable interest in the buyer and passage of property. However, in this case goods were lost before the risks attached).

Wetherell,[75] approved. Thus, partial delivery or shipment tends to complicate further passage of property and risk and consequently the determination of insurance obligations in FOB.

3.17 Passage of Property And Insurance Obligations at Common Law

The English, Canadian and US authorities on the subject have been discussed. The position in Australia[76] and New Zealand are not dissimilar to that of the English and older US decisions.[77] There are no significant cases in South Africa and other jurisdictions. Elsewhere in the Common Law jurisdiction, the only notable reported authority is the Indian case of *Marwa Tent Factory v Union of India and Others*.[78] Although decided as a FOR case (FOR now subsumed into FCA under Incoterms 2020), nevertheless the principle of passage of property and risk are the same as in FOB. The facts of this case are as follows. In 1968 Marwa Tent Factory ('the sellers'), trading from Jodpur, entered into a contract to supply consignments of tents by rail to the Directorate of General of Supplies and Disposal in Kanpur ('the buyer').

Under Clause 11 of the contract, the appellant would supply the consignments FOR at Jaipurite buyer would pay 95% of the price after inspecting the goods at a seller's premises in Jadpur and on proof of despatch from Jadpur. The remaining 5% would be paid on receipt of the goods in good condition in Kanpur. In October 1968, a consignment arrived in in Kanpur without 224 of the tents. The trial judge found on the evidence that the seller had delivered the full amount of the consignment to the railway company at Jadpur, but that the railway company had failed to deliver the 224 tents to the buyer. The decision was upheld by the Indian High Court but reversed by the Indian Supreme Court that it was the seller's liability to place the goods free on board the rail as the place of delivery and therefore the property and the risk belonged to the buyer. Accordingly, it was his obligation to take out insurance.

---

[75] 9 B.& C.387 (as in Colonial Insurance the property and therefore risks had passed to the buyer when the loss occurred).

[76] See the case noted in footnote 28 above, a marine insurance policy in which goods were insured on a "lost or not lost" clause, and where goods were stolen before loading. The same case is discussed by Andrew James, with regard to whether an FOB consignee has insurable interest in goods prior to shipment (loading, in *International Business Lawyer* (IBL) 1993, Vol.21, No.9 pp. 423–424.

[77] For the older American position see, again, Richard E. Speidel and Others, *Commercial Law*, West Publishing Co, 4th Edition, Chapter at pp.650-60, and the cases cited and discussed therein.

[78] *Marwa Tent Factory v Union of India and Others* [1991] LRC (Comm.) 427 (IND).

3.18 Effect of Special Contractual Circumstances

Returning to the 'pendulum swing' debate arising from *Pyrene and Scindia* case, in determining the passage of property and risk in FOB contracts certain factors stand out. First, it is noted that the principle developed when loading was still by the use of slings still rules today, well into the container and multimodal transport age or when goods may be loaded up-country near the seller's inland-depot facility. Despite that advancement in transport technology, the concept of the ships' rail remains current. Secondly, in many commercial contracts the question of risk is dealt with by specific terms. For example, the contract may be uncertainty or silence in the contract on the parties' intentions, in which case sections 20, 20A and 20B of the *SGA* 1979 will apply. A significant number of merchants (and insurers) are unaware of the significance of this aspect of the transfer of property and the effect that receipt of goods may have upon insurance. It has been demonstrated that seller by retaining title may wish to make certain that the buyer insures the goods. However, while he may stipulate this in the contract of sale, default in obtaining adequate cover may mean that the buyer is unprotected by insurance. It is therefore better, and practical, in such a case, for the seller to insure and add the premium to the contract price.[79]

Finally, parties, especially the buyer, need to be aware of the effect of s. 20(1), when read together with s.33 of the *SGA* 1979. The former[80] provides that when goods are transferred to the buyer, they are at his risk whether delivery has been made or not. Section 33(1) provides that where the seller of goods agrees to deliver them at his own risk at a place other than where they are when sold, the buyer must nevertheless (unless otherwise agreed) take the risk of deterioration in the goods necessarily incident to the course of transit. There are modern cases on this section but *Mash and Murrell Ltd. v Joseph I Emmanuel* (Joseph)[81] (I) was decided under an identical section in its predecessor the *SGA 1893*.

However, *Beer v Walker*[82] (on whether merchant liable for deterioration of goods in transit) and *Bull v Robison*[83] (on deterioration necessarily incident to transit) predate the 1893 codification of the Act and are presumably based on the precodification common law. And the latter[84] puts the onus on the buyer even where the seller had undertaken to deliver at his own risk at a distant place other than where

[79] For details on the effect of the retention of title or *Romalpa Clause*, see, generally, Borden (UK) v Scottish Timber Products and McNicol Brownlie Ltd. [1979] 2 Lloyds Rep 168 (and on appeal) [1980] 1 Lloyds Rep.160 and *Re Highway Foods International Ltd (in Administrative Receivership)* [1995] 1 BCC 271 (where the risk in both cases was the uncertainty caused by inclusion in the contract of the retention of title clause); See also Note 33 supra.

[80] The section [s.20(1)] See also *Halsbury's Laws of England*, 4th Edition, Vol. 4. para. 142 et seq; and, cf. s 55(1) of the *SGA* 1979.

[81] *Mash and Murrell Ltd. v Joseph I Emmanuel Ltd* [1961] 1All ER 485 (reversed [1962] 1 All ER 77n).

[82] *Beer v Walker* (1877) 46 LJKB 677.

[83] *Bull v Robison* (1854) 10 Exch. 342.

[84] The section [s.33].

goods were situated or the sale conducted. Although both sections open with, and include the proviso, "unless otherwise agreed", in their texts, they seem to put the buyer at a disadvantage.

3.19 Nature of Other Related Contracts

3.19.1 Ex-Ship Contracts

Of the remaining "Free" contracts only FAS, FOR and Ex-Ship (subsumed into EXW) contracts have had common law interpretations. The DDU, DDP, etc., have not had judicial interpretation. Under an ex-works sale contract, the seller undertakes to have the goods available for collection by the buyer at the seller's premises, for instance, factory, warehouse or mine. From that viewpoint in resembles the FOB in making goods available free from a particular point. It will be apparent from Incoterms 2020, that under EXW the seller must provide packaging required for the transport of the goods, at his/her expense. Before the sale is concluded, the seller should also make the buyer aware of the circumstances relating to the transport. The buyer has to make arrangements to take delivery and for cargo, insurance cover, obtaining export licenses and import licenses. Risk and property pass to the buyer from delivery. The seller will be required, under the Incoterms 2020, to render any assistance in obtaining an export license at the buyer's request, risk and expense. Here, the seller makes the goods available on his own premises and the buyer bears costs for loading on vehicle, transport and insurance. Not an Incoterms. For insurance see Chap. 6 (post).

3.19.2 *Ex-Works* Contracts

Ex Works is a common law contractual term. EXW means that the seller fulfils his obligation to deliver when he has made the goods available at his premises (i.e. works, factory, warehouse, etc) to the buyer. In particular, he is not responsible for loading. The buyer bears all costs and risks involved in taking the goods from the seller's premises to the desired destination. Three aspects should be noted in this context. First, Ex Works is an English concept and remains so. Secondly, the term thus represents the minimum obligation for the seller. Thirdly, the term should not be used when the buyer cannot carry out directly or indirectly the export formalities. In such circumstances, the FCA term should be used. Fourth, and finally, it is now known as an Incoterms EXW. For insurance coverage see Chap. 6 (post).

3.19.3 C&F/CNF Contracts

The C&F, also known as the CNF, is the older and common law versions of the modern Incoterms CFR. It means that the seller must pay the costs and freight necessary to bring the goods to a named port of destination and must also procure marine insurance against the buyer's risk or loss to the goods during the carriage. When used as the three letters CNF together, with regards to shipping, the acronym stands for "Cost Net Freight." It's a shipping agreement where the seller pays for delivering the item to the port closest to the buyer, but it doesn't include the cost of insurance. C&F stands for cost and freight and is always stated as C&F port of importation. Cost and Freight (C&F), commonly referred to as CFR or CNF, is very similar to CIF. The only difference is that the seller doesn't cover the insurance. The seller chooses the ship himself and cover the freight costs. When the cargo reaches the LA port, you assume all the costs. CIF (Cost, Insurance and Freight) and CFR (Cost and Freight, sometimes called C&F or CNF) are widely used international shipping terms or Incoterms. The seller pays for everything up to and including the freight to a named destination port, the first charge to the buyer is the terminal handling at the destination port [For insurance under common law see Para 4.23.1 (post)]

3.19.4 Free Alongside Ship (FAS) Contracts

FAS is an Incoterm describing a term of sale that details the responsibilities of the buyer and seller for the international trade transaction.[85] Under this term, the seller fulfils his obligation to deliver when the goods have been placed alongside the vessel on the quay or in lighters at the named port of shipment. *Yusen Karim v Ramjbam Serowgee*[86] dealt with the delivery aspects of the contract. It was clearly indicated in this case that the seller delivers the goods into the possession of the employees of the ship owners. The seller does this on behalf of the buyer, not on his own behalf, otherwise he might become liable as a shipper vis a vis ship owner.[87]

The case should, however, be compared to the description of the FAS contract in *Grill and Duffus Landauer Ltd v London Export Corpn. GmbH*,[88] which decided that the buyer has to bear all costs and risks of loss of or damage to the goods from that moment. Otherwise Justice Megaw, in *Anglo-African Shipping Co of New York Inc v J Mortimer Ltd*[89] determined that it is the buyer's duty to engage shipping space and to give the seller sufficient notice, in so far as the contract does not itself indicate, when, within the contract, and where goods are to be ready alongside what ship: "on an FAS contract it is for the buyers to arrange for shipping space and it is for the buyers to tell the sellers to what point, and by what date, the goods are to be brought to that place. Until the suppliers, the sellers, are so informed by or on behalf

---

[85] See *Halsbury's Laws of England* (5th Edn 2012) at paragraph 372.

[86] *Yusen Karim v Rajmjbam Serowgee* [1938] 2 All ER 285.

[87] Ibid at 290–293 PC.

[88] Ibid; see also *Grill and Duffus Landauer Ltd v London Export Corpn GmbH* [1982] 2 Lloyds Rep 627.

[89] *Anglo-African Shipping Co of New York Inc v J Mortimer Ltd* [1962] 1 Lloyds Rep 81.

of the buyers, the sellers are under no obligation, and cannot be under an obligation, to move the goods.[90]

The buyer must clear the goods for export. Can only be used for sea or inland waterway transport. FAS is a less commonly known or used Incoterm. It is used most commonly in sales of bulk cargo such as grains, oil, etc. In FAS the seller/exporter arranges to have the goods placed alongside the vessel at the named port of origin. Please note that FAS is ONLY used for ocean or inland waterway transport. The named place of origin in the sales contract will always be "domestic" to the seller. For example, if I was selling grain from Germany, I might sell it to an importer in New York on "FAS-Free Alongside Ship Port Bremen, Germany". It would not be advisable to use "FAS Port Le Havre, France" that would be an incorrect usage of FAS. Under FAS terms, the seller's risk and responsibility end the moment the goods are delivered alongside the vessel at the named port of origin. Its treatment under Incoterms is covered in Chap. 9 (post).

3.20 Arrival Contracts

Essentially a to arrive contract is an agreement to lock in the only the futures price portion of the contract. This is an agreement for a specific amount of a commodity to be delivered in the future for cash. The basis may be set at a later date, but it must take place before delivery of the contract. This was simply a contract for the purchase of goods upon their arrival. For example, ship cargoes were often sold before their arrival in port on a "to-arrive" The best examples of these contracts are where the seller does not contract for carriage (the free family) and contracts for goods sold and bought afloat.

3.21 The Older Related Contracts

3.21.1 Free on Rail (FOR)

Although discontinued under modern Incoterms since 1980, it is still subject of common law interpretation. In a Free on Rail contract, the seller is required to deliver the goods on board the rail. The Court of Appeal in *Young (Thomas) & Sons Ltd v Hobson*[91] decided that under FOR contracts, the duty of the sellers to make a reasonable contract with carrier means delivery into railway wagons or at the station (depending on the practice of the railway), at his own expense and (commonly) to make such a contract with the railway on behalf of the buyer as is reasonable in the

[90] Ibid at 92 per Megaw J; affirmed [1962] 1 Lloyds Rep 610 at 615, 618 CA; cf. the judgment of Lord Diplock at 623.

[91] *Young (Thomas) & Sons Ltd v Hobson* (1949)65 TLR 365 CA where goods were sent at owner's risks.

circumstances. Accordingly, it was unreasonable to send goods forwards in this case, by rail 'at owner's risk' rather at the company's risk.

Thus, the seller has to bear all expenses up to and including shipment of goods on behalf of the buyer. Once the goods are put on board on rail, the property in the goods passes to the buyer and they are at the risk of the buyer, who is responsible for their freight, insurance and subsequent expenses. Thus, in *Underwood Ltd v Burgh Castle Brick Cement*,[92] where the risk and expense involved in dismantling and delivering the engine in question safely on rail was emphasized, it was nevertheless held by Lord Justice Bankes that property of goods damaged while loading had passed. Considering that the risk and expense involved in dismantling and moving this engine, he had no hesitation in holding that the proper inference to be drawn is that the property was not to pass until the engine was safely placed on rail in London,[93] following *Pyrene v Scindia* principle.

3.21.2 Free on Truck (FOT)

However, this case should be contracted with *Healy v Howlett & Sons*[94] where there was no appropriation of specific goods at the time of delivery on rail, but it was held by Justice Ridley that property and risk had passed. "There are insuperable difficulties in holding that the property has passed in the present case It is impossible to say which consignee is to bear the loss caused by the deterioration of any particular boxes of the mackerel. The essence of the authorities which decide that appropriation of goods to the contract by delivery to the carrier at the beginning of the transit may be sufficient to pass the property is that it should be known to whom the goods are appropriated, and not that the question as to who is to bear any loss that may happen should be open to any discussion or be determined by accident.".[95]

Although it is still perfectly possible to conclude contracts for the sale of goods on FOR terms, it is now more common for parties who might previously have contracted on such sale terms to incorporate the FCA since Incoterms 2010.[96] However, FCA was first introduced in Incoterms 1990,[97] replacing the Free on Rail/Free on Truck named departure point (FOR/FOT) contained in Incoterms 1980.[98] The FCA has been retained in both Incoterms 2000[99] and Incoterms 2010.Not an Incoterm but parties free to use at Common Law

[92] *Underwood Ltd v Burgh Castle Brick Cement* [1921] All ER Rep 515; [1922] 1 K.B. 343.

[93] Ibid at p. 345.

[94] *Healy v Howlett & Sons* [1917] 1KB 337 DC.

[95] Ibid at pp. at pp. 344, 345.

[96] Incoterms 2010 at pp pp. 23–31; Incoterms 2020 (ICC Doc.No723E) at pp. 29–39.

[97] Incoterms 1990 FOR at pp. 24–31.

[98] Incoterms 1980 FOR/FOT at pp. 22–27.

[99] Incoterms 2000 at 33–39.

3.22 Other *EX-Ship* Contracts

Ex Ship is the modern and Incoterm version of the discarded DES a term of sale that details the responsibilities of the buyer and seller for the international trade transaction. Under this term, the seller fulfils his obligation to deliver when the goods have been made available to the buyer on board the ship uncleared for import at the named port of destination. The seller has to bear all costs and risks involved in bringing the goods to the named port of destination. This contract was also sometimes known in Incoterms 2010 as Delivered Ex Ship.[100] Among these types of contracts are arrival contracts. As arrival contracts, at common law they predated Incoterms. As early the eighteenth century, the case of *Boyle v Siffkin*[101] treated it so. In *Hollis Bros & Co Ltd v White Sea Timber Trust Ltd*,[102] where goods were sold subject to contract and the seller exercised the option to ship, his short delivery was judged by Justice Porter a breach of contract. He said: "My view is that if they have shipped the goods the sellers are obliged, at any rate if they have not been shipped in fulfilment of other contracts, to supply them under this contract."[103]

And in *Hong Guan & Co Ltd v Jumabhoy & Sons Ltd*,[104] Lord Morris of Borth-Y-Gest ruled that these contracts are subject to the continental European force majeure or English frustration. "…it must furthermore be borne in mind that the clause now under consideration is not 'subject to shipment' but 'subject to force majeure and shipment.' There is, therefore, a double-barrelled condition in which there is a juxtaposition of 'force majeure' and of 'shipment.' So far as the clause deals with force majeure it appears to be designed to protect the respondents from liability in the event of their being prevented from performing the contract by circumstances beyond their control.".[105] For insurance under Incoterms see Chap. 8 (post)

3.23 Further Food for Thoughts

3.23.1 Confusion Over the Multiplicity of Rules

There are a number of concerns about the FOB and this group of contracts in which parties do not have obligations to insure. First, is the confusion over its multiplicity. For instance, is it necessary to have the many variations in FOB?. Are they just academic or have practical significance? Doesn't it confuse the respective insurance obligations (see next chapter). The relationship between FOB and the related contracts is not based on the "Free" aspects such as the FCA and FAS but also on the

[100] For detailed treatment see Halsbury's Laws of England (5th Edn 2012) at paragraph 373.

[101] *Boyle v Siffkin* (1809) 2 Cam 326, where the vessel arrived empty.

[102] *Hollis Bros & Co Ltd v White Sea Timber Trust Ltd* [1963] 3 All ER 895.

[103] Ibid at pp.

[104] *Hong Guan & Co Ltd v Jumabhoy & Sons Ltd* [1960] A.C. 684.

[105] Ibid at pp. 699–700.

related characteristics which includes the old C (CPT, CFR, CPT), the old D (DAP, DDP and DPU) and the old E categories (Ex-W).

3.23.2 The Cost Escalation

Secondly, although, it is generally thought to be cheaper to deal in these contracts, for instance compared to the CIF and the CIP in which parties provide insurance, in practice, buyers might find that usually find that the unit prices of goods to be provided under FOB terms and related contracts is higher than if you're looking at EXW shipments. However, this doesn't necessarily mean the overall cost will be higher, as this price includes some transport costs. Parties will usually find that the unit prices of goods to be provided under FOB terms is higher than if you're looking at Ex Works (also called EXW) shipments. However, this doesn't necessarily mean the overall cost will be higher, as this price includes some transport costs.

Thirdly, despite the designations free on board for the FOB for instance, the seller actually takes responsibility for loading the goods onto the ship like any other contracts. Once the goods are onboard, risk and costs are divided between the buyer and the seller. The seller pays costs, including freight and insurance. But as soon as the goods are loaded onto the ship, all risk transfers to the buyer. Buyer will not be held responsible for any loss in-transit. Certain disadvantages of FOB Destination are: 1. Sellers will not be able to recover any loss once the goods have been on-boarded.

3.23.3 Undue Burden on Parties

Fourth, for a new buyer—especially with international shipping, FOB might not be the option best suited for them. FOB places a lot of responsibility on the buyer, as they need to comprehend the complexity involved with international shipments. There are plenty of opportunities for penalties, delays, and other problems to occur if you don't have a good handle on the complete overseas shipping landscape. Accordingly, and especially for new shippers and buyers who are looking for the right advice on how to handle international shipments, consulting or depending on the experience of a proven third-party logistics provider like LTX is a smart idea destination to which the buyer will take them.

3.23.4 Delayed Transfer of Risks

Fifth, as noted in the Commentary to Incoterms 2020, there are two extremes in these contracts. At the other extreme in DAP, DPU and DDP, the delivery point is the same as the destination point to which the seller or its carrier will carry the goods. In the rest, the EXW, risk transfers before the transport cycle even starts; in the second, the D rules, risk transfers very late in that cycle. Again, in the rest, the

EXW and, for that matter, FCA (seller's premises), the seller performs its obligation to deliver the goods whether or not they actually arrive at their destination. In the second, the seller performs its obligation to deliver the goods only if they actually arrive at their destination.[106] This could lead to mis-delivery or late delivery with dire insurance consequences.

3.23.5 Better Alternatives!

Sixth, the Commentary [continues] that the two rules at the extreme ends of the Incoterms rules are EXW and DDP. However, traders should consider alternative rules to these two for their international contracts. Thus, with EXW the seller has to merely put the goods at the buyer's disposal. This may cause problems for the seller and the buyer, respectively, with loading and export clearance. The seller would be better advised to sell under the FCA rule. Likewise, with DDP, the seller owes some obligations to the buyer which can only be performed within the buyer's country, for example obtaining import clearance. It may be physically or legally difficult for the seller to carry out those obligations within the buyer's country and a seller would therefore be better advised to consider selling goods in such circumstances under the DAP or DPU rule.[107]

3.24 Concluding Remarks

The history of an export contract term determines nature of FOB contracts. That in turn determines the parties' respective duties regarding delivery, carriage contracts, passage of risks, passage of property and eventually liabilities. At the bottom of this food chain is insurance. The FOB contract has a long history; it can be found as early as the beginning of the nineteenth century. The contract was developed in an era when:

(a) parties were both self-insured and ship-owners and own bankers;
(b) it became and was customary for a merchant to charter a ship and travel with it to trade at various ports, the merchant would require the persons from whom he bought goods to place them 'free on board' his vessel;
(c) eventually the buyer assumed that position as a carrier; and
(d) the buyer also assumed the position of insurance responsibilities.

It has remained useful and popular with the emergence of charter party era and oil companies and large exporting/importing houses with own departments of shipping and insurance. The FOB and all other common law and Incoterms contractual terms in this chapter either belong to the 'F' group or the 'Ex' group in which the seller's

[106] Incoterms 2020, Introduction, paras 21–26 at para 21.
[107] Ibid para 22.

obligations do not include provision of insurance unless otherwise provided for in the contract. Like the CIF and all the other Incoterms, it has both a legal and commercial context: the former relating to parties' rights and obligations and the latter to quoting and price function of the contract. (More Text to Come-including all topics discussed in the chapter and make reference to insurance).

3.25 Further Reading

Books
- Sassoon, David: CIF and FOB Contracts, Sweet and Maxwell, Reuters, (10th edn 2011),
- Wooldridge, "The Kinds of FOB Contracts", in Law and International Trade (Festschrift fur Clive M Schmitthoff) Frankfurt, 1973
- Carr, Indira, Law of International Trade, Taylor and Francis, Informa, (5th edn, 2018)
- Schmitthoff, Clive: Export Trade, Sweet and Maxwell, Reuters, (12th edn, 2010)
- Scmitthoff, Clive: International Trade Usages, [1987] Institute of International Business Law.
- XX Halsbury's Laws of England, (5th edn, 2012) Vol.91 (Sale and Supply of Goods and Services)
- Bridge, Sale of Goods, [2014] OUP
- Benjamin on Sales,
- Hermann, International Trade Terms: Standard Terms for Contracts for International Sale of Goods [1993] Graham and Trotman/M Nijhoff

Clauses
- Ademuni-Odeke 'Insurance of FOB Contracts under Anglo-American and Other Common Law Jurisdictions Revisited' *Tul. Mar. Law Journal Vol.31 No.1 pp. 425-462 (2007).*
- Bennet, 'FOB contracts: substitution of vessels' [1990] LMCLQ 466
- Davis, "The Various types of FOB Contracts", 1956 JBL XX
- Sassoon, "Application of FOB and CIF Sales in Common Law Countries" [1981] ETL 50
- Evans, "FOB and CIF Contracts" [1993] *ALJ* 844;
- Gower, "FOB Contracts", (1956) 19 *MLR*, 417;
- Sassoon, "The Origin of FOB and CIF: Terms and Factors influencing choice" [1967] *JBL*32
- Treitel, 'Time Shipment in fob contracts', [1991] LMCLQ 147
- Eckersley, 'International Sale of Goods, licenses and export prohibitions' [1975] *LMCLQ*, 265
- Reynolds, "towing, trimming and their effect on delivery, risk, property in sales 'FOBS', 'FOBT' and 'FOBST' [1994] *LMCLQ* 119

Reports

- Institute of Maritime Law, Law School, Southampton University, CIF and FOB Courses 2013
- Linkstalors Solicitors, London, Report of CIF and FOB Seminar, 2012

Websites

- Reed Smith LLP, "FOB contracts: shipment/delivery periods", ***http://www.lexology.com/library/detail.aspx?g=112292da-8588-434e-94ca-b74b29499f7b***
- Reed Smith LLP , "Shipment/delivery periods in FOB contracts: confusion explained", ***http://www.lexology.com/library/detail.aspx?g=18ad4940-9628-4cbb-a8e1-4e4f0ff8c4c0***
- Law and Sea, "Sale Contracts. FOB Terms". ***http://www.lawandsea.net/COG/COG_SaleContracts_FOB.html***
- Rami Al - Tal "NOMINATION OF VESSEL FOB CONTRACTS" ***http://www.tamimi.com/en/magazine/law-update/section-7/may-6/nomination-of-vessel-fob-contracts.html#sthash.D7wH2AhG.dpuf***
- Law and Sea, "Sale Contracts. Three types of FOB contract", ***http://www.lawandsea.net/COG/COG_SaleContracts_Types_of_FOB.html.***

Insurance of Contracts that Exclude Sellers' Obligations to Provide Insurance to Buyers at Common Law

4

Abstract

This chapter continues discussions of the subject under common law. It focuses on actual insurance obligations under these types of contracts. Topics covered include insurable interest, comparisons with the opposed contracts (CIF and CIP) where there is mandatory obligation for the seller to insure, exceptions of insurance risks under the institute cargo clauses, uncertainties caused by the FOB classifications, insurance of standard and classic FOB, confusions over insurance of extended contracts, potential problems of seller providing insurance as an agent in extended, comparison of fob and CIF insurance, requirement for insurance notice under s.32(2) of the UK *Sale of Goods Act 1979* (*SGA* 1979), application of the section to Scotland and Northern Ireland, whether incoterms 2020 alters the common law rule on notice. Other contracts discussed include American FOB and FAS contracts and C&F & and Ex Works contracts. Also covered are damages for failure to insure, tender documents and providing insufficient insurance. Leading authorities such as *Pyrene v Scindia*, *Northern Steel v John Batt*, and *Wimble v Rosenberg* are covered in details. Also covered are FOT, FOR, FOB(A) and other considerations such as war risks, tender, commodities contracts. While "Further Food for Thoughts" include: caution to both parties, specific caution to sellers, specific cautions to buyers and theoretical v practical scenarios of export insurance.

Since the buyer bears the risk of destruction to the goods (from the moment of delivery FOB), he will normally seek to protect himself against their loss or damage by way of insurance. In the ordinary course of events, this insurance will cover, apart from the contract price, the freight and margin of profit, as well as the insurance premium. Frequently, provision is also made for perils other than marine (i.e., war, seizure, strikes, etc.) that the goods may encounter on their sea journey.

P. Ademuni-Odeke, *Insurance of International Sales' Contracts under Incoterms*, Law for Professionals, https://doi.org/10.1007/978-3-031-75136-3_4

However, unless there is an agreement to the contrary, the buyer cannot be under any obligation to procure such cover.[1] This might be a source of serious concern to the seller. For, so long as he remains 'unpaid' his fears that in the absence of insurance recovery of the price may be prejudiced, where loss or damage has ensued, are by no means idle. In order to overcome this undesirable situation, the seller therefore frequently inserts a provision in the contract, whereby the buyer undertakes to confirm his insurance before loading commences.[2] Occasionally, the buyer agrees to hold the policy at the seller's disposal and to deposit it with him until the price has been tendered.[3]

Moreover, in some cases where the seller acts as the buyer's agent for procuring insurance, he may even be allowed to procure a policy of his own, which will be assigned to the buyer only upon the termination of his interests in the goods.[4] Where the seller is acting in this capacity, the question may arise whether he is under a duty to tender any particular form of policy (see the case of the sale of CIF).[5] Whatever authority exists on the matter appears only to indicate that the contract will probably be satisfied by a certificate or letter of insurance and that FOB contracts are not necessarily subject to the rules which govern CIF contracts.[6]

4.1 Introduction

As in Chap. 3 above, this chapter is dominated by the FOB contract as the leading contract in this category. The above opening quotation from Sassoon sums up the gist of the FOB seller's and, consequently, the buyer's insurance position and needs, and forms the basis of discussion for this and subsequent chapters. This chapter deals with the insurance of FOB and related contracts that do not require the seller to provide insurance for the seller at common law. The related contracts are the Ex-Works and C&F contracts. The chapter builds on the previous chapter, which provides the background, nature and characteristics of these contracts under English, American UCC, and common law.

The FOB is not only the dominant contract in this group but is also one of the major export contracts, whereby the seller does not have to take out a policy as part of his obligations to the buyer. It also belongs to the 'F' category of Incoterms contracts, in which neither the main carriage nor the insurance is paid by the seller. It is also in that context that it differs from the 'C' category, such as CIF and CIP, in

[1] These agreements would include extended FOB (FOB with additional duties) or any other FOB variant where the seller would be required to contract for shipping and/or insurance.

[2] Such arrangements and undertakings now include provisions of Clauses A7 and B7 of FOB Incoterms 2010, requiring notice from both parties to each other.

[3] A type of surety provided by and/or akin to the Reservation of Title clause.

[4] Such as is anticipated by the extended FOB (FOB with additional duties); see also where Sassoon cites *The Exporters' Yearbook* 1953.

[5] This is because such arrangements might affect the type of policy that is to be tendered under the contract; for details of such documents see Chap. 11 of this book.

[6] Sassoon (1984), para. 661, p. 472; Sassoon (1995), para. 661, pp. 511–512. The statement is missing in the 5th edn., 2012, by Filippo Lorenzo. In the quotation, Sassoon also cites *The Sorfareren* (1916) 114 LT 46; *Muller Maclean Co v Leslie Anderson* (1921) 8 LL.LR 328 and 'Export Documentation', *Export* (March 1948) pp. 41–60 at p. 44.

which the seller contracts for and pays for the main carriage and takes out insurance as part of his obligations to the buyer. However, it does not mean that the FOB seller does not have to take out any insurance in all circumstances. This caution is highlighted throughout this chapter and the rest of the book. The FOB seller has to take own insurance[7] for the following reasons:

First, because he is still on risk until goods pass the ship's rail at common law pursuant to *Pyrene v Scindia* and until he has shipped the goods in Incoterms.[8] He should, therefore, take out cover for pre-shipment risks between his premises/warehouse and completion of the loading process.

Secondly, he does have to take out contingency or seller's insurance to cover himself for all sorts of eventualities, including his possible breach of the contract to the buyer.

Thirdly, he has to cover himself for post-shipment contingency risks, such as non-payment by the buyer for various reasons including insolvency, trade embargoes, sanctions and exchange regulations.

Fourthly, he should cover himself for damage and/or loss caused by the carrier and other third-party negligence.

Fifthly, the contract imposes on him other obligations, such as the duty to give notice to the buyer and on time to enable the latter to take out a policy.[9]

Finally, if he does undertake insurance such as in FOB with additional services, then that becomes part of his express contractual duties, putting him on almost the same footing as the CIF and CIP seller.

The insurances referred to in the second to fifth categories above are further detailed in Chap. 10 post of this book.

However, those insurance requirements arise out of the seller's additional undertakings rather than his/her original contractual package, while the former is voluntary and for his/her own benefit.

4.2 General Duty to Insure at Common Law

It is evident from Chap. 3 that determining the point at which property and risks pass in FOB contracts is only part of the tasks of assessing when, and by whom, insurance is affected. This is because of the *flexibility* of an FOB contract which, unlike a CIF contract, has many variants. Although the basic concepts as to delivery, passage of property and risks are common to all contracts, including FOB and CIF, it will be consistently maintained in this book that the extent of insurance obligation varies. The variations are more apparent in those FOB insurance incidents arising from flexible relationships between parties and depending on the parties' intentions as determined by express contractual terms and the surrounding circumstances.

[7] Ademuni-Odeke (2007), pp. 425–462.

[8] Clause A5 Incoterms 2020.

[9] See *Wimble, Sons & Ltd. v. Rosenberg & Sons* [1913] 3 KB 743 CA; *Northern Steel and Hardware Co Ltd v John Batt & Co (London) Ltd* (1917) 33 TLR 516.

Although procurement of insurance is not one of the FOB seller's common law duties,[10] the FOB seller fulfils his insurance obligations only when he has provided and shipped goods:

1. in conformity with the contract;
2. on the nominated ship and port at the scheduled time; and
3. obtained the proper documents and tendered them to the buyer at the right time and given place, and in a manner provided for in the contract; failing of which leads to breach and consequently insurance implications.

Otherwise, apart from a few exceptions regarding the responsible party's obligations, an FOB policy should be largely the same as a CIF one with regard to insurers, scope of cover, duration, additional cover, value and currency.[11] In addition, unless otherwise provided, the seller should insure personally rather than relying on agents to do so. This is because of the general view that there is no obligation on the forwarding agent, for instance, to cover goods from the seller's warehouse to the ship's rail. Justice Pilcher in *WLR Traders (London) Ltd. v British and Northern Shipping Agency Ltd*[12] suggested that it is ordinary practice for the seller himself to cover the goods. This case is further discussed under the requirement of notice.[13] However, *Hepburn v A Tomlinson (Hauliers) Ltd.*[14] thought that there was no conflict between that and the forwarding agent insuring his part of the interest or the whole interest in trust for the seller. Once more, the difficulty with FOB insurance obligations is due to the bifurcation of FOB contracts.[15]

4.3 FOB-CIF Insurance Cost Comparisons

CIF is considered a more expensive option when buying goods. This is because the seller uses a forwarder of his or her choice who may charge the buyer more in order to increase the profit on the transaction. Communication can also be an issue because the buyer relies solely on people who are acting on behalf of the seller. And the

[10] For detailed discussions on insurance of FOB contracts, see, generally, Lorenzo (2012), Ch. 12; Schmitthoff's *Law and Practice of International Trade*, pp. 23–24 and chapters 25 and 26 on general export insurance; *Benjamin's Sale of Goods*, paragraph 20-043 at pp. 1811–1812.

[11] See, generally, Ademuni-Odeke (1995), pp. 86–92 (Ademuni-Odeke, "Insurance Elements in CIF and CIP"); cf. the comparison of CIF and FOB contracts at para. 4-030 post and the texts thereunder; CIF Incoterms 2020, Clause A5.

[12] *WLR Traders (London) Ltd. v British and Northern Shipping Agency Ltd.* [1955] 1 Lloyds Rep.554 at 557.

[13] See para 4.10 post on notice and the texts thereunder.

[14] *Hepburn v A Tomlinson (Hauliers) Ltd.* [1966] AC 451.

[15] See Chap. 3.

buyer may still have to pay additional fees at the port, such as docking fees and customs clearance fees, before the goods can be cleared. FOB is frequently the preferred method of shipping goods. The products are considered delivered once they cross the ship's rail. The buyer can therefore negotiate a cheaper price for the freight and insurance with a forwarder of his or her choice. In fact, some international traders seek to maximize their profits by buying FOB and selling CIF.

4.4 Insurable Interests in the Contracts

Like all other insurance contracts, the FOB insured must have insurable interest in the subject matter in order to insure same.[16] Indorsees and other assignees of the policy deride their interests from him Otherwise it would be relegated to a wagering and gaming contract. The full nature and extent of cargo insurable interests are covered elsewhere in this book apply to FOB contracts.[17] The rules in this context can be summarised thus:

(a) The interest may be full or partial interests;[18]
(b) They are vested in the seller until the goods pass the ships rail when property and risks pass to the buyer;
(c) After which they transfer to the buyer or subsequent buyers in the event of selling and buying afloat;
(d) They, may however, be subject to stoppage of goods in transit rules;
(e) Unascertained goods;
(f) Claims may be an exception to the "lost or not lost" rule;
(g) Contingency insurance;
(h) American variation; and
(i) Varied by Credit Insurance

4.5 Formation of the Insurance Contracts

Just as with the omission of the detailed mechanisms for effecting insurance, the actual extent of the cover, detailed discussions on the parties' bargain and the nature and circumstances of each contract are also omitted from this chapter. Briefly,

---

[16] See ss.6–16 (especially 5(1)–5(2), 6(1)–(2) and 7(1)) of MIA 1906; see also Lorenzo (2012), Chapter 12.

[17] See Chapter 1 paragraph 2.9 (on applicable principles to the FOB and CIF contracts); chapter 13 (on the effect on claims) and the ICC 'Insurable Interest Clause', *ante*.

[18] See *The Colonial Insurance Co of New Zealand v The Adelaide Marine Insurance Co* (1887) L.R.12 App Cas128.

however, the usual insurance requirements, akin to those in CIF, are also applicable to FOB, such as the:

(a) Need for possession or acquisition of insurable interest by the parties;
(b) Validity of the policy or other evidence of cover;
(c) Requirement for effecting insurance with reputable insurers;
(d) Scope of cover is on terms and policy acceptable;
(e) Duration of cover—to cover whole transit;
(f) Sufficiency of value of cover—full cost of contract;
(g) Provision of minimum insurance, unless provided otherwise;
(h) Need for additional cover when required or needed (e.g., war, civil commotion, riots); and
(i) Synchronisation of main contract and currency of insurance.

Furthermore, because of the uncertainty in an FOB insurance contract arising from the numerous FOB classifications (see below), both parties should be aware of the need for, and provision of, adequate cover for the following additional risks and eventualities:

(a) Seller's interest policy;
(b) Buyer's interest policy;
(c) Contingency insurance;
(d) Consequential loss insurance;
(e) Institute cargo clauses requirements;
(f) Institute cargo clauses' exceptions;
(g) Commodity contracts insurance;
(h) War risks insurance;
(i) Export credit insurance;
(j) Government war insurance;
(k) Government terrorism insurance; and
(l) Miscellaneous insurance.

These mechanisms are each discussed elsewhere in this book.[19] Not all FOB risks are insurable in a general policy. The guidelines are those of the Institute Clauses, in which exceptions are reinstated by additional cover and/or extension clause. The practise applies to FOB contracts.

---

[19] See Chap. 9 (post) on notice and the text thereunder.

4.6 Insurable Risks Under Institute Clauses

4.6.1 Introduction

Parties to FOB contracts have the choice to provide either an insurance clause within their contract, or to adopt the Incoterms 2010 guidelines, or insure under either the GAFTA terms or the Institute Cargo Clauses, *inter alia.* The Institute Clauses (as the Institute Cargo Clauses are commonly known) form the most widely used global system in export import trade insurance. However, for this to apply, the parties have to expressly provide so within their sales and/or insurance contract, whichever is applicable.

4.6.2 Application of Institute Clauses to FOB Insurance Contracts

Although the insurance and institute clauses are not as prominently emphasised in FOB as in CIF, the party responsible for insurance should be aware that FOB insurance is also subject to the Institute Cargo Clauses. With slight differences between them, Cargo Clauses (A)–(C)-1/1/09, apply to FOB insurance contracts and do contain the same inclusions and exclusions. For these exclusions, the party insuring would need the reinstating cover under the respective clauses. Like all other export policies, not every risk is insurable in FOB. Although sections 1–3 of the MIA 1906 outline the insurable marine risks, maritime adventures and maritime perils, Cargo Clauses (A)–(C), however, contain those risks which are covered by the clauses and those which are excluded. Any excluded risks can be included by either the express agreement of the parties' indorsements to the policy or customs, or the use of any of the numerous clauses supplementing Cargo Clauses.

4.6.3 Main FOB Risks Covered by Cargo Clauses

Unless otherwise provided, risks covered by an FOB policy will be those contained in Clauses 1–3 of Cargo Clauses (A)- (C)- 1/1.09.[20] For instance, the relevant Clauses 1–3 in Cargo Clauses (A) provide that:

[20] See Dunt, Chapters 8 and 9, for detailed treatment of risks covered by the clauses.

Risks Covered
1. - **Risks Clause**

This insurance covers all risks of loss of or damage to the subject matter insured except as provided in Clauses 4, 5, 6 and 7 below.

2. - **General Average Clause**

This insurance covers general average and salvage charges, adjusted or determined according to the contract of affreightment and/or the governing law and practice, incurred to avoid or in connection with the avoidance of loss from any cause except those excluded in Clauses 4, 5, 6 and 7 or elsewhere in this insurance.[21]

3. - **"Both to Blame Collision" Clause**

This insurance is extended to indemnify the Assured against such proportion of liability under the contract of affreightment "Both to Blame Collision" Clause as is in respect of a loss recoverable hereunder. In the event of any claim by shipowners under the said Clause the Assured agree to notify the Underwriters who shall have the right, at their own cost and expense, to defend the Assured against such claim.

The wording of Clause 1 supposes that all other risks in addition to losses arising from the general average, salvage charges and 'Both to Blame collisions', except the exclusions in Clauses 4–10 of the Cargo Clauses, are 'insurable',[22] Otherwise the rest of the Clauses are self-explanatory.[23]

4.6.4 Further FOB Risks Covered by Cargo Clauses

Further coverage available also includes permission to change voyage on prompt notice, forwarding charges arising from the interruption, constructive total loss and increased value. These are found in Clauses 10–14 of Cargo Clauses (A)–(C). The relevant text in cargo clauses (A), for instance, provide that:

[21] The clause also includes General Average Act and general average loss in s.66 of the MIA 1906.

[22] These are discussed in detail in Chap. 1.

[23] Discussed in details in Chap. 1.

Cargo Clauses (A)–(C)
10. **Change of Voyage Clause**

Where, after attachment of this insurance, the destination is changed by the Assured, held covered at a premium and on conditions to be arranged subject to prompt notice being given to the underwriters.[24]

11. Insurable Interest [omitted]

12. **Forwarding Charges Clause**

Where, as a result of the operation of a risk covered by this insurance, the insured transit is terminated at a port or place other than that to which the subject-matter is covered under this insurance, the Underwriters will reimburse the Assured for any extra charges properly and reasonably incurred in unloading, storing and forwarding the subject-matter to the destination to which it is insured hereunder. This Clause 12, which does not apply to general average or salvage charges, shall be subject to the exclusions contained in Clauses 4, 5, 6 and 7 above, and shall not include charges arising from the fault negligence insolvency or financial default of the Assured or their servants.

13. **Constructive Total Loss Clause**[25]

No claim for Constructive Total Loss shall be recoverable hereunder unless the subject-matter insured is reasonably abandoned either on account of its actual total loss appearing to be unavoidable or because the cost of recovering, reconditioning and forwarding the subject-matter to the destination to which it is insured would exceed its value on arrival.[26]

14. **Increased Value Clause**[27]

14.1 If any Increased Value insurance is effected by the Assured on the cargo insured herein the agreed value of the cargo shall be deemed to be increased to the total amount insured under this insurance and all Increased Value insurances covering the loss and liability under this insurance shall be in such proportion as the sum insured herein bears to such total amount insured. In the event of claim, the Assured shall provide the Underwriters with evidence of the amounts insured under all other insurances.[28]

---

[24] See also ss.45(1) and 45(2) of the MIA 1906.

[25] Constructive total loss is only recoverable when the insured has met the conditions therein which include giving the notice of abandonment and in a manner prescribed in accordance with s.64 of the MIA 1906 covered. Although not specifically mentioned, actual total loss (see s.60 of MIA 1906) is also covered.

[26] See also ss.60(1) and 60(2) of the MIA; Chaps. 1 and 2.

[27] See s.16 of the MIA 1906.

[28] See s.16 of the MIA 1906.

> 14.2 Where this insurance is on Increased Value the following clause shall apply: The agreed value of the cargo shall be deemed to be equal to the total amount insured under the primary insurance and all Increased Value insurances covering the loss and effected on the cargo by the Assured, and liability under this insurance shall be in such proportion as the sum insured herein bears to such total amount insured. In the event of claim, the Assured shall provide the Underwriters with evidence of the amounts insured under all other insurances.[29]

Parties should be aware that Increased Value Insurance is closely related to insured value, valued policies and unvalued valued policies. Successful claims under this heading therefore depend on proof of loss or damage at the claims stage. This is also self-explanatory.[30]

4.7 Institute Cargo Exclusions Affecting Insurance Contracts

The Cargo Clauses do not provide positively for risks insured. Instead, they provide by the process of elimination (or negatively) for aspects of risks not covered in Clauses 4–10, leaving the insured to surmise by deduction for risks covered. This, in turn, warns the insured to either extend cover by extension clauses or additional cargo clauses to the contract, or decide to self-insure (not recommended) for the excluded risks.

4.7.1 General Exclusions

The first exclusion is the general exclusion clause, which includes losses caused by wilful misconduct, ordinary leakage, insufficient packaging, inherent vice, delay, carrier's insolvency and atomic weapons. These are contained in Clause 4 of Cargo Clauses (A)–(C). Clause 4 in Cargo Clauses (A) provides that:

[29] The values vary depending on whether the calculation is made on insurance on the ship, freight, goods or merchandise, or any other subject matter insured.

[30] See Chap. 1.

4. - General Exclusion Clause
In no case shall this insurance cover

4.1 loss, damage or expense attributable to *wilful misconduct of the Assured*[31]

4.2 *ordinary leakages*, ordinary loss in weight or volume, or ordinary wear and tear of the subject-matter insured

4.3 loss, damage or expense caused by *insufficiency or unsuitability* of packing or preparation of the subject-matter insured (for the purpose of this Clause 4.3 "packing" shall be deemed to include stowage in a container or liftvan but only when such stowage is carried out prior to attachment of this insurance or by the Assured or their servants)[32]

4.4 loss, damage or expense caused by *inherent vice* or nature of the subject-matter insured[33]

4.5 loss, damage or expense proximately caused by *delay*, even though the delay be caused by a risk insured against (except expenses payable under Clause 2 above)[34]

4.6 loss, damage or expense arising from insolvency or financial default of the owner's manager's charterers or operators of the vessel[35]

4.7 loss, damage or expense arising from the use of any weapon of war employing atomic or nuclear fission and/or fusion or other like reaction or radioactive force or matter.[36]

Although excluded under this clause, this category of risks is insurable either as an additional insurance or additional clause to the policy for an additional premium. The exclusions are discussed elsewhere in the book.[37]

---

[31] Dunt, p. 153; s.52(1) of the MIA 1906; Justice William Watkins in *Midland Insurance Co v Smith* (1881) 6 QBD 561 at 568.

[32] Dunt, p. 147.

[33] Dunt, p. 144; s.52(2) of the MIA 1906.

[34] Dunt, p. 156; s.48 of the MIA 1906.

[35] Cf. 'Not to inure' clause.

[36] See Chap. 11 on War.

[37] See Chap. 1.

4.7.2 Unseaworthiness and Unfitness[38] Exclusion

The second exclusion relates to the unseaworthiness and unfitness of the cargo for the contemplated voyage. These are contained in Clause 5 of Cargo Clauses (A)–(C), which provide that:

> **5. - Unseaworthiness and Unfitness Exclusion Clause**
> **5.1** In no case shall this insurance cover loss, damage or expense arising from unseaworthiness of vessel or craft, unfitness of vessel craft, conveyance container or liftvan for the safe carriage of the subject-matter insured, where the Assured or their servants are privy to such unseaworthiness or unfitness, at the time the subject-matter insured is loaded therein.
>
> **5.2** The Underwriters waive any breach of the implied warranties of seaworthiness of the ship and fitness of the ship to carry the subject-matter insured to destination, unless the Assured or their servants are privy to such unseaworthiness or unfitness.[39]

This exclusion applies principally to the unseaworthiness of the vessel, but may also include unseaworthiness of the cargo itself, the first being the responsibility of the carrier and the latter that of the shipper/cargo owner. The exclusion is reinstated elsewhere.[40]

4.7.3 War Exclusions

The third set of exclusions relates to war risks.[41] War in this context includes actual war, civil war, revolution, rebellion, insurrection, civil strife, hostilities, capture and seizure, arrests, derelict mines, torpedoes, bombs and other derelict weapons of war. These are contained in Clause 6 of Cargo Clauses (A)–(C). Clause 6 of Cargo Clauses (A) provides as follows:

---

[38] See ss.14–16 of the *SGA* 1979 on fitness for purpose of goods sold both in domestic and international trade; ss.39(1)–(5) of the MIA 1906.

[39] Dunt, p. 161.

[40] See Chaps. 1 and 11.

[41] Ibid.

6. - War Exclusion Clause[42]
In no case shall this insurance cover loss damage or expense caused by

6.1 war civil war revolution rebellion insurrection, civil strife arising therefrom, or any hostile act by or against a belligerent power

6.2 capture seizure arrest restraint or detainment (piracy excepted), and the consequences thereof or any attempt thereat

6.3 derelict mines torpedoes bombs or other derelict weapons of war.

Once again, although excluded here, these war risks are covered under a number of clauses. Insurance of FOB and CIF war risks and piracy are discussed elsewhere in this book.[43]

4.7.4 Strikes Exclusion[44]

The fourth set of exclusions is an extension of war and hostilities and deals with strikes, which include strikes, lock-outs, riots, civil commotion, terrorism and persons acting from political and religious motives.[45] These are contained in Clause 7 of Cargo Clauses (A)–(C). Clause 7 of Cargo Clauses (A) provides as follows:

7. - Strikes Exclusion Clause
In no case shall this insurance cover loss damage or expense

7.1 caused by strikers, locked-out workmen, or persons taking part in labour disturbances, riots or civil commotions

7.2 resulting from strikes, lock-outs, labour disturbances, riots or civil commotions

7.3 caused by any terrorist or any person acting from a political motive.[46]

Risks arising from strikes and labour lock-outs are part of war insurance.[47] These exclusions are covered by the addition of specialist Cargo Clauses under the relevant headings and are detailed elsewhere in this book.[48]

---

[42] Dunt, Chapter 10; *Pesquerias y Secaderos de Bacalao de Espana SA v Beer* (1949) 82 Ll. LRep 501 at 514, HL, per Lord Morton.

[43] See Chap. 10.

[44] Dunt, p. 205.

[45] Ibid.

[46] Details in Chaps. 1 and 10.

[47] See, again, *Nishina Trading Co Ltd v Chiyoda Fire and Marine Insurance Co Ltd* [1969] 1 Lloyds Rep 293 at 298 CA per Lord Denning MR.

[48] Details in Chap. 10.

4.7.5 Termination of Contract Exclusion[49]

The fifth set of exclusions deals with losses resulting from termination of the voyage and transit charges and expenses resulting therefrom.[50]

> **9. - Termination of Contract of Carriage Clause**
> If owing to circumstances beyond the control of the Assured either the contract of carriage is terminated at a port or place other than the destination named therein or the transit is otherwise terminated before delivery of the goods as provided for in Clause 8 above, then this insurance shall also terminate unless prompt notice is given to the Underwriters and continuation of cover is requested when the insurance shall remain in force, subject to an additional premium if required by the Underwriters, either
>
> **9.1** until the goods are sold and delivered at such port or place, or unless otherwise specially agreed, until the expiry of 60 days after arrival of the goods hereby insured at such port or place, whichever shall first occur, or
>
> **9.2** if the goods are forwarded within the said period of 60 days (or any agreed extension thereof) to the destination named herein or to any other destination, until terminated in accordance with the provisions of Clause 8 above.[51]

These come under the heading of 'duration of the policy', which includes their commencements, transit and termination. They are, therefore, covered under various categories, including 'door-to-door' or 'warehouse-to-warehouse' policies, in the book.[52] They are more pronounced in CIF contracts.

4.7.6 Change of Voyage Exclusion

The sixth exclusion concerns losses resulting from change of voyage. However, the exclusion applies only where notice is not given during and after change of voyage for reasonable grounds. Unlawful and unreasonable change of voyage is not covered.[53] This is now contained in Clause 10 of Cargo Clauses (A)–(C). Clause 10 of Cargo Clauses (A) provides that:

[49] See the Transit Clause, Cl.18; cf., 'warehouse to warehouse clause'.

[50] See Transit Clause in Cargo Clauses (A)–(C); Dunt, p. 147.

[51] This would amount to change of voyage. See footnote 24.

[52] Dunt Chapter 11; Chap. 7 post (CIF Insurance).

[53] See s.45(1) and s.45(2) of the MIA 1906.

10. - Change of Voyage Clause[54]
Where, after attachment of this insurance, the destination is changed by the Assured, held covered at a premium and on conditions to be arranged subject to prompt notice being given to the Underwriters.[55]

This exclusion is operational only where the insured fails to give 'prompt notice' to the insurers following the change. The exclusion clause gives the insured the opportunity to do so at an extra premium and whatever conditions the insurers impose.

4.7.7 Deviation Exclusion

The seventh and final exclusion concerns deviation. Deviation can arise from an unauthorised change of voyage or deliberate deviation itself.[56] However, agreed deviation, lawful deviation or reasonable deviation (e.g., to save life, to answer distress) would not lead to exclusion. This exclusion arises from the operation of maritime law rather than Cargo Clauses 1/1/09.[57]

4.8 Uncertainties Caused by Multiple Contract Classifications

The nature and characteristics of the variants were covered earlier, in Chap. 3. This chapter will relate to the effect of these classifications on insurance. Unlike the other types of Incoterms and other export contracts, it is probably only the FOB that has as many types or classifications. The CIF, on the other hand, has only variants, not classifications or types. Insurance duties in each FOB circumstance further depend on each of the three or four types of FOB contract.[58] As outlined by Justice Devlin in *Pyrene v Scindia*[59] and followed by Lord Donaldson in *The El Amria* and *The El Amnia*,[60] are the three known FOB types or variants: 'classic', 'extended' or 'with additional duties', but not 'strict' or 'simple',[61] each with slightly different insurance requirements.[62] Parties' respective insurance duties will, consequently, depend

[54] Dunt, pp. 251 and 259.

[55] Ibid.

[56] See ss.46 (1)–7) and s.49.

[57] See also change of voyage, transit and war risks clauses.

[58] The agreed types are strict, simple and extended or with additional duties. It is unclear whether strict is a separate fourth variant or the alternative name of the classic.

[59] *Pyrene v Scindia* [1954] 2QB 402.

[60] *The El Amria* and *The El Amnia* [1982] 2 Lloyd's Rep. 28.

[61] See paragraphs 4.9–4.13 (post).

[62] See paras. 4.90 and 4.120 post; Schmitthoff's *Law and Practice of International Trade*, p. 23.

on which of these three or four types they opt for. 'Classic' is the first type where the seller may be required to have insurance.

4.9 Insurance of '*Classic*' Contracts

The first FOB variant noted by Justice Devlin in *Pyrene v Scindia* is 'classic' FOB.[63] Justice Mocatta in *Scandinavian Trading Co.* further considered this classic type of FOB contract where provision of the ship is the duty of the buyer in *A/B v Zodiac Petroleum S.A and William Hudson Ltd. (The Al Hofuf)*.[64] In this case, the classic FOB was varied by the custom of the oil trade to the extent that the buyer must give, in succession, notices of expected time of arrival of the vessel at the refinery or lifting port in question, 72, 48 and 24 h in advance of the anticipated date of arrival. Although Justice Mocatta did not do say so, this variation extends the seller's notice obligations to the buyer for insurance purposes beyond *Wimble* v *Rosenberg* and *Northern Steel v John Batt* (see paras 414–419 post). This variant, where the buyer and not the seller is the party to the contract of carriage, was also considered by Lord Denning in *President of India v Metcalfe Shipping Line (The Dunelmia),*[65] *a case involving shipment of urea fertilisers FOB Ravenna, Italy, to Madras, India.* However, Lord Denning limited himself to the variants and did not delve into issues of insurance obligations.

Such FOB variations might change insurance obligations and introduce further sub-issues, albeit theoretical ones. This can cause problems. First, parties' duties in *classic,* compared for instance to *strict* FOB, are not clearly defined. Consequently, insurance obligations, where applicable, are made even more complicated and unpredictable.

Secondly, the nature of the duties and obligations in the *classic* variant could involve the seller taking out carriage and insurance contracts which would equate it to the extended FOB (FOB with additional duties) (para 4.10 and 4.11post) without admitting it. This, in turn, introduces the issue of whether, in such eventualities, agency principles would be applicable in the transaction, with the buyer as principal and the seller as agent for shipping and insurance purposes. What has escaped the scrutiny of many authors and commentators is that the issue of agency re-occurs in all but the 'strict' type of FOB contracts and is also a major factor in the comparison between the 'extended' and the FOB 'with additional duties' and the CIF is rather confusing.[66]

---

[63] Different authors number them differently, but the general method is 'classic' or 'strict', 'simple' and 'extended'. This chapter uses 'classic', 'simple' and 'extended', with a question as to whether or not 'strict' is the fourth.

[64] *Scandinavian Trading Co. A/B v Zodiac Petroleum SA and William Hudson Ltd., (The Al Hofuf)* [1981] 1 Lloyd's Rep. 81.

[65] *President of India v Metcalfe Shipping Line* [1970] 1 QB 289.

[66] See *Benjamin on Sale of Goods*, paras. 20-007–20-013, see also para 4.10 and 4.11 post.

Finally, it is noted that, for the seller to fulfil all of his general including insurance obligations under 'classic' FOB, the seller must comply with all the necessary FOB terms, namely:

(a) The contract must be with the agreed, nominated or designated ship;
(b) Goods must be stowed in a manner according with any stipulations in the contract; in the absence of any in the manner customary for that type of goods;
(c) The contract must be such that the ship will sail within the agreed shipping period;
(d) Transit must comply with the stipulations as to route in the contract of sale. If no route is specified, then the carriage must be on the route customary, if none the reasonable route; and;
(e) Unless deviation is permitted by the terms of the contract of sale, the contract of carriage must be for direct transit to the port of destination.

Although not his duty to insure, failure to observe these general obligations can lead to breach of the contract and consequently add to the seller's insurance problems. Some of the CIF insurance requirements (see Chap. 7, *post*) may also apply to FOB insurance. To avoid these problems, parties should provide expressly whether the seller should take out insurance on behalf of the buyer. He should, of course, take out some cover for himself and pass on the costs as miscellaneous charges to the buyer. Otherwise, it is the courts with hind knowledge, rather that the parties themselves no party is able to determine whether a contract is *classic* or *strict*. However, these may be theoretical rather than practical issues. That would account for the absence of any litigation on the subject.

4.10 Insurance of '*Extended*' Contracts

The second type of FOB contract, also noted by Justice Devlin in *Pyrene v Scindia*, is the FOB *with additional duties* or *extended* FOB.[67] This is a much clearer variant, as both parties would know where they stand and can willingly add duties as they so wish only where they so specify. Thus, after 'classic', this is the other type that may require the seller to insure. In this type of contract, the seller is asked to make the necessary shipping arrangements and the contract may then provide for his taking the bill of lading in his own name and obtaining payment against the transfer, as in classic FOB or CIF contract. He may also be asked to take out insurance. However, this differs from the 'classic' FOB in two essential aspects: first, the seller makes the contract of carriage as principal, the buyer is not a party unless he becomes so by operation of *COGSA 1992*[68] and, secondly, it is the seller who nominates the ship. It

[67] See Schmitthoff's *Law and Practice of International Trade*, p. 20; Lorenzo (2012) p. 260; Benjamin on Sale of Goods, para. 20-007 at p. 1657.

[68] *COGSA, 1992* (CAP 50). The Act repeals and replaces the *Bills of Lading Act,* 1855 and enacts new provisions relating not only to bills of lading but also to seaway bills and ships' delivery

however leaves 2 questions unanswered. First, how does this variation affect the assumption that in FOB contracts, the buyer is always the shipper? In addition, how does that affect agency-related shipping and insurance issues it creates?

Sassoon clarifies the effect of additional duties on risks and insurance thus:

> For presentation purposes these differences are probably best reflected in the seller's capacity while performing certain (additional) services, which according to the "strict" definition is regarded as the responsibility of the buyer. Where the seller undertakes these as agent of, and for and on behalf of the buyer, *the latter assumes the cost and risk, and the ultimate liability therefore.* On the other hand, where the seller as principal undertakes these additional obligations, the position is reversed. He personally bears responsibility therefore, and unless exempted by virtue of the operation of some legal doctrine (e.g., frustration, illegality, etc) or protected by an appropriate exception clause, is therefore liable for any failure of performance.[69] (*Emphasis added*).

It is confusions such as these expressed by Sassoon above that makes identifying parties' insurance obligations in FOB contracts unpredictable and not as easy as it first appears.

However, identification of the tasks alone does not determine the parties' insurance obligations. If anything, it may further complicate them. However, of interest for this chapter, the extension of the seller's duties may include an obligation to procure insurance and carriage, or, indeed, both. In that respect, two further factors need considering.

First, as in *classic* FOB above, there has to be an express request from the buyer to the seller to take out insurance and an acceptance by the seller to do so on agreed terms; the courts will not imply such undertakings unless they have to.

Secondly, once agreed, the undertaking becomes a binding obligation (on par with his original/other contractual undertakings) on the part of the seller to provide the insurance.

Third, and finally, is once again the possible conflict of interests where the seller is both a shipping and an insurance agent with a dual interest in the success or failure of the venture. Where he does so, where and when does his interest start and end? Does he take the policy in his own name or in that of the buyer? What about where he, in turn, uses an insurance or freight-forwarding agent in breach of the rule that an FOB buyer insure personally? Apart from a few guidelines, as regards the insurance agent's duties to obtain the policy,[70] there are no authorities from either

orders. The Act reforms and updates the law in respect of rights of suit relating to contracts for carriage of goods by sea. At the core of the Act is section 1, which sets out the shipping documents to which the Act applies. The need for reform and the relevance of the Act to this clause, was made greater by the fact that a large number of contracts for the carriage of goods by sea are expressly governed by English law even though the ships, cargoes and ports involved may have no connection with the UK.

[69] Sassoon (1984), pp. 401/477 (omitted in later editions).

[70] For the general duties of an insurance agent as to the policy, see *Friedman's Law of Agency*, 6th edn., Butterworth, London, 1990, p. 139; Bowstead *On Agency*, 19th edn., Sweat and Maxwell, London, 1990, para 9-011 at pp. 549–550.

maritime, export trade or agency law, the nearest being of a bailee in *A. Tomlinson (Hauliers) Ltd v Hepburn*,[71] which is, however, an authority that goods may be insured by a person with an interest in them so as to cover the interest of others. In support of that, *Re E Dibens & Sons Ltd.*[72] went further to suggest that in such cases the agent would account to the seller or buyer in trust. It gets worse when complex agency issues are mixed with those of trusteeships.

The potential issues that would need clarification are therefore:

(a) seller's insurance agent's liabilities to the buyer/principal or third parties; or
(b) the buyer's/principal's rights against the seller/insurance agent (outside the main sales contract); and
(c) the buyer's/principal's liabilities to third parties are all issues that would need further investigating.

An example discussed in paragraph 4.10 below is the risks where/when the seller simply substitutes and assigns his own (seller's) interests and/or contingency insurance policy to the buyer. The danger is that such policies, even where suitable for the seller's limited interests, may not cater for the buyer's wider interests. The guiding principles in *classic* and *additional duties or extended* FOB being that the policy procured and tendered must be adequate to cover all the export risks (including war where applicable) involved.

4.11 Potential Problems of Sellers as Buyers''Shipping and Insurance Agents'

A possible scenario in *classic* (ante) and *extended* FOB is where the seller takes out insurance on the buyer's behalf and thereby brings himself into an agency situation. This is not same as a typical insurance agent or broker.

First, among the sub-issues raised by the scenario is the legal situation where the seller was negligent in either failing to obtain, or obtaining a wrong or insufficient, insurance and the buyer suffered a loss as a consequence.

Secondly, further issues relate to what type of insurance document the seller-agent should tender and, if so, when and how? Once again, there is no reported authority, but that does not mean the issue has never arisen in practice. It remains a speculation.[73]

[71] *A. Tomlinson (Hauliers) Ltd v Hepburn* [1965] 1 Lloyd's Rep. 1, Court of Appeal; [1966] 1 Lloyd's Rep. 309, House of Lords.

[72] Re E Dibens & Sons Ltd [1990] B.C.L.C 577.

[73] See *Benjamin on Sale of Goods*, paras. 20-002–20-006; Schmitthoff, pp. 22 and 37; "Who is an agent?", *Insurance Law Monthly*, Informa Law, London, Vol. 17, No. 9, September 2005, p. 6, dealing with the ECJ's decision in *Staatssecertaris van Fiasneien v Arthur Andersen & Co* (Case C-472/03).

Thirdly, as already indicated above, there is the likelihood of a conflict of interest for the seller, already party to the sales contract, to also be the buyer's insurance agent, since the seller would have interest to be paid as:

(a) a seller;
(b) a shipping agent; and
(c) an insurance agent.

The question is does he present an invoice itemising cost of the goods, freight, premium and commission for both freight and insurance agencies? Once more, there is no reported common law authority on this and the possible conflict. It would appear, however, that this too is not a practical problem, since there is neither case law nor academic views on the subject. Until then, parties should be aware of the potential pitfalls regarding insurance of, especially, classic FOB. The same issues would arise in 'extended' or FOB 'with additional duties'.[74] It is also probable that, in such cases, the strict requirements of agency liability to the principal and third parties, agency's duty of care and standard of duty, principal's obligations to third parties, etc., would not be strictly applied, as they would simply complicate matters further where goods are sold afloat and the policy is assigned. Would the cost of the premium be transferred to the buyer within the invoice or separately? Since this would not be your normal agency relationship, it raises further questions. For instance, how would breach by the seller or his agent of the duty of utmost good faith affect the validity and tender of the policy?

Finally, although in theory the seller be personally liable, sellers in this situation sometimes employ freight forwarders to handle shipments of goods on their behalf. They may also outsource insurance to agents. These circumstances would also import sub-delegation of agency duties, a scenario which would further conflict with the agency principle of *delegatus non-potest delegary* (delegate cannot sub-delegate). The exception to that would be where the buyer agrees to the sub-delegation through actual consent or knowledge of the facts or of trade practice or custom. Such consent would be done by fax, telephone or e-mail, considering the possible urgency involved. But how often and how practical? What would happen if the sub-agent were negligent in a case where the buyer/principal has not consented to the sub-delegation? Thus, especially for insurance purposes, classic and extended FOB might be most difficult to handle. Worse still, since they might not be apparent, merchants have to use their wits to determine whether the contract is a *classic* rather than a *strict* or *extended* type. In contrast, however, and by its nature, *extended* FOB insurance would be relatively easier.

[74] *Benjamin on Sale of Goods*, paras. 20-002–20-006.

4.12 Comparison of *Extended* and Standard Contracts' Insurance Obligations

Where the seller assumes insurance and freight functions, especially in extended FOB, this type of FOB will be almost the same as the CIF; the only differences being in the computation of the price, the invoicing and tender of the documents including the insurance ones.[75] In the *extended* FOB, the price would not include the cost of insurance within the same invoice. The seller would make the contract of insurance for the buyer's account and would invoice him separately for the costs and expenses incurred. Benjamin sums up the differences that, in such cases, the seller's duties in relation to a shipment are distinguishable from a CIF contract in that the cost of freight and insurance are for the buyer's account. This will be so even if the seller is, under the contract of carriage or of insurance, liable to pay these sums to the carrier or to the underwriter of both. As between the parties to the contract of sale, the buyer bears the ultimate responsibility for these payments, and he takes the risk of any variation in, for example, freight rates which may occur between the time of the sale and the making of the contract of affreightment.[76]

Sassoon, on the one hand, supports this position in the last paragraph of the statement quoted at the opening of this chapter:

> Moreover, in some cases where the seller acts as the buyer's agent for procuring insurance, he may even be allowed to procure a policy of his own, which will be assigned to the buyer only upon the termination of his interests in the goods. Where the seller is acting in this capacity, the question may arise whether he is under a duty to tender any particular form of policy (see the case of sale of CIF). Whatever authority exists on the matter appears only to indicate that the contract will probably be satisfied by a certificate or letter of insurance and that FOB contracts are necessarily subject to the rules which govern CIF contracts.[77]

Being an agent in the three aspects, the seller would presumably charge the buyer agency commissions for freight and insurance; he would certainly send at least two invoices, possibly four (one each for the costs, insurance and freight) compared to only one for the CIF. The need for notice to the buyer under s.32 (3) of the *SGA 1979* would therefore not arise. However, further on, Sassoon adopts a somewhat different and, perhaps contradictory, view when he writes:

> The view that the seller invariably acts as agent of the buyer in undertaking any duties beyond those presented under the "strict" definition finds no support in jurisprudence or commercial practice. This view is tenable only where the question of procuring shipment (and/or of prepaying for the freight and insurance) is considered. It follows, therefore, that the seller's capacity in securing the shipping space provides the key for differentiating

[75] See also *Benjamin on Sales*, paras. 20-008–20-013.

[76] Ibid, paras 20-007 at p. 1773. He discusses FOB contract with addition duties (para. 20-007), FOB contracts distinguished from CIF contracts (para. 20-008), effects of distinction between FOB and CIF contracts (para. 20-009) and FOB contract distinguished from contract to deliver at dock or alongside (para. 20-010).

[77] Sassoon (1984), p. 473, also cited at the opening of this chapter.

between FOB contract and other shipping contracts. This distinction is, however, often overlooked.[78]

Another distinction is that either way the total cost of the extended FOB contract would remain overall cheaper than that of the CIF. Property and risks would pass on shipment. It should also be legitimate to raise here once more the issue of agency law and conflicts of interests discussed in the preceding paragraphs. The above comparisons notwithstanding, the essential characteristics of both FOB and CIF contracts should not be compromised and the general rule is that the buyer remains the shipper and the party responsible for insurance in FOB contracts.

4.13 Insurance of '*Simple*' Contracts

The third or fourth type [depending on one's placement order] of FOB contract is the 'simple'. Although not generally agreed by all leading academic authorities, the third type of FOB contract is the simple FOB.[79] As indicated, some regard it as the third (or '*simple*', since it is when the buyer contracts with the carrier), others as a fourth and separate ('*strict*'). Schmitthoff does not assign it any name, but just calls it FOB (buyer contracting with seller).[80] However, both Lorenzo[81] and Schmitthoff[82] prefer '*simple*', as does Chua.[83] Notwithstanding that debate, under this type of FOB the buyer or his agent nominates and/or charters the ship; in other words, enters into a contract of carriage with the ship owner. The seller loads the goods on board, collects the mate's receipts from the vessel and gives them to the buyer or his agent, who obtains a bill of lading from the master in exchange for it. In this case, the buyer and not the seller is the party to the contract of carriage. This separation of duties provides a clear distinction between the "simple" FOB and the extended or FOB with additional duties. In the former the seller is not party to the contract of carriage; whereas he is in the latter. This is the type of FOB discussed by Lord Denning in *President of India v Metcalfe Shipping Line.*[84]

Despite disagreement between leading authors, unless otherwise provided, this is the *usual* or *normal* or *strict* FOB contract, hence the confusion whether there are only three or four categories of FOB. However, the problem is that the *usual* or *normal* FOB also happens to be the *strict*. The general rule is that unless otherwise provided the default principle would be for the *usual*, or *normal* or *strict* FOB contract It is also the type used in Clause A5 of FOB Incoterms 2020. In this type of

[78] Ibid, p. 402.

[79] For details of the strict FOB see Schmitthoff's *Law and Practice of International Trade*, paras 2-007.

[80] Ibid.

[81] Lorenzo 2012, chapter 6.

[82] Benjamin on Sale on Goods, 7th edn., 2006, para 2-007.

[83] Chua, International Trade Law, paras. 2.16–2.29.

[84] *President of India v Metcalfe Shipping Line* [1970] 1 QB 289.

contract, the shipping arrangements are made by the buyer or his agent who books space on a particular ship and the seller discharges his duty by putting the goods on board, obtains a mate's receipt and hands it over to the buyer's (forwarding) agent to enable him (the agent) to obtain the bill of lading. He is neither party to the contract of carriage, nor is he the shipper. The buyer remains the shipper. This third type of FOB contract differs from the classic FOB in several respects. Firstly, the seller nominates the ship and makes the contract of carriage in his own name—as principal. Secondly, the seller and not the buyer arranges the insurance. An example of this type of FOB contract is considered by Lord Donaldson in *The El Amria and El Minia.*[85]

Sassoon, in particular, highlights the diverging views on strict FOB contracts generally and insurance obligations therein that, from a purely academic point of view, the 'strict' interpretation has perhaps much to commend itself as the most satisfactory definition of the term 'FOB'. He points out that circumstances have, however, rendered this interpretation unsuitable in many cases and that a practice has consequently developed whereby the respective obligations are adjusted somewhat. Accordingly, because judicial pronouncements have seldom gone much beyond the general statement that in an FOB contract the seller bears all the charges and responsibilities, ranging from barely putting the goods on board to CIF terms (with or without pre-payment of freight insurance) remains a matter of doubt in many instances, and the subject of conflicting opinions. The result of this situation is reflected in the diversity of views about the precise interpretations of the FOB term.[86] He should perhaps have added consequential insurance complications.

In this FOB the seller has no function in the making of the contract of carriage whether as agent for the buyer or as principal, so agency principles and conflicts do not arise. Neither is he responsible for insurance of the goods on the buyer's behalf except for his own purposes. The buyer nominates the ship and port and is responsible for his own shipping and insurance. Again, property and risk pass on shipment. This is also the case in an FOB contract[87] in which the buyer would be entitled to notice from the seller in order to enable him to take out insurance under s.32(3) of the *SGA 1979.*[88] Schmitthoff[89] and Sassoon[90] hold slightly differing views on the above three divisions of the FOB; however, these diverging views have no bearing on the parties' insurance duties and will not therefore be considered further here.

[85] *The El Amria and El Minia* [1982] 2 Lloyd's Rep. 28.

[86] Sassoon (1984), p. 401.

[87] See FOB in Incoterms 2000 at p. 50 (English version) and p. 182 (French version).

[88] The case was actually decided on the basis of s.32(3) of the Sale of Goods Act 1893. However, the repealing and replacement *SGA* 1979 contains an identical s.32, hence the reference here to the *SGA* 1979 rather than the *SGA* 1893. See also *Wimble, Sons & Co Ltd v Rosenberg & Sons* and *Northern Steel & Hardware Company (Limited) v John Batt & Company (London) Limited.*

[89] Professor Schmitthoff is the proponent of the three divisions, see *Schmitthoff's Law and Practice of International Trade*, pp. 19–23.

[90] Professor Sassoon on the other hand subscribes to the 'strict' and the 'additional services', but calls the third 'shipment to destination', see Sassoon (1984), para. 441 at p. 333.

Thus, other than protecting his *post*- and *pre*-shipment interests and other eventualities through mechanisms such as seller's interest, contingency insurance, export credit and retention of title insurances,[91] the seller need not worry about insurance under simple FOB.

4.14 Is There a Fourth (*Strict*) Category of FOB Contracts?

The questions persist: are there three or four types of FOB? In other words, are the *simple* FOB and *strict* FOB the same or are they different? Generally, though, unless the contract clearly provides otherwise or there is an agreement or the contract is on an Incoterms 2020, when there is a dispute, often the parties will not know which of the three FOB contracts is involved until the court's decision, by which time it will probably be too late. Therefore, if and when not sure, a merchant should take out the above listed additional insurance, as the dangers of double or over insurance, if any, is better than that of having no insurance at all. Subject to the debate above whether this is a fourth and, therefore separate FOB, the 'strict' FOB is the type contemplated in Incoterms 2020[92] Unless otherwise provided in a contract, this is the default FOB where the seller just provides and loads the goods and presents the documents to the buyer. The buyer being solely responsible for the contract of carriage and insurance.[93]

4.15 Requirement for Notice Under s.32 (3) of *SGA* 1979: The *Wimble* Decision

Where it is not the seller's duty to insure, such as in the *strict* or *simple* FOB, it is nevertheless his duty to give such notice to the buyer as may enable him (the buyer) to insure the goods during their sea transit and, if the seller fails to do so, the goods are deemed to be at his risk the during transit.[94] The basis for this position is section 32 of the *SGA 1979*,[95] s.32(1) of which provides that delivery of goods by the seller to the carrier be *prima facie* deemed a delivery of the goods to the buyer. It is generally agreed that section 32(3) of the *SGA 1979* applies to FOB contracts but not to CIF. However, the problem arises from the reading of s.32(1), which presumes that delivery to a carrier is delivery to the buyer. The subsection provides that:

---

[91] Discussed in Chap. 5.

[92] Clause A5 (seller) and Clause B5 (buyer) Incoterms 2020.

[93] See *Benjamin on Sales*, para. 20-007; Schmitthoff, para. 2-007.

[94] See Clause A5 CIF Incoterms 2020.

[95] This Act [cap 54/1979] provides for the consolidation of the law relating to sale of goods. It replaces the earlier Sale of Goods Act 1893 which had almost identical s.32. Part III of the Act (ss.27–37) in which s.32 falls; it concerns performance of the contract, within which the relevant s.32 provides for delivery to a carrier.

> (1) Where, in pursuance of a contract of sale, the seller is authorised or required to send the goods to the buyer, delivery of the goods to a carrier (whether named by the buyer or not) for the purpose of transmission to the buyer is *prima facie* deemed to be a delivery of the goods to the buyer.

This is because the most important function of the FOB contract is the physical delivery of the contract goods on board the nominated vessel rather than their symbolic delivery by tender of shipping documents in the CIF. The FOB has traditional been a cash against goods contract compared to the cash against documents CIF although that distinction is disappearing in the performance of modern contracts. Furthermore, because property and risks pass at the crossing of the ships rail, that point determines delivery, the carrier being the buyer's agent. An instance which might involve liability to a seller under FOB with additional duties or either of the other two where the seller contracts or enables shipping is subsection 32(2), which provides that:

> Unless otherwise authorised by the buyer, the seller must make such contract with the carrier on behalf of the buyer as may be reasonable having regard to the nature of the goods and the other circumstances of the case; and if the seller omits to do so, and the goods are lost or damaged in course of transit, the buyer may decline to treat the delivery to the carrier as a delivery to himself or may hold the seller responsible in damages.

This introduces a further distinction between the FOB and CIF insurance of the requirement of notice. Specifically, and with regard to insurance, subsection 32(3) provides that:

> Unless otherwise agreed, where goods are sent by the seller to the buyer by a route involving sea transit, under circumstances in which it is usual to insure, the *seller must give such notice to the buyer as may enable him to insure them during their sea transit,* and if the seller fails to do so, the goods are at his risk during such sea transit.[96] (Emphasis provided)

The third subsection has produced varying interpretations. In the leading case of *Wimble, Sons & Co Ltd v Rosenberg & Sons*[97] where, in goods sold FOB Antwerp, the buyers sent instructions for the shipment leaving the selection of the ship to the sellers. The sellers shipped the goods but did not insure them and the cargo was lost at sea. The majority decision of the Appeal Court was that although *dispatch* is different from *delivery*, nevertheless the seller has to perform both functions to bring him under the operation of s.32(1). However, Lord Hamilton dissented from Lord

[96] Cf. *Vienna Convention on Contracts for the International Sale of Goods*, Art 32(3), which requires the seller to give the buyer the requisite information only "at the buyer's request". Clause 32(3) provides that "If the seller is not bound to effect insurance in respect of the carriage of the goods, he must, at the buyer's request, provide him with all available information necessary to enable him to effect such insurance". That might be preferable to the equivalent provision in the *Sale of Goods Act*. For general notice containing no provisions as to notice or rate of loading para 20-031 pp. 1407–1408.

[97] *Wimble, Sons & Ltd. v. Rosenberg & Sons* [1913] 3 KB 743 CA.

Williams and Lord Buckley, in that s.32(3) applied to FOB contracts since the seller only puts goods on the ship for dispatch. He said:

> ...in spite of the use of the same verb 'to send,' it does not necessarily follow that a contract involving sending, if within sub-s. 1, must therefore also be within sub-s. 3. It is well settled that, on an ordinary FOB. contract, when 'free on board' does not merely condition the constituent elements in the price but expresses the seller's obligations additional to the bare bargain of purchase and sale, the seller does not 'in pursuance of the contract of sale' or as seller send forward or start the goods to the buyer at all except in the sense that he puts the goods safely on board, pays the charge of doing so, and, for the buyer's protection but not under a mandate to send, gives up possession of them to the ship only upon the terms of a reasonable and ordinary bill of lading or other contract of carriage. There his contractual liability as seller ceases, and delivery to the buyer is complete as far as he is concerned. In such a case the goods are not 'sent by the seller to the buyer', though they then begin a journey, which will end in the buyer's hands. In law, as between buyer and seller, they are then and there delivered by the seller to the buyer, and thereafter it is by the buyer and his agent, the carrier, and not by the seller, that the goods are 'sent' to their destination. It is in this sense that I understand the words of [first instance Judge] Bailhache J., 'what one generally understands by an FOB. contract is that the goods are not sent by sea by the vendor but are delivered by him at the rail of the ship and are then taken over by the shipowner nominated by the buyer and conveyed by him across the sea'.[98]

His Lordship added that *dispatch* in this context refers to action at the beginning, while delivery is the reverse with the latter ensuring physical arrival of the cargo. Having held that the section applied, Lord Buckley nevertheless thought that, in this case, the seller was not liable since the buyer already had *sufficient* information to enable him to insure if he so wished. It seemed to him that no notice to 'enable' the buyer was wanted, for he already had ability; he had all the materials necessary to enable him to insure and that those words of the section, therefore, which require the seller to give notice, do not apply, for no notice was wanted to enable the buyer to insure. However, although he conceded that if this was not so and the seller was under an obligation to give him such notice, he maintained that the contract itself of 27 June 1912 was a sufficient notice as it gave the buyer knowledge of all the necessary particulars other than knowledge, which rested with himself, or was determinate by himself, namely, first, the port of discharge, and, secondly, the name of the ship. For these reasons His Lordship was of the opinion that, although subsection 3 is applicable to this case notwithstanding that the contract was an FOB contract, the seller had not failed to do anything which by subsection 3 he was bound to do.[99]

Thus, if the buyer had not had sufficient information, the seller would be liable. The decision revolved around the issue that the buyer had knowledge of the port of loading and discharge and what the freight was; the only missing information was the ship's name, which under the circumstances Their Lordships thought was not material to effecting insurance. There appears to be is no decided case where notice was needed because the buyer did not have sufficient information of all the relevant facts. Notice in this instance is implied, not necessarily express.

---

[98] Ibid at 756–757.

[99] Ibid at 754, 755.

Lord Williams, on the other hand, thought that such construction would destroy the efficacy of s.32 (3) of the *SGA 1979*, since it is always possible for the buyer to insure goods by a general cover policy. However, what constitutes a general cover policy was not defined; it probably means and includes an open cover and/or a blanket policy. Accordingly, His Lordship could not agree with the argument of the plaintiffs that the contract of sale itself was notice within the meaning of subsection 3, arriving at this conclusion not only on the ground that the contract did not afford sufficient information to enable the buyer to insure the purchased goods during their sea transit, but also on the ground that knowledge of the buyer, actual, inferred or assumed, which would enable the buyer to insure, does not dispense with the statutory obligation of the seller, where the route involves sea transit under circumstances in which it is usual to insure, to give such notice to the buyer as may enable him to insure the goods during their sea transit.[100]

As to the specific obligation, quality and extent of the notice required, Lord Williams continued and clarified that:

> The obligation, unless dispensed with by the agreement, - and in this case there was no dispensing agreement - on the seller is to give such notice, with such details, to the buyer as may be necessary to effect insurance of the goods during sea transit. It is to my mind impossible to construe the words as meaning that the obligation to insure does not arise in case the buyer happens to have sufficient information from some other source than the statutory notice to enable him to insure the goods. I have only to add that, whichever of the suggested constructions relieving the seller from obligation to give the statutory notice in the case of an FOB. contract is adopted, the practical utility and application of sub-s. 3 of s. 32 are reduced to nil. I think this appeal should be allowed and judgment given for the defendants.[101]

Furthermore, although Lord Buckley had sympathy for the argument that the mere fact that the buyer can take out a general cover policy would not affect the operation of s.32(3), he too was, however, satisfied that in this case the buyer had sufficient information to enable him to effect a particular insurance.

4.16 Requirement of Notice Under S.32 *SGA* 1979: The *Northern Steel* Decision

Wimble v Rosenberg was followed by the subsequent leading American case of *Northern Steel & Hardware Company (Limited) v John Batt & Company (London) Limited*,[102] which was also decided on the basis of the fact that the buyer had had *actual* or *constructive* knowledge or information to effect insurance before the loss that gave rise to the claim. *Northern Steel* is an Anglo-American decision on which we shall dwell at length due to its importance on the subject (i.e., what constitutes notice) and for being Anglo-America. In this case, the plaintiffs sold to the defen-

[100] Ibid at 751.

[101] Ibid.

[102] *Northern Steel and Hardware Co Ltd v John Batt & Co (London) Ltd* (1917) 33 TLR 516.

dants a quantity of nails to be delivered FOB New York, for shipment to the destination as specified by the defendants on receipt of shipping instructions from the defendants, for cash against shipping documents. In June 1916, the defendants sent an order under the contract and specified the shipping marks. On 16 August, the plaintiffs gave notice to the defendants that shipment of the goods would shortly be made. The goods were shipped on a vessel, which sailed from New York on 24 August. Two days later, on 26 August, the ship owners notified the defendants that the ship had sailed, and 2 weeks later by 6 September the defendants knew that the goods had been shipped. Three weeks later, on 18 September, the ship was torpedoed and the goods were lost. The defendants had not insured the goods.

In an action for the purchase money, there was evidence that the defendants could have effected insurance before they knew of the loss. In addition to finding that the *SGA 1893*, s.32(3)[103] applied to the contract for sale of goods FOB, the trial court had no difficulty in holding that the defendants had sufficient knowledge of the facts and, therefore, did not need further notice to enable them to insure the goods. The plaintiffs were therefore entitled to recover the purchase price as the property and risk had passed to the defendants, sold FOB New York, shipped from there on 24 August 1916 and lost when the carrier's ship was struck by a submarine's torpedo on 18 September. The Court of Appeal (*Chief Justice Reading, Lord Scrutton and Lord Neville*) sympathised with the dissenting reasoning of Lord Hamilton to the contrary, but felt obliged to follow the majority decision in *Wimble v Rosenberg* that the section applied to FOB contracts and that where the contract itself gave the buyer sufficient notice, to give further notice would be superfluous.

Equally in *Northern Steel v John Batt*, further notice was felt unnecessary, the facts of the shipment having been communicated to the buyers at least 14 days before the loss. The result of these cases is that although the subsection in theory applies to FOB contracts, in practice it will rarely be of much comfort, because in most cases the buyer will already have had sufficient information to enable him to insure the goods. There are no other prominent American nor other common law cases; however, *Northern Steel* should serve for North American authority as it involved a sale from New York to London. This should be compared with the judgment of Lord Hamilton in *Wimble, Sons & Co. Ltd. v Rosenberg & Sons*,[104] who dissented on the application of what is now the *SGA 1979*, s.32(3).

4.17 Importance of the *Wimble* and *Northern Steel* Decisions

The two common law authorities on FOB insurance are therefore *Wimble v Rosenberg* and *Northern Steel v John Batt*. These two decisions have formed the basis of common law precedence on this subject. However, based on these two decisions, a buyer who had neither information nor notice would recover. Other than dissenting judgements in the two cases and related ones, the lack of contrary

[103] Which is identical to the same under the *SGA 1979*.

[104] At pp. 755–764, supra.

decisions makes it difficult to determine fully what would have been the decision had the buyers not had knowledge. There are two competing arguments. One is that the seller should be liable for failure to give notice even though the goods arrive safely. The other is that he should not be liable in such a scenario. Therein lies the nature and extent of the seller's dilemma and indirectly of his insurance obligations. Benjamin is of the view that:

> The stated consequence of the seller's failure to give such notice is that the goods shall be deemed to be at his risk during such sea transit. It does not seem that the subsection imposes a contractual duty to give notice to the buyer, for breach of which the buyer can reject or claim damages. Thus, if the goods arrive safely the seller's failure to give notice will have no legal consequences; and his position should be contracted with the consequences of a CIF's failure to tender a policy of insurance.[105]

Benjamin seems to treat failure to give notice as a minor breach of the contractual warranty, which entitles the buyer only to nominal damages, rather than a fundamental breach, giving rise to repudiation of the contract and damages thereof. According to this line of thought, if the goods never arrived then the buyer could only sue under the main contract for failure to deliver instead of failure to give notice. It is the author's view that Benjamin's argument is untenable and would greatly undermine s.32 of the *SGA 1979* and business efficacy. Two important factors need to be borne in mind here.

First, the requirement to give notice applies only to the seller and not to agents but only where the seller is not party to the shipment and/or insurance contract. It was determined by Justice Pilcher in *WLR Traders (London) Ltd v British and Northern Shipping Agency Ltd.*[106] that there was no obligation on the forwarding agent to cover the goods from the seller's warehouse to the ship's rail and that it was the ordinary practice for the seller to cover the goods himself in a fashion that he thought appropriate. In the course of delivering his judgment, Justice Pilcher said:

> I am perfectly satisfied that where a commercial transaction of this nature is concerned there is no obligation whatsoever upon a forwarding agent to cover the goods from the seller's warehouse to the ship's rail, and that it is the ordinary practice for the seller to cover the goods himself in any fashion that he thinks appropriate.[107]

Secondly, Justice Rowlatt in *Law and Bonar Ltd v British American Tobacco Co Ltd.*[108] determined that the rule does not apply to CIF contracts. He said that:

> The buyers paying CIF terms were actually paying for the insurance against all contemplated risks from the moment of shipment. It seems to me that a term that, for a period after shipment, the goods were to be at the risk of the seller is repugnant to that, and the clause to that effect printed on the form used in this case is inapplicable to the transaction that

[105] 20-043 at p. 1811.

[106] *WLR Traders (London) Ltd v British and Northern Shipping Agency Ltd* [1955] 1 Lloyds Rep 554.

[107] Ibid at 557.

[108] *Law and Bonar Ltd v British American Tobacco Co Ltd* [1916] 2 KB 605.

> actually was entered into. The next question is whether s. 32, sub-s. 3, of the Sale of Goods Act, 1893, applies to this case. ...It does not apply because the contract CIF provides for all the insurance that is contemplated or usual and the seller is to effect it. That was the nature of this contract when made. It dealt exhaustively and expressly with all the insurance that was in view.[109]

Thirdly, Lord Ellenborough in *Clarke v Hutchison*,[110] a case involving transhipment between seaports, was of the view that the responsible party may need to insure goods in transit where the carrier's liability is limited. Another decision, arrived at independently in *Cathy v Tute*,[111] a case where the carrier's notice of liability limitation on land carriage was posted on the gate, is an authority for this proposition. It is thought that on the basis of *Wimble v Rosenberg* and *Northern Steel v John* Batt authorities, the requirement for notice would not apply to Ex Ship contracts. The modern equivalent of the Ex-Ship contract is Delivered Ex-Ship (DES).

4.18 Application of S.32 *SGA* 1979 to Scottish Jurisdiction

Although the whole Act applies to England, Northern Ireland and Wales, pursuance to subsection 32(4),[112] subsections (1)–(3) of the Act do not apply to Scotland in consumer contracts. With regard to this, the subsection provides that:

> In a case where the buyer deals as consumer or, in Scotland, where there is a consumer contract in which the buyer is a consumer, subsections (1) to (3) above must be ignored, but if in pursuance of a contract of sale the seller is authorised or required to send the goods to the buyer, delivery of the goods to the carrier is not delivery of the goods to the buyer.

Neither is delivery of goods to the carrier equivalent to delivery of the goods to the buyer in Scotland. Where does that leave the Scottish seller and his buyer regarding delivery of goods in FOB contracts which are not consumer contracts? More importantly, do the provisions relating to notice and therefore *Wimble v Rosenberg* and *Northern Steel V Batt* apply to Scotland?

Even in the remaining UK jurisdictions, since subsection 32(2) requires that any contract of carriage unilaterally arranged by the seller must be reasonable having regard to the nature of the goods and the circumstances of the case, sellers are put on notice that the buyer has remedy where the contract of carriage is not reasonable. Accordingly, English, Northern Irish and Welsh FOB sellers would be well advised to have regard to these factors when making a contract of carriage as well as to the terms and conditions of the carrier. This is in addition to the impact on the

[109] At p. 608.

[110] *Clarke v Hutchison* (1811) 14 East, 475; 104 ER 683; applied in *Pointing v Porrier* (1885) 49 JP 199. However, the seller had to exercise reasonable precautions to ensure delivery to the buyer.

[111] *Cathy v Tute* (1811) 3 Camp 129;170 ER 1329.

[112] s.32(4) inserted (31.3.2003) by S.I. 2002/3045, reg. 4(3).

obligations imposed by the *Unfair Contract Terms Act 1977*. This seems to be the implication of the decision in *Thomas Young & Sons Ltd v Hobson & Partners*.[113]

4.19 Application of S.32 *SGA* 1979 and Case Law to Northern Ireland

The position in Wales is treated as English law jurisdiction. Although the s 32(1) to s 32(3) do not apply to Scottish jurisdiction when parties are trading as consumers, the Act is silent when it comes to its application to Northern Ireland jurisdiction on this subject. What are we to make of this?

That notwithstanding, it must be stressed that even in the other three UK jurisdictions where subsections (1) to (3) apply, while delivery to the carrier is treated as delivery to the buyer, the delivery to the carrier does not deny the buyer's right to examine the goods for conformity with the FOB contract as well as subsections 14–16 of the Act. These factors may have enormous implications on the seller's breach of contract and consequently further insurance repercussions.

4.20 Whether Incoterms Alters the Common Law Rule Relating to Notice and "Minimum Cover"?

Incoterms 2020 seems to have formalised the provision of notice for insurance purposes in FOB. This is now contained in Clauses A5, B5, A10 and B10 of FOB Incoterms 2020 (see Chap. 5 post). However, this time the obligation relates to both parties, not just the seller as under common law.

4.20.1 Introduction

In FOB with additional duties, and other circumstances where the FOB seller has to insure, he only has to provide the minimum cover which, *inter alia*, excludes war risks. Parties can always vary this requirement. This is also the same for both common law CIF and CIF under Incoterms. In this context, the term 'minimum cover' does not include sufficient cover.

4.20.2 Minimum Cover

The minimum amount of FOB cover is a matter between the parties. Failing that, the CIF common law position, Clause A5 of CIF/CIP Incoterms 2020 and relevant case

[113] *Thomas Young & Sons Ltd v Hobson & Partners* (1949) 65 TLR 365.

law therein on the subject in Chap. 7 (below) would be suitable guidelines.[114] The position on commodity trade contracts (see Sect. 4.23.5 below) might be different.

4.20.3 Sufficient FOB Cover

For the above reasons CIF and Incoterms 2020 text in Chap. 7 (below) on the subject would be persuasive.

4.20.4 Maximum FOB Cover

For the reasons outlined under minimum and sufficient cover above, Chap. 7 would be a useful fall-back position.

4.21 Insurance of American FOB and FAS Contracts

4.21.1 Introduction

As discussed in Chap. 3, North American FOB is always different from common law FOB.[115] Due to its large landmass and the long distance between east and west coasts, it is more akin to the European continental FOB, which is used for both import and export.[116] Furthermore, unlike the English common law and mainstream FOB Incoterms, the American FOB is codified being contained in §2-319(1) (FOB and FAS terms) of the American UCC[117]

4.21.2 Carriage and Delivery Obligations

With regard to carriage, delivery and insurance obligations, §2-319(1) of the UCC (FOB and FAS terms) provides that:

[114] See Chap. 7.

[115] See Commentary to the Ohio Revised Code 2006 at para 6.

[116] See, for example, generally, Reynolds (2020).

[117] The UCC treats FOB and FAS as the same, which is not quite right, as the normal FOB requires that the seller loads the goods whereas, unless otherwise provided, the FAS simply requests him to provide goods alongside the ship for the buyer's loading.

§2-319(1)
Clause (Section 2-504) and bear the expense and risk of putting them into the possession of the carrier; or "(1) Unless otherwise agreed the term FOB (which means "free on board") at a named place, even though used only in connection with the stated price, is a delivery term under which

(a) when the term is FOB--, the place of shipment, the seller must at that place ship the goods in the manner provided in this

(b) when the term is FOB--, the place of destination, the seller must at his own expense and risk transport the goods to that place and their tender delivery of them in the manner provided in this Clause (Section 2-503);

(c) when under either (a) or (b) the term is also FOB vessel, car or other vehicle, the seller must in addition at his own expense and risk load the goods on board. If the term is FOB vessel the buyer must name, the vessel and in an appropriate case the seller must comply with the provisions of this Clause on the form of bill of lading (Section 2-323)".

It is also apparent from this statute that American law does not make a distinction between FOB and FAS contracts, just as it doesn't between the CIF and C&F, both of which are treated the same. That is a marked difference from English common law, which makes the distinction. Except in minor changes, the American FOB sellers' and buyers' obligations are not very different from those of English common law.

4.21.3 Passage of Property and Risks

The American §2-319(1) of the UCC above is almost the same as those of the English common law and indeed the Incoterms. It does not provide for when property and risks pass, but presumes this is on delivery of the contract goods to the carrier (shipment).

4.21.4 Insurance Obligations

The American UCC has no reference to FOB insurance. Information on this is discernible only from commentaries. For instance, Reynolds, a leading authority, opines that:

> Neither party is required to insure FOB. However, common sense dictates otherwise, and insurance should be covered outside of the Incoterms. This is important to the buyer, since the seller has discharged his or her responsibility before main carriage transportation takes place. It is also important to the seller if he or she is shown as 'shipper' on the vessel transportation document, because of the GA peril.[118]

---

[118] Reynolds (2020), Commentary No. 9, p. 68.

This explanation is much clearer and more helpful than the basic requirement under Clause B5 of FOB Incoterms 2020, which simply provides that the buyer has no obligation to the seller to make a contract of insurance. From this, it would appear the American interpretation of the insurance obligations is not very different from the mainstream FOB.[119]

4.22 Insurance of Other Related Contracts

4.22.1 General

In doing so, in addition to the above list, this chapter will introduce the following FOB-related contracts in the 2020 Incoterms to be covered in the next chapter (Chap. 5): Unlike the FOB itself, to the best of the author's knowledge, none of these remaining FOB-related 2020 Incoterms or those below have had judicial interpretations and are not, therefore, included in this chapter. Reasons for lack of judicial reference could range from the absence of reported disputes, reliance on solution through arbitration and other confidential dispute resolution mechanisms and their relatively young age compared to that of the FOB

4.22.2 FOT and FOR

"F.O.R." and "F.O.T." mean "free on rail" or "free on truck." Both refer to goods being carried by rail, although "Truck" could include lorries (road). As in the main FOB, unless otherwise provided the buyer is responsible for insurance. FOR and FOT are no longer in use under English common law but are still in use in Indian and other common law jurisdictions. However, they are included in this book partly for historic reasons and partly because of their possible continued use by some parties in other jurisdictions. These too are covered in the next chapter (Chap. 5). They were subsumed into FCA under İncoterms 2020.

4.22.3 FOB (AIR)

FOB (Air) or FOB (Airport) is very similar to the FOB term but used only for air cargo. The seller fulfils his obligation by delivering the goods to the aircraft or their cargo handling agents at an airport and is responsible for insurance. This too is no longer in use under English common law but may be still functional in other common law jurisdictions. Likewise, they are now part of the FCA in Incoterms 2020

[119] See also the Ohio State Code Commentary in Chap. 7.

4.23 Other Insurance Considerations

4.23.1 Introduction

As indicated above, unless otherwise provided, the contract requires provision of only the minimum cover. This has a number of implications. First, additional cover would have to be expressly requested and then provided by the seller. Secondly, any additional cover would be at the buyer's request and expense. Finally, both parties would be advised to provide their own additional insurance to cover contingencies not anticipated in the contract, as discussed below.

4.23.2 FOB and Related Incoterms War Risks Insurance

War insurance for FOB and related contracts is not different from those of any other export contracts. With a few exceptions, it would not be different from those of CIF. However, this chapter does not include discussions on insurance war risks for FOB and related contracts.[120]

4.23.3 Tender of Insurance Documents in FOB

The FOB policy, together with the other documents, should be tendered to the buyer in the same way as in any other export policies. Although there is less emphasis on insurance in FOB contracts, the tender requirements and procedures are not much different from those of the CIF.[121] [see Chap. 11].

4.23.4 FOB Insurance and the Letters of Credit Under UCP 600

Although initially designed for use with CIF contracts, the UCP applies to FOB and all other export contracts. For purposes of tender for letters of credit payments, UCP 600 does not distinguish between the CIF and FOB nor their related contracts. In fact, it does not refer to any specific contract [see Chap. 11].

[120] For these reasons, the subject has been consolidated into one chapter (Chap. 10).

[121] See Chap. 11 for details.

4.23.5 Insurance of FOB-GAFTA Contracts

4.23.5.1 Clause-1.3 GAFTA Insurance for FOB

4.23.5.1.1 Clause-1.3.1 Buyers' Insurance Obligations

GAFTA has no standard insurance terms for FOB, equivalent to the CIF *GAFTA Insurance Terms No.72*. This is instead effected through, for example under Clause 9 of the Contract for the delivery of goods *Central and Eastern Europe in Bulk or Bags Terms*, providing that:

> Marine and war risk insurance including strikes, riots, civil commotions and mine risks to be effected by Buyers with first class underwriters and/or approved companies. Buyers shall supply Sellers with confirmation thereof at least 5 consecutive days prior to expected readiness of vessel(s). If Buyers fail to provide such confirmation, Sellers shall have the right to place such insurance at Buyers' risk and expense (***emphasis provided***)

Reference to "***first class***" underwriters is in contrast to "insurance companies of good repute" in Clause A5 of Incoterms CIF/CIP 2020. The former can be confusing as it might suggest different levels of cargo underwriters. For those reasons, the latter is preferable as it reflects underwriters' honour records rather than their class in the pecking order.

4.23.5.1.2 Clause-1.3.2 Sellers' Insurance Obligations

There are no equivalent FOB provisions for sellers as they don't have such obligations at common law, Incoterms and or commodity trade contracts. The educated advice would use the sellers' interest insurance and other facilities discussed (ante).

Finally, although Incoterms 2020 CIF/CIP insurance Clauses (A5/B5) refer to provision of insurance policy and/or evidence, they do not detail the tender process. These are instead covered under the UCP600 (Chap. 11 post).

4.24 Insurance of C&F Contracts

4.24.1 General

Other contracts where, unless otherwise provided, sellers are not responsible for similar insurance include the C&F contracts. As discussed in Chap. 5 (post), at common law, the seller is responsible only for costs and freights. Consequently, it is clear that insuring of C&F contracts is the buyer's responsibility. Of the two principle common law cases on the subject, *The Pantanassa*[122] and *The Galatia*,[123] the latter dealt with the.

[122] **Efploia Shipping Corporation, Ltd. v. Canadian Transport Company, Ltd. (The "Pantanassa.")** [1958] 2 Lloyd's Rep. 449 **Queen's Bench Division. (Commercial Court.)** Before Mr. Justice Diplock.

[123] **Golodetz & Co. Inc. v. Czarnikow-Rionda Co. Inc. (*The "Galatia"*).** [1979] 2 Lloyd's Rep. 450 **Queen's Bench Division (Commercial Court)** Before Mr. Justice Donaldson.

(a) the obligations of the seller regarding the type and use of the bill of lading [customary in the trade; and
(b) the tender of the policy in the process.

On the former, Lord Megaw on appeal from Justice Donaldson at the arbitration, decided on the first issue that there was no evidence of non-acceptability of such a bill of lading in the trade. He (Judge) said:

> However, [the buyer], as I have said, submits that, on the construction of the award as a whole and by reference to various documents that passed between the parties and, I think he also submits, as a matter of ordinary good sense, the arbitrators ought, by way of necessary inference, to be taken as saying that the bill of lading was not 'clean' in the sense that it was not a document that would ordinarily and properly have been accepted in the trade as being an appropriate document. That there is such a requirement in relation to bills of lading is, I think, sufficiently clear...Donaldson J. [at first instance] unreservedly accepted that proposition. He said that, if the arbitrators had found that a bill of lading in this form was not acceptable in the trade, his decision 'would, of course, have been different' ... In that event, he would have upheld their decision on this issue. But he found himself unable to take the view that that was what the arbitrators were to be treated as having said, either by the words that they had used or by any inference that could properly be drawn in respect of them from the award as a whole or any relevant matters referred to therein.[124]

On the second issue whether the policy tendered was not one which was usual or merchantable in the trade, he said: 'For myself, I find that view supported by the fact that, in the second award dealing with what has been called the 'insurance' issue, the self-same arbitrators, in dealing with the question whether a policy of insurance taken out by the buyers was in accordance with the contract, made an express finding, first, that the policy was defective in certain stated respects, and then went on to say: 'We further find and/or hold that the policy was not one which was usual or merchantable in the trade. 'The arbitrators, therefore, when they were minded to find that a document was not one that was usual or merchantable in the trade, were prepared to express that view specifically.

4.24.2 Under English Common Law

That lends strength, in my view, to the conclusion reached by Donaldson J. I would agree with him, in any event, that here it cannot be assumed or accepted, even on a balance of probability (if that were the appropriate test), that the arbitrators were intending to say: 'We, having considered this matter, find here that this document is one that was unusual and that was not merchantable in the trade.' In my judgment, accepting the conclusion of Donaldson J., the arbitrators here must be taken, incorrectly as a matter of law, to have held that the bill of lading in question was not 'clean' by reason of the notation referred to. If the arbitrators have not found that this bill of lading, with its notation, is not reasonably and readily fit to pass current

---

[124] Ibid.

in commerce, there is no reason for the court so to hold. No other grounds are now put forward in favour of the buyers on this issue. I am satisfied that the decision of Donaldson J. was correct on this issue."

His Lordship made a distinction between the acceptable bill of lading and the unacceptable policy in the same case. Thus, The Galatia followed the earlier decision in *The Pantanassa* in determining that it was the buyer's duty to take out insurance in C&F contracts. Although insurance is not part of the seller's obligations, where, however, he is requested to and agrees to, he is liable if he fails to do so. Thus, although the case turned on whether a certificate is acceptable tender instead of the policy, *Muller, MacLean & Co v Leslie and Anderson*,[125] decided that in such instance the seller satisfies his obligations by tendering a certificate instead of a policy of insurance. In dismissing the buyer's contention for non-acceptance of the tender of the certificate, Justice Roche said: "Whatever the rule may be with regard to a c.i.f contract, I know of no such rule in connection to the contract for cost freight and freight only".[126] The seller would of course take out his own seller's interest and contingency insurance but these are neither contractual to nor are they for the benefit of the buyer. The same position applies to the new CFR Incoterms, in Chap. 9 below.

4.25 Insurance of American C&F Contracts

4.25.1 Under the UCC

The American UCC treats the C&F as equivalent to the CIF save for the absence of seller's insurance obligations to the buyer. The Commentary to the Ohio State Revised Code (chapter 7 above) shades more light on the American insurance context and differences, where applicable, to English and other common law jurisdictions. C& F under US law is treated as if it were a CIF. It is codified under the US UCC§ 2-320 (1) which provides that: "The term C. & F. or C.F. means that the price so includes cost and freight to the named destination" and under UCC 2-320(3) that "Unless otherwise agreed the term C. & F. or its equivalent has the same effect and imposes upon the seller the same obligations and risks as a C.I.F. term except the obligation as to insurance". and under US UCC§ 2-320(4) that:

> Under the term C.I.F. or C. & F. unless otherwise agreed the buyer must make payment against tender of the required documents and the seller may not tender nor the buyer demand delivery of the goods in substitution for the documents.

The UCC and Incoterms for Americans both treat the C&F as the same as the CFR. Those documents include insurance documents. Thus, the insurance obligations are the same as under English common law.

[125] Muller, Maclean and Co v Leslie and Anderson (1921) 8 Lloyd's List Law Rep 328.

[126] Ibid.

4.25.2 Carriage Risks

These are the same as the common law C&F/CFR/CIF for both parties. These risks have implication on parties' and, therefore, liabilities insurance needs and obligations.

4.25.3 Delivery Risks

These are the same as the common law C&F/CFR/CIF for both parties. These risks have implication on parties' and, therefore, liabilities insurance needs and obligations.

4.25.4 Passage of Property

These are the same as for the common law C&F/CFR/CIF for both parties. These risks have implication on parties' and, therefore, liabilities insurance needs and obligations.

4.25.5 Passage of Risks

These are same as for the common law C&F/CFR/CIF for both parties. These risks have implication on parties' and, therefore, liabilities insurance needs and obligations.

4.25.6 Requirement for Information and Notice

These are the same as for the common law C&F/CFR/CIF. These risks have implication on parties' and, therefore, liabilities insurance needs and obligations.

4.25.7 Insurance Obligation

The seller has no obligation to provide insurance for the buyer, the same as for common law and Incoterms' C&F for both parties. The insurance obligations are therefore the same as in CFR, FOB, FAS and FCA above

4.26 Insurance of *EXW*

The EXW is such a unique contract that, unless otherwise agreed, the seller is concerned with only the provision of the contract goods at its premises or depot. Risks and property pass at that point. He is not concerned with either carriage or delivery matters beyond that point. Least of all, the seller is not concerned with insurance matters. The buyer is responsible for all those matters from taking delivery. This rule places minimum responsibility on the seller, who merely has to make the goods available, suitably packaged, at the specified place. From that viewpoint there is not much difference between the common law and Incoterms EXW. The same principles and obligations apply to EXW Incoterms.

4.27 Damages for Breach of Insurance Obligations

4.27.1 Difference Between General and Insurance Breaches

There is a difference between breach of failure to insure and other breaches; the former leaves goods uninsured or under-insured. Secondly, it is only in FOB with additional duties or extended FOB that the issue may arise. Where the seller undertakes to insure contract goods under an extended FOB (FOB with additional duties) or any other FOB variant imposing additional duties, he will be liable for damages for breach of the undertaking. Although not part of the original obligations, once agreed on, the assumption of any additional duties becomes a term of the contract as if it had been the customary terms thereof.

4.27.2 Failure to Take Out Insurance

One of the breaches leading to damages includes failure to take out the policy for whatever reason. Considering the essential nature of insurance in export/import trade, this would amount to a fundamental breach of the contract, with dire consequences to the wrongdoer. The contract goods would be unprotected. The buyer would be entitled for double relief: for breach of the insurance obligations which leaves the goods exposed; and breach of the insurance term of the contract.

4.27.3 Damages for Failure to Tender Documents

Insurance is not part of the FOB seller's obligations unless specifically provided such as in the extended FOB. These are matters of agreement between the parties. However, when so agreed and provided, then the seller's duty extends to tendering the policy together with the other export documentation. In that case, failure to tender the insurance policy would be a breach of contract in the same way as it is for CIF.[127] Even if that were not the case, the buyer normally tenders documents anyway for payment purposes under letters of credit. Just as in CIF contracts, in the same fashion there would be breach of sales, insurance and letters of credit contracts. So, the three subjects here—tender, UCP and damages—should be read together.[128] It will be recalled that in *Northern Steel*, the defendants forgot to insure and lost, but could have succeeded had the contract been an FOB with additional duties.

4.27.4 Damages for Provision of Insufficient Cover

Since insurance is not the seller's responsibility in classic, strict and simple FOB, then the issue does not arise. However, in extended FOB (which includes insurance), then he would be in breach of contract. Such a contract would stipulate the amount of cover requested or necessary. This would amount to under-insurance rather total failure to insure. However, the seller might take leaf from the CIF contracts in Chap. 7 *post,* where insurance is inbuilt.

4.27.5 Damages for Failure to Tender Policy

Comments above regarding classic, strict and simple FOB apply in this respect. The seller is not responsible, so the issue does not arise. However, he still has to tender the remaining documents as per contract. Extended FOB would be a different matter. Where insurance is included, then the position is the same as in CIF contracts. For tender of documents see Chap. 11 (post).

4.28 Further Food for Thoughts

4.28.1 Caution to Both Parties

Although it is suggested that the FOB contract has its advantages, that is depends on whether one is viewing from the sellers' of buyers; viewpoint. Misreading of such provisions can have catastrophic effects on the party liabilities and therefore insurance obligations

First, from both parties' points of view the divisions between the several FOB variations into classic, etc may not make sense from a practical point of view. For instance, apart from may be the extended FOB or the FOB with additional duties,

[127] See tender of policy and other documents in Chaps. 5, 7 and 8.

[128] See Lorenzo (2012), Chapter 10.

often parties cannot tell the others, and is normally only the courts are able to do so at which point it would be too late for the losing party to remedy. And even the extended FOBs, the parties will have to provide so expressly in the contract. In any case that option is not available to parties contracting under Incoterms and or commodity trade standard term contracts

Secondly, still for both parties, regarding the extended FOB, as indicated in paragraph 4.10 above, where the buyer takes on extra responsibilities, he may be liable for failure to perform those extra obligations. Besides the obligations will depend on whether it is assumption of shipping contracts with the shipowner or the insurance company. In the former, the buyer could breach it or even where he doesn't, he probably becomes a shipping agent in which he incurs a conflict-of-interest problems when he is both the seller and the shipper. Can the buyer sue him as both the contractual party to the main contract and as a principal for the agency contract? And where does leave what Schimitthorf describes as the FOB where the seller undertakes to contract for shipping.

Thirdly, as demonstrated at length under paragraphs 4.14–418 above the requirements of notice between the parties pursuant to ss. 32 of the *SGA* 1979 and the *Wimble v Rosenberg* and *Northern Steel v John Batt*, the issue of notice remains a problem. The only reason why the seller was not liable for not providing notice was because the buyer had had sufficient information under the circumstances. There is no authority to cover instances where the buyer had not had constructive notice.

4.28.2 Specific Caution to Sellers

First, for the seller, with regard to the additional obligations being insurance, the same issues as above arise. The seller charges for the insurance commission and other insurance charges. Does he send one invoice and several representing each of the additional duties. In this case does the seller take on the full liability as an insurance agent for this purpose. What about where the seller further sub-contracts on insurance (despite the common law discouraging such sub-contracts by requiring the seller does so personally). The same problems as above arise; can the buyer sue the seller both as a contractual party to the mail sales contract and as an insurance agent. Do the normal agency rules follow that the buyer would be liable for his agent's liabilities to third parties for breaches? At this stage things then get messy.

Secondly, continuing for the seller, Seller still has to arrange the export permits. Seller still has to transport the merchandise from their warehouse until it crosses the rail of the vessel. This includes the custom clearance and the terminal handling charge. Seller cannot recover any loss if the merchandise is already on board the vessel. Seller cannot recover the price if the buyer failed to nominate a suitable vessel, which eventually makes the BL date to miss the agreed pricing window, and the future price is dropping. Buyer will not be responsible for any shipping costs of the goods and their damage if happens. Buyer will not be held responsible for any loss in-transit. Accordingly, the sellers will not be able to recover any loss once the goods have been on-boarded

4.28.3 Specific Caution to Buyers

First, from the buyer's point of view, there are other disadvantages of trading under FOB which may impact on his/her insurance obligations. For instance, if one is a new buyer especially with international shipping, FOB might not be the option best suited for him/her. This is because the FOB places a lot of responsibility on the buyer, as they need to comprehend the complexity involved with international shipments. There are plenty of opportunities for penalties, delays, and other problems to occur if you don't have a good handle on the complete overseas shipping landscape. For those new shippers and buyers who are looking for the right advice on how to handle international shipments, consulting or depending on the experience of a proven third-party logistics provider like LTX is a smart idea.

Secondly, for the buyer, there are further twin problems of passages of property and risks. Unless otherwise provided risks normally follow property and the person having property (title to) in the goods bears risks and corresponding insurance obligations. In the former case, under the FOB contract, when the goods are placed on board the vessel, the buyer has a title of the goods, because property in goods passes at the same time. Another reason of this, he becomes a shipper of the goods after shipment and he has a contractual relationship with the carrier. In the latter case, pursuant to *Pyrene v Scindia,* authority, the principle of the FOB contract is that property and risk passes to the buyer, who bears all the other costs, when the goods cross the ship's rail. The transfer of risk in CIF (Costs, Insurance and Freight) contracts is conditioned to transfer of property.

4.28.4 Theoretical vs Practical Scenarios

Are the numerous FOB divisions merely academic or do they have practical implications? Are the divisions helpful to contractual parties for insurance purposes? Authors are not even agreed as to the exact definitions and number of the variations. Is it always clear where and when the insurance obligations arise in the various FOBs? Are the guidelines for when notice is required by the buyer, under s 32 *SGA* 1979 and the leading authorities therein, helpful for insurance purposes? Doesn't it cause confusion on when to and when not to provide the notice? Doesn't it cause confusions on agency relationships when the seller contracts for freight and takes out insurance in extended FOBs? Despite the theoretical discourses does the FOB insurance obligations of extended FOB differ from CIF in practice? See also under "Food Thoughts" chapter 7 (CIF Insurance) and all relevant chapter.

4.29 Concluding Remarks

The general rule is that it is the buyer's responsibility to secure insurance and carriage in FOB and related contracts at common law. This rule is, however, subject to the following exceptions and modifications.

First, this may be modified by the extended FOB or FOB with additional duties, where both insurance and carriage contract responsibilities might revert to the buyer.

Secondly, case law has shown that the seller may be required to notify the buyer in reasonable time to enable the latter to take out the policy. This requirement of notice is now included in Clauses A5, B5, A10 and B10 of FOB Incoterms 2020. This qualification to the seller's insurance obligations makes sense as, between the two parties, the seller is best placed to gauge if and when the loading process is affected.

Finally, both parties would, in addition to their contractual obligations, be advised to take out additional insurance to cater for contingencies. For these reasons, it is not entirely accurate to assume that it is only the buyer's duty to insure in FOB contracts at common law.

4.30 Further Readings

Books

- Sassoon, David: *CIF and FOB Contracts*, Sweet and Maxwell, 10th edn., 2011, Chapter 12.
- Wooldridge, Frank: "The kinds of FOB contracts", in *Law and International Trade* (Festschrift fur Clive M. Schmitthoff) Frankfurt, 1973 p.383.
- Carr, Indira: *Law of International Trade*, Taylor and Francis, Informa, 5th edn., 2014, Chapter 14.
- Schmitthoff, David M.: *The Law and Practice of International Trade*, Sweet and Maxwell, Reuters, 12th edn., 2010, Part IV Chapters 19 and 20.
- *Halsbury's Laws of England*, (5th edn., 2012) Vol.91 (Sale and Supply of Goods and Services) paras. 300–393 at 363.
- Dunt, John, *Marine Cargo Insurance*, Informa Law, 2012, generally.
- Vishwanath, Krishna S.: *Insuring Cargo* [Practical Guide to the law and practice], Witherby, 2010, generally.
- Chuah, Jason: *Law of International Trade (Cross-Border Commercial Transactions)*, 5th edn., 2013, Sweet & Maxwell, Chapter 10.
- Benjamin, Judah Philip: *Benjamin on Sale of Goods*. Chapter 20.
- Reynolds, David: *Incoterms for Americans 2020*.
- Bridge, Michael: *International Sale of Goods*, Chapter 3.
- Crockford, Neil (ed.): *Insuring Foreign Risks*, Sweet and Maxwell, London, 2013.
- Jimenez, Guillermo: *ICC Guide to Export-Import Basics*, ICC Pub. No.453 (E), 1997, pp. 187–190.

- Ewan McKendrick *F.O.B. Contracts*, Imprint Informa Law from Routledge1st Edition, 2000
- "**Laytime and demurrage in CIF and FOB contracts**", Chapter X in *International Trade and Carriage of Goods by* Baris Soyer, Andrew Tettenborn (edited) 1st Edition, 2016 Imprint Informa Law from Routledge
- Reynolds, Frank: Incoterms Rules for Americans (Rewritten for Incoterms 2020 Rules), International Projects, Inc. Toledo, OH, US 2019

Selected Clauses

- Davis: "The Various types of FOB Contracts", 1956 *JBL.*
- Sassoon, David: "Application of FOB and CIF Sales in Common Law Countries" [1981] ETL 50.
- Evans, Paul: "FOB and CIF Contracts" [1993] *ALJ* 844.
- Gower, Laurence Cecil Bartlett: "FOB Contracts", (1956) 19 *MLR*, 417.
- Sassoon, David: "The Origin of FOB and CIF: Terms and Factors influencing choice" [1967] JBL 32.
- International: "Insurance of FOB Contracts in Anglo-American and Common Law Jurisdictions Revisited",), *International* Vol.31 No.1 pp. 425–462 (2007).
- John Williamson: "FOB Contracts: An Examination of Their Principles and Practical Application in Internal Trade" *Auckland University Law Review pp.476–493*
- Liang Zhao: "FOB seller under Chinese law and privity of contract in carriage of goods by sea" **Orcid** Icon Pages 286–305 | Received 18 Apr 2019, Accepted 10 Sep 2019, Published online: 23 Dec 2019
- UK Essays: "Comparing CIF and FOB Contracts", https://www.lawteacher.net/free-law-essays/international-law/comparing-cif-and-fob-contracts-international-law-essay.php
- Law Teacher: "Critical assessment of the rules on risk in relation to CIF and FOB contracts", https://www.lawteacher.net/free-law-essays/contract-law/cif-and-fob-contracts.php
- Michael Bridge: "Chapter 9: CIF and FOB contracts in English law: current issues and problems" https://www.elgaronline.com/view/edcoll/9781786436146/9781786436146.00019.xml
- Choi, Myung- Kok: "Insurable Interest under the Traditional FOB Contracts", *The International Commerce and Law Review,* Vol.11,1998, pp. 185–204
- Choi, Myung- Kok The International Commerce and Law Review "Problems on Validity of the Goods Conformity Clauses in FOB Contracts- -The Mercini Lady" Vol. 58, 2013, pp. 35–58
- Aleksei Yurievich Churilov, "Classification of CIF and FOB Contracts and its Role," *Russian Foreign Economic Journal,* Russian Foreign Trade Academy Ministry of economic development of the Russian Federation, Issue 1, January, 2021.pages 44–50.

- "F. O. B. Contracts" *The Modern Law Review*, Vol. 19, No. 4 (Jul., 1956), pp. 417–419
- -Aubrey L. Diamond "Opening the Credit in F. O. B. Contracts", The *Modern Law Review*, Vol. 21, No. 4 (Jul., 1958), pp. 430–433

Theses

- Al-Anbaki, Majid H. K: *Passing of property in C.I.F. & F.O.B. contracts (comparative study).* PhD thesis Glasgow University (1978) http://theses.gla.ac.uk/3990

Reports

- See also under Reports in other chapters.

Websites

- Reed Smith LLP, "FOB contracts: shipment/delivery periods", http://www.lexology.com/library/detail.aspx?g=112292da-8588-434e-94ca-b74b29499f7b
- Reed Smith LLP , "Shipment/delivery periods in FOB contracts: confusion explained", http://www.lexology.com/library/detail.aspx?g=18ad4940-9628-4cbb-a8e1-4e4f0ff8c4c0
- Law and Sea, "Sale Contracts. FOB Terms". http://www.lawandsea.net/COG/COG_SaleContracts_FOB.html
- Rami Al-Tal "Nomination of vessel FOB contracts" http://www.tamimi.com/en/magazine/law-update/section-7/may-6/nomination-of-vessel-FOB-contracts.html#sthash.D7wH2AhG.dpuf
- Law and sea, "Sale Contracts. Three types of FOB contract", http://www.lawandsea.net/COG/COG_SaleContracts_Types_of_FOB.html.
- Benjamin, Insurance of Transportation, 21-047-21-106
- Ohio State Revised Code 2006 (1302.35. corresponding to UCC 2-322), para.4 http://law.justia.com/codes/ohio/2006/orc/jd_130233-53fb.html
- Ufuo Asanwana and Okor Efombruh: "Understanding FOB and CIF Contracts: And When Property and Risk Pass in These Transactions" 13 Pages Posted: 28 Nov 2018 **The Law Hall**; University of the West of England University of the West of England, Date Written: November 5, 2018 https://papers.ssrn.com/sol3/papers.cfm?abstract_id=3278642
- Patrick McGonigal: *UK: FOB Contract - Rights and Obligations of Buyer and Seller Re-Examined,* Barlow Lyde & Gilbert LLP, 21 September 2010 (This Article was first published in *Maritime Risk International*, April 2010)
- UK Essays: "The Definition And Essence Of F O B Contract", https://www.ukessays.com/essays/law/the-definition-and-essence-of-f-o-b-contract-international-law-essay.php

References

Ademuni-Odeke (1995) Insurance element in CIF and CIP incoterms. T I L &P 4(4):86–92
Ademuni-Odeke (2007) Insurance of FOB contracts in Anglo-American and common law jurisdictions revisited. Tul. MLJ 31(1):425–462
Lorenzo F (2012) CIF and FOB contracts, 5th edn
Reynolds F (2020) Incoterms for Americans
Sassoon DM (1984) CIF and FOB contracts, 3rd edn. Stevens & Sons, London
Sassoon DM (1995) CIF and FOB contracts, 4th edn. Stevens & Sons, London

5 Insurance of FOB and Related Contracts that Exclude Seller's Insurance Obligations to the Buyer Under Incoterms

Abstract

This chapter deals with **[Insurance of FOB and Related [9 Contracts] that Exclude Sellers' Insurance Obligations to the Buyer Under Incoterms]** and follows the same pattern of Chaps. 4 and 5. The contracts covered are the FOB, CFR including the old C&F, CPT, FCA, FAS, DAP, and DPU including their corresponding American versions under the UCC and Incoterms for Americans Guidelines. Prior to the main discourse the chapter puts the latest and applicable Incoterms 2020 in perspectives in relations to: at glance, insurance clauses, and comparisons with previous Incoterms. In relation to the FOB insurance the chapter delves into the requirement for notification by the seller to the buyer upon shipment as the seller has no obligation to insure. For each of all the nine contracts concerned under this category the chapter summarises the parties' obligations in carriage, delivery, risks and passage of property whose breaches have implications on insurance. The chapter also covers other relevant insurance factors which the parties need to consider regarding these contracts, namely: problem of the recurring "**No Obligation**" to insurance statement; necessity for insurance notices and information; need for maximum insurance for international transport costs; carriage/delivery and security notices and information; sellers' and buyers' interest insurance; buyers' and sellers' contingency insurance; restrictive state insurance practices; and external factors and considerations. For ease of the readers' convenience the chapter also contains a comparative table of parties' Passage of Risks, Sellers Insurance and Buyers Insurance Obligations.

P. Ademuni-Odeke, *Insurance of International Sales' Contracts under Incoterms*, Law for Professionals, https://doi.org/10.1007/978-3-031-75136-3_5

5.1 Introduction

Chapter 3 dealt with the general nature and characteristics of contracts that exclude seller's obligations to provide insurance for the buyer at common law while Chap. 4 covered their insurance aspects at common law. This chapter concerns insurance aspects of the same contracts under Clause A5/B5 of Incoterms 2020. In general, the rules are silent on the matter of insurance so the buyer and the seller each have to decide whether they wish to insure the cargo and if so for that part of the journey for which they bear the risk of loss or damage. The class of Incoterms contracts in this instance here is purely in relation to the absence of seller's insurance obligations and are listed alphabetical. The classification has no reference to their transportation[1] mode or the C,[2] D,[3] E[4] and F[5] classifications as in previous Incoterms. Not all common law contracts are included in Incoterms. The chapter inevitably includes only those contracts in Incoterms 2020.

They may, therefore, differ from categorizations used in other Incoterms publications. Contracts in which seller's insurance obligations are exclude in this context, include the CPT, CFR, DAP, DDP, DPU, EX WORKS, FCA, FAS and FOB. They are a mixture of C, D, E and F classifications. In this family of contracts, the letter F signifies that the seller must hand over the goods to a nominated carrier free of risk and expenses to the buyer. However, the common thread is that the buyer bears risk and is, therefore, responsible for insurance from that point. For a better appreciation of the insurance needs, the chapter includes summarises of carriage and delivery obligations risks, passage of property risks and passage of risks themselves before considering their respective impacts on insurance. This is because breach of those obligations gives rise to liability and, therefore, need for coverage.

At the risk of repetitions, the chapter includes discussions on and requirements of notice and information for insurance purposes and consequences of "No Obligations" aspects before embarking on discourses on insurance obligations. This is to provide a background to and demonstrate relationship between the breach of those duties and insurance liabilities of both parties. Furthermore, the Incoterms insurance provisions are paraphrased where they are short and quoted for clarity where they are long. There is also coverage of insurance obligations under the American UCC and "Incoterms for Americans" respectively. Inevitably, the chapter starts with, and is dominated by, the FOB contract. The chapter opens with the treatment of insurance under Incoterms.

Parties trading under FCA, FAS, FOB, CFR AND CPT Terms should note that although the transfer of responsibility for damage or loss is clearly defined in INCOTERMS, insurance questions often arise when damage or loss occurs before the buyer is responsible and before coverage attaches under his insurance policy. If

---

[1] E.g., Sea, Land, Air and Multimodal.

[2] E.g., C& F, CFR, CIF, CIP.

[3] E.g., DAP, DDP, DPU.

[4] E.g., EXW.

[5] E.g., FCA, FAS.

there is any doubt in the buyer's mind about whether or not he will have proper recourse against the seller for loss or damage during his responsibility, the buyer may wish to review these doubts with his insurer and arrange additional coverage in the form of "contingency" insurance. (See Chap. 9 post).

5.2 Insurance Obligations in Incoterms 2020

5.2.1 Incoterms 2020 Insurance at a Glance

Incoterms and its insurance clauses have had to adapt to developments in the technological, transport and communications aspects of international trade practices. The latest Incoterms, Incoterms 2020, published in September 2019 and entering into force on 1 January 2020, has kept face with that ever-evolving global trade landscape. As noted above, it is divided into those (7) deliverable by any means of any transportation and (4) carried by sea and inland waterways transport. It is worth noting that among the differences between the 2010 and the 2020 version was the removal of DAT in favour of DUP. Furthermore, there is re-emphasis of parties' provision of notices and information to the other for purposes of the contractual and additional insurance (Clause A5/B5) as well as delivery arrangements. The allocation of cost elements of insurance for both CIF and CIP (Clause A9(f)/B9(d)) and their relation delivery (Clause A10/B10) are also included.

Before Incoterms 2020, carriage and insurance were contained in Clauses A3(a)/B3(a) and A3(a)/B3(b) respectively. These reverted to the format of Incoterms 1953 numberings with the removal of (a) and (b) and the separation of Clause A4/B4 (Carriage) from Clause A5/B5 (Insurance) respectively. Although rather repetitive in drafting, the insurance Clause A5 is now more extensive and more elaborate than the equivalent (Clause A3(b)) in Incoterms 2010. Apart from those superficial changes, the basic insurance obligations remain largely unchanged in Incoterms 2020 from those of Incoterms 2000 and 2010.

5.2.2 Insurance Clauses in Incoterms 2020

Incoterms' insurance clauses have had a long history of evolution and progressive developments. Like Incoterms, themselves, the Insurance Clause has come a long way since Incoterms 1953. The ICC too has come a long way since 1895 when it was conceived, 1919 when it materialised, 1936 when Incoterms was first published, and 1953 when the Insurance Clause first appeared. In their current forms, both Incoterms and the Insurance Clauses have been influenced and shaped by financial, technological, transport and transport developments, inter alia, in the broader remits of International Trade. Thus, both Incoterms and the Insurance Clause have had to adapt to commercial and other global environments such as the introduction of the new Cargo Clauses and developments of containerisation, emergence of rail, air, road and multimodal transport. The insurance clauses were either non-existent or did not feature much in the earliest Incoterms prior to 1953.

However, Incoterms 2020 has not altered the basic terms in which CIF and CIP sellers' insurance obligation were compulsory in Incoterms 2000 and Incoterms 2010. So, the position remains that, with the exception of CIF and CIP rules, Incoterms place no obligation on the seller or buyer to provide insurance cover to the other or for themselves in all the remaining nine rules. However, depending on the actual term used for each shipment, the seller or buyer bears responsibility for loss or damage to the goods: pre-shipment, post-shipment and during transit. Prudence would, therefore, dictate that risk exposure during those gaps be insured against. To sum up, Incoterms' position is that in two rules (CIF and CIP) the seller must provide only the minimum insurance and in the remaining Incoterms 9 rules the seller does not have to.

However, it does not mean that both parties to those Incoterms 9 rules should not make some insurance arrangements for themselves or for those in CIF and CIP to provide more than the minimum cover. Clause A5 in the two contracts is only a guideline. That notwithstanding, they cannot provide lesser cover unless otherwise agreed in the CIF and CIP. Although not addressing the subject directly, the Explanatory Note for Incoterms 2020 draws attention to the possibility of restrictive insurance practices at destination.[6] That notwithstanding, there are still similarities and differences between Incoterms 2020 and its immediate 2010 predecessor. Clause A5/B5 is discussed in details below.

5.2.3 Comparison of Incoterms 2020 with Predecessors

5.2.3.1 Main Similarities

Aesthetically, a decade on from the last revision, Incoterms 2020 text now has a very different layout and a more user-friendly style of presentation. Incoterms 2020 features many changes to the sequencing and presentation of the rules, simplified presentation and providing a welcome expansion of the explanatory notes within the Incoterms rather than in a separate publication as before. Guide for users is now contained within n the same publication compared to previous ones which were in a separate publication. All-in-all, in its lay-out, Incoterms 2020 now is easier to follow and, therefore, more user friendly. As indicated above, the insurance clause reverses to its original A5/B5 format and in Incoterms 1953 from Clauses A3(b)/B3(b) numberings used between Incoterms 1976 and Incoterms 2010. Nevertheless, these are only cosmetic changes. Other than those, there have been very few substantive changes from Incoterms 2010. There are still eleven rules. They are still divided into four restricted to "water" rules and seven "inter-modal" rules that can be used with any transport mode. No rules have been removed or added, and only one rule has been renamed from DAT to DPU. The separation of the English from the French texts, started in Incoterms 2010, is continued.

[6] "Introduction to Incoterms 2020", Incoterms 2020, pp. 1–17.

5.2.3.2 Implications for Commercial Practice

However, even the minor changes between the 2010 and 2020 rules have had commercial implications. It seems authors of the Incoterms 2020 have clearly intended to make it an effective, practice and teaching document as well as a reference work. Nevertheless, the very limited changes from Incoterms 2010 do not provide much incentive for its adoption, especially where Incoterms 2010 has been incorporated into complex trading agreements. Still, as always, trading partners remain free to adopt the Incoterms Revision of their choice by specifying it in their commercial contracts. Although backdating several years back is inadvisable, that means contracts under Incoterms 2010 and others before it, as far back as is contractually possible, are still theoretically applicable where parties expressly so provided in their contract. On the constructive side, since the Incoterms 2020 changes are minimal, businesses and organisations that have already established a good Incoterms 2010 practice do not need to undertake a major retraining exercise for Incoterms 2020.

Once more, Incoterms are neither exhaustive nor perfect, so parties should beware and take it as it is, manoeuvre around it and improvise.[7] So, the above backdrops are intended for appreciation of the trading partners' obligations below.

5.3 Insurance of the FOB Incoterms

The FOB related Incoterms is in the F Class which involve free carriage elements, the others being the FCA and FAS. Those in D Class (including those now discontinued) which do not involve carriage are DAP, DDP, and DPU. Normally this D categorisation would not include those with the F family but are grouped for their common insurance obligations. Others might have different categorisation but the thread running through their relation with FOB is the absence of insurance obligations on the seller. Under the relevant Clause A5 and Clause B5, the Incoterms provide that the seller/buyer has no obligation to make the contract of insurance or simply carries the phrase "**No Obligation**". Although the transfer of responsibility for loss or damage is clearly defined in Incoterms, parties should be aware that insurance questions often arise when loss or damage occurs before the buyer is responsible and before coverage attaches under his insurance policy. Thus, if there is any doubt in the buyer's mind about whether or not he will have a proper recourse against the seller for loss or damage during his responsibility, the buyer may wish to review these doubts with his broker or insurer and arrange additional coverage in the form of "contingency" insurance. Most policies do, however, provide automatic

[7] See Chap. 11 (post) dealing with these and related issues; "Incoterms 2020 Sellers and Buyers Beware! What The New Rules Do Not Tell You About Overall Insurance Obligations" [2021] *J.B.L.*, Issue 8 pp. 674–699; "The insurance clause in INCOTERMS 2020: The latest stage in its evolution and a progressive development 1980–2020 Part II" *The European Insurance Law Review* 2/2020, pp. 45–57 www.erevija.org "The insurance clause in INCOTERMS 2020: The latest stage in its evolution and a progressive development 1980–2020 Part I" *The European Insurance Law Review* 1/2020, pp. 28–38 www.erevija.org.

contingency coverage which may apply in these situations or are subject of practical and regular liaison between the parties.

5.4 Insurance of FOB Under Incoterms 2020

5.4.1 Parties' General Duties Affecting Insurance

As transpired from Chaps. 1–4 above, the term FOB under Incoterms 2020 means "FOB Vessel" at a named port of shipment e.g., FOB London. This clarification is important as the FOB has many variations. As detailed below, failure to clarify can, therefore, lead to confusions and damaging uncovered risks. The term can only be used for vessel shipments by water by sea or inland water transport,[8] under which responsibility for the shipment transfers from exporter to importer when shipment is loaded aboard the vessel. But under the American UCC FOB includes multimodal but not air transport, the latter now covered under FCA.

Otherwise, under FOB incoterms, the seller must load the goods onto the ship. Centuries of maritime tradition suggested that the FOB point is the "Ship's Rail", also referred to as "Freight on Board." If the freight falls while loading, however, it is the exporter's responsibility if it lands on quay as was the case in *Pyrene vs Scindia*, but it is the importer's responsibility if it lands on ship. The documentation of delivery is normally the ocean bill of lading or sea waybill, although both parties can agree on other types. The parties' duties are covered in Clauses A1–A4 and A6–A10 for seller and Clause B1–B4 and B6–B10 for the buyer respectively. The seller agrees to deliver the goods on board the overseas vessel at the named port of shipment, including during lighterage and during loading onto the vessel.

For those reasons, FOB insurance under Incoterms is not much different from that under common law, on which it is based. As will be apparent later, with the exception of CIF and CIP terms, Incoterms place no obligation on the seller or buyer to provide insurance. This is more so with the contracts under this chapter. However, depending upon the actual term used for each shipment the seller or buyer bears responsibility for loss or damage to the goods at some point during transit. Prudence would dictate that this exposure to financial loss be insured against. This is same as the common law's 'FOB classic' discussed earlier in Chaps. 3 and 4 above. Accordingly, the authorities covered therein would apply here too. The seller's general duties are covered in clauses A (1)–A (4) while the buyers are in the corresponding Clauses B/1–B/4 of Incoterms 2020. Compared to the younger CIF, FOB is the older maritime term of trade. The Incoterm FOB equivalent of the Common Law FOB is the "FOB Classic" or "Strict FOB".[9] Incoterms 2020 does not take into consideration the other common law divisions of the FOB discussed above

[8] *See Also:* Freight Collect, Incoterms® rule *Compare:* Free On Board—UCC.

[9] Schmitthoff (2012), pp. 19–22 for general aspects thereof; Ademuni-Odeke (2007), pp. 441–442 for insurance aspects thereof.

such as, "FOB with additional duties" or "Extended FOB",[10] sometimes also referred to as "FOB with additional services" and "Simple FOB".[11] Thus, unless qualified, the common law 'FOB strict' (FOB Vessels) is the Incoterms FOB covered herein.

5.4.2 Issues of FOB Insurance Under Incoterms

Unlike the CIF there is a lack of not just clarity but also judicial authority in FOB Incoterms. Ramberg in fact commented that:

> First, in this area too, there are no guidelines due to lack of reported cases. Precautionary, and as a matter of practice, however, when selling FOB sellers can safeguard their interests by arranging adequate insurance whilst goods are still at their risk, bearing in mind that where the consignee affects insurance, the seller has no claim under such insurance for loss or damage up to FOB.[12]

This is what Sassoon was alluding to, *inter alia*, in his observation in the opening quotation to Chap. 4 above. The Guide to (the earlier) Incoterms 2000 seemed to be in agreement with this position, at least with regard to premature transfer of risks.

> In some cases, the risk can be transferred from the seller to the buyer even before the seller has fulfilled his delivery obligation. This could happen because of (1) the buyer's failure to do what is required of him to enable the seller to deliver the goods to him, or (2) the buyer's failure to take delivery of the goods (Clause B5).[13]

With regard to the requirement for notice from the seller to the buyer, he (Ramberg) concluded that, therefore, the buyer must give such notice to the seller as the latter requires preparing the delivery,[14] or the buyer must nominate the carrier under F-terms and accept the goods from the carrier as agreed. Moreover, a buyer having undertaken under DDU to clear the goods for import must fulfil his obligation to do this within the agreed time so the seller can proceed with the on-carriage of the goods to destination as intended. If the buyer fails to do this, he must bear all additional risks of loss of or damage to the goods resulting from his failure.[15]

Other insurance and commercial considerations under, especially, Incoterms 2020 are where shipment duties are split between the buyer and the seller such as in *Strict* or Extended FOB or when parties use FCA instead of FOB. In this case, Incoterms notes that problems could arise when the transportation risk is split between the seller and the buyer at some intermediate point. In this case, the seller

[10] Schmitthoff (2012), p. 20; Ademuni-Odeke (2007), pp. 443–444.

[11] Ibid.

[12] *ICC Guide to Incoterms 2000,* p. 61; see also paragraph (e) below on requirement of notice for.

[13] Ibid.

[14] Then Clause B7.

[15] Ibid.

has no insurable interest after he has reached the pointed noted in the delivery (Clause A4) of Incoterms, while the buyer has no insurable interest before that point. This means that an FOB buyer has no insurable interest before the goods have crossed the ship's rail, and that, accordingly, the FOB seller remains at risk until that point has been reached.

However, if the parties use FOB when FCA should have been used instead, the seller remains at risk even after the goods have been handed over to the carrier nominated by the carrier's terminal or at a place other than the ship itself. Normally, sellers have general insurance arrangements (so-called open or blanket cover) which protect them in such cases. Nevertheless, a seller who fails to cover himself adequately in these situations will not normally benefit from the buyer's interest insurance, even if that insurance contains a so-called transit clause to the effect that the insurance protection last from warehouse to warehouse, thereby covering the period before the goods on board. There two reasons for this: first, the FOB-seller is not a contracting party to the FOB-buyer's insurance contract; and second, the FOB-buyer has no insurable interest before the goods have passed the ship's rail.[16]

However, to guard against such eventuality, the parties would find it prudent to use the door-to-door insurance. Although the original creature of the CIF contract, this type of transit insurance also seems highly recommended by freight forwarders and other shipping agents. A buyer who is unsure of which insurance should, therefore, contact his brokers or insurers or better still take out a contingency insurance.

In order to provide a wholistic view, it is also helpful to consider parties' carriage, delivery, passage of property and passage of risks obligations which may have bearings on liabilities and, therefore, insurance and obligations[17]

5.4.3 Carriage Obligations

5.4.3.1 Seller's Obligations

Pursuant to Clause A4, the seller has three different functions under carriage obligations. First, he has no obligation (negative obligation) to the buyer to make a contract of carriage.

Secondly, however, the seller must provide the buyer, at the buyer's request, risk and cost, with any information in the possession of the seller, including transport-related security requirements, that the buyer needs for arranging carriage. This tallies with insurance information below. The provision of the information is not automatic: it must be expressly requested by the buyer; it is at the buyer's risk; at the buyer's cost; and only if the information is in the buyers' possession. Conditions as to the buyers' risk and cost should be straightforward: the seller cannot ask for advance from the buyer for those costs; and bears the risks where the information cannot be provided for reasons mentioned above. However, requirement regarding information could be problematic if the buyer does not have the information in his

[16] ICC Guide to Incoterms 2010, *supra*, p. 26.

[17] This approach is taken for purposes of insurance in all Common Law and Incoterms in this book.

possession when requested. Incoterms is void of any guidelines where this may be the case.

Third, the statement, "If agreed, then the seller must contract for carriage on the usual terms at the buyer's risk and cost" is novel. Unlike in previous Incoterms, the carriage clause (A4) not only permits for the parties to vary the term by allowing the seller to provide carriage and charge the buyer separately, but also introduces the common law possibility of both different FOB classifications such as Schmithoff's FOB where the sellers' contracts with the shipowner,[18] but also of 'Extended FOB' or 'FOB with Additional Duties'.[19] As was apparent in Chap. 4 and the introduction to this chapter, the seller's other obligations can affect his overall insurance needs and/or obligations. Except for 'FOB with Additional Duties' at common law, the seller's only Incoterms obligation is to deliver goods.

Fourth, the seller must in addition comply with any transport-related requirements as to delivery,[20] failure of which could result into breach and therefore insurance claims.

For the above reasons, it is apparent that on this pint Incoterms and common law are converging. For instance, the pultimate sentence above envisages additional duties similar to those of 'Extended FOB'. However, the sentence could, in addition to insurance complications, cause problems where the parties are not fully acquainted with their respective carriage duties; which would consequently impact further on liability for passage of risks and, therefore, insurance requirements and obligations.

5.4.3.2 Buyers Obligations

Like the seller, the buyer's general obligations too can have a bearing on his overall insurance obligations and needs. The buyer has two principal obligations: first, contract for freight and secondly, receive the goods when delivered by the seller. On contract of carriage, under Clause B4 the buyer must contract at its own cost for the carriage of the goods from the named port of shipment, except where the contract of carriage is made by the seller as provided for in Clause A4.[21] The implications of "*at own cost*" is discussed under sellers' obligations above. The highlighted text implies that the buyer cannot ask for an advance from or set-off against the sellers' accounts. As in Clause A4, Clause B4 allows the parties to vary the terms of this provision with the same consequences as described therein. Either way parties should be aware of their potential liabilities and insurance consequences of their variation of the Clauses.

---

[18] Schmitthoff (2012), chapter 2, para 2-007, pp. 19–22 at 20.

[19] Extended FOB-See Chap. 4 above which complicates insurance obligations.

[20] Incoterms 2020, p. 108; security-related requirements were introduced by the Incoterms 2020. The last paragraph is a change by Incoterms 2020, by which, for the first time Incoterms getting closer to the common law FOB classic and with additional duties (Extended FOB). The clause numbering has remained A4.

[21] Ibid, p. 106; remains unchanged.

5.4.4 Delivery Obligations

5.4.4.1 Sellers Obligations

On delivery, pursuant to Clause A2:

> **Clause A2**
> The seller must deliver the goods either by placing them on board the vessel nominated by the buyer at the loading point, if any, indicated by the buyer at the named port of shipment or by procuring the goods so delivered.
>
> The seller must deliver the goods.
>
> 1. on the agreed date
>
> or
>
> 2. at the time within the agreed period notified by the buyer under B10
>
> or
>
> 3. if no such time is notified, then at the end of the agreed period
>
> and
>
> 4. in the manner customary at the port
>
> If no specific loading point has been indicated by the buyer, the seller must select the point within the named port of shipment that best suits its purpose[22]

Thus, under this term, used only for vessel shipments, the seller agrees to deliver the goods on board the overseas vessel at the named port of shipment, including during lighterage and loading onto the vessel. Unless requested the seller is not responsible for freight but is responsible for loss or damage until the goods "pass the ship's rail", same as at common law.[23] This makes no reference to completion of delivery when the goods pass the ship's rail as at common law. Clause A2 also introduces the hitherto only CIF concept of sellers not actually shipping but buying and presenting goods already shipped- the so called buying and selling afloat. Attention needs to paid, under the provision, to the seller's obligations to give notice and information to the buyer. Under Clause A10 he must give the buyer sufficient notice either that the goods have been delivered in accordance with Clause A2 or that the vessel has failed to take delivery within the time agreed.

Delivery of the documents include delivery of the documents (transport, insurance, etc.) accompanying those goods. Clause 28 of UCP 600 provides details for contracts paid or financed by letters of credit. Without the latter the seller will not have legally delivered the goods.

---

[22] Ibid, p. 106; Note that (a) the clause is much changed in wordings and (b) detailed content than in Incoterms 2010, (c) ports customary loading manner is introduced, and (d) delivery of goods is now separated by delivery of documents in Clause A6.

[23] As *Pyrene Co Ltd v Scindia Steam Navigation Company Ltd* [1949] 2QB 405, followed in the *EL Minia and El Amria* [1982] 2 Lloyds Rep28.

5.4.4.2 Buyers Obligations

On delivery, there is no equivalent provision to Clause A2.[24] The buyer is responsible from that point on for transport, loss and damages to the contract goods and, therefore, insurance.[25] Again, as in the seller's obligations, the buyer also needs to pay attention to the provision of on notice and information to the seller, failure of which could lead to breach of contract and consequently, payment by his insurers. However, his obligations relate to security-related arrangements rather than simply delivery. Thus, under Clause B10 he must give notice of any transport-related security requirements, the vessel name, loading point and, if any, the selected delivery date within the agreed period. Delivery in this case meanings the buyer accepting delivery of the goods themselves as well as accepting delivery of documents relating to those goods. These include bills of lading (transport documents), insurance policy (insurance documents) and other accompanying documents. In practice accepting of documents has the additional meaning of paying for the goods.

5.4.5 Passage of Property and Title for Both Parties

Passage of property risks have a direct effect on insurance; except in certain circumstances, the party with property bears the risks of loss and should therefore insure. The position on passage of property in FOB at Common Law is different from that under Incoterms. As already indicated, unlike Incoterms 2010 and others before it, Incoterms 2020 eliminated the Clause on passage of property. However, that does not change the fact that property passes from the seller to the buyer when goods have passed the ship's rail in accordance with the Pyrene *v Scindia* principle.

It is, however, debatable whether from Incoterms 2000, the rule in Delivery (Clause A4)/Taking Delivery (Clause B4) has displaced the common law rule of the goods crossing the "ships rail" That notwithstanding, the delivery provisions in Incoterms 2020 are similar to those of Incoterms 2000 and Incoterms 2010. However, the seller's obligation is now to place the goods "on board the vessel," rather than over the ship's rail at the loading port indicated by the buyer. The "ship's rail" as the point of delivery has been omitted in preference for the goods being delivered on board the vessel in order to more closely reflect modern commercial reality and to avoid costly disputes over when exactly the goods pass the "ship's rail". It is unclear whether that displaces the common law 'ships rail' established in *Pyrene vs Scindia* and, therefore, whether Incoterms disputes arising therefrom can use *Pyrene v Scindia* a default position.

Thus, the current position is, if no specific loading point has been indicated by the buyer, the new terms make it clear that the seller may select the point that best suits the seller's purpose. In practice, it would be sensible to include an express provision enabling the seller to choose the loading point if that is what is agreed. Finally, the new Terms clarify that the seller may now perform its delivery

[24] Ibid, p. 107; there is no equivalent provision to Clause A2; the previous Clause had provided that "the buyer must take delivery of the goods when they have been so delivered as envisaged in A2".

[25] Ibid; changed from Clause A3(a) Incoterms 2010, p. 88.

obligation by procuring delivered goods as opposed to deliver goods itself. This aligns the FOB to the CIF in the buying and selling afloat practice. This simply reflects the current accepted practice in string sales.

5.4.6 Passage of Risks

5.4.6.1 Sellers Risks

Passage of risk is contained in Clause A3, namely that he (the seller) bears all risks of loss of or damage to the goods until they have been delivered in accordance with Clause A2 (*Delivery/Taking delivery*) with the exception of loss or damage in the circumstances described in Clause B3 (Transfer of risk to buyer). In this respect seller's obligations also includes requirement for notice to the buyer under Clause A10 in which the seller must give the buyer sufficient notice either that the goods have been delivered in accordance with Clause A2 or that the vessel has failed to take the goods within the time agreed. The importance of Clause A10 cannot be over emphasised in relation to insurance obligations below especially resulting from failure to give that information where the vessel has failed to load.

5.4.6.2 Buyer's Risks

Just as at common law, the seller is responsible for loss or damage until the goods "pass the ship's rail". The buyer being responsible from that point on. There are, therefore, fewer burdens on the seller and more on the buyer who according to Clause B3.

> **Clause B3**
> "The buyer bears all risks or loss or damage to the goods from the time they have been delivered under A2".
>
> If:
>
> (a) the buyer fails to notify the nomination of a vessel in accordance with B10; or
>
> (b) the vessel nominated by the buyer fails to arrive on time to enable the seller to comply with A2, is unable to take the goods, or closes for cargo earlier than the time notified in accordance with B10; then, the buyer bears all risks of loss of or damage to the goods:
>
> (i) from the agreed date, or in the absence of an agreed date,
>
> (ii) from the date notified by the seller under B10 within the agreed period, or, if no such date has been notified,
>
> (iii) from the expiry date of any agreed period for delivery,
>
> *provided that the goods have been clearly identified as the contract goods*[26] (***emphasis provided***)

[26] Incoterms 2020, p. 107; remains fundamentally the same but with slight changes.

The highlighted text demonstrates the link between carriage, delivery, risk and insurance liabilities not only in Incoterms but also for all export-import contracts. Furthermore, it should be recalled that the buyer's further risk-related obligations also include those under Clause B10 regarding notice to the seller. He must give the seller sufficient notice of any transport-related security requirements, the vessel name, loading point, if any, the selected delivery date within the agreed period. Failure to comply with Clause B10 could lead to him bearing risks to the loss or damage, and, therefore, his insurer's liabilities to goods irrespective of fulfilment of the actual delivery. As Clause B10 above provides, the buyer must give the seller sufficient notice of any transport related security requirements, the vessel name, loading point and, if any, the selected delivery date within the agreed period.

How do the above carriage, delivery, passage of property and passage of risks reflect on the parties' insurance requirements and obligations?

5.4.7 Insurance Obligations

5.4.7.1 Seller's Obligations

Unless otherwise provided (e.g., in Extended FOBs which include insurance) the FOB Incoterms' seller's insurance obligations are the same as under common law. Hence the requirements of Clause A5 of Incoterms 2020 that the seller has no obligation to the buyer to make a contract of insurance. The buyer has no obligation to the seller to make a contract of insurance. However, the seller must provide the buyer, at the buyer's request, risk, and cost, with information in the possession of the seller that the buyer needs for obtaining insurance.[27] The implications of the information were analysed under carriage, delivery, and risks obligations above. It will be remembered this equates to the common law position and requirements of s.20 of the *SGA* 1979, the *Wimborne* Case[28] and the *Northlands Case.*[29]

In theory, the seller has no obligation to provide insurance[30] (hence "**No Obligation**" under Clause A5 of Incoterms 2010 and Incoterms 2020) but must provide the buyer at the buyer's request, risk, and costs with information which the buyer might need to obtain insurance.[31] This requirement for information makes the obligation almost same as at common law[32] and was no doubt further influenced by common law practice and statutory requirements under s.*32(3)* of *SGA* 1979 and the judicial decision in *Wimble v Rosenberg and Sons*[33] case. Finally, the seller should note the mandatory requirements under Clause A10 to give the buyer sufficient notice either that the goods have been delivered in accordance with Clause A2 or

---

[27] Ibid, p. 108.

[28] [1913] 3KB 743, for details see p. 4.15 in Chap. 4.

[29] [1917] 33TLR 516, for details see p. 4.16 in Chap. 4.

[30] Incoterms 2020 Clause A5 at p. 108.

[31] Ibid.

[32] Information or Notice are also repeated at Clauses A10/B10, Incoterms 2020 at p. 110.

[33] *Wimble v Rosenberg* and Sons [1913] 3KB743; *Northern Steel & Hardware Co v John Batt & Co* (London) [1917] 33TLR516.

that the vessel has failed to take the goods within the time agreed; such a failure to fulfil which could have bearings on his insurance liabilities. Note that delivery of insurance documents (Clause A5/B5) are part of the obligations to deliver goods (Clause A4/B4).

5.4.7.2 Buyer's Insurance Obligations

This term requires the seller to pay all origin charges (including loading onto the vessel). After this, however, responsibility shifts to the buyer who is responsible for freight, insurance and all charges thereafter. Therefore, for insurance coverage, the buyer is required to consider insurance under the FOB term given they are responsible for loss or damage during the 'main carriage' of the voyage. Buyers take on the risk once the goods "pass the ship's rail" (a phrase used in the Incoterms to refer to when the goods are loaded onto a vessel and, effectively, 'pass' their rail). Insurers typically insure under this term from the date the On-Board bill of lading is issued. Thus, under provision Clause B5 of Incoterms 2020 that the buyer has no obligation to the seller to make the contract of insurance.[34]

Because the buyer is responsible for loss or damage during the "main carriage", FOB shipments would be insured under his own policy. Insurance, under Incoterms, would attach once the goods "pass the ship's rail" which, unless otherwise provided, falls on the buyer from then on.[35] Because the buyer is responsible for loss or damage during the "main carriage" FOB shipments would be insured under his ocean cargo policy. In practice most insurers use the date on which the On-Board bill of lading is issued. To enable the seller, avoid such risks, the buyer must, under Clause B10, give the seller sufficient notice of any transport related security requirements, the vessel name, loading point and, where necessary, the selected delivery time within the agreed period.

In practice, however, most insurance companies use the date on which the "On Board" Bill of lading is issued and buyers generally request this additional service depending on their circumstances. Although the rules also provide that the buyer has no obligation to seller to make a contract of insurance,[36] this is rather misleading because the nature of FOB is that he is responsible for risks[37] and therefore insurance after the ship's rail. Were it to be permitted under Incoterms, the Common Law "Extended FOB" or "FOB with additional services" classifications would involve the seller contracting for freight and insurance where such services were one of the extended or additional duties. That would put the FOB in the CIF league.[38] There is

[34] Incoterms 2020, Clauses B5, p. 109.

[35] A position now upheld by the common law in *Glencore Grain Rotterdam BV v Lebanese Organisation for International Commerce* (LORICO) [1997] 2 Lloyds Rep 386 CA.

[36] See Ibid, Clause B3 Incoterms 2020 p. 107

[37] Transfer of Risks are also repeated in, Ibid, Clause B3, pp. 106 and 107.

[38] Ademuni-Odeke (2007), pp. 44–445, for a comparison of between FOB Extended and CIF Insurance.

clearly a difference between the requirement of notice for insurance purposes under FOB and for information for same objective under the non-CIF/CIP C group as well as the E, F and D groups. However, by introducing the requirement for information under the latter, Incoterms is now trying to synchronise insurance requirements and bridge the gap between itself and the Common Law.

5.4.7.3 The Requirement of Notice and Information

5.4.7.3.1 Comparisons with the Common Law

From the foregone, although provision of notice was a limited requirement at common law (see Chap. 4 above), it is now explicit requirement under Incoterms, as outlined below.

5.4.7.3.2 Under Incoterms 2020

The information requirement now runs through the insurance clause (Clauses A5/B5), as a requirement through the delivery of the goods (Clauses A2/A10/B10), and delivery of transport documents (Clause A). Finally, as indicated above, the right to the information is not automatic: the buyer has to: specifically request; bear the risks and cost thereof; and demonstrate need for the information. It will also depend on seller having the information. Accordingly, both parties should be aware of the new requirement for notice under Incoterms. Thus, the requirement for notice for insurance purposes under the FOB is no longer the preserve of the common law. (see also Chap. 10 on wider implications). Can the parties vary this condition by inserting the FOB Attachment Clause in their contracts?

5.4.8 FOB Institute Attachment Clause

The FOB Institute Attachment Clause provides that:

> **F.O.B. Attachment Clause**
> Notwithstanding anything contained herein to the contrary, the risks covered hereunder shall not attach to the interest hereby insured prior to being on board the overseas vessel at the port of shipment.
>
> In case, however, the assured have to bear the risks of the interest hereby insured, under their F.O.B. or C. & F. contract with the shipper, from the time when it has effectively passed the rail of the overseas vessel at the port of shipment, the risks covered hereunder shall attach from that time

It would appear they can.
Does the American law and practice vary the traditional Incoterms on this?

5.4.9 American FOB

5.4.9.1 Under the UCC

Subject to discussions under Chap. 4 above, the US position remains the same as in normal Incoterms below? However, the American law under the UCC seems to treat FAS the same as with FOB. Thus, as in FOB above, the American Common Law and Statutory FAS is contained § 2-319(2)–(4). (F.O.B. and F.A.S. Terms) and provides thus:

> (2) Unless otherwise agreed the term F.A.S. vessel (which means "free alongside") at a named port, even though used only in connection with the stated price, is a delivery term under which the seller must
>
> (a) at his own expense and risk deliver the goods alongside the vessel in the manner usual in that port or on a dock designated and provided by the buyer; and
>
> (b) obtain and tender a receipt for the goods in exchange for which the carrier is under a duty to issue a bill of lading.
>
> (3) Unless otherwise agreed in any case falling within subsection (1)(a) or (c) or subsection (2) the buyer must seasonably give any needed instructions for making delivery, including when the term is F.A.S. or F.O.B. the loading berth of the vessel and in an appropriate case its name and sailing date. The seller may treat the failure of needed instructions as a failure of cooperation under this Clause (Section 2-311). He may also at his option move the goods in any reasonable manner preparatory to delivery or shipment.
>
> (4) Under the term F.O.B. vessel or F.A.S. unless otherwise agreed the buyer must make payment against tender of the required documents and the seller may not tender nor the buyer demand delivery of the goods in substitution for the documents.

The American FAS general delivery obligations follow closely those of the American FOB above which in turn resemble those of the mainstream American FOB.[39] The insurance obligations are, therefore, identical to the American FOB Insurance Obligations above[40]

5.4.9.2 Under "Incoterms for Americans Guidelines"

IFA guidelines agree with the above contention and provides that:

> Neither party is required to insure. However, common sense dictates otherwise and insurance should be addressed outside of the rule. Sellers are risk until the goods are placed on board the vessel (check with your insurers about FAS/FOB coverage). Buyers are risk thereafter[41]

---

[39] Likewise, the American Common Law and Statutory FAS is contained § 2-319(2)–(4). (F.O.B. and F.A.S. Terms) same as above.

[40] Reynolds, Frank: Incoterms for Americans Guidelines 2020, p. 83, note 6.

[41] Reynolds: Incoterms for Americans Guidelines, p. 83 Note 6; see also generally, chapter 8 (Insurance), pp. 33–37 of the same book.

5.5 Insurance of *EX-WORKS*

5.5.1 Introduction

This is the only E category contract in Incoterms. It is an Incoterms rule under which the price that the seller quotes apply only at the point of origin. Their attraction to the seller being that the E category is the only such a contract in which the seller's obligations are at a minimum. However, parties could agree to vary those conditions. Unless otherwise agreed, the buyer takes possession of the shipment at the point of origin and bears all costs and risks associated with transporting the goods to the destination. This Incoterms rule is regarded as the most open-ended. There is generally nothing specific regarding delivery. EXW contract is the same as in FOB except that the points of incidents are at the arrival since this forms part of the sale of goods on arrival (hence an arrival contract) and unloading rather than at the loading port.

5.5.2 Comparisons with the Common Law EXW

A comparison with the common law position might shade some light on its general and insurance obligations. Since it was decided in *Boyd v Siffkin*[42] that in contracts for the sale of goods by a particular ship, meaning on the arrival of the goods which the ship is expected to bring arrival, if the ship arrives empty, without any default on the part of the seller, he is not liable to the purchaser for non-delivery of the goods, then the purchaser has recourse against his insurers. However, according to *HR & S Sainsbury Ltd v Street*,[43] this does not apply to future sales, which carry implied conditions that such contracts are discharged if the crop fails.

The decision in *Islamic Republic of Iran Shipping Lines v Mutual Underwriting Association (Bermuda) Ltd*,[44] in which *Sainsbury v Street* was considered, has a further bearing on parties' liabilities and, therefore, insurance obligations in Ex Ship and Arrival contracts. However, expression of probability does not amount to a contract. In that respect, in the Canadian case of *Cummings Grain Co v Butcher*[45] decided correctly that: "Where in a negotiation for the sale of oats by the carload, the seller says, 'I am not sure whether I can procure more than two cars; I undertake to let you have two cars and I may be able to let you have three cars', the buyer is not entitled to bind the seller to the delivery of three cars, and if the buyer attempts to do so, and the seller dissents, there is no contract even for two cars".

---

[42] *Boyd v Selkin* (1809) 2Camp326; 170 ER1172, NP.

[43] *HR & S Sainsbury Ltd v Street* [1972] 1WLR 834.

[44] *Islamic Republic of Iran Shipping Lines v Steamship Mutual Underwriting Association* (Bermuda) Ltd, [2010] EWHC 2661; [2011] 2All ER (Comm) 609; [2011] 1 Lloyds Rep195; [2010] All ER (D) 261(Oct).

[45] *Cummings Grain Co v Butcher* (Cummings) (deceased) (1922) 66 DLR 462;17 Alta LR 122; [1922] 1 WWR 243; *The Modern Law Review*, Vol. 50, Index to Volumes 1–50 (1988), pp. 171–252.

How does that affect parties general and insurance obligations under Incoterms 2020?

5.5.3 Carriage Obligations

5.5.3.1 Seller's Obligations

Once more, carriage and obligations affect insurance responsibilities. The relevant Clause A4 does not impose any obligations on the seller to make a contract of carriage for the buyer. But the seller must provide the buyer, at the buyer's request, risk, and cost, with any information in the possession of the seller, including transport-related security requirements, that the buyer needs for arranging carriage.[46] Note that, as explained above, the buyer must request the information, bear the costs and risks of such request therein and the seller is mandated to provide such information only when in his possession. This is the same as under FOB and other contracts above. However, note also that Clause A10 requires the seller to give the buyer any notice needed to enable the buyer to take delivery of the goods.

Thus, for carriage purposes, the seller simply makes the goods available to the buyer at his premises on a specified date or within a specified time period. Unless specifically agreed to, the seller is not responsible for loading the goods onto the conveyance at his premises. Consequently, the seller has no carriage contract obligations to the buyer. He or she simply makes the goods available to the buyer at his premises on a specified date or within a specified time period.[47] His only responsibility would be where the goods appropriate to the contract are damaged while in his workshop or warehouse. That makes EXWORKS the contract where the seller has the least obligations and therefore less exposed insurance wise. The buyer takes full responsibility for shipping the goods from their origin to their final destination. The supplier isn't on the hook for any aspect of the shipping process. EXW can benefit sellers, because they have minimum obligations in the transaction and therefore take on less risk.

5.5.3.2 Buyers Carriage Obligations

Equally, under the corresponding Clause B4, the buyer has no obligation to the seller to make the contract of carriage.[48] Instead, the clause provides simply that it is up to the buyer to contractor arrange at its own cost for the carriage of the goods from the named place of delivery. However, although he is not obligated to provide notice or information to the seller the clause must be read in conjunction with the corresponding notice requirement under Clause B10 requiring that he must, whenever he is entitled to determine the time within an agreed period and/or the point of taking delivery in the named port of destination, give the seller sufficient notice thereof. Note that he is obligated to do so only where he is entitled to determine the

[46] CF. Incoterms 2010, p. 16.

[47] Incoterms 2020 p. 24

[48] Ibid, p. 25

time and/or point of delivery. Apart from its mandatory nature, the clause does not provide any penalties for failure to give the notice or for late or improper notice.

5.5.4 Delivery Obligations

5.5.4.1 Sellers Obligations

The seller must deliver the goods by placing them at the disposal of the buyer at the agreed point, if any, at the named place of delivery, not loaded on any collecting vehicle. If no specific point has been agreed within the named place of delivery, and if there are several points available, the seller may select the point that best suits its purpose. The seller must deliver the goods on the agreed date or within the agreed period. Under EXW the buyer pays for all aspects of the shipping process. This includes loading charges, delivery to port, export duties and taxes, origin terminal charges, loading on carriage, carriage charges, destination terminal charges, delivery to destination, and import duty and taxes.

5.5.4.2 Buyers Obligations

Just as in carriage obligations above, the Ex works buyer has the most onerous obligations. The buyer must take delivery of the goods when they have been delivered by the seller outside his premises under Clause A2 and notice given under Clause A10. One major disadvantage of EXW to buyers is related to customs clearance. One major disadvantage of EXW to buyers is related to customs clearance. According to the EXW terms, sellers are required to facilitate the paperwork for export clearance. If sellers' information is inaccurate, the buyers are still responsible for the additional cost and results of delays. According to the EXW terms, sellers are required to facilitate the paperwork for export clearance. If sellers' information is inaccurate, the buyers are still responsible for the additional cost and results of delays.

5.5.5 Liability for Risks

5.5.5.1 Seller Risks

Of the two parties, the seller bears the main delivery obligations in accordance with Clause A2 providing that the he (the seller) must deliver the goods by placing them at the disposal of the buyer at the agreed point, if any, at the named place of delivery, not loaded on any collecting vehicle. However, if no specific point has been agreed within the named place of delivery, and if there are several points available, then the seller may select the point that best suits its purpose. Nevertheless, the seller must deliver the goods on the agreed date or within the agreed period seller must deliver the goods on the agreed date or within the agreed period.[49]

---

[49] Incoterms 2020 p. 26.

Having fulfilled carriage and delivery obligations, the seller still has to address the requirements of Clause A10, requiring him to give notice the buyer any notice needed to enable to the buyer to take delivery of the goods.[50] Failure to fulfil this requirement can and may have consequences on the seller's liability for insurance purposes. As for passage of risks, under Clause A3 the seller bears all the risks of loss of or damaged to the goods until they have been delivered in accordance with Clause A2, with the exception of loss or damage in the circumstances described in Clause B3. Responsibility for loss or damage follows passage of risks. Unless specifically agreed to, the seller is not responsible for loading the goods onto the conveyance at his premises. Since this term can be used with any mode of transportation including multimodal.

The buyer becomes responsible for loss or damage to the goods on the agreed upon date, or when the goods are picked up within the specified time period, or on expiration of the specified time period. The seller should pay attention to Clause A10 for requirement for notice to the buyer that he (the seller) must give the buyer sufficient notice as to when and where the goods will be placed at his disposal. Consequently, the seller may be liable if he fails to or gives wrong or insufficient information and as a consequence the buyer incurs loss or damage directly resulting from the wrong act or omission. The common law position in the case of *Pyrene v Scindia* and subsequent decisions might provide some guidance in the present context as the duties are not very different and since Incoterms is largely based on the common law. In an EXW agreement, the buyer is at the risk of damage and loss of goods during the loading process. Although the seller loads the goods as a common procedure, it is the buyer who bears the damage to the goods, if any.

5.5.5.2 Buyers Risks

Under B3, the buyer must take delivery of the goods when they have been delivered by the buyer under A2 and received notice from the seller under Cause A10. However, he should note that under Clause B10, he must, whenever it is agreed that the buyer is entitled to determine the time within an agreed period and/or the point of taking delivery within the named place, give the seller sufficient notice. For the buyer, the corresponding Clause B3 provides that The buyer bears all risks of loss of or damage to the goods from the time they have been delivered under Clause A2. If the buyer fails to give notice in accordance with Clause B10, then the buyer bears all risks of loss of or damage to the goods from the agreed date or the end of the agreed period for delivery, provided that the goods have been clearly identified as the contract goods.[51] The highlighted text in Clause B3 suggests that the risks pass to the buyer under those conditions only the goods had been appropriated to the contract implying possible problems buyer fails to give notice and/or appropriate the goods or both.

This is another new development in Incoterms 2020, as till then appropriation was normally associated with CIF and FOB and even then, only at common law.

[50] Incoterms 2020, p. 24.

[51] Ibid, p. 25.

This provision is more detailed and more explicit than those for the seller above. The buyer becomes responsible for loss or damage to the goods on the agreed upon date, or when the goods are picked up within the specified time period, or on expiration of the specified time period. Above all a breach of any of the above obligations can lead to liabilities needing insurance coverage. The buyer must, whenever it is agreed that the buyer is entitled to determine the time within an agreed period and/or the point of taking delivery within the named place, give the seller sufficient notice.

5.5.6 Passage of Property and Title

As in all contracts, risk follows property. All Incoterms up to 2010 had provisions on the subject. However, passage of property is not covered by Incoterms 2020 and is therefore determined by the common law, national laws, and the general rules of contract that risk follows property. [With regard to passage of property, comments under sellers' obligations above also apply].

5.5.7 Insurance Obligations

5.5.7.1 Seller's Obligations

Sellers' insurance obligations are covered under Clause A5 of Incoterms 2020 namely that the seller has no obligation to the buyer to make the contract of insurance. However, he must provide the buyer, at the buyer's request, risk, and costs, with information that the buyer needs for obtaining insurance.[52] Needless to emphasise that the information has to be requested and the costs and risks therefrom borne by the buyer; and the seller is only obliged to do so if and when he has the information. This is the same as under all the nine Incoterms (except for CIF and CIP) where the seller does not provide insurance for the seller. Furthermore, as in all other contracts under Incoterms, although the seller has no insurance obligations to the buyer to make a contract of insurance, he must provide the buyer, at the buyer's request, risk, and expense (if any), with information that the buyer needs for obtaining insurance. Ramberg[53] concurs on this point. Otherwise, the seller's insurance obligations are the same as in especially FOB, FCA and FAS.[54] Accordingly, when purchasing goods EXW the buyer should seek an insurer that will provide coverage during these situations.[55] Fortuitously, most cargo insurance policies automatically insure these exposures. Liability and, therefore, insurance consequences of failure to fulfil the notice requirements in Clause A10 should be considered by the seller.

---

[52] Ibid.

[53] Ibid.

[54] Ibid.

[55] On EXW and the seller's assistance see Ramberg, Jan, p. 22.

Thus, the seller does not have the risk beyond the delivery point so it has no obligation to the buyer to arrange a contract of insurance. However, if the buyer requests, at its risk and cost, the seller must provide the buyer with information in its possession that the buyer needs to arrange its insurance.

In summary, because the buyer is responsible for loss or damage during the "main carriage" EXW shipments would be insured under the buyer's cargo policy. However, the buyer should be aware that since few cargo policies attach on individual shipments when they leave the warehouse of origin (i.e. The Warehouse To Warehouse provisions of the Open Policy), the buyer may not have insurance for the period of time the goods may be on the premises of the seller, or during loading onto the conveyance, or after loading while awaiting transit even though he is responsible for loss or damage. Therefore, before choosing EXW contracts the buyer choose an underwriter that will provide coverage during these situations. Failing that the buyer should seek advice from reputable brokers.

5.5.7.2 Buyer's Obligations

Clause B5 follows the normal Incoterms 2020 pattern that the buyer has **No Obligation** to the seller to make a contract of insurance in this contract category.[56] There is no buyer's obligations to provide information unlike the seller. However, because the buyer is responsible for loss or damage during the "main carriage" EXW shipments would be insured under the buyer's ocean cargo policy. Since most ocean cargo policies attach on individual shipments when they leave the warehouse of origin (i.e., The *Warehouse-To-Warehouse* provisions of the Open Policy), the buyer may not have insurance for the period of time the goods may be on the premises of the seller, or during loading onto the conveyance, or after loading while awaiting transit even though he is responsible for loss or damage. Therefore, when purchasing goods EXW the buyer should seek an insurer that will provide coverage during these situations. Other than those circumstances the seller has no insurance obligations to the buyer and his insurance provisions under Clause A5 are, therefore, identical to those of the FOB seller. Consequences of notice under Clause B3/B10, regarding requirement of notice, are also relevant in this instance. How does the English and Incoterms position different from those under American EXW contracts?

The buyer has all the responsibility under the EXW term. The seller must make the goods available at a specific location but the buyer has to organise the collection, freight, delivery, tax payments and more. When the buyer collects goods from the premises, they are responsible for everything until the goods arrive at their final delivery point. For insurance purposes, under this term, is responsible for loss and damage under the so-called 'main carriage' of the journey. Freight is covered under an insurance policy for this. Few marine cargo insurance policies, however, automatically cover for the time when goods are on the seller's premises or after loading and awaiting transit (even though buyers are responsible). It's, therefore, important for the buyer his insurance policy to ensure he is covered for all parts of the journey.

---

[56] Incoterms 2020 p. 25.

5.5.8 American EXW Insurance Obligations

5.5.8.1 Under the UCC

The American EXW under the UCC is not that different from those of the common law or Incoterms 2020. In both cases the seller is not required to tender a bill of lading or the insurance policy since it is not his duty to insure the goods. The *Commentary to the Ohio State Revised Code* 2006 confirms this, providing that:

> A contract fixing a price "ex ship" with payment "cash against documents" calls only for such documents as are appropriate to the contract. Tender of a delivery order and of a receipt for the freight after the arrival of the carrying vessel is adequate. The seller is not required to tender a bill of lading as a document of title nor is, he required to insure the goods for the buyer's benefit, as the goods are not at the buyer's risk during the voyage.

Accordingly, unless otherwise provided by the contract, tender of the delivery order and freight receipt after vessels arrival is sufficient. The parties' carriage and delivery obligations as well as property, risk and insurance liabilities are the same as in FOB, FCA and FAS below[57]

5.5.8.2 Incoterms for Americans Guidelines

IFA provides that:

> Neither party is required to insure. However, common sense dictates otherwise and insurance should be addressed outside of the rule. Sellers are risk until the goods are placed on board the vessel (check with your insurers about FAS/FOB coverage). Buyers are risk thereafter[58]

5.6 Insurance of CFR

5.6.1 Introduction

Originating from and based on the common law C&F contract discussed above, the CFR is a relatively new Incoterm, that replaced the C&F, describing a term of sale that details the responsibilities of the buyer and seller for the international trade transaction. Accordingly, the C&F principles and case laws in Chap. 4 above would apply to the CFR. Under this term, the seller must pay the costs and freight necessary to bring the goods to the named port of destination but the risk of loss of or damage to the goods, as well as any additional costs due to events occurring after the time the goods have been delivered on board the vessel, is transferred from the seller to the buyer when the goods pass the ship's rail in the port of shipment. The seller must clear the goods for export. Although it has not had common law interpretations, however, since this term has replaced or is regarded as the variation of

---

[57] Reynolds, Incoterms for Americans Guidelines 2020, Commentary No. 7, p. 44.

[58] Ibid., p. 41, Note 6; see also generally, Chapter 8 (Insurance), pp. 33–37.

C&F it follows that the latter's case law above applies to it. For the reasons given therein the C&F common law cases below would apply to the CFR.

This term can be used only for sea or inland waterway transport shipments. Although the seller agrees to pay all costs and freight to the named port of destination, his responsibility for delivery ends when the goods "pass the ship's rail" at the port of shipment. Like in all the carriage paid "C" categories, the seller performs his contract by handing over goods to the carrier as specified in the contract not when they reach their destinations. It is therefore advisable to emphasize either the port of shipment or port of destination, as that will determine when the risks attach, and therefore, insurance obligations begin. The seller is responsible for loss or damage until the goods "pass the ship's rail" at the port of shipment. The buyer is responsible for loss or damage to the goods from that point onwards. This is essentially the same as CIF/CIP without the "I" but with "F". CFR should only be used for non-containerized sea-freight and inland waterway transport; for all other modes of transport it should be replaced with CPT.

5.6.2 Relationship Between Common Law C&F and Incoterms CFR

There is confusion whether the new CFR replaces the old C&F which mean the same thing. However, Lorenzon,[59] Schmitthoff[60], Benjamin[61] and other texts continue to treat both as different. The common law still uses the C&F while Incoterms now uses CFR. It is an Incoterms describing a term of sale that details the responsibilities of the buyer and seller for the international trade transaction. Under this term, the seller must pay the costs and freight necessary to bring the goods to the named port of destination but the risk of loss of or damage to the goods, as well as any additional costs due to events occurring after the time the goods have been delivered on board the vessel, is transferred from the seller to the buyer when the goods pass the ship's rail in the port of shipment. The seller must clear the goods for export. Technically there is no common law interpretation of CFR insurance. However, since it is s replacement of the C&F, above, *The Galatia,*[62] *The Pantanassa,*[63] and *Muller and MacLean v Leslie and Anderson*[64]principles would apply. The American position on CIF discussed above applies to C&F; the UCC treats the CIF and C&F as the same contract except for insurance requirements in the latter. The buyer is not responsible for carriage contracts. It is the seller who is required to arrange for the carriage of goods by sea to a port of destination and provide the buyer with the documents necessary to obtain the goods from the carrier.

---

[59] Lorenzo CIF and FOB Contracts.

[60] Export Law and Practice para 2-039, pp. 51–52.

[61] Benjamin on Sales.

[62] *Golodetz & CO. Inc v. Czanikow-Rionda CO. Inc.* (*The "Galatia"*) [1980] 1 Lloyd's Rep. 453CA.

[63] *Norsk Bjergningskompagni A/S v Owners of the Pantanassa* (*The Pantanassa*) [1970] 1 All ER 848.

[64] *Muller and MacLean v Leslie and Anderson* (1921) 8 Ll.L.Rep. 328 KB.

5.6.3 Carriage Obligations

5.6.3.1 Sellers Obligations

If the quantity of the clause is anything to go by then the CFR ranks among those most burdened by carriage. Pursuant to Clause A4 the seller must contract or procure a contract for the carriage of the goods from the agreed point of delivery, if any, at the place of delivery to the named port of destination or, if agreed, any point at that port. Furthermore, the contract of carriage must be made on usual terms at the seller's cost and provide for carriage by the usual route in a vessel of the type normally used for the transport of the type of goods sold. The seller must comply with any transport-related security requirements for transport to destination. Through the use of the highlighted text, the contract leaves the parties with wide lee-ways regarding customs and usages of the particular trade. See also under delivery in FOB contracts above.

5.6.3.2 Buyers Obligations

The buyer has no obligation to the seller to make a contract of carriage. CIF or CRF import freight terms are more expensive than Ex Works or FOB. There will be a cost for arranging the shipping that the seller has to pass on. Further, the shipping becomes a cost of sale for the seller.

5.6.4 Delivery Obligations

5.6.4.1 Seller's Obligations

On delivery A2 provides that the seller must deliver the goods either by placing them on board the vessel or by procuring the goods so delivered. In either case, the seller must deliver the goods on the agreed date or within the agreed period and in the manner customary at the port.[65] The seller pays for the carriage of the goods up to the named port of destination. The contract of carriage must be made on usual terms at the seller's expense and provided for carriage by the usual route in a vessel of the type normally used for the transport of the type of goods sold.[66] The Shipper is responsible for origin costs including export clearance and freight costs for carriage to named port. His delivery obligations are also same as in CIF and are contained in Clause A2.[67] See also under delivery in FOB contracts above.

5.6.4.2 Buyer's Obligations

The buyer has no obligation to the seller to make a contract of carriage. However, the buyer must take delivery of the goods when they have been delivered under Clause A2 and receive them from the carrier at the named port of destination. It is the buyer rather than the shipper who is responsible for taking delivery at the final

[65] Manner and customs dealings at a particular port could vary the terms and therefore affect performance of the contract.

[66] The types of goods involved could equally the above.

[67] Making everything about the CIF and CFR the same except for the insurance components.

destination from the port (generally the buyer's facilities), or for buying insurance. See also under buyer's delivery obligations in FOB contracts above. The buyer must not only take delivery of the goods when the seller has delivered them on board the vessel but also receive them from the carrier at the named destination port. Most importantly, delivery occurs when the goods are released from the seller's direct control, not when the goods reach the destination.

5.6.5 Passage of Property and Title

Passage of property is not covered by Incoterms 2020. The rule regarding passage of property is probably same as in CIF and CIP.

5.6.6 Passage of Risks

5.6.6.1 Sellers Risks

A3-The seller bears all risks of loss of or damage to the goods until they have been delivered in accordance with Clause A2, with the exception of loss or damage in the circumstance described in Clause B3. See A10 on requirement for notice. the risk of loss passes to the buyer when the goods are received. When documents that can transfer title, or ownership, represent existing, identified goods, the buyer has property interest, but not title, and an insurable interest in such goods at the time and place of contacting for their sale. Risk will usually pass when property in the goods passes. One practical consequence is that the party that has a property right (or a right to possession) can make a claim in tort for the damage or destruction of the goods.

5.6.6.2 Buyer's Risks

The buyer bears all risks of loss of or damage to the goods from the time they have been delivered under Clause A2. If the buyer fails to give notice in accordance with Clause B10, then it bears all risks of loss of or damage to the goods from the agreed date or the end of the agreed period for shipment, provided that the goods have been clearly identified as the contract goods. The goods have to be appropriated for the risks to kick in. Note also that under Clause B10 the buyer must, whenever it is agreed that the buyer is entitled to determine the time for shipping the goods and/or the point of receiving the goods within the named port of destination, give the seller sufficient notice. What is sufficient notice was covered by common law FOB in Chap. 4 above.

5.6.7 Insurance Obligations

5.6.7.1 General

For insurance purposes, this contract has the same characteristics as the CIF except for insurance, which are not the seller's obligations. The buyer, therefore, provides the insurance for himself but not for the buyer. Although there is no obligation on the seller to provide insurance, Incoterm makes mandatory for him to provide the buyer at the buyer's request, risk, and expense (if any), with information the buyer needs for obtaining insurance, which equates CFR to FOB contracts. As neither party have insurance obligations, identical duties are placed on the buyer under the corresponding Clause B5. For same reasons as for the CFR above, both parties must need the provisions of Clause A5 for the seller and Clause B5 for the buyer, regarding passage of risks. Thus, like FOB and all the other contracts where the buyer does not provide insurance, the buyer is entitled to notice from the seller to enable him take out cover. The only problem is that s. 32 (3) of SOGA 1979 on requirement of notice or information does not apply to the CIF, CIP, CFR, CPT, and C&F contracts as it does the FOB, Clause A10/B10.

5.6.7.2 Seller's Obligations

The seller has no obligation to the buyer to make a contract of insurance under Clause A5, he must provide the buyer, at the buyer's request, risk, and expense (if any), with information in his (buyer's) possession that the buyer needs for obtaining insurance. It is evident that, in keeping with the aim of Incoterms is to make it clear to the parties; their respective obligations have been laid out in some particularity. If the buyer does require the seller to obtain insurance, the Incoterm CIF should be considered. See comments under "**No obligation**" above. The seller has no obligation to the buyer to make a contract of insurance. See also under seller's obligations in FOB contracts above. The Buyer is responsible for all costs related to importing the shipment into the country of destination. Since the Seller is not responsible for insuring the shipment, the buyer needs to arrange insurance for the shipment.

5.6.7.3 Buyer's Obligations

B5 provides that the buyer has no obligation to the seller to make a contract of insurance. Neither does he have the obligation give notice and/or provide information relating thereto. But he would be advised to procure cover for himself. Incoterms 2010 had provided that the buyer must provide the seller, upon request, with the any information necessary for the seller to obtain insurance. This requirement has been removed from Incoterms 2020. However, this does not mean that having provided the pertinent information the buyer need not consider the question of insurance further.

First, it is necessary to examine the seller's duty in a little more detail. Because the buyer is responsible for loss or damage during the "main carriage" (see above) CFR shipments would be insured under his insurance policy. There is no obligation to make a contract of insurance. The buyer may, however, make it at his own cost and risk. In addition, the seller bears the risk (as well as loss or damage to the goods) only until the goods are on board the vessel.

This makes CFR similar to FOB shipments where insurance under Incoterms attaches once the goods "pass the ship's rail". It is for this reason that Incoterms 2010 now provides for seller's information to the buyer (upon buyer's request, risks, and expenses where applicable) to enable him take out insurance. That has been a significant improvement to Incoterms from the insurance perspective. In practice, however, most insurance companies use the date on which the On-Board Bill of Lading is issued. The buyer must, whenever it is agreed that the buyer is entitled to determine the time for shipping the goods and/or the point of receiving the goods within the named port of destination, give the seller sufficient notice.

See also under buyers' obligations in FOB contracts above. The seller has more responsibility under these terms, as they have to pay all charges up until the port of destination. The buyer, however, assumes risk when the goods are loaded on the vessel. Any charges at the final destination also must be paid by the buyer. This has a bearing on insurance coverage. Since the buyer is responsible for loss or damage during the 'main carriage' of the voyage and are therefore should consider insurance. The buyer assumes risk once goods "pass the ship's rail" (much like under FOB terms). Similar to FOB shipments, insurance, under INCOTERMS definition would attach once the goods "pass the ship's rail". In practice most insurance companies use the date on which the On Board Bill of Lading is issued.

5.6.8 Insurance of American CFR

5.6.8.1 Under the UCC

This is the same as in Chap. 4 above.

5.6.8.2 Under Incoterms for Americans Guidelines

IFA provides that:

> Neither party is required to insure. However, common sense dictates otherwise and insurance should be addressed outside of the rule. Sellers are risk until the goods are placed on board the vessel (check with your insurers about FAS/FOB coverage). Buyers are risk thereafter[68]

Note the relationship with FAS, FOB, and related contracts in which there are no obligations for the seller to provide insurance for the buyer or for each party to the other. Secondly, these are matters outside the contract where common sense and practical considerations prevail.

5.7 Insurance of C&F

5.7.1 General

As discussed under common law above, the term cost and freight means that the seller must provide to the buyer two things; first, the goods themselves, loaded on the vessel (the "cost"), and secondly, the transportation of the goods to the discharge

[68] Incoterms Rules for Americans Guidelines 2020, p. 104, paragraph 6.

port (the "freight"). However, the C&F is not an Incoterm contract anymore; it is the equivalent to the new CFR above. It is sometimes shortened to CNF. CNF is similar to CIF, except insurance is not included. If a supplier quotes to the buyer a CNF Felixstowe (UK) price, it means that the price includes shipping of the goods via sea freight to the Felixstowe port. However, there is confusion whether C&F means the same as CNF. And if so, whether CNF includes insurance?.

5.7.2 C&F Insurance

This is because technically the three letters CNF together, with regards to shipping, the acronym stands for "Cost Net Freight." It's a shipping agreement where the seller pays for delivering the item to the port closest to the buyer, but it doesn't include the cost of insurance, otherwise that would make it a CIF contract.

5.7.3 Under American UCC

See under Chap. 4 and Sect. 5.6.7.1 above.

5.7.4 Under "Incoterms for American for American Guidelines"

See under Chap. 4 and under Sect. 5.6.7.2 above.

5.8 Insurance of CPT

5.8.1 Introduction

CPT is an Incoterm describing a term of sale that details the responsibilities of the buyer and seller for the international trade transaction. When goods are bought or sold "Carriage Paid To" (CPT) it means that the Seller delivers the goods to a destination previously agreed to by the seller and the buyer. It can also be the handoff to the preferred carrier of the buyer. Under this term, the seller pays the freight for the carriage of the goods to the named destination. The risk of loss of or damage to the goods, as well as any additional costs due to events occurring after the time the goods have been delivered to the carrier, is transferred from the seller to the buyer when the goods have been delivered into the custody of the carrier. The seller must clear the goods for export. Like the CIP, it has not yet formed part of the common law. Its insurance obligations are covered in Chap. 8 ahead.

5.8.2 Carriage Obligations

5.8.2.1 Sellers Obligations

The seller must contract or procure a contract for the carriage of the goods from the agreed point of delivery, if any, at the place of delivery to the named place of destination or, if agreed, any point at that place. The contract of carriage must be made on usual terms at the seller's cost and provide for carriage by the usual route in a customary manner of the type normally used for carriage of the type of goods sold. If a specific point is not agreed or is not determined by practice, the seller may select the point of delivery and the point at the named place of destination that best suit its purpose. The seller must comply with any transport-related security requirements for transport to the destination.

The major difference between CIF and CPT is that the shipping term CPT is used in all modes of transport, whereas CIF terms of shipping is used only for sea and inland water transport. The carriage contractual position is same as under CIP. The delivery position is also the same as for CIP. See also under seller's obligations in FOB contracts above.

5.8.2.2 Buyers Obligations

The buyer has no obligation to the seller to make a contract of carriage. Cf. buyers' obligations under FOB contracts above.

5.8.3 CPT Delivery

5.8.3.1 Sellers Obligations

CPT makes the seller responsible for export packing, loading charges, delivery to port/place, export duties and taxes, origin terminal charges, loading on carriage, carriage charges, and destination terminal charges. Despite the three letters "CPT" being followed by the destination place, delivery occurs when the seller gives the goods to its carrier contracted to take them to that destination. It is at that delivery point in the seller's country that the risk transfers from the seller to the buyer.

5.8.3.2 Buyers Obligations

Despite the three letters "CPT" being followed by the destination place, delivery occurs when the seller gives the goods to its carrier contracted to take them to that destination. It is at that delivery point in the seller's country that the risk transfers from the seller to the buyer.

5.8.4 Passage of Property and Title

Incoterms 2020 does not deal with passage of property. The situation regarding passage of property is same as for CIF and CIP.

5.8.5 Transfer of Risks

5.8.5.1 Sellers Risks

As for passage of risks, Clause A3 provides that the seller bears all the risks of loss of or damaged to the goods until they have been delivered in accordance with Clause A2, with the exception of loss or damage in the circumstances described in Clause B3. Responsibilities for loss or damage to good are the same as for FCA terms[69] It would be equivalent to EXW where the delivery at the sellers' premises.

5.8.5.2 Buyer's Risks

The buyer bears all risks of loss of or damage to the goods from the time they have been delivered under Clause A2. If the buyer fails to give notice in accordance with Clause B10, then the buyer bears all risks of loss of or damage to the goods from the agreed date or the end of the agreed period for delivery, provided that the goods have been clearly identified as the contract goods. At what point does the risk pass to the buyer in the CPT CIP CFR or CIF Incoterms? The risk of damage or loss to the goods is transferred from the seller to the buyer as soon as the goods have been delivered to the carrier. The seller is responsible only for arranging freight to the destination and not for insuring the shipment of the goods during transport.

5.8.6 Insurance Obligations

5.8.6.1 Introduction

The CPT is a relatively new Incoterms and is unknown to common law. It describes a term of sale that details the responsibilities of the buyer and seller for the international trade transaction. Under this term, the seller pays the freight for the carriage of the goods to the named destination. The risk of loss of or damage to the goods, as well as any additional costs due to events occurring after the time the goods have been delivered to the carrier, is transferred from the seller to the buyer when the goods have been delivered into the custody of the carrier. The seller must clear the goods for export. It is therefore the buyer's responsibility to contract for insurance. Other than that, both the Common Law and its American variants are silent on the CPT.

5.8.6.2 Seller's Obligations

The seller arranges export clearance and also makes goods available alongside the vessel at the relevant port of departure. They're also responsible for origin charges. However, the buyer is responsible for loading the vessel and any charges following loading. Therefore, the buyer will be responsible during the 'main carriage'. Buyers take on the risk of the cargo when the goods are placed alongside the vessel or after the goods are loaded.

---

[69] Although the CPT is a "C" and not an "F" (Free Carrier) type of Incoterms; Incoterms 2020 p. 44.

Otherwise, Clause A5 provides that the seller has no obligation to the buyer to make a contract of insurance. However, the seller must provide the buyer, at the buyer's request, risk, and cost, with information in the possession of the seller that the buyer needs for obtaining insurance. Thus, the seller has no insurance obligations to the buyer, same as for FCA terms. He is the shipper but not the insured. The notice or information is only upon requested by and the buyer's risk and expenses. The only problem here is the question of timing, that is that although the transfer of responsibility for loss or damage is clearly defined in Incoterms, insurance questions often arise when loss or damage occurs before the buyer is responsible and before coverage attaches under his insurance policy. Of course, the seller is responsible for his own insurance needs (see Chap. 9) See also under sellers' obligations in FOB contracts above.

5.8.6.3 Buyer's Obligations

The corresponding B5 provides that the buyer has no obligation to the seller to make a contract of insurance. However, if there is any doubt in the buyer's mind about whether or not he will have proper recourse against the seller for loss or damage during his responsibility, the buyer may wish to review these doubts with his insurer and arrange additional coverage in the form of "contingency" insurance. He is nevertheless responsible for his own insurance needs (see Chap. 9). Otherwise, most insurance policies will provide automatic contingency coverage which may apply in these situations. Does CPT incoterm include insurance? No. The buyer is required to purchase freight insurance, as it is not included in the terms of the contract in a CPT incoterm agreement. See also under buyer's obligations in FOB contracts above. The seller is responsible for making goods available at a place of destination. The buyer then must arrange any further transportation, and pay any duties and taxes. The buyer also then is responsible for arranging insurance during transit. Insurance is the same for CPT as it is FCA. See comments under that term.

5.8.7 American CPT Insurances

5.8.7.1 Under the UCC

The UCC has provisions for FOB, FAS, C&F and CIF contracts but not for CPT. It, therefore, follows it has no provisions for CPT insurance obligations. The assumption, therefore, is that the best guiding principle is that contained in the "Incoterms for Americans Guidelines" (below), namely that neither party is obliged to provide insurance to the other-except perhaps for themselves.

5.8.7.2 Under the "Incoterms for Americans Guidelines"

This is the same as for American insurance obligations under the C class (except CIF and CIP), D, E and F terms above. Where in doubt for Americans, attention is drawn to "Incoterms for Americans Guidelines" which provides that: "Neither party is required to insure under CPT. However, common sense dictates otherwise, and the buyer should consider insuring outside the rule"[70]

5.9 Insurance of FCA

5.9.1 Introduction

Together with FAS and FOB, FCA belonged to the F Incoterm 2010 category of contracts characterised by the main carriage being paid. Free Carrier (named place) is term can be used with any mode of transportation including multimodal. This term subsumed the previous FOB (A), FOB (T) and FOB (R), representing air, truck, and rail aspects of the FOB. It is the term that most resemble FOB. An Incoterms rule under which seller delivers goods, cleared for export, to the buyer-designated carrier at a named location. Used for any mode of transport. Seller must load goods onto the buyer's carrier. The key document signifying transfer of responsibility is receipt by carrier to exporter. This term is useful for trade between countries in large continental mass such as Africa, Europe (especially the European Common Market), Asia and North America (e.g., between the US border on the one hand and the Canadian and Mexican borders on the other).

5.9.2 Carriage Obligations

5.9.2.1 Seller's Obligations

The FCA insurance effect of the seller's breach of carriage and delivery obligations is the same as for the FOB and EXW above. On contract of carriage, Clause A4 provides that the seller has no obligation to the buyer to make a contract of carriage. However, the seller must provide the buyer, at the buyer's request, risk and cost, with any information in the possession of the seller, including transport-related security requirements, that the buyer needs for arranging carriage. If agreed, the seller must contract for carriage on the usual terms at the buyer's risk and cost. The seller must comply with any transport-related security requirements up to delivery.

Hence, under this contract the seller agrees to deliver the goods into the custody of the carrier selected by the buyer either at his premises or at a named point or place,[71] or to a party acting on the carrier's behalf (a freight forwarder or freight terminal, for example). In that context the FCA would be almost the same as EXW (post). The actual point of delivery can be anywhere in the country of origin, including at the seller's premises. The contract of sale must clearly state to where and to whom the goods are to be delivered. See also under sellers' obligations in FOB contracts above.

[70] Reynolds, Incoterms for Americans Guidelines 2020, p. 90, Note. 6.

[71] Incoterms 2020 p. 34.

5.9.2.2 Buyer's Obligations

Clause B4 follows the normal Incoterm pattern that the buyer must contract, at its own expense for the carriage of the goods from the named port of shipment, except where the contract of carriage is made by the seller as provided for in Clause A4.[72] Once more, this makes FCA almost the same as for FOB and EXW above.

5.9.3 Delivery Obligations

5.9.3.1 Sellers Obligations

On delivery, Clause A2 provides that:

> **Clause A2**
> The seller must deliver the goods to the carrier or another person nominated by the buyer at the named point, if any, at the named place, or procure goods so delivered.
>
> The seller must deliver the goods
>
> 1. on the agreed date or
>
> 2. at the time within the agreed period notified by the buyer under B10(b) or,
>
> 3. if no such time is notified, then at the end of the agreed period.
>
> Delivery is completed either:
>
> a) If the named place is the seller's premises, when the goods have been loaded on the means of transport provided by the buyer;
>
> or
>
> b) In any other case, when the goods are placed at the disposal of the carrier or another person nominated by the buyer on the seller's means of transport ready for unloading.
>
> If no specific point has been notified by the buyer under B10(d) within the named place of delivery, and if there are several points available, the seller may select the point that best suits its purpose.

This is however further subject to notice in Clause 10 providing that:

[72] Ibid, 35.

Clause 10

The buyer must notify the seller of

a) the name of the carrier or another person nominated within sufficient time as to enable the seller to deliver the goods in accordance with A2;

b) the selected time, if any, within the period agreed for delivery when the carrier or person nominate will receive the goods;

c) the mode of transport to be used by the carrier or the person nominated including any transport-related security requirements; and

d) the point where the goods will be received within the named place of delivery.

See also under sellers' obligations in FOB contracts above.

5.9.3.2 Buyer's Obligations

B2 provides that the buyer must take delivery of the goods when they have been delivered as envisaged in Clause A2.[73] The seller agrees to deliver the goods into the custody of the carrier selected by the buyer at a named point or place, or to a party acting on the carrier's behalf (a freight forwarder or freight terminal, for example). The actual point of delivery can be anywhere in the country of origin, including at the seller's premises. The contract of sale must clearly state to where and to whom the goods are to be delivered. See also under buyers' obligations in FOB contracts above. Thus, the seller has no obligation to the buyer to make a contract of carriage. However, if requested by the buyer or if it is commercial practice to do so and the buyer does not give instruction to the contrary in due time, the seller may contract for carriage on usual terms at the buyer's risk and expense. In either case, the seller may decline to make the contract of carriage and, if it does, shall promptly notify the buyer. This is the same as in FOB. Note that parties can vary this obligation and that the carriage notice extends to security-related issues.

5.9.4 Passage of Property Risks

As intimated above, Incoterms 2020 make no provision on passage of property leaving it to contract or common law as a fullback position. This is the same as for CIF and CIP.

5.9.5 Passage of Risks

5.9.5.1 Seller's Risks

Clause A3 provides that the seller bears all the risks of loss of or damaged to the goods until they have been delivered in accordance with Clause A2, with the

[73] Ibid, 32.

exception of loss or damage in the circumstances described in Clauses B3[B5[74]/2010]. This makes the FCA seller's duty the same as FOB and EXW above. The general rule being that the seller is responsible for loss or damage until the goods are delivered to the carrier at the named point or place. He may also have to clear goods at export customs but not import customs. However, the seller should note the elaborate requirements of Clause A7 for requirement of notice to the buyer.

5.9.5.2 Buyer's Risks

Comments on all the FOB and EXW Incoterms regarding property above apply here too. However, on passage of risks in Cause B3 is a little more elaborate than their FOB and EXW equivalents, providing that:

> **Cause B3**
> The buyer bears all risks of loss of or damage to the goods from the time they have been delivered under A2.
>
> If:
>
> a) the buyer fails to nominate a carrier or another person under A2 or to give notice in accordance with B10; or
>
> b) the carrier or person nominated by the buyer under B10(a) fails to take the goods into its charge, then, the buyer bears all risks of loss of or damage to the goods:
>
> (i) from the agreed date, or in the absence of an agreed date,
>
> (ii) from the time selected by the buyer under B10(b); or, if no such time has been notified,
>
> (iii) from the end of any agreed period for delivery, provided that the goods have been clearly identified as the contract goods.[75]

Other than that, the buyer becomes responsible thereafter, which is the same as in FOB and EXW. Like the buyer should be aware of the insurance obligations of the breach of the above obligations as well as the requirements of Clause B10 on prerequisite for notice to the seller and.

5.9.6 Insurance Obligations

5.9.6.1 Seller's Obligations

Insurance of FCA at common law was covered under Chap. 4 of this book above. Under Clause A5 of the Incoterm, the seller has no obligation to the buyer to make the contract of insurance. However, the seller must provide the buyer, at the buyer's

[74] Ibid, p. 34.

[75] Ibid, p. 35.

request, risk, and cost, with information that the buyer needs for obtaining insurance,[76] which is the same as for FOB. Thus, the seller's obligations under A5 are identical to those of the FOB term. The difference with the FOB is that the buyer has no obligation to the seller to contract for insurance under Clause B5. The uncertainty in the seller-buyer's obligations makes FCA insurance a little more complex and requires some explanations. Because the buyer is responsible for loss or damage during the "main carriage" FCA shipment insurance are primarily the buyer's responsibilities during that carriage. Insurance attaches at the time the goods are delivered to the carrier as agreed either at the seller's premises or the border between the two party's countries. See also seller's obligations under FOB contracts above.

5.9.6.2 Buyer's Obligations

5.9.6.2.1 General Obligations

Correspondingly the buyer, under Clause B5, has no obligation to the seller to make a contract of insurance.[77] However, as indicated above, because the buyer is responsible for loss or damage during the "main carriage" FCA shipments would be insured under his policy. Insurance would attach at the time the goods are delivered to the carrier as agreed. When buying goods FCA it is important for the buyer to understand that in allowing delivery at a place other than the port or airport of shipment he is extending his exposure to loss or damage to additional hazards of transportation which may be unique to the country of origin, such as: additional storage, additional handling exposures, exposure to the elements and exposure to theft, hijack or pilferage.

Depending upon the country the goods are being shipped from these additional hazards can be severe and loss or damage can adversely affect the placement and costs of insurance. Therefore, before agreeing to FCA terms it may be in a buyer's interest to review the parties' country exposures with their insurer. The seller under these terms must make goods available to a carrier which the buyer nominates. The buyer assumes all responsibility and costs thereafter. The buyer also must arrange for export clearance. Therefore, for insurance coverage, the buyer is responsible during the 'main carriage' so FCA shipments require the importer to organise a marine insurance policy. Insurance would cover a buyer when the goods are delivered to the carrier.

5.9.6.2.2 Precautionary Obligations

The buyer should note first that, should he operate under this term, he will be exposing his freight to further risk as you're delivering to a place other than a port. Check the country of origin's exposures (including exposure to risk or hijacking) and insure accordingly if need be. One advantage to a buyer in using FCA terms is when he uses FCA Seller's Warehouse versus EXW. As commented on in EXW above, the buyer is responsible for loss or damage during loading of the goods onto the

[76] Ibid, p. 24.

[77] Ibid, p. 25.

conveyance at the place of origin, an exposure not usually covered by ocean cargo policies. By selecting FCA Seller's Warehouse the responsibility for loading is placed on the seller. The seller is responsible for loss or damage until the goods are delivered to the carrier at the named point or place. The buyer becoming responsible thereafter. See also buyer's obligations under FOB contracts above.

Secondly, he should note that because is responsible for loss or damage during the "main carriage" FCA shipments would be insured under his policy. Insurance would attach at the time the goods are delivered to the carrier as agreed. Thus, when buying goods FCA it is important for the buyer to understand that in allowing delivery at a place other than the port or airport of shipment he is extending his exposure to loss or damage to additional hazards of transportation which may be unique to the country of origin, such as: additional storage, additional handling exposures, exposure to the elements and exposure to theft, hijack or pilferage. Depending upon the country the goods are being shipped from these additional hazards can be severe and loss or damage can adversely affect the placement and costs of insurance. Before agreeing to FCA terms it may be in a buyer's interest to review the country exposures with their insurer.

However, one advantage to a buyer in using FCA terms is when he uses FCA Seller's Warehouse versus EXW. As commented on in EXW, the buyer is responsible for loss or damage during loading of the goods onto the conveyance at the place of origin, an exposure not usually covered by ocean cargo policies. By selecting FCA Seller's Warehouse the responsibility for loading is placed on the seller.

5.9.7 FCA Institute Attachment Clause

FCA institute Attachment Clause provides that:

> **Free Carrier Attachment Clause**
> Notwithstanding anything contained herein to the contrary (excepting coverage against War Risks), it is understood and agreed that this insurance shall not attach to the interest hereby insured prior to being delivered into the charge of or the custody of the carrier at the point or place named in the policy for the commencement of the transit

This is the same position as for the FOB.

5.9.8 American FCA Insurance Obligations

5.9.8.1 Under the UCC

The American FCA insurance obligations are the same as in American FOB and American FAS Insurance Obligations above[78] which are now in turn based on the mainstream FCA in Incoterms 2020. See also Chap. 4 above.

[78] See Reynolds, Frank, Incoterms for Americans 2020, and Commentary No. 7, pp. 52–53.

5.9.8.2 Under Incoterms For Americans Guidelines

IFA guidelines provide that:

> Neither party is required to insure under FCA. However, common sense dictates otherwise, and insurance should be addressed outside of the rule. This is particularly important for buyers because the seller delivers prior to any transportation[79]

5.10 Insurance of FAS

5.10.1 Introduction

Another of the former F category, Free Alongside Vessel (FAS) is to named port of shipment. This term can only be used for maritime trade vessel shipments including inland waterways. Free alongside ship (FAS) is a contractual term used in the international export business that stipulates that the seller must arrange for goods to be delivered to a designated port and next to a specific vessel for easier transfer in the Incoterms rules for FAS (short for "Free Alongside Ship"), the seller clears goods for export and places them alongside the vessel at the named port of departure. The named port of departure location can be a loading dock or a barge, but not a container terminal.

5.10.2 Carriage Obligations

5.10.2.1 Seller's Obligations

With regard to contract of carriage, under Clause A4, the seller has no obligation to the buyer to make a contract of carriage. However, the seller must provide the buyer, at the buyer's request, risk and cost, with any information in the possession of the seller, including transport-related security requirements, that the buyer needs for arranging carriage. If agreed, the seller must contract for carriage on the usual terms at the buyer's risk and cost. The seller must comply with any transport-related security requirements up to delivery. Thus, if requested by the buyer or if it is commercial practice and the buyer does not give instruction to the contrary in due time, the seller may contract for carriage on usual terms at the buyer's risk and expense. In either case, the seller may decline to make the contract of carriage and, if it does, shall promptly notify the buyer[80] Making it the same as for FOB, EXW and FCA above. See also seller's obligations under FOB contracts above.

5.10.2.2 Buyer's Obligations

The buyer must contract at its own cost for the carriage of the goods from the named port of shipment, except when the contract of carriage is made by the seller as

[79] Ibid; p. 56, Note 6; see also chapter 8 (Insurance), pp. 33–37.

[80] Incoterms 2020, p. 98.

provided for in Clause A4;[81] making FAS same as FOB, EXW, FCA. See also buyer's obligations under FOB contracts above. The buyer is responsible for loading the goods on their transport and everything else necessary to get the goods to the final destination. The risk or liability for the goods transfers from the seller to the buyer when the goods are alongside the ship, and the buyer bears costs from that point forward.

5.10.3 Delivery Obligations

5.10.3.1 Sellers Obligations

Clause A2 of the Incoterm provides that:

> **Clause A2**
> The seller must deliver the goods either by placing them alongside the vessel nominated by the buyer at the loading point, if any, indicated by the buyer at the named port of shipment or by procuring the goods so delivered.
>
> The seller must deliver the goods
>
> 1. on the agreed date or
> 2. at the time within the agreed period notified by the buyer under B10 or,
> 3. if no such time is notified, then at the end of the agreed period and
> 4. in the manner customary at the port.
>
> If no specific loading point has been indicated by the buyer, the seller may select the point within the named port of shipment that best suits its purpose

If the parties have agreed that delivery should take place within a period, the buyer has the option to choose the date within that period.[82] This is the same as FOB save for the additional highlighted text.

In this contract, the seller agrees to deliver the goods alongside the vessel (e.g., on a quay or a barge) nominated by the buyer at the named port of shipment ready for loading onto the overseas vessel;[83] or until loaded onto lighters if customary to the port. The seller agrees to deliver the goods alongside the vessel at the port of shipment ready for loading onto the overseas vessel; or until loaded onto lighters if customary to the port. Under this arrangement, the supplier agrees to deliver the goods in proper condition alongside the vessel. See also sellers' obligations under FOB contracts above.

[81] Ibid, p. 99.

[82] Ibid, p. 96.

[83] Ibid.

5.10.3.2 Buyer's Obligations

As for delivery the buyer must, Clause B2 provides that the buyer must take delivery of the goods when they have been delivered under Clause A2.[84] See also buyers obligations under FOB contracts above.

5.10.4 Passage of Property and Title

Comments on passage of property above applies here too. Otherwise, Incoterms 2020 does not deal with passage of title and property issues. However, that does not mean it is not important.

5.10.5 Transfer of Risks

5.10.5.1 Seller's Risks

Under Clause A3, the seller bears all the risks of loss of or damaged to the goods until they have been delivered in accordance with Cause A2, with the exception of loss or damage in the circumstances described in Clause B3.[85] The seller is responsible for loss or damage until the goods are delivered to the port as agreed. The buyer being responsible from that point on. The buyer assumes all subsequent risks and expenses after delivery to the pier. The provisions of Clause A10, on notice, also applies here. The buyer takes the goods after delivered. All risk of loss/damage from the time or end of the period agreed for delivery. If the buyer fails to nominate a carrier, or if the carrier doesn't arrive, the risk is under the buyer. No obligation to make a contract of carriage. The risk of loss of or damage to the goods transfers when the goods are alongside the ship, and the buyer bears all costs from that moment onwards.

5.10.5.2 Buyer's Risks

On passage of risks Clause provides that:

> **Risks Clause**
> The buyer bears all risks of loss of or damage to the goods from the time they have been delivered under A2.
>
> If:
>
> a) the buyer fails to give notice in accordance with B10; or
>
> b) the vessel nominated by the buyer fails to arrive on time to enable the seller to comply with A2, fails to take the goods, or closes for cargo earlier than the time

[84] Ibid, p. 97.

[85] Ibid, p. 82.

notified in accordance with B10; then the buyer bears all risks of loss of or damage to the goods:

(i) from the agreed date, or in the absence of an agreed date,

(ii) from the date selected by the buyer under B10, or, if no such date has been notified,

(iii) from the end of any agreed period for delivery, provided that the goods have been clearly identified as the contract goods.

Thus, the buyer bears risk[86] of loss and property when the goods are alongside the vessel rather than when they cross the ship's rail as in mainstream FOB above. The buyer is responsibility for loss or damage after that. Unless requested by the buyer the seller has no obligation to contract for freight. This term is almost the same as the FOB save that the FAS seller wishes to have nothing to do with contracting for freight. Reference should also be made to Clause B10 on corresponding notice between the parties.

5.10.6 Insurance Obligations

5.10.6.1 Seller's Obligations

As in all other Incoterms, under Clause A5 the seller has no obligation to the buyer to make the contract of insurance. However, the seller must provide the buyer, at the buyer's request, risk, and cost, with information that the buyer needs for obtaining insurance.[87] Neither party has insurance obligations to the other. Accordingly, the insurance provisions of Clause A5 for seller and Clause B5 for buyer are identical to those of the FOB seller and buyer. However, because the buyer is in practice responsible for loss or damage during the "main carriage" FAS shipments would be covered under his ocean cargo policy. Insurance would attach either at the time the goods are place alongside the vessel or after being loaded onto lighters if customary to the port. Quite often insurance companies use the date of issuance of a Dock Receipt or a "Received for Shipment" Bill of Lading, or similar document issued by the carrier, to determine when risk of loss passes from the seller to the buyer. The seller is not free from the obligations of Clause A10, relating to delivery notice, which might have a bearing on his insurance liabilities. See also seller's obligations under FOB contracts above.

5.10.6.2 Buyer's Obligations

The seller arranges export clearance and also makes goods available alongside the vessel at the relevant port of departure. They're also responsible for origin charges. However, the buyer is responsible for loading the vessel and any charges following

---

[86] Ibid p. 83.

[87] Ibid, p. 98.

loading. Regarding insurance coverage, the buyer will be responsible during the 'main carriage'. Buyers take on the risk of the cargo when the goods are placed alongside the vessel or after the goods are loaded. A5 provides that the buyer has no obligation to the seller to provide a contract of insurance,[88] which is the same as under FOB. However, as is always the case with commercial transactions, the party bearing risks for loss and damage of property is also the one charged with insurance if they so wish. Thus, because the buyer is responsible for loss or damage during the "main carriage"

FAS shipments would be his insurance responsibility from delivery alongside ship. Insurance would attach either at the time the goods are placed alongside the vessel or after being loaded onto lighters if customary to the port require. Hence the expression "No Obligation" under Clause A5 for insurance. However, like in all Incoterms categories, except for CIF and CIP, the seller must provide the buyer, at the buyer's request, risk, and expenses (where applicable) with information that the buyer needs for obtaining insurance. In practice, however, quite often insurance companies use the date of issuance of a Dock Receipt or a Received for Shipment Bill of Lading, or similar document issued by the carrier,[89] to determine when risk of loss passes from the seller to the buyer. Otherwise, sellers and buyer's insurance obligations are identical to those of the FOB above.[90]

This is irrespective of the fact it also introduces the *s.32 (3) SGA* 1979 and the *Wimble v Rosenberg* scenario. The seller arranges export clearance and also makes goods available alongside the vessel at the relevant port of departure. They're also responsible for original charges. However, the buyer is responsible for loading the vessel and any charges following loading. Insurance coverage: Once again, the buyer will be responsible during the 'main carriage'. Buyers take on the risk of the cargo when the goods are placed alongside the vessel or after the goods are loaded. See also buyer's obligations under FOB contracts above.

Thus, the seller is responsible only for loss or damage until the goods are delivered to the port as agreed. The buyer being responsible from that point on. Because the buyer is responsible for loss or damage during the "main carriage" FAS shipments would be covered under the buyer's policy. Insurance would attach either at the time the goods are place alongside the vessel, or after being loaded onto lighters if customary to the port. Most insurers use the date of issuance of a Dock Receipt or a Received For Shipment Bill of Lading, or similar document issued by the carrier, to determine when risk of loss passes from the seller to the buyer.

5.10.6.3 F.A.S. Attachment Clause

The FAS Institute Clause provides as follows:

---

[88] Ibid, p. 99.

[89] For these are other carriage documents see Clause 27 of the UCP 600.

[90] Ibid; Clause A3(a), p. 80 and Clause B3(b), p. 81; CF Clause A3(a) and Clause B3(b), p. 88 regarding the obligations as well as requirements for seller to give buyer notice so as to take out insurance. (R)

F.A.S. Attachment Clause
Notwithstanding anything contained herein to the contrary, the risks covered hereunder shall not attach until the title of the interest hereby insured is duly vested in the assured alongside the overseas vessel at the port of shipment under their F.A.S. contract with the shipper

This is the same as for FOB and FCA above.

5.10.7 American FAS

5.10.7.1 Under the UCC

This is the same as at common law. See also under Chap. 4 above.

5.10.7.2 Under Incoterms for Americans Guidelines

IFA Guidelines provide that:

> Neither party is required to insure under FAS. However, common sense dictates otherwise, and insurance should be addressed outside the rule. Sellers are at risk until the goods are delivered next to the vessel (Check with your insurer about FAS/FOB coverage). Buyers are at risk thereafter.[91]

5.11 Insurance of DAP

5.11.1 Introduction

DAP is a Shipping Incoterm that means "Delivered at Place," where the seller is responsible for all costs and risks associated with the delivery of the goods to the final agreed-upon place, usually the buyer's premises. Originally another D Incoterms category, it is a new rule in Incoterms 2020 under which the seller delivers goods to the buyer's facility or another named location (other than a terminal) in the destination country. The buyer is responsible for import clearance and any further in-country carriage. This term is one of two terms considered to be replacement terms for the DDU, which is eliminated from both Incoterms 2010 and Incoterms 2020 rules. It should be compared to DPU and DDP. Under the contract, the buyer is responsible for import clearance and any further in-country carriage. The term may be used for any mode of transport including multimodal transport.

[91] Reynolds: Incoterms for Americans Guidelines, p. 74, Note. 6; see also chapter 8 (Insurance), pp. 33–37 of the book.

5.11.2 Carriage Obligations

5.11.2.1 Seller's Obligations

The seller has two principal duties: carriage contract and delivery. On the contract of carriage, Clause A4 provides that the seller must contract at its own expense for the carriage of the goods to the named place of destination or to the agreed point, if any, at the named place of destination. If a specific point is not agreed or is not determined by practice, the seller may select the point at the named place of delivery which best suits his purpose. The seller must comply with any transport-related security requirements for transport to the destination (added 2020).[92] See also sellers' obligations under FOB contracts above.

5.11.2.2 Buyer's Obligations

The buyer has just one obligation to take delivery. On carriage Clause B4 provides that the buyer has no obligation to the seller to make a contract of carriage[93] See also buyers obligations under FOB contracts above.

5.11.3 Delivery Obligations

5.11.3.1 Sellers Obligations

On delivery, under Clause A2 the seller must deliver the goods by placing them at the disposal of the buyer on the arriving means of transport ready for unloading at the agreed point, if any, at the named place of destination or by procuring the goods so delivered.[94] In either case the seller must deliver the goods on the agreed date or within the agreed period. The contract requires that the seller procures the freight contracts delivers when the goods are placed at the disposal of the buyer on arriving means of transport ready for unloading at the named port of destination.[95] For insurance purposes, below, it is essential the point of delivery is described clearly in the contract. The seller may have to clear goods for export but not necessarily for import. Where clearing goods for import are also involved, parties should use the DDP term instead. Requirement of notice under Clause A10 is relevant here. See also sellers' obligations under FOB contracts above.

5.11.3.2 Buyers Obligations

On delivery, Clause B2 provides that the buyer must take delivery of the goods when they have been delivered in accordance with Clause A2.[96] Requirement for notice under Clause B10 is relevant here. See also buyers' obligations under FOB contracts above.

---

[92] Incoterms 2020, p. 66.

[93] Ibid, p. 67.

[94] Ibid, p. 66.

[95] Incoterms 2010 Clause A3(a), p. 62.

[96] Incoterms 2020, p. 66.

5.11.4 Passage of Property and Title

These are the same as above.

5.11.5 Transfer of Risks

5.11.5.1 Sellers Risks

The seller bears all risks of loss of or damage to the goods until they have been delivered in accordance with Clause A2, with the exception of loss or damage in the circumstances described in Clause B3. Apart from when the goods are held waiting for import clearance the seller has the risk of loss or damage to the goods. The seller has no obligation to the buyer to provide insurance and the buyer has no insurable risk in the goods until delivered at the named place.

5.11.5.2 Buyers Risks

Clause A3 provides that:

> **Clause A3**
> The buyer bears all risks of loss of or damage to the goods from the time they have been
>
> delivered under A2.
>
> If:
>
> a) the buyer fails to full its obligations in accordance with B7, then it bears all resulting risks of loss of or damage to the goods; or
>
> b) the buyer fails to give notice in accordance with B10, then it bears all risks of loss of or damage to the goods from the agreed date or the end of the agreed period for delivery,
>
> provided that the goods have been clearly identified as the contract goods.
>
> Note that failure to give notice unwraps everything.

5.11.6 Insurance Obligations

5.11.6.1 Seller's obligations

The seller has no obligation to the buyer to make the contract of insurance. This relates to Clause 3(b) of Incoterms 2010 which provided that; however, the seller must provide the buyer, at the buyer's request, risk, and expense (if any), with Information that the buyer needs for obtaining insurance.[97] Since he was responsible

[97] Ibid.

for risks of loss and damage up to that point, the seller was responsible for his own insurance up to the point of delivery. Other than that, the seller had no insurance obligations to the buyer to insure the goods. Hence the expression then of "**No Obligation**" there and now under Clause A5 of Incoterms 2020 for insurance. However, he must provide the buyer at the buyer's request, risks and expenses (if any), with information that the buyer needs for obtaining insurance.[98] That makes the seller's insurance obligations identical to those of the FOB, FAS and FCA. See also under seller's obligations under FOB contracts above.

5.11.6.2 Caution on Sellers' Insurance Obligations

Although technically the seller is not responsible for DAP insurance, there may be times when he may. This is because the seller will be responsible for the risk of cargo damage up to the door of destination (but is not obliged to insure cargo) under DAP. The seller should also be aware that he is responsible for all charges up until the goods are delivered to the end destination. The buyer only assumes responsibility for unloading the goods and any duties or taxes. Accordingly, a seller who is unsure should take out at least a contingency policy.

5.11.6.3 Buyer's Obligations

However, there is a difference with regards the DAP buyer's insurance obligations. Although he has no obligation to the seller to provide insurance to the seller, he must provide the seller, at the seller's request, risk and cost, with information that the seller needs for obtaining insurance. This is a complete reversal of parties' insurance obligations in FOB, FAS, FCA and xx above; first he should have his own insurance. It is these similarities that led to the categorization of the F and D under one roof in this clause. The buyer should be aware of the provisions of Clause B10 that he must, whenever it is agreed that he is entitled to determine the time within an agreed period and/or the point of taking delivery within the named place of destination, give the seller sufficient notice. This text is different from all the corresponding texts in related contracts above. See also buyer's obligations under FOB contracts above.

5.11.7 American DAP Insurance Obligations

5.11.7.1 Under the UCC

There is no longer an American UCC equivalent of DAP so it would be difficult to envisage the parties' insurance obligations; but one would imagine its obligations are similar to those of FOB, FAS, and FCA above.

[98] Ibid, p. 67; CF Incoterms 2010 Clause A3(b), Incoterms 2010 p. 62.

5.11.7.2 Under "Incoterms for Americans Guidelines"

IFA provides that: "Neither party is required to insure under DAP. However, common sense dictates otherwise, and sellers should consider insurance outside the rule"[99]

5.12 Insurance of DDP

5.12.1 Introduction

This is an Incoterms 2020 rule under which seller (exporter) is responsible for all costs involved in delivering the goods to a named place of destination and for clearing customs in the country of import. It can be used for any mode of transportation including multimodal. Seller provides literally door-to-door delivery, including customs clearance in the port of export and the port of destination. Thus, seller bears the entire risk of loss until goods are delivered to the buyer's premises. Delivery takes place when exporter places goods at disposal of importer in city of delivery. There is no corresponding transportation document, although bill of lading is usually used. It should be compared with DPU, EXW, FOB (UCC), and DAP. Sadly, DDU disappeared from the Incoterms 2000 and replaced by either DAT or DAP under Incoterms 2010 and now Incoterms 2020. However, the DDP is essentially the same as DDU except that the seller agrees to pay duty and taxes.[100] It has been retained by Incoterms 2020.

5.12.2 Carriage Obligations

5.12.2.1 Seller's Obligations

The seller bears two principal obligations-contracting for carriage and delivering. On carriage, under Clause A4, he (the seller) must contract at its own expense for the carriage of the goods to the named place of destination. If a specific point is not agreed or is not determined by practice, the seller may select the point at the named place of destination which best suits his purpose.[101] The seller must comply with any transport-related security requirements for transport to the destination. The highlighted texts could cause problems. See also sellers' obligations under FOB contract above.

---

[99] Reynolds, Incoterms for Americans Guidelines 2020, p. 118, Note 6.; see also generally chapter 8 (Insurance), pp. 33–37 of the same book.

[100] Ramberg ICC *Guide to Incoterms 2000,* p. 176; *Introduction to Incoterms* 2000 paragraph 10, p. 19.

[101] Incoterms 2020, p. 86.

5.12.2.2 Buyer's Obligations

His only obligation to the seller is to take delivery. On carriage**,** in accordance with B3, the buyer has "**No obligation**".[102] This is essentially the same as DPU below. See also buyer's obligations under FOB contract above.

5.12.3 Delivery Obligations

5.12.3.1 Sellers' Obligations

On delivery pursuant to Clause A2 the seller must deliver the goods by placing them at the disposal of the buyer on the arriving means of transport ready for unloading at the agreed point, if any, at the named place of destination or by procuring the goods so delivered. In either case the seller must deliver the goods on the agreed date or within the agreed period. Thus, the buyer must place the goods at the disposal of the buyer or at that of other person named by the buyer, on any arriving means of transport, not unloaded at the named place of destination on the date or within the agreed period for delivery.[103] This includes delivery of transport documents under Clause A6 and their corresponding receipt under Clause B6. See also seller's delivery obligations under FOB contract above-where the seller has an additional duty of notifying the buyer!?.

5.12.3.2 Buyers' Obligations

When goods are bought or sold "Delivery at Place" (DAP) it means that the Seller delivers the goods to a place previously agreed to by the seller and the buyer. This can be any location. The agreed place of delivery (e.g. the terminal) needs to be specifically named. However, for delivery, under Clause B2, the buyer must take delivery of the goods when they have been delivered under Cause A2.[104] Again, essentially the same as the others FOB, FCA, FAS, etc., except that the seller agrees to pay duty and taxes. See also buyer's obligations under FOB contracts above.

5.12.4 Passage of Property and Title

Passage of property is the same as all the above contracts. Incoterms has no provision.

[102] Ibid, p. 87.

[103] Ibid, p. 86.

[104] Ibid, p. 87.

5.12.5 Transfer of Risks

5.12.5.1 Sellers Risks

On risk, under Clause A3, the seller must, subject to the provisions of Clause A2, The seller bears all risks of loss of or damage to the goods until they have been delivered in accordance with Clause A2, with the exception of loss or damage in the circumstances described in Clause B3.[105] See comments under DPU below which apply to DDP shipments also. Responsibility for loss or damage to the goods is the same as in DPU; comments under DPU above also apply to DDP shipments.

5.12.5.2 Buyer's Risks

On passage of risks, Clause B3 provides that:

> **Clause B3**
> The buyer bears all risks of loss of or damage to the goods from the time they have been delivered under A2.
>
> If:
>
> a) the buyer fails to full its obligations in accordance with B7, then it bears all resulting risks of loss of or damage to the goods; or
>
> b) the buyer fails to give notice in accordance with B10, then it bears all risks of loss of or damage to the goods from the agreed date or the end of the agreed period for delivery,
>
> provided that the goods have been clearly identified as the contract goods.[106]

Comments under DPU, above, apply to DDP shipments too. However, these are subject to fulfilment of Clause B7 (assistance with export and transit clearance as well as import clearance) and Clause B10 (provision of notice for delivery purposes). Also subject to Clause A6 (delivery of documents).

5.12.6 Insurance Obligations

5.12.6.1 Seller's Obligations

The seller has no insurance obligations towards the buyer under Clause A5.[107] As in the, DPU above the DDP shipments contract[108] of sale must clearly show the place to which goods are to be delivered; especially if it is a location other than the buyer's warehouse. It is therefore advisable that the full name of the location, Street Address, City, State/Province (for federal states such as Australia, Canada, Nigeria and the

---

[105] Ibid, p. 86.

[106] Ibid.

[107] Ibid.

[108] See under DDU Rules, at pp. 73–83; also discussed below

USA), and Country (where applicable and possible) are clearly shown in the contract. This is so because left to chance, insurance coverage may attach or cease prematurely at an inappropriate place. For the reasons given above insurance comments on DPU and DDP shipments also apply. Other than that, the seller has no insurance obligations to the buyer; hence "No Obligation" under Clause A5 of the Incoterm. However, as in DPU, the seller does must provide information to the buyer under the Clause to enable the latter to take out insurance. Comments under DPU which apply to DDP shipments too. Seller should also bear in mind Clause A10 on requirement of delivery notice to the buyer. See also under seller's obligations under FOB contracts above.

5.12.6.2 Uncertainty over the Sellers' Insurance Obligations

For the same reasons as for DAP above, the DDP seller should be cautious and where unsure seek broker's/insurer's advice and/or take out a contingency policy. This is because, as indicated above, the seller will be responsible for the risk of cargo damage up to the door of destination (but is not obliged to insure cargo). Although this is arguably the most buyer-friendly term, nevertheless, sellers are responsible for practically the whole shipment. They are responsible for import clearance and must ensure goods arrive at the end destination. All buyers have to do is pay to unload the goods when they arrive.

5.12.6.3 Buyer's Obligations

The buyer too has no insurance obligations towards the seller. However, he must provide the seller, at the sellers' request, risk and cost, with information that the seller needs for obtaining insurance.[109] In practice in the USA, the contract of sale must clearly show the place to which goods are to be delivered; especially if it is a location other than the buyer's warehouse. As for seller above parties should consider showing the full name of the location, Street Address, City, State/Province, and Country (as above, where applicable). If left to chance, insurance coverage may cease at an inappropriate place. See comments under DDU which apply to DDP shipments also. Buyer should note Clause B10 on further 'notice to the seller'. See also seller's obligations under FOB contracts above.

Otherwise DDP is essentially the same as DDU except that the seller agrees to pay duty and taxes. See comments under DDU which apply to DDP shipments and responsibility for loss or damage. However, because of uniqueness, under this term, the contract of sale must clearly show the place to which goods are to be delivered, especially if it is a location other than the buyer's warehouse, otherwise insurance coverage may cease at an inappropriate place.

[109] Ibid, p. 87.

5.12.7 American DDP Insurance Obligations

5.12.7.1 Under the UCC

This is almost the same as for DPU above.

5.12.7.2 Under Incoterms for Americans' Guidelines

IFA Guidelines provide that: "Neither party is required to insure under DDP. However, common sense dictates otherwise, and the seller should consider insurance outside the rule"[110]

Reynolds' adds to that view that:

> Neither party is required to insure under DDP. However, the seller should insist that insurance is covered outside of the Incoterm (preferable by his or her own insurer)
>
> After all, it is the seller who must provide import-cleared delivery to the buyer
>
> The norm of insuring at 110% of the CIP or CIF value and may not provide adequate coverage. Sellers should make sure that the amount of insurance is sufficient to also cover the cost of any required on-carriage[111]

5.13 Insurance of DPU

5.13.1 Introduction

Another of the former D categories under Incoterms 2010, this term, DPU, can be used with any mode of transportation including multimodal. It is an Incoterms rule under which seller bears the risk and expense of getting the goods to a named destination, but excluding duties, taxes and other official charges payable on import. Some variations on DDU are possible if the seller is to pay some of the import charges. Delivery takes place when the exporter places goods at the disposal of the importer in city of delivery. There is no corresponding transportation document, although a bill of lading is usually used. Used for any mode of transportation. DDU is almost the same as the discontinued DEQ, except that the buyer and seller can specify delivery of the goods to a warehouse or other destination point. Seller must arrange for ground transport in the buyer's country. Buyer bears responsibility for import customs duties.

---

[110] Reynolds, Incoterms for Americans Guidelines 2020, p. 132, note 6; see also generally chapter 8 (Insurance), pp. 33–37 of the same book.

[111] Ibid., Commentary No. 6, p. 114.

5.13.2 Carriage Obligations

5.13.2.1 Seller's Obligations

The seller has two principal duties-carriage contract and delivery. On carriage, under Clause A4, the seller must [The seller must contract or arrange at its own cost for the carriage of the goods to the named place of destination or to the agreed point, if any, at the named place of destination.[112] If a specific point is not agreed or is not determined by practice, the seller may select the point at the named place of destination that best suits its purpose. The seller must comply with any transport-related security requirements for transport to the destination.] contract or arrange at its own cost for the carriage of the goods to the named place of destination or to the agreed point, if any, at the named place of destination. This (highlighted) sentence is ambiguous and can cause problems so parties should be very careful. See also sellers' obligations under FOB contracts above.

5.13.2.2 Buyer's Obligations

The buyer has no obligation to the seller to make a contract of carriage. The buyer's only obligation to the seller is to take delivery of the goods on arrival in accordance with Clause A2. Thus, on the contract of carriage, Clause B4 confirms that the buyer has: "**No obligation**".[113] See also buyers' obligations under FOB contract above.

5.13.3 Delivery Obligations

5.13.3.1 Sellers' Obligations

On delivery, Clause A2 provides that the seller must unload the goods from the arriving means of transport and must the deliver them by placing them at the goods at the disposal of the buyer at the agreed point, if any, at the named place of destination or by procuring the goods so delivered. In either case the seller must deliver the goods on the agreed date or within the agreed period.[114] This is straightforward. The seller agrees to deliver the contract goods to an agreed upon point in the country of destination. In most cases this will be the buyer's premises, but it could be any other place in the country of destination. This remains the same as for Incoterms 2010. Rules about delivery of transport documents under Clause A6 applies here too.

---

[112] Incoterms 2020 p. 76. See also note 11 above at p. 114; A corresponding provision in Incoterms 2010 provided that "The seller must contract at its own expense for the carriage of the goods to the named quay (wharf) at the named port of destination. If a specific quay (wharf) is not agreed or is not determined by practice, the seller may select the quay (wharf) at the named place of destination which best suits his purpose" This had pinpointed a quay or wharf but 2020 thought that unfair to the seller for arrival ship purposes.

[113] Ibid, p. 77; Cf. Incoterms 2000, p. 115.

[114] Ibid, p. 76.

5.13.3.2 Buyers' Obligations

The buyer must take delivery of the goods when they have been delivered under Clause A2.[115] See also buyer's obligations under FOB contract above. Delivered at Place Unloaded (DPU) (formerly referred to as DAT for "Delivered at Terminal") requires the seller to deliver the goods at the disposal of the buyer after they've been unloaded from the arriving means of transport.

5.13.4 Passage of Property and Title

Property passage rules are the same as above- incoterms 2020 is silent.

5.13.5 Transfer of Risks

5.13.5.1 Seller's Risks

As for risks, under Clause A3, the seller bears all risks of loss or damage to the goods until they have been delivered in accordance with Clause A2, with the exception of loss or damage in the circumstances described in Clause B3 (buyers' risks obligations). For above reasons the seller is responsible for loss or damage during the "main carriage."

With the DPU Incoterm, the seller assumes all costs and risks until the goods are unloaded at the agreed named place at destination. In this case, the buyer is responsible for import customs formalities. DPU can apply to any mode of transport or multiple modes of transport.

5.13.5.2 Buyers' Risks

On passage of risks, Clause B3 provides that:

> **Clause B3**
> The buyer bears all risks of loss of or damage to the goods from the time they have been delivered under A2.
>
> If:
>
> a) the buyer fails to full its obligations in accordance with B7, then it bears all resulting risks of loss of or damage to the goods; or
>
> b) the buyer fails to give notice in accordance with B10, then it bears all risks of loss of or damage to the goods from the agreed date or the end of the agreed period for delivery,
>
> provided that the goods have been clearly identified as the contract goods[116]

Thus, the buyer being responsible from that point on for all costs (including delivery duties) and risks for loss or damage to goods from that point onwards.

[115] Ibid, p. 77.

[116] Ibid, p. 76.

However, these are subject to: fulfilment of B7 (assistance with export and transit clearance as well as import clearance); Clause B10 (provision of notice for delivery purposes). Also subject to Clause A6 (delivery of documents); and appropriation of the goods.

5.13.6 Insurance Obligations

5.13.6.1 Seller's Obligations

The seller has no insurance obligations towards the buyer to make a contract of insurance. Clause A5 confirms that the seller has "**No obligation**".[117] DPU shipments would, therefore, be insured by the seller up to that point of delivery and by the buyer from there on since he is responsible for the risk of loss or damage to the goods from that point. This is primarily because in DPU insurance usually attaches when the goods leave the place of origin and ceases when the seller's responsibility ceases upon delivery at the agreed place.[118] Because the seller is responsible for loss or damage during the "main carriage" DPU shipments would be insured under his cargo policy. Insurance usually attaches when the goods leave the place of origin and ceases when the seller's responsibility ceases upon delivery at the agreed place. Clause A10 in relation to notice of Clauses A5/B5 is relevant. See also sellers' obligations under FOB contract above.

5.13.6.2 Caution on Sellers' Insurance Obligations

Once more, and as in DAP and DDP above, the seller will be responsible for the risk of cargo damage up to the door of destination, he should (but is not obliged to insure cargo). This is a new Incoterm, having replaced Delivered at Terminal (DAT). DPU permits sellers to deliver goods after they've been unloaded from the transport and obligates them to unload goods at the place of destination. The seller agrees to deliver the goods point agreed upon in the country of destination. In most cases this will be the buyer's premises, but it could be any other place in the country of destination.

So, the seller is responsible for loss or damage until the goods are deliver to the agreed place. The buyer being responsible from that point on. Because the seller is responsible for loss or damage during the "main carriage" DDU shipments would be insured under his ocean cargo policy. Insurance usually attaches when the goods leave the place of origin and ceases when the seller's responsibility ceases upon conveyance at the agreed place.

5.13.6.3 Buyer's Obligations

The buyer too has no insurance obligations towards the seller. Clause B5 provides that the buyer has: "**No obligation**".[119] However, the buyer must provide the seller, at the seller's request, risk and cost, with the information that the seller needs for obtaining insurance. But should be aware of the expression "**No Obligation**".

[117] Ibid, p. 76.

[118] Ibid.

[119] Ibid, p. 77.

Clause B10 in relation to notice of Clauses A5/B5 are relevant. See also buyer's obligations under FOB contracts above.

5.13.7 American DPU Insurance Obligations

5.13.7.1 Under the UCC

This is almost the same as in CIF and CIP below. However, Reynolds cautions on extra insurance for DPU far and beyond even the CIF/CIP value because of DPU's uniqueness. Thus, he opines that neither party is required to insure DPU. Keep in mind, however, that the seller is responsible for the goods until they are delivered to the stipulated place. In other words, the seller bears the transit risk, usually right up to the buyer's premises. For this reason, the seller should insist that adequate insurance be covered outside of the Incoterm (preferably by his or her own insurer).[120] The term of insuring at 110% of the CIP or CIF value may not provide adequate coverage. Sellers should make sure that the amount of insurance is sufficient to also cover the cost of on-carriage[121]

5.13.7.2 Under Incoterms for Americans Guidelines

Incoterms for Americans Guidelines provide that: "Neither party is required to insure under DDU. However, common sense dictates otherwise, and the seller should consider insurance outside the rule"[122]

5.14 Further Food for Thoughts

Parties trading under the above nine contracts, under which there are no sellers' obligations or provide insurance to buyers, should consider the following consequential issues.

5.14.1 Doubts on Sellers' Insurance of DAP, DDP and DPU

Despite the doubts expressed above, caution dictates that insurance is the seller's responsibility under all of the above terms. It's not required, but sellers are likely to purchase insurance on behalf of their buying customers to cover the wide range of circumstances for which they are responsible. It's important to specify the exact 'place' the goods are to be delivered to in the sale contract—i.e. the exact street address if possible. This will avoid disputes between the parties in the future.

---

[120] Contingency insurance, the type discussed in Chap. 9 ahead.

[121] Ibid, Commentary No. 6, p. 106.

[122] Reynolds: Incoterms for Americans Guidelines 2020, p. 124 Note 6; see also, generally, chapter 8 (Insurance), pp. 33–37 of the same book.

5.14.2 The Problem of "No Obligations" Incoterms Clauses

The fact that neither party is under obligation to provide insurance contracts to the other does not relieve them of all insurance obligations and liabilities. This is a relatively new Incoterms requirements and is more to the sellers' rather than the buyers' benefit. A5 simply means that the buyer is primarily responsible for insuring the goods. However, allows parties to vary this term but is subject to specific agreements at the buyers' risks, costs and only where the seller is able to provide the insurance. The seller too has to take care of own insurance needs. Furthermore, they are subject to the sellers and buyers interest policies below. This is further detailed in Chap. 11 below.

5.14.3 Insurance Notice and Information

Parties should also be aware that even where they have such obligations to themselves, most rules under this category require that they, where possible, provide notice and/or information to each other to enable the other take out the insurance under A5/B5. This too is subject to the express request of the other party, cost, risk and availability at the relevant time of the required information by the requested party. On this point Incoterms seems to getting closer to the Common Law rules especially in relation to the FOB contract discussed in Chap. 4 above. Further explanations are contained in Chap. 11 below.

5.14.4 Maximum Insurance for International Transport Contracts

As indicated under Further Food for Thoughts in Chap. 2 above, parties should ensure that they provide maximum insurance coverage for especially manufactured goods involving international transit transport. This is irrespective of Clause A5 for CIF requiring only cargo clause C and Clause A5 of CIP which requires coverage under cargo clause A. In that case the maximum coverage would be either an All Risks policy or, to be safe coverage under at least cargo clause A+War Clause+ Strike Clause.[123] This is because cargo clauses A excludes War and Strikes risks is, therefore, neither a maximum or an *All Risks* policy.

5.14.5 Carriage/Delivery and Security Notices and Information

Both parties, their agents and assignees should also be aware of this new Incoterms' requirements. Although based on delivery Clauses (A2/B2), transfer of risks Clauses (A3/B3), carriage Clauses (A4/B4) and notices Clauses (A10/B10) rather than

[123] See Global Negotiator: Incoterms 2020, Obligations, Costs and Risks, 2020, London, pp. 139–140.

insurance Clauses (A5/B5) clauses, the requirements are couched in the same phrases as for the insurance ones and are subject to the same terms and conditions. However, failure to observe and fulfil them affects parties' liabilities and consequently insurance obligations.

5.14.6 Sellers Interest Insurance

Although they are not primarily responsible for insuring the cargoes, sellers should also bear in mind that they need to take care of their own insurance interests. They should close any other loops by considering sellers interest insurance. These too are detailed in Chap. 10 below.

5.14.7 Buyer's Interest Insurance

The opposite of the sellers' interest insurance, is the buyers' interest insurance, both covering same risks and issues. This too is detailed in Chap. 10 below.

5.14.8 Contingency Insurance for Both Parties

In addition to sellers and buyers interest insurance, both parties should take out cover against contingency losses. Among such risks are pre-shipment, post shipment, buyer's failure to take delivery and/or pay for the goods due to related problems from their country's intervention and/or bankers' default or bankruptcy. This is also detailed in Chap. 10 below.

5.14.9 Restrictive Practices and Other External Factors

Both parties should bear in mind external factors, not covered by Incoterms or general export/import insurance requirements. These include state interventions in shipping, governmental restrictive insurance practices, See Chap. 10 below.

5.14.10 Sanctions, Embargoes and Other Considerations

Other insurance considerations that both parties and their assignees and agents need to bear in mind are effects of sanctions on export/import trade generally and insurance obligations in particular. See Chap. 11 below.

5.15 Concluding Remarks

A number of conclusions can be drawn from this chapter that Incoterms and all export/import merchants, their carriers and insurers need to consider.

First, being influenced by common law, Incoterms generally follow the common law in most of its guidelines on terms and conditions of the contract. That includes insurance contracts.

Secondly, although some are more related to C and D classes or classifications pre-Incoterms 2020, the contracts included here are those in which the seller has no obligation to insure in the latter. It means sellers in this category have no obligation to provide insurance to the buyer. This can of-course be tweaked slightly to allow the reverse. In that case they more resemble the Extended FOB or FOB with additional duties, where one or both of the additional duties includes insurance. That being so the problems of agency insurance discussed in chapter comes into play. The dominant in the category is FOB- either because they contain "free" in carriage, delivery and insurance or simply predominantly have the same FOB characteristics.

Thirdly, as mentioned in Chaps. 3 and 4 above, unless otherwise provided the FOB Incoterms is the traditional FOB at common law, I which case the insurance obligations are the same in both contracts.

Fourth, the seller has a duty in some of the nine contracts to provide information and/or notice to the buyer in insurance as well as carriage and delivery obligations. This is in the form of the insurance clauses themselves as well as carriage (Clauses A4/B4), delivery (Clauses A2/B2) and general notice (Clauses A10/B10) and (Clause A7 and Clause B7) in all Incoterm contracts making it mandatory for the parties to provide notice to each other. Although initially in relation to carriage and delivery duties, this has, nevertheless a direct correlation to insurance liabilities due to the possible breaches thereof. In other words, it gives rise to indirect insurance requirements e.g., in the form of contingency rather that a direct contractual obligation. This is possibly a sign of the times that the common law and Incoterms are merging in their approaches to parties' contractual obligations. It is also possibly an indication that both systems are embracing common sense and practice as they are shaped by practical experiences of merchants in the field.

Conditions for the notice and information are indicated therein. This would bring these contracts to the remit of FOB common law requirements in the *Wimble* and *Northern Steel* decisions on the requirement for notice from the seller to the buyer to enable the buyer take out a policy now seems acceptable to Incoterms 2020.

Fifth, the seller has a duty to cover himself for seller's interest insurance: pre-shipment, post shipment and contingency insurance. These are covered in Chaps. 9 and 10.

Sixth, and finally, the seller has to consider external factors, [such as state intervention in the insurance market, sanctions] not covered by either Incoterms and the traditional insurance. Equally the buyer is responsible for own insurance save where the function has been passed to the seller. He is also responsible for buyers' interest insurance the type described in Chaps. 9 and 10.

5.16 Further Readings

- Incoterms 1980 ICC Publication No.
- Guide to Incoterms 1980 ICC Publication No
- Incoterms 1990 ICC Publication No
- Guide to Incoterms 1990 ICC Publication No.
- Debattista, Charles, Incoterms in Practice, ICC, Paris, 1995
- Incoterms 2000 ICC Publication No.
- Guide to Incoterms 2000 ICC Publication No.
- ICC Incoterms 2010 ICC Publication No.
- Guide to Incoterms 2010 ICC Publication No.
- Incoterms 2020, ICC Publication No.
- **Global negotiator**: INCOTERMS 2020-Obligations, Costs and Risks, Global Marketing Strategies SL, London 2020
- Linklators, Incoterms 2010: all changes or some changes for commodities and shipping, Report of Seminar, Thursday 14 February 2013
- Gillermo Jimenez (edt), ICC Incoterms 1990 Questions and Answers
- Reynolds, Incoterms 2020 for Americans
- Southampton University, Institute of Maritime Law, CIF and FOB Course

5.17 Parties' Insurance Responsibilities in Incoterms Contracts Excluding Parties' Insurance Obligations to Each Other

Incoterm contract	Passage of risk	Sellers insurance	Buyer's insurance
CFR	The seller bears all risks of loss of or damage to the goods until they have been delivered in accordance with A2, with the exception of loss or damage in the circumstance described in B3.	(a) The seller has no obligation to the buyer to make a contract of insurance. (b) However, the seller must provide the buyer, at the buyer's request, risk and cost, with information in the possession of the seller that the buyer needs for obtaining insurance. (c) Seller is advised to take out pre-shipment insurance up to delivery (d) Seller is also advised to take out post-shipment and contingency insurance	(a) Buyer has no obligation to the seller to make a contract of insurance (b) However, the buyer bears all risks of loss of or damage to the goods from the time they have been delivered under A2. If the buyer fails to give notice in accordance with B10, then it bears all risks of loss of or damage to the goods from the agreed date or the end of the agreed period for shipment, provided that the goods have been clearly identified as the contract goods. (c) Accordingly buyer should take out insurance to cover goods during international transit (post-delivery and post-passage of risk) (d) For that the buyer should consider using CIF which is equivalent to CFR but with transport insurance taken out by the seller though in the case of damage the beneficiary of the insurance is the buyer.
American CFR	CFR treated similar to CIF		
Under UCP			
Under IFA	See under Sellers insurance next door	"Neither party is required to insure. However, common sense dictates otherwise, and insurance should be considered outside the rule. Sellers are at risk until the goods are placed on board the vessel (check with your insurers for FAS/FOB insurance). Buyers are at risk thereafter"	Buyers have no obligations. However, risks pass to them when goods have been placed on board the vessel

Incoterm contract	Passage of risk	Sellers insurance	Buyer's insurance
CPT	Ships Rail	(a) Neither party has obligation to take out insurance (b) Seller advised to take out pre-shipment insurance (c) Seller advised to take out post-shipment and other contingency insurance covers	(a) Neither party has obligation to insure the goods (b) Seller advised to take out insurance to cover the goods during international transit (c) For this buyer should consider using CIP which is equivalent to CPT but with transport insurance taken out by the seller though in the case of damage the beneficiary of the insurance is the buyer
American CPT			
Under UCC	N/A, UCC does not have a CPT		
Under IFA		"Neither party is required to insure. However, common sense dictates otherwise, and insurance should be considered outside the rule"	"Neither party is required to insure. However, common sense dictates otherwise, and insurance should be considered outside the rule"
DAP		(a) The seller has no obligation to the buyer to make a contract of insurance (b) But must provide information to buyer when requested to enable buyer take out insurance-(Clause A5) (c) Seller advised to take out pre-shipment insurance (d) Seller advised to take post-shipment and other contingency insurance	(a) Buyer has obligation to provide for the goods. (b)However, buyer is entitled to information from seller but upon his request, risks and expenses where applicable-(A5) (c) Buyer strongly advised to take out insurance to cover the international transport aspects of the goods. (d) "The buyer has no obligation to the seller to make a contract of insurance. However, the buyer must provide the seller, at the seller's request, risk and cost, with information that the seller needs for obtaining insurance".
American DAP	N/A, UCC does not have a DAP		
Under UCC			

Incoterm contract	Passage of risk	Sellers insurance	Buyer's insurance
Under IFA Guidelines		"Neither party is required to insure under DAP. However, common sense dictates otherwise, and insurance should be considered outside the rule"	"Neither party is required to insure under DAP. However, common sense dictates otherwise, and insurance should be considered outside the rule"
DDP		(a) Seller has no obligation to insure goods on behalf of the buyer (b) However, seller must provide information to buyer when requested to unable buyer take out insurance. Clause A5. (c) Seller advised to take out pre-shipment insurance (d) Seller should also take out shipment policy to the point of delivery unloaded (e) Seller should also take out post-shipment/post-delivery insurance from goods delivery unloaded and contingency insurance.	(a) Buyer has obligation to insure the goods. (b) However, buyer is entitled to information from seller but upon his request, risks and expenses where applicable (Clause A5 (c) By implication of (b) above, buyer should, and is advised to take out insurance (c) The buyer has no obligation to the seller to make a contract of insurance. However, the buyer must provide the seller, at the seller's request, risk and cost, with information that the seller needs for obtaining insurance".
American DDP	N/A, UCC does not have a DDP		
Under UCC			
IFA Guidelines		"Neither party is required to insure under DDP. However, common sense dictates otherwise, and insurance should be considered outside the rule"	"Neither party is required to insure under DDP. However, common sense dictates otherwise, and insurance should be considered outside the rule"

Incoterm contract	Passage of risk	Sellers insurance	Buyer's insurance
DPU		(a) Seller has no obligation to provide insurance to the buyer (b) Seller has no duty to provide information to buyer (c) However, seller should take out insurance to cover goods up to the delivery place unloaded (see Note (d) below). (c) "The seller has no obligation to the buyer to make a contract of insurance". (d) Note: This provision is rather confusing for although the seller is not obliged to insure under A/5, the seller is nevertheless entitled to information from the buyer under B/5 to enable insurance	(a) Buyer no obligation to provide insurance to the seller or the goods (b) However, buyer must provide information to seller to enable the seller take out insurance-(B5) (c) Buyer advisable to take out insurance to cover goods from when they are delivered at a place unloaded. (d) "The buyer has no obligation to the seller to make a contract of insurance. However, the buyer must provide the seller, at the seller's request, risk and cost, with information that the seller needs for obtaining insurance".
American DPU			
Under UCC	N/A, UCC does not have a DPU		
IFA Guidelines		"Neither party is required to insure under DPU. However, common sense dictates otherwise, and insurance should be considered outside the rule"	"Neither party is required to insure under DPU. However, common sense dictates otherwise, and insurance should be considered outside the rule"
EXWORKS	Sellers Premises. Multimodal Transport	(a) None. (b) But must provide information to buyer when requested to unable buyer take out insurance (A5) (c) "The seller has no obligation to the buyer to make a contract of insurance. However, the seller must provide the buyer, at the buyer's request, risk and cost with information in the possession of the seller that the buyer needs for obtaining insurance"	(a) The buyer has no obligation to the seller to make a contract of insurance. (b) However, should take out insurance to cover at least the international transport aspects of the contract. (c) Buyer is entitled to information from seller upon request and at own risk and expense (A5)
American EXWORKS			
Under UCP			

Incoterm contract	Passage of risk	Sellers insurance	Buyer's insurance
IFA Guidelines		"Neither party is required to insure under Ex-Works. However, common sense dictates otherwise, and insurance should be considered outside the rule. This is particularly important for buyers because the seller delivers prior to loading or any transportation"	"Neither party is required to insure under Ex-Works. However, common sense dictates otherwise, and insurance should be considered outside the rule. This is particularly important for buyers because the seller delivers prior to loading or any transportation"
FAS		(a) Seller has no obligation to provide insurance. (b) However, seller must provide information to buyer when requested to enable buyer take out insurance-(Clause A5) (c) Seller is advised to take out pre-shipment insurance (d) Seller is also advised to take out post-shipment and other contingency covers where possible (e) "The seller has no obligation to the buyer to make a contract of insurance. However, the seller must provide the buyer, at the buyer's request, risk and cost, with information in possession of the seller that the buyer needs for obtaining insurance".	(a) Buyer has obligation to insure goods. (b) However, seller is entitled to information from seller upon request and at own risks and expenses where applicable A5 (c) This implies, and the seller is advised to take out insurance for the goods at least post shipment. (d) "The buyer has no obligation to the seller to make a contract of insurance".
American FAS			
Under UCC	FAS treated similar to FOB		
IFA Guidelines		"Neither party is required to insure under FAS. However, common sense dictates otherwise, and insurance should be considered outside the rule"	"Neither party is required to insure under FAS. However, common sense dictates otherwise, and insurance should be considered outside the rule"

Incoterm contract	Passage of risk	Sellers insurance	Buyer's insurance
FCA	Only sea or inland waterways transport. Ships Rail. Multimodal	(a) None. (b) But must provide information to buyer when requested to enable buyer take out insurance Clause A5 (c) "The seller has no obligation to the buyer to make a contract of insurance. However, the seller must provide the buyer, at the buyer's request, risk and cost, with information in the possession of the seller that the buyer needs for obtaining insurance"-A/5	(a) Buyer has no obligation to make a contract of insurance for the goods (b) Buyer is entitled to information from seller upon his request, risks and expenses where applicable. Clause A5 (c) It is advisable that the buyer takes out insurance to cover at least the international transport as of the goods
American FCA			
Under UCC	N/A, UCC does not have a FCA		
IFA Guidelines		"Neither party is required to insure under FCA. However, common sense dictates otherwise, and insurance should be considered outside the rule"	Neither party is required to insure under FCA. However, common sense dictates otherwise, and insurance should be considered outside the rule
FOB			
Main Stream FOB	(a) Only sea or inland waterways transport. (b) Ships Rail. Clause A5 (c) Leading Cases. *Pyrene v Scindia; The ElMinia & El Amria*	(a) Seller has no obligation to insure goods. (b) However, the seller must provide information to buyer when requested under A5 to enable the buyer to insure. (c) Seller is advised to take out pre-shipment insurance (d) Seller also advised to take out post-shipment and contingency insurance (e) See also Statute and cases opposite (f) "The seller has no obligation to the buyer to make a contract of insurance. However, the seller must provide the buyer, at the buyer's request, risk and cost, with information in the possession of the seller that the buyer needs for obtaining insurance"	(a) Buyer has no obligation insure goods. (b) However, buyer is entitled to information from seller but upon request and risks to enable buyer to take out insurance -Clause A5 (c) Buyer is advised to take out from shipment and for international transits (e) Buyer also advised to take out pre-shipment to cover possible failure or late nomination of the vessel. (f) See also: S32 (2) Sale of Goods Act 1979; (g) Useful case: *Wimble v Rosenberg* (h) The buyer has no obligation to the seller to make a contract of insurance.

Incoterm contract	Passage of risk	Sellers insurance	Buyer's insurance
Simple FOB		Seller not obliged to take out insurance	
Extended FOB		Seller may be requested to provide insurance if part of the additional duties	
American FOB			
Under UCC	Same as at common law	(a) Seller not responsible for insuring the goods (b) Seller should consider taking out own pre-shipment insurance (c) Seller should consider post-shipment contingency insurance	(a) No obligation to provide insurance for the buyer (b) Buyer is responsible for insuring goods (c) Buyer responsible for additional insurance
IFA Guidelines		"Neither party is required to insure under FOB. However, common sense dictates otherwise, and insurance should be considered outside the rule. Sellers are risk until the goods are placed on board the vessel (check with your insurers about FAS/ FOB insurance)"	"Neither party is required to insure under FOB. However, common sense dictates otherwise, and insurance should be considered outside the rule. Sellers are risk until the goods are placed on board the vessel (check with your insurers about FAS/FOB insurance"

References

Ademuni-Odeke (2007) Insurance of FOB contracts under Anglo-American and other common law jurisdictions revisited. Tul Mar Law J 31(1):425–462

Schmitthoff C (2012) The law and practice of international trade, 12th edn. Sweet and Maxwell

Part III

Nature and Characteristics of Contracts Which Include Selle's Obligations to Provide Insurance to the Buyer at Comon Law and Under Incoterms

6 Nature and Characteristics of Incoterms Contracts Which Include Seller's Obligations to Provide Insurance to the Buyer at Common Law

Abstract

In the reverse to Part II, this Part III deals with **Insurance of Contracts Which Include Seller's Obligations to Provide Insurance for the Buyer**. As in Chap. 3, this chapter discusses the general Nature and Characteristics of the only contract in this category: the CIF. The chapter covers it under: Introduction; The General Nature of CIF Contracts; "Variants" of CIF Contracts as opposite to "Variations" in FOB; Shipment of Goods; Physical and Symbolic Delivery of Goods; Tender of Documents; Payments for Goods; Other Essential Characteristics; Importance of Documents; Whether the contract is for Sale of Documents or Sale of Goods!?; Importance of Appropriation in CIF Contracts; Passage of Property; Passage of Risks; The Two Rights of Rejection-of documents when tendered and goods when delivered-the only contract providing these remedies to the buyer; Importance of Insurance-the very essence of the contract; Examples of Insurance Clauses; Comparative Status in International Trade; Comparisons with the older FOB Contract; Under the American UCC and Incoterms for Americans Guidelines; Comparison with C&F Contract; Remedies under CIF and Related Contracts; Frustrations of CIF Contracts; "Further Food for Thoughts"; Concluding Remarks; References; and Further Readings.

6.1 Introduction

The only established common law contract in this category is the CIF. The CIP, the only other Incoterms in which the seller provides insurance is not an established common law contract. As outlined in Chap. 2 (ante), insurance is one of the most innovative risk management mechanisms ever devised by commerce. Despite no compulsion to insure, in practice only an idiot transacts business without it. The two leading export contracts, FOB and CIF, differ from each other and prescribe rights

P. Ademuni-Odeke, *Insurance of International Sales' Contracts under Incoterms*, Law for Professionals, https://doi.org/10.1007/978-3-031-75136-3_6

and obligations on the parties. Each contract has a purpose and imposes duties and obligations on exporters and importers. As discussed below (Chap. 7), one such obligation is to insure goods in transit against marine and export risks. The nature and extent of those duties depend on the nature, history and development of the two contracts. Although in many respects from the FOB, two distinct characteristics of the CIF is the emphasis on insurance on the role documents generally and insurance in particular. It is for those reasons that it is sometimes dubbed a sale of documents rather a sale of goods contract. Otherwise, both contracts are governed by common law, customs and usages, Incoterms, Institute Clause, or Commodity Trade Terms e.g., GAFTA, FOSFA, etc.

Thus, following coverage of FOB at common law in Chap. 3 and FOB Insurance at common law in Chap. 4 above, this chapter introduces the CIF contract, and examines parties' CIF insurance obligations under Anglo-American and other Common Law Jurisdictions. It contrasts CIF with FOB Insurance and selected Civil Law Jurisdictions. The chapter focuses also on and summarises only those CIF factors and parties' obligations that are relevant to insurance and thereby lays the foundation for the subsequent discourses on CIF insurance at common below (Chap. 7) and under Incoterms (Chap. 8). However, a detailed treatment of the nature, development and parties' obligations are beyond the scope of this chapter and book which focuses on insurance aspects. The reader is, therefore, advised to look at those advanced and specialist publications on the general law governing the CIF contract. Some of those are listed at the end of the chapter. Adequate bibliography is provided at the end of the chapter for that purpose. Insurance aspects of the contract at common law are covered in Chap. 7, under incoterms in Chap. 8, and of its war risks in Chap. 10.

6.2 The General Nature of CIF Contract

In order to determine parties' duties and obligations in CIF, it is essential to understand the exact definition and therefore nature of the contract.[1] The CIF contract is a form of sale of goods used in overseas trade. It names the port of destination and the price quoted by the seller includes cost of the goods, insurance and freight. It is a rigid contract often referred to as three contracts in one or the "holy trinity". More modern and popular than the FOB it is based on modern institutional developments (banking, insurance, shipping, letters of credit and technology)

The CIF seller has specific duties different from those of FOB or any other export contracts. The seller must ship or buy afloat goods of the contract description. If they are unascertained goods, he must normally give notice of appropriation. On or after shipment he must obtain a proper bill of lading and insurance policy. He performs the contract by transferring the shipping documents—bill of lading, insurance policy and invoice to the buyer on the 'prompt', the date fixed for payment. When payment is being made by banker's comer. Lord Porter in *Comptoir d'*

[1] See *Halsbury's Laws of England,* (5th edn 2012) Vol. 91 para 335 for nature of the contract.

Achat et de Vent du Boerenbond Belge SA v Luis de Ridda Limitada (The Julia)[2] pronounced that the CIF seller must put the buyer in a position where he can:

(a) take delivery of the goods;
(b) resale the goods afloat and; and failing that;
(c) claim directly from the insurers in the event of loss or damage,[3] where he said:

> …the obligations imposed upon a seller under a C.I.F. contract are well known, and in the ordinary case include the tender of a bill of lading covering the goods contracted to be sold and no others, coupled with an insurance policy in the normal form and accompanied by an invoice which shows the price and, as in this case, usually contains a deduction of the freight which the buyer pays before delivery at the port of discharge. Against tender of these documents the purchaser must pay the price. In such a case the property may pass either on shipment or on tender, the risk generally passes on shipment or as from shipment, but possession does not pass until the documents which represent the goods are handed over in exchange for the price. In the result the buyer after receipt of the documents can claim against the ship for breach of the contract of carriage and against the underwriter for any loss covered by the policy.[4]

Pursuant to *The Julia* principle, now acceptable to Incoterms 2020 and the commodity market, the purpose of the CIF being to deal with goods afloat[5]

6.3 Variants of CIF Contract

Whereas the FOB has types or classifications, the CIF has no types but instead has variants.[6] There are many variants and types of CIF. With regard to variants, first is:

(a) C&F contracts which are similar except the buyer arranges insurance. There is doubt whether this is an independent contractual in its own right or a variant or type of CIF. In this book it is treated as a related but separate contract and discussed below. A common one is the C & F contract, which lays the responsibility to insure on the buyer. This is a positive responsibility, and not merely a discharge of the seller's obligation to insure, because sometimes the seller himself is interested in the insurance. For example, if the buyer does not pay or goes bankrupt and the seller is left to reclaim the goods;
(b) In 'C.I.F. and C.' variant the additional c indicates the price, includes agent's commission;
(c) In 'C.I.F and I' the additional i includes banker's interest and commission;

---

[2] *Comptoir d' Achat et de Vent du Boerenbond Belge SA v Luis de Ridda Limitada* (*The Julia*) [1949] AC 293 (House of Lords).

[3] Ibid.

[4] ibid, at p. 309.

[5] See *Halsbury's Laws of England*, 5th edn 2012, Vol 91, para 340 for legal incidents of the CIF contract.

[6] See Lorenzo (2012), pp. 54–64.

(d) In C.I.F. and E, "E" includes exchange rates;
(e) C.I.F.& F.O, "FO" includes Foreign Exchange;
(f) CIF delivered contracts;
(g) CIF Out-Turn Contract, both are normally used in the bulk oil trade;
(h) Other variants of CIF contract arise when the buyer agrees to pay, in addition to cost, insurance, and freight, for some extra items such as commission, exchange above;
(i) American CIF has more variations;
(j) More variations are covered by Schmithoff,[7] Sassoon,[8] Reynolds[9] and Halsbury's Laws[10]

The seller has to provide insurance for categories (b)-(j) above

It will be recalled that that in *The Julia,* Lord Porter thought that even though a contract is stated to be C.I.F. it, it may be found to be ex ship or arrival contract if that is the real relation. However, according to Mr. Justice Graham in *Morton-Norwich v Intergren,*[11] true C.I.F. contracts are not used in carriage by air; although that is probably now an antiquated view. He commented that:

> The contract was expressed to be a C.I.F. contract, but can, it seems to me, hardly be regarded as a normal C.I.F. contract... In view of the air carriage and the short period of time the goods were likely to be in transit, and the fact, as I am told, that the principal document, the air waybill, is not negotiable, it can hardly have been contemplated that the seller was intending to retain the property in the goods for such purposes as obtaining credit by way of a charge on the goods and the policy of insurance.[12]

6.4 Shipment, Delivery of Goods and Tender of Documents

The CIF names the port of destination and the price quoted by the seller includes cost of the goods, insurance and freight. The seller's principal common law obligations are to ship or buy afloat goods of the contract description.[13] If they are unascertained goods, sellers must normally give notice of appropriation. On or after shipment they must obtain a proper bill of lading and insurance policy or equivalent documents.[14] The seller performs the contract by transferring the shipping documents bill of lading, insurance policy and invoice to the buyer on the 'prompt', the date fixed for payment through assignments.[15] In *Re Denbigh Cowan & Co & R*

[7] Schmitthjoff Export Trade, Para 2-039.

[8] Lorenzo (2012).

[9] Reynolds, Incoterms for Americans Guidelines, 2020.

[10] *Halisbury's Laws of England*, 5th Edn 2012 Vol 91 para 339.

[11] *Morton-Norwich v Intergren* [1976] FSR 513.

[12] Ibid at pp. 526, 527.

[13] See Sassoon, Chapter 4.

[14] For tender of documents in CIF see Halsbury's Laws (5th edn 2012) Vol. 91 para 351.

[15] See *Halsbury's Laws of England*, (5th edn 2012) Vol 91, para 353-6 for time of payments.

Archery& Co,[16] following the landmark case of *The Julia,*[17] Lord Banks[18] at the English Appeal Court re-emphasizes the sellers' common law obligation to provide and tender insurance documents under CIF contract namely that "[The seller] admits that the document there referred to are the documents which are ordinarily required under a C.I.F. contract-the invoice, bill of lading and policy of insurance-and that admission, it appears to me, stamps the contract as in its essentials a C.I.F. contract."[19] without which buyers can refuse to take delivery of the goods.[20]

6.5 Delivery and Payments: UK Sale of Goods Act 1979[21]

The above-described position may be different under statutory law. For instance, since under s.28 of the *SGA* 1979, payment and delivery are concurrent conditions and delivery in a CIF contract means delivery of shipping documents. In *Clement Horst v Biddle Bros Horst,* Earl Loreburn L.C. held that the buyer (unless there is contrary agreement) cannot refuse to pay[22] until he is able to examine the goods,[23] s. 34 thus being excluded. He opined that "...the Sale of Goods Act says in effect that payment is to be against delivery. Accordingly, we have supplied by the general law an answer to the question when this cash is to be paid. But when is there delivery of goods which are on board ship? That may be quite a different thing from delivery of goods on shore. The answer is that delivery of the bill of lading when the goods are at sea can be treated as delivery of the goods themselves, this law being so old that I think it is quite unnecessary to refer to authority for it"[24]

This does not exclude his right to reject the goods if they do not conform to the contract on arrival (see Rejection in paras 6.12.2 and 6.21.5 ahead). S. 32 (1) providing that delivery to a carrier is *prima facie* delivery to the buyer, does not apply to FOB as it does CIF, nor does s. 32 (3) as there are always terms as to insurance, but s. 32 (2) requiring a seller to make a reasonable contract with a carrier, does apply.

---

[16] *Re Denbigh Cowan & Co & R Archery& Co* 125 LT 388, [1921] All ER Rep 245 CA; 90 LKJB 836; (1921) 6 Ll. L. Rep. 383.

[17] *Comptoir D'Achat et De Vente Du Boerenbond Belge SA v Luis De Ridder, Limitada, The Julia* [1947] 2All ER 443.

[18] Scrutton LJ and Atkin LJ concurring, *at 384*, reversing the judgment of Rowlett J.

[19] *Re Denbigh Cowan & Co & R Archery & Co* at p. 384.

[20] For detailed discussions of the tender of documents at common law, under Incoterms and UCP see Chap. 11 post.

[21] Although the principles of the *Marine Insurance Act 1906* and the *Sale of Goods Act* 1979, as amended, apply to CIF policies there is no specific UK statute applicable to CIF contracts. The only such a statute in the Common Law jurisdictions is the US UCC. The new UK *Insurance Act 2015* has not made any difference to the *Marine Insurance Act 1906* in this respect.

[22] For time of payment see *Halsbury's Laws of England* (5th edn 2012) Vol. 91 para 353 and for payment by acceptance of bills of exchange 54.

[23] *Clement Horst v Biddle Bros Horst* [1912] AC 18.

[24] Ibid at 22, 23.

As in the FOB a contract, *The Julia,*[25] suggests that property normally passes on delivery of the shipping documents but in *The Albazero,*[26] Lord Justice Roskill at the Court of Appeal, was of the view that in special circumstances, this may be displaced. He added that although the letters C.I.F. are used, other terms of the contract may show that the property is intended to pass on shipment and not upon tender of and payment against the documents so tendered or though the letters f.o.b. are used, other terms may show that the property was not intended to pass on shipment but upon tender and payment.[27]

Lord Roskill's judgment approved by Approved by Lord Diplock in the House of Lords.[28] Risk normally passes 'on shipment or as from shipment'[29] so that s. 20 of the *SGA*,1979, linking property with risk, is displaced. He repeated Lord Roskill's observations above[30] adding that the bill of lading must normally be transferable, cover the voyage continuously over an agreed or customary route, state the goods are shipped and not merely received for shipment, be genuine in stating correct dates and not containing forgery, cover only the contract goods, be valid and effective and be 'clean', that is not contain any adverse comment on the good order or condition of the goods.

The insurance policy must be assignable,[31] legally effective (not an honour policy), cover only the contract goods continuously over the route and be usual in the trade or as specified in the contract. *Groom v Barber*[32] is authority for the fact that if it is usual or agreed sellers will not be in breach if they fail to cover other risks, e.g. war risks. The invoice must at least enable the buyer to relate it to the contract but more detail may be required by the contract;[33] the requirements as to documents may be modified by the contract, e.g. allowing a delivery order on the ship of a 'received for shipment' bill of lading or a certificate of insurance instead of a policy. The contract may also require other documents such as certificates of origin, quality, testing and the like. The contract may require the seller to give notice of appropriation[34] of goods to the contract or to 'declare' a shipment within a given time and these documents may be added to the shipping documents. Such notice transforms hitherto unascertained goods into specific goods, and the contract binding.

---

[25] *The Julia,* [1919] AC 293.

[26] *The Albazero* [1977] AC 774.

[27] Ibid.

[28] Ibid at 840.

[29] Ibid at p. 809.

[30] See notes 22 and 23 above

[31] See Note 47 below; see also *Halsbury's Laws of England,* (5th Edn 2012), Vol. 91 Note 7.

[32] Ibid; See also *Groom v Barber* [1915] 1 KB 316; INCOTERMS 2010, Note 24, Clause A3(b).

[33] On Invoice see *Halsbury's Laws of Emngland* above para. 349.

[34] Ibid—For notice of appropriation see *Halsbury's Laws* of England, above, para 359.

6.6 Other Essential Characteristics

On essential characteristics of the CIF, Lord Wright in *Smyth v. Bailey*[35] supplementing that the special feature of the C.I.F. contract is the importance attached to the documents. In his view, in this course of business, the general property in the goods remains in the seller until he transfers the bills of lading. These rules, which are simple enough to state in general terms, are of the utmost importance in commercial transactions.[36] These are the bill of lading, the invoice and insurance policy. With regard to insurance, according to Justice Rowlatt in *Orient Co v Brekke and Howlid,*[37] if insurance is not effected the buyer may reject the goods even though they arrive safely, but according to Justice Atkin in *Groom v Barber*[38] if proper documents (including a proper policy) are tendered the buyer must accept and pay for them even though the goods are lost.[39]

He opined that it was also clear that [the seller] can make an effective tender even though he possesses at the time of tender actual knowledge of the loss of the ship or goods. For the purchaser in case of loss will get the documents he bargained for; and if the policy be that required by the contract, and if the loss be covered thereby, he will secure the insurance moneys. He also noted that the contingency of loss is within and not outside the contemplation of the parties to a C.I.F. contract and confidently concluded that in his feeling the views he expressed were in full accord with the observations of Atkin J. in *C. Groom, Ltd. v. Barber* as to the requirements of a C.I.F. contract.[40]

Justice Atkin was right as his decision was followed by Justice Maccardie in *Manbre v Corn Products.*[41] In his judgment *Orient Co v Brekke and Howlid*, Justice Rowlatt thought that:

> I cannot doubt that ordinarily it is the duty of the vendor under a C.I.F. contract to deliver not only a bill of lading but also a policy of insurance. The respondents contend that the goods arrived safely and that, therefore, there was no longer any occasion to deliver a policy… What is meant by saying that the goods have 'arrived'? To the buyer it means only that the ship has arrived which he is told contains the goods. The bill of lading must be given to him and, further than that, he is entitled to say that he will not pay the price unless a policy of insurance is handed to him along with it so that if anything has gone wrong with the goods, he may acquire his rights under the policy in lieu of the goods themselves. Even if it could be made out that he had waived the actual tender of a policy, that alone would not help the seller. What has to be shewn is that he waived the insurance itself. It is impossible to hold that he is to be called upon to pay for goods which have been shipped uninsured.[42]

[35] *Smyth v Bailey* [1940] 3 All ER 60.

[36] Ibid at p. 68.

[37] *Orient Co v Brekke and Howlid* [1913] I KB 531 at pp. 536, 537.

[38] *Groom v Barber* [1915] 1 KB 316.

[39] Ibid.

[40] Ibid at, [1919] I KB 198, at p. 204. [1919] I KB 198, at p. 204.

[41] *Manbre v Corn Products* (1919) 1KB 198.

[42] *Orient Co v Brekke and Howlid* [1913] I KB 531 at pp. 536, 537.

On the often-made assumption that the C.I.F. contract is a sale of documents rather than goods, he clarified that it may rather be a contract of sale of goods, to be performed by delivery of documents since a contract for the sale of specific goods C.I.F. is void if at the time of the sale the goods had perished even though a policy relating to them was in existence.[43] In the particular circumstances of this case, His Lordship opened that:

> ...looking to the contract itself alone, it appears to me clearly that what the parties contemplated, those who bought and those who sold, was that there was an existing something to be sold and bought, and if sold and bought, then the benefit of insurance should go with it... I think the full benefit of the insurance was meant to go as well to losses and damage that occurred previously to the 15th of May, as to losses and damage that occurred subsequently, always assuming that something passed by the contract of the 15th of May. If the contract of the 15th of May had been an operating contract, and there had been a valid sale of a cargo at that time existing, I think the purchaser would have had the benefit of insurance in respect of all damage previously occurring. The contract plainly imports that there was something which was to be sold at the time of the contract, and something to be purchased. No such thing existing, I think the Court of Exchequer Chamber has come to the only reasonable conclusion upon it, and consequently that there must be judgment given by your Lordships for the Defendants in Error.[44]

So also, when a seller bought what he believed were goods afloat covered by regular documents and re-sold them it was held by Justice Kerr in *Hindley v East India Produce Co*[45] that he did not fulfil the contract by handing over an apparently regular set of shipping documents when the goods had never existed. He added that:

> It ... is indeed a matter of elementary law - that a c. & f. or C.I.F. contract is to be performed by the tender of documents covering goods which have been shipped either by the seller or by someone else in accordance with the terms of the contract. If no goods have in fact been shipped the sellers have not performed their obligation. I cannot see any basis for the distinction which the sellers here seek to draw between a seller who is also the shipper and a seller who is not the shipper[46]

So, despite the contention that such contracts are akin to contracts for the sale of documents rather for sale of goods, the goods have to exist at some stage in the first place which excludes incidences of simply fabricating documents for goods which never existed.

---

[43] *Couturier v Hastie* (1856) 5 HLC 673.

[44] Ibid at, per The Lord Chancellor at pp. 681, 682.

[45] *Hindley v East India Produce Co.* [1973] 2 Lloyd's Rep 515.

[46] Ibid at p. 518.

6.7 Importance of Documents

The foregone discussions have demonstrated the importance of documents in CIF contracts. Although there are two deliveries in the contract, goods and documents, the most important function in CIF is delivery (tender) of the documents by seller to buyer, contrasting FOB which is the physical delivery of the goods on board a vessel.[47] Therefore, contrary to FOB contracts, s. 32 (1) of the *Sale of Goods Act* 1893, providing that delivery to a carrier is prima facie delivery to the buyer, does not apply to CIF contracts, nor does s. 32 (3) as there are always terms as to insurance, but s. 32(2) requiring a seller to make a reasonable contract with a carrier, does apply. The purpose of the CIF contract is to enable dealing with goods afloat. If payment transfer is being made by banker's commercial credit the documents will in practice tender to a bank making the payment. The special feature of the CIF contract is the importance attached to the documents *Smyth v Bailey.*[48] Justice Scrutton in *Arnold Karberg & Co v Blythe, Green, Jourdain & Co*[49] summarised the problem in his often-quoted judgment that:

> …I am strongly of opinion that the key to many of the difficulties arising in C.I.F. contracts is to keep firmly in mind the cardinal distinction that a C.I.F. sale is not a sale of goods, but a sale of documents relating to goods. It is not a contract that goods shall arrive, but a contract to ship goods complying with the contract of sale, to obtain, unless the contract otherwise provides, the ordinary contract of carriage to the place of destination, and the ordinary contract of insurance of the goods on that voyage, and to tender these documents against payment of the contract price. The buyer then has the right to claim the fulfilment of the contract of carriage, or, if the goods are lost or damaged, such indemnity for the loss as he can claim under the contract of insurance. He buys the documents, not the goods, and it may be that under the terms of the contracts of insurance and affreightment he buys no indemnity for the damage that has happened to the goods. This depends on what documents he is entitled to under the contract of sale. In my view, therefore, the relevant question will generally be not 'what at the time of declaration or tender of documents is the condition of the goods?'… but 'what, at the time of tender of documents, was the condition of those documents as to compliance with the contract of sale?'[50]

Insurance can technically affect delivery. Thus, in *Orient Co. v Bekke and Howlid,*[51] where the seller failed to insure, it was held that if insurance is not effected the buyer may reject the goods even though they arrive safely. However, and giving rise to the supposition that the contract is a sale of documents rather than goods, the importance of buying and selling afloat and the two separate rights of rejection, both *Groom v. Barber*[52] *and Manbre v. Corn Products*[53] suggest that if proper documents

---

[47] For the bill of lading and other essential documents, see Lorenzo, Chapter 5 and 7.

[48] *Smyth v Bailey* [1940] 3All ER 60; See also Ademuni-Odeke (1993).

[49] *Arnold Karberg & Co v Blythe, Green, Jourdain & Co* [1915] 2 KB 379.

[50] *Arnold Karberg & Co v Blythe, Green, Jourdain & Co.*

[51] *Orient Co. v Bekke and Howlid* [1913]1KB531.

[52] *Groom v. Barber* [1915]1KB316.

[53] *Manbre v. Corn Products* [1919]1KB 198.

(including the policy or equivalent) are tendered the buyer must accept and pay for them even though the goods are lost. Hence the supposition that the CIF is a sale of documents rather than goods.

6.8 Sale of Documents or Sale of Goods?

Following on *Groom v. Barber and Manbre v. Corn Products*, *Hindley v East India Produce Co,*[54] rationalises that, it is these CIF characteristics that have led to the suggestion that a CIF contract is a sale of documents rather than goods but it may be rather a contract of sale of goods,[55] to be performed by delivery of documents. However, this suggestion should be contrasted with that in *Couturier v Hastie*[56]*(*please source judge and citation where possible*)* that a contract for the sale of specific goods CIF is void if at the time of sale, the goods had perished even though a policy relating to them was in existence. He said:

> ...looking to the contract itself alone, it appears to me clearly that what the parties contemplated, those who bought and those who sold, was that there was an existing something to be sold and bought, and if sold and bought, then the benefit of insurance should go with it... I think the full benefit of the insurance was meant to go as well to losses and damage that occurred previously to the 15th of May, as to losses and damage that occurred subsequently, always assuming that something passed by the contract of the 15th of May. If the contract of the 15th of May had been an operating contract, and there had been a valid sale of a cargo at that time existing, I think the purchaser would have had the benefit of insurance in respect of all damage previously occurring. The contract plainly imports that there was something which was to be sold at the time of the contract, and something to be purchased. No such thing existing, I think the Court of Exchequer Chamber has come to the only reasonable conclusion upon it, and consequently that there must be judgment given by your Lordships for the Defendants in Error.[57]

Thus, in this case, when sellers bought what they believed were goods afloat covered by regular documents and re-sold them it was held they did not fulfil the contract by handing over an apparently regular set of shipping documents when the goods had never existed.[58] The US position seems to mirror those of the English common law. In *Smith & Co v Morano,*[59] where 2 days after shipment the ship sank with the barrels of oil, the buyer's refusal to accept the documents was rejected by the court on the basis that since the goods had been shipped and the documents were in order, risks in the CIF contract had passed to the buyers. This authority is clearly distinguishable from *Couturier v Hastie* where goods had perished before shipment and reconcilable with *Groom V Barber*, *Manbre v Corn Products* and *Hindley v East*

[54] *Hindley v East India Produce Co* [1973] 2 Lloyd's Rep 515.

[55] See Ademuni-Odeke (1993), pp. 158–176.

[56] *Couturier v Hastie* (1856) HLC 673.

[57] Ibid per The Lord Chancellor at pp. 681, 682.

[58] Ibid.

[59] *Smith & Co v Morano* (1920, Pa)110 Atl 94.

India Produce where the loss alleged loss (where applicable) occurred after shipment.

6.9 Appropriation

Another essential characteristic, but which may not be the preserve of the CIF, is the need for appropriation and the requirement of notice thereof. Appropriation is more important in CIF than in any other contracts.[60] This has a knock of effect on passage of property and therefore risks below. The contract may require the seller to give notice of appropriation of goods to the contract or to 'declare' a shipment within a given time and these documents may be added to the shipping documents. Such notice transforms hitherto unascertained goods into specific goods, and the seller is then bound to deliver those goods only in rendering performance but does not transfer property. In *Karlsham Oljefabriker v Eastport, (The Elafi),*[61] it was held by Justice Mustill that when contracts cover a whole bulk shipment, goods under one of these contracts may be ascertained for passing of property without being physically allocated and when the goods for that contract are ascertained by exhaustion there is no need for appropriation. He said:

> ...what would have been the position if the entire cargo had been sold to the claimants under a single contract? Here, since the contract was on C.I.F. terms, it is very probable that the property would have passed to the claimants when the shipping documents were negotiated, for the cargo was ascertained and appropriated from the outset, and the general rule is that under a C.I.F. contract the property passes with the documents. The only cause for uncertainty is the fact that the claimants had a right to reject goods in excess of the stipulated quantity, so that it would not be possible to know during the voyage whether any individual portion of cargo might not ultimately revert to the vendors. I believe, however, that in such a situation the property in the entire cargo would pass conditionally to the claimants, subject to a retransfer of any excess if the claimants so elected, and that this would be sufficient to found a claim in tort in respect of all such cargo as the claimants chose to accept.[62]

Appropriation determines when property pass at contract.

6.10 Passage of Property and Title

Passage of property and risks are important to assessing risks and therefore insurance liabilities. This is more so than in CIF which involves buying and selling afloat. According to Lord Porter in *Comptoir d' Achat v Luis de Ridder Limitada, The*

---

[60] See *Halsbury's Laws of England,* (5th edn) Vol. 91, para 359 for notice of appropriation in CIF contracts.

[61] *Karlsham Oljefabriker v Eastport, (The Elafi)* [1982]1 All ER 208, at pp. 212, 213.

[62] Ibid at pp. 212, 213.

Julia,[63] property normally passes on delivery of the shipping documents. However, as already discussed, in *The Albazero*[64] Lord Justice Roskill in the CA (please cite where possible unless already done so on the same point above) opined that in special circumstances this may be displaced. In addition to passage of property Lord Scrutton added that risk normally passes 'on shipment or as from shipment',[65] so that s. 20 of SOGA 1979, linking property with risk, is displaced. Although initially only an FOB authority, *Pyrene v Scindia*[66] determined passage of property[67] and therefore risks which now applies to all export shipping contracts, passage of risks in CIF has specific rules.[68] These is namely that:

(a) Risks pass to the buyer as from shipment;[69]
(b) Buyer of goods damaged before discharge cannot sue carrier;[70]
(c) Buyer of goods damaged before receipt of bill of lading sues in tort;[71]
(d) Seller does not warranty existence of goods at time of tender;[72]
(e) Goods can be shipped or bought and sold afloat;
(f) Most important function is tender of documents rather than goods;
(g) Sometimes treated as sale of documents rather than goods; and
(h) Tender with knowledge of lost goods is good tender.[73]

The basis for the above characteristics being that any loss is underpinned by insurance policy to compensate any party in the chain that suffers losses and/or damages.

---

[63] *Comptoir d'Achat v Luis de Ridder Limitada,* (The Julia) [1949] AC 293.

[64] *The Albazero* [1977] AC 774.

[65] *Comptoir d'Achat v Luis de Ridder Limitada,* (The Julia) [1949] AC 293.

[66] *Pyrene Co Ltd v Scindia Navigation Co Ltd* [1954] 2 QB 402.

[67] Discussions on passage of property and reservations of right of disposal are omitted here; see *Halsbury's Laws of England, (5th Edn 2012),* Vol. 91, Note 7, para. 356.

[68] Ibid, para. 357.

[69] *E. Clemens Horst v Biddell Bros* [1912] AC 18 HL, reversing SC sub nom *Biddell Bros v E Clemns Horst* [1911]1KB934 CA; *The Julia* [1949] 1 All ER 269; *The Galatia* [1980] I All ER 501.

[70] *Margarine Union GmbH v Cambay Prince SS Co Ltd* [1967] 3All ER 775-ditinguished in *The Elafi* [1982] 1 All ER 208, not followed in the *Irene Success* [1982] 1 All ER 218, followed in *The Aliakmon* (1986) Financial Times, 29 April.

[71] *Schiffart und Kohlen GmbH v Chelsea Maritime Limited, The Irene Success* [1982] 1 All ER 218 followed in *The Aliakmon* [1986] 2 All ER 145.

[72] *Groom (c) v Barber* [1915] 1 KB 316; Re Weis & Co Ltd & Credit Colonial et Commercial, Antwerp [1916] 1 KB 346.

[73] *Mambre Saccharine Co Ltd v Cord Products Co* [1919] 1KB 198 *sub nom Mambre Saccharine Co v Corn Products* (1919)88 LJKB 402, applied in *Diamond Alikali Export Corpn v FL Buourgeoise* [1921] 3 KB 443; Halsbury Laws of England, Vol 91, para. 356.

6.11 Passage of Risks

Passage of risks in the contract has been partly mentioned above. In sale of goods contracts, like most contracts, there is a presumption that unless otherwise provided, risks normally follow property. In FOB, the risk passes when goods have been successfully delivered,[74] i.e., after loading.

> The seller shall he responsible for all the risk of loss of damage to the goods until such time as they have the passed the ships rail at the said port of shipment. The seller shall also bear the risk to the goods until they have been delivered as aforesaid including costs of loading the goods on boat the ship and charges for unloading at the port of discharge which may be levied by the shipping line when contracting for carriage and also pay all customs charges for exportation as well as all duties taxes and other Government charges payable on exportation.[75]

Although *Pyrene v Scindia* emphasised the passage of risks over the ships rail in FOB contracts, it is not clear whether the same emphasis applies in CIF contracts. Rather the latter focuses on passage of risks during the completion of loading rather than over the ship's rail in that process. This might have something to do with the importance of the physical delivery of goods in FOB contracts compared with the symbolic delivery of documents in CIF contracts.

6.12 The Two Rights of Rejection

6.12.1 Rejection of Documents

The discussions in the role of documents and whether CIF is a sale of documents or goods leads to the two rights of rejection.[76] *Kwei Tek Chao v British Traders*[77] is among the authorities lending support to the principle that there are separate rights to reject documents and goods if they are not in conformity with the contract. Justice Devlin held that:

> Here, therefore, there is a right to reject documents, and a right to reject goods, and the two things are quite distinct. A C.I.F. contract puts a number of obligations upon the seller, some of which are in relation to the goods and some of which are in relation to the documents. So far as the goods are concerned, he must put on board at the port of shipment goods in conformity with the contract description, but he must also send forward documents, and those documents must comply with the contract. If he commits a breach the breaches may in one sense overlap, in that they flow from the same act. If there is a late shipment, as there was in this case, the date of the shipment being part of the description of the goods, the seller has not put on board goods which conform to the contract description, and therefore he has broken that obligation. He has also made it impossible to send forward a bill of lading

[74] See para 357 for incidents of risks in FOB contracts.

[75] *Pyrene v Scindia*; Clause A3(a) Incoterms 2010.

[76] See *Halsbury's Laws of England*, opct, para 358 on right to reject in CIF contracts.

[77] *Kwei Tek Chao v British Traders* [1954] 2 QB 459.

> which at once conforms with the contract and states accurately the date of shipment. Thus, the same act can cause two breaches of two independent obligations. However, that may be, they are distinct obligations, and the right to reject the documents arises when the documents are tendered, and the right to reject the goods arises when they are landed and when after examination they are found not to be in conformity with the contract. There are many cases, of course, where the documents are accepted but the goods are subsequently rejected. It may be that if the actual date of shipment is not in conformity with the contract, and the error appears from the documents, the buyer, by accepting the documents, not only loses his right to reject the documents, but also his right to reject the goods, but that would be because he had waived in advance reliance on the date of shipment.[78]

However, *Pancahaud v General Grain*[79] suggests that if the buyers take up without objection documents, which do not conform, they will be precluded from rejecting them later.

6.12.2 Rejection of Goods

Once more the lynch-pin here being the insurance policy. In the case Lord Denning thought:

> If the buyers choose not to read the documents, they must put up with the consequences. They must be treated as if they had read them. This was clearly the view of the Committee of Appeal of the London Corn Trade Association Ltd.... By taking up the documents and paying for them, they are precluded afterwards from complaining of the late shipment or of the defect in the bill of lading... The buyers are precluded, by their conduct, from relying on the late shipment as a ground for rejecting the goods. Reading this award [in London Corn Trade Association Ltd] broadly, I feel no doubt that the Committee of Appeal held that the buyers, by their conduct in taking up these shipping documents without exception and paying for them, are precluded from rejecting the goods on the ground of late shipment or defective bill of lading: because a reasonable and fair examination of those documents would have led any businessman to know that the goods were in fact shipped late.[80]

In CIF contracts, there are separate rights to reject documents and goods, if they are not in conformity with the contract.[81] However, if the buyer takes up without objection documents which do not conform, he will be precluded from rejecting them later.[82] Since under the Sale of Goods Act 1893, s.28 payment and delivery are concurrent conditions and delivery in a C.I.F. contract means delivery of shipping documents, the buyer (unless there is contrary agreement) cannot refuse to pay until he is able to examine the goods,[83] s. 34 thus being excluded (revise delivery in sale

---

[78] Ibid at pp. 480, 481.

[79] *Panchaud v General Grain* [1970] 1 Lloyd's Rep 53.

[80] Ibid per Lord Denning, MR at p 58.

[81] *Kwei Tek Chao v British Traders* [1954] 2 Q B 459.

[82] *Panchaud v General Grain* [1970] I Lloyd's Rep 53.

[83] *Clements v Horst Brothers* [1912] AC 18.

of goods). This does not exclude his right to reject the goods if they do not on arrival conform with the contract.

6.13 Importance of Insurance in CIF

The role of insurance which includes the policy or insurance documents is adequately covered above. However, suffice to reiterate that the insurance policy plays a crucial role in the documentation process of the CIF contract.[84] This must be listed in and accompany the commercial invoice.[85] Prepared by the seller to inform of costs of the goods provided, charges incurred, and additional services rendered. Not legal, but important customary, commercial and practical, documents. There may be provisional or final invoices; the former when by the buyer to estimates or application for foreign currency. The second document that accompanies the insurance policy or certificate of insurance and the invoice is the bill of lading.[86] The bill of lading must normally be transferable, cover the voyage continuously over an agreed or customary route, state the goods are shipped and not merely received for shipment be genuine in stating correct dates and not containing forgery, cover only the contract goods, be valid and effective and be 'clean', that is does not contain any adverse comment on the good order or condition of the good

6.14 Example of CIF Insurance Clauses

The third and most important document is the policy. As to the policy itself, it is not every policy that meets the CIF requirements. Rather the CIF insurance policy must be assignable, legally effective (not an honour or ppi policy), cover only the contract goods continuously over the route and be usual in the trade or as specified in the contract. If it is usual or agreed the seller will not be in breach if it fails to cover other risks, e.g. war risks.[87] The invoice must at least enable the buyer lo relate it to the contract but more detail may be required by the contract.

A sample CIF insurance would read like this:

> The seller shall obtain at his own costs cargo Insurance for the price of the goods plus 10% so that the buyer shall able to the claim directly from the insurance provide the buyer with the Insurance policy or other evidence of insurance cover. The insurer shall be of good reputed and the Insurance shall be in accordance with maximum cover of the cargo clauses embed by the institute of underwriters. The declaration of the insurance shall be from the delivery of the goods on board the ship at the port of shipment namely ….

[84] *Halsbury' Laws of England*, (5th edn 2012), Vol. 91 paras 347 and 348; (3rd edn *re issue*) case no 3359 (assignment of policy).

[85] For commercial invoice see *Halsbury's Laws of England,* (5th edn 2012), Vol. 91 para. 4349.

[86] Ibid.

[87] *Groom v Barber* (1915)1 KB 316, per Justice Atkin at p. 322.

This sample is taken from/based on Clause A5 of Incoterms 2020. Cargo clauses and commodity trade standard contracts have adopted similar clauses.

As already indicated, the insurance policy and the other documents (the bill of lading and invoice) may be substituted. The requirements as to documents may be modified by the contract, e.g. allowing a delivery order[88] on the ship of a 'received for shipment' bill of lading or a certificate of insurance[89] instead of a policy. The contract may also require other documents such as certificates of origin, quality, testing and the like. Depending on the nature of the particular contract, a number of other documents may accompany the CIF contract tender. These may include but are not necessarily limited to the following:

(a) Certificates [inspection, health, agricultural, etc.];
(b) Export and Import Licenses; and
(c) Declarations.

6.15 Comparative Status in International Trade

The CIF is one of the two principals in international sales' transactions; the other being FOB. The two have different variations and characteristics. Among the minor differences are the distinct characteristics and manner of performance and among the similarities are points of passage of property and risks and converging contemporary practices in tender of documents for payments. The FOB is thought to be the older of the two although now the less popular, accounting for about 40%, compared to 60% for CIF, in proportion of international sales' transactions carried by them. The principal difference between them is the insurance provision and the emphasis therein in each. Except for FOB, "with additional duties" or Extended FOB, the usual (*Classic* or *Strict*) FOB is devoid of freight and insurance obligations[90] whereas those functions are essential part of the CIF seller's duties.

To conclude, CIF and FOB contracts are the most important contracts in the field of International Trade. Both of them resemblance each other. However, CIF contract has a very significant difference from FOB contract. Mainly, under the CIF contract, the parties have to deal with delivery of documents and not actual physical delivery of goods by the seller. As a matter of fact, FOB contract is known as a flexible instrument which could be useful to International Trade companies while on the other hand, CIF contract is in demand much more than FOB contracts by companies in the field of International Trade.

---

[88] Delivery Order, see *Halsbury's Laws*, Vol. 91 para 339.

[89] Certificate of insurance in Halsbury's Laws of England, Vol. 91 see para 339.

[90] Sassoon (1967), p. 32; Wooldridge (1973), p. 383; Davis (1956); Sassoon (1981), p. 50; Evans (1993), p. 844; Gower (1956), p. 417.

6.16 Comparisons with the FOB Contracts

For a comparison of the CIF and FPB contracts see Chap. 3 FOB

6.16.1 With Classic, Strict and Simple FOB Contracts

In terms of their nature, CIF or CIP are both different from the FOB. As indicate above, historically the FOB was the first contract developed when there were no separate and independent insurance, shipping and banking institutions or facilities. Hence, at the time, the FOB buyer was the ship-owner and self-financier and self-insured. He paid for the goods in cash himself, was responsible for the freight and took upon himself the risks involved. It follows therefore that both the freight and insurance duties were redundant. Apart from a few changes in the "FOB *Classic*" and "*Extended FOB*" regarding shipping duties, those principal duties remain basically the same; that is in the normal FOB Classic, such as one contained in the INCOTERMS 2000, the seller does not have to take out either the shipping or the insurance contracts.[91] The parties' insurance obligations in the second category, simple (buyer contracting with carrier) FOB *Erg Raffinerie Mediterranee Spa v Chevron USA Inc*[92] and *Scottish and New Caste International Ltd v Othon Ghallanos Ltd*[93] are same as in strict or classic FOB.

6.16.2 With Extended and Other Social FOB Contracts

Where both insurance and freight form part of the additional duties, the "FOB with additional duties" or the "Extended FOB", will all but resemble the CIF contract. However, certain fundamental differences remain such as the CIF unique characteristics of almost being a contract for sale of documents rather than a sale of goods *Arnold v Blythe.*[94] In this case, Justice Scrutton opined that the CIF contract is not a sale of the goods themselves, but of the documents relating to the goods.[95]

The emphasis on delivery (tender) of documents rather than physical delivery of the goods and the availability of separate and independent remedies for rejection of goods and rejection of documents being the other distinguishing factors. There are many other ways by which, especially, the CIF differs from the FOB but these are

[91] See generally, Davis (1956); Ademuni-Odeke (2007), pp. 440–449; Schmitthoff (2012), pp. 19–22.

[92] *Raffinerie Mediterranee Spa v Chevron USA Inc* [2007] EWCA Civ. 494 (check page).

[93] *Scottish and New Caste International Ltd v Othon Ghallanos Ltd* [2008] 2 Lloyds Rep 662 (Ibid, at p. 20 check); see also *Erg Raffinerie Mediterranee Spa v Chevron USA Inc* [2007] EWCA Civ. 494 and *Scottish and New Caste International Ltd v Othon Ghallanos Ltd* [2008] 2 Lloyds Rep 662 both of which followed *Pyrene Co Ltd v Schindia Navigation Co Ltd* [1954]2 QB 402 at 424 and *The El Amria and El Minia* [1982]2 Lloyds 28 at 32 on the nature and types of FOB contracts.

[94] *Arnhold v Blythe* [1915] 2KB 379; Crawford (1995), p. 396; Ademuni-Odeke (1993), pp. 158–176.

[95] *Arnhold v Blythe* at 388.

beyond the remits of this book and have been ably dealt with elsewhere by this author.[96] Where the additional duties are only two (Carriage and Insurance) are involved then the FOB contract with additional duties would bear resemblance to CIP contract. It is also possible that these additional duties could form part of the FOB classic. Once again, the author has dealt with this subject elsewhere under "Extended" or "Additional Duties" FOB where the additional duties include freight and insurance in which those FOB insurance obligations nearly resemble those of the CIF contract.[97] Where the additional duties include freight and insurance; those FOB insurance obligations nearly resemble those of the CIF contract.[98]

6.17 Under, 'Incoterms for Americans Guidelines'

Although North American concepts differ slightly from the common law position, US and Canadian law and practice, regarding delivery obligations and risks, is not very different from those of the English law. As indicated immediately above, US CIF Insurance, for instance, is under the UCC[99] and Canadian law by case law. The US Incoterms insurance obligation is also almost the same as in normal UK/Europe above.[100] However, in his explanations, Reynolds explains that:

> Insurance is a seller's obligation under CIF. However, only minimum cover (commonly 'free of particular average') is required by the Incoterm. Since this is inadequate in most situations, the buyer and seller should agree to additional coverage outside the Incoterm.
>
> If both seller and buyer have insurance in place to cover their respective pre-carriage and on-carriage risks, a form of 'with average' insurance covering main- carriage only may be sufficient. However, this is risky in that one or the other party may slip up.
>
> "All Risk" coverage provides excellent coverage. It is usually written warehouse to warehouse (pre-carriage, main-carriage, and on-carriage). However, it should be called "almost all risks" since it usually doesn't cover war or strikes and civil commotion. Both of this supplemental coverage is available, usually at a very modest additional cost. The amount of should be 110% of the CIF value, unless both parties agree to a different amount.[101]

In *St. Paul Guardian Insurance Company and Travelers Insurance Company*, as subrogees of *Shared Imaging, Inc., Plaintiffs v. Neuromed Medical Systems & Support, GmbH, et al.*, Defendants,[102] a contract governed by the CISG, was held it

[96] See Ademuni-Odeke (2007).

[97] Ibid, at pp. 440–449.

[98] Ibid, at pp. 443–445.

[99] Ibid.

[100] Reynolds (2010) (Reynolds, "*Incoterms for Americans*", Commentary No 9, p. 80).

[101] Ibid.

[102] *United States District Court for the Southern District of New York 00 Civ. 934* (SHS) 26 March 2002, http://www.cisg.law.pace.edu/cases/020326u1.html.

to be sufficient to validly incorporate the term 'CIF' as defined by the Incoterms into the contract.

6.18 Comparison with the C& F Contract

The common law C&F[103] is also known as CFR under Incoterms 2020 This means cost and freight and is where the seller is providing a price which includes the cost of the goods and of the freight, but NOT insurance. The seller's obligations were considered by Justice Donaldson in *M Golodetz & Co Inc v Czanikow-Rionda Co Inc (The Galatia):*[104]

> As between the shipowner and the shipper (including those claiming through the shipper as holders of the bill of lading) the crucial time is shipment. The shipowner's prime obligation is to deliver the goods at the contractual destination in the like good order and condition as when shipped. The cleanliness of the bill of lading may give rise to an estoppel and the terms of the bill of lading contract may exempt the shipowner from a breach of this obligation, but everything stems from the state of the goods as shipped. As between seller and C.I.F. or c. & f. buyer, the property and risk normally pass upon the negotiation of the bill of lading but do so as from shipment. Thus, the fact that the ship and goods have been lost after shipment or that a liability to contribute in general average or salvage has arisen is no reason for refusing to take up and pay for the documents.[105]

In payment of the freight, except insurance, in *Norsk Bjergningskompagni A/S v SS Pantanasa (Owners), her cargo & freight, (The Pantanassa),*[106] *the* C&f contract was treated the same as the CIF by Justice Brandon thus:

> In my view, the payment of freight contemplated by the contracts of sale is, as in other cif or c & f contracts under which freight collect bills of lading are used, payment of bill of lading freight to the ship against delivery of the goods and not payment to the charterers or the charterers' bank, in case delivery should never take place..[107]

Therefore, it is similar to CIF but does not include insurance of the goods on their journey to the buyer. Term of sale signifying that the price invoiced or quoted by a seller for a shipment does not include insurance charges, but includes all expenses up to a named port of destination. In comparison, CPT terms include all transport charges (but not insurance) up to a named place (usually the buyer's warehouse) of destination. See also CIF. The seller pays for the carriage of the goods up to the named port of destination. Risk transfers to buyer when the goods have been loaded on board the ship in the country of Export. The shipper is responsible for origin

[103] *Halsbury's Laws of England* (5th edn 2012) Vol. 91 para. 361.

[104] *M Golodetz & Co Inc v Czanikow-Rionda Co Inc (The Galatia)*, [1979] 2 Lloyd's Rep. 450.

[105] Ibid at p. 856 per Justice Donaldson at p. 510.

[106] *Norsk Bjergningskompagni A/S v SS Pantanasa* (Owners), her cargo & freight (*The Pantanassa*) [1970]1 All ER 848.

[107] Ibid at 855.

costs including export clearance and freight costs for carriage to named port. The shipper is not responsible for delivery to the final destination from the port (generally the buyer's facilities), or for buying insurance. If the buyer does require the seller to obtain insurance, the Incoterm CIF should be considered. CFR should only be used for non-containerized seafreight; for all other modes of transport it should be replaced with CPT. Note that the American UCC treats the C&F the same as the CIF. Its insurance obligations are covered in Chaps. 7 and 8 (post).

6.19 Frustration of CIF Contracts

Frustration under English law and force majeure under continental civil laws affect CIF contracts in the way that differs from other contracts. At one time export bans could not be pleaded as a ground of frustration in C.I.F. contracts since the seller could always purchase goods afloat to perform,[108] but purchase afloat seems now rare so that such bans may now frustrate the contract. Lord Denning MR added to this in *Tradax v Andre*[109] that: "A prohibition of export is well within the term 'force majeure'...provided that the sellers proved the prohibition did prevent their fulfilling the contract."[110] as did Viscount Dilhorne in *Czarnikow v Rolimpex*[111] that:

> It is in my opinion clear beyond all doubt that delivery of the sugar in pursuance of the contracts within the delivery time was prevented by the intervention of the government of Poland. It is, I think, equally clear that the action taken by the government was beyond Rolimpex's control. Rule 18(a) [of the Rules of London Refined Sugar Association] clearly requires it to be established if the force majeure relied on is government intervention. It does not stipulate that, if there is such intervention, one has to go on to consider for what purpose the intervention was made.[112]

However, the effect of frustration and force majeure may be affected by parties' negligence. For instance, a C.I.F. buyer who is unable to sue in contract because he is not holding the bill of lading may sue in negligence for damage to the cargo.[113]

6.20 Remedies Under CIF and Related Contracts

The first remedy of a CIF buyer is rejection.[114] First, he has a right to reject the documents when they arrive, normally before the goods. Among reasons for rejection of documents are: non-conformity with letters of credit, *The Julia* type examples

[108] *Vantol v Fairclough v Dodd* [1956] 3 All ER 750.

[109] *Tradax v Andre* [1976] 1 Lloyd's Rep 416.

[110] Ibid at p. 421.

[111] *Czarnikow v Rolimpex* [1978] 2 All ER 1043, at pp. 1049, 1050 (*Force Majeure*).

[112] Ibid at pp. 1049, 1050 (*Force Majeure*).

[113] *Shiffart unds Kohlen v Chelsea Maritime, (The Irene Success)* [1982] I All ER 218.

[114] See para. 360 for remedies for breach of CIF contracts and 358 for right of rejection.

where the insurance policy does not enable the buyer to sue the carrier for loss or damage or to claim directly from the insurer.[115]

Secondly, and without losing the right to reject documents, he can independently reject the goods when they arrive.[116] Among possible reasons for rejection of the goods are: non-delivery, short delivery, late delivery, miss-description, and other general non-conformity with the contract contained in s.12–14 of the *SGA* 1979. Thirdly, he can still sue for damages where he was tricked to accept wrong documents. The buyer can also plead frustration, or force majeure in Europe, of the contract. Furthermore, according to Justice Lloyd in *Shiffart und Kohlen v Chelsea Marine (The Irene Success),*[117] a CIF buyer who is unable to sue in contract because he is not holding a bill of lading may sue in negligence for damages to the cargo.

Justice Lloyd said:

> The plaintiffs cannot sue in contract, since they never became holders of the bill of lading. The question is whether they can sue in tort, even though they were not the owners of the goods when the damage was caused... Thus, the first question is whether there is a sufficient relationship of proximity between the plaintiffs as cif buyers and the defendants as ocean carriers, such that the defendants ought reasonably to have contemplated that carelessness on their part in carrying the goods would be likely to cause damage to the plaintiffs. It seems to me that the answer to that first question can only be Yes.[118]

The *Hadley v Baxendale*[119] principle that an injured party may recover those damages reasonably considered to arise naturally from a breach of contract, or those damages within the reasonable contemplation of the parties at the time of contracting damages, apply to CIF contracts.

6.21 Further Food for Thoughts

6.21.1 General-Advantages

The advantages of the CIF over all other contracts are overwhelming. However, there are aspects that needs food for thoughts which might affect especially the seller's rights for which he might not necessarily have recourse to insurance or other immediate remedies. Babu, for instance, thinks one of the problems is that moreover sometime the CIF term in contract seems to be very vague, while determining whether it is a CIF contract or not. For example, where the goods are shipped in bulk and remain unascertained until the ships arrival, in that case the documents cannot

[115] Ibid, for a more detailed discussion on remedies in CIF contracts, see *Benjamin on Sale of Goods*, paragraphs 19-144–19-220 at pp. 1574–1652.

[116] See Note 113 above.

[117] *Shiffart und Kohlen v Chelsea Marine (The Irene Success)* [1982] 1All ER 218.

[118] Ibid at per Justice Lloyd at pp. 220, 221.

[119] *Hadley v Baxendale* (1854) 9 Ex 341.

cover the goods sold. In those scenarios the question arises whether this is an CIF contract after passing of documents or is it an 'arrived' or ex ship contract.

6.21.2 Passage of Risks and CIF Insurance

The seller has the advantage of receiving the transacting money well in before the goods actually reach the buyer. The advantage of the buyer is that he has a substantial right once he gets the documents of sale and he may still reject the goods on their actual delivery if they turn out to be not in conformity with the standards he had prescribed. The risk which he takes is that the loss or damage of goods may not be covered by the bill of lading or insurance policy. The main disadvantages of CIF contract are that risk passes to the buyer at the time of contract. S20 of the *SGA* 1979 provides that, after delivery of the goods risk passes to the buyer, but in the CIF contract risk passes to the buyer at the time he Pays and takes up the document.

On the other hand, risk passes to the buyer when the seller ships the goods. However, if the contract is made after the shipment risk passes at the time of contract. This seems to be very harsh on the buyer. Moreover, the risk passes to the buyer at the time of shipment, if the goods are damaged while loading into the cargo or the goods are lost in the sea, though the seller knew that, the goods might be lost when he tenders the shipping document. Where the goods are unascertained and shipped in bulk in that case the documents can not identified the goods sold. Hence the CIF contract sometimes seems to be very vague.

6.21.3 Passage of Property and CIF Insurance

According to the general rule, the property and the risk passes at the same time but this is not the usual case in a C.I.F. contract. Under a C.I.F. contract, the buyer is in effect the insurer, as of the time of shipment. The transfer to him of the bill of lading and the policy of insurance giving him the right of action in respect of loss or damage to the goods has the effect of placing the goods at his risk on and after shipment. But the property in the goods may not, and generally does not, pass on shipment. It very often will not pass until tender and payment. The moment at which the property passes is entirely a matter of intention which can be gathered from the terms of the contract, the parties' conduct and according to the circumstances of the case.

6.21.4 Sale of Goods or Documents

The importance of the documents in CIF contracts is illustrated by the rule that allows the seller to tender documents even after the goods they represent have been damaged or lost. It seems incredulous that such a rule could exist and even if it did exist that the sale was for the goods and not the documents. If the goods were utmost importance and were to all intents and purpose the subject matter of the contract then this rule would not exist. It seems impossible to argue otherwise than that a CIF is a sale documents when we consider that the documents are key to all elements of the contract and they are central to shaping parties' duties, defining when risk passes, and determining the condition of the goods. It is this document on which the entire contract is based. The importance of the documents in CIF contracts is illustrated by the rule that allows the seller to tender documents even after the goods damaged or lost. It seems unbelievable that such a rule could exist and even if it did exist that the sale was for the goods and not the documents.

If the goods were utmost importance and were to all intents and purpose the subject matter of the contract then this rule would not exist. It seems impossible to argue otherwise than that a CIF is a sale documents when we consider that the documents are key to all elements of the contract and they are central to shaping parties' duties, defining when risk passes, and determining the condition of the goods. The seller has the advantage of receiving the transacting money well in before the goods actually reach the buyer. The advantage of the buyer is that he has a substantial right once he gets the documents of sale and he may still reject the goods on their actual delivery if they turn out to be not in conformity with the standards he had prescribed. The risk which he takes is that the loss or damage of goods may not be covered by the bill of lading or insurance policy.

Thus, due to its nature (sale and purchase afloat and dependence on insurance and documentation), CIF has been likened to a sale of documents rather than that of goods.[120] As the effectiveness of the CIF contract depends on the transfer of the documents which give the buyer control, and a right of disposal of the goods, and rights to recover compensation if they are damaged due to the default of the carrier[121] or due to some insured peril it is concluded that this is fact a sale of documents[122]

6.21.5 Effect of the Two Rights of Rejection on CIF Insurance

A buyer can reject documents which do not comply with the contract for instance, if the bill is claused, showing that the goods were not in good condition when loaded, dated outside the shipment period or discloses deficiencies in quantity; or if an insurance certificate is tendered instead of policy. It is difficult to think of other sales contracts of any description which are akin to this procedure. The right to reject the document is lost if the byer takes up the documents, even though inaccurate and pays the price without objection. Moreover, if a defect in the goods is

[120] Ademuni-Odeke: Law of International Trade; "CIF Contracts: is it a sale of goods or documents", para 3.6 pp. 72-84.

[121] Ibid; see also: Bridge (1999); Bradgate (2003); Chuah (2001); Ademuni-Odeke (1999); Sealey and Hooley (2003). Journal Clauses: Treitel (1984), p. 565; Treitel (1988), p. 457.

[122] On Critical Evaluation Whether a CIF Contract Is a Contract for the Sale of Documents or a Sale of Goods Related in International Trade Law, see: https://www.lawteacher.net/free-law-essays/general-law/saleofdocuments.php.

apparent on the face of the documents, the byer who accepts the documents will also be unable to reject the goods themselves on arrival for that defect. A byer cannot reject his property on completion if on exchange of contracts that defect was obviously contend in the contract, so for example if the price was incorrect this should have been raised at exchange of contract as opposed to completion. Unsurprisingly the rights of the buyer to reject goods in a CIF are a lot less meaningful than those relating to the documents.

Shamin reasons rightly that the right to reject in CIF really is a right to reject documents and not goods.[123] The buyer will accept the document if he deals with them before the goods arrive, for instance, by using them to resell or pledge the good. A buyer who deals with the documents in this way therefor loses the right to reject the goods themselves for defects apparent from the documents.[124] Although all the c.i.f. advantages, there are certain problems or disadvantages that must be noted. Since the buyer must pay upon presentation of proper documents, he will generally be unable to reject the documents on the grounds that non-conforming goods were shipped. On the other hand, he will be in a position to reject non-conforming documents even when the seller has shipped conforming goods. While it is true to say that the seller does not assume an obligation physically to deliver the goods to the buyer, it is not true to say that the seller does not owe the buyer any duties in relation to the conformity of the goods with the terms of the contract. It is accepted that the buyer has two rights of rejection, namely the right to reject the documents and the right to reject the goods.

6.22 Concluding Remarks

Unlike the FOB, the CIF is a much later creature whose development was determined by technological and other developments in transportation (shipping), communication (telegraph), insurance (emergence of insurance companies) and banking especially the emergence of letters of credit, inter alia. For those reasons it became reliant on the:

(a) Symbolic transfer of goods by documents rather than the physical delivery of goods as in the FOB;
(b) Buying and selling afloat;
(c) And dependence on insurance which underpins the whole lot;
(d) In the process it acquired other related characteristics such as need for appropriation;
(e) Two independent and separate rights of rejections (documents and goods);

[123] Shamin: Critically Evaluate Whether a CIF Contract Is a Contract for the Sale of Documents or a Sale of Goods Related in International Trade Law—https://www.lawteacher.net/free-law-essays/general-law/saleofdocuments.php.

[124] Ibid.

(f) Purchase and sale afloat and, therefore, the notoriety of sale of documents rather than goods;
(g) Rigidity and certainty; and
(h) Variants rather than types of classes.

These quite different characteristics in the two contracts are evident in the two principal representative cases of *Pyrene v Scindia (followed in El Amria and El Minia)* and *The Julia*. These distinct characteristics was to later shape the parties' respective insurance obligations (Chaps. 4–5 above for the FOB) and (Chaps. 7–8 ahead for the CIF) such as the requirement for seller to provide insurance and quite elaborate common last rules now embodied in Clause A3(b) of all Incoterms since their inceptions.

6.23 Further Readings

Major Publications

- Sassoon, CIF *and FOB Contracts,* (5th edn 2012) Sweet & Maxwell/ Thomson Reuters
- Schmitthoff, Export Trade
- Benjamin's Sale of Goods (7th edn 2006), Sweet & Maxwell/Thomson Reuters
- Halsbury's Laws of England (5th edn 2012), Vol.91 (Sale of Goods and Supply of Services)
- Halsbury's Laws of England (5th edn 2012), Vol.60 (Insurance)
- Indira, International Trade Law, (5th edn, Routledge 2014), [Taylor and Francis Group] chapter 1
- Chuah, J. Law of International Trade. (London: Sweet & Maxwell, 2001) second edition
- Crockford, Neil (General Editor): Insuring Foreign Risks (Loose-leaf), Sweet & Maxwell Thomson-Reuters, London 2013.
- John Dunt, Marine Cargo Insurance, Informa Law, 2009
- K.S. Insuring Cargoes, A practical guide to the law and practice, Witherby Insurance, 2010, Edinburgh
- Bridge, M. The International Sale of Goods: Law and Practice. (Oxford: Oxford University Press, 1999)
- Bradgate R Commercial Law (London: Butterworths Lexis-Nexis 2003)
- Ademuni Odeke Law of International Trade. (London: Blackstone Press, 1999)
- Sealey, L.S. and R.J.A. Hooley Commercial Law Text, Cases and Materials. (London: Butterworths, 2003) third edition
- Ewan McKendrick C.I.F. Contract, 1st Edition 2000 Imprint Informa Law from Routledge

Journals

- David Sassoon, "The Origin of FOB and CIF: Terms and Factors influencing choice" [1967] JBL 32
- David Sassoon, "Application of FOB and CIF Sales in Common Law Countries" [1981] ETL 50
- Evans, "FOB and CIF Contracts" [1993] *ALJ* 844;
- Gower, "FOB Contracts", (1956) 19 *MLR*, 417;
- Peters, "Remedies for Breach of Contracts Relating to the Sale of Goods under the Uniform Commercial Code: A Roadmap for Clause Two" *The Yale Law Journal*, Vol. 73, No. 2 (Dec., 1963), pp. 199-287
- Philip W. Thayer, "C. I. F. Contracts in International Commerce" *Harvard Law Review* Vol. 53, No. 5 (Mar., 1940), pp. 792-826.
- Oduntan, Gbenga, *"C.I.F. Gatwick' and Other Such Nonsense Upon Stilts: Incoterms and the Law, Jargon and Practice of International Business Transactions",* International Company and Commercial Law Review, 21 (6). (2010) pp. 214-223.
- Grewal, Shivbir S., "Risk of Loss in Goods Sold during Transit: A Comparative Study of the U.N. Convention on Contracts for the International Sale of Goods, the U.C.C., and the British Sale of Goods Act", 14 *Loy. L.A. Int'l & Comp.* L.J. 93 (1991-1992)
- Tetley, William, "Who May Claim or Sue for Cargo Loss or Damage - Part II"; 17 J. Mar. L. & Com. 407 (1986)
- Treitel, "Damages for breach of a CIF contract", [1988] LMCLQ 457
- Treitel, "Rights of rejection under a CIF sale", [1984] LMCLQ565
- Crawford, Henry Paine "Analysis and Operation of a C.I.F. Contract", 29 Tul. L. Rev. 3 (1954-1955)
- Crawford, Note, "Analysis and operation of CIF Contract" [1995] Tulane LR 396;
- Ademuni-Odeke, "The Nature of CIF Contract- Is it a Sale of Documents or Goods?" 6(2) JCL, pp. 158-176 (1993)
- Ademuni-Odeke, "CIF and CIP under Incoterms 1990", (check)
- K.N.L. "C. I. F. Contracts in American Law", *The Yale Law Journal* Vol. 32, No. 7 (May, 1923), pp. 711-720
- Sakshi Agarwal (Cost, Insurance and Freight) CIF Contracts October 17, 2018 https://lawtimesjournal.in/cif-contracts
- Law Teacher: "Critically Evaluate Whether a CIF Contract Is a Contract for the Sale of Documents or a Sale of Goods Related in International Trade Law" https://www.lawteacher.net/free-law-essays/general-law/saleofdocuments.php
- M. G. Bridge "Documents and cif contracts" Amicus Curiae, 1998 (3). pp. 4-6. https://journals.sas.ac.uk/amicus/article/view/1622
- "CIF Contracts in International Commerce", *53 Harv. L. Rev.* 792 (1939-1940)
- L. C. B. Gower C. I. F. Contracts *The Modern Law Review* Vol. 12, No. 2 (Apr., 1949), pp. 241-245 (5 pages)
- Aedit Abdulla, "Issues in the Transfer of Risks in CIF Contracts" 14 Sing. L. Rev. 151 (1993)

- U Asanwana, & O Efombruh, "Understanding FOB and CIF Contracts: And When Property and Risk Pass in These Transactions" Available at SSRN 3278642, 2018 - papers.ssrn.com
- M Darabpour, "CIF Contracts and the Terms Contrary to Their Standards" *Journal of Private Law Research*, 2013 - jplr.atu.ac.ir

Theses

- Galdes, M. (2001). The obligations of the seller in C.I.F. contracts (Master's dissertation). University of Malta

Websites

- Tariq Idais, "CIF CONTRACTS IN INTERNATIONAL SALES OF GOODS", http://www.tamimi.com/en/magazine/law-update/section-5/july-august-2/cif-contracts-in-international-sales-of-goods.html#sthash.47PQaB1F.dpuf
- *M. G. Bridge* "Documents and cif contracts" DOI: https://doi.org/10.14296/ac.v1998i3.1622
- Law Teacher, "Critically assess the rule on the relation to CIF and FOB contracts", http://www.lawteacher.net/free-law-essays/contract-law/cif-and-fob-contracts.php#ixzz3fKCGpGAr
- Stuart Shepherd, Jane Fitzgerald "Delivery Obligations under CIF Contracts", *International Trade & Commodities* incelaw.com/en/knowledge.../delivery-obligations-under-cif-contract
- Dionysios Flambouras, "Transfer of Risk in the Contract of Sale involving Carriage of Goods: A Comparative Study in English, Greek Law and the United Nations Convention on Contracts for the International Sale of Goods", www.jus.uio.no/pace/transfer_of_risk_contract.../_13.html
- Rami Al Tal, "United Arab Emirates: The Nature of CIF Contracts", www.mondaq.com/x/117852/cycling.../The+Nature+Of+CIF+Contracts
- Alastair C.L. Mullis, "Termination for Breach of Contract in C.I.F. Contracts Under the Vienna Convention and English Law; Is There a Substantial Difference?" www.cisg.law.pace.edu/cisg/biblio/mullis.html
- "The Essence of the CIF Contract Law", www.uniassignment.com, Essay Samples
- Ademuni-Odeke, "The Nature of the CIF Contract, whether it is a Sale of Documents or Goods" [1993] JCL
- Sales. "'C.I.F' Contracts. Risk of Shipment on the Buyer" *The Yale Law Journal*, Vol.30, No.1 (Nov., 1920), pp. 90-

References

Ademuni-Odeke (1993) The nature of CIF contract- is it a sale of documents or goods? JCL 6(2):158–176

Ademuni-Odeke (1999) Law of international trade. Blackstone Press, London

Ademuni-Odeke (2007) Insurance of FOB contracts in Anglo-American and common law jurisdictions revisited. Tul MLJ 31(1)
Bradgate R (2003) Commercial law. Butterworths Lexis-Nexis, London
Bridge M (1999) The international sale of goods: law and practice. Oxford University Press, Oxford
Chuah J (2001) Law of international trade, 2nd edn. Sweet & Maxwell, London
Crawford N (1995) Analysis and operation of CIF contract. TLR 396
Davis (1956) The various types of FOB contracts. JBL
Evans (1993) FOB and CIF contracts. ALJ 844
Gower (1956) FOB contracts. MLR 19:417
Reynolds F (2010) Incoterms for Americans. International Projects Inc., Toledo
Sassoon (1967) The origin of FOB and CIF: terms and factors influencing choice. JBL 32
Sassoon D (1981) Application of FOB and CIF sales in common law countries. ETL 50
Sassoon (2012) CIF and FOB contracts, 5th edn. Sweet & Maxwell
Schmitthoff C (2012) The law and practice of international trade, 12th edn. Sweet and Maxwell
Sealey LS, Hooley RJA (2003) Commercial law – text, cases and materials, 3rd edn. Butterworths, London
Treitel (1984) Rights of rejection under c.i.f. sales. LMCLQ 565
Treitel (1988) Damages for breach of a c.i.f. contract. LMCLQ 457
Wooldridge F (1973) The kinds of FOB contracts. In: Law and international trade. Festschrift fur Clive e M Schmitthoff, Frankfurt

Insurance of Contracts that Include the Seller's Obligations to Provide Insurance to the Buyer at Common Law

7

Abstract

Like Chap. 4, this chapter is dedicated to the sellers' obligations to provide insurance to the buyer at common law, which makes the obligations the same as under Incoterms. The chapter treats the subject under the following Insurance Policy; Other role of the policy; Insurance as a Marine Cargo Policy; Insurable Interest in the Policy; American CIF Policy under Acceptant of the Common Law Obligations; Preliminary Issues in the CIF Policy; Assignment of the CIF Policy; The *Minimum Cover* vs the "All Risks" Policy; Express vs Implied Value Cover; Implied vs Sufficient Value; The *Minimum* 110% vs *Maximum* Coverage Policy; The Included vs the Excluded Policy Costs; The Arrival vs Shipment Value; Whether CIF Buyer is entitled to Notice to insure unusual risk; Duration of the CIF Policy; Relationship of Domestic to Foreign Policy; Constitution of the Valid vs Approved Policy; Other Insurance Considerations; Damages for Breach of Insurance Obligations; "Further Food for Thoughts"; Concluding Remarks; References; and Further Readings.

7.1 Introduction

The previous chapter (Chap. 6) laid the background of the nature and characteristics of the CIF and related contracts which ultimately affects the parties' insurance obligations. That was a forerunner to discussions on CIF insurance in this chapter. This chapter covers the subject under the principal sub-headings listed above. It also includes some comparisons of the practice between the Anglo-American and other common law jurisdictions. As will be apparent in Chap. 8 (post), these common law traditions and principles influenced Incoterms. Once more, the only contract under this category is the CIF, the CIP being a relatively new invention.

P. Ademuni-Odeke, *Insurance of International Sales' Contracts under Incoterms*, Law for Professionals, https://doi.org/10.1007/978-3-031-75136-3_7

7.2 Central Role of the Policy

7.2.1 Policy Central to the Contract

What makes the CIF contract unique, in contrast to the FOB and related contracts, is the pivotal role of insurance. It is the linchpin of the contract. Although the bill of lading is regarded as the most important document for the symbolic delivery of the goods, nevertheless the fabric of the CIF contract is the underpinning provided by the insurance policy. It is for those reasons, and only those reasons, that sellers were able to tender documents, in *The Galatia,*[1] *Groom v Barber,*[2] *Manbre v Corn Products*[3] and related cases on goods even though lost or damaged after shipment.[4] It is also due to the protection provided by insurance that parties are allowed to buy and sale afloat. In addition, and naturally, it is due to that feature that law and practice puts emphasis on the documents and which gives rise to the assumption that the CIF could be a sale of documents rather than goods. Hence, the principle of the *Julia*[5] that, inter alia, in the CIF contract the seller must put the buyer in a position that he can claim directly by himself from the insurer or from the carrier in the event of damages, with subrogation rights to the insurers. If he fails to then he has not performed the CIF contract.

7.2.2 The Essence of the CIF Insurance

Since insurance is of the essence in CIF contracts, this chapter focuses on the subject at length, touching on both responsibilities to insure, liability for failure to and other breaches. Responsibility for insurance arises from contractual obligations but liability for failure to do so, insufficient insurance or breaches of other contractual obligations might vary. For those reasons, the CIF sale contract should clearly state the functions to be performed and the type of insurance to be provided. Otherwise, the CIF is one of only two Incoterms which contains an obligation to provide insurance. The other term is CIP. However, that raises three paradoxes (below) First, although the seller agrees to pay all costs and freight to the port of destination, his responsibility for delivery ends when the goods have been delivered on board the overseas vessel at the port of shipment. There is, therefore, an apparent conflict between the end of shipment and the arrival of the goods at destination. And yet it is technically not an arrival contract. The same situation is the same for FOB and CFR terms.

---

[1] *Golodetz (M) & Co v Czarnikow-Rionda Co Inc* (*The Galatia*) [1979] 2 All ER 726.

[2] *Groom (C) Ltd v Barber* [1915] 1KB 316.

[3] *Manbre Saccharine Co Corn Products Co* [1919] 1KB 198; see note 35 below for details (check).

[4] See Chap. 3 on tender of documents for lost goods and *Groom v Barber*; *The Galatia and Manbre v Corn Products*.

[5] *The Julia* [1949] AC 293.

Secondly, although the buyer is responsible for loss or damage during the "main carriage", under CIF terms the seller agrees to provide insurance for the buyer's account. Therefore, CIF shipments are in effect insured under the seller's rather than the buyer's policy. And yet it should normally be the other way round.

Thirdly, as will be apparent in Chap. 8 (post), Incoterms provides that "lacking agreement, minimum cover of the Institute Cargo Clauses be provided". This reflects the common law position too. However, this is essentially only "named perils" or "minimal coverage" which is rarely adequate for the needs of the buyer, a position only corrected by additional insurance through contractual extensions or at the buyer's request. Thus, the provision for insurance in CIF contracts can lead to possible conflicts.[6]

However, areas of non-conflicts include that insurance must also be in negotiable form enabling losses to be payable to the buyer or other party having an insurable interest in the shipment at the time of loss. Proof, or evidence, of insurance is required which is usually accomplished by issuance of the policy, certificate of insurance, letters of insurance, cover note (for proof only, not for tender) and related documents[7] by the seller or his insurer. In addition, insurance should cover the shipment from the place of origin to the final destination of the buyer.

7.2.3 Formation of the CIF Policy

The CIF insurance policy like any insurance and every other contract, is formed when there is an offer made, that offer is accepted, and consideration (payment or a promise to pay premium) is given. In a diversity action, a federal court must apply the choice-of-law rules of the forum state. Formation and sources of CIF insurance is the same as for the FOB above[8]

7.2.4 Application of Institute Clauses to CIF Insurance

Institute Clauses' application to the CIF insurance is also the same as for the FOB insurance.[9] However, there are specific characteristics of the CIF policy at common law as listed below.

First, it is a marine cargo policy.

---

[6] See Chap. 8 which deals with other insurance considerations intended to solve the problem.

[7] Some of the documents are covered under this chapter and others under Chap. 10 on tender of the documents.

[8] See para 2.13 for sources of the export insurance and para. 4-17 ante, for formation of the contract.

[9] See paras 4-005–4-014.

7.3 Insurance as a Marine Cargo Policy

7.3.1 The CIF Policy Is a Marine Cargo Policy

A CIF policy is a marine policy. As noted in Chap. 2, marine insurance against perils is an important aspect of international commercial transactions. In the event of loss or damage to cargo due to hazards during voyage, an insured party will be able to recover losses from the insurer. The type of insurance required depends on the mode of transport agreed between parties to transport the cargo. Such insurance forms include marine, aviation and land. The type of insurance contract depends on the common law or Incoterms, commodity trades and Institute Cargo Clauses adopted by the parties in a sale contract. A CIF sale contract requires the seller to obtain insurance cover for the voyage. This is in contrast to the FOB contract however places no obligation on the buyer or seller to obtain insurance, although it is prudent for the buyer to protect against potential losses. Although it is not uncommon for the FOB buyer to request the seller to arrange insurance on an understanding that they will reimburse the insurance costs incurred. It will be apparent below that the insurance obtained must cover only those goods that are being sold and stipulated in shipping documents. The insurance must also cover the entire voyage of the sale contract. Where it covers only party of the transit, the buyer will be able to reject the documents upon tender.

Marine insurance contracts, the mainstay in the CIF export/import insurance, may be divided into hull, aviation or cargo insurance all of which affect export trade insurance. Although UNCTAD attempted to introduce one,[10] there is no uniform law or convention for international marine insurance. However, commercial customs, usage and practices in international marine insurance have played a significant role in regulating marine insurance internationally. Thus, the marine insurance contract, basis of FOB/CIF insurances, is subject to both general principles of contract law and relevant domestic marine insurance law. Other export trade transportation modes use the marine insurance principles and documentation. That is why aviation, road, rail and multimodal transports (principal CIF conveyors) insurance contracts all include marine cargo insurance. The various transport modes of apply own international transport conventions. These conventions together provide guidance to domestic and international export insurance ranging from FOB, CIF and related contracts. The insurance may be issued to independent exporters and importers or to those transacting on commodity trade rules.

Secondly, the general principles of marine insurance apply to the CIF.

7.3.2 Application of Marine Insurance Principles to the Policy

The general principles of insurance applicable to FOB and CIF were dealt with in Chap. 2 above. Others are covered in Chap. 13 on Claims and Settlements. It should

[10] See generally, UNCTAD Secretariat (1982).

be added that in the UK and most common law jurisdictions, export policy is governed by the principles of the MIA 1906 either in its original form or as modified. MIA 1906 applies to CIF insurance. As such, the CIF policy is subject to all the principles, doctrines and rules contained in the Act. For instance, both the CIF seller and buyer should have insurable interests in the subject matter insured, capacity to contract and make marine insurance contracts. They are also bound by the utmost good faith duties of disclosure and non-disclosure, representations and misrepresentations. Furthermore, the CIF policy is subject to other marine insurance principles such as proximate cause, conditions and warranties, payment of premium, types and rules as to policies, types and rules as to losses, doctrine of abandonment, subrogation in claims process and related insurance principles. The rest of the chapter is devoted to CIF insurance and case law thereto, while Chap. 8 deals with CIF insurance at Incoterms.

Thirdly, the CIF policy is subject to insurable interest rule.

7.4 Insurable Interest in CIF Policy

As in all insurance contracts both CIF seller and buyer should at some point have insurable interest in the shipment; the seller until delivery and the buyer and his assignees after that. Risks pass at shipment and property at tender of the document in which case the seller's interest might continue up to this point. The buyer and sub-buyers in sales afloat derive their interest from the original buyer. This in contrast to the FOB contract, where risks and property pass at shipment when sellers interest also terminates. This rule might be varied by the seller exercising retention of tile clause.

The Canadian and most common law jurisdiction follow English common law. How does that compare to the American law?

7.5 American CIF Insurance Policy

7.5.1 Federal Level: Parties' General Obligations Under the UCC

The US law[11] and practice is not very different from those of the UK law except for the former's codification into the UCC; and the codification making no distinction between the CIF and C&F or C.F. On the nature and definition of the CIF and C&F s 2-30(1) of the UCC provides that:

[11]The US CIF is covered in U.C.C. Clause 2—Sales (2002) "Part 3. General Obligation and Construction Of Contract" § 2-320. C.I.F. and C. & F. Terms. § 2-320. C.I.F. and C. & F. Terms.

S 2-30(1) of the UCC

"(1) The term C.I.F. means that the price includes in a lump sum the cost of the goods and the insurance and freight to the named destination. The term C. & F. or C.F. means that the price so includes cost and freight to the named destination"

(2) The seller must:

(a) (omitted)

(b) (omitted)

(c) (omitted)

(d) prepare an invoice of the goods and procure any other documents required to effect shipment or to comply with the contract; and

(e) forward and tender with commercial promptness all the documents in due form and with any indorsement necessary to perfect the buyer's rights.

(3) (Omitted)

(4) Under the term C.I.F. or C. & F. unless otherwise agreed the buyer must make payment against tender of the required documents and the seller may not tender nor the buyer demand delivery of the goods in substitution for the documents.

The section captures the gist of the English common law provisions on the nature, insurance, payments, documentation and tender in CIF contracts.

7.5.2 Federal Level: Parties' Insurance Provisions

With specific reference to insurance s.2-30(2) of the UCC, once more closely follows English common law practice in providing that:

S.2-30(2) of the UCC

(2) Unless otherwise agreed and even though used only in connection with the stated price and destination, the term C.I.F. destination or its equivalent requires the seller at his own expense and risk to:

(a) (Omitted)

(b) (Omitted)

(c) obtain a policy or certificate of insurance, including any war risk insurance, of a kind and on terms then current at the port of shipment in the usual amount, in the currency of the contract, shown to cover the same goods covered by the bill of lading and providing for payment of loss to the order of the buyer or for the account of whom it may concern; but the seller may add to the price the amount of the premium for any such war risk insurance

Most states have adopted the Federal Code. One particular example, which will be used for guidance in this chapter, is that of the *Ohio State Revised Code* 2006.[12]

7.5.3 State Level: The Ohio Revised Code 2006—1302.32

The *Ohio State Revised Code's* insurance provision is the same as that at federal level.[13] This in turn largely mirrors the position below under English common law and Incoterms' law and practice with regard to the:

(a) seller's obligations;
(b) role of the policy and certificate of insurance;
(c) extent of the war risk insurance;
(d) terms current at port of shipment;
(e) currency of the policy;
(f) limitation of the policy to only contractual goods; and
(g) minimum nature of the coverage and buyers' costs for war and any other additional insurance.

However, the Commentary to the *Ohio State Revised Code* demonstrates some important aspects in which the US may differ from the English common law.

[12] http://law.justia.com/codes/ohio/2006/orc/jd_130233-53fb.html.

[13] Ohio State Revised Code, 2006-1302.33. (UCC 2-320) C.I.F. and C. and F. terms.

7.6 Extent of Common Law Obligations

7.6.1 Extent of the Common Law Obligations

The fullest extent of CIF insurance should be considered against five major criteria:
(a) Seller's express contractual obligations;[14]
(b) Seller's implied contractual obligations;[15]
(c) Amount of cover;[16]
(d) Terms of the policy;[17]
(e) War Risks Cover;[18] and
(f) An 'All Risks' Cover.[19]
Some of these headings are summarised below.

The common law is very strict with regard to all contractual obligations. This is more so with obligations to take out CIF insurance. For instance, delivery of the documents without the policy is not valid delivery or tender. For those reasons *Orient Co Ltd v Brekke & Howlid,*[20] decided that when goods are sold under CIF, but the seller does not affect insurance upon them for the transit, they are not delivered in accordance with the contract although they arrive safely at their destination, and that the buyer is not bound to accept them or to pay the price.

Justice Rowlatt explained that:

> What is meant by saying that the goods have 'arrived'? To the buyer it means only that the ship has arrived which he is told contains the goods. The bill of lading must be given to him and, further than that, he is entitled to say that he will not pay the price unless a policy of insurance is handed to him along with it so that if anything has gone wrong with the goods, he may acquire his rights under the policy in lieu of the goods themselves. Even if it could be made out that he had waived the actual tender of a policy, that alone would not help the

[14] *CIF and FOB Contract,* 5th edn, 2015, pp. 161–162 including cover as per contract, requirements under Incoterms 2020, conflicts between Incoterm 2020 and other forms, and the duty under UCP 600.

[15] Ibid, at pp. 163–174 including necessity of insurance policy, effect of customs and usages, consequences of failure to insure and/or tender policy, relation of certificates to policy, need for stating policy terms, indemnity in lieu of policy, role of broker's cover note and c and f insurance.

[16] Ibid, at pp. 175–179 covering judicial approach, minimum amount under Incoterms 2020/UCP 600, implied amount, minimum amount (110%), sufficient amount, and freight considerations.

[17] Ibid, at pp. 179–182 covering trade and customs, meaning of ordinary policy, policy terms under Incoterms 2020, relevance of ICC definition, and policy terms under UCP 600.

[18] Ibid, at pp. 182–186 covering excluded war risks, institute war risks clauses, express stipulations as to, free of war risks, and responsible part. War risks are discussed in Chap. 10.

[19] Ibid, at pp. 186–202 covering express stipulations on, meaning of, certainties, customary exclusions, meaning and exclusion of inherent vice, attachment or risks, particular contractual stipulations, notice for additional insurance and shipment, confinement to contractual goods, coverage of entire transit, transit clause, effect s.44 MIA 1906, loss between warehouse & ships rail, buyers and sellers insurable interests, tender of foreign policy, effect of statements in certificate, policy for buyer's benefit, validity of policy, other policy forms, assured's identity, insurers insolvency, right to excess insurance, increased value policy, and effect of failure to insure.

[20] *Orient Co Ltd v Brekke & Howlid* [1913] 1KB 531.

> seller. What has to be shewn is that he waived the insurance itself. It is impossible to hold that he is to be called upon to pay for goods which have been shipped uninsured.[21]

This not only expands the concept of delivery but also gives automatic right to rejection. It tantamount to strict liability. It is that serious.

7.6.2 Relationship Between the Common Law and Incoterms

The seller's common law obligations consist mainly of case[22] law, MIA 1906 provisions and related statutes as outlined below. The common law has, however, been influenced by, and now partly 'codified' into Incoterms since its introduction in 1957, latest being Clause A5 of CIF-CIP 2020 Incoterms analysed in paragraph 8.4 ahead.[23] With scant information on the common law influence on the history and development of Incoterms, it is fair to assume that pre-1936 common law decisions, as laid out in this chapter, influenced Incoterms establishment in 1936.[24] That notwithstanding, case law pre- and post- 1936 has interpreted this Incoterms provision as amended from time to time. Case law on CIF commenced as early as the sixteenth to seventeenth centuries. Thus, just as Incoterms has 'codified' common law, the common law has consequently interpreted Incoterms. This should be regarded as a progressive development of the common law. Case law discussed in the rest of the chapter reflects that position. Thus, Clause A5 of the CIF/CIP Incoterms 2020 represents a refinement of common law and practice before and after 1957.

That refinement is summarised in the preliminary issues on the policy below.

7.7 Preliminary Issues on the CIF Policy

As a preliminary issue, there are at least seven requirements that a CIF policy must meet at common law. First, the English policy should be one in the sales contract.

---

[21] Ibid at p. 537.

[22] For insurance policy under CIF see *Halsbury's Laws of England* (5th Edition Reissue) Vol. 11 paras. 333, 331, 33-1; for insurance see, Ibid, Insurance, Vol. 29 (2nd Edition Reissue) no 2031 et sea (assignment of policy).

[23] Clause A5 (*emphasis added*); See also Ramberg, *Guide to Incoterms* 2010, Note 24, pp. 200–201. Identical commentary appeared in Ramberg's *ICC Guide to Incoterms* 2000 at pp. 120–121.This text varies slightly as indicated therein from that of Incoterms 2000, ICC Pub. No 560 and Incoterms 2010 ICC Pub. No.715E.

[24] Although the ICC itself was established in 1919, Incoterms were not introduced until 1936, first revised in 1957 and then almost at every 10 years at the end of a decade, thereafter.

7.7.1 The English CIF Policy Should Be One Agreed in the Contract

The starting point for any commercial transaction is to look at the terms and conditions of the contract to determine what the parties agreed and therefore their intentions. Thus, in *Yull & Co v Scott-Robson,*[25] where a CIF contract for shipment of cattle from Argentina to South Africa provided for an 'all risks policy', it was judged that that term was not fulfilled by tender of a policy containing an 'fc and s' clause, i.e., warranted free of capture, seizure and detention and therefore their consequences; a decision affirmed on appeal.[26] Half a century later, *Reinhart & Co v Joshua Hoyle & Sons Ltd,*[27] a case dealing with pre-shipment risks in the cotton trade, reached same conclusion. Thus, the seller must effect the insurance policy on the terms and conditions agreed by the parties. Unless there are compelling reasons, courts will endeavour to effect the parties' intentions as provided in their written contract. Accordingly, parties should not substitute or change the terms of the agreed policy. There are, however, American variations to this.

7.7.2 American Variation: 'Usual' and 'Current' at Port of Shipment

In addition to the English law requirement that the contract should be that agreed in the contract, the American one adds the term 'usual' and 'current' and requests seller to take out policy covering both marine and war risks. As the Ohio Commentary suggests: "The requirement that unless otherwise agreed the seller must procure insurance "of a kind and on terms then current at the port for shipment in the usual amount, in the currency of the contract, sufficiently shown to cover the same goods covered by the bill of lading," applies to both marine and war risk insurance. As applied to marine insurance, it means such insurance as is usual or customary at the port for shipment with reference to the particular kind of goods involved, the character and equipment of the vessel, the route of the voyage, the port of destination and any other considerations that affect the risk.

It is the substantial equivalent of the ordinary insurance in the particular trade and on the particular voyage and is subject to agreed specifications of type or extent of coverage. The language does not mean that the insurance must be adequate to cover all risks to which the goods may be subject in transit. There are some types of loss or damage that are not covered by the usual marine insurance and are excepted in bills of lading or in applicable statutes from the causes of loss or damage for which the carrier or the vessel is liable. Such risks must be borne by the buyer under Clause A5 of CIF/CIP contracts in Chap. 8.

---

[25] *Yull & Co v Scott-Robson* [1907] 1 KB 685; for detailed discussion see para. 7.102 ante.

[26] *Yull & Co v Scott-Robson* [1908] 1 KB 270.

[27] *Reinhart & Co v Joshua Hoyle & Sons Ltd* [1961] 1 Lloyds Rep 346.

Otherwise, according to Chubb Worldwide Ocean Cargo Insurance, a leading provider, the general policies available in the US are:

(a) Ocean/Air Transit Insurance for goods in international trade, as well as domestic coastwise trade
(b) Controlled Master Programs with locally written underlying policies where required and permitted by law
(c) Multiline coverage when combined with other Chubb products
(d) Shippers Interest Cargo
(e) Project Cargo
(f) Bailee Liabilities, including Non Vessel Operating Common Carrier (NVOCC) and Air Cargo Legal
(g) Alternative risk transfer/retention options
(h) Tailored engineering, including marine risk management services
(i) Global risk transfer options for large, complex financial requirements, including:
(j) Dedicated team of specialists in global marine program structures
(k) Customized risk transfer options, as well as risk retention options through deductible and retrospective rating structures and use of captive reinsurers[28]

Insurance secured in compliance with a C.I.F. term must cover the entire transportation of the goods to the named destination".[29]

The Commentary to the *Ohio State Revised Code* 2006, on the section:

(a) elaborates on what constitutes customary practice in the US trade;
(b) like the English common law, confirms that the policy must cover the entire CIF transit;
(c) unlike the provisions of Clause A5 of Incoterms and the English common law, it specifically includes war risks to the seller's duties with the proviso that the seller can include premium in the price; and
(d) unlike under English law, it is equivocal on the adequacy or sufficiency of the policy.

The commentary realises, rightly, that it would be impractical to expect the seller to foresee and provide for all possible risks that CIF shipment may be exposed. Accordingly, the Commentary appreciates that there are risks, which may need to be covered by the buyer himself. This is a common-sense approach and one that does not put intolerable and onerous burdens on the seller. Any additional insurance is, rightly, left to the discretion of the buyer. All in all, the American law seems to adopt a sensible and a practical approach.

7.7.3 The CIF Policy Should Be Those Current in the Particular Trade

Secondly, the English policy must not only be that agreed between the parties but must also be that current in a particular trade. What that is 'current in a particular

[28] https://www.chubb.com/us-en/business-insurance/worldwide-ocean-cargo-insurance.html.

[29] Commentary to The Ohio State Revised Code 2006, para 6.

trade' depends on the facts of each case, the prevailing circumstances and customs and usages at the time. Justice Mathew in *Borthwick* v *Bank of New Zealand*,[30] involving practice in the frozen meat trade at the time, supports the supposition. This is so whether the contract is for an 'All Risks' CIF policy or covering war and other risks separately. Terms of the policy will also depend on a particular trade and current practice therein. However, Schmitthoff is of the view that:

> "The parties should not place too much reliance on the customs of trade, which sometimes varies at the ports of shipment and destination and may be interpreted differently by merchants and courts",[31] and instead, he advises, that: "they should, in appropriate cases agree in the contract of sale on the nature of the insurance policy which the seller has to tender, for example whether the policy should be an all risks policy in the form of an Institute of Cargo Clauses to Lloyds Marine Policy or should cover war risks".[32]

Thus, there seems to be a marked difference between legal theory and practice on the one hand and between trade customs and common sense on the other.

There is, once again, a slight variation to this in American law.

7.7.4 American Variations: Policy Should Be 'Usual' and 'Sufficient'

The American requirements go further than that stipulated in English Law. As the Commentary to the Ohio State Code adds, it must not only be 'usual' in the trade but must also correspond with the bill of lading. It also includes issues covered above such as covering only the buyer's goods, only goods in the bill of lading, sufficiency, nature and the role of American certificates. The Commentary provides that:

> Insurance 'for the account of whom it may concern' is usual and sufficient. However, for a valid tender the policy of insurance must be one which can be disposed of together with the bill of lading and so must be "sufficiently shown to cover the same goods covered by the bill of lading." It must cover separately the quantity of goods called for by the buyer's contract and not merely insure his goods as part of a larger quantity in which others are interested, a case provided for in American mercantile practice by the use of negotiable certificates of insurance which are expressly authorized by this section. By usage these certificates are treated as the equivalent of separate policies and are good tender under C.I.F. contracts. The term "certificate of insurance", however, does not of itself include certificates or "cover notes" issued by the insurance broker and stating that the goods are covered by a policy. Their sufficiency as substitutes for policies will depend upon proof of an established usage or course of dealing. The present section rejects the English rule that not only brokers' certificates and "cover notes" but also certain forms of American insurance certificates are not the equivalent of policies and are not good tender under a C.I.F. contract.[33]

---

30 *Borthwick v Bank of New Zealand* (1900) 17 TLR 2.

31 Schimitthoff, *The Law and Practice of International Trade*, Chapter 2, para. 2-023, p. 37.

32 Ibid.

33 Commentary to *The Ohio State Revised Code*, 2006, para. 9.

Otherwise, reference in the Commentary to assignability 'for the account of to whom it may concern', coverage of only the contract goods and sufficiency of the policy resonates with English law. However, the Commentary's elaboration on the rationale for the requirement for 'only the buyer's goods' is helpful. Further exposition on the unique and different role of the certificate in the American customary law is a striking difference from English law and is, therefore, considered 'a rejection of English law'. So is the American non-acceptance of the cover note as valid tender, which English law accepts as valid tender.

Thirdly, the CIF policy should cover only the contract goods sold.

7.7.5 Policy Should Cover Only the Contract Goods Sold

It will be recalled that the CIF policy should cover only goods sold. This is augmented by further stipulations that the beneficiary should be named and that the tender must include the insurance policy or other alternative insurance document. *Orient Co Ltd v Brekke & Howlid* decided that omission of the required documents constitutes breach. A further authority for the principle, including the rule of omission of documents, is *Hickox and Another v Adams,*[34] where the plaintiffs (New York exporters) contracted to sell and deliver 1000 quarters of wheat to defendants, at Bristol, upon the terms, "cost, freight and insurance". However, by mistake the plaintiffs shipped by a sailing vessel, a cargo of 2000 quarters of wheat to a buyer's agent at Bristol. They also forwarded to the agent by steamer a bill of lading and policy of insurance of the whole cargo of wheat shipped. The policy was "free from particular average". The agent at the request of the plaintiffs accepted a bill of exchange drawn by the seller upon him in their favour for the price of 2000 quarters. The defendants afterwards refused to accept the 1000 quarters from the agent.

In an action against defendants for breach of a contract to accept the 1000 quarters the court held that the plaintiffs were not "ready and willing" to deliver the 1000 quarters to defendants within the terms of their contract. The Lord Chancellor, Lord Mellish,[35] thought that the English firm was not bound to accept the bill of lading for the goods without the policy of insurance. It is noteworthy that the issue of estoppel against the buyers' agents was not raised against the buyers. The buyers could have accepted the whole cargo if they wished but were not obliged to. That notwithstanding the Lord Chancellor's decision was correct, the sellers did not tender contract goods. There is a whole difference between 2000 quarters and 1000 quarters. Although it does not nor necessarily follow, the tendered policy for 2000 quarters might have cost more premium than the stipulated one for 1000 quarters. The 100% margin between the ordered and the delivered cargo extinguished any possibility for the court did exercise the discretion of the de minimis rule and allow the tender. Justice McCardie, in the leading case of *Manbre Saccharine Co Cord Products Co,*

[34] *Hickox v Adams* (1876) 34 LT 404, the policy must refer to and cover the buyer; also, authority for covering only goods sold and omission of documents.

[35] Ibid, at 407.

followed *Hickox and Adams,* on this point.[36] Fifty years earlier, Lord Justice Turner in *Ralli v Universal Marine Insurance Co,*[37] concerning shipment of wheat CIF from Odessa to England had come to the same conclusion.[38]

However, it was Lord Sumner who, 3 years later, rationalised the situation and emphasised the importance of the documents in *Hansson v Hemel & Holey Ltd*[39] when he said: "Those documents have to be handled by banks, they have to be taken up or rejected promptly and without any prolonged inquiry, they have to be such as to be re-tendered to sub-purchasers, and it is essential that they should conform to the accustomed shipping documents as to be reasonably and readily as to pass current in commerce".[40] It is due to mistakes like this or avoidance of possible frauds that this strict CIF rule exists. Its other functions are to prevent the unscrupulous seller substituting or tendering a wrong policy, which does not cover the contract goods. In this case, Lord Sumner was also reiterating the doctrine of strict compliance in letters of credit transactions. Otherwise, the American law is the same on this point.

There appears to be no American or other variations from a common law jurisdiction.

Fourth, the CIF policy must clearly identify the seller or buyer.

7.7.6 Policy Must Clearly Identify the Seller and/or Buyer

Although this requirement is obvious to avoid confusion and/or fraud, one way to ensure that the policy is valid is that it must clearly identify the insured as well as the beneficiary following indorsement. This is in line with the requirements of the policy in s.23 of MIA, 1906. Subsection 1 provides that a marine policy must specify the name of the assured, or of some person who effects the insurance on his behalf. Sub-s. (2) through to (5) have been repealed.[41]

Pursuant to *Biddell Bros v E Clemens Horst R Co,*[42] these details should be easily available both in the documents of sale such as the invoice and the bill of lading as well as the policy itself. That authority was followed in *Johnson v Taylor Bros & Co Ltd.*[43] The need for identity of the assured was further affirmed by Lord Hirst, in a recent decision of *Colonia Versicherung AG v Amoco Oil Co (The Wind Star),*[44] an FOB-turned CIF for oil shipment from Texas to England which provided a bearer

[36] *Manbre Saccharine Co Cord Products Co* [1919] 1 KB 198.

[37] *Turner in Ralli v Universal Marine Insurance Co* (1862) 6 LT 34.

[38] Ibid at p. 37.

[39] *Hansson v Hemel & Holey Ltd* [1922] 2 AC 36.

[40] Ibid, at p. 46.

[41] s. 23(2)–(5) was repealed as to instruments made or executed after 1.8.1959 by the Finance Act 1959 (c. 58), Sch. 8 Pt. II.

[42] *Biddell Bros v E Clemens Horst R Co* [1911] 1 KB 214 at 220.

[43] *Johnson v Taylor Bros & Co Ltd* [1920] AC 144 at 156.

[44] *Colonia Versicherung AG v Amoco Oil Co (The Wind Star)* [1997] 1 Lloyd's Rep 261.

certificate naming numerous but unidentified beneficiary. However, in practice the assured's name in the policy could be replaced by the agent's name where the policy is taken out by the latter. The rationale was to avoid the antiquated practice of leaving the insured's name blank which, although facilitates transfer and assignment, can lead to misuse and/or fraud. American law does not expressly require the identity of the seller and/or buyer.

Once more there are no common law variations to the requirement.

Fifth, the CIF policy must be for the benefit of the buyer only, buyer in this context including sub-buyers and other assignees.

7.7.7 English Policy Must Be for the Benefit of the Buyer

Requirement for the identity of the assured follows supplements another that the policy must also be for the benefit of the buyer. That is what CIF contracts are all about. *The Julia* had already ruled impliedly that the policy should not only be for the benefit of the buyer but must also allow him to claim directly from the insurers. If, however, the buyer sales afloat and indorses the documents then his assignees become the new buyer beneficiaries. Accordingly, *Colonia Versicherung v Amoco Oil Co (The Wind Star)* remains the good authority for both propositions that the seller must not only ensure that the policy is for the buyer's benefit but also that the buyer should be identified with certainty.

Lord Justice Hirst citing an explicit House of Lords judgment in *Boston Fruit Co. v. British and Foreign Marine Insurance Co. Ltd.*,[45] with reference to similar wording in a marine policy opined that where it has been established that the person claiming was not such a person as those who effected the policy had in contemplation, courts have disallowed his claim, though he might be within the description.[46] In modern contracts, insistence on the strict requirement 'for the benefit of the buyer' might not amount to much. It would, for instance, in practice exclude the possibility of buying and selling afloat from what might have been a long contract chain. For those reasons 'for the benefit of the buyer' should include the benefit of the buyer and the buyer's and subsequent assignees.

However, there are American variations to this fifth requirement.

7.7.8 American Variations: 'Policy for the Buyer's Benefit'

The American law tallies with English law on the requirement that the policy be for the buyer's benefit. However, the requirement forms an American 'ordinary mercantile meaning' which implies first that that the seller pays for the insurance upfront and secondly that it is for the buyer but not the seller's benefit. The relevant Commentary provides that:

---

[45] *Boston Fruit Co. v. British and Foreign Marine Insurance Co. Ltd* [1906] A.C. 336 at 339.

[46] Ibid at pp. 271–272.

> 3. The insurance stipulated by the C.I.F. term is for the buyer's benefit, to protect him against the risk of loss or damage to the goods in transit. A clause in C.I.F. contract "insurance - for the account of sellers" should be viewed in its ordinary mercantile meaning that the sellers must pay for the insurance and not that it is intended to run to the seller's benefit.[47]

Although the author has not come across any American authority, it is possible that *The Wind Star* and other English cases cited above would be persuasive in that jurisdiction.

Sixth, the CIF policy contains this cardinal principle that it and the whole contract must enable the buyer to claim directly from the insurer, a principle since adopted by Incoterms.

7.7.9 Policy Must Enable the Buyer to Claim Directly from the Insurers: *The Julia*

As summarised by Lord Porter in *The Julia,*[48] it is one of the fundamental requirements in the CIF seller's obligations that he must not only take out the insurance, but that the policy he provides must put the buyer, as an assignee/transferee, in a position that he can sale the goods and indorse it, or claim from the carrier in the event of damage or directly from the insurers and in his own name in the event of loss or damage. It will be remembered one of the reasons *The Julia* failed as a CIF contract was because of all the numerous times the parties had traded, the buyer was never permitted to claim directly from the insurers; instead, the seller claimed from the insurers and passed the proceeds to the buyer less expenses. A CIF policy that does not accord those facilities is not valid policy under the CIF. This fact is now included in Clause A5 of CIF-CIP Incoterms 2020. Enabling the buyer or his assignee to sue the insurer directly and in his or her own names is a further reason why the policy should be for the buyer's benefit. Although not expressly provided, this position is implied in the America law.

Seventh, and finally but not least the seller-obtained policy does not warrant the solvency of the insurer. Indeed, no party would do that.

7.7.10 Seller-Obtained Policy Does Not Warrant Solvency of the Insurer

Although the identity of the insurer forms part of the requirements for a policy with a reputable insurer (below), the authorities are not clear whether that includes the seller warranting the solvency of the insurer. Indeed, no one commercial entity in real life or practice can warrant such an undertaking. Taking out an 'approved'[49]

[47] Commentary to the Ohio State Revised Code, 2006, para. 3.

[48] *The Julia* [1949] AC 293.

[49] See para. 7-086 and 7-088.

policy with a 'reputable'[50] and 'responsible'[51] insurer would be sufficient for the seller to discharge his insurance obligations. Those three would provide sufficient checks and balances. Warranting the insurer's insolvency would be stiffer requirements would be onerous and an intolerant burden on the seller. It is therefore not surprising that, when faced with the decision, Lord Eady in *Arnhold Karberg v Blythe, Green, Jourdain & Co*[52] avoided dealing with the issue. Otherwise, this warranty is different from that required of the assured under ss.33–41 of MIA 1906[53] relating to the terms and conditions of the policy.

In addition to the above seven preliminary requirements, there are a further four CIF common law requirements for the assignment of the policy.

The first one goes without saying that the policy must in the first instance be assignable.

7.8 Assignment of the CIF Policy

7.8.1 CIF Policy Must Be Assignable

Like most commercial and export insurance policies, CIF insurance should of course be assignable.[54] It follows from the above that a valid CIF must be capable of transfer by assignment or other customary means of transfer to a lawful assignee or transferee of the goods. To do so the valid must valid, i.e., fulfil all the above requirements relating to the one agreed on, in the name the buyer, current in the trade and cover the consignments for the whole transit. Only then will that policy meaningful be assignable. The requirement for assignment is now contained in s.15 (assignment of interest), s.50 (when and how assignable and s. 51 (exceptions on) of MIA 1906, defines and provides the manner of transfer of the insurance policy. The American position on the assignment is the same.

There are no other common law variations of the requirement.

Secondly, the assignment relates to and relinquishes the assignor's interest.

7.8.2 Assignment of CIF Interest

When the CIF seller goods and assigns the policy, he relinquishes his interests in the merchandise and policy. This is embodied in s.15 of MIA 1906, which provides that where the assured assigns or otherwise parts with his interest in the subject-matter insured, he does not thereby transfer to the assignee his rights under the contract of insurance, unless there be an express or implied agreement with the assignee to that

[50] See paras. 7-087–7-090.

[51] Ibid.

[52] *Arnhold Karberg v Blythe, Green, Jourdain & Co* [1916] 1 K.B. 495 at 508.

[53] Warranty in the FOB and CIF policy is covered in Chap. 1 ante.

[54] See *Halsbury's Laws* Vol. 91, Note 7, para. 32.

effect. However, the provisions of this section do not affect a transmission of interest by operation of law.

However, the provision also contains some outdated common law that the policy could transfer the subject matter of the contract but not the right to sue under the policy itself. This is now changed by allowing for assignment by express or implied agreement of the parties or the operation of the law such as a court order.

Consequently, this enabled assignment of policy concerning sale of ship can be assigned to the purchaser in *Powles v Innes*[55] while. *North of England Pure Oil v Archangel*[56] did the same for the sale of cargo. However, the interest whether in the vessel or cargo cannot be transferred until property in the subject matter had passed to the buyer. Hence the ruling in *Yangtze Insurance v Lukmanjee*[57] that property in the contract goods could not be assigned until the property and therefore risk in them had passed to the buyer. In that case the cargo which was on transit, was lost during but before completion of the loading process. The authority is also important for providing the contrast between ex-ship and CIF contracts. Lord Esher in *Rayner v Preston*[58] commented that: "Where the subject matter of insurance is sold during the running of the policy, no interest under the policy passes unless it is made part of the contract of purchase and sale, so that it would be considered in the court of equity as assigned"[59]

Although this is probably no longer good law, interpretation of the section in *Strass v Spillers*[60] includes the fact that a CIF seller can retain 'increased value' interest in the cargo despite the assignment. This would be contrary to the principle that on sale of goods and transfer of the policy, the seller relinquishes all rights in both the goods and the policy to the buyer or his assignees. To hold otherwise would be a retrograde position. However, the other interpretation of the that the provision, by *Hibbert v Carter*[61] that, assignment needn't be for the whole interest, even partial interest is assignable, is probably still good law on the basis that one might own only a part of the property.

There are no variations from other common law jurisdictions.

Thirdly, there are specific times and methods of assigning a CIF policy.

7.8.3 When and How a Policy Is Assigned

There are rules on the terms and conditions, effects and mechanisms on assignment of the CIF policy. These are contained in s. 50 of MIA 1906. On when the policy is assignable, subsection 50(1) provide that a marine policy is assignable unless it

[55] *Powles v Innes* (1841) 11 M&W 10.

[56] *North of England Pure Oil v Arcangel* (1875) LR 10 QB 49.

[57] *Yangtze Insurance v Lukmanjee* [1918] AC 585.

[58] *Rayner v Preston* (1881) 18 Ch D at 12.

[59] Ibid at p. 12.

[60] *Strass v Spillers* [1911] 2 KB 759.

[61] *Hibbert v Carter.*

contains terms expressly prohibiting assignment. It may be assigned either before or after loss. Where the policy expressly prohibits assignment under certain conditions, those conditions must be observed. Such conditions include prohibition for allowing cancellation of the policy following sale of the subject matter (ship) to a new management, as was in *Pynam v Martine.*[62] However, *Lawrie v West Hartlepool Indemnity Association*[63] contradicted that authority by holding that once the conditions are met, such policies can still be assigned either before or after loss. Although the case was a P&I and a ship rather that goods policy, the authority would still be persuasive.

On the effect of assignment s.50(2) provides that where a marine policy has been assigned so as to pass the beneficial interest in such policy, the assignee of the policy is entitled to sue thereon in his own name; and the defendant is entitled to make any defence arising out of the contract which he would have been entitled to make if the action had been brought in the name of the person by or on behalf of whom the policy was effected.

The highlighted text reinforces the position taken by Lord Porter in the Julia that the 'cardinal' principle of the CIF insurance is that the buyer (assignee) should be put in a position where he can sue claim and/or sue in his own name.

However, contrary to s.50(2), *Swan v Marine Insurance Co,*[64] held that even when the mortgagee is satisfied, the mortgagor can still sue for his residual interest.[65] Nevertheless, this view is not supported by *Williams v Atlantic Assurance Co Ltd*[66] in which Lord Greer[67] (Lord Slesser concurring[68]) construed that the words 'beneficial interests' mean the whole beneficial interest. dissented from the majority decision in the case.[69] On the other hand, Justice Hirst in *The Black King Shipping Corporation v Massie*[70] *(The Litsion Pride)* held that the right to sue in his name does not include a fraudulent claim by a mortgagee.[71] Thus, it appears that residual interests are not extinguished by the subsection. And on how assignment is effected, subsection 50(3) provides that a marine policy may be assigned by indorsement thereon or in other customary manner.

The method of assignment was indorsed in *Compania Colombiana de Seguros v Pacific Steam Navigation Co.*[72] This is the same method as chose in action in

---

[62] *Pynam v Marten* (1906) 13 Com Cas 64 CA; CF *Sparkes v Marshall* (1836) 2 Bing NC 761; *Lloyd v Fleming* (1872) LR7 QB 299 (action by executor of assignee).

[63] *Lawrie v West Hartlepool Indemnity Association* (1899) 15 TLR 486.

[64] *Swan v Marine Insurance Co* [1907] 12 Com Cas 79.

[65] Ibid at 79, 80.

[66] *Williams v Atlantic Assurance Co Ltd* [1933] 1 KB 81 Marine.

[67] Ibid, at 100.

[68] Ibid, at 105.

[69] Ibid, at 97-8.

[70] *The Black King Shipping Corporation v Massie* (*The Litsion Pride*) [1985] 1 Lloyds Rep 437.

[71] Ibid, at 519.

[72] *Compania Colombiana de Seguros v Pacific Steam Navigation Co* [1964] 1 All ER 216.

accordance with s.136 *Law of Property Act 1925.*Otherwise according to *Baker v Adam,*[73] it is now customary to do so by mere delivery.[74] On when and how the policy is assigned, Lord Scrutton in *J Aron & Co Inc v Miall*[75] said: "On the policy there is an assignment in the ordinary form in which policies are assigned in England, that is to say, the brokers who effected the policy have signed their name and the agent of the first seller has signed his name; and that indorsement in blank according to custom of marine insurance in England assigns all claims on the policy to the holder of the policy"[76]

This rather antiquated practice has probably been overtaken by modern arrangements.

Fourth and finally, but not least, only an assured with insurable interest in the goods can assign the CİF policy.

7.8.4 Only an Assured with Interest Can Assign

It is common sense that one cannot assign what one does not own or have a legitimate interest in. To do otherwise would be illegal if not fraudulent. That fact is now enshrined in s.51 of the MIA 1906 which provides that 'Where the assured has parted with or lost his interest in the subject-matter insured, and has not, before or at the time of so doing, expressly or impliedly agreed to assign the policy, any subsequent assignment of the policy is inoperative'. Thus, an assured who has no interest cannot assign. However, nothing in this section affects the assignment of a policy after loss.

This section applies to CIF contracts and should be read together with s.15 above on assignment of interest and the cases cited therein.[77] Those authorities are supported by the *North of England Pure Oil Cake Co Ltd v Archangel Maritime Bank and Insurance Co Ltd*[78] on the main provision of this section regarding assignment of interest. This was rather an intriguing case. The sellers (the Vagliano Brothers) who were abroad (Greece) insured cargo of linseed being shipped on the brig, the Fanny 'including all risk of the craft' from Constantinople (then part of Greece) to Stockton-on Tees (England). While the cargo was still afloat, the seller's agent (Edwards & Co) sold the cargo to a buyer (plaintiffs) but the seller retained the policy, as the cargo was not to be paid for until arrival.

However, part of the cargo (in 1 lighter) was damaged after being loaded in the buyer's lighters. However, after the seller's interests had ceased, the seller assigned

[73] *Baker v Adam* (1910) 15 Com Cas 227.

[74] Ibid, at p. 230.

[75] *J Aron & Co Inc v Miall* (1928) 34 Cam Cas at 20.

[76] Ibid, at p. 20.

[77] Especially *Hibbert v Carter* on assignment o partial interest and *Strass v Spillers* and *Baker* on the right of assignors to retain 'increased value policies'.

[78] *North of England Pure Oil Cake Co ltd v Archangel Maritime bank and Insurance Co ltd* (1875) LR 10 QB 249; Asp. Mar. Law Cases vol. ii 1873–1876, p. 571.

he policy to the buyer. The buyer sued unsuccessfully on the policy. Chief Justice Cockburn (Justices Lush and Quain concurring) held that the buyers could not recover on the policy as the policy had not passed to them by the contract of sale; that the sellers interests ceased on the delivery to the lighter and therefore that the subsequent assignment was void. The decision seems to have centred on the act that the property passed on arrival not on contract when goods were afloat.[79] This was not a typical contract of sale afloat as in CIF but sale on arrival (arrival contract). There is some resemblance to *The Julia* in this case. On the proviso to the section 50 and in relation to s 50(1), Justice Blackburn in *Lloyd v Flemming*[80] affirmed that s.51 does not affect assignment after loss.

7.9 The *"Minimum Cover"* vs the *"All-Risks"* Policy

Although the CIF provides for a minimum cover, unless otherwise provided, a higher or an all-risk policy would be preferable. However, the nature and extent of an all-risk CIF policy never really been determined nor has its inclusions.

7.9.1 What Is an *'All Risks'* Policy?

An 'all-risks' policy, a type of insurance designed to protect the insured against loss or damage however caused, is the ideal and preferable policy. However, an 'all-risks' policy is not the preserve of CIF contracts, a CIF All risks policy should therefore be considered as part of the much wider 'All risks insurance'.[81] Normally associated with property all risks coverage; an all-risks policy covers loss arising from any fortuitous cause except those that are specifically excluded. This is in contrast to named perils coverage, which applies only to loss arising out of causes that are listed as covered. An all-risk cargo insurance policy is the broadest form of shipping insurance and will cover any physical loss/damage from any external cause.

An all-risk policy will list any exclusions that are not covered, which can be added on to the policy as an additional clause. The next few paragraphs are devoted to various aspects of this type of policy and its application in CIF contracts. However, it will be apparent that there is no such a thing as an 'all-risks' policy; that is only achievable by additional cover to make up for the exceptions and top up for

[79] *Lloyd v Flemming* (below) distinguished *Tamvaco v Lucas* (above) affirmed and reversed *Ralli v The Universal Marine Insurance Co.*

[80] *Lloyd v Flemming* (1872) LR 7 QB 299.

[81] See Sassoon, pp. 186–202 and all the authorities cited therein. These types of policies are not restricted to export or CIF, but rather are used in general marine insurance, jewellery insurance, contractors' insurance and cash or goods in transit policies insurance and cash or goods in transit policies.

additional requirements. By inclusion of the war risks within the seller's duties,[82] the American law is nearer an 'all-risks' policy than the English counterpart.

7.9.2 An "*All Risks*" CIF Policy Should Be Inclusive

7.9.2.1 What Constitutes the Policy

In relation to CIF contracts, in *Groom(C) v Barber*[83] Lord Atkin[84] pronounced on what constitutes the nature and terms of an 'All Risks' policy. As the title suggests, this type of policy should cover all risks, including war risks without any exceptions. He said that in a contract on c.i.f. terms the seller has, as stated by Hamilton J. in *Biddell Brothers V. E. Clemens Horst Co.*, to arrange for an insurance on the terms current in the trade which would be available for the buyer. Accordingly, he was satisfied, in this case, that at the time this contract was made the terms current in the trade were terms which excluded war risk; in other words that the policy would contain the f. c. and s. clause, and therefore, apart from the special terms of this contract, a policy in such terms would be in order.[85]

And, on the seller's duties, role of the policy and time of tender of the policy Lord Atkin continued that in his opinion the result is that the contract of the seller is performed by delivering to the buyer within a reasonable time from the agreed date of shipment the documents, ordinarily the bill of lading, the invoice, and the policy of insurance, which will entitle the buyer to obtain on arrival of the ship delivery of goods shipped in accordance with the contract, or in case of loss will entitle him to recover on the policy the value of the goods if lost by a peril agreed in the contract to be covered, and in any case will give him any rightful claim against the ship in respect of any mis delivery or wrongful treatment of the goods.[86]

Further judicial authority on the relationship between the CIF policy and the 'all risk' policy is *Yuill & Co v Robson,*[87] in which Lord Alverstone CJ[88] gave three guidelines as to "All Risks" policy, upholding Justice Channell's judgment at the lower court.[89]

---

[82] See para 7.5 above; see also para 7.7.2, 7.7.4 and 7.7.8.

[83] *Groom(C) v Barber* [1915] 1 KB 316 (effect of validity of tender for goods lost in transit; however, distinguished in *Arnold Karberg & Co v Blythe, Green, Jourdain and Co, Schneider & Co v Burgett & Newsman* [1915] 2KB379); see also *Vincentelli Co v Rowlett & CO* (1911)105 LT 411 on the extent of vendor's obligations on All Risks Insurance.

[84] *Groom v Barber*, per Lord Atkin, at 321, 322.

[85] Ibid, at 321 and 322.

[86] Ibid, at 324.

[87] *Yuill & Co v Robson* [1908] 1 KB 270.

[88] Ibid, at 274, Buckley LJ and Kennedy LJ concurring.

[89] *Yuill & Co v Robson* [1907] 1 KB 685.

7.9.2.2 Meaning of the Policy

First, on the meaning of the terms 'all-risks' generally, he said: "The question turns on the meaning of the stipulation in the contract that the cattle were to be insured by the defendant against all risks. On the defendant's contention in this case that that the expression "all risks" must be subject to some limitation, expressing his own views, he disagreed that it is necessary, in deciding this case, to say whether or not that proposition might not be correct in certain cases. On considering the meaning of the words as used in this contract he confessed inability to do better than adopt the language of Channell, J. that no doubt the evidence clearly shews that an insurance broker would expect a policy against all risks to contain the warranty against capture, seizure, and detention.

However, on the question as between the buyer and seller of goods is a very different one indeed, and he very much doubted the admissibility of the evidence given on behalf of the defendant. He concluded that in the present case the expression covers insurance against a risk so obvious to parties buying and selling live cattle for shipment as that of the cattle being prevented from landing at their destination by reason of the apprehension of the authorities of the importation of disease. Such a prohibition is very usual, and the risk would naturally be present to the minds of persons in the position of the plaintiffs and the defendant.[90]

Secondly, on whether the 'all-risks' policy has acquired secondary meaning he could only express entirely agreement with that statement. Addressing the specific cattle trade practice, he opined that the words 'insurance against all-risks' have acquired a secondary and special signification, and that the parties to this contract must be taken to have known that an insurance against all risks would not include all risks, but would exclude the particular risk of a prohibition against the landing of the cattle by an order of the authorities in the country to which they were to be sent. He noted, further, that there were two kinds of policy in use, one of which does not contain the free of capture, seizure, and detention warranty, and that, if a policy in that form is desired, an additional premium has to be paid.

As to the situation where the slip does not contain the words 'no free of capture, seizure, and detention warranty,' he agreed with the then underwriters' practice to insert the clause in the policy as very reasonable and proper practice, despite his reservation that to a great extent it negatives the suggestion that the words 'all-risks' have acquired a special secondary meaning binding on the parties to this action.[91] He in fact concluded that there was no such acquired secondary meaning in the 'all-risks' policy; any such qualification would negate it being an 'all-risks' policy.

7.9.2.3 Efficacy of the Policy

Thirdly, and finally, on the efficacy of the 'all risks livestock clause', he noted that the policy, which was tendered, and which was assumed by both parties to be an all-risks policy, contained what are known as the 'all risks livestock clauses,' one of which, the 'mortality' clause, contained certain stipulations limiting the insurer's

[90] *Yuill & Co v Robson* [1908] 1 KB 270 at 273–275.

[91] Ibid, at 274.

liability in certain events. Accordingly, the argument for the defendant had not satisfied him that the words 'insurance against all-risks' in this contract must be read subject to a limitation. In any case, he agreed with Channell J. that it was necessary in order to comply with the contract to tender a policy which would protect the assured against the whole venture being frustrated by reason of a prohibition against the landing of the cattle at Durban. The policy which was in fact tendered contained the warranty against capture, seizure, and detention, and the cattle having been prevented from landing by the authorities at Durban, the case of *Miller v. Law Accident Insurance Co.* decides that that loss was not recoverable under a policy in that form. For the reasons which his opinion on the main point was that the plaintiffs were not bound to accept the policy which was tendered.[92] Accordingly, a policy which includes a warranty of 'f c&s' is not an all risks a policy.

The case decided that inclusion of a "free from capture and seizure" (fc and s) clause in the "*All Risks*" CIF policy is a breach of such a policy. In the case, a contract was made at Buenos Aires for the sale and shipment of cattle from Buenos Aires to Durban at a price which included cost, freight, and insurance, the insurance to be 'against all risks,' The seller obtained and delivered to the purchasers an ordinary Lloyd's 'all risks livestock' policy, which contained the clause 'Warranted free of capture, seizure, and detention, and the consequences thereof.' During the voyage, foot and mouth disease broke out amongst the cattle, and the authorities at Durban refused to allow the vessel to enter the port, with the result that the cattle were slaughtered on board and sold at a considerable loss. The underwriters refused to pay upon the policy, except for losses by death during the voyage, on the ground that they were protected by the "free of capture and seizure" clause.

In an action by the purchasers against the seller Justice Atkins held that the seller, in procuring an insurance which did not protect the purchaser against the risk of the landing of the cattle being prohibited by the authorities, had broken his contract to procure an insurance, 'against all-risks', and was therefore liable for the loss. Besides, evidence was not admissible to show that a policy containing the "free of capture and seizure" clause was a performance of the contract to procure an insurance against all risks. *Yuill* was considered on this point, and in the same year, *in Upjohn v Ford*[93] by Lord Warrington[94] and Lord Scrutton,[95] affirming the decision of Justice Roche.[96] Where no "All Risks" policy is provided, the CIF seller provides only the minimum cover under common law, Incoterms and all other rules.

[92] Ibid *Yuill & Co v Robson* [1908] 1 KB 270 at 273–275.

[93] *Upjohn v Ford* [1918] 2 KB 48; *sub nom* see also Upjohn v Hitchens [1917–18] 24 TLR 412 alias *Upjohn v Ford*—although the policy was to do with exceptions of war risks in a *Landlord and Tenant Aircraft Risks* rather than CIF or international trade risks.

[94] Ibid, at 55 and 56; Lord Pickford giving a separate judgment.

[95] Ibid, at 60 and 61.

[96] *Upjohn v Ford* [1918] 1 KB 171.

7.9.3 The "*All Risks*" Policy vs. The "*All Clauses*" Insurance

The extent of vendor's obligation in an all risks policy, was also the subject of *Vincentelli & Co v John Rowlett & Co*,[97] an earlier case involving a contract for the sale of goods on CIF terms which contained the following terms 'insurance to be effected by (sellers) all-risks', Justice Hamilton[98] opined that on the construction of the contract, the sellers' obligation was to effect an insurance to cover all risks in the sense of the entire quantity of damage, and not to cover the assured against all causes of accident, e.g. damage done to the goods in consequence of the shipowners committing a breach of the contract of carriage by improperly stowing them on deck instead of below deck. There is a major difference between insurance against all risks and against all causes. The question remains whether under such a contract of sale it is sufficient for the seller to procure protection for the buyer against all risks partly by means of the contract of carriage and partly under the contract of insurance.[99]

7.10 The Express and the Implied Value of the CIF Cover

There are also issues surrounding the value of a CIF policy between an express and an implied one. Furthermore, the implied value can be by either the underlying sales contract or policy contract or custom.

7.10.1 Express Provision of Stated Amount

Being only advanced contracts, insurance contracts generally and FOB and CIF insurance in particular are subject to the general principles of contract law. This is namely that unless otherwise provided, the courts will honour the wishes of the parties in contracts where contracts expressly include those intentions. At least *Biddell Bros v E Clemens Horst Co*,[100] *C Groom Ltd v Barber*[101] *and Johnson v Taylor Bros & Co Ltd*,[102] are examples of two principal authorities where have not sought to deviate from that principle.

What about where the parties have not provided so expressly?

---

[97] *Vincentelli & Co v John Rowlett & Co* (1911) 105 LT 411.

[98] Ibid at 415.

[99] For the minimum and maximum amounts in CIF policy see Lorenzon, *CIF and FOB Contracts*, 5th edn?, pp. 175–179.

[100] *Biddell Bros v E Clemens Horst Co* [1912] AC 18 at 220 and 956.

[101] *C Groom Ltd v Barber* [1915] 316 at 324.

[102] *Johnson v Taylor Bros & Co Ltd* [1920] AC 144 at 149, 156.

7.10.2 Implied Amount on Insured Value

7.10.2.1 Where Parties Have Not Provided

It is also the principle of contract law that where the parties have not provided their intentions expressly, the courts will nevertheless try to discover their intentions from other sources such as implied references, customary practices and contractual history, if any, between the parties, etc. Only where there are no clues will the courts give up. Once again FOB and CIF in particular insurance contracts and insurance contracts generally will abide by these rules, and, in this case with regards to the insurable values. Thus, in *Tamvaco v Lucas*[103] and *Johnson v Taylor*,[104] the courts have held that in the absence of express stipulations as to the precise amount of the minimum CIF cover required, the reasonable value of the goods must be insured. In the case Justice Blackburn said the question turned on the construction of this contract, which, as he read it, was a contract to supply a cargo afloat of a particular description, and to furnish the shipping documents in exchange for the price.

Since the cargo itself is not shipped when the contract is made, nor is it known what will be the name of the ship, it was merely a contract to supply such a cargo as described and so he perfectly agreed with the defendants that they would not be bound to pay the stipulated price, unless proper shipping documents were given to them, by which it meant, not only a proper bill of lading and the proper charter party applicable to such a cargo as that which is described in the contract, but also a policy of insurance for the proper amount. Furthermore, since the number of quarters of grain that were to constitute the cargo are stipulated for in the contract; and the time and manner in which it was to be supplied were fixed by the contract, on these points he believed there was no doubt whatever that the amount of the policy which the parties contemplated at that time was not, in express terms, mentioned in the contract at all.[105]

7.10.2.2 Where the Shipping Price Is Fixed

Touching on the issue of shipping from start, rather than buying afloat, being one of the objectives of the CIF contracts, Justice Blackburn noted that the objection taken at the trial was that, by fixing the price at which the vendors, the plaintiffs, were to supply this cargo afloat, they also fixed the amount to cover which the policy ought to be made out: and, if that were so, the defendants would be right in saying that the policy tendered was not sufficient. But he agreed with the rest of the Court in thinking that that is not the true construction of the contract. If this had been the case of a contract for selling afloat a cargo already shipped in a specific ship (which was originally the more common way in which these transactions were carried on), and the plaintiffs had, as is usual in the market, sold the same cargo from one to another, the contract only varying in price, each vendor in succession stipulating to furnish the shipping documents, he took it to be quite plain, for the reasons which [his

---

[103] *Tamvaco v Lucas* (1861) 121 E.R. 683; the case is discussed in details below.

[104] *Johnson v Taylor* [1920] AC 144.

[105] Ibid; Blackburn J, p. 691.

learned brother] Crompton had given, that the amount of the policy, which was originally the proper shipping document of such a cargo, could not vary from time to time, according to the different prices which were inserted in the different contracts by the different persons who were passing it from one to the other[106]

Whereas on the undesirable effect of variation and/or flexibility on the CIF insurance value, he concluded that to say that the policy must so vary, would be to make its amount dependent on the market and the Corn Exchange of this country, and cause that amount to fluctuate with the fluctuations of the corn market; which would certainly be very inconvenient. Accordingly, this, then, being a contract to supply a cargo afloat, the documents which were furnished would be such as would fairly belong to such a cargo when afloat; and the amount of the policy, as I said before, must depend, not upon the contract price in this country for which the contractor is to furnish such a cargo, but on the nature and kind of the cargo itself. The amount of the policy must be such as would fairly and truly cover and protect that cargo so described.[107]

7.10.2.3 Reasonable Insurable Value

Although in another decision, *(Johnson v Taylor),* Lord Birkenhead further commented on the seller's duties to ship CIF goods, provide reasonable insurance and to tender the insurance policy together with the other documents to the buyer as soon as possible when he said:

> There is nothing at all unusual in the provisions of this contract. It is an ordinary contract for the sale of goods upon cost, insurance, freight, or more shortly c.i.f. terms. Under such a contract, as is well known, the seller undertakes various obligations. He is bound in the first place to ship goods of the contract description on board a ship bound to the contract destination. He is bound in the second place to tender to the purchaser within a reasonable time after shipment the shipping documents, e.g., the Bill or Bills of Lading and a Policy of Insurance reasonably covering the value of the goods.[108]

Although what is a reasonable value is a matter of fact in each case, in *Harland & Wolf v Burstall,*[109] however, that was inferred to mean the value at shipment not at destination and would normally include reasonable amount of anticipated profit and the cost of forwarding charges such as freights and customs duties. That notwithstanding, *Manbre Saccharine Co Ltd v Cord Products Co Ltd,*[110] on the other hand suggests that, if everything fails, in the absence of an express stipulation the cost price of the goods should be the best guideline as a fall-back situation.

---

[106] Ibid, at 692.

[107] Ibid.

[108] *Johnson v Taylor Bros & Co Ltd* [1920] AC 144 at 149, 156 per Lord Birkenhead L.C. at p. 149.

[109] *Harland & Wolf v Burstall* (1901) 6 Com. Cas. 113 at 117.

[110] *Manbre Saccharine Co Ltd v Cord Products Co Ltd* [1919] 1 KB 198.

7.10.3 Implied and Trade Customs' Value

A further guideline on the required documents and insurable value is to refer to implied trade customs and usages of merchants at a particular port, region or jurisdiction. Although, they related more to the terms and documentations in the policy respectively, that is the reading one gets from the authorities of *Manbre Saccharine Co Ltd v Corn Products Co Ltd,*[111] *Wilson, Holgate & Co v Belgian Grain and Produce Co Ltd*[112] and *Ireland v Livingston.*[113] However, where the contract is silent, trade customs value is not the only source of guide as to the implied amount.

The American position on this varies slightly from the English (above).

7.11 Implied v Sufficient Amount: The *Tamvaco vs Lucas* Decision

7.11.1 *Tamvaco v Lucas*

In addition to what amounts to implied and trade customs value, there is also the issue of whether implied amount means sufficient amount. The issue whether 'implied amount' meant 'sufficient amount' and where 'implied amount' conflicts with sufficient amount was once again the subject of *Tamvaco v Lucas,*[114] a rather complicated case which involved complex calculations of profits, freights, insurable value but with the central issue being whether the value insured was sufficient. Detailed facts of the case are covered above. The gist of the facts was the difference of £24, 10s between the provisional invoice value of £4, 626 and the insured value of 3600, after deducting freight. The contract was for the purchase of 1800–2000 quarters of wheat at Taganrong CIF safe port in the UK, payment 'cash in London in exchange for shipping documents. Policy tendered was for 1850 quarters, policy was sufficient to cover shipment. The plaintiffs sue for non-payment and the defendants pleaded that the plaintiffs were 'not ready and willing to tender, nor did they tender the usual shipping documents according to the contract'.

7.11.2 Summary of the Judgment

After long deliberations the Chief Justice Coburn (Justices Crompton and Blackburn concurring) decided that what is a reasonable insurable amount is a question of fact to be decided by the jury, whether from all the circumstances of each case, the

[111] *Manbre Saccharine Co Ltd v Corn Products Co Ltd* [1919] 1 KB 198 at 205.

[112] *Wilson, Holgate & Co v Belgian Grain and Produce Co Ltd* [1920] 2 KB 1 at 7–9.

[113] *Ireland v Livingston* (1872) LR 5 HL 395 at 406.

[114] *Tamvaco v Lucas* (1861) 121 E.R. 683 on appeal; (1859) 1 E & E 58, 592; subnom *Tamvaco v Lucas* (1859) 28 LJKB 150, 301;1 LT 161; Jur NS 731, 1258; 7 WR 568 at trial court-(30 LJQB 234; (1861) 31 LJQB 296.

policy was a sufficient shipping document within the meaning of the contract.[115] The court held, rightly, probably on the *de minimis* principle, that the small difference was no reason to reject the documents.[116] The court also held that freight did not constitute part of the value to be insured. Chief Justice Coburn, Justice Crompton, and Justice Blackburn delivered concurring judgments.

7.11.3 Chief Justice Cockburn: 'Insufficient Amount', Excludes Freight

7.11.3.1 Role of the Documents

There were three leading and concurring judgments in the case. All the three judgments discuss further facts to the case and also raised issues not included in the summary of facts and judgments above.

First, Chief Justice Cockburn decided, *inter alia*, that the policy forms part of the shipping documents and should be sufficient to provide protection to the buyers. In his opinion the rule for entering a verdict for the defendants must be discharged. The case was presented to them in this shape. It was admitted that the defendants were liable, having received commission which made them responsible as del credere agents, if the buyers of this cargo of wheat were bound to accept the shipping documents tendered, and to fulfil the contract by payment.

However, it was alleged that there was a defect in one of the shipping documents, viz. the policy of insurance, in consequence of it not being for an amount sufficient to afford the buyers of the cargo such an indemnity against the loss of the cargo as they were entitled to. The question was put as one of pure law, on these very simple and short facts. The terms of the contract being that the payment should take place on the production of the shipping documents, and when the cargo would still be at sea, a provisional invoice was sent in to the defendants, or rather to the buyers of the cargo, which invoice, framed upon the bill of lading, stated the quantity of wheat at a given amount; but the cargo did not realize that amount, for it turned out considerably less.

When the policy of insurance was produced, it turned out to be of less amount than the sum at which the total value of the cargo appeared in the provisional invoice and the bill of lading. It was also said that the buyers would be entitled to take advantage of that circumstance, and to refuse to accept the shipping documents, or to pay according to the terms of the contract; inasmuch as the policy of insurance was included in the shipping documents, on the delivery of which payment was to be made, and the policy of insurance was not sufficient to satisfy the provisions of the contract, being of less amount than the value of the cargo as represented in the provisional invoice.

---

[115] See the judgments of Cockburn CJ at 238, Crompton J at 241, and Blackburn J at 243 on the 30 LJKB 234 report.

[116] (1862) 3 B&S 89; F&F 110; 31 LJKB 296; 6 LT 697; 10 WR 733; 1 Mar LC 231; 122 ER 34, Ex Ch.

7.11.3.2 Total Value of the Cargo

The total value of the cargo, as appearing on the provisional invoice, included the amount of £10,001 and 10s. for freight; and it was said, on the part of the plaintiffs, that at all events the insurance was not to cover the freight, but only the value of the cargo, as compounded of the cost of the cargo at the place of shipment, the shipping of it, and the commission and other charges which would be incidental to the shipping of such a cargo, and also the premiums of insurance; and that, if the sum of £10,001 and 10s. were therefore deducted, as it ought to be, from the price as per invoice, there would remain uncovered by the policy the comparatively insignificant sum of £241 and 10s[117] That, in his Lordship's view, did not provide sufficient reasons for rejection.

Secondly, Chief Justice Cockburn decided that in this instance what constituted the 'fair amount' of the CIF insurance did not include freight. He continued that:

> The first question is whether that is a correct view of the matter, and whether the freight ought to be deducted, as not meant to be included in the policy of insurance and covered by it. I think that is the correct view; and, when we are dealing with a policy of insurance as one of the shipping documents to be delivered by the seller to the buyer in order to protect the buyer, I am of opinion that the freight, which the buyer will not have to pay until the cargo has arrived, need not be covered by the policy of insurance. There still remains, however, when the freight has been deducted, a sum of 241.10s. unprotected by the policy. Mr. Smith has argued that a further deduction should be made on the score of discounts. In that view I cannot concur, because I think the true period of payment is that fixed by the terms of the contract, and that the discount is only matter of subordinate and independent arrangement between the parties, whereby, in consideration of a speedier payment by the one party than that which the contract would in strictness require, the other party agrees to make an abatement of a portion of the purchase money. I do not think, therefore, that that touches the difficulty in the case.[118]

Thus, if the difference had been higher, rejection would have been possible.

Thirdly, Chief Justice Cockburn decided, on the *de minimis* principle, that the small amount of the discrepancy in the value contracted and presented did not warrant rejection by the buyer of the tender. On the question, whether the deficiency of 241.10s. was a matter which could fairly be objected to on the delivery of such a shipping document as this, he thought as it is presented to them, he thought their decision ought to be in favour of the plaintiffs. This is because, the contract provided for payment by the buyers on the delivery of the shipping documents. By that he understood the ordinary and usual shipping documents, as they are understood in contracts of this nature by members of the mercantile community but not outsiders. The policy of insurance is undoubtedly one of these; and, if the policy, instead of being such as is contemplated as an ordinary and usual shipping document, turns out substantially a defective one, and such as would not afford the buyer a reasonable protection and indemnity against risk, which he is entitled to under the terms of such a contract, and the shipping documents be accordingly rejected, and the

---

117 Ibid, at 688–689.

118 Ibid.

performance of the contract resisted on that ground, However, he was far from saying that such ground would not be sufficient to justify a buyer in refusing to fulfil the terms of the contract of purchase and sale, although it became a very different question whether the present small and comparatively insignificant deficiency may be made a mere pretext for a departure from the contract, when substantial and bonâ fide protection is afforded to the buyers by means of the policy.

7.11.3.3 Question of Law in the Circumstances

The defendants submitted the question on this part of the case for the court's consideration, as a mere question of law on this short point. The policy, when produced, turned out to be somewhat less in amount than what appears on the provisional invoice to be the value of the cargo; and it is said that, on that mere simple fact, without more, as a matter of law, the defendants were entitled to say that the buyers were not bound to perform their part of the contract; and that therefore the defendants, who have insured the performance of the contract by their principals, are not bound either. His Lordship could not concur in that proposition taken as a matter of law, for as he said before, there may be facts in any particular case which would justify a buyer in refusing to accept a policy of insurance as one of the shipping documents, if the policy of insurance was substantially inoperative to protect the buyer against the possibility of loss or damage by perils of the sea; but no such question was here submitted as a matter of fact for the consideration of the jury.

It was not proposed that it should be submitted to the jury, whether, in the present instance, the policy of insurance was substantially effective as a shipping document, as satisfying that which the buyers had reasonably a right to expect. The question is submitted to the court was a mere question of law on the facts as they appear to us on evidence; and, as he had said before, he could not come to a conclusion that the defendants' contention is correct. If the objection could avail them anything, it would only be on the ground that this was not a compliance with the terms of the contract, reference being had to all circumstances of the case, and to how far this policy of insurance was, substantially and practically, a protection to the buyer against sea risk. Accordingly, the defendants not having asked to have the question left to the jury, the court was compelled had to take it, as against them, that this was substantially a good policy of insurance, and one which would have satisfied the exigencies of this contract, as being a shipping document on the production and the delivery of which the buyers would have been bound to pay.[119]

For some reason the court sought to compare sufficient policy to a bona fide and an illusory policy.

---

[119] Ibid, at 688–689.

7.11.4 Justice Compton: A 'Fair, Bona Fide and Illusory Policy' in CIF-Afloat Contracts

7.11.4.1 *Bona Fide* Policy

In the course of his judgment, Justice Compton introduced the phrases bona fide policy and illusory policy in addition to the sufficient policy, he thought that in this in this contract the plaintiffs undertook to insure the defendants as to their interest with reference to the contract price, and with reference to the apparent interest of the buyer under the contract. He did not think that, in point of law, that was so. Although he admitted that there was some evidence in the case that the policy was one which would be sufficient as a policy on the shipment and that and probably the jury would have found in the affirmative, if that point had been left to them. He, therefore, concluded that on this issue the defendants must be confined strictly to the objection which is made the ground of their rule, and which really comes to this: they undertook to insure the plaintiff's interest in the cargo with reference to this contract price; that is, to insure the interest to the extent of 50s. per quarter. The validity of that objection depends on the nature of the contract. This is not a contract, as his lordship understood it, for the seller to ship free on board a particular ship to be found by the vendee; but it is one of the usual contracts to sell a cargo which is to come by a ship sailing at a particular time, and is covered by the usual policy that would be taken in such a case.

He did not think the construction of the contract is that these parties engaged to ship the cargo: if it had been to be shipped by these particular parties' other questions might arise; and, as it was argued, it might be an ingredient, if the contract had been so worded, that they should ship and insure in accordance with their knowledge that the value to the buyer was this precise amount. He doubted very much whether that would be so; but, in the present case, he was of the opinion that the plaintiffs were at liberty to buy a cargo in the market of any wheat corresponding with that mentioned in the contract, which should be shipped from the 1st of October to the 15th of November, not in any particular ship, but in any ship answering the description "A 1 English or a first-class foreign vessel, not Greek or Turk." Therefore, he thought it was clear that the present case was one of those in which a person is bargaining for a cargo or which shall answer the description on its shipment, or which shall answer the description on the seller ordering it to be shipped in a particular manner, or by buying a shipment which is already at sea.[120]

7.11.4.2 Policy Existence Pre-requisite

Furthermore, Justice Compton re-emphasized the fact that the CIF policy required first that there be a policy in place at the beginning, although he was prepared to accept that the policy could be taken later in London. Secondly, that the policy must relate to the contract and contract goods. Thirdly, that it must be a policy to cover the full price of the shipment. And, finally, as in *The Julia*, he emphasized the rationale of the policy in CIF contracts to enable goods to be bought and sold afloat

[120] Ibid, at 688–691.

several times where possible; noting that that being the contract, the court was obliged to see how this supposed obligation to insure to the extent of the interest of the parties on that contract, that is, to the amount of the contract price, including the freight, can arise.

He thought it very true that this contract is for a shipment which had to be insured, because the price of 50s. "including freight and insurance;" it had, therefore, be a cargo by a ship which is bringing goods on freight, and there must be a bill of lading, there must be the charter party, and there must be a policy of insurance; and the question is, what is the meaning of that word "insurance," coupled with the phrase "cash in London in exchange for shipping documents"? He did not think that, on this contract, the seller himself was bound to insure. Rather it was one of those contracts in which the insurance "runs," as it has been expressed, as the bill of lading, and the charter party runs, with the interest in the cargo, as one of the three shipping documents.

Furthermore, he thought that, if the original shipper had insured, which he ought to have done, or, if the person who knew of the shipments had insured in London, in either of those cases the policy so effected would be the one to which such a contract as this would refer. Accordingly, appeared unanswerably to be the true view, when the court considered that these documents went along with the property, into whosoever hands it may come. The object was to have these kinds of cargoes saleable in the market; and that, although the cargo has not arrived, the owner may realize his money, and the cargo be sold over and over again before it comes to this country. It seemed to him a monstrous thing to say, with reference to every contract of sale of this description, that there must be a policy to cover the full price. The phrase "shipping documents," he thought, showed that the policy connected with the shipping and effected at that time would be the document meant. He did not mean to say that if, by any accident, there were no insurance when the cargo was shipped, the contract might not be answered by making a policy in London; but he thought the contract contemplated a policy made with reference to the shipment.[121]

7.11.4.3 *Bona Fide* vs *Genuine* Policy

Finally, Justice Compton introduced the interesting concept of a 'bona fide' policy, presumably meaning a 'genuine' policy. Although having a generic same meaning, there is a slight difference in the meaning. 'Bona fide' is a legal term that is often inserted in documents to indicate that any errors it contains are accidental and will be corrected. Bona fide is a Latin phrase that means "in good faith." To make the point he contrasted a "bona fide" policy with an 'illusory insurance', i.e., a deceptive or misleading policy, noting that "I quite agree with what my Lord has said, that the policy must be a bone fide policy. I take it that, if there was an illusory insurance, that would not do; because the contract is for a price covering freight and insurance. It appears to me, as I said before, to contemplate, not only that the cargo shall come on freight, but that it shall come in one of the particular class of ships named, and be insured; and therefore if there was an illusory insurance I think the buyer might

[121] Ibid, at 691.

say, "You have not sent it insured."[122] He thought, therefore, that the terms of the contract relate to the policy on the shipment; that the insurance must cover the value of the goods, and the cost of the insurance, as at the port of loading; but that it need not include the freight or profit at the port of discharge. The buyer buys what the seller sells, and puts himself, in effect, in his shoes.

On the other hand, 'genuine' things are true or authentic. When you're talking about people, being genuine has to do with being sincere. This word has to do with things and people that are true. A genuine blonde is a real blonde—no hair dye involved. A genuine friend is a real friend you can trust when the chips are down. He added that the first man, if he buys from the original shipper, puts himself in his shoes, as it were, and takes the policy from him—supposing the policy is a right policy with regard to the first shipper, and whether it be or not is not determined by the value which the buyer thinks the goods will bear when they come to England. That being so, the only question was one of fact. Was this a document fairly to be taken as a shipping document, accompanying the rest of the papers, and a bonâ fide policy?. He thought that no point was made as to that at the trial. There was some evidence on which the jury might have so found, but no point having been made of it, the court would be doing wrong if they were to send the case down for a new trial on account of any doubt of that kind, the objection at the trial being merely that the plaintiffs ought to have calculated the amount of insurance so as to cover the cost of 50s. For those reasons, he thought that justice was done in this case, and that the point of law on which the defendants insisted was against them. Accordingly, therefore, the rule had to be discharged.[123]

The remaining issue of the amount of the policy in relation to the shipment was taken up by Lord Justice Blackburn.

7.11.5 Justice Blackburn: 'The Amount of the Policy Must Be such as Would 'Fairly and Truly' Cover and Protect that Cargo So Described'

Justice Blackburn, on the other hand introduced the idea of the policy 'fairly and truly' covering the contract goods. He also supported the other judges' contention that the value should be definite rather than allowing to vary in accordance with the market forces. In his opinion the question turns on the construction of this contract, which, as h read it, was a contract to supply a cargo afloat of a particular description, and to furnish the shipping documents in exchange for the price. The cargo itself is not shipped when the contract is made, nor is it known what will be the name of the ship; it is merely a contract to supply such a cargo as described. He, therefore, and he perfectly agreed with the defendants that they would not be bound to pay the stipulated price, unless proper shipping documents were given to them. By which he meant, not only a proper bill of lading and the proper charter party applicable to

[122] Ibid at 691.

[123] Ibid, at 691.

such a cargo as that which is described in the contract, but also a policy of insurance for the proper amount. On these points there was no doubt whatever in his Lordship's mind that the number of quarters of grain that were to constitute the cargo are stipulated for in the contract, and the time and manner in which it is to be supplied are fixed by the contract. Furthermore, that the amount of the policy which the parties contemplated at this time was not, in express terms, mentioned in the contract at all.

The objection taken at the trial was, that, by fixing the price at which the vendors, the plaintiffs, were to supply this cargo afloat, they also fixed the amount to cover which the policy ought to be made out: and, if that were so, the defendants would be right in saying that the policy tendered was not sufficient. Nevertheless, he agreed with the rest of the Court in thinking that that was not the true construction of the contract. If this had been the case of a contract for selling afloat a cargo already shipped in a specific ship (which was originally the more common way in which these transactions were carried on), and the plaintiffs had, as is usual in the market, sold the same cargo from one to another, the contract only varying in price, each vendor in succession stipulating to furnish the shipping documents, he took it to be quite plain, for the reasons which his learned brother [Crompton] had given, that the amount of the policy, which was originally the proper shipping document of such a cargo, could not vary from time to time, according to the different prices which were inserted in the different contracts by the different persons who were passing it from one to the other.[124]

7.11.6 The CIF Policy Is for a Fixed Price

Secondly, Justice Blackburn emphasized the need for the CIF policy to be of a fixed price rather than leaving it dependant on the market, noting that 'The amount of the policy must be such as would fairly and truly cover and protect that cargo so described'.

> To say that the policy must so vary, would be to make its amount dependent on the market and the Corn Exchange of this country, and cause that amount to fluctuate with the fluctuations of the corn market; which would certainly be very inconvenient. This, then, being a contract to supply a cargo afloat, the documents which were furnished would be such as would fairly belong to such a cargo when afloat; and the amount of the policy, must depend, not upon the contract price in this country for which the contractor is to furnish such a cargo, but on the nature and kind of the cargo itself. The amount of the policy must be such as would fairly and truly cover and protect that cargo so described. He agreed with [his learned brother] Hill, whose reasons he did not repeat, has pointed out that, at the trial, there was evidence enough on which the jury might have found that this policy was quite sufficient to cover the cost of the cargo at the port of loading, and of the insurance; and the point taken at the trial not being a question of fact, but merely a question of law, viz. whether the construction of the contract compelled the plaintiffs to make a policy covering the larger sum, the defendants are not entitled to have the rule made absolute on any doubtful point not left to the jury, and on which they were not asked to decide.

[124] Ibid at 692.

Accordingly Lord Blackburn agreed with "what ha[d] fallen from the other members of the Court", that the policy was not to include the freight, which never was at the risk of the defendants, for the reason that if the ship had gone down, they would not have been called upon to pay the freight, and therefore to say that they were entitled to a policy which, in the event of the ship going down, would enable them to recover the value of the freight, which they had not paid, would be, in my opinion, an argument ad absurdum, and a contradiction of all the cases from *Baillie v. Moudigliani.*[125]

For those reasons his Lordship discharged the Rule.[126]

The following three observations are necessary here. First, the CIF is always thought to be for a fixed price, hence the 110% value to cushion any adverse outcomes. Secondly, however, *Tamvaco* was considered on that point (that seller may not go outside margin where the contract stipulated for 'about' and 'more or less amount in *Anderson & Co v Weil Bros & Co*[127] Thirdly, is whether the 110% is the minimum or only the recommended. And if so whether parties could provide for a higher sum.

7.12 The *Minimum* 110% v the *Maximum* Coverage

7.12.1 The Issue of the Minimum 110% of the Contract Price

Although Clause A5 of Incoterms 2020 recommends 110% as the acceptable CIF and CIP normal insurable value, there is no clear guideline for CIF insurance at common law. Case law has scatted around the issue by using 'sufficient', 'reasonable', 'expectations' and 'market value', but none has dared tackle the question whether it is lawful or reasonable to insure for more than 110%. The nearest the judiciary has come to committing itself was in the High Court's advice for flexibility in *Plaimar Ltd v Waters Trading Co Ltd,*[128] a case concerning shipment of Zanzibar cloves via Singapore CIF Fremantle, Australia. The cloves disappeared while in transit in Singapore. In a preliminary issue, it was found that the stipulation that the value should not exceed 110% did not invalidate the CIF contract.

However, one can see the court's rationale for flexibility and reluctance to wade in as there may be unique markets and rare circumstances where 20% profit (i.e., 120%) is acceptable. In any case Incoterms' 110% are only guidelines and there is therefore nothing to stop parties from agreeing higher figure in a unique market.

---

[125] (1 Park on Insurance, 8th ed. p. 116) downwards.

[126] Ibid, at 692.

[127] *Anderson & Co v Weil Bros & Co* [1912] 1 KB 574.

[128] *Plaimar Ltd v Waters Trading Co Ltd* (1945) 72 C.L.R 304.

7.12.2 Whether "Maximum Amount" Can Exceed 110% of the Contract Price?

Although the maximum amount insurable would be the upper limit of the value of the cargo plus 10%, the issue as to whether the parties can exceed that also came up for decision in the Australian case of *Plaimer Ltd v Waters Trading Co Ltd.*[129] The Australian High Court too avoided the decision whether:

(a) 110% was possible;
(b) the CIF stipulation that that 'insurance was not to exceed 10%' was sufficient; and
(c) and if so, whether it would be for the benefit of the seller rather the buyer.

In the end they thought so since CIF is to destination the policy would be for the benefit of the buyer. On the first and second issues they simply left it to the parties to determine what in their view and judgment was a reasonable sum to insure. However, they advised that the addition of ten per cent, or some other percentage, to cover the buyer's profit or the increased value to him is a not uncommon practice, and, on the whole, it looks as if the clause is to express a limit of the amount of the responsibility of the seller to insure but, subject to that limit, to leave him under the same obligation of effecting a reasonable insurance as well as to amount as to other terms includes other goods, he can await the ship's arrival, obtain a delivery order and tender that instead of a bill of lading. It does not alter the conditions which the seller must fulfil if he chooses to tender a bill of lading and the obligations of the buyer if that course is taken. This judgement is in line with the Incoterms' ethos; it is only a guideline providing the minimum course of action leaving parties to exceed it if they wish and depending on the circumstances of the case.

There is more cogency in the argument founded on the words "net landed weight." If the landing of the goods must be awaited, how can the conditions imported by CIF terms be complied with and how can the responsibility for risks ever arise[130]

On whether the clause constituted an 'indispensable' condition in the CIF policy, he opined that:

> The provision is, of course, based on the assumption that the purpose of the contract will be fulfilled, and the goods will be available for weighing. The real question is whether it imports an indispensable condition into the contract. It seems clear that one way open to the seller of performing his obligations under the contract is to hand over a bill of lading against payment. The goods could not be weighed before delivery to the consignee which, of course, means that the bill of lading is spent, even if not surrendered. It is evident that the weighing may be after payment of the price has been made against the bill of lading. In other words, just as under a c.i.f. contract examination of the goods for condition and quality must take place after the delivery of the bill of lading, so under contract may the final computation of the quantity and adjustment of the price. It is a fair inference that arrival and weighing were not intended to be a condition of or precedent to liability.[131]

---

[129] *Plaimar Ltd v Waters Trading Co Ltd* (1945) 72 CLR 304.

[130] Ibid, at p. 313.

[131] Ibid, at 314.

The lesson of the case seems to be that where there is ambiguity, then the 110% assumes a default position.

7.12.3 Otherwise, the 'Minimum Cover' Is a Default Position

That from the foregone, unless otherwise notified and requested by the buyer, the CIF seller is bound to provide a policy with only the minimum coverage. The obvious omission here is war risks. It is up to the buyer to either provide extra coverage or request extra coverage at additional costs or provide one himself. Alternatively, this problem could be solved by a provision in the contract stipulating the nature of insurance, e.g., that the seller provides an All-Risk Policy.[132] This is also the case now with Incoterms.[133] What the buyer requests will depend on various factors including but necessarily limited to his circumstances, availability of insurance services at home and sometimes government regulations requiring insurance with domestic insurance companies[134] in what is known as policy considerations[135] in or government regulation or interference[136] with insurance.

What remains is what is included and excluded in the 110% CIF insured value.

7.13 The *Included* v the Excluded Policy Costs

7.13.1 Inclusion of Freight into the Policy Value

Tamvaco (above) decided that freight should not be included in the insurable value. The issue as to whether the CIF insurable value should include the cost of freight also came up for decision in another Australian case of *Loders & Nucoline v The Bank of New Zealand,*[137] involving the sale of copra from Australia to London. It was to include the contract price plus 5% for freight. Justice Wright had no difficulty in deciding that it did and should in the case.[138] The reason being that in this particular case a policy on goods valued at the contract price including freight no doubt may involve a possible profit to the buyer if he obtains possession of the documents and is entitled to recover on the policy without having paid the freight, which he attributed to being merely an ordinary incident in business life. He admitted that although as has been pointed out many times, the purpose of marine insurance is to

132 See under *War Risk Policy* (Chap. 10) of this book below, and the authorities cited therein.

133 See e.g., Clauses A5 and B5 of CIF Incoterms 2020, discussed above at Note 68.

134 For the list of countries applying such policy see, Winkler (1995), Chapter 5, pp. 92–94.

135 Ibid; for policy considerations, see Sassoon, "Origin of CIF and FOB Contracts", Note 1; Battista, Note 86, Chapter 5, pp. 92–94 and 96.

136 Ibid, and Annex 2 at p. 96 for list of countries with compulsory national insurance (State Regulation of Export trade insurance).

137 *Loders & Nucoline v The Bank of New Zealand* (1929) 33Ll. L. Rep 70.

138 Ibid, at 76.

give an indemnity, the effect of a valuation may be to give much less than an agreed indemnity.

Besides, it may be that, though the insured has not had to pay the freight but has had to take the documents and therefore make a profit on the insurance to the extent of the freight, he may yet be a very heavy loser indeed, notwithstanding the profit that he has got through collecting the whole insured value under those circumstances, because the market may have risen to such an extent that he is a very heavy loser. Accordingly, he concluded that: "It is an ordinary business risk, and in my opinion, it is quite legitimate within the ordinary principles of marine insurance law that goods under a c.i.f. contract should be valued as this contract provides-a contract of a very well-known trade association-and I see nothing objectionable in any sense in this valuation."[139]

However, it is not clear whether the decision was based on the law or the fact that this was a valued policy in which case, barring fraud, the value would stand. Way back then (1929), 105% seems to be the going rate, which has only risen by 5% in 80 years to Incoterms 2010. Justice Blackburn summed it quite well in *Tamvaco v Lucas* that:

> I need hardly say that I quite agree with what has fallen from the other members of the Court, that the policy was not to include the freight, which never was at the risk of the defendants; for, if the ship had gone down, they would not have been called upon to pay the freight, and therefore to say that they were entitled to a policy which, in the event of the ship going down, would enable them to recover the value of the freight, which they had not paid, would be, in my opinion, an argument ad absurdum, and contradiction of all the cases from *Baillie v Moudigliani* (1 Park on Insurance, 8th ed p. 116) downwards[140]

However, neither case indicated whether the 5% freight charge is part of the 110% or is additional. Nevertheless, the 110% value includes profits.

7.13.2 Inclusion of Profits in the Insurable Value Calculations

It would be prudent and indeed common sense, to include profits in the calculation of insurable value to any mercantile contract. After all s. 3(2) (b) of MIA 1906 includes the earning of profits as legitimate insurable marine adventures and maritime perils. Furthermore, Lord Blackburn in *Mackenzie v Whitworth*[141] rationalised this on the basis that: "The 'subject matter insured', is generally described very concisely as being so much 'on ship', 'on goods', 'on freight', 'on profit on goods', 'on advances on coolies', 'on emigrant money', and son on".[142] Besides, one of the advantages of CIF over FOB is the ability to include profits and transfer other charges to the buyer. Quite often, CIF pricing includes hidden supplier profits on

[139] Ibid.

[140] *Tamvaco v Lucas* (1861) 121 E.R. 683 per Justice Blackburn, at 692.

[141] *Mackenzie v Whitworth* (1875) 1 Ex D 40.

[142] Ibid, at 40.

transportation. These profits inflate the buyer's overall cost of goods unnecessarily but that is the risk he takes in going for the CIF as a package deal. However, the computation should be for reasonable profits. Subject to the nature of the trade and circumstances of a particular transaction, excessive profits might impute fraud on the part of the seller.

Profits and freight charges do not seem to include unusual charges.

7.13.3 Inclusion of Any Other 'Unusual Costs and Charges'

Apart from the ability to transfer profits to the buyer's account the other is to transfer any unusual charges to him. International trade being volatile and commercial transactions unpredictable, being what it is, it would not be out of place to include any unusual expenses in the insurable value for purpose of insurance. For the CIF buyer that means the ocean transportation and insurance costs are normally included in the sales price and are worst still they are subject to duties and fees. What constitutes unusual charges is difficult to predict and should therefore depend on the circumstances and facts of each case. It should however include charges that would not be contemplated by the market or policy. American law is in line with this position.

Since the CIF contract shipment can be resold several times afloat leading to differences in value, how does that affect any apparent differences between shipment and arrival value?

The following guidelines seem to provide some answers to that question.

7.14 The *Arrival* vs the *Shipment* Value

7.14.1 Policy Must Cover Reasonable Value at Shipment

Although that value might rise and fall during transit, in accordance with market fluctuation, nevertheless the CIF policy must cover reasonable value at shipment. In *Johnson v Taylor Bros& Co Ltd,*[143] a case dealing predominantly with service out of jurisdiction, decided so. Likewise, in *Tamvaco v Lucas,*[144] a case which contained a term providing that the value should be 'about' 'more or less' a certain value, the courts used the principle of the *de minimis* rule of construction to decide that seller may not go outside the margin. Similar position was taken in *Law & Bonar v British American Tobacco Co Ltd*[145] and *Wimble v Rosenberg*. Nevertheless, the CIF insurance policy should cover not only the goods sold but also reasonable value at shipment; although the destination value might vary depending on a number of factors including market forces.

[143] *Johnson v Taylor Bros& Co Ltd* [1920] AC 144.

[144] *Tamvaco v Lucas* (1859) 28 LJQB 150; see Note 114 above and 147 below for the full facts of the case.

[145] *Law & Bonar v British American Tobacco Co Ltd* [1916] 2 KB 605.

American law is in line with English law on this point.[146]
But what is reasonable value?

7.14.2 What Is "Reasonable Value at Shipment"?

Tamvaco v Lucas[147] is also the main common law authority for the proposition that the CIF policy should cover value at shipment. It will be recalled that in this case, the defendants had become responsible, as *Del Credere* agents,[148] for the purchase of a cargo of wheat of from 1800 to 2000 quarters, to be shipped at the price of 50s per quarter FOB at Taganrog, 'and including freight and insurance to any safe port in the UK. 'Payment cash in London in exchange for shipping documents.' The plaintiffs tendered the following shipping documents of a cargo answering the description in the contract: a charterparty, a bill of lading and provisional invoice, in both of which the cargo was stated to be 1850 quarters, at 50s per quarter, totalling £4626, less freight, at 10s 9d per quarter, £1001 10s and a policy of insurance effected on the cargo valued at £3600.

Evidence was given, for the plaintiffs which was not contradicted, that the policy tendered was sufficient to protect the interest of the shipper of the cargo at the time of shipment. In an action against defendants for not paying or procuring from their principal payment of the price of the cargo, they pleaded that the plaintiffs were not "ready and willing"[149] to tender, nor did they tender, 'the usual shipping documents' according to the contract. It was held that whether plaintiffs had so tendered was a question for the jury; it was not a question of law but of fact for the jury, whether, in all the circumstances, the policy was a sufficient shipping document within the meaning of the contract.

However, these were obiter dicta observations as the court had decided that the insurance, whether CIF or FOB, should cover value at shipment although that value may subsequently change. Nevertheless, the court left open the issue of what amounts to reasonable value. That notwithstanding, this requirement is not unique to CIF and applies to all export trade and shipment contracts. On the other hand, the case is no authority for value at delivery which might have appreciated or depreciated according to market fluctuations.

7.14.3 Reasonable Value at Arrival

The question of reasonable value at arrival remains unanswered.

---

[146] See paras.7-011–7-014 ante.

[147] *Tamvaco v Lucas* (1862) 31 LJQB 296.

[148] *Del Credere* Agents are agents who undertake or warranty additional risks and are important players in international trade law; see Chuah, Note 6, para. 2-013 at p. 32.

[149] A statement echoed in Hickox v Adams 187634 LT 404, where the defendants were in breach of the CIF contract by tendering a policy which included other non-contract goods.

7.14.4 American Variation: Must Cover Value at Shipment

On this position the American law tallies with English common law. The *Commentary on the Ohio State Revised Code*, 2006, explains that:

> The C.I.F. contract calls for insurance covering the value of the goods at the time and place of shipment and does not include any increase in market value during transit or any anticipated profit to the buyer on a sale by him.
>
> The contract contemplates that before the goods arrive at their destination they may be sold again and again on C.I.F. terms and that the original policy of insurance and bill of lading will run with the interest in the goods by being transferred to each successive buyer. A buyer who becomes the seller in such an intermediate contract for sale does not thereby, if his sub-buyer knows the circumstances, undertake to insure the goods again at an increased price fixed in the new contract or to cover the increase in price by additional insurance, and his buyer may not reject the documents on the ground that the original policy does not cover such higher price. If such a sub-buyer desires additional insurance, he must procure it for himself.
>
> Where the seller exercises an option to ship "freight collect" and to credit the buyer with the freight against the C.I.F. price, the insurance need not cover the freight since the freight is not at the buyer's risk. On the other hand, where the seller prepays the freight upon shipping under a bill of lading requiring prepayment and providing that the freight shall be deemed earned and shall be retained by the carrier "ship and/or cargo lost or not lost," or using words of similar import, he must procure insurance that will cover the freight, because notwithstanding that the goods are lost in transit the buyer is bound to pay the freight as part of the C.I.F. price and will be unable to recover it back from the carrier.[150]

The American law includes freight in the policy value unlike the English and other common law jurisdictions.

7.14.5 Contrasts with Incoterms and UCP Guidelines on Value

Unlike earlier versions, both Incoterms 2020[151] and UCP 600[152] are now explicit on value-it is 110%. Thus, the 110% coverage of the value of the goods is now the minimum allowable in both instruments. However, they do exclude the above value, if the parties so wish. Other guidelines might implied terms from customs such as in commodities trade contracts.

---

150 Commentary to The Ohio State Code, 2006, para. 8.

151 Clause A3(b) leading the 110%, but only as a guideline, see Chap. 8 ahead.

152 Clause 28(f) (ii), also 110, and also as a guideline, see Chap. 11 ahead.

7.14.6 Commodities Contracts Guidelines on Value

There are no standard requirements for the value of CIF policy. Incoterms and the UCP provides for 110% or thereabouts. Different commodity agreements may well provide different values. Clause 20(c)[153] of GAFTA Contract, for instance, details requirements for value, although it puts it 102%. There is lack of English case law on the subject.[154] The subject is discussed in details elsewhere in the book[155]

7.15 Whether CIF Buyer Entitled to Notice and Information to Enable Insuring 'Unusual Risks'?

7.15.1 Introduction

It is established that CIF seller and FOB buyers are responsible for insurance. It is also established in *Wimble v Rosenberg* and *Northern Steel v John Batt* that the FOB buyer is entitled to notice from the seller to enable them to take out insurance.[156] However, the CIF buyer appears not entitled to such communication, except for unusual risks. *Re Weis & Co & Credit et Commercial Colonial (Antwerp)* decided that where the buyers already had notice of the shipment, there is no need for one from the sellers. However, it should be noted that this decision is restricted to notice of the shipment (applicable to CIF and C&F and CIP) and not for insurance purposes (applicable in FOB and related contracts) although one might affect the other.

The issue whether a CIF buyer is also entitled to notice in order to take out insurance came up in the renowned case of *Law and Bonar v British American Tobacco.*[157] The case involved shipment of Calcutta hessian on the British Vessel *The City of Winchester* CIF Smyrna to arrive by September 1914 just before the beginning of the Second World War. The bill of lading being issued on 20 July 1914. Two days later on 6 August 1944, 2 days after the declaration of war, The City of Winchester was captured and sank by a German cruiser before the notice of shipment was given. The buyers sued for failure to deliver and failure to give notice. One of the issues was whether s.32 (3) of the *SGA 1893* applied. It was, however, held by Justice Rowlatt, first, that s 32(3) of the *SGA 1893,*[158] which requires notice to the buyer,

[153] "20 (c) Insurable Value - Insured amount to be for not less than 2% over the invoice amount, including freight when freight is payable on shipment or due in any event, ship and/or cargo lost or not lost, and including the amount of any War Risk premium payable by Buyers".

[154] But see American case of *I.T.N. Consolidators, Inc. v. Northern Marine Underwriters Ltd.* 464 Fed. Appx. 788 C.A.11 Dealing frozen clauses although the insurable value was one of the issues involved.

[155] See Chap. 11 post.

[156] See generally, Ademuni-Odeke (2007), pp. 425–462.

[157] *Law and Bonar v British American Tobacco* [1916] 2 KB 605, approved in The *Julia* Case.

[158] (Cap 71), now replaced by the *SGA 1979* (cap 54) although the relevant section has not changed; *Wimble Sons & Co v Rosenberg & Sons* [1913] 3 KB 743, at 747–48 and *Northern Steel &*

does not apply to a contract on CIF terms entered into in time of peace, inasmuch as the contract itself provides for all the insurance that is contemplated or usual at the time when it is made,[159] and secondly, that the s 32(3)[160] does not impose any new obligation on the seller to give notice to the buyer so as to enable the buyer to insure against war risks if, after the date of the contract, war becomes imminent.[161]

Justice Rowlatt left it open that the requirement might apply during wars and/or hostilities.

However, he summed it up in this case thus:

> The next question is whether s. 32, sub-s. 3, of the Sale of Goods Act, 1893, applies to this case. It clearly does not apply to a c.i.f. contract in times when no one contemplates war, and when, therefore, war is not being usually insured against. It does not apply because the contract c.i.f. provides for all the insurance that is contemplated or usual and the seller is to effect it. That was the nature of this contract when made. It dealt exhaustively and expressly with all the insurance that was in view. But now it is said that, on war becoming imminent, another form of insurance emerged and the contract ceased to be one which dealt exhaustively with the question of insurance and a new obligation arose for the seller. I cannot agree. This sub-section annexes a term to the contract, and the question whether it is applicable or not falls to be decided as at the time when the contract is made. I say nothing as to whether the sub-section could apply to a contract c.i.f. made at a time when insurances other than those to be provided by the seller - e.g., against war risks - are usual. That point does not arise. In this case I do not think there is any real evidence that it was usual to insure against war risks at any material time. Even the buyers themselves in their letter of August 4, referring to the question of insurance against war risks, wrote that, if they were advised of the lowest rates, they would give the matter their consideration. I am not at all certain that they themselves had made up their minds whether they would insure against war risks or not.[162]

Is it reasonable to read that the subsection applies to:
(a) only contracts entered into in peace time;
(b) in unusual circumstances; and
(c) if war becomes imminent?
What happens if t war is not imminent and the circumstances do not involve an unusual insurance risk? The *SGA* 1893 was replaced by the *SGA*, 1979, itself amended or affected several times by subsequent legislation,[163] although the issue of notice is not affected. Indeed, *The Julia* decided in peacetime in 1949 approved *Law and Bonar v BAT.*

Hardware Co v John Batt & Co (London) [1917] 33 TLR 516 at 516 discussed by the author in Note 17 at pp. 448–449.

[159] Ibid.

[160] Now retained as same section in the *SGA 1979* that repealed and replaced the *SGA 1893.*

[161] However as to notice of shipment for addition insurance of CIF contracts see Lorenzo, *CIF and FOB Contracts 2012*, Note 3, at pp. 190–191.

[162] Ibid, at pp. 608, 609.

[163] Such as the *Supply of Goods and Services Act 1982* (cap 29), Carriage of Goods by Sea Act 1992 (cap 50), Sale and Supply of Goods Act 1994 (cap 35) and the Sale of Goods Amendment Act 1995 (cap 28).

However, the common law position may be different from either practice or Incoterms,[164] where under certain circumstances it may be helpful for the seller to provide notice especially with regard to unusual risks. This reinforces, Clause A5, of Incoterms 2020 that the seller must provide the buyer, at the buyer's request, risk and expense (if any), with information that the buyer needs to procure any additional insurance. This also takes this requirement nearer that of an FOB seller, and therefore putting it in the *Wimble v Rosenberg*[165] and *Northern Steel v John Blatt*[166] realms.

7.16 Duration of CIF the Policy

The duration of the CIF policy does not seem to pose much problem and is in line with most export policies, as summarised below.

7.16.1 Policy Must Cover Goods for the Entire Transit

To be a valid CIF policy, it must cover the shipment for the entire journey. In other words, it should be equivalent of the warehouse to warehouse or door to door policy. *Landauer & Co v Craven and Speeding Bros*[167] did not meet such a criterion. It was, therefore, not good CIF tender because it did not include documents for the contract of affreightment from Manila to Hong Kong and Hong Kong to London in a contract which involved transhipment in Hong Kong. *Lascelles & Co Ltd v George Willis & Co Ltd*[168] went further and held that the requirement applies to certificates of insurance too. That sentiment was echoed in *LindonTricotagefabrik v White & Meacham.*[169] However, this is not a departure from case law as the Court of Appeal in *Belgian Grain Produce & Co v Cox & Co Ltd*[170] had settled the issue nearly half a century before that the CIF policy must be cover the whole adventure. However, what constitutes "entire transit" in CIF contracts?

[164] See Clauses A5 and B5 of CIF Incoterms 2020, compared to the common law position as discussed herein

[165] *Wimble & Sons v Rosenberg & Sons* [1913] 1 KB 279; affirmed [1913] 3 KB 743 CA.

[166] *Northern Steel and Hardware v John Batt & Co (London) Ltd* (1917) 33 TLR 516 CA.

[167] *Landauer & Co v Craven and Speeding Bros* [1912] 2 KB 94.

[168] *Lascelles & Co Ltd v George Willis & Co Ltd* (1921) 21 S.R. (NSW) 773.

[169] *Lindontricotagefabrik v White & Meacham* (1974) 118 Sol Jo 752; see Note 115 below for the facts of the case.

[170] *Belgian Grain Produce & Co v Cox & Co Ltd* [1919] W.N.308.

7.16.2 What Amounts to the "*Entire Transit*"?

Entire transit means the whole transit; hence the CIF policy should cover whole transit. This was the subject of *LindonTricotagefabrik v White & Meacham*[171] decision. In this case, the plaintiffs delivered a consignment of pullovers to the defendants' London office under a CIF contract. The invoice and correspondence specified 'CIF customer's warehouse London'. However, the goods were stolen before they could be transferred to the defendants' warehouse in Ealing, West London. The plaintiffs claimed the contract price. Lord Denning in the Appeal Court, approving Justice Peck's ruling,[172] disagreed with the plaintiffs for the reasons that holding that the plaintiffs could not succeed:

> I look at it in this way: the sellers were allowed to depart from their pleading so as to rely on a c.i.f. contract. Having been allowed that concession, the defendants were entitled to take any legitimate point to defeat it. They are entitled to take it in this Court. On this fresh way of putting it, the defendants have a complete answer. No policy of insurance was tendered to cover goods to warehouse. So, the plaintiffs are not in a position to sue for the price of the goods. They very likely have an action against All Transport Ltd. for misdelivery. But that does not arise before us. As between seller and buyer, it seems to me the buyers are not proved to have been liable for the price and I would allow the appeal accordingly.[173]

The court's reasoning was that under a CIF contract the seller was bound to tender an insurance policy covering the goods through to the buyer's warehouse. Therefore, since the plaintiffs had not pleaded a CIF contract but had relied on it as an alternative in the county court the onus was on them to prove such tender, and this they had failed to do. Once again, this requirement is not unique to CIF but applies to all export shipmen contracts.[174]

However, a policy in a contract which clearly allowed for transhipment in the bill of lading, such in *Belgian Grain and Produce Co v Cox & Co Ltd,*[175] was judged by the court of appeal to be sufficient. Equally, in *Lascelles & Co Ltd v George Wills & Co Ltd*[176] a certificate of insurance was adjudged to have covered the goods for the whole transit. The buyer's contention that there was a breach due to deviation of the ship was rejected on the grounds that it was a single continuous voyage anticipated in the contract of carriage.[177] Is *entire transit* equivalent to warehouse to warehouse or door to door policy?

---

[171] *LindonTricotagefabrik v White & Meacham* [1975] 1 Lloyds Rep 384 CA sub norm *Lindontricotagefabrik v White & Meacham* (1974) 118 Sol Jo 752; applied *Manbre Sachran Co v Corn Products* [1919] 1 KB 798.

[172] *LindonTricotagefabrik v White & Meacham* [1975] 1 Lloyds rep 384CA.

[173] Ibid at p. 386 col. 1; Lord Justices Orr and Brown concurring.

[174] Where such policies must cover the whole transit on "warehouse to warehouse" or contain a "transit clause"-see for instance Sassoon, Note 1, at pp. 192–194.

[175] *Belgian Grain and Produce Co v Cox & Co Ltd* [1919] W.N. 308 CA.

[176] *Lascelles & Co Ltd v George Wills & Co Ltd* (1921) S.R. (N.S.W) 773.

[177] See, again, *Landauer & Co v Craven and Speeding Bros* [1912]2 KB 94 where it was held that the tender of documents was not valid tender because it did not include all the documents for con-

7.16.3 *"Warehouse to Warehouse"* or *"Door to Door"* Policy

Modern policies now include transit clauses and are issued 'warehouse to warehouse' or "door to door" to avoid problems arising out of interpreting entire transit. This is normally achieved by inclusion of a warehouse-to-warehouse clause. This is a clause in an insurance policy that provides for coverage of cargo in transit. A warehouse-to-warehouse clause usually covers cargo from the moment it leaves the origin-warehouse until the moment it arrives at the destination-warehouse. Separate coverage may be necessary to insure the cargo while it is being stored in either warehouse. However, such transit clauses require continuation in the coverage to validate the policy. Thus, in *Idle & Christie v Chalmers & White,*[178] damage by fire of jute from Calcutta to Dundee insured under the old Institute Clauses, was not considered by Justice Kennedy to have broken the chain link while the cargo was awaiting for unloading at the destination. Consequently, the buyer's contention that the jute was not covered since it had not reached the warehouse but was waiting in a shed at the wharf, was rejected. The transit provision is now contained in Cargo Clauses (A)-1/1/09.

7.16.4 Reconciling the Statutory and Institute Clauses' Transit Provision

The courts, in a recent case of *Nima SARL v Deves Insurance Public Co Ltd (The Prestrioka)*,[179] had the opportunity to consider the effect of insurance warehouse-to-warehouse under a modern Institute Clauses which seems to apparently conflict with s.44 of MIA 1906, titled "Sailing for a different destination", and which provides that where the destination is specified in the policy, and the ship, instead of sailing for that destination, sails for any other destinations, the risk does not attach. Also, under consideration in the case was Rule 2 of the Rules for Construction of the Policy,[180] which provides that where the subject matter is insured from 'from' a particular place, the risk does not attach until the ship starts on the voyage insured.

In the case,[181] Lord Potter thought that it was the plain import of the judgment in the Simon Israel case that, despite the effective extension of the voyage insured 'from' the moment of sailing back to the moment of leaving the warehouse for the purposes of the attachment of risk, the overall voyage or adventure assured is still properly characterized as a voyage from A to B and, if that adventure is never in fact embarked upon, the insurer will not be liable. Accordingly, he did not accept Mr. Dunning's [defendants counsel] argument that, if the goods have been appropriated by the hand and act of an innocent seller or shipper to carriage in the vessel named

tracts of affreightment between Manila to HK and HK to London.

[178] *Idle and Christie v Chalmers and White* (1900) 5 Com Cas.210.

[179] *Nima SARL v Deves Insurance Public Co Ltd* (*The Prestrioka*) [2003] 2 Lloyd's Rep 327.

[180] First Schedule to the *Marine Insurance Act*, 1906.

[181] *Nima SARL v Deves Insurance Public Co Ltd* (*The Prestrioka*) [2003] 2 Lloyd's Rep at 350.

in the policy which he believes and intends will occur, that is sufficient to avoid the effect of s. 44 if the vessel in fact sails on a different voyage. Rather, he thought it was clear from the authorities that where an insurer invokes s. 44, the Court will conduct an ex post facto exercise to determine not simply the contractual, but the actual, destination of the ship at the time of sailing, which exercise depends upon the acts and intentions of the owners and/or master at the time of its departure.[182]

Referring to ss. 44 and 46 of MIA 1906, on deviation and change of voyage, Lord Porter opined that if the Court determines that, at the time of sailing, vessel and cargo were in truth bound for a terminus ad quem other than that identified in the policy as definitive of the voyage insured, then s. 44 will apply and the risk which prima facie attached when the goods left the warehouse will in the event be held not to have attached. Referring to *Hewitt v. London General Insurance Co. Ltd*[183] and s. 46 of MIA1906 Act, he retorted that the position is to be contrasted with that where the prior intention is merely to deviate. In that event, provided the terminus ad quem remains unaltered, the policy will attach; however, at the point when deviation occurs (without lawful excuse) the insurer will be discharged from liability.[184]

However, in the end he thought that the provision did not apply to goods lost between the warehouse and the ship's rail.[185]

7.17 Relationship of Domestic to Foreign Policy

7.17.1 Must a UK Policy Be Effected with a UK Underwriter?

This is an obscure legal requirement in the CIF Commodities' Contract that the insurance should be taken out with a UK insurer. The GAFTA Standard Term Contract provides that:

> (b) Insurers - The insurance to be effected with first class underwriters and/or companies who are domiciled or carrying on business in the United Kingdom or who, for the purpose of any legal proceedings, accept a British domicile and provide an' address for service of process in London, but for whose solvency Sellers shall not be responsible.[186]

This is now also supported by a phrase in Clause A5 of both the CIF and CIF that the seller should provide cover commensurate with those in Cargo Clauses (A) and (C) respectively "or any similar clauses". However, both the GAFTA and Incoterms Clauses must be read with caution.

---

[182] Ibid.

[183] *Hewitt v. London General Insurance Co. Ltd.*, (1925) 23 Ll.L. Rep. 243.

[184] See Note 180.

[185] Ibid.

[186] Gafta Contract Series No. 100 (Effective 1st September 2010).

First, it appears this may be so only where the issue is adjudicated in but not outside the UK.

Secondly, it is more of an English Law Applicable Clause as contained in Clause 19 English Law and Practice Clause of the Cargo Clauses[187] providing that "This insurance is subject to English law and practice", rather than a CIF insurance principle.

Thirdly, in view of the opening of the UK insurance market to the rest of the European Union market and general liberalisation where anyone can establish an insurance business in the UK, this requirement could be challenged or at best be open to challenge for restrictive practices. That said, it is doubtful whether the provision affects tender of UK policy overseas and vice versa.

7.17.2 Foreign Policy May Be Acceptable in England

Foreign policy must be acceptable to the UK and vice versa. Being truly global and the City of London and the Lloyds of London Insurance being the Centre of International Insurance, international trade would be impractical of this was not the case. Every day hundreds, if not thousands of foreign policies are tendered both here and overseas. Furthermore, international standards are more or less uniform and international merchants speak the same 'language'. *Malmberg v HJ Evans & Co*[188] decided that an English buyer is not entitled to demand an English policy from a foreign seller unless the contract expressly provides so. Presumably because of the unreasonability of the suggestion the question was left open on appeal.[189] Malmberg was followed, on this point, by *AC Harper & Co Ltd v Mackechinie & Co.*[190]

That notwithstanding, the CIF policy should be valid at place of shipment although there are no implications it should be at destination.

Thus, that the policy should not only cover goods for the whole transit but should also be valid at place of shipment, was the subject of the seminal CIF case of *Malmberg v HJ Evans & Co*[191] which, Lord Scrutton decided, confirmed the issues first that the policy must specify clearly the protection available to the buyer. Affirming Justice Bailhache's decision,[192] at first instance, he said:

> It appears that this insurance company have a policy which, written out in full, contains a number of conditions and clauses, but that policy was not tendered with this document, nor was any copy of it tendered to the buyers. The document goes on to say: 'And the rules of the said in insurance company.' It appears that in Sweden there is a document called an insurance plan, which is, I believe, accepted by most of the insurance companies, and, in addition, this insurance company, and, I suppose, the others too, have rules of their own.

---

[187] See Clause 19 of the Cargo Clauses (A)–(C) where the identical text is deployed.

[188] *Malmberg v HJ Evans & Co* (1924) 29 Com Cas 235.

[189] *Malmberg v HJ Evans & Co* (1924) 30 Com Cas 107 at 115–116 CA235.

[190] *AC Harper & Co Ltd v Mackechinie & Co* [1925] 2 KB 423.

[191] (1924) 41 TLR 38, (1924) 20 Ll. L. Rep. 40.

[192] *Malmberg v HJ Evans & Co* (1924) 29 Com Cas 235.

> It is quite clear, therefore, that nobody looking at this policy, if I may so call it, could find out, without a very great deal of research, and looking at all sorts of documents and the marine laws of Sweden, what sort of perils are insured against, and under what conditions.[193]

For those reasons, His Lordship concluded that the document therefore signally fails to answer what is necessary to make it in itself a complete insurance policy, that is to say it does not give the assured knowledge of the particular perils against which he is insured, and it is conceded that if this document had been tendered to the buyers on the first occasion of these people doing business together, it is a document the buyers would have been entitled to reject.[194] He was, therefore, not prepared to hold, and neither did he think it was the law, that any objection can be taken to this policy on the ground that it is a policy of a Swedish company. It seemed to him that inasmuch as we under common law CIF contracts as sellers always provide our policy, we are also, when we are buyers in this country, bound to take as a policy to which no objection can be taken a policy issued by a company or underwriters in the country from which the goods come and where the seller carries on business. So far as that objection is concerned, he did not think there was anything in it.[195]

To solve the problem, *Promos SA v European Grain & Shipping Ltd*[196] suggests inserting specific clauses involving reputable insurers, currency of the policy and application of UK law.

7.17.3 Validity of a Foreign Policy in the UK

The Court of Appeal having dodged the issue in *Malmberg*, there is nothing to suggest that foreign policy may not be valid tender in the UK.[197] International trade practice being fairly standard the reverse is probably true. Otherwise, *Malmberg* was considered on that point by Lord Caldcote in *FinaskaCellulosaforeningen v Westfield Paper Co.*[198] He said:

> The judgment of Mr. Justice Bailhache in the case of Malmberg v. H. J. Evans & Co., 29 Com. Cas. 235, 19 Ll.L.Rep. 25 was cited. There the contention was made that buyers could not take objection to the form of a policy of insurance merely because there had been a large number of previous transactions in which they had accepted the particular kind of policy without objection. Mr. Justice Bailhache rejected this contention, but the decision throws no light on the facts of this case. I accept [the defendants'] submission that a bill of lading

[193] Ibid.

[194] Ibid; [1924] 19 Ll. L. Rep. 25, at p. 25.

[195] *Malmberg v HJ Evans & Co* [1924] 19 Ll. L. Rep. 25, Bailhache J at p. 26.

[196] *Promos SA v European Grain & Shipping Ltd* [1979] 1 Lloyds Rep 375.

[197] On the position of tender of foreign policies in the UK and vice versa, see Sassoon, *CIF and FOB Contracts*, Note 3, at pp. 196–197.

[198] *FinaskaCellulosaforeningen v Westfield Paper Co* [1940] 4 All ER 473, (1940) 68 Ll. L. Rep. 75.

> tendered under a c.i.f. contract must be, as in the case of the policy of insurance, in a form usual or current in the trade.[199]

That in turn raises the question what constitutes a valid and/or invalid CIF policy within the MIA 1906. *Reuter v Sala*[200] suggests that such dilemma is solvable by the buyer taking out an open or floating policy to cover himself. *The Promos*-type suggestions above would go a long way to providing viable and practical solutions. If foreign policies were not acceptable in other jurisdictions, trade would grind to a halt.

7.17.4 Policy Must Be Valid at Place of Shipment

A plausible assumption from *Malmberg* is that for foreign policy to be valid in the UK, the policy should be valid at place of shipment. An educated assumption is made here as this issue was not really discussed much in the Court of Appeal decision, as the sellers had admitted that the document was not good tender. Could a foreign policy valid at shipment not be valid under English law and vice versa?

That notwithstanding, the Appeal Court in *Malmberg* had this to say:

> Whereupon each of the parties gets on his strict rights, and in this particular case the goods are rejected because there is not a document which complies with the original terms, unless there was some course of business to alter them. I am not able, and the learned Judge was not able, to infer from that state of facts, though the document had been tendered and accepted in cases where no question whatever arose about it, an agreement in a case where each party was standing on his strict rights-even though that position was occasioned by the buyers putting forward a perfectly untenable claim-that the strict rights must not be enforced; and if you are on strict rights then, according to the admission, this is not a document that can be tendered… I can see that there are serious questions arising as to whether Swedish insurance policies are good tender. I can see that in a case where there is not an admission, and where the case arises under somewhat different facts, there may be very serious questions for this Court. I can only suggest to Swedish sellers that they should alter the terms of their contract. It is quite obvious that you may contract on the terms that a document of this sort shall be a good tender; it may be a good tender even without such a term; but this case I decide on the ground, firstly, that there is an admission that it is not a good tender unless there is some course of business, or waiver or estoppel; and, secondly, that the facts of this case do not amount to such evidence of course of business or waiver or estoppel as to terminate or destroy the original position.[201]

It having been admitted that in the absence of some evidence of course of business or waiver of estoppels, the issue in *Malmberg*[202] was whether the policy of insurance tendered by the seller was not a good tender under a CIF contract. The court found that there was no evidence of course of business between the parties, or waiver or

---

[199] Ibid, at 81.

[200] *Reuter v Sala* (1879) 4CPD 246 CA.

[201] *Malzberg v HJ Evans & Co* (1924) 20 Ll. L. Rep. 40, at 43.

[202] Ibid.

estoppel on the part of defendants, which would entitle them to set up the defence that the document in question was not a compliance with the terms of the written contract. What *Malmberg* or any other decision before and after it does not answer, however, is whether it is a sufficient compliance with a CIF contract if the seller tenders a policy, which is valid in the country in which the seller is carrying on business and on which the seller ships the goods. *Malmberg* and *Promos SA v European Grain &Shipping Ltd,*[203] where Justice Parker considered the status of tender of the cover note.[204] He said:

> I take the cover note first. This is no more than a certificate that a contract of insurance on unspecified terms has been effected for the sellers. It may or may not have been on terms which cover other people than the sellers; it may or may not have included appropriate or usual conditions; it may or may not have been one which was transferable by endorsement or anything of that sort. It is no more than a statement by some brokers that an insurance has been affected... It was submitted that there is no material difference between this document and a certificate of insurance but that appears to me to be an unsustainable contention. In the one case the underwriters are bound to the holder of the certificate provided that it is properly endorsed; here there is no undertaking by the underwriters of any sort whatever and that document does not, in my judgment, avail.[205]

Surely, a foreign policy should be tendered in the UK otherwise international trade would not function.

7.18 Constitution of 'Valid' Policy and 'Approved' Policy Within the MIA 1906[206]

7.18.1 Policy Must Be an 'Approved' Policy

An added difficulty to the debate on the 'reputable' and 'responsible' insurer (below) is the reference or use of 'approved' insurer or approved policy. That term first appeared in Clause A5 of both the CIF and CIP only in the Incoterms 2020. However, the approved policy is not defined by the Clause on anywhere else. In plain English "approved" means authorised or agreed by custom. It is synonymous with 'acceptable', 'agreed', 'permitted', and 'official'. Approved policy does not appear in a Marine Insurance policy but does in Employment Insurance policy. Bennett is of the view that in terms of the *Employment Liability (Compulsory Insurance) Act* 1969, s.1 (3) (a) an approved policy is a policy which is not subject to 'prohibited conditions' (qv). These are certain conditions (specified in the General Regulations), which would, if not complied with by the insured employer allow the insurer to repudiate a claim under the policy. There is no objection, however, to

[203] *Promos SA v European Grain &Shipping Ltd* [1979] 1 Lloyd's Rep 375.

[204] Ibid.

[205] Ibid, at p. 388.

[206] For a discussion limited to section 44 of the Act and the *Institute Cargo Clauses*' "*Warehouse to Warehouse*", see Lorenzon, Sassoon, *CIF and FOB Contracts*, 5th edn 2012 at p. 193.

conditions that enable the insurer, in specified circumstances, to reclaim from the insured the amount of any compensation (including incidental costs and expenses) paid by the insured to the injured employee. The insurer issues a certificate to indicate that the policy is approved in accordance with the Act.[207] A policy from a 'responsible' and/or 'reputable' insurer an essential CIF insurance requirement (below) might go a long way to establishing an approved policy.

7.18.2 Policy Should Be Procured from a 'Responsible' and "Reputable" Insurer

Both the common law and Incoterms 2020 provide that the CIF policy must be procured from "an insurance company of good repute", reputable insurer. However, case law also provides that the policy should be procured from a 'responsible' insurer. That notwithstanding, it does not define what a 'responsible insurer' is. The two terms are not defined. However, in plain English, 'responsible'[208] denotes 'accountable', 'in charge', 'dependable' and 'conscientious', while 'reputable'[209] means 'of good repute', 'highly regarded', 'well thought of', 'trustworthy', 'sound', 'upright', 'honest' and 'decent'. A reputable insurance company or person therefore means a reliable company or person and can be trusted. In the final analysis it means a well-known insurance company with proven trading record and reputation in meeting its claims obligations. It would follow that a reputable insurer is most likely to meet the responsible insurer requirement. In *Cantiere Mecannico Brindisno v Constant*[210] Justice Scrutton affirmed that the policy must be taken from a responsible insurer,[211] a decision affirmed by the Court of Appeal.[212] So, the ordinary meaning of the words should be adopted.

However, this does not include a ppi policy which has been avoided by the insurers.[213]

[207] The Act meaning the Marine Insurance Act 1906—Bennet (1992), p. 24.

[208] There is no known legal definition of responsible insurer, dependable and conscientious being the nearest.

[209] Ibid re 'reputable' insurer but the above reflects the spirit if not the letter of reputable.

[210] *Cantiere Mecannico Brindisno v Constant* (1912) 17 Com Cas 182.

[211] Ibid at 192.

[212] *Cantiere Mecannico Brindisno v Constant* (1912) 17 Com Cas 332.

[213] *Strass v Spillers & Bakers Ltd* [1911] 2 KB at 759 at 768 and 773.

7.18.3 What Constitutes, "Approved", 'Responsible', and 'Reputable' Insurer?

Both the common law and the 2020 Incoterms,[214] but not UCP 600,[215] provide for a reputable insurance company and/or approved policy but without defining or providing what constitutes reputable or approved. It is once more left to case law to fill in the gaps. And the answer is emphatic: CIF and CIP cover should be with an "approved insurance company". *Scott (Donald H) & Co v Barclays Bank Ltd,*[216] where bankers issued a letter of credit to English sellers of tons of steel plates to Dutch buyers, supports the principle that CIF insurance should be within an approved policy and more. But what is an approved insurance policy? It was considered in the case that an approved 'insurance policy is one to which no reasonable objection can be made'. Under the terms of the letter of credit, in this case, the bankers agreed to honour the sellers' draft for the amount of the purchase-money, which included freight and insurance to Rotterdam, provided the draft were accompanied by an approved insurance policy covering the shipment of the goods.

The sellers presented their draft accompanied by a certificate of insurance, which neither contained nor offered any means of ascertaining the full terms of the insurance. In an action by the sellers against the bankers for not honouring the draft, Lord Bankes held that the certificate of insurance was not an 'approved insurance policy' within the meaning of the letter of credit, and that the bankers were justified in refusing to honour the draft.[217] He thought courts should ask two supplementary questions on the form of the document before answering this question. First, is whether the document contains sufficient information to enable any one reading it to ascertain whether it reaches the standard of an 'approved insurance policy'? Second, is whether the expression 'approved insurance policy,' occurring in a letter of credit issued by an English bank to an English trading firm, means a policy of insurance in the English form valid according to English law and enforceable in England.[218]

For those reasons he thought it unnecessary to decide that question in this case and rested his decision upon the fact that the document tendered was one of which no one could assert that it did or did not fall within the terms of the letter of credit. It is a certificate of insurance which only indicates that a policy has been issued by this company; but the terms of that policy, the risks insured against, and the conditions imposed by the policy respecting shipment can only be ascertained by reference to some document which did not accompany the certificate and of which the

---

214 Incoterms 2020 CIF Clause A5.

215 UCP 600, Note 20, Clause 28 is silent on the issue.

216 *Scott (Donald H) & Co v Barclays Bank Ltd* [1923] 2 KB 1.

217 For tender of documents under UCP 600 see Chap. 11 below.

218 Where would that leave Scotland and Northern Ireland?.

appellants could know nothing. On this point he felt guided by McCardie J. in *Diamond Alkali Corporation v. Bourgeois,*[219] where dealing with a certificate in the same form as the document in this case the learned judge said a certificate is not a policy. It does not purport to be a policy. It is a certificate, in this case, that a policy was issued to D. A. Horan, and it incorporates the terms of that policy. Those terms I do not know, nor is there anything before me to indicate that the buyers knew them.[220]

7.18.4 Documentation in Approved Policy

On the relation between a certificate and a policy for purposes of tender in this particular case he explained that the certificate does not show whether that policy was in a recognized or usual form or not and, therefore, does not therefore contain all the terms of the insurance. Those terms have to be sought for in two documents—namely, the original policy and the certificate. But even if this document is not a policy yet the sellers say it is 'equivalent to a policy.' In connection with that phrase, he quoted from another part of the judgment of Bailhache J. in *Wilson & Co. v. Belgian Grain Co*[221] *that* the buyer—cannot be compelled to take a document which is something like that which he has agreed to take but is entitled to have a document of the very kind which he has agreed to take, or at least one which does not differ from it in any material respect.

Consequently, as to whether the document before him differs in any material respect from a policy of insurance, he could not see how the buyer here could know whether the document he got was of a proper character (one he was bound to accept) unless he saw the original policy, and examined its conditions, whether usual or otherwise. For those reasons it seemed conclusive answer to the claim of the respondents that they had tendered an approved insurance policy. Accordingly, he was content to decide this case upon this single point in accordance with the opinion of McCardie J.[222]

Scott (Donald H) remains good law and was applied the following year in *Malmberg.*[223] So the test of an approved policy is that of the reasonable man. Under English law and practice, a *Lloyd's Marine Policy*[224] or the Insurance *Company's Marine Policy*[225] would fulfil both the 'approved' and 'reputable' criteria. The aim

---

[219] *Diamond Alkali Corporation v. Bourgeois* [1921] 3 K. B. 443, 455.

[220] Ibid, at pp. 12 and 13.

[221] *Wilson & Co. v. Belgian Grain Co* [1920] 2 K. B. 1, 9.

[222] Ibid.

[223] See paras.7-083–7-084 ante.

[224] Developed in 1982 and used by Lloyds Insurance to replace the old Ships and Goods (SG) Policy that had lasted nearly 400 years; For reasons for change see generally, Legal *and Documentary Aspects of Marine Insurance Contract* TD/B/C.4/ISL/27/Rev 1. Report by UNCTAD Secretariat (1982).

[225] Ibid, but used only by the non-Lloyds Insurance Companies but covering same risks.

of his requirement is to protect the buyer for goods sold afloat by ensuring that the seller does not provide either non-existent or some cow-boy back street insurer who might not be capable of meeting their obligations. Perhaps the best clarification is that of the GAFTA Contract which provides:

> The insurance to be effected with first class underwriters and/or companies who are domiciled or carrying on business in the UK or who, for the purpose of any legal proceedings, accept a British domicile and provide an' address for service of process in London, but for whose solvency Sellers shall not be responsible[226] (*emphasis added*).

Thus, a UK 'approved insurers' must not only be with 'first class' insurers, but should also be UK domiciled or UK based business, provide a London or UK address and be solvent. However, sellers are not responsible to the buyers for the solvency of such insurers from whom they procure cover. First class underwriters were also used in a Chinese contract[227]

7.18.5 Policy Must Be a "Valid Policy"

To fulfil his obligations, the seller must also tender a valid policy. What amounts to a valid policy not defined but will depend on the facts of the case and the surrounding circumstances. A literal meaning of the term in relation to an argument or point, means having a sound basis in logic or fact; reasonable or cogent. In terms of criticism, the term is synonymous with well founded, sound, well grounded, reasonable, rational, logical, justifiable, defensible, defendable, supportable, sustainable, maintainable, workable, arguable, able to hold water, plausible, telling, viable, bona fide; More cogent, effective, powerful, convincing, credible, believable, substantial, forceful, strong, weighty, authoritative, reliable; and rarevindicable. Legally, the term means legally binding due to having been executed in compliance with the law. While "a valid contract" is synonymous: correct, authentic, legally acceptable, proper, bona fide, genuine, official, signed and sealed. In insurance law, however, the policy must be that stipulated in the contract of sale.

And if issued in the UK it must conform to the requirements of MIA1906 and related legislations, the UK Cargo Clauses of the LIU. Other guidelines appear in Justice Scrutton's judgment in *Cantieri Meccanico Brindisino v Constant.*[228] These are, inter alia, that:

> The clause 'seaworthiness admitted' is put into these insurances of floating docks and river steamers not ordinarily engaged in sea voyages to avoid the doubtful and difficult inquiry

---

[226] Paragraph (b) of *the Gafta Contract, Series No. 100* (Effective 1st September 2010).

[227] See the Annex (GAFTA Contract No 72) to this book, which uses the same words.

[228] *Cantieri Meccanico Brindisino v Constant (Janson)* [1912] 2 KB 112.

> whether sufficient temporary strengthening for an unusual service has been applied to a subject-matter not originally intended for that service; and in my view the proposal of such an insurance to an underwriter, while requiring the disclosures I have already suggested, puts him on inquiry as to the actual construction, and strengthening if any, of the subject-matter if he wants to investigate it. The defence of concealment in my view therefore fails.[229]

However, the argument on behalf of the plaintiffs in the case that the insurer does not warrant the validity of the policy was rejected by Justice Scrutton.

7.18.6 Policy Must Not Be a PPI or 'Honour Policy'

Although the policy proof of interest (ppi) is generally similar to the wagering and gambling policies discussed below, it is, nevertheless, quite different in other aspects. Although ppi policies might not necessarily be illegal or unlawful the CIF policy should not be a ppi or honour policy or other wagering policy in contravention of s.4 (2) (b) quoted below of MIA 1906. Justice Hamilton J in *Strass v Spillers* and Baker Ltd[230] defined and provided explained the workings of the ppi policy.[231] However, the best example comes from Bennett's definition of the ppi. as:

> A term which applies to a policy which agrees to pay the insured whether or not he has an insurable interest (qv). By s.4(2) of the Marine Insurance Act 1906 such a policy is deemed to be a gaming or wagering contract and therefore unenforceable in a court. In practice, in maritime ventures it may be difficult to establish the existence of an insurable interest at any given time. Consequently, it has become the custom to attach a PPI to the policies to obviate the need to prove insurable interest. As these policies are legally void and unenforceable, they are known as 'honour policies' as payments under them is dependable on the honour of the insurers. These policies are peculiar to marine insurance[232]

Lord Scrutton in *Thomas Cheshire & Co v Vaughan Bros & Co*[233] thought that a policy containing a ppi clause is void even though the assured has, in fact, an insurable interest.[234] Justice Lawrence in *Re London County Commercial Reinsurance Office Ltd*[235] supports the contention that a policy containing a detachable ppi clause is void even though at the time of the claim under it the clause may have been detached by the assured;[236] while Justice McCardie in *John Edwards & Co v Motor*

[229] Ibid, at 117.

[230] *Strass v Spillers and Baker Ltd* [1911] 2 KB 759.

[231] Ibid, at 768.

[232] Bennet (1992), p. 259.

[233] *Thomas Cheshire & Co v Vaughan Bros & Co* (1920) 123 LT 487.

[234] Ibid at 493.

[235] Re *London County Commercial Reinsurance Office Ltd* (1922) 127 LT 20.

[236] Ibid, at 26.

Union Insurance Co Ltd,[237] supposed there was no subrogation under the ppi. policy.[238] It is evident from these authorities that the ppi policy is not only void but is also not suitable for CIF insurance.

7.18.7 The Policy Must Not Be a Wagering Policy

Although part of the generic wagering policy, and are therefore contained in the same legislative provision, there is a slight difference between a ppi or honour policy and the general wagering policies. A wagering policy is contained in s.4 of MIA 1906 as follows:

> **S.4 of MIA 1906**
> 4 Avoidance of wagering or gaming contracts.
>
> (1) Every contract of marine insurance by way of gaming or wagering is void.
>
> (2) A contract of marine insurance is deemed to be a gaming or wagering contract—
>
> (a) Where the assured has not an insurable interest as defined by this Act, and the contract is entered into with no expectation of acquiring such an interest; or
>
> (b) Where the policy is made "interest or no interest," or "without further proof of interest than the policy itself," or "without benefit of salvage to the insurer," or subject to any other like term:

Provided that, where there is no possibility of salvage, a policy may be effected without benefit of salvage to the insurer.

A wagering policy is the same as a gambling policy below, which is equally unenforceable.

7.18.8 Policy Must Not Be a Gambling Policy

A gambling policy is one whose purposes to bet rather than to insure legitimate commercial risks. Gambling policies are now outlawed by the *Marine Insurance (Gambling Policies) Act* 1909 and the *Gambling Act 2005.*

[237] *John Edwards & Co v Motor Union Insurance Co Ltd* (1923) 128 LT 276.

[238] Ibid, at 278.

Marine Insurance (Gambling Policies) Act 1909 and the Gambling Act 2005
1. Prohibition of gambling on loss by maritime perils.

(1) If—

(a) any person effects a contract of marine insurance without having any bonâ fide interest, direct or indirect, either in the safe arrival of the ship in relation to which the contract is made or in the safety or preservation of the subject-matter insured, or a bonâ fide expectation of acquiring such an interest; or

(b) any person in the employment of the owner of a ship, not being a part owner of the ship, effects a contract of marine insurance in relation to the ship, and the contract is made "interest or no interest," or "without further proof of interest than the policy itself," or "without benefit of salvage to the insurer," or subject to any other like term, the contract shall be deemed to be a contract by way of gambling on loss by maritime perils, and the person effecting it shall be guilty of an offence, and shall be liable, on summary conviction, to imprisonment, . . . F1 for a term not exceeding six months or to a fine not exceeding [F2level 3 on the standard scale], and in either case to forfeit to the Crown any money he may receive under the contract.

(2) Any broker or other person through whom, and any insurer with whom, any such contract is effected shall be guilty of an offence and liable on summary conviction to the like penalties if he acted knowing that the contract was by way of gambling on loss by maritime perils within the meaning of this Act.

PPI policies would come within the ambits of gambling policies[239] and is, therefore, an invalid policy under CIF.

7.18.9 What Constitutes Tender of an 'Invalid' CIF Policy

Legally an invalid policy would be an incorrect or provable or not legally recognized policy. It will be recalled that in the seminal case of *Diamond Alkali,*[240] Justice McCardie determined impliedly that a CIF policy is invalid if not within MIA 1906. In his MIA 1906 deals with marine policies only. It does not cover other documents, although they may be said to be the 'business equivalent' of policies. Neither did he think that MIA 1906 covered the document then before him, as in his humble view a document of insurance was not a good tender in England under an ordinary CIF

[239] See also-*Biddell Bros v Clemens Horst-Cantieri v Constant-Strass v Spillers* (not an honour policy).

[240] *Diamond Alkali Export Corporation v Bourgeois* [1921] 3 K.B. 443; see also under tender in Chap. 8 below.

contract unless it was an actual policy and unless it falls within the provisions of MIA1906, as to assignment and otherwise.[241]

Impliedly because the case actually concerned whether a 'Received for shipment', bill of lading was acceptable in CIF contract. Under a contract for the sale of goods to be shipped from American Eastern seaboard CIF Gothenburg, the sellers tendered, with an invoice for the goods:

(a) a document purporting to be a bill of lading, in the following form, 'Received in apparent good order and condition from DA to be transported by the steamship All glia now lying in the Port of Philadelphia or failing shipment by said steamer in and upon a following steamer, 280 bags Dense Soda; and,
(b) a certificate of insurance issued by an American insurance corporation, which, as the certificate declared, 'represents and takes the place of the policy and conveys all the rights of the signed policy holder, as surely as if the property was covered by a special policy direct to the holder of this certificate'

Lord Scrutton in *Koskas* agreed with the buyers that they were entitled to reject on the ground that proper documents had not been tendered by the sellers in conformity with the contract. Two reasons were given for the decision: first because the document tendered did not acknowledge shipment, and was therefore not a bill of lading within the CIF contract; and secondly, because the tender of insurance certificate was not good tender in England under an ordinary CIF contract unless it is an actual policy, and unless it falls within the MIA 1906. *Diamond Alkali,* still good law, was followed on this point in *Donald H Scott Co Ltd v Barclays Bank Ltd,*[242] but distinguished on a different issue by Lord Banks and Lord Scrutton in *Koskas v Standard Marine Insurance.*[243] So, it would appear the common law as codified by the MIA 1906 is very strict. This issue ties up with the need for an 'approved policy' above.

7.19 Other Insurance Considerations

7.19.1 Common Law vs. Incoterms Insurance

Although the common law has had opportunities to interpret CIF contracts, nevertheless common law rules for CIF Insurance may differ from those of incoterms (*post*) which it predates. However, the results might be different if CIF incoterms are incorporated into the contract. The courts had the opportunity recently to deliberate on the effect of the incorporation of Incoterms into the common law (contract). *Stora Enso OYJ v Port of Dundee*[244] was such a case which incorporated the substance of Clause A5 of Incoterms 2020. The same Clause in Incoterms 2010 was

---

[241] Ibid, at 457. As a general rule, the buyer is entitled to a policy of insurance and nothing else will suffice.

[242] *Donald H Scott Co Ltd v Barclays Bank Ltd* [1932] 2 KB 1.

[243] *Koskas v Standard Marine Insurance* (1927) 137 LT 165.

[244] *Stora Enso Oyj v Port of Dundee* [200] CSOH 40; [2006] 1 CLC 453.

more substantial than that of Incoterms 2000.[245] It has been retained by Incoterms 2020 (see Chap. 8 post).

7.19.2 CIF Insurance and the UCP 600

The provisions of the UCP600 relate more to tender of documents for payments under letters of credit than with regards to substantive law on the subject. These tender rules are contained in Clauses 34 of UCP 500[246] and Clause 28 of UCP 600.[247]

7.19.3 CIF War Risks' Insurance[248]

English War risks policy for the FOB, CIF and all other contracts discussed in this book is consolidated in Chap. 11 below.

7.19.4 American Changes to the Common Law

The American CIF differs from the English CIF in that the former includes coverage for war risks which is chargeable separately to the seller. Commentary to the Ohio Revised Code makes that point thus:

> An additional obligation is imposed upon the seller in requiring him to procure customary war risk insurance at the buyer's expense. This changes the common law on the point. The seller is not required to assume the risk of including in the C.I.F. price the cost of such insurance, since it often fluctuates rapidly, but is required to treat it simply as a necessary for the buyer's account. What war risk insurance is "current" or usual turns on the standard forms of policy or rider in common use[249]

For other insurance considerations see chapter (below).

---

[245] *The Stora Enso OYJ v Port of Dundee* case is covered in details in Chap. 6 above. Insurance of CIF and related contracts under Incoterms is the subject of Chaps. 8 and 11 post.

[246] UCP 500 (1993). ICC Doc. No. 516E.

[247] UCP 600 (2007), ICC Doc. No. 680E. Tender of the policy at common law is covered above while those under the UCP 500 and UCP 600 form part of the detailed discussions under Chap. 11 below.

[248] This subject is covered together with insurance of FOB in Chap. 10 below.

[249] *Commentary on the Ohio Revised Code* 2006 at p. 7.

7.20 Damages for Breach of Insurance Obligations

7.20.1 Failure to Insure

Failure to insure contract goods can lead to untold damages and other consequences as detailed below in this paragraph and in Chap. 11 (post).

7.20.2 Insufficient Cover

The CIF seller would be liable for taking out insufficient cover for the shipment. What constitutes sufficient cover under the CIF policy is adequately covered (above)-meaning not enough or inadequate. *Tamvaco* and other authorities on 'sufficiency' and 'amount' of policy (above) also apply here. Sufficiency would be provided for either in the contract or through request. Failing that guidelines should be sought customs and usages as well as from commodity trade insurance requirements. It will be a question of fact in each case whether the seller has provided sufficient cover. The *Orient & Co v Brekke* decision determined that what constitutes sufficiency is a matter of fact to be determined in each case. Insufficient cover for own seller's interest and contingency policy would amount to under insurance and therefore self-insurance for the rest. This applies only to the contractual policy taken for the buyer's benefit. To the buyer insufficiency would not be a breach of contract covered by contingency insurance. The American law provided for sufficient cover but without indications of the consequences for failure to provide sufficient insure.

7.20.3 Failure to Tender: English Law

One of the distinct features of CIF contracts is that the buyer is required to pay against the tender of documents listed in the sale contract. If the seller fails to tender the policy among the documents, then he does not only forfeit payment but would be in fundamental breach of the contract: it is the policy which holds the contract together. A CIF contract is an agreement to sell goods at a price which is inclusive of the cost of ... The purchaser is obliged to pay against the tender of the documents ... as per the insurance policy, but not against the vendor under the contract of sale. ... 'a contract which contains such conditions as will render the seller liable for the (See also under Chap. 11).

7.20.4 Failure to Tender: American Law

The same rules apply in the US an elsewhere. He must not only tender the policy among the documents but it must also be a valid policy. As indicated above, a valid tender the policy of insurance must be one, which can be disposed of ... by the buyer's contract and not merely insure his goods as part of a larger quantity in the buyer, did not impose any new obligation on the seller to give notice. (See under Chap. 11).

7.21 Further Food for Thoughts

7.21.1 General Considerations

The advantages of the CIF over all other contracts are overwhelming. However, there are aspects such as insurance implication of passage of risks, property; insurance implications of whether the contract is a sale of goods or documents and of the two rights of rejection; and the problem of notice, that needs food for thoughts which might affect especially the seller's rights for which he might not necessarily have recourse to insurance or other immediate remedies. These are discussed in details below. Babu, for instance, thinks one of the problems is that moreover sometime the CIF term in contract seems to be very vague, while determining whether it is a CIF contract or not.[250] For example, where the goods are shipped in bulk and remain unascertained until the ships arrival, in that case the documents cannot cover the goods sold. In those scenarios the question arises whether this is an CIF contract after passing of documents or is it an 'arrived' or ex ship contract;[251]

7.21.2 Insurance Implications of Passage of Risks

The seller has the advantage of receiving the transacting money well in before the goods actually reach the buyer. The advantage of the buyer is that he has a substantial right once he gets the documents of sale and he may still reject the goods on their actual delivery if they turn out to be not in conformity with the standards he had prescribed. The risk which he takes is that the loss or damage of goods may not be covered by the bill of lading or insurance policy. The main disadvantages of CIF contract are that risk passes to the buyer at the time of contract. S20 of the *SGA*1979 provides that, after delivery of the goods risk passes to the buyer, but in the CIF contract risk passes to the buyer at the time he pays and takes up the document.

On the other hand, risk passes to the buyer when the seller ships the goods. However, if the contract is made after the shipment risk passes at the time of contract. This seems to be very harsh on the buyer. Moreover, the risk passes to the buyer at the time of shipment, if the goods are damaged while loading into the cargo or the goods are lost in the sea, though the seller knew that, the goods might be lost when he tenders the shipping document. Where the goods are unascertained and

[250] Source: Abu Naser Bablu: http://abunaserbablu.blogspot.com/2010/11/c-i-f-contract-problems.html accessed on 21/10/2020.

[251] e.g. *Comptoir d'Achat v Luis de Redder* [1949] 1 LL E.R. 269(H.L.) (*The Julia*).

shipped in bulk in that case the documents can not identified the goods sold. Hence the CIF contract sometimes seems to be very vague.[252]

7.21.3 Insurance Implications of Passage of Property and Title

According to the general rule, the property and the risk passes at the same time but this is not the usual case in a C.I.F. contract. Under a C.I.F. contract, the buyer is in effect the insurer, as of the time of shipment. The transfer to him of the bill of lading and the policy of insurance giving him the right of action in respect of loss or damage to the goods has the effect of placing the goods at his risk on and after shipment.[253] But the property in the goods may not, and generally does not, pass on shipment. It very often will not pass until tender and payment. The moment at which the property passes is entirely a matter of intention which can be gathered from the terms of the contract, the parties' conduct and according to the circumstances of the case.

7.21.4 Insurance Implications Whether CIF Is a Sale of Goods or Documents Contract

The importance of the documents in CIF contracts is illustrated by the rule that allows the seller to tender documents even after the goods they represent have been damaged or lost. It seems incredulous that such a rule could exist and even if it did exist that the sale was for the goods and not the documents. If the goods were utmost importance and were to all intents and purpose the subject matter of the contract, then this rule would not exist. It seems impossible to argue otherwise than that a CIF is a sale documents when we consider that the documents are key to all elements of the contract and they are central to shaping the parties' duties, defining when risk passes, and determining the condition of the goods. It is this document on which the entire contract is based. The importance of the documents in CIF contracts is illustrated by the rule that allows the seller to tender documents even after the goods damaged or lost. It seems unbelievable that such a rule could exist and even if it did exist that the sale was for the goods and not the documents.

If the goods were utmost importance and were to all intents and purpose the subject matter of the contract, then this rule would not exist. It seems impossible to argue otherwise than that a CIF is a sale documents when we consider that the documents are key to all elements of the contract and they are central to shaping the parties' duties, defining when risk passes, and determining the condition of the goods. The seller has the advantage of receiving the transacting money well in before the goods actually reach the buyer. The advantage of the buyer is that he has a substantial right once he gets the documents of sale and he may still reject the

[252] Carr and Stone (2005), p. 7.

[253] [*Tregelles v. Sewell* (1862) 7 H&N. 574].

goods on their actual delivery if they turn out to be not in conformity with the standards he had prescribed. The risk which he takes is that the loss or damage of goods may not be covered by the bill of lading or insurance policy.

7.21.5 Insurance Implications of the Two Rights of Rejections

A buyer can reject documents which do not comply with the contract for instance, if the bill is claused, showing that the goods were not in good condition when loaded, dated outside the shipment period or discloses deficiencies in quantity; or if an insurance certificate is tendered instead of policy. It is difficult to think of other sales contracts of any description which are akin to this procedure. The right to reject the document is lost if the byer takes up the documents, even though inaccurate and pays the price without objection. Moreover, if a defect in the goods is apparent on the face of the documents, the byer who accepts the documents will also be unable to reject the goods themselves on arrival for that defect. A byer cannot reject his property on completion if on exchange of contracts that defect was obviously contend in the contract, so for example if the price was incorrect this should have been raised at exchange of contract as opposed to completion. Unsurprisingly the rights of the buyer to reject goods in a CIF are a lot less meaningful than those relating to the documents.

Shamin is of the view, rightly, that the right to reject in CIF really is a right to reject documents and not goods.[254] The buyer will accept the document if he deals with them before the goods arrive, for instance, by using them to resell or pledge the good. A buyer who deals with the documents in this way therefor loses the right to reject the goods themselves for defects apparent from the documents.[255] Although all the c.i.f. advantages, there are certain problems or disadvantages that must be noted. Since the buyer must pay upon presentation of proper documents, he will generally be unable to reject the documents on the grounds that non-conforming goods were shipped. On the other hand, he will be in a position to reject non-conforming documents even when the seller has shipped conforming goods. While it is true to say that the seller does not assume an obligation physically to deliver the goods to the buyer, it is not true to say that the seller does not owe the buyer any duties in relation to the conformity of the goods with the terms of the contract. It is accepted that the buyer has two rights of rejection, namely the right to reject the documents and the right to reject the goods.[256]

[254] K.H. Shamin http://khsharmin.blogspot.com/2010/11/disadvantages-of-c-i-f-contract.html.

[255] D'Arcy et al. (2000), p. 45.

[256] The implied terms in sections 13–15 of SOGA-79 are applicable to c.i.f. contracts.

7.21.6 The Problem of Notice in CIF Insurance

Although it has transpired in paragraph 7.15 above that unlike the FOB buyer, the CIF buyer is not entitled to notice to enable him take out insurance, there are persisting problems.

First, he is only allowed notice for unusual risks. What amounts to unusual risks can be problematic?

Secondly, he is allowed notice only in times of hostilities or war but not peaceful times. This too can be problematic determined when such period is where hostilities might have broken out unknown to the buyer.

Third, a buyer might wish to take out additional cover for himself which wishes to keep secret from the seller. He might require notice to assess his additional requirements.

Fourth, the relevant section 32(1) of *SGA* 1979, as amended does not apply to Scotland anyway. So where does that leave Scottish parties to the CIF contract?

Finally, this day and age there is not much difference between FOB regarding most aspects including insurance. So, this principle may be redundant.

That is why Incoterms 2020 now makes requirement for notice for both contracts.

7.22 Concluding Remarks

This chapter in insurance CIF at common law attracts a number of comments.

First, the general comments on insurance of FOB at common law in Chap. 4 apply here too.

Secondly, since the CIP is not a common law contract, CIF remains the only export common law contract that explicitly provides for the seller to provide insurance on the contract to the buyer.

Thirdly, and above all, unlike in the FOB the importance of insurance in CIF cannot be more emphasized. It is what binds the contract and underpins most of its characteristics.

Fourth, although quite detailed in itself, the common law provision on CIF insurance is only a general guideline. This chapter has shown that that general rule is only a theoretical approach subject to practical and common-sense requirements such as both parties having to take own additional contingency policies.

Fifth, and finally, but not least, this chapter has further demonstrated that the said general rule is subject to additions and clarifications such on: "cif policy", "valid policy", "invalid policy", "minimum insurance", "sufficient value", "shipment value", "approve insurers", "responsible insurers", "reputable insurers", etc. It is also significant that Clause A5 and B5 of CIF Incoterms 2020 and (ante and in Chap. 8 post) both contain what amount substantially to a "codification" of CIF common law (more on this!). It has been retained by Incoterms 2020.

7.23 Further Readings

Major Publications

- Sassoon, CIF and FOB Contracts, 5th edn, 2012, Sweet & Maxwell, Part II chapter 6
- Schmitthoff, Law and Practice of International Trade Chapters 19 and 20
- Benjamin's Sale of Goods 7th edn, 2006, Sweet & Maxwell, chapter 19 (chapter 20 for FOB)
- Bridge, The Sale of Goods, 2nd edn 2009, OUP, (para 4.18 FOB Wimble; para 422-3 cif
- Halsbury's Laws of England, 5th edn, *Reissue* 2012, Vol.91 (Sale of Goods and Supply of Services)
- Halsbury's Laws of England, 5th edn, *Reissue* 2012, Vol.60 (Insurance)
- Carr, Indira, International Trade Law, 5th edn, Routledge, 2014, Chapter 1 (contracts) chapter 14 (marine insurance)
- Chuah, Jason C. T, Law of International Trade, 4th edn, Sweet & Maxwell, 2009, Chapter 12
- Crockford, Neil (General Editor): Insuring Foreign Risks, Sweet & Maxwell, London 2013.
- Dunt, John, Marine Cargo Insurance, Informa Law, 2009
- K.S. Insuring Cargoes, A practical guide to the law and practice, Witherby Insurance, 2010, Edinburgh
- Soyer, Warranties in Marine Insurance, 2nd edn, 2005, Cavendish Publishing.
- Bridge, M. The International Sale of Goods: Law and Practice, OUP, 1999, Chapter 4
- P S Atiyah, John N Adams, Hector MacQueen, Atiyah's Sale of Goods, 12th edn, Pearson Educational 2010
- Michael Connolly, Brief Case Commercial Law, 2nd edn, Cavendish Publishing Limited,1998
- LS Sealy and RJA Hooley, Commercial law: text, cases, and materials, 4th edn, OUP, 2009
- Michael Furmston, Principles of Commercial Law,2nd edn, Cavendish Publishing Limited, 2001
- Dunt, John, Marine Cargo Insurance (generally)
- Crockford, Neil: (General Editor): Insuring Foreign Risks (Loose-leaf), Sweet and Maxwell (Reuters), London 2013.
- Jimenez, Guillermo: ICC Guide to Export-Import Basics, ICC Pub.No.453 (E). 1997, pp. 187-190
- Thomas A. Cook, Series Editor, The Global Warrior: Mastering the Business of Global Trade: Negotiating -Competitive Advantage Contractual Best Practices, Incoterms, and Leveraging Supply Chain Options.

Journal Clauses

- David Sassoon, "The Origin of FOB and CIF: Terms and Factors influencing choice" [1967] JBL 32
- David Sassoon, "Application of FOB and CIF Sales in Common Law Countries" [1981] ETL 50
- Evans, "FOB and CIF Contracts" [1993] *ALJ* 844;
- Gower, "FOB Contracts", (1956) 19 *MLR*, 417;
- Ellen A. Peters, "Remedies for Breach of Contracts Relating to the Sale of Goods under the Uniform Commercial Code: A Roadmap for Clause Two" *The Yale Law Journal*, Vol. 73, No. 2, 1963, pp. 199-287
- Philip W. Thayer, "C. I. F. Contracts in International Commerce" *Harvard Law Review* Vol. 53, No. 5, 1940, pp. 792-826.
- Oduntan, Gbenga, *"C.I.F. Gatwick' and Other Such Nonsense Upon Stilts: Incoterms and the Law, Jargon and Practice of International Business Transactions", International Company and Commercial Law Review, 21 (6), 2010, pp. 214-223.*
- Grewal, Shivbir S., "Risk of Loss in Goods Sold during Transit: A Comparative Study of the U.N. Convention on Contracts for the International Sale of Goods, the U.C.C., and the British Sale of Goods Act", 14 Loy. L.A. Int'l & Comp. L.J. 93 (1991-1992)
- Reitel, "Damages for breach of a CIF contract", [1988] LMCLQ 457
- Treitel, "Rights of rejection under a CIF sale", [1984] LMCLQ565
- Crawford, Henry Paine "Analysis and Operation of a C.I.F. Contract", 29 Tul. L. Rev. 3 (1954-1955)
- Crawford, Note, "Analysis and operation of CIF Contract" [1995] TLR 396;
- Ademuni-Odeke, "The Nature of CIF Contract- Is it a Sale of Documents or Goods?" 6(2) JCL, pp. 158-176 (1993)
- Ademuni-Odeke, "Insurance Element in CIF and CIP INCOTERMS", *4 (4) T I L &P pp. 86-92.*
- Ademuni-Odeke, "Windfall in Marine and Export Credit Insurance Contracts in Anglo-American and Other Common Law Jurisdictions", *Part II, The European Insurance Law Review, 1/2018, pp. 8-44, April 2018,* www.erevija.org
- Ademuni-Odeke, "Windfall in Marine and Export Credit Insurance Contracts in Anglo-American and Other Common Law Jurisdictions", Part I, *The European Insurance Law Review, 4/2017, pp. 6-44, 2017,* www.erevija.org
- Ademuni-Odeke, "Insurance of CIF and Related Contracts under Incoterms and Anglo-American Common Law", Part II, *The European Insurance Law Review, 4/2016, 2016, pp. 1-44 (English and Serbo-Croat),* www.erevija.org
- Ademuni-Odeke, "Insurance of CIF and Related Contracts under Incoterms and Anglo-American Common Law", Part I, *The European Insurance Law* Review, 3/2016, 2016, pp. 1-34 (English and Serbo-Croat) www.erevija.org

- Ademuni-Odeke, "Insurance of FOB Contracts in Anglo-American and Common Law Jurisdictions Revisited", 2007, Tul.MLJ Vol.31, No.1, pp. 425-462
- Ademuni-Odeke, "The Insurance Clause In Incoterms 2020: The Latest In The Evolution And A Progressive Development 1980-2020 Part II", *The European Review of Insurance Law* 2/2020 pp. 38-48
- Ademuni-Odeke, "The Insurance Clause In Incoterms 2020: The Latest In The Evolution And A Progressive Development 1980-2020 Part I", *The European Insurance Law Review*, 1/2020, 1/2020 pp. 28-38, www.erevija.org
- Ademuni-Odeke, "Incoterms 2020: Sellers And Buyers Beware: What The Rules Do Not Tell You About Insurance Obligations In The New Incoterms", Journal *of Business Law, Issue 8, 2021, pp. 673-700*
- Dillon, C. "Cif and fob contracts". *South African Law Journal*, 103(1), 1986, pp. 166-168.

Reports

- UNTAD: Report on Incoterms Insurance, 1982[details]
- UNCTAD: Legal Aspects of International Trade, 1976[details]
- See Other UNCTAD Reports in other Chapters

Websites

- Tariq Idais, "CIF contracts in international sales of goods", http://www.tamimi.com/en/magazine/law-update/section-5/july-august-2/cif-contracts-in-international-sales-of-goods.html#sthash.47PQaB1F.dpuf
- *M. G. Bridge* "Documents and cif contracts" DOI: https://doi.org/10.14296/ac.v1998i3.1622
- Law Teacher, "Critically assess the rules on risk in relation to CIF and FOB contracts",http://www.lawteacher.net/free-law-essays/contract-law/cif-and-fob-contracts.php#ixzz3fKCGpGAr
- Stuart Shepherd, Jane Fitzgerald "Delivery Obligations under CIF Contracts", International Trade & Commodities incelaw.com/en/knowledge.../delivery-obligations-under-cif-contract
- Dionysios Flambouras, "Transfer of Risk in the Contract of Sale involving Carriage of Goods: A Comparative Study in English, Greek Law and the United Nations Convention on Contracts for the International Sale of Goods", www.jus.uio.no/pace/transfer_of_risk_contract.../_13.html
- Rami Al Tal, "United Arab Emirates: The Nature of CIF Contracts", www.mondaq.com/x/117852/cycling.../The+Nature+Of+CIF+Contracts
- Manfred Galdes, "The obligation of the seller in c.i.f contracts, University of Malta, 2001, https://www.google.com/search?q=seller's+duty+under+cif+contract&aq=f&oq=seller's+duty+under+cif+contract&aqs=chrome.0.57j62l2.14057&sourceid=chrome&i.e., =UTF-8

References

Ademuni-Odeke (2007) Insurance of FOB contracts in Anglo-American and common law jurisdictions revisited. *Tul MLJ* 31(1):425–462
Bennet C (1992) Dictionary of insurance. Pitman (Longman Group)
Carr I, Stone P (2005) International trade law, 3rd edn. Cavendish, London
D'Arcy L, Murray C, Cleave B (2000) Schmitthoff's export trade the law and practice of international trade, 10th edn. Sweet & Maxwell, London
UNCTAD Secretariat (1982) Report of: *Legal and documentary aspects of Marine Insurance Contract*. United Nations. New York
Winkler KB (1995) Incoterms and insurance. In: Debattisa C (ed) *Incoterms in practice*, ICC Pub. Doc.No.505 (E)

Insurance of Contracts That Include Seller's Obligations to Provide Insurance to the Buyer Under Incoterms

8

Abstract

As in Chap. 5, this chapter is dedicated to the treatment of insurance under the only two contracts [CIF and CIP] under Incoterms that include the sellers' obligations to provide insurance to the buyer. The sub-headings covered are: Introduction; Insurance of CIF Incoterms; Insurance and Carriage Contracts; Insurance of CIP Incoterms; Insurance of American CIP Contract; Practical Implications of the CIF/CIP Insurance Obligations; Differences between CIF and CIP Insurance Clause A5 and Clause B5; Other Implications of the CIF and CIP Insurance Clause A5 and Clause B5; Cautions on the Wider Incoterms' Insurance Perspectives; Requirement of Notice and Information; Related Contracts under Civil Law and Other Jurisdiction; Further Food for Thoughts; Concluding Remarks; References Used; Further Readings; and a Comparative Table 2.

8.1 Introduction-the Contracts

The only two contracts in this chapter are the CIF and CIP. Having discussed the role of the ICC, Incoterms and insurance in international trade (Chaps. 1 and 2 above), nature of the CIF (Chap. 6) and insurance of CIF under common law (Chap. 7), this chapter treats the CIF and its variants and related contract (CIP) that include sellers' obligations to insure goods on behalf of the buyer under Incoterms 2020. In its contents and coverage, the chapter follows the same pattern as of those in which sellers have no obligation to provide insurance to buyers under Incoterms (See Chap. 5 post). The chapter begins with the CIF itself, the oldest and dominant of the two contracts, followed by the CIP.

The chapter also briefly covers parties' obligations on carriage, delivery, passage of property and risks and requirement for notice as breaches of these duties impact

P. Ademuni-Odeke, *Insurance of International Sales' Contracts under Incoterms*, Law for Professionals, https://doi.org/10.1007/978-3-031-75136-3_8

on the parties' contractual liabilities and consequently necessity for insurance to cater for breaches of obligations.

8.2 Separation of Carriage and Other Obligations from Insurance Obligations

Incoterms rules mention carriage and other obligations in relation to insurance contracts. However, the parties (of especially CIF and CIP contracts) should be aware that the rules do not deal with them in detail. The rules only mention the need for those other obligations and which of the parties (seller or buyer) organises them and or insures the goods. The rules leave it to the parties to deal with how and where to obtain those services. For those treasons, in addition to expressly adopting Incoterms as the mode of their sales contracts, parties need to make separate contracts for carriage and insurance. The terms of the Incoterms rules do not bind carrier or the insurer to the parties on those contracts. They are kept separate from the insurance obligations and or contracts.

Those separations of especially the carriage and delivery from the insurance contracts can have consequences. First, the terms of the carriage contracts and delivery obligations bind only the seller (consignor) and his assignee-buyer (consignee) and the carrier. The carrier is only bound to issue a transport document as required by the carriage contract it makes with the other party to the contract. It is not bound to issue a transport document complying with the Incoterm rules, to which they are not party, unless specifically notified.

Secondly, and equally, insurance contract binds only the insured seller and his assignee-buyer, at a later stage, with the insured. Accordingly, the insurer is bound to issue a policy or insurance documents to the level and in the terms agreed with the party purchasing the insurance. It does not have to be a document or policy which makes references to or complies with the Incoterms rules to which they are not party, unless specifically requested.

8.3 Insurance of CIF Incoterms

8.3.1 Importance of Insurance to the CIF Incoterms

The nature of Incoterms and role of insurance in international trade were covered in Chaps. 1 and 2, insurance at Common Law was covered in Chap. 7 *ante*. A5/B5 of CIF Incoterms is not dissimilar to the common law position; the latter simply codified the former. In other aspects, the CIF Incoterms rule is similar to C&F and CFR where goods are considered to be "delivered" (and buyer assumes risk of loss) when they pass the ship's rail in the port of shipment. The seller is responsible for clearing the goods for export and for costs and freight to bring the goods to the destination port. The central issue is that under CIF the seller must also obtain marine insurance against buyer's risk of loss or damage in transit. It is only one of two Incoterms, where the seller takes out insurance for the benefit of the buyer.

These characteristics reflect Incoterms rules on the CIF and CIP. It was evident from Chap. 6 and that at common law the seller does not perform his CIF obligations until he has contracted for shipment and provided insurance and put the buyer in a position where he can claim directly from insurer. Incoterms reinforces that common law position putting insurance at the centre of the CIF contract. CIF only applies to maritime shipments (not air freight). Under these terms, sellers assume responsibility for the goods and insurance up until the goods arrive at the destination port. The responsibility then shifts to the buyer when the goods arrive. If shipping is on CIP or CIF terms, buyers should check that their insurance cover is for the total cost of goods rather than just a portion of it.

8.3.2 Carriage Obligations

8.3.2.1 The Seller's Obligations.

Under Clause A4, the seller must contract or procure a contract for the carriage of goods from the agreed port of delivery, if any, at the place of delivery to the named port of destination, or if agreed, any point at that port. The contract of carriage must be made on usual terms at the seller's cost and provided for carriage by the usual route in a vessel of the type normally used for the transport of the type of goods sold. The seller must comply with any transport-related security requirements for transport to the destination.[1] The underlined phrase does not appear in the CIP's version of Clause A4 which is in any case more extensive. So, the buyer has two locations in which to take delivery, at the port of shipment and destination unless he buys and sales them afloat in which case he is covered by the expression, "if any". Furthermore, the seller has to two types of notices' duties under Clause A10, first he is required to notify the buyer that the goods have been delivered in accordance with Clause A2; and secondly to give the buyer any notice required to enable the buyer to receive the goods.

8.3.2.2 The Buyers Obligations

The buyer has no obligation to the seller to make a contract of carriage under Clause B4.[2] This provision is redundant as it is simply declaratory. However, this duty can be altered by parties' agreement to vest part of it on the buyer. That reversal imposes an obligation to provide notice. Accordingly, the buyer must comply with Clause B10 imposing a mandatory obligation, whenever it is agreed that he (the buyer) is entitled to determine the time for shipping the goods and/or the point of receiving the goods within the named port of destination, give the seller sufficient notice. Sufficient notice is not defined leaving it to a question of fact in each case. Failure to do so might incur liability and have insurance implications.

[1] Incoterms 2020 at p. 123.

[2] Ibid, 127.

8.3.3 Delivery Obligations

8.3.3.1 Sellers Obligations

Under Clause A2, the seller must deliver the goods either by placing them on board the vessel or by procuring the goods so delivered. In either case the seller must deliver the goods on the agreed date or within the agreed period and in the manner customary at the port.[3] However, this is only in theory. In practice the seller may have to take care of the goods beyond the port of destination to an inland final destination. An example is the CIF "*Door to Door*" and/or CIF "*Warehouse-to-Warehouse*". Although the seller agrees to pay all costs and freight to the port of destination, his responsibility for delivery ends when the goods have been delivered on board the overseas vessel at the port of shipment. So, this Clause, like all the others in all Incoterms are for guidelines only or are on the basis of unless otherwise provided. In accordance with the importance of insurance, documents and two delivery obligations, the sellers' obligations include delivery of the documents first, then later delivery of the goods when they arrive. Breach of each those deliveries attract separate and independent breaches and damages.

8.3.3.2 The Buyer's Obligations

For his part the buyer must take delivery of the goods when they have been delivered under Clause A2 and receive them from the carrier at the named port of destination.[4] However, once again the seller's duty to deliver and the buyer's obligations to take delivery might be extended beyond the port of arrival to an inland destination in a "door to door" and/or "warehouse-to-ware house" CIF. Following from the sellers' deliveries above, the buyer too has separate obligations to take delivery of documents followed by taking delivery of goods when they arrive. Pursuant to Chap. 7, the buyer cannot reject the documents because the goods haven't arrived, neither can he do so simply the goods they relate are lost or damaged after shipments. Certain aspects of the sellers' obligations affect the buyers' ones.

8.3.4 Passage of Property and Title

Incoterms does not provide for when property passes. However, that does not mean that passage of property or title is not important in the contract, which, as a matter of fact, passes at the delivery of the documents to the buyer and not at the loading process or delivery of the goods to the carrier or buyer. Nevertheless, it is evident from common law sales of goods version that this is when goods have been loaded

---

[3] Incoterms 2020 at p. 126.

[4] Ibid at p. 127.

and/or pass the ship's rail. The same positions apply to Incoterms. From the foregone property passes to the buyer when he accepts the documents tendered to him by the buyer. This will be so regardless of wrongful rejection of the documents and goods. The position regarding when property passes to the buyer is the same as for the seller above.

8.3.5 Transfer of Risks

8.3.5.1 Sellers Risks

Th transfer of risks is provided for in A3 under which the seller bears all the risks of loss of or damaged to the goods until they have been delivered in accordance with Clause A2, with the exception of loss or damage in the circumstances described in B3.[5] It would, therefore, appear that property passes then. This is crucial as it determines when the risk attaches and, therefore, when insurance should be taken and/or commence. Note that the sellers on the seller's liability for failure to give the 2 sets of notices pursuant to Clause A10.

8.3.5.2 Buyers Risks

There are more onerous risk burdens on the buyer under Clause B3. However, responsibility for loss or damage is the same as for FOB and CFR terms. The seller is responsible for loss or damage until the goods are delivered on board the overseas vessel at the port of shipment. Under the clause the buyer bears all risks of loss or damage to the goods from the time they have been delivered as envisaged under Clause A2. However, if the buyer *fails to give notice in* accordance with Clause B10, then it bears all risks for loss of or damage from the agreed date or the expiry date of the agreed period for shipment, provided that the goods have been *clearly identified* as the contract goods.[6]

Nevertheless, this raises two further issues. First, "failure to give notice" constitutes a contingency for which the buyer may need contingency or any of the additional insurances discussed under Seller's Interest Insurance.[7] Secondly, "clearly identified" goods refer to goods appropriated to the contracts, a requirement of the CIF contract. The buyer has to ensure the goods in question are appropriated before he gives notice otherwise risks will not pass to the buyer. Thus, any failure to fulfil the carriage, delivery and transfer of risks requirements might be detrimental to the buyers general and consequently, insurance obligations.

---

[5] Ibid at 126.

[6] Ibid at p. 127.

[7] The text, '((A) or (B) of the Institute Cargo Clauses', are omitted since Incoterms 2000; otherwise, this additional cover would raise the minimum to almost "all risk policy", but not quite as it only restores some of those exceptions in Clauses 4–7 of the Cargo Clauses A-C.

8.3.6 Insurance Obligations

8.3.6.1 Importance of Insurance in CIF

As noted, CIF is one of the two Incoterms where the seller undertakes to insure the cargo as part of his contractual obligations. The other being CIP. Since its invention, insurance has always been an essential and central aspect of the CIF contract. This is more, so the contract being a document-based and possible buying and selling contract thereby lending itself to the notion that it is a contract for sale of documents rather than goods. The insurance policy underpins that concept. Thus, although the buyer is responsible for loss or damage during the "main carriage", under CIF terms the seller agrees to provide insurance for the buyer's account. Therefore, CIF shipments are insured under the seller's ocean cargo policy. They are also the only Incoterms which provide for sellers' insurance duties in Clause A5 thereof; all the other Incoterms providing "No Obligation" under Clause A5 and Clause B5 for the buyer. However, as will be evident below, the insurance obligations are more onerous on the seller than the buyer.

8.3.6.2 Seller's Insurance Obligations"[8]

The sale contract should clearly state the type of insurance to be provided. CIF and CIP sales impose obligations on the seller to take out insurance. The CIP insurance should be for any mode of transport (multimodal) and the CIF insurance should be for sea and inland water transport only except where the contract is for warehouse to "warehouse". Incoterms state that "lacking agreement, minimum cover of the Institute Cargo Clauses be provided". This is essentially "named perils" coverage which is rarely adequate for the needs of the buyer. Insurance must also be in negotiable form enabling losses to be payable to the buyer or other party having an insurable interest in the shipment at the time of loss. The seller must provide the seller with notification of the delivery of goods to the carrier and their estimated arrival at port destination pursuant to Clause A10. The Clause is analysed in details. Comments on the seller's delivery obligations for goods (above) apply in this instance too. See also Chap. 7 (post) on CIF at common law and Chap. 9 (post) on tender of documents for all Incoterms contracts. CIF also requires insurance to be taken out by the seller. However, the level of cover required is Institute Cargo Clause (C), which is more restrictive and generally the most affordable option.

Clauses A5/B5 of Incoterms 2020 now represent the latest stage of the evolution and progressive developments of the Insurance Clause in Incoterms. The CIF and CIP Seller's insurance obligations, now contained in Clause A5 for both contracts, provides that:

---

[8] Incoterms 2020, p.128. Cf Incoterms 2010 Clause A3(b); Ramberg Jan, *ICC Guide to Incoterms 2010*, pp. 200–201 where he: compares CIF to CFR insurance obligations; explains the seller's need to provide minimum insurance cover; explains duration of cover; deals with risks which require additional insurance; and explains the amount of insurance cover. Identical commentary appeared in Ramberg's *ICC Guide to Incoterms* 2000 at pp. 120–121. (Tidy this up)-Incoterms 2010 at p. 110.

Clause A5

Unless otherwise agreed[9] or customary[10] in the particular trade,[11] the seller must[12] obtain, at his own cost[13] cargo insurance[14] complying at least with the minimum cover[15] as provided by Clauses (C)[16] of the Institute Cargo Clauses (LMA/IUA) or similar clauses.[17] The insurance shall be contracted with underwriters or an insurance company of good repute[18] and entitle the buyer, or any other person having an insurable interest[19] in the goods, to claim directly from the insurer.[20]

When required by the buyer,[21] the seller shall, subject to the buyer providing any

[9] This is significant as it implies that the rules are flexible and that insurance clause terms could be displaced express agreement between the parties.

[10] The Clause does not define or provide any guidelines as to what is customary. So, what is a trade custom?. In the technical language of the Uniform Commercial Code, a trade custom is defined as: "any practice or method of dealing having such regularity of observation in a place, vocation or trade as to justify an expectation that it will be observed with respect to the transaction in question.?

[11] . Phrase not contained in the equivalent Incoterms 2010 provision- Clause A3(b). The rules can be displaced by particular trade practice such those pertaining to GAFTA, FOSFA, Energy (Oil and Gas Trade, Coal), etc.

[12] Note that once agreed the seller's duty to provide the insurance becomes mandatory.

[13] Note the change from "expenses" to "costs" from Incoterms 2010. Whether this is significant at all, it marks a return nearly 70 years back to Incoterms 1953 when that word was first appeared in the Incoterms Insurance Clause. Although he eventually gets reimbursed once the policy and other documents have been tendered and paid for, the seller cannot ask for the premium and related costs upfront. The duty costs of the goods may be calculated against a specific Incoterm: for example, in India and Jordan, duty is calculated against the CIF value of the goods, and in South Africa the duty is calculated against the FOB value of the goods. These calculations may have no bearing the 110% CIF-CIP value.

[14] Changed from "marine insurance" to "cargo insurance" to keep up with developments in International Trade Practices.

[15] The concept of minimum cover goes back to Incoterms 1953; for details of what constitutes minimum cover see Note above.

[16] The equivalent CIP's Clause A5 is "Clauses (A)"; the only difference between CIF Clause A5 and CIP Clause A5 is thus the provision of higher insurance cover in the latter; see also paragraph 2 immediately below.

[17] The principle that the insured or consignee or any other transferee of sales afloat should cover directly from the insurance was established at common law by the House of Lords in the seminal case of *Comptoir d'Achat et de Vente du Boerenbond Belge S/A v. Luis de Ridder Limitada (The Julia)* House of Lords, [1949] A.C. 293.

[18] To cater for consignees, transferees and other buyers afloat, a common characteristics of modern trade practices.

[19] Ibid.

[20] Provision of additional cover is not automatic, has to be requested by the buyer at which the term when agreed binds the seller. However, the manner and nature of the request is not provided or whether it becomes part of the request for notice and information between the parties.

[21] [This in turn depends on: (a) request by the buyer and becomes mandatory on both parties' agreement, hence the use of "shall" in the text; and (b) the buyer providing the "necessary information"].

necessary information[22] requested by the seller, provide at the buyer's cost[23] any additional cover, if procurable,[24] such as cover[25] complying[26] with the Institute War Clauses and/or Institute Strikes Clauses[27] (LMA/IUA) or any similar clauses,[28] (unless such cover is already included with the cargo insurance described in the preceding paragraph)[29]

The insurance shall cover, at a minimum, the price provided in the contract plus 10% (i.e., 110%) and shall be in the currency of the contract

The insurance shall cover the goods from the point of delivery set out in A2[30] to at least the named place of destination

The seller must provide the buyer with the insurance policy or certificate or any other evidence of insurance cover.

---

[22] Ibid; however, compared to Note 21 above, the buyer seller can request these costs upfront although in practice they are included in the Invoice and payable on tender of documents This in turn depends on:

(a) request by the buyer and becomes mandatory on both parties' agreement, hence the use of "shall" in the text; and
(b) the buyer providing the "necessary information".

[23] Note that the additional cover is to be provided only if procurable, so they are not mandatory; however commercial practice requires exchange of information on this, hence the new emphasis on Notice and Information since Incoterms 1980.

[24] Word 'as provided by Clause(A) or (B) of", between the word 'cover' and the word 'complying' from Incoterms 2010 are omitted. Ibid.

[25] [Ibid].

[26] The text, '((A) or (B) of the Institute Cargo Clauses', are omitted since Incoterms 2000; otherwise, this additional cover would raise the minimum to almost "all risk policy", but not quite as it only restores some of those exceptions in Clauses 4–7 of the Cargo Clauses A-C "and/or cover" between "similar clauses" and "complying" in Incoterms 2010 are omitted; otherwise see Note 24 above what amounts to "similar clauses".

[27] "and/or cover" between "similar clauses" and "complying" in Incoterms 2010 are omitted; otherwise see Note 24 above what amounts to "similar clauses".

[28] The text, '(complying with the Institute War Clauses and/or Institute Strikes Clauses (LMA/IUA) or any similar clauses)', from Incoterms 2010 has been rearranged.

[29] Compared to the previous 'A4 and A5' in Incoterms 2010.

[30] First time 'certificate' is mentioned. This is to synchronise Incoterms with Clause 28(a) of the UCP 600 which allows for the tender of the certificate in lieu of the policy. Furthermore, 'any other' is also mentioned for the first time. This is also in line with Clause 28(a) of the UCP 600 which permits tender of a certificate or 'a declaration under an open cover'. Furthermore, the use of the phrase 'such as' implies that the list of acceptable insurance documents is not exhaustive. However, 'An insurance policy is acceptable in lieu of an insurance certificate or a declaration under an open cover'- Clause 28(d).

Moreover, the seller must provide the buyer, at the buyer's request, risk and cost,[31] *with information that the buyer needs to procure any additional insurance.*" (***Emphasis provided***).

Other than the highlighted texts and commentaries therein, the insurance Clauses (A5/B5) of the CIF and CIP rules of Incoterms 2020 are almost identical to those of the corresponding Clauses A3(b)/B3(b) of the CIF and CIP rules in Incoterms 2010.

In their current form, Incoterms 2020 is intended to last until Incoterms 2030. Clause A5 is analysed below.

8.3.6.3 Buyer's Insurance Obligations

If shipping is on CIP or CIF terms, buyers should check that their insurance cover is for the total cost of goods rather than just a portion of it. Under the corresponding Clause B5 the buyer has no obligation to the seller to make a contract of insurance. This is the same as for contracts which exclude sellers' obligations to provide insurance to the buyer under Chap. 5 above. Accordingly, comments there and in and in Chap. 10 (post) on "No Obligations" applies in this case too; it applies only to the buyer's obligations towards the seller. However, the buyer must first take care of his own insurance needs; and secondly, provide the seller, upon request, with the any information necessary for the seller to procure any additional insurance requested by the buyer as envisaged in A5.[32] Two clarifications are called for here.

First, the seller provides only the minimum insurance which unless otherwise provided excludes war cover, *inter alia* (see minimum in Chap. 8). Secondly, either the buyer then purchases additional insurance himself, or decides to be self-insured for those risks. It might be prudent though for him to have all these done under one roof by the seller. For that he needs to request the seller and then provides all necessary information. Incoterms is silent on the nature and extent of this information but proof, or evidence, of insurance is required which is usually accomplished by issuance of a Special Cargo Policy or Certificate of Insurance by the seller or his insurer. Insurance should cover the shipment from the place of origin to the final destination of the buyer. Failure to comply with requirement for notice on shipment and delivery under Clause B10 might involve liability and therefore have insurance implications.

---

[31] The word 'cost replaces 'expense'; and 'if any' between 'cost' and 'with' in Incoterms 2010 is omitted. The replacement of expense with cost might not be significant as the two invoke the same meaning depending on the context. In economics, production, research, retail, and accounting, a cost is the value of money that has been used up to produce something or deliver a service, and hence is not available for use anymore. In business terms, the cost may be one of acquisition, in which case the amount of money expended to acquire it is counted as cost. To an ordinary individual, an expense is an expenditure is an outflow of money to another person or group to pay for an item or service, or for a category of costs. Buying food, clothing, furniture or an automobile is often referred to as an expense. For a tenant, rent is an expense. For students or parents, tuition is an expense. However, it does not make any difference to the seller who recoups the costs or expenses from the buyer as an invoice item. The significance of notice and information is dealt with below.

[32] Incoterms 2020 at 129.

8.3.7 Potential Areas of Conflicts in CIF Insurance

One potential area of conflict, between the requirements of CIF terms and insurance coverage is when insurance actually ceases. By definition CIF refers to the port of destination. CIF also obligates the seller to provide insurance covering the buyer's risk of loss or damage which in almost all cases extends until the goods are delivered to his place of destination. Banks are usually involved in the financing of CIF shipments. If a Letter of Credit stipulates CIF port of destination and the insurance certificate stipulates another place, the bank may reject the certificate. Conversely, if the certificate shows the port of destination as the final place of insurance in order to comply with the Letter of Credit, the buyer will have no insurance for transit beyond the port of destination. Therefore, it is important for the actual place of insured destination to be shown clearly in the sales contract, invoice, letter of credit instructions and the certificate.

A suggestion to overcome the above problems would be inclusion in the insurance and delivery details of the: Name of Buyer's Warehouse, Street Address, City, State/Province, Country, or other appropriately identified location. Interpretation of this Clause at common law, including case law, are contained in Chap. 7 (ante).

The only other Incoterm in which the seller provides insurance to the buyer is the CIP.

8.3.8 American Perspective

8.3.8.1 Under the UCC

This is the same as under common law; see Chap. 7 above.

8.3.8.2 Under "Incoterms for Americans Guidelines"

IFA Guidelines provides that: "The seller is supposed at least minimum cover insurance (FPA American or Institute Cargo Clauses C). Additional coverage should be considered".[33] Free of Particular Average (FPA) policy is cargo policy provision that eliminates all coverage for any partial loss of cargo. From shipping perspective, it includes particular average- a partial loss or damage to a ship or its cargo that affects only the ship owner or one cargo owner. Thus, the insured should bear in mind that the policy covers losses borne by the owners of the ship or cargo due to direct damage to their property only. It includes named perils coverage meaning that the policy will only cover losses resulting from specifically named causes.

This makes American cover equivalent to that under CIF Incoterms 2020.This simply summarises and emphasizes the provisions of Clause A5/B5 of Incoterms 2020, without adding much. Like the CIF Incoterms, it allows parties to provide for additional cover. American exporters and importers parties are well advised to purchase and study Reynolds Incoterms Rules for Americans especially the general

[33] Reynolds: Incoterms Rules for Americans, pp. 109–112 at p. 10 Note 6; see also, generally, this chapter (Insurance), pp. 33–37 of the same book.

Chap. 8[34] on insurance and the specific insurance advice in Chap. 6[35] on Getting Goods from Seller to buyer.

8.4 insurance of CIP Incoterms

8.4.1 The CIP Incoterms

This is an Incoterms rule under which seller delivers goods to seller-designated carrier, pays cost of carriage to named destination and must obtain insurance to cover buyer's risk of loss in transit. Buyer bears risk of loss and any additional costs after seller's delivery to carrier, protected by seller's insurance. Used for any mode of transportation; same as CPT, but seller pays for insurance and names buyer as beneficiary. This has not become part of the common law. Rather, it is still an Incoterm describing a term of sale that details the responsibilities of the buyer and seller for the international trade transaction.

Under this term, the seller pays the freight for the carriage of the goods to the named destination. The risk of loss of or damage to the goods, as well as any additional costs due to events occurring after the time the goods have been delivered to the carrier, is transferred from the seller to the buyer when the goods have been delivered into the custody of the carrier. In addition, the seller must procure cargo insurance against the buyer's risk of loss of or damage to the goods during the carriage. The seller must clear the goods for export. There is no English common law interpretation of this term or of its insurance. Nevertheless, since it resembles the CIF in having identical A5 and B5. For this purpose, the relevant CIF insurance cases above, now part of the common law, should with modifications apply to CIP.

However, in the recent Scottish case of *Stora Enso OYJ v Port of Dundee*,[36] Lord Clark held that the use of the expression CIP in a contract for the sale of goods is not, in itself, determinative of when risk passes. That however, left the issue of insurance open as Lord Clarke did not touch on it in his short ruling although the insurance taken out by the plaintiffs covered goods until delivery to the defendant's warehouse. He was required to make an order as whether the CIP or General Wood Rules governed the contract, and, consequently whether property had passed to the buyer at the time of loss. His duties did not extend to ruling on insurance.[37]

Carriage and Insurance Paid To, named place of destination. This term can be used with any mode of transportation.

[34] pp. 33–37.

[35] Getting Goods from the Seller to the Buyer, Chapter 6 pp. 25–28 at p. 27 (How about Insurance) and p. 28 (Insurance Contracts) where to purchase them.

[36] *Stora Enso OYJ v Port of Dundee* [2006] 1 CLC 453; s CSOH 40; (2006) *Times*, 11 April (SCOT).

[37] Ibid, at 464.

8.4.2 Carriage Obligations

8.4.2.1 Seller's Obligations

Under CIP, the seller assumes responsibility for making the goods available at a place of destination. They also have to arrange insurance to cover the goods during transit. All the buyer has to do is arrange further transport, duties or taxes upon the goods' arrival. The CIP seller appears to have more to do under the carriage obligations that the CIF seller. The respective duties are also slightly different. A4 provides that the seller must contract or procure contract for the carriage of the goods from the agreed point of delivery, *if any*, at the place of delivery to the named place of destination or, if agreed, any point at that place. The contract of carriage must be made on usual terms at the seller's cost and provide for carriage by the usual route in customary manner of the type normally used for carriage of the type of goods sold. If a specific point is not agreed or is not determined by practice, the seller may select the point of delivery and the point at the named place of destination *that best suit its purpose*. The seller must comply with any transport-related security requirements for transport to the destination.

The underlined indicates the difference in wording between CIF and CIP carriage contracts. The following phrase, "which suits in a vessel of the type normally used for the transport of the type of goods sold" appeared at the end of the 2010 version but was replaced by the above emphasized in the latter. The use of the phrase "if any", leaves for buying and selling afloat just as in CIF.

Unlike the CIF, however, this term can be used with any mode of transportation including multimodal. It is essentially the same as CIF except that the seller pays all costs and freight to deliver the goods to a named place in the country of destination (vs. port of destination under CIF terms), and the seller agrees to deliver the goods to the carrier, or party acting on his behalf, at a named point or place in the country of shipment (vs. on board the overseas vessel at the port of shipment under CIF).[38] Responsibilities for loss or damage to the goods are the same as under FCA and CPT terms. The term is attractive to a buyer who has or can arrange his or her own freight compared to the CIF buyer who wants a total package but at a higher price. This is essentially the same as the CIF except for absence of seller's freight responsibilities.[39] The choice between the two or other terms will depend on the parties' circumstances and other prevailing conditions.

8.4.2.2 Buyers Obligations

Unlike for the CIF, on carriage, the CIP buyer has no obligation to the seller to make a contract of carriage,[40] under Clause B4. See also Clause A10.

---

[38] *Incoterms 2020*, at p. 126.

[39] However, apart from the fact that the CIP seller tenders only the invoice and insurance policy excluding the bill of lading, there may be other qualitative difference in the performance of the two contracts as the CIF is a special contract with unique characteristics.

[40] Incoterms 2020 at p. 127.

8.4.3 Delivery Obligations

8.4.3.1 Sellers Obligations

As to delivery Clause A2 provides that the seller must deliver the goods by handing them over to the carrier contracted in accordance with Clause A4 or by procuring the goods so delivered. In either case, the seller must deliver the goods on the agreed date or within the agreed period.[41] Note the difference between handing over to the contracted carrier in CIP to delivering on board a contracted vessel in CIF (Clause A10). Thus, the seller must contract or procure a contract for the carriage of the goods from the agreed point of delivery, if any, at the place of delivery to the named place of destination or, if agreed, any point at that place. The contract of carriage must be made on usual terms at the seller's cost and provide for carriage by the usual route in a customary manner of the type normally used for carriage of the type of goods sold. If a specific point is not agreed or is not determined by practice, the seller may select the point of delivery and the point at the named place of destination that best suit its purpose. The seller must comply with any transport-related security requirements for transport to the buyer. Although the CIF and CIP are technically different their delivery performance are not that different.

8.4.3.2 Buyer's Obligations

As to delivery, under Clause B4 the buyer must take delivery of the goods when they have been delivered under Clause A2 and receive them from the carrier at the named place of destination or if agreed, at the point within that place.[42] The buyer must take delivery of the goods and documents when in order. However, the CIP buyer does not have the two separate rights of rejecting goods and documents as the CIF buyer does.

8.4.4 Passage of Property and Title

As for the CIF Incoterms does not provide for when property passes to the seller. However, can the same assumption be made since the Common Law has no equivalent of the CIP. With regard to passage of property, comments under the seller above apply here. See Clause A10 for notice to the buyer.

8.4.5 Passage of Risks

8.4.5.1 Sellers Risks

Under Clause A3 the seller bears all risks of loss of or damage to the goods until they have been delivered in accordance with Clause A2, with the exception of loss

[41] Ibid, 126.

[42] Ibid, 127.

or damage in the circumstance described in Cause B3."[43] This is essentially the same as CIF except that in this case the seller pays all costs and freight to deliver the goods to a named place in the country of destination (vs. port of destination under CIF terms), and the seller agrees to deliver the goods to the carrier, or party acting on his behalf, at a named point or place in the country of shipment (vs. on board the overseas vessel at the port of shipment under CIF). Responsibility for loss or damage: The same as under FCA and CPT terms.

8.4.5.2 Buyer's Risks

Under Clause B3 the buyer bears all risks of loss of or damage to the goods from the time they have been delivered under Clause A2. However, if the buyer fails to give notice in accordance with Clause B10, then the buyer bears all risks of loss of or damage to the goods from the agreed date or the end of the agreed period for delivery, provided that the goods have been clearly identified as the contract goods.[44] It will be recalled that Clause B10 provides that the buyer must, whenever it is agreed that the buyer is entitled to determine the time for dispatching the goods and/or the point of receiving the goods within the named place of destination, give the seller sufficient notice. This Clause and obligation demonstrate the interconnections between the carriage and delivery obligations to the risks and consequently insurance obligations.

8.4.6 CIP Insurance Obligations

8.4.6.1 General Comments

As mentioned above, CIP requires insurance to be taken out for the buyer. The terms under which insurance must be taken out are those under Clauses (A) of the Institute Cargo Clauses. This is a recent change introduced in Incoterms® 2020. This is the least restrictive clause and has quite an expansive coverage (therefore, it's generally more expensive). CIP terms obligate the seller to provide insurance on behalf of the buyer and therefore as in the CIF shipments would be insured under the seller's ocean cargo policy. Like the CFR, the CIP was a relatively new in Incoterms 2010 (and now Incoterms 2020) contract for which the common law has not yet developed either principles or case law. However, its close proximity to CIF regarding insurance means CIF case law (but not other CIF duties and principles) discussed under CIF above would apply to the CIP.

[43] Ibid at 126.

[44] Ibid, 127.

8.4.6.2 Insurance Obligations

8.4.6.2.1 Seller's Obligations

A5 on insurance obligations is identical to that of Clause A5 of CIF above,[45] except for inclusion of Cargo Clauses A in the latter instead of Cargo Clause C in the former. Thus, as in the CIF, under the CIP terms the seller charges for the goods (C) and provides insurance (I) on behalf of the buyer as part and parcel of the contract to the named place of destination. Therefore, CIP shipments would be insured under the seller's policy, which are then transferred on tender to the buyer or the buyer's agents or indeed any subsequent sellers and buyers of the same goods afloat. Furthermore, although there is a slight variation in other obligations, those relating to insurance are the same and so the comments under same above would apply. The seller's insurance obligations are the same as in the CIF insurance clause above. See also comments on CIF.[46] However, both parties should be aware that Clause A5 in both CIF/CIP Incoterms, the minimum cover may not be suitable for all cargo; e.g., manufactured goods.[47] But first, the seller must contract for insurance, pay the premium, obtain the insurance documents and tender to the buyer with all other documents pursuant to Clause 28 of the UCP 600.

As under freight obligations above, the choice between CIF and CIP would depend on the availability of freight and insurance markets on either side of the sales contract as well as national policy restrictions on both services, where applicable-Clause A10. Clause A5 is analysed below. Under Incoterms 2020, the CIP, the seller must now obtain an increased level of cargo insurance. It will be recalled that under Incoterms 2010, a CIP seller had to purchase cargo insurance on Cargo Clauses (C) terms, which provides cover for a limited number of risks. Under Incoterms 2020, however, a CIP seller must purchase insurance on Cargo Clauses (A), which is the nearest to an "all risks" policy but for the exceptions.[48] This is the only major distinction between the CIF and CIP sellers' insurance obligations. Other than that, the rest of the wording in Clause A5 is identical for both CIF and CIP. The status of CIP seller's insurance obligations is almost back to that of Incoterms 1953 when the level of CIP terms was higher than that of the CIF. There are at least two further issues at this point. First, the seller must contract for insurance cover against the buyer's risk of loss of or damage to the goods from the point of delivery to at least the point of destination.

However, this may cause problems where the destination country requires insurance cover to be purchased locally (see restrictive practices). To avoid this dilemma, parties may be advised to instead contract and ship CPT which would avoid provision of insurance to destination. Secondly, parties should also not note the unusual situation under this Incoterms where the seller is required to provide the more extensive cover complying with Cargo Clauses (A) in the CIP rather than with more

---

[45] Ibid, 128.

[46] Ibid, and Note 41 above.

[47] See Ramberg's Comments at Note 18 below.

[48] Incoterms 2020, p.128.

limited cover under Cargo Clauses (C) for the CIF. Despite that, the contract keeps the parties' option to provide a less favourable insurance coverage consequential from "unless otherwise agreed" or "customary in a particular trade" expressions in A5. This contradicts and might cause problems with tender of insurance documents under Clause 28 of the UCP 600 (see Part VI(C) below) requiring tender of exact and conforming documents. Accordingly, although there are no significant changes, both CIF and CIP now allow for variance of the insurance obligations by parties' agreements and by customs of a particular trade.

Further details of the variations are discussed immediately post.

8.4.6.2.2 CIP Buyer's Insurance Obligations

Clause B5 on insurance obligations is identical to that of Clause B5 of CIF above. Accordingly, any guideline to both parties therein, are relevant. Needless to emphasize, at the risk of repetitions, that the above narratives apply only to the two rules CIF and CIP, not the remaining 9 Incoterms. These relate only to obligations to the seller, not to themselves (see post). How do these CIP buyers' obligations differ from those in the remaining 9 Incoterms' rules? No, they do not. The differences are in turn determined by the further divisions of said 9 into 3 for unimodal (sea and inland waterways) and 6 for multimodal (any modes) transports.

8.4.6.3 American Perspectives

8.4.6.3.1 Under the UCP

These are the same as in the American UCC[49] and main ICC Incoterms 2020.[50]

8.4.6.3.2 Under "Iconterms for Americans Guidelines"

"Incoterms for Americans' Guidelines" provide that:

"The seller is required to provide Institute Cargo Clauses A (so called "All Risk" in American) coverage".[51] This is the same as under Incoterms 2020.

8.5 Practical Implications of CIF/CIP Sellers' Insurance Obligations

8.5.1 Relationships with Cargo Clauses

The Incoterms 2020 sellers' insurance CIF/CIP obligations are covered in Clauses A5/B5 for sellers and buyers respectively. Like the 2010 version, the 2020 ones are also still based on Cargo Clauses. It will be remembered that on the equivalent 2010 Clauses A5/B5, Ramberg Commented that:

[49] See para XX for American UCCXXX.

[50] See also -Reynolds, Frank *Incoterms 2010 for Americans*, Commentary No.9 at p.80; CF Incoterms 2020, p128.

[51] Reynolds: Incoterms Rules for Americans Guidelines 2020, pp. 97–101 at p. 99, Note.6.

> There are only two terms which deal with insurance, namely CIF and C1F. Under these terms the seller is obliged to procure insurance for the benefit of the buyer. In other cases, it is for the parties themselves to decide whether and to what extent they want to cover themselves by insurance. Since the seller takes out insurance for the benefit of the buyer, he would not know the buyer's precise requirements. Under the Institute Cargo Clauses drafted by the Institute of London Underwriters, insurance is available in "minimum cover" under Clause C, "medium cover" under Clause B and "most extended cover" under Clause A.[52]

Thus, the CIF/CIP insurance obligations are intrinsically with their terms and conditions- the Cargo Clauses. They have also heavily influenced the commodities contracts and respective insurances on which they are also based.

8.5.1.1 Comparisons with Commodities' Contracts

However, the provisions of Clause A5 may be varied by parties' express agreement to lower or extend the covered above that. It could also be varied by trade customs such as those of GAFTA[53] contracts in the commodity trade. He adds that: "Since in the sale of commodities under the CIF term the buyer may wish to sell the goods in transit to a subsequent buyer who in turn may wish to resell the goods again, it is impossible to know the insurance cover suitable to such subsequent buyers and, therefore, the minimum cover under CIF has traditionally been chosen with the possibility for the buyer to require the seller to take out additional insurance. Minimum cover is however unsuitable for sale of manufactured goods where the risk of theft, pilferage or improper handling or custody of the goods would require more than the cover available under Clause C. Since CIP, as distinguished from CIF, would normally not be used for the sale of commodities, it would have been feasible to adopt the most extended cover under CIP rather than the minimum cover under CIF".[54]

8.5.1.2 Effect on the "On minimum" Cover

Thus, unless otherwise provided to the contrary by either the parties express provisions or commodities and customs, then the seller is obliged to provide on the minimum cover, which would be Cargo Clauses C for the CIF and Cargo Clauses A for the CIP. He continues and cautions thus: "But to vary the seller's insurance obligation under CIF anti CIP would lead to confusion and both terms therefore limit the seller's insurance obligation to the minimum cover. It is particularly important for the CIP-buyer to observe this: should additional cover be required, he should agree with the seller that the latter could take out additional insurance or, alternatively, arrange for extended insurance cover himself.

There are also particular instances where the buyer may wish to obtain even more protection than is available under Institute Clause A, for example insurance against war, riots, civil commotion, strikes or other labour disturbances. If he wishes

---

[52] *Introduction to Incoterms 2000,* Paragraph 9(3) on CIF/CIP insurance reproduced at p. 184 ICC Guide to Incoterms 2000 and p.94 of Incoterms 2000, A Forum of Experts.

[53] See GAFTA, pp XXX post.

[54] Ibid. [cif commentaries]

the seller to arrange such insurance, he must instruct him accordingly in which case the seller would have to provide such insurance if procurable".[55]

For both CIF and CIP, the seller's obligation is provided in identical terms in Clause A5. The seller must obtain at his own expense cargo insurance as agreed in the contract, that the buyer, or any other person having an insurable interest in the goods, shall be entitled to claim directly from the insurer and provide the buyer with the insurance policy or other evidence of insurance cover.

The persisting problems is the minimum cover. The Clause provides that the insurance *shall* (not will or should) cover at a minimum the price provided in the contract plus ten percent (i.e., 110%). The requirement of the insurance to be in the currency of the contract is clear enough and poses no problems. The price + ten percent does. *First,* does the 10% represent profit margin or level of damage in the event of a claim and therefore the replacement of the goods? *Secondly*, does the 100% or 110% represent the contract price alone or does it include insurance premium and freight? The German approach seems to point to the insured value at the port of loading,[56] i.e., the commercial value at the beginning of the insurance when the goods are shipped + insurance premium + expenses incurred until the time when goods are delivered to the carrier + freight definitely paid.

Third, is another possible scenario. If the contract is excessively high wont this give rise to over insurance? And if so what about the consideration that the excess is not normally valid except in case of an agreed value policy. Does that make the CIF and CIP insurance an agreed value policy? And if so, how does that accommodate sale of commodities which either appreciate and depreciate after the sales contract? However, all these scenarios might be theoretical and/or speculation as, to the best of the author's knowledge, no reported case has arisen in actual practice.

8.5.1.3 Comparison Between CIP with CFR and CIF

Both CFR and CIF have identical Clause B4 provisions on taking delivery. The corresponding Clause A4 referred to above concerns delivery by the seller to the carrier. These two paragraphs embody the obligations very concisely, and it is necessary to examine each point in turn in order to flesh out the obligations placed upon the seller. However, it should be noted that, although the parties have decided, by

---

[55] Ibid. [minimum cover]

[56] Insurance Contract Act 2008 (VVG) Section 136.

"Section 136 Insurable value

(1) The insurable value of the goods shall be deemed to be the common market value and, for lack of that value, the common value of the goods at the place of shipping at the commencement of the insurance, plus insurance costs, costs arising up until the time when the transporter takes receipt of the goods and the final amount of freightage paid.
(2) The value determined in accordance with subsection (1) shall also be deemed to be the insurable value upon occurrence of the insured event.
(3) Where goods are damaged upon arrival at their place of delivery, their value at that place in their damaged state shall be deducted from the value which they would have at that place in an undamaged state. The fraction of the insurable value corresponding to the ratio between the reduction in value and their value in their undamaged state shall be deemed to be the amount of damage".

contracting Incoterms CIF or CIP, that their respective rights and obligations are to be determined according to the relevant Incoterms provisions rather than by an examination of the common law cases, nevertheless, if the contract is governed by English law, it will remain subject to the relevant English statutes. The primary piece of legislation in this context is, of course, the MIA 1906.[57]

8.6 Differences Between CIF and CIP Insurance Clauses

8.6.1 The Main Differences

From the foregone, despite its later development, insurance coverage in CIP is much higher than those of the older CIF. Thus, as indicated above, in Incoterms CIP the seller is under the obligation to take out under contract transport insurance in favour of the buyer with extensive coverage, which corresponds to Clause (A) of the Cargo Clauses (IUA/LMA). Nevertheless, parties may agree to take out insurance which offers reduced coverage (Clause (C) of the Cargo Clauses) although that is unlikely. In CIP, the risk of goods passes from the seller to the buyer at the destination port, whereas in CIF the risk is transferred to the buyer once the goods are loaded by the seller on the vessel port.

In the CIF, on the other hand, the seller is only under the obligation to take out under contract insurance with minimum coverage, which corresponds to Clause (C) of the Cargo Clauses (IUA/LMA). This difference with CIP is justified on the basis that as the CIF is commonly used for bulk maritime transport (raw materials, minerals etc.) whose price per kilo is very low and the requirement of insurance with maximum coverage which would drive up considerably the policy premium, making it much more expensive, and which is detrimental to margin for negotiation of the sellers. In either event, comparable CIP to and CIF, parties may agree to take out insurance which offers broader coverage (e.g., Clause (A) of the Cargo Clauses) which will be compulsory, if the sales' payment is made by means of a letter of credit.

8.6.2 Other Superficial Changes in the Insurance Clauses

On the minor side, as indicated ante, there is more preference for use of buyers' costs[58] rather than expenses[59] in the drafting. That notwithstanding, this view provides the rationale for the differences in cover which also tallies with comparative practitioners' position some of who have opined that:

[57] For a copy see Annex XVII [MIA on English Law].

[58] See again Note 4(CIP) and 8(CIF) Incoterms 2020, ICC Document No. 723E at p. 52 and pp. 124–125 respectively.

Ademuni-Odeke "Insurance Elements in CIF and CIP Incoterms", supra.

This is a reverse of the provision in EXW, see below.

[59] The difference is only academic; in practise costs are expenses and are both chargeable.

> Under Incoterms 2010, the seller was required to obtain the minimum coverage under Institute Cargo Clause C in both CIF and CIP contracts. In Incoterms 2020, the ICC has responded to feedback that in practice, these two terms often call for different levels of cover. CIF is a maritime-only term and is therefore more typically used for trading bulk cargoes for which Institute Cargo Clause C level coverage is sufficient. However, CIP is a multimodal term, often used for manufactured goods which may require a higher level of cover. It remains open to the parties to decide on the appropriate level of insurance cover for their trade; this can be provided for expressly in the contract. Parties should be aware, however, that under Incoterms 2020, the default position under CIP is that the seller must procure the level of cover provided for in Institute Cargo Clause A.[60]

Exhaustive comparative analysis of the two Incoterms is beyond the scope of clause. However, this opinion is also in line with comprehensive examination of the differences between expenses and costs in Incoterms 2010[61] and Incoterms 1990[62] provisions in earlier publications. These relate only to obligations to the buyer not themselves (see post).

Are there any reasons for these differences? The answer is in the affirmative.

8.6.3 Justification for the Differences

There are legal and commercial rationale for the above different CIF-CIP approaches. On the different levels of insurance between the CIF and CIP which has been retained in Incoterms 2020. Noting that point, the ICC has opined that:

> Under the CIF Incoterms rule, which is reserved for use in maritime trade and is often used in commodity trading, the Institute Cargo Clauses (C) remains the default level of coverage, giving parties the option to agree to a higher level of insurance cover. Taking into account feedback from global users, the CIP Incoterms rule now requires a higher level of cover, compliant with Cargo Clauses (A) or similar clauses".[63]

That view and its rationale is also backed by practitioners thus:

> As well as the reallocation of all insurance obligations from former clauses A3/B3 to new clauses A5/B5, the default minimum level of insurance cover required under the CIP Incoterm has increased, from Institute Cargo Clauses (C), to Institute Cargo Clauses (A). Under Incoterms 2010, both CIF and CIP Incoterms required the seller to procure insurance cover which conformed with Institute Cargo Clauses (C) as a minimum, which covers certain limited listed risks, subject to listed exclusions. Institute Cargo Clauses (A) is by comparison an "all risks" cover but subject again to listed exclusions. The amendment reflects a better understanding of the types of goods commonly transported under the two Incoterms: while CIF is a Maritime Rule, used predominantly for maritime commodity trades, CIP is

---

60 Ibid; either way the seller includes them in the invoice and is reimbursed for the costs or expenses when he tenders the documents for payment.

61 HFW: ICC INCOTERMS 2020 – AT A GLANCE https://www.hfw.com/downloads/001487-HFW-Incoterms-2020-At-a-Glance-and-Commentary.pdf.

62 *Ademuni-Odeke, "Insurance of CIF I" supra.*

63 See ICC, "What's new about Incoterms®2020?" Updates, Wednesday 29 April 2020.

a Multi-Modal Rule, more commonly used in the sale of high-value, manufactured goods. Sellers will therefore need to factor in the increased cost of the additional insurance premium that is required under CIP.[64]

Buyers' insurance obligations are fundamentally different from those of sellers (see post).

8.7 Other Implications of the Insurance Clauses

8.7.1 Meaning of "Cargo Insurance at Sellers' Cost"

The seller's obligation is to obtain cargo insurance, that is, insurance to cover the risks to which the goods, as cargo, will be subject as his own costs. What is the implication of the provision that the seller must obtain insurance at his own costs? The cargo insurance must comply with cover provided by Cargo Clauses A or similar clauses as appropriate to the means of transportation used. This means the cover must comply with Cargo Clauses A or similar clauses but must not be narrower that Cargo Clauses A. Otherwise (for example) Clauses 16.1 and 16.2 (duties imposed on the insured for minimising losses) or Clause 18 (duty to avoid delays) or Clause 19 (subjecting the insurance contract to English Law and Practice) do not need to be incorporated.

This term has changed from "expenses" in Incoterms 2010 to "costs" throughout Incoterms 2020.However, all it means in practice is that the seller pays upfront and is then reimbursed when he tenders the documents. He cannot ask the buyer for advance payment. This particular requirement is important to note since, as in any contract for the sale of goods, among the many risks to which the transaction is subject is the possibility that, for example, payment of the price may not be made because of the bankruptcy of the buyer, or a moratorium on payments, or any of a number of possible reasons.

These risks may be insured against by taking out credit or political risks insurance. However, the procurement of this type of cover is merely to protect the seller's interest and is neither in pursuance of his obligation under the contract, nor for the benefit of the buyer. On the other hand, the obligation here is mandatory, and requires that the seller takes out insurance to protect the goods against loss or damage during the course of the journey, i.e., during such time they constitute cargo. Such cover is to protect the buyer's insurable interest in the goods, which he acquired upon their crossing the ship's rail or being handed to the carriers.[65] On the question of insurable interest, see again MIA1906, s 5, which provides that subject to the

[64] Ibid; Clyde & Co LLP: A Practical Overview of ICC Incoterms 2020, para 2(ii), https://www.lexology.com/library/detail.aspx?g=a6d530f0-f180-4973-8092-4dbfee36b1de.

[65] The buyer necessarily acquires an insurable interest in the goods at this stage, even though the property may not have passed to him, since the goods henceforth are held at his risk.

provisions of the Act, every person has an insurable interest who is interested in a marine adventure.

The insurance must be procured at the seller's own expense, and although the cost, being included in the overall contract price, is recouped from the buyer, the seller cannot, for example, request an advance to cover the expense of the insurance premium. This expense is incurred as a necessary part of the performance of his contractual obligations and so must be borne by the seller himself. Moreover, the cost of the premium must appear as an item in the invoice that the seller is obliged to tender to the buyer as part of the shipping documents.

8.7.2 Implications of "Allowing for Direct Claims by Anyone with Insurance Interest Against Insurers"

In taking out the insurance cover, the seller does not act as the agent of the buyer, unlike in FOB, but as a principal, and he becomes an original party to the insurance contract. However, the fact that the cover is for the buyer's benefit means that the seller's rights under the contract must be transferred to the buyer. Ordinarily, transfer of insurance cover is not automatically achieved when the goods are themselves transferred or assigned. As s. 15 of MIA 1906 makes clear: "Where the assured assigns or otherwise parts with his interest in the subject-matter insured, he does not thereby transfer to the assignee his rights under the contract of insurance, unless there be an express or implied agreement with the assignee to that effect".

However, the fact that in a CIF or CIP contract the seller procures insurance cover for the benefit of the buyer means that in such contracts the agreement to transfer such rights is clearly present. The seller may take out the policy, in his own name, or, in order to facilitate this transfer, take it out in the buyer's name. However, even in this case, he must ensure that the policy is transferable in order to allow for such transfers down the line. It is quite likely that even before he receives delivery of the goods, the buyer may wish to sell all or part of it to sub-buyer(s), and they in turn do other buyers. This is the process known as buying and selling *'afloat'*.

Such sub-buyers would also wish to have the benefit of insurance cover, and if, as is likely, the goods were sold on to them on CIF or CIP terms, the sellers (i.e., the original buyers) would be required to ensure that they were insured. It is in order to facilitate this on-sale of goods that the terms of the insurance must be such that the policy is capable of being transferred not only to the first, but also to all such subsequent buyers. As mentioned above S.5 of MIA 1906 provides that enables every person directly affected by the loss of the subject matter of the contract to acquire an insurable interest who is interested in a marine adventure. These would include the sellers and buyers themselves as well as carriers, bankers and subsequent buyers and/or their agents and assignees.

See also under Common Law (Chap. 5) above and Tender under UCP (Chap. 9) below. Having obtained the required insurance cover, the seller must then, 'provide the buyer with the insurance policy or other evidence of insurance cover'. Since the original as well as all subsequent buyers are to be given the right to claim directly against the insurers, it is necessary that they be particular a person is interested in a marine adventure where he stands in any legal or equitable relation to the adventure or to any insurable property at risk therein, in consequence of which he may benefit by the safety or due arrival of insurable property, or may be prejudiced by its loss, or by damage thereto, or by the detention thereof, or may incur liability in respect thereof.' See also s 7 of the MIA1906.

See also under insurable interest below where the same mechanism can be achieved through the "cut through clause" A cut-through clause is a provision in a contract of insurance which typically purports to afford protection to a policyholder against the insolvency of its insurer. It is also known as the cut through endorsement, a reinsurance contract endorsement providing that, in the event of the cedent's insolvency, the reinsurer will pay any loss covered by the reinsurance contract directly to the insured. Also called an "assumption endorsement."

8.7.3 Assignability of the CIF/CIP Policy

The requirement that the policy should be transferable should not present any difficulties, since s.50(1) of MIA 1906 provides that:

> **s. 50(1) of MIA 1906**
> (1) A marine policy is assignable unless it contains terms expressly prohibiting assignment. It may be assigned either before or after loss. 'If the insurance was procured in the buyer's name, no formalities are necessary, and the seller simply tenders the policy or other document together with the other shipping documents. If it was in his own name, therein at the time of tendering the shipping document the seller will endorse the policy to the buyer, usually in blank so that it may be further transferred down the line. A policy in the buyer's name may similarly be transferred to sub-buyer by endorsement.

S.50(3) provides that: '(3) A marine policy may be assigned by endorsement thereon or in other customary manner.' Sub-buyers are encompassed in the Incoterms provision either by the term 'buyer' or by the term 'any other person having an insurable interest in the goods. The latter phrase is, however, wide enough to cover not merely sub- buyers, but also others, for example, creditors of buyers who may be in receivership. Such persons should clearly have a right to claim under the policy, should the goods be lost or damaged because of a risk against which they were insured.

8.7.4 Requirements for Insurable Interests

Both CIF and CIP require that the insurance provided must entitle the buyer or any other person having an insurable interest in the goods to claim directly from the insurer. That means, *inter alia*, that the seller must take out an insurance to the benefit of the third party, namely the seller or his assigns. German law expresses it better in *Versicherung fur femde Rechnung* as do the French in *assurance pour le compte d'autrui.* The law may provide that under certain circumstances the policy holder, who took out insurance to cover the interest of another (the 'assured' or 'insured'), may nevertheless claim directly from the insurer.[66] This is what Incoterms seemingly tried to avoid.

Insurance to whom it may benefit (*assurance pour le compte de qui il appartiendra* and *Verischerung fur Rechnungwen es angeht)* falls into this category. If the seller takes out insurance 'warehouse to warehouse 'to cover all the carriage and has an insurable interest in part of it (for instance from its premises to the port of loading) this insurance may be an insurance 'to whom it may benefit'. In such a case for the portion of the carriage where the seller bears the risk the seller will be also deemed to be an insured and entitled to claim directly from the insurers for loss or damage occurring in that carriage portion.

Insurable interests are also covered under Chap. 1 (Introduction) above and Chap. 14 (Claims Procedures) below. Although concept of 'insurable interest' is potentially very broad, and it is questionable whether the seller will know who such persons are, provided they are able to satisfy the insurers that they are such a person, the seller is not concerned with who they are, and is simply required to take out a policy that covers such persons. Any such individual to whom the policy is subsequently transferred or who otherwise has an insurable interest in the goods must be able to claim 'directly' from the insurers, that is to say, without having to join the seller or any other party to the claim or action. Again, under s.50(2) of MIA 1906 it is provided that: 'Where a marine policy has been assigned so as to pass the beneficial interest in such policy, the assignee of the policy is entitled to sue thereon in his own name; and the defendant is entitled to make any defence arising out of the contract which he would have been entitled to make if the action had been brought in the name of the person by or on behalf of whom the policy was effected.'

This requirement that the policy 'stand on its own', is essential if the cover is to be worthwhile, for the parties will invariably be based in different countries, and if it was necessary to join a person in another country in order to bring a claim under the policy, not only would the possibility arise that such other party may cease to exist, or be uncooperative, but the sheer time, cost and general inefficiency of it would mean that the CIF or CIP term would never be used.

In CIF contracts the buyer's insurable interest (with regard to carriage) exists until the warehouse in cases where is situated far from the named port of

---

[66] *Insurance Contract Act 2008* (VVG) section 45(2) and (3).

"Section 45 Rights of the Policyholder

(1) The policyholder may dispose of the rights to which the insured person is entitled on the basis of the contract of insurance in his own name.
(2) If an insurance policy has been issued, the policyholder shall only be authorised to receive benefits from the insurer and to assign the rights of the insured person without the agreement of the insured person if he is in possession of the insurance policy.
(3) The insurer shall only be liable towards the policyholder if the insured person has given his consent to the insurance".

destination. But the seller is allowed to take out insurance only up to the named port of destination. Additional coverage (until inland warehouse) upon request of the buyer. Under, those conditions, it might be better for parties to contract CPT instead of the CIP.

8.7.5 Inconsistencies Arising from "Insurance Policy or Other Evidence"

Together with the delivery of the goods or delivery of transport documents (Clause A6).

In other words, in addition to tendering the insurance policy or other document evidencing the insurance cost, the cost of the insurance must also be separately presented in the invoice. This is in contrast to the FOB where, except for extended FOB, the seller is the agent for the buyer and might request payments for the premium in advance provided with some sort of document under which the insurer makes the undertaking to be liable thus. The authoritative document in which the underwriter undertakes to cover the risk is the insurance policy. The policy is not only the prime insurance document, it is also, unlike certificates of insurance, broker's cover notes, letters of insurance, memoranda, etc, directly admissible in court as evidence of the terms of the cover.[67]

S. of MIA 1906 provides that: 'Subject to the provisions of any statute, a contract of marine insurance is inadmissible in evidence unless it is embodied in a marine policy in accordance with this Act. The policy may be executed and issued either at the time when the contract is concluded or afterwards". Nevertheless, the reference to 'other evidence of insurance cover' makes it clear that the policy itself need not be tendered, but that another appropriate document would suffice.

The phrase is vague, perhaps deliberately so, and draws no distinction between the various alternatives, but should be seen in the context of insurance documents acceptable as tender to businessmen who regularly trade on CIF and CIP terms, and not be taken as meaning any other evidence of cover. As will be apparent shortly, it is quite likely that the letter of credit contract (where payment is being made by that method), would permit only tender of certificates of insurance as substitutes for the policy, and disallow cover notes, letters, or memoranda of insurance. By allowing evidence of insurance cover rather than the policy to be tendered, the provision accommodates the widespread practice of insuring goods under open cover whereby the seller declares the nature and value of the shipment under a pre-existing arrangement with his brokers who undertake subsequently to issue duly executed policies within the terms of the cover. Meanwhile the seller will be issued with a certificate of insurance, which he can then tender, to the buyer. The policy should be with reputable insurers.

The problem is when should the policy, certificate or any other evidence be provided?

---

[67] S 22 of the *Marine Insurance Act* 1906.

8.7.6 Inferences of the "Reputable Insurers" Requirements

The situation under Common Law was discussed in Chap. 3 above? Whilst the requirement that the insurance be contracted with 'an insurance company of good repute' is in itself quite clear, what may not be so straightforward is the question of whether a particular insurance company is of good repute or not. Does the insurance of good repute refer to domestic or international repute? Secondly, does it include reinsurance cases? Otherwise in cases where the benefit of reinsurances is assigned to the buyer, this condition might not be necessary and can be left out if reinsurers have a good repute. Since Lloyds of London Insurance dominates this market, national and international repute would not come bigger than that. Or similarly when the insured is entitled to claim directly from the reinsurers of good repute on the basis of 'cut through clause'.

For policies emanating from the UK, a Lloyd's policy would certainly satisfy this criterion, and though it may be considered 'second best', so too would a policy issued by an insurance company registered under the *Insurance Companies Act* 1982[68] (as amended) (such registration being prima facie evidence of good repute). Given that, these are the only two sources of insurance cover within the UK and both are of good repute, then effectively any policy underwritten within the UK will almost satisfy this requirement.

As for policies issued by underwriters in other countries, whether such underwriters are of good repute or not is essentially a quasi-factual question, upon which opinions might quite legitimately differ. There is no requirement that the insurers be of international repute, although in the context of international trade, to be of good repute invariably means international standing. However, if the requirement is read so as to entail the seller having to procure insurance from insurers of good repute in the international commercial world, it may present a problem for some exporters. A number of developing countries require not only that their exporter's trade on CIF or CIP terms, but also those they insure with domestic insurance companies.[69] Such countries are unlikely to have well-established insurance industries, or companies that could be said to be of 'good repute' simply because they are not known in the commercial world. It seems only natural in such cases, that good repute be taken to refer to repute within the country of the exporter.

8.7.7 Institute Scope of Cover

Unless expressly agreed in the underlying contract (incorporation into the written contract would be the best means of demonstrating this agreement, but does not appear to be specifically required), the insurance must be in accordance with the minimum cover of the Institute Cargo Clauses or a similar set of clauses. The *Institute Cargo Clauses* to which the provision refers are sets of clauses that

[68] There is an assumption that an insurance company registered under the Act is reputable.

[69] Incoterms placed the number of such countries at over 40 as of 1991.

accompany the new *Lloyd's Marine Policy* introduced in 1982. The essence of the new policy is that it allows for varying degrees of cover to be provided according to which clauses are used. There are three main clauses, which provide general cover: *Institute Cargo Clauses* A, B and C, together with a number of subsidiary clauses, which provide cover against specific risks: e.g., *Institute War Clauses (Cargo)* and *Institute Strikes Clauses (Cargo).* Of the three main clauses, Clause A provides the most comprehensive, or 'all-risks' cover—although it does not actually provide cover against all risks;[70] Clause B provides less cover than Clause A; and Clause C provides the least, or 'minimum cover'. Nevertheless, the cover provided under Clause C is sufficient to satisfy Incoterms, since 'minimum cover' is all that is required.

Provided there is express agreement to the contrary, the cover procured may be other than minimum cover. Thus, the parties may agree to use Clause A or B, or even, though unlikely, agree less cover than is available under Clause C. The cost of insurance will, of course, vary according to which clause is used. However, given the fact that cover ought to be on Clause C failing express agreement to the contrary, if it is agreed that insurance should be on Clause A or B, there is no indication of which party ought to bear the increased expense. It would appear that this fall on the seller,[71] and the additional cost thus included in the contract price. The seller will, of course, factor the increased expense into the invoiced price he agrees with the buyer.

Although widely used in international trade, the *Institute Cargo Clauses* are by no means the only such clauses available, and other clauses, provided they are 'similar', may be used in their place. As long as this similarity condition is met, there does not seem to be any need for an express agreement between the parties in order to permit their usage.

8.7.8 Duration of Cover

Duration of cover does not pose much problem. Both CIF and CIP provide that the insurance shall cover the goods from the point of delivery to at least the named port of destination. In CIF it should be insurance complying with the cover provided by cargo clause C and in CIP it should comply with coverage provided under cargo clause A. However, cargo clauses A provide for "warehouse to warehouse" insurance coverage. Nevertheless, both CIF and CIP cover are subject to insurable interest clause. In that case there is no need to buy insurance covering carriage, if any, up to shipment point. However, to be safe, the seller might purchase additional pre-shipment insurance and the buyer additional post-shipment insurance.

---

[70] Certain risks, for example, loss, damage or expense caused by 'wilful misconduct of the Assured', 'insufficiency or unsuitability of packing or preparation', 'inherent vice', 'delay', 'insolvency or financial default of the owner's managers charters or operators of the vessel', etc. are all risks which are excluded under Clause A.

[71] Based on the distinction between the silences of the provision on this point, as against the stipulation further on that the expense for additional cover for war, strikes, etc. is to be borne by the buyer.

See also under Common Law (Chap. 7) above. The best guide for thus requirement is Incoterms, which constitute an inter-related set of rights and obligations, and so in order to make sense of the reference to CIF Incoterms 2020 [Clause A3/B3] it is, necessary to examine these provisions. The provision of B5 varies slightly between the CIF and CIP term. In relation to the CIF term, it states that the seller must bear all risks of loss of or damage to the goods until they have been delivered in accordance with Clause A2[72] with the exception of loss or damage in the circumstances described in Clause B3. Clause B3 on the other hand provides that the buyer bears all risks of loss of or damage to the goods However, it goes further than Clause A3 by providing that should he fail to give notice in accordance with Clause B10, the it bears all risks of loss of or damage to the goods from the agreed date or the end of the agreed period fixed for shipment provided, that the goods have been clearly identified as the contract goods.

In relation to CIP, it states that the seller bears all risks or loss of or damage to the goods until they have been delivered in accordance with Clause A2, with the exception of loss or damage in circumstances described in Clause B3. Should he fail to give notice in accordance with Clause B10, bear all risks of the goods from the agreed date or the end of the agreed period for delivery provided, that the goods have been clearly identified as the contract goods. Clause B10 requires that whenever the seller is entitled to determine the time for shipment of the goods or the port of destination, he gives the seller sufficient notice thereof.

In a CIF contract, this will be from the time that goods cross the ship's rail; in a CIP contract, at the earlier time of when the seller delivers goods to the carriers. It also provides that where the buyer is entitled to determine either the time of dispatch and/or port of destination and fails to give sufficient notice to the seller thereof, then, provided the seller has duly appropriated goods to the contract, the risk of loss of or damage to the goods passes to the seller at either the agreed date, or the expiry of the period fixed for shipment. In other words, under B3 there are two points at which risk may pass: one based on the premise that the parties have fulfilled their respective obligations promptly, the other on the contingency that the seller has failed to fulfil a certain obligation. This duality renders the requirement that 'the duration of insurance cover shall be in accordance with Clause B3'[73] slightly problematic, for the seller knows that he needs to procure cover that begins, at the latest, from the time the goods cross the ship's rail or are delivered to the carriers—this being the time from which goods are (ordinarily) held at the buyer's risk.

Clause B2 provides that the buyer must take delivery of the goods when they have been delivered under Clause A2 and receive them from the carrier at the named place of destination or if agreed, at the point within that place. See Clause A2 to

---

[72] The equivalent provision in the Incoterms 2010 provided that "from the time they have passed the ship's rail at the port of shipment".

[73] Clause B4 prevision in both CIF and CIP is the same.

which it refers merely provides that the seller must deliver the goods on board or to the carriers within the stipulated period. However, if his duty is taken to consist of the more general obligation to ensure that the goods are covered from the time the risk passes to the buyer, rather than specifically from the time they are delivered on board, or to the carriers, then should he procure cover that begins at the latter point, a subsequent breach of an obligation by the buyer that serves to pass the risk prior to this time would have the effect of 'wrong-footing' the seller and rendering him in breach of his insurance obligation. This can hardly be right. It therefore seems likely that ensuring the duration of cover is 'in accordance with Clause B5' means ensuring cover, not from the time the risk passes to the buyer, but from the time the goods are delivered on board or to the carriers.

8.7.9 Passage of Risks Revisited

Passage of risks at Common Law was discussed in Chap. 6 above. This chapters revisits the same at Incoterms. Where risk passes to the buyer at an earlier point because of his own default, it would be a matter for him, and not the seller, to worry about. Indeed, it would render it ineffective as a penalty for the buyer's failure to give timely notice to have the risk pass to him yet make it the seller's responsibility to provide cover against the risk in such eventuality. Clause A5 provision makes it the responsibility of the seller to bear all risks of loss of or damage to the goods until such time as they have passed the ship's rail or been delivered to the carriers. However, this provision is expressly made subject to Clause B5. Thus, if goods have not been put on board or delivered to the carriers because of the buyer's fault, Clause A5 is overridden in favour of the risk falling on the buyer.

Clause B2' provides that if the seller delivers goods to the carriers within the shipment period, the buyer must accept delivery of the goods, and receive them from the carriers at the named port of destination. The requirement that the duration of the insurance cover shall be in accordance with Clause B2, thus simply means that the seller must ensure cover until such time as the buyer accepts delivery of the goods. It is clear that cover does not terminate upon arrival at the port of destination but continues in effect during the course of the unloading, during which time the goods are subject to as much, albeit different, risk as when they were at sea. However, upon receipt of the goods from the carriers, the question of insurance becomes a matter solely for the buyer, and the seller is not required to procure insurance that covers the goods to their final destination within the buyer's country. Although the seller needs to ensure the goods are covered until the point at which they are delivered to the buyers, it should be stressed that the risk does not thereby lie with the seller until that point: it passed to the buyer well before the vessel embarked on its journey. If the buyer wrongfully rejects the goods, they remain held at his risk, and without any insurance cover whatsoever, since that procured by the seller will have terminated once the goods were tendered to the buyer.

8.7.10 Cautions in Relation to the "*Minimum Cover*"

Unless provided otherwise, Incoterms require the seller to take out only minimum cover. What is the legal implication of this? The fact that the seller is only obliged to provide minimum cover means that if goods become lost or damaged because of a risk materialising against which the minimum cover clause offers no protection, the buyer must bear the loss. Provided the insurance obtained by the seller satisfied the minimum cover requirement, he cannot be held liable, and indeed, would still be due the full contract price—even though the buyer has received damaged goods or nothing at all. It may therefore be prudent for the buyer to ensure that the seller on the buyer's behalf insures the goods against a wider range of risks than that available under Cargo Clause C. Cover for such additional risks may either be obtained by the buyer himself, or if so, requested by the buyer. However, the cost of such insurance does not constitute part of the contract price, and the increased expense incurred must be borne by the buyer in addition to the contract price. Given that it does not form part of the contract price, the cost must appear as a separate item in invoice or be invoiced separately.[74]

Certain heads of additional insurance are specifically mentioned in Incoterms, and the obligation to provide such cover is therefore mandatory, provided it is procurable, i.e., the seller cannot refuse to provide such cover on the grounds of, say, inconvenience or unwillingness. If, on the other hand, it is simply unobtainable, the seller will not thereby breach his contractual obligations, although it is recommended that he notifies the buyer as soon as possible in order that the buyer may make alternative arrangements. The risks specifically mentioned are the following.

8.7.11 Need for Additional Cover Revisited

Since both cargo clauses A (for CIP) and cargo clauses C (for CIF) are not all risk policies, parties may, if they wish, purchase additional coverage. Additional cover required by especially the buyer such as cover against war risks or other risks such as strikes, lock-out labour disturbances, riots, civil commotions, terrorism, loss or damage caused by political, ideological or religious motives. However, Clause B5 (buyers' obligations) provides that the buyer must provide any information necessary to that effect. Thus, the seller must take out the additional cover insurance if the buyer provides the necessary information. Costs and risks must be borne by the buyer. However, neither Incoterms provide any further details r guidelines as to whether these costs are invoiced ales contract costs or paid separately. In the former the seller cannot ask for advance payments.

[74] It may be the case that whereas the seller procures the 'basic' insurance as a principal, i.e. it is done pursuant to his primary obligation under the contract, in the case of such additional insurance he acts as an agent of the buyer, since it is the latter's responsibility to obtain such cover and the seller is not obliged to obtain it for him.

A contract might require the seller to take out additional cover. In the absence of an all-risks' policy, this normally means taking out war risks. However, war risks are an umbrella provision, which include civil war, strikes, riots, civil war, civil commotion, insurrection and rebellion. This is partly pertinent in current unstable global environment. Neither Incoterms nor the UCP define what war, strikes, riots or civil commotion. We have, therefore, to fall back to the general principles of common law, generally and insurance law in particular, for help regarding their meanings. We will attempt to define each of these in turn.

8.8 Caution on the Wider Incoterms' Insurance Perspectives

8.8.1 Legal and Commercial Effects of Insuranve Limitations

It is established that neither Incoterms nor its Insurance Clauses are as exhaustive as we are meant to believe. Instead, they only a codification of guidelines to exporters and importers. That Incoterms limitation has legal and commercial repercussions as they. For those reasons, it is common for contracts for exports to these countries to use these Incoterms, even when they are not suitable for the chosen mode of transport. What if the destination country requires insurance cover to be purchased locally? This is known as "*fronting*"—in a fronting programme, an insurance company (the *fronting carrier*) issues a policy and transfers some or all of the risk back to the insured. It is the acceptance of insurance or reinsurance with the intention of passing it wholly to another insurer or reinsurer.

Most fronting programmes utilise a reinsurance cession to the insured's captive to secure the risk participation required by the insured. Can such policies be taken out locally in the destination country by the seller using an agent? Such a method would not defeat the aims of the restrictive policy to earn foreign currency and boost local shipping and insurance industries. Alternatively, do such state interventions discharge the seller from obtaining insurance? Or is the obligation complied with only if the seller takes out insurance in his own country? Otherwise, parties would be better advised in those circumstances to contract CPT instead of CIF or CIP. However, where that where one party is a US citizen or resident, parties should be aware that fronting is disapproved of in the US jurisdiction for tax and supervisory reasons unless purposes unless the fronting company retains a reasonable share of the risks.

The above restrictions might affect the formation or use of fronting companies in the US jurisdiction. This is a company where an insurer or a reinsurer engaged in fronting by placing business with another insurer or reinsurer. The scheme is particularly popular with insurance and reinsurance companies formed offshore by foreign brokers and/or insurers to handle large risks arising in countries which lack domestic insurance facilities and markets. It is such countries which tend to resort to restrictive marine insurance and shipping practices.

If this is the case, then great care must be exercised to ensure that the points at which costs and risks pass are clarified with the customer. This has a direct bearing and consequence on insurance of Incoterms sales. Accordingly, parties are recommended to consider wider implications, other than those provided in CIF and CIP insurance clauses which might have cost bearings on their contractual as well as additional insurance requirements. One of those is the implications of NO OBLIGATION both in the CIF-CIP and the other 9 Incoterms rules (See also Chap. 9).

8.8.2 Caution on "NO OBLIGATION" To Insure Clauses

As established above, with the exception of the CIF and CIP, the remaining 9 of the 11 Incoterms rules do not deal with sellers' insurance obligations. In those 9 rules, all Incoterms up to Incoterms 2020 simply provide **'NO OBLIGATION'** under both parties' contractual insurance obligations. This can be misleading. Both parties should, therefore, be very careful about this provision in Incoterms especially in relation to insurance. Otherwise, they might be left exposed or left under insured in both their contractual, additional, and own insurance requirements. For insurance purposes, the expression may imply, but not necessarily mean, that the party in question should not bother about other/and or with indirect insurance requirements. All it means is that the concerned party does not owe the other a duty to contract for insurance, but still have to cater own insurance.

Furthermore, sellers could even agree to provide the cover on buyers' request, risk and expenses. In that case those sellers should, however, ensure that they have adequate contingency cover for their own exposure arising from breach of contractual duties relating to delivery, property passage, passage of risks both before and during delivery to the buyer. That means even when they feel they have performed their obligations adequately; they should still also take out contingency insurance to cover any contingencies such pre- and post-shipment eventualities such premature passage of risk. The rationale behind the drafting of Incoterms insurance provisions in their current form may be understood by seasoned traders acquainted with Incoterms and insurance, but not to novices. For those reasons, perhaps there needs to a warning to all parties, in red and capitals as is in rules governing exclusion of liabilities in contract law, to all parties along the lines that, "YOU MAY WISH TO AND/OR ARE STRONGLY ADVISED TO INSURANCE YOUR OWN RISKS AND ANY POSSIBLE BREACHES ON YOUR PART". The dilemma has been around and was explained in commentaries to earlier Incoterms.[75]

> As appears from the expressions "the seller must", and "the buyer must" Incoterms are only concerned with the obligations which the parties owe to each other. The words "no obligation" have therefore been inserted whenever one party does not owe an obligation to the other party. Thus, if for instance according to A3 of the respective term the seller has to arrange to pay for the contract of carriage we find the words "no obligation" under the heading "contract of carriage in B3 setting forth the buyer's position. Again, where neither party

[75] For instance, paragraph 10 (The Expression **"No Obligation"**) of Ramberg J, Introduction to Incoterms 2000, ICC Doc No 560 pp. 5–22 at p. 19.

> owes the other an obligation, the words "no obligation will appear with respect to both parties, for example, with respect to insurance.
>
> In either case, it is important to point out that even though even party may be under "no obligation towards the other to perform a certain task, this does not mean that it is not in his interest to perform that task. Thus, for example, just because a CFR buyer owes his seller no duty to make a contract of insurance under B4, it is clearly in his interest to make such a contract, the seller being under no such obligation to procure insurance under A4[76]

Thus, although Incoterms is extensively used globally, it does not follow that it is equally widely and commonly understood. Once more the rules do not go into details and nature of the notice and information. However, the requirement for notice and information seem to supplement the "NO OBBLIGATION" scenarios.

8.9 Requirement for Notice and Information

8.9.1 Notice and Information Relating to Insurance

One of the developments in Incoterms practices, generally and insurance in particular, are the twin requirements for both parties. Additionally, the latest three Incoterms (1990, 2000 and 2020), introduced a requirement for notices and information liaisons between the parties to deal with shipment and insurance issues. This is important because at common law only the FOB contract required the seller to provide the buyer with notice to enable him take out the policy except where the buyer already had or should have had the information.[77] The rationale for this being that, except in extended or FOB with additional duties (where the extended duty included shipment and insurance), it is the buyers' duties to take out the policy.

This is in marked contrasts to both CIF and CIP rules. Hence, the requirements for notice and information were never necessary for CIF and consequently CIP. Unlike the other 9 rules, sellers are responsible for and therefore in possession of all the necessary information. So, by gradually introducing the concept of such requirements, Incoterms is now trying to standardise international trade practices thereby chipping away on the main historical differences between the FOB and related contracts and the CIF-CIP. Is the provision of information in buyers' possession of the same standard as in Clause A5 of the CPT for instance?

First, except under CIF and CIP rules, parties must to give notice to each other to enable the shipment and to provide information to enable the other to take out insurance as well as additional insurance, where applicable. This is significant development for Incoterms as such notice was required only in FOB[78] and related contracts

[76] Reproduced at Ramberg J, ICC Guide to Incoterms 2000, ICC Pub.No.620, at 194.

[77] See Ademuni-Odeke, "Insurance of FOB Contracts", pp. 445–447 and the cases discussed therein.

[78] Ibid, pp. 447–449; Wimble Sons & Co. v. Rosenberg & Sons, [1913] 3 K.B. 743, 747–748; Northern Steel & Hardware Co. v. John Batt & Co. (London) [1917] 33 T.L.R. 516, 516.

at common law but not in CIF and later CIP, under s.32(3) of the UK *SGA* 1979.[79] Secondly, this points to the fact that in practice the difference between the "Free Family" (FOB and related contracts) and the CIF-CIP is quickly disappearing in this and other respects of export trade. As detailed immediately below, 4 particular aspects of notice require parties' attention: nature of the risks involved, sufficiency of the notice, consequences of failure to give notice and extent of the requirements.[80]

8.9.2 Nature, Sufficiency, form of and Failure to Give Notice of

First, the nature of the risks involved. Clause A5/B5 is silent on these details. However, information relating to insurance depends on the nature of the risks, need for addition insurance and market restrictions in the buyers' country, where applicable.[81] Secondly, is the sufficiency of the notice. As usual, there are no guidelines on this in Incoterms. The rules only state that the notice must be "sufficient". However, they should be adequate such as to enable the other party to act accordingly. Sufficient here has both the ordinary and legal meanings. Third, as to the form, there are again no special requirements in Incoterms that notice be given in a particular form e.g., such as by letter, telex or telefax. However, resort to the principal means of communication used in the underlying sales contract might a be goo guide as to the nature and means of the notice too. Failing that, common sense suggests that any of the social or mass media could apply.

Fourth, the rules do not provide for consequences of giving insufficient notice or failure to provide notice at all. It can only be conjectured that such failure to provide the prerequisite notice can lead to breach of contract giving either party the right to cancel and terminate the contract or for loss and damage arising from such failure such as in the premature passage of risks (Clause B5) below or the liability to pay additional costs. Finally, another noticeable Incoterms development (since Incoterms 2000) is the emphasis on requirement for notice. However, this is not restricted to the insurance clause. Hence their inclusion not only in the CIF-CIP Insurance Clauses (A5/B5) but are also in: Clauses A3/B3 (Transfer of Risks for EXW, CPT,

[79] s32(3) of the UK *SGA* 1979, as amended, provides that:

> Unless otherwise agreed, where goods are sent by the seller to the buyer by a route involving sea transit, under circumstances in which it is usual to insure, the seller must give such notice to the buyer as may enable him to insure them during their sea transit; and if the seller fails to do so, the goods are at his risk during such sea transit.

Case law (e.g., Wimble v Rosenberg and Northern Steel v John Batt above) has suggested that the provision applies only to FOB but not apply to CIF (and by deductions to CIP) contracts: see, also, Ademuni-Odeke, "Insurance of CIF II", supra, pp. 28–29; Ademuni-Odeke, "Insurance of FOB Contracts", supra pp. 443–445.

[80] See *ICC Guide to Incoterms* 1990, ICC Pub No.461/90 at p. 37. Market restrictoions.

[81] Market restrictions. See para 10.19 on **State Restrictions on Export Insurance**, para 10.20 on **Other Insurance considerations**, and paras 10.28.1-28.3 on **External Considerations Affecting Insurance Obligations**, below.

DAP, DPU, DDP, FAS, FOB and CFR); and in Clause A10/B10 (Taking Delivery at Shipment and at Destination) in all the rules. That takes us back to the standardization of notice and information requirements.

8.9.3 Importance of Standardization of Notice and Information

Although originally the preserve of especially FOB at common law, requirement for notice and information is becoming standard for Incoterms and all export contracts. For Incoterms that standardization is now contained, with the 4 conditions for the notice and information, in Clause B10 of FCA especially with reference to Clause A2 (Delivery) thereof.[82] Thus, although, they have NO OBLIGATION to provide insurance, sellers in EXW, FCA, CPT, FAS, FOB and CFR must however provide the buyer, at buyer's request, risks and costs, with information in their (sellers) possession that the buyer requires to take out insurance (Clause A5).

Consequently, only those sellers in DAP, DDP, and DPU do not have to provide the information or give notice under Clause A5. Equally, buyers in DAP, DPU, and DDP have to provide the information or give notice under Clause B5. This would now equate their position to those of CIF and CIP buyers regarding the requirement for notice and information with the exception that the latter have to also insure and provide the information both contractual and in relation to additional insurance. While buyers in EXW, FCA, CPT, FAS, FOB and CFR do not have to either insure or provide the information or give notice under Clause B5.

Both parties should also be aware of the exceptional circumstances affecting liability such as pre-mature transfer of, pre-shipment and post-shipment, risks.

8.9.4 Effect of Law Applicable in Loss and Damage

8.9.4.1 Law Applicable

Although Incoterms avoids dealings with jurisdictional issues, nevertheless there are residual problems resulting from its references to related insurance topics. For instance, CIF uses cargo clauses C and CIP cargo clauses A. However, there are more than one version of the Cargo Clauses. So which edition is applicable-1982 or 2009? Clause 19 of the 2009 version of the cargo clauses provides that "This insurance is subject to English Law and Practice" Is it a requirement to adhere to this choice of law? If in the affirmative what about the MIA 1906 provisions which also point to English Law and Practice? What practice do Clause 19 of the Cargo Clauses 2009 refer to? And what customary law does the MIA refer to-English customary law or commercial/trade usage?

---

[82] Ibid. Revisit.

8.9.4.2 Risk of Loss or Damage Covered by *'All Risks'* Insurance

Does Cargo Clauses A cover *'all risks'* in the CIP policy as it claims or only the named peril? Equally does Cargo Clauses C in CIF policy cover more than the named perils. That notwithstanding, in *'all risks'* insurances the burden of proof, that the risks materialised does not fall within the scope of the cover, but lies with the insurer. The policyholder or the insurer must prove that the risk that materialised is a carriage risk which occurred within the time and geographical limits of the insurance contract. Thereafter, the insurers -in order to escape liability-must then prove that the risk is due to one or more excepted cases.

8.9.4.3 The Loss or Damage Risk Covered by *'Named Perils'* Insurance or the Insured, Whichever Is Applicable, Has to Demonstrate:

(a) in addition to conformity to time and general geographical limits;
(b) that the loss resulted from one of the perils mentioned in the insurance clause
(c) in CIF contracts, the buyer covered in accordance with cargo clauses C must prove that the cause of all-risks' the loss or damage is one of the followings:
  (i) fire or explosion
  (ii) vessel or craft being stranded, grounded, or sunk;
  (iii) overturning or derailment of land conveyancing;
  (iv) collision or contact of vessel or craft or conveyance with any external object other than water;
  (v) discharge of cargo at port of distress; and
  (vi) general average sacrifice or jettison.
(d) in cargo clauses C, after the above evidence is brought about one or more of the named perils, the burden of proof will shift and the insurer will to demonstrate one of the excepted cases or a behaviour, for example breach of duty, that discharges the insurer.

8.9.5 Other Lingering Issues

There are four lingering problems:

(a) effect of the seller contracting in own name, for the insurance, on the transfer of risks; and the so called "To Whom it May benefit policies" taken to avoid problems arising in the former;
(b) To Who it may benefit Policies;
(c) Goods Bought and Sold in Transit; and
(d) Cash Against Documents (CAD) and Cash Against Goods (CAG) Contracts.

8.9.5.1 Effect of Contracting in Own Name on Transfer of Risks

The seller that has concluded an insurance on its own behalf in in breach of Incoterms CIF and CIP that require an insurance to be taken out on behalf of the buyer. This is because transfer of risk to the buyer means:

(a) if the seller did receive the sale price, it shall not be required to return it, neither wholly or partly, upon loss or damage during transit. This might have effect on subrogation to; and

(b) if seller did not receive the sale price yet, it will still be entitled to claim it regardless of the loss or damage during transit.

Therefore, legally speaking, the loss or damage during transit does not adversely affect the CIF seller and possibly the CIP seller too. This is because the risk of non-payment of the sale price by the buyer, including non-payment as a result of delivery of the goods at destination not in sound condition or refusal of the goods, can and should be covered by a credit (trade receivable) insurance contract. That is why insurance is so crucial in especially CIF contracts. That is also the case at common law, hence the notion that the CIF is a sale of documents rather than a sale of goods.

Second the status of the so called "To Whom It may Benefit Policies".

8.9.5.2 "To Who It May Benefit" Policies

English common law is either silent or is not clear on this issue. However, German law seems to have a satisfactory if not a better solution. This is covered by the *Versicherung fur femde Rechnung* concept (Insurance for someone else's account) contained in the German Insurance Act 2008(VVG = Versicherungsvertragsgesetz).[83] These are covered in sections 43, 45, 46 and 48 of the German Act. Section 45 providers that

> **Section 45 Rights of the Policyholder**
>
> (1) The policyholder may dispose of the rights to which the insured person is entitled on the basis of the contract of insurance in his own name.
> (2) If an insurance policy has been issued, the policyholder shall only be authorised to receive benefits from the insurer and to assign the rights of the insured person without the agreement of the insured person if he is in possession of the insurance policy.
> (3) The insurer shall only be liable towards the policyholder if the insured person has given his consent to the insurance.

[83] For the English translation of the (VVG = Versicherungsvertragsgesetz)see: https://www.gesetze-im-internet.de/englisch_vvg/.

Section 48 deals with (*Verischerung fur Rechnungwen es angeht* [sic] (Insurance for the account of "whom it may concern" and provides that:

Section 48 Insurance for the Account of "Whom It May Concern"
If the insurance is taken out for the account of "whom it may concern" or if the contract provides in another manner that it is to remain unspecified whether an own interest or the interest of another is to be insured, sections 43 to 46 shall apply if it can be concluded from the circumstances that the interest of another is insured.

Section 43 (Definition) under "Division 4 Insurance for the account of a third party" provides that:

Section 43-Definitions

(1) The policyholder may make the contract of insurance in his own name for the account of another with or without naming the insured third party (insurance for the account of a third party).
(2) If the contract of insurance is made for another, it is assumed in cases of doubt, even if the third party is named, that the policyholder is not acting as his agent but in his own name for the account of a third party.
(3) If the circumstances do not indicate that the contract of insurance is to be concluded for another, it is deemed to have been made for the policyholder's own account.

And Section 46 provides that:

Section 46-Rights Between the Policyholder and the Insured Person
The policyholder shall not be obligated to hand over the insurance policy to the insured person or, in the event of insolvency proceedings having been opened with regard to his assets, to the insolvency estate, until his claims against the insured person have been satisfied with regard to the insured thing. He may satisfy these claims from the claim for compensation against the insurer and, after it has been collected, from the compensation paid before the insured person and the latter's creditors.

8.9.5.3 Goods Bought and Sold in Transit

Although originally a preserve of the CIF contract, especially at common law, Incoterms is now catching up by permitting the practice in FOB, etc. This might, however, cause insurance problems.

(a) for goods sold in transit, what happens if the insurance contract, or a law applicable to the insurance contract, provides that the acquirer of the goods will not benefit from the insurance? Does such an insurance contract conform with CIF and CIP Incoterms?

(b) Yet Clause A5 of both the CIF and CIP provides that, "This insurance shall entitle the *buyer, or any other person having insurable interest in the goods* to claim directly from the insurers"
(c) Yet Clause A6(second paragraph) of the CIP Incoterms provides that, "if agreed or customary, the (transport)document must also enable the buyer to sell the goods in transit by the transfer of the document or by notification to the carrier".
(d) That is repeated in principle in Clause 6(second paragraph) of the CIF Incoterms by the phrase, "unless otherwise agreed"

8.9.5.4 Cash Against Documents (CAD) and Cash Against Goods (CAG) Contracts

CAD[84] and CAG[85] contracts might introduce further confusions into especially the insurance aspects of CIF and CIP contracts. For instance, a recent Turkish Court of Cassation ruled that:

(a) In CIF or CIP contracts, the seller shall have an insurable interest until the sale price is paid. This is due to the seller's interest discussed above.
(b) Therefore, from the above, it follows that in CIF and CIP sales contracts the unpaid seller that has concluded the insurance on its own behalf shall be entitled to claim from the insurer for losses or damage occurring during the carriage, yet the same seller claims directly from the buyer even if the loss or damage have occurred after shipment!
(c) It is submitted that the above scenarios may be the case for example if the contract provides for CAD and or CAG payments which are quite legal and common practice
(d) For those reasons there is widespread opinion that CAD and CAG clauses override the transfer of the risks clause (A4/B4)

8.10 CIF and Related Contracts Under Civil and Other Jurisdictions

8.10.1 The Nordic Countries

8.10.1.1 The *Nordic Plan*

Export insurance generally and CIF insurance in particular in civil and other jurisdictions are affected almost on the same principles as those of the Anglo-American and other Common Law Jurisdictions. The common land practice is now same as

[84] Payment terms used in bank collections that require the drawee to pay before receiving certain documents. Typically, the drawer will send these documents to the drawee's bank with instructions that it secure payment before releasing them. Also called payment at sight.

[85] In the Cash Against Goods payment method, the exporter submits, free of charge, the documents representing the goods to the importer either directly or through the bank, and the importer makes payment for the goods at a date after the goods are cleared through the customs.

international practice. The Norwegians,[86] for instance, use the *Nordic Marine Insurance Plan* (The *Norwegian Plan)*. Equally the *Norwegian Plan*[87] is conducted on the basis almost identical to those of the English MIA 1906. Chapter 2, on a comparative analysis of the exclusion for deck cargo, delay, and temperature, of the Marine exclusions in the Scandinavian cargo insurance conditions, puts cargo insurance in context. Among the topics covered are: what is cargo insurance, the need for cargo insurance, the relationship with the sales contract, and the carrier liability versus cargo insurer liability.[88]

8.10.2 CIF and Related Contracts in Other Major Trading Nations

8.10.2.1 Germany

The German position has been covered by the discussions on *Versicherung fur femde Rechnung* and *Verischerung fur Rechnungwen es angeht* above.

8.10.2.2 Switzerland

The leading European continental trading countries such as France,[89] Germany,[90] Italy[91] and Switzerland (look for) apply the same Common Law principles despite having own commercial and insurance codes.

8.10.2.3 The Peoples Republic of China

Similar Plans exist in China.[92] The Chinese CIF Contract for Chinese importer provides that:

> **Chinese CIF Contract for Chinese Importer**
> The Seller shall effect insurance against all risks, war risk and on deck risk if applicable, with a ***first-class insurance company*** covering 110% of the invoice value of the Contract Equipment with the Buyer as the beneficiary. The insurance has to be covered in the Contract Currency showing claims payable in China and with no deductible clause

[86] The latest being the Nordic *Marine Insurance Plan 2013* based on the *Norwegian Marine Insurance Plan 1996* (2010 Version) and the 1964 Plan and Relevant *Nordic Insurance Contracts Acts* (Nordic ICAs); see also Trine-Lise Wilhemsen and Hans Jacob Bull, Chapter 12 in John Dunt, Note 8, pp. 405–439, It is not clear whether it applies to Denmark, Finland and Sweden.

[87] Ibid.

[88] A comparative analysis of the exclusion for deck cargo, delay and temperature damage Kandidatnummer: 686 Leveringsfrist: 25.05.2020 Antall ord: 15 903, https://www.duo.uio.no/bitstream/handle/10852/79047/1/686.pdf.

[89] Gildas Rostain, "Marine Buzulier and Maxine de La Marionerie", Chapter 12 in *John Dunt*, Note 8, pp. 371–404.

[90] Joachim Bartels, Chapter 10 in *John Dunt*, Note, 8, pp. 311–372.

[91] John Dunt, Note 8, Chapter 9.

[92] For mainland China, see Liu Guiming, Liang Jian and Cai Dongdong, "XXX", Chapter 13 in *John Dunt* pp. 441–464; for Hong Kong Special Economic Zone see Colin Wright and Caroline

> In case the Contract Equipment are lost and/or damaged in the ocean transportation, the Seller shall assist the Buyer to apply to the insurance company for compensation or lodge claims against the insurance company on behalf of the Buyer and effect, upon the Buyer's request, supplementary supply of the same at the original Contract Price[93]

Section 2(Clauses 33–51) of the *Insurance Law of the People's Republic of China*[94] deals with property insurance which includes cargo insurance. In particular Clause 35 on Cargo insurance provides that: A cargo insurance contract or an insurance contract for the carrier's voyage shall not be terminated by the parties thereto subsequent to the commencement of insurance liability.

The Chinese policy has all the requirements of the common law ones which also include: all risks, war risk, reputable insurance (first class insurance company), the 110%, currency of the contract, payable in China, and no deductibles. The only difference with the common law is, assistance required of the seller to "lodge claims on behalf of the Buyer". This runs counter to the principles of *The Julia* where the seller should put the buyer in a position where the latter can sue in own name and in a direct claim from the insurer.

8.10.2.4 Japan

Similar position applies in Japan.[95] Nakaide relates that "The *Commercial Code* contains special provisions on marine insurance from Clauses 815 to 841–842. These provide, inter alia, definition of marine insurance, indemnity principle, insurable value, period of cover, marine insurance policy, change of voyage or other alteration of risks, exclusions, partial loss, unavoidable sale of cargo, abandonment, and application to mutual insurance. Most of these provisions are considered discretionary. The *Commercial Code* was enacted in 1899 and has had no major revision since then. The government just launched a thorough revision of the Code in April 2014 to reflect the change in marine insurance business as well as its legal environment."[96]

Thomas, Chapter 4 in John Dunt Note 8, pp. 111–128; Johanna Hjalmarsson, Dingjing Huang (Editors) *Insurance Law in China*, 1st Edition, Informa Law from Routledge, 2015 (paperback 2020).

[93] Art.5.15 of a CIF Model Contract for Importation of Complete Plant from overseas into China.

[94] Adopted at the 14th Meeting of the Standing Committee of the Eighth National People's Congress on June 30, 1995, promulgated by Order No. 51 of the President of the People's Republic of China, and amended in accordance with the Decision on Amending the Insurance Law of the People's Republic of China adopted at the 30th Meeting of the Standing Committee of the Ninth National People's Congress on October 28, 2002.

[95] See John Dunt, Note 8, pp. 145–171; Satoshi Nakaide "Marine Insurance Law in Japan A Structure Based on a Combination of Civil Law and English Marine Policy Wordings", https://core.ac.uk/download/pdf/144444276.pdf p. 6.

[96] Nakaide, ibid.

He also provides that "Cargo insurance contracts used in Japan are also divided into two types:

(i) Cargo insurance policy with Japanese conditions written in Japanese. Contracts based on these conditions include a Japanese jurisdiction clause and Japanese governing law clause; and.
(ii) English policy with Institute Cargo Clauses or other standard clauses used in London.

He also opines that "These policies are for international trade. The clause below, known as the Foreign Governing Law Clause, is added to the clause, reading: Notwithstanding anything contained herein or attached hereto to the contrary, this insurance is understood and agreed to be subject to English law and practice only as to liability for and settlement of any and all claims".[97]

8.10.2.5 Thailand

The Latin American countries also use the Civil Law systems introduced by the Portuguese in Brazil, the Dutch, and the French in their former colonies and by the Spanish in the rest. However, there is evidence that these countries use the common law principles and in some the spirit of the English MIA 1906.

8.11 Further Food for Thoughts

8.11.1 See Also Nature of CIF

The uncertainty as to whether the CIF is a sale of documents or sale of goods (see Chap. 6 above (characteristics of contracts which necessitate the seller to provide insurance) could persist in this instance as food for thought. Comments under Food for Thought in chapter would therefore be relevant in this chapter.

8.11.2 See also Insurance of CIF at Common Law

For the same reasons as in paragraph 8.11.1 comments under Food Thoughts in Chap. 7 (Contracts which require the seller to provide insurance at Common Law).

8.11.3 Requirement of Notice Requirements

Discussions on the nature and consequences of the requirement of notice discussed above are relevant and applicable here too. However, this is rather contradictory. Although Clause A5 in both CIF/CIF and the others, mandate the seller to provide that information; first it must be requested by the buyer; secondly the buyer bears the risks and costs of the request and; finally, it is only if the seller has the information. If he doesn't then the provision is superfluous.

---

[97] Ibid.

8.11.4 Problems of the Minimum Cover in CIF and CIP

1. The minimum cover provision in Clause A5 is only dependant on if:
   (a) parties do not agree otherwise.

This implies that parties can agree otherwise to provide insurance on higher terms. However, they cannot agree on lower terms than the minimum or not provide insurance cover at all.

   (b) it is not inconsistent with customs.

Clause A5 is silent on what constitutes customs. The educated guess is that it is either sales or insurance trade customs or shipping customs at the port of shipment

2. Even the additional insurance is also subject to:
   (a) buyer's request and costs.

It is silent on whether the request should be express or implied, oral or in writing. They should make the request and not assume that the seller will do so. Costs here refers to upfront costs; the buyer cannot ask for credit from the seller. However, in practice the cost is normally payable by the seller and reimbursed at the tender of documents and payments thereto

   (b) buyer's provision of the necessary information requested by the seller.

The seller's provision of additional insurance further in turn depends on if the buyer provides the seller with the necessary information such as the final destination of the insured cargo if different from the contractual destination. The seller has to request this information. Once more Clause A5 is silent on the nature, mangoade and extent of the request. If the seller does not request then either this sub-contract is off or there is an assumption he is in possession of and does not need the information.

   (c) only where insurance procurable by the seller.

Even if the above conditions are met, there is no guarantee that the seller will provide the additional insurance. That in turn depends on if and whether the additional insurance is procurable. If it is not then that would be the end of the matter save that common sense dictates that the seller should notify the buyer of the inability to do so, so that the buyer makes other arrangements.

8.11.5 Inconsistencies in Passage of Risks and Duration of the CIP/CIF

Until such point as risk in the goods passes to the buyer, the goods are at the seller's risk and the seller is responsible for them. This means that if the goods are damaged or destroyed, the seller will remain responsible for providing replacement goods on the terms set out in the agreement.

8.11.6 Other Considerations for CIP and CIF

The following problems have also been identified in the CIF and CIP insurance:

(a) Once the goods have been taken in charge by the carrier (or loaded on board the ship), the buyer is "on risk", and so must deal with the insurance company in order to make a claim. This has implications for the insurance document that the seller provides—it may need to be appropriately endorsed.
(b) Some sellers have global freight insurance policies covering all their consignments. This often creates problems for the use of e.g., CIP. (For a single consignment, how can the insurance be costed, and how can arrangements be made allowing a buyer to make a claim?)
(c) Some sellers find the requirement for the buyer to claim under the insurance policy unsatisfactory from a customer service perspective. In such cases, the seller may agree to take care of claims. A letter of subrogation can be supplied (seller takes over right to claim under the policy)
(d) Even the highest of the Institute Cargo Clauses—Clauses A—excludes risks that the buyer may think are important—for example War and Strikes (for which a standard Institute clause exists)"[98]

8.11.7 The "No Obligations" Caution Regarding (C&F, CFR and CPT)

The "no obligation" aspects relate to buyers in all the 11 Incoterm rules: 9 contracts covered in Chap. 7 above where there are no obligations to insure under Clause A5 and the 2 contracts (CIF AND CPT) in this chapter; not to CIF and CIP sellers, under Clause A5. Pursuant to the discussions in paragraph 8.7.2, although under no obligations to do so for the seller's benefits, the buyers concerned should ignore this and instead take out contingency policies for their own benefits.

8.11.8 Inconsistencies in Between Incoterms and UCP 600 on Documentation

Clause A5 of both CIF and CIP provide among other things that "The seller must provide the buyer with the insurance policy or certificate or certificate or *any other evidence of insurance coverage*". However, Clause A5 does not define or provide guide as to "evidence of insurance coverage" What constitutes the evidence of the insurance? Evidence of insurance means written or printed statements evidencing the applicability and effectiveness of insurance coverages, including, but not limited to, policy forms, certificates, cover notes, binders and other traditionally acceptable

[98] Incoterms Explained.Com:*Freight Insurance-Incoterms Rules and Freight Insurance* https://www.incotermsexplained.com/freight-insurance/ (accessed 23/11/2022).

evidences of insurance. These would be acceptable under Clause A5 but only the policy, certificate of insurance and declaration under open cover would be acceptable under Clause 28 of the UCP 600. However, that might be acceptable in contracts not involving payments for or finance by letters of credit.

For the latter, however, Clause 20 of the UCP 600 only expressly allows for tender of the policy or certificate of insurance. Even brokers covernotes are not acceptable tender under Clause 28(c) UCP 600. However, there is a leeway in Clause 28(a) providing that "An insurance document, *such as an insurance* policy, an insurance certificate or *a declaration under an open cover*, must appear to be issued and signed by an insurance company, an underwriter or their agents or their proxies". So, it would appear the evidence of cover here would include declarations under open covers or blanket policies or even letters of insurance. The expression "such as" seems to point to that direction.

8.11.9 Security Concerns-What Are These?

Like all Incoterms under Clause A4, "The seller must comply with any transport-related security requirements for transport to the destination" First, these are not defined. Secondly what happens if the seller fails to comply!? If that means or leads to default, would he be covered by the policy?

8.11.10 Potential Problem Areas of CIF/CIP Insurance

Thus, the seller must also contract for insurance cover against the buyer's risk of loss of or damage to the goods from the port of shipment to at least the port of destination. As pointed out above and in Chap. 11 below, this may cause difficulty where the destination country requires insurance cover to be purchased locally: in this case the parties should consider selling and buyer under CFR or even CPT instead of CIF or CIP. Furthermore, the buyer should also note that under CIF Incoterms 2020 rule the seller is required to obtain limited insurance cover complying with Institute Cargo Clauses C or similar clause, rather than with the more extensive cover under Institute Cargo Clauses (A) required for CIP insurance. It is, however, still open to the parties to agree on a higher level of cover.

8.11.11 Failure to Check the Level of Insurance

Use of CIP or CIF without checking whether the level of insurance in force matches the requirements of the commercial contract could lead to unintentional under insurance and disastrous consequences. In some instances, these Incoterms rules only require a minimal level of cover, which may be inadequate. This is something that both parties may have to revisit. Failing that they should always take contingency insurance both pre- and post-shipment.

8.11.12 Parties Beware-Check Your Coverage

A leading international underwrite cautions that "Insurers are becoming more and more risk-averse, with the complexities of international shipping contributing to what's been called the 'hardening' of the insurance market. This means premiums are becoming more expensive and the cover is harder to secure".[99]

8.11.13 Some Recommendations

For the above reasons the said underwriter proffers the following recommendation to the parties:

First, "Always clarify with the insurer what your insurance actually covers. The Institute Cargo Clauses, of which most freight insurance policies in Australia are based, have plenty of exclusions. You don't want a policy excluding something fundamental to your shipment".

Secondly, "Consider what term you're buying on so you don't double up on insurance cover. You don't want to take out the same insurance policy twice with both the importer and exporter paying a set of fees".

Thirdly, "Make sure you have end-to-end coverage. Shipowners are obligated under what's called the 'Hague Visby Rules' to compensate you if your goods are damaged on a maritime voyage. But this liability is limited. It's critical to attain the extra insurance, otherwise, you could lose a significant value of your goods".

Fourth, and finally, "Understanding the Incoterms underpinning your sales contract and the insurance that covers you is critical when engaging in domestic and international shipments. Use your forwarder to manage your marine insurance and request a certificate of currency to outline your policy".[100]

8.12 Concluding Remarks

This chapter set out to examine the incidents of the obligation laid out in Incoterms 2020 with regard to the procuring of insurance in contracts where the seller has no obligation, namely Incoterms CIF and CIP contracts. Although no attempt was made to compare the obligations with those that exist under the common law CIF term, it is self-evident that the basic outline of the duty remains the same as under the common law term. Clause A5 is a reflection of the common law precedents on CIF insurance. Nevertheless, the fact that parties' contract on Incoterms CIF or CIP rather than CFR or CPT simplicities is significant, for it means that their rights and

[99] ICECargo-CUSTOMS "Incoterms Insurance Responsibilities Explained: Who Insures What", 28 OCTOBER, 2022 https://icecargo.com.au/incoterms-insurance-responsibitlies/.

[100] Ibid.

obligations must be determined by examining the current edition of Incoterms,[101] rather than dated common law cases. It should be noted that only a few cases concerning Incoterms have come before the English courts, and none involve a discussion of Incoterms itself, so it is hard to predict the court's approach to the matter. However, the CIF case law precedents covered in Chap. 7 would be a good guideline.

However, the clear manner in which Incoterms is presented, and a full understanding by both sellers and buyers of their Incoterms duties should ensure that the matter never reaches the unfortunate stage of having to be interpreted by a court of law. As far as the obligation to procure insurance in Incoterms CIF and CIP contracts is concerned, it is clearly laid out in the Incoterms provision, and corresponds closely with the UCP requirement pertaining to the tender of insurance documents. Both the current Incoterms and the UCP are recent editions and their (combined) usage by businessmen is a clear indication of the progress that the international business community is making in regard to the formalisation and standardisation of the terms upon which they trade: a trend which reduces the likelihood of misunderstandings and subsequent disputes.

8.13 Further Readings

Books

- See under Books for all other chapters; and in addition; see 2–8 below
- Donna Bude: Export/Import Procedures and Documentation, 5th Edition,
- Robert (Bob) Rona: A Commentary on Incoterms 2020 Rules, Kindle Edition
- Global Negotiator: INCOTERMS 2020: Obligations, Cost& Risks, Kindle Edition, Global Marketing Strategies SL, London, 2020
- Sameer Varun: A Practical Guide to Shipping and Freight Forwarding: Your key to success in the shipping industry, Kindle Edition, 2019
- Corinne Campbell: Made Easy E-Guide to Incoterms 2020 Rules-Kindle Edition
- Rupanarayan Bose: Letters of Credit: Theory and Practice: Incoterms 2020 and Marine Insurance
- John J. Capela: Import/Export Kit for Dummies, John Wiley & Sons Inc. Hoboken, New Jersey 2016

Clauses

- John A. Spanogle: "Incoterms and UCC Article 2—Conflicts and Confusions" *The International Lawyer* Vol. 31, No. 1 (SPRING 1997), pp. 111–132 (22 pages)
- John Vogt and Jonathan Davis: "The State of Incoterm® Research", *Transportation Journal* Vol. 59, No. 3 (Summer 2020), pp. 304–324
- Jonathan Davis and John Vogt "Incoterms® 2020 and the missed opportunities for the next version", *International Journal of Logistics Research and Application*

[101] I.e. the edition current at the time they contracted. In the event that the edition is revised after the parties have contracted, but before performance of the contract, the former edition governs.

- Ademuni-Odeke: 1. "Incoterms 2020 Sellers and Buyers Beware! WHAT The New Rules Do Not Tell You About Overall Insurance Obligations" (2021), *Journal of Business Law Issue* 8, pp 673–700
- ---- "The insurance clause in INCOTERMS 2020: Th e latest stage in its evolution and a progressive development 1980-2020-Part II" *The European Insurance Law Review* 2/20, pp. 45–57 December 2020 www.erevija.org
- ---- "The insurance clause in INCOTERMS 2020: The latest stage in its evolution and a progressive development 1980-2020-Part I", The European Insurance Law Review 1/20 pp. 28–38 December 2020 www.erevija.org
- ----: Windfall in Marine and Export Credit Insurance Contracts in Anglo-American and Other Common Law Jurisdictions", Part II, *The European Insurance Law Review*, 1/2018, pp. 8–44, April 2018, www.erevija.org
- ----: "Windfall in Marine and Export Credit Insurance Contracts in Anglo-American and Other Common Law Jurisdictions", Part I, *The European Insurance Law Review*, 4/2017, pp. 6–44, December 2017, www.erevija.org
- ----: "Insurance of CIF and Related Contracts under Incoterms and Anglo-American Common Law", Part II, *The European Insurance Law Review*, 4/2016, December 2016, pp. 1–44 (English and Serbo-Croat), www.erevija.org
- ----: "Insurance of CIF and Related Contracts under Incoterms and Anglo-American Common Law", Part I, *The European Insurance Law Review*, 3/2016, October 2016, pp. 1–34 (English and Serbo-Croat) www.erevija.org
- ----- "The Insurance Element in CIF and CIP Incoterms' Contracts", *Tolley's Insurance Law and Practice*, Vol. 4 No. 4, 1995, pp. 17–25.

Website based sources

- "Incoterms® rules 2020 released! Are you prepared for the next century of global trade?"
- David Noah: "Incoterms 2020: Here is what is new", https://www.shippingsolutions.com/blog/incoterms-2020-heres-whats-new
- Joanna Kadus: "The Significance of the Incoterms Rules in the Freight Forwarding Services Market" http://www.worldscientificnews.com/
- Thomas J. Schaefer: "Incoterms® Use in Buyer-Seller Relationships: a Mixed Methods Study" https://irl.umsl.edu/cgi/viewcontent.cgi?article=1666&context=dissertation
- See further readings in Chaps. 3–7.
- ICECARGO: "Incoterms Insurance Responsibilities Explained: Who Insures What" 28, OCTOBER, 2022 https://icecargo.com.au/incoterms-insurance-responsibitlies/
- CHUBB Insurance: "Ocean Cargo INCOTERMS and Insurance", https://www.chubb.com/ca-en/business-insurance/ocean-cargo-incoterms-insurance.html

8.14 Table 2 Summary of Parties' CIF and CIP Incoterms Insurance Responsibilities

Incoterm Contract	*Carriage, Delivery, Passage of property and passage of risk*	*Sellers Insurance*	*Buyer's Insurance*
CIF Contract	(a) Useable for only sea or inland waterways transport and multimodal transport. (b)Carriage (c) Delivery (d) (i)No provision for passage of property (ii) However, property passes with delivery (e) Risks pass when goods are loaded.	(a) Insurance is a central function of the contract (b) Provision of insurance is one of the seller's 3 principal obligations (c) One of the only 2 Incoterms (the other being CIP) in which the seller provides insurance (d) The extensive Clause A5 is reproduced below, providing terms and conditions. (e) Same obligations apply at common principles on which A5 is based (see *the Julia* case) (f) Seller also advised to take out pre-shipment or "door to do" or "All Risk" policy. (g) Seller also advised to take out post-shipment and contingency insurance-also coverable by door to door or "All Risk".	(a) Buyer has no obligation to take out insurance 1. No obligation. 2. But minimum cover 3. Additional at own costs and risks 4. Policy must enable buyers' direct claim from insurers 5. Takes care of own interest insurance 6. Beware of external factors

Incoterm Contract	*Carriage, Delivery, Passage of property and passage of risk*	*Sellers Insurance*	*Buyer's Insurance*
		Clause A5 provides that: "The Seller must obtain at his own expense cargo insurance complying at least with the minimum cover as provided by Clauses (C)[102] of the Institute Cargo Clauses (LMA/IUA) or similar clauses. The insurance shall be contracted with underwriters or an insurance company of good repute and entitle the buyer, or any other person having an insurable interest in the goods, to claim directly from the insurer. When required by the buyer, the seller shall, subject to the buyer providing any necessary information requested by the seller, provide at the buyer's expense any additional cover, if procurable, such as cover provided by Clause (A) or (B) of the Institute Cargo Clauses (LMA/IUA) or any similar clauses, and/or cover complying with the Institute War Clauses and/or Institute Strikes Clauses (LMA/IUA) or any similar clauses. The insurance shall cover, at a minimum, the price provided in the contract plus 10% (i.e., 110%) and shall be in the currency of the contract. The insurance shall cover the goods from the point of delivery set out in A4 and A5 to at least the named place of destination. The seller must provide the buyer with the insurance policy or other evidence of insurance cover. Moreover; the seller must provide the buyer, at the buyer's request, risk and expense (if any), with information that the buyer needs to procure any additional insurance."	Clause B5 provides that buyer has no obligation to provide insurance to the seller or himself. However, he would be well advised to take out additional cover for himself
American CIF		The seller has obligation to provide insurance covering transport at least from the port of loading to the port of destination	(a) If the buyer wants additional cover above the required minimum, the buyer should specifically agree with the seller. (b) Failing the agreement, the buyer should out own policy

[102] Clause (A) for CIP.

Incoterm Contract	*Carriage, Delivery, Passage of property and passage of risk*	*Sellers Insurance*	*Buyer's Insurance*
Under UCC	Ships Rail	(a) See S2-13 UCC (b)See Incoterms for Americans (below) (c) Same as Incoterms 2020	(a) See S-2013 UCC (b) Same as Incoterms
Under IFA Guidelines		The seller is required to provide at least minimum cover insurance (FPA American or Institute Cargo Clauses C). Additional coverage should be considered as the minimum is only recommended by Incoterms and not conclusive	(a) Seller has no insurance obligations (b) However, seller is advised to take out own contingency insurance
CIP Contract	Ships Rail. Multimodal	(a) Yes. (b) Same as CIF A5 (c) Except on higher Cargo Clauses A (d) See *The Julia* case	(a) None. (b) But policy must enable buyers' direct claim from insurers 3. But Note information 4. Additional on request and at own risks and costs
American CIP		The seller is required to provide Institute Cargo Clauses A (so called American "All Risk" in America) coverage.	Buyer has no obligations to provide insurance to himself, but would be advised to take out additional cover.
Under UCC	N/A, UCC has no CIP contract	N/A, UCC has no CIP contract	N/A, UCC has no CIP contract
Under IFA		The seller is required to provide Institute Cargo Clauses A (so called "All Risk" policy in America), coverage.	

Part IV

Tender of Policy and Other Insurance Considerations

9 Insurance of Common Law and Incoterms War and Piracy Risks

Abstract

This first chapter, of **Part IV [Insurance of Piracy, War Risks and Other Insurance Considerations**], is dedicated to insurance of international sales contracts for war, piracy and terrorism. Among the sub-headings covered are the: Introduction; Selected List of War Risks; War Risks and the Insurance Concept of "*Minimum* Cover"; War Risks Insurance as an Additional Cover; Nature of the Common Law and Incoterms' War Risks; War Risks Policy under Institute Cargo Clauses; Insurance Clauses and War Risks; War Risks under Institute Causes and Commodity Cluses' Policy; Exclusion of War Risks under Clauses A, B and Coward Risks Reinstatement Clauses Meaning of War Risks; Civil Commotions and Hostilities; Meaning of Strikes; Civil Commotions and Insurrections; Civil Commotions and Insurrections; Terrorism and Piracy Acts; "Food for Further Thoughts"; Concluding Remarks; and Further Readings.

9.1 Introduction

This chapter deals with war risks insurance for both the FOB, CIF and related contracts under common law and Incoterm. The chapter outlines and discusses judicial pronouncements of the various categories of war risks policy (war, civil war, civil commotion, strikes, piracy, etc.) the way it has never been done before. Although there are minor differences in the various insurances, this has been grouped together because the general principles are applicable to all. War risk insurance is coverage provided on losses resulting from events such as war, invasions, insurrections, riots, strikes, and terrorism. War risk insurance is offered as a separate policy as it is excluded from standard insurance policies due to the high risks involved. This includes passive war risks cover. Passive War means a situation where the Insured Person is not actively involved in War whether declared or

P. Ademuni-Odeke, *Insurance of International Sales' Contracts under Incoterms*, Law for Professionals, https://doi.org/10.1007/978-3-031-75136-3_9

not, or any Warlike operations, including use of military force by any sovereign nation to achieve economic, geographic, nationalistic, political, racial, religious or other ends.

The war risks covered here also apply to all export and import contracts. However, instances where the FOB and CIF insurance are clearly applicable, this is indicated. This separate discussion is necessary because the general cargo and hull insurance does not cover the risks of a vessel sailing into a war zone.

A typical example is the current risk to a tanker or dry-cargo ship sailing in the Somali coast or previously in the Persian Gulf during the first and second Gulf War. For the UK market, the war risks areas are established by the London-based Joint War Committee, which recently moved to include the Malacca Straits as a war risks area due to piracy. If an attack is classified as a "riot" then it would be covered by war-risk insurers.

The terms of the war risks policy normally include the various Institute Clauses. In the UK, US and other major trading nations, war risks are also partly covered by the state under circumstances and schemes described below.

In the UK War Risks are covered by the:

(a) *Marine Insurance Act* 1906;
(b) *Restrictions of Advertisement (War Risks Insurance) Act* 1939;
(c) *The Marine and Civil Aviation (War Risks) Act* 1952;
(d) *The Reinsurance (Acts of Terrorism) Act* 1993;
(e) *The Merchant Shipping and Maritime Security Act*, 1997;
(f) *The Terrorism Act 2000*;
(g) *The Aviation and Maritime Security Act*, 1997, UK;
(h) *The Terrorism Risk Insurance Act* (TRIA), US;
(i) *The Terrorism Risk Insurance Act*, 2002;
(j) *The Terrorism Risk Insurance Program Reauthorization Act of 2007*, effective January 1, 2008 (the "Act"), US; and
(k) *The Terrorism Insurance Act 2003*, Australia.

In addition to UKEF insurance, war risks are the other only class of export insurance where the state provides support. Apart from the London and UK Institute Clauses, other major trading nations like the US, Japan and the Scandinavians, to mention but a few have equivalent Institute Clauses which are comparable and would be acceptable in the London and UK market. For the first time ever, the chapter attempts to define what constitute these offences.

9.2 Selected List of War Risks

There are many risks insurable under export policies generally and FOB, CIF and related contracts in particular. The most common ones are:

1. War;
2. Warlike operations;
3. Hostilities;
4. Civil War;
5. Civil Commotions;
6. Arrests, Restraints;
7. Detainments of princesses;
8. Insurrection;
9. Rebellion;
10. Revolution;
11. Strikes;
12. Lock-out workmen;
13. Participants in labour disturbances;
14. Pirates;
15. Thieves and Rovers;
16. Terrorism;
17. Persons acting from political motives;
18. Hostile use of any weapon or device employing atomic or nuclear fission and/or fusion or other like reaction or radioactive force or matter;
19. Derelict mines torpedoes bombs or other weapons of war; and
20. Other War Risks

The above list is not conclusive. Furthermore, they are not exclusive to FOB, CIF and related Incoterms contracts' exports and important. Rather, they apply to all exports and imports and some instances to domestic sales where such risks exist. It is not possible to cover insurance of all the above risks in details. However, some of the risks and case law applicable thereto, are discussed below.

9.3 War Risks and the Insurance Concept of '*Minimum Cover*'

Unless otherwise provided the seller provides only the minimum cover. Marine cargo policies normally contained a fc&s (Free of Capture & Seizure) clause, which excludes war risks, strikes, riots, strikes, civil commotions and similar risks. A specific agreement had to be made for an additional premium to be paid if these perils are to be insured. There are three Institute War Clauses covering cargo, air cargo, and postal shipments. War Risk rates are set by the London Market War Risks Rating Committee or the American Market War/SR&CC Schedule. The political and social climates of a given country determine the rates. The aforementioned committees keenly monitor these forces and update the war rates frequently as conflicts often arise suddenly.

9.4 'War Risks' Insurance an Additional Cover

Normal policies under Institute Cargo Clauses A-C except war risks and for provision of minimum cover. They are also excluded by the free from capture and seizure (f&c) clauses where applicable. A contract might require the seller to take out additional cover. In the absence of an all-risks' policy, or specific requests for one, this normally means taking out war risks cover. However, war risks are an umbrella provision, which include civil war, strikes, riots, civil war, civil commotion, insurrection and rebellion covered under the various Institute War Clauses listed below. This is partly pertinent in current unstable global environment. Neither Incoterms the UCP define what war, strikes, riots or civil commotion. We have, therefore, to fall back to the general principles of common law, generally and insurance law in particular, for help regarding their meanings. We will attempt to define each of these below in turn.

9.5 Nature of the Common Law and Incoterms' War Risks Policy

The nature of the CIF War risks policy[1] was the further subject of *Oulu Osakayetio of Oulu, Finland v Arnold Lever & Co Ltd*,[2] an authority which best demonstrates this point. The clause will dwell at length on the case for the reason that ironically here goods were shipped in vessel of a belligerent. By CIF contracts dated October 6 and 7, 1938, Finnish merchants contracted to sell to British buyer's parcels of timber to be shipped in November 1938, from Pateniemi to Hull. By clause 6 of the contracts the sellers, before or as soon as tonnage was secured, were to insure the timber for the voyage to Hull against (inter alia) war risks, and any increase in premium payable for covering those risks in respect of the country of destination in excess of the rates ruling at September 26, 1935, was to be for buyers' account. The exchange rate on September 26, 1935, was three pence per £100. The sellers chartered a Spanish steamship to carry the timber, and there was no evidence that any other suitable vessel was available.

At the material time the prevailing rate of war risks premium for all steamships other than those flying the Spanish or Greek flags was 2s 6d per £100, the premiums for Spanish and Greek ships being left to the discretion of individual underwriters. At the beginning of November 1938, due to Spanish civil war, the war risks premiums demanded for cargo in Spanish ships rose abnormally, and the sellers, fearing the rates would rise still higher, as they in fact did, insured the timber with Lloyds' underwriters at a premium of £5 per cent. They then claimed the difference between 3d and £5 per £100 from the buyers, who repudiated liability.

---

[1] For War Risks generally see *Halsbury's Laws of England*, Vol.60 (5th Edition) 2012 pp. 557–565 at 559–562.

[2] *Oulu Osakayetio of Oulu, Finland v Arnold Lever & Co Ltd* [1940] 2 All ER 243; [1940] 1 KB 750; 109 LJKB 669; 162 LT 415; 56 TLR 545; 84 Sol. Jo 453; 45 Corn Cas 193, CA.

However, on judgment from Justice Atkinson,[3] Lord Justice Slesser[4] had no difficulty in finding that the contract provided for a comparison being made between like and like, i.e., between the general market rate current at September 26, 1935 and the general market rate ruling at the material date in 1938 and holding that the buyers were only liable for the difference between 3d and 2s 6d per £100. The court agreed with the sellers that they (*semble* that) (the sellers) were entitled under the contract to charter a belligerent ship, but with a proviso that if they chose to do so they could not hold the buyers to account for the abnormal premiums asked in respect of such a vessel.

Thus, under CIF the sellers are not only obliged to insure but should do so the war circumstances notwithstanding and have discretion how they do it.

9.6 CIF 'War Risks' Under Institute and Commodity Clauses Policy

Finally, an all-risks policy, whether CIF or otherwise, is best and is now affected under the Institute Cargo Clauses A. However, even then merchants should be careful as the Institute Cargo Clauses A is not really a true "All Risks" policy since it has exclusions such as war, civil commotions and strikes, which are then covered by additional clauses separately accordingly. That notwithstanding, and as indicated above, unless otherwise provided the CIF seller's common law and INCOTERMS 2020 (Clause A5) duty is to provide a minimum cover which does not include war and/or strikes cover. A reasonable merchant should therefore add the Institute Cargo Clauses (War Risks) and the Institute Cargo Clauses (Strikes) and any other excluded risks, separately and additionally, to ensure fulfilling obligation to provide a War

[3] *Oulu Osakayetio of Oulu, Finland v Arnold Lever & Co Ltd* [1939] 4 All ER 88(243).

[4] "In my view, … it is not necessary here to invoke the principle of *The Moorcock or of Hamlyn & Co v Wood & Co*, or to import into the contract what is not there. I think that the actual language of the contract requires the comparison of a ruling rate with a ruling rate, and, in so far as there was no ruling rate for Spanish ships at the time when the comparison was said to have been made, I think that the contract has no application as regards this part of the clause, and, therefore, the claim must fail.

I would add—since I think that the judge is perhaps mistaken in one way in which he looks at this case—that the question of the reasonableness or propriety of chartering a Spanish ship has nothing to do with the case. It may well be that under this contract as a whole the sellers were fully entitled to charter either a belligerent ship or a non-belligerent ship. The question I have to consider is whether or not, having done so, they have established a right to hold the buyers to account for the difference between the rate which they paid for insurance on chartering such a ship and the rate prevailing at 26 September 1935. For the reasons I have stated, I think that they had no such right, and that the judge was right on the case stated in holding that the arbitrator was wrong in the view to which he came." [1940] 2 All ER 243 at pp 246, 247, Lord Justices Luxmore and Goddard concurring at 247 et seq.

Risks Policy under CIF.[5] Otherwise, a Non-All Risks policy can also be contracted for instance through the Institute Cargo Clauses B and C.

Equivalent Institute Clauses exist in Japan, the US and in other major common law jurisdictions[6] as well as civil law jurisdictions.[7] With regard to CIF commodities policy, Clause 20(h) of Grain and Feed Trade Association (GAFTA) instance provides that the "Sellers' obligation to provide War Risk Insurance shall be limited to the terms and conditions in force and generally obtainable in London at time of shipment".[8] Other trades will have their own rules and guidelines for and above common law, GAFTA and Incoterms. Because war risks are common to both FOB and CIF and related contracts, these are discussed together in chapter in this chapter.

9.7 Institute Clauses and War Risks

Cargo insurance is underwritten on the Institute Cargo Clauses, with coverage on an A, B, or C basis, A having the widest cover and C the most restricted. Valuable cargo is known as specie. Institute Clauses also exist for the insurance of specific types of cargo, such as frozen food, frozen meat, and particular commodities such as bulk oil, coal, and jute. Often these insurance conditions are developed for a specific group as is the case with the Institute Federation of Oils, Seeds and Fats Associations (FOFSA) Trades Clauses which have been agreed with the Federation of Oils, Seeds and Fats Associations and Institute Commodity Trades Clauses which are used for the insurance of shipments of cocoa, coffee, cotton, fats and oils, hides and skins, metals, oil seeds, refined sugar, and tea and have been agreed with the Federation of Commodity Associations.

Ordinary Institute Cargo Clauses do not cover war; to which they are an exception. Rather War, piracy, strikes, terrorism and related war risks are covered by specific clauses. These Institute War Clauses, their numbers and starting dates include:

1. Institute War Clauses (Air Cargo) 01/01/2009 CL388;
2. Institute War Clauses (Cargo) 01/01/2009 CL385;
3. Institute War Clauses (Air Cargo) 01/01/2009) CL388;
4. Institute Strikes Clauses (Air Cargo) 01/01/2009 CL389;
5. Termination of Transit Clause Terrorism 2009 JC2009/056;
6. Institute War Clauses (Sendings by Post) 01/03/2009 CL390;
7. Institute Strikes Clauses (Air Cargo) 01/01/2009 CL389;
8. Institute War Clauses (Sendings by Post) 01/03/2009 CL390;

[5] For a more detailed discussion of War Risks in CIF Contracts see, Sassoon, *CIF and FOB Contracts*, Note 3, at pp. 182–186.

[6] Such as Australia, Canada, New Zealand, South Africa, Singapore and Nigeria.

[7] Such as the *Norwegian Plan;* France, Germany and Switzerland being the other leading Civil Law countries; see Notes 227–233, *infra*.

[8] GAFTA Contract No. 48 in Annex XII below.

9. Institute Strikes Clauses (Cargo) 01/01/2009 CL386;
10. Institute Strikes Clauses (Cargo) 01/01/2009 CL386;
11. Institute War Clauses (Cargo) 01/01/2009 CL385;
12. Institute War and Strikes Clauses (Hulls-Time) cl 14-15;
13. Institute War and Strikes Clauses (Hulls-Voyage) cl1-4-1.5;
14. Institute War and Strikes Clauses (Freight-Time) cl 1.2.1-1.2.2; and
15. Institute War and Strikes Clauses (Freight-Voyage) cl1.2.1-1.2.2.

The above list is by no means exhaustive. Furthermore, they relate to all export insurances rather than just the FOB, CIF and related contracts.

9.8 CIF War Risks' Policy Under Institute Cargo Clauses

Finally, an all-risks policy, whether CIF or otherwise, is best and is now affected under the Institute Cargo Clauses A. However, even then the merchant should be careful as the Institute Cargo Clauses A is not really a true "All Risks" policy since it has exclusions such as war and strikes, which are then covered by additional clauses separately accordingly. That notwithstanding, and as indicated above, unless otherwise provided the CIF seller's duty is to provide a minimum cover which does not include war and/or strikes cover. A reasonable merchant should therefore add the Institute Cargo Clauses (War Risks) and the Institute Cargo Clauses (Strikes) and any other excluded risks, separately and additionally, to ensure fulfilling obligation to provide a War Risks Policy under CIF.[9] Otherwise, a Non-All Risks policy can also be contracted for instance through the Institute Cargo Clauses B and C. Equivalent Institute Clauses exist in the US and in other major common law jurisdictions[10] as well as civil law jurisdictions.[11] However, for the UK GAFTA Contracts, for instance, Clause 20(h) of GAFTA provides that the: "Sellers' obligation to provide War Risk Insurance shall be limited to the terms and conditions in force and generally obtainable in London at time of shipment".[12]

9.9 Exclusion of War Risks by Institute Clauses A, B and C

The reason why war risks are covered separately is because they are accepted by both the Institute Cargo Clauses A-C as well the free from capture (fc&s) clauses included in most marine cargo and hull policies. A normal or an "all risks" policy

[9] For a more detailed discussion of War Risks in CIF Contracts see, Lorenzo, CIF and FOB Contracts, at pp. 182–186.

[10] Such as Australia, Canada, New Zealand, South Africa and Nigeria.

[11] Such as the *Norwegian Plan*. France, Germany and Switzerland being the other leading Civil Law countries.

[12] GAFTA Contract No.48.

will only be presumed to cover war risks if the exceptions in Clauses 6-7 in the cargo clauses are crossed out and endorsed and the fc&s clauses are omitted from the policy. The two exceptions and judicial approach to the whole subject are discussed below.

9.9.1 In the Institute Cargo Clauses A, B and C

In the Institute Cargo Clauses, A, B and C, war risk is an exception. It does not mean it is not insurable, rather that it is done in a separate contract or indorsement by war clause. Alternatively, crossing out the exception Institute Cargo Clauses A, but not B and C, will reinstate war coverage. Clauses 6 and 7 of Institute Clauses A and B provide that:

Clauses 6 and 7 of Institute Clauses A and B

6. In no case shall this insurance cover loss damage or expense caused by

6.1 war civil war revolution rebellion insurrection, or civil strife arising therefrom, or any hostile act by or against a belligerent power

6.2 capture seizure arrest restraint or detainment (piracy excepted), and the consequences thereof or any attempt thereat

6.3 derelict mines torpedoes bombs or other derelict weapons of war.

7. In no case shall this insurance cover loss damage or expense

7.1 caused by strikers, locked-out workmen, or persons taking part in labour disturbances, riots or civil commotions

7.2 resulting from strikes, lock-outs, labour disturbances, riots or civil commotions

7.3 caused by any act of terrorism being an act of any person acting on behalf of, or in connection with, any organisation which carries out activities directed towards the overthrowing or influencing, by force or violence, of any government whether or not legally constituted

7.4 caused by any person acting from a political, ideological or religious motive

9.9.2 By the Free from Capture and Seizure (f c&s) Clause

In addition to the above Clauses and 6 and 7 of the Institute Cargo Clauses A-C above, war risks were originally excluded by the free from capture and seizure clause (fc&s) inserted in all hull and cargo clauses. When included in a marine insurance policy the clause exempted the underwriter from liability caused by war risks. It provides that:

> Warranted free of capture, seizure, arrest, restraint or detainment, and the consequences thereof or of any attempt thereat; also from the consequences of hostilities or warlike operations, whether there be a declaration of war or not; but this warranty shall not exclude collision, contact with any fixed or floating object(other than a mine or torpedo), stranding, heavy weather or fire unless caused directly (and independently of the nature of the voyage or service which the vessel concerned or, in the case of a collision, any other vessel involved therein, is performing) by a hostile act by or against a belligerent power; and for the purpose of this warranty "power" includes any authority maintaining naval power, military or air forces in association with a power. Further warranted from the consequences of a civil war, revolution, rebellion, insurrection, or civil strife arising therefrom, or piracy.

This type of fc&s clauses was in use by the SG Policy and the old institute clauses, a position was changed by the move to the Lloyds Mar and Companies Mar Policies and the new institute clauses in 1982.

9.10 War Risks Reinstatement Clauses

9.10.1 Inclusion by Ordinary War Clause

War clauses can be included through the inclusion in the policy of a war clause or the insertion of a number of the Institute War Clauses and Institute Strikes Clauses. The War Clause reintroduces war clauses into the policy that had been excepted either by the older method of fc&s or the newer method of Institute Cargo Clauses A, B and C. War Clauses also cover loss or damage to the subject matter insured caused by: "(a) hostilities, warlike operations, civil war, revolution, rebellion, insurrection or civil strife arising therefrom; (b) mines, torpedoes, bombs or other engines of war". But the War Clauses do not cover loss or damage proximately caused by delay, inherent vice or loss of market. These headings are each discussed below.

9.10.2 Inclusion of War Risks by the Institute War Clauses

All the war risks exclusions by Clauses 6 and 7 of the Institute Cargo Clauses A, B and C are reinstated by Clauses 1and 2 of the Institute War Clauses (Cargo) and Air Cargo)), Institute Strikes Clauses (Cargo (Cargo)

Clauses 1 and 2 of the Institute War Clauses (Cargo) and Air Cargo))
Institute War Clauses (Cargo)

War Clauses

RISKS COVERED

1. Risks Clause

1 This insurance covers, except as provided in Clauses 3 and 4 below, loss of or damage to the subject-matter insured caused by

1.1 war civil war revolution insurrection, or civil strife arising therefrom, or any hostile act by or against a belligerent power

1.2 capture seizure arrest restraint or detainment, arising from risks covered under 1.1 above, and the consequences thereof or any attempt thereat

1.3 derelict mines torpedoes bombs or other derelict weapons of war.

2. General Average Clause

2 This insurance covers general average and salvage charges, adjusted or determined according to the contract of affreightment and/or the governing law and practice, incurred to avoid or in connection with the avoidance of loss from a risk covered under these clauses.

9.10.3 Inclusion by the Institute Strikes Clauses

Institute Strikes Clauses (Cargo 1/1/09)
Strikes Clauses

RISKS COVERED

1. Strikes Clauses.

1. This insurance covers, except as excluded by the provisions of Clauses 3 and 4 below, loss of or damage to the subject-matter insured caused by

1.1. strikers, locked-out workmen, or persons taking part in labour disturbances, riots or civil commotions

1.2. any act of terrorism being an act of any person acting on behalf of, or in connection with, any organisation which carries out activities directed towards the overthrowing or influencing, by force or violence, of any government whether or not legally constituted

1.3. any person acting from a political, ideological or religious motive.

3.7. loss damage or expense arising from the absence shortage or withholding of labour of any description whatsoever resulting from any strike, lockout, labour disturbance, riot or civil commotion

3.8. any claim based upon loss of or frustration of the voyage or adventure.

Similar or equivalent provisions exist in Institute War Clauses (Cargo) (Sending by Post)) and Institute Strikes Clause (Cargo) (Sending by Post).

9.11 Meaning of War, Civil Commotions and Hostilities' Risks

9.11.1 Meaning of "War" Risks

Unless otherwise provided, FOB, CIF and other export policies do not normally define what constitutes war and war risks. These meanings are therefore gathered from the Marine Insurance Act 1906, legalisations dealing with marine and war risks, common law and case law. From the foregone, for insurance purposes, war includes civil war. At common law, war and/or war risks refers to the group of perils that generally have their origin in political and similar matters capable of causing widespread damage beyond the scope of private enterprise insurers. These risks are in effect fundamental risks. In *Pesquerias y Secaderos de Bacalao de Espana SA v Beer*[13] Lord Morton held that the term includes civil war unless the context makes it clear that a different meaning should be given to the word.[14] War risks are excluded from material damage policies covering property on land and as such are more properly covered under the central government schemes such as the Export Credit Guarantee Department (ECGD-now UKEF) insurance. The perils that are grouped in this way include: war, civil war, rebellion, insurrection, usurped powers, military or usurped powers, civil commotion and martial law.

9.11.2 "Warlike Operations"

For some reasons war is legally different from warlike operations. Presumably the former means actual war whereas the latter refers to operations that are akin to war but not amounting to war. In contrast to Lord Morton's decision in *Pesquerias y Secaderos de Bacalao de Espana SA v Beer*[15] above, Justice Atkinson in *Clan Line Steamers Ltd v Liverpool and London War Risks Insurance Association Ltd*[16] opined that:" 'Warlike operations' means one which forms part of an actual or intended belligerent act or series of acts by combatant forces; that part may be performed preparatory to the actual act or acts of belligerency, but there must be a connection

[13] *Pesquerias y Secaderos de Bacalao de Espana SA v Beer* (1948–1949) 82 Lloyd's Rep 501.

[14] "I desire to say quite plainly that in my view the word 'war' in a policy of insurance includes civil war unless the context makes it clear that a different meaning should be given to the word. There is no such context in the policy now under consideration. I can see no good reason for giving to the word 'war' a meaning which excludes one type of war." Per Lord Morton, at p.514, HL.

[15] See Notes 14 and 15 above.

[16] *Clan Line Steamers Ltd v Liverpool and London War Risks Insurance Association Ltd* [1942]2 All ER 367.

sufficiently close between the act in question and the belligerent act or acts to enable a tribunal to say with at least some modicum of common sense. That it formed part of the acts of belligerency".[17] Since the industry maintains intelligence on and publishes periodic lists of areas and regions of war and warlike operations, they would be in a better situation establish the difference between the two including when warlike operations have developed into a full war.

9.11.3 Hostilities[18]

Equally hostilities would seem to be different from war but probably closer in definition and characteristics to warlike operations. The definition of hostilities was discussed by the US case of *Woodruff v. Wentworth.*[19] The principal case is a further application of the general rule. In addition to there. In the UK Lord Wrenbury, in *Britain SS Co Ltd v R*[20] thought that: "Hostilities, does not mean the existence of the state of war but means act of hostility or operation of hostility".[21] However, Justice Bailhache, in *Atlantic Mutual Insurance Co v King,*[22] added that: "Such acts or operations must be committed by people acting as agents of an enemy government or of an organised rebellion, and not by private individuals acting entirely on their own initiative".[23] While Justice Mustil in the seminal case of *Spinny's (1948) Ltd v Royal Insurance Co Ltd,*[24] where a contract involving Lebanese exporters excluded war risks, thought is associated with rebellion, civil war and actions of belligerents, thus: "The term 'hostilities' refers to acts or operations of war committed by belligerent. There seems no reason to doubt that the exception applies to acts committed in the course of a civil war; and perhaps also to an organised rebellion"[25] These headings are considered separately below, where Spinney's case will continue to feature.

9.11.4 Meaning of "Civil War"

Further to the foregone, legal and insurance meaning of civil war is that which pertains at common law. As indicated above, at common law, "war" generally includes "civil war". Ordinarily war means combat between two or three external states.

---

[17] Ibid at 374.

[18] Insurance. Marine Insurance. "Hostilities", Meaning in F. C. and S. Clause *Harvard Law Review* Vol. 32, No. 7 (May, 1919), pp. 859–860.

[19] I33 Mass. 309, 314.

[20] *Britain SS Co Ltd v R* [1921]1 AC 99.

[21] Ibid at 133.

[22] *Atlantic Mutual Insurance Co v King [1919] 1KB 307.*

[23] Ibid, at 310.

[24] *Spinny's (1948) Ltd v Royal Insurance Co Ltd* [1980]1 Lloyd's Rep 406.

[25] Ibid at 437.

However, on its own a civil war simply means a war which has the characteristic of being a civil war, i.e., and internal rather external war.[26] Furthermore, Jones,[27] defines civil war as: "War between two or more portions of a country or state, each contending for mastery of the whole and each claiming to be the legitimate government. The term is also sometimes applied to war or rebellion when the rebellious portions of the state are contiguous to those containing the seat of government".[28] He further opines that. "This special characteristic means that certain features of an international war are absent. Nevertheless, a civil war is still a war. The words do not simply denote a violent internal conflict on a large scale. It does however seem to me that a decision on whether such a war exists will generally involve a consideration of three questions".[29]

These distinctions are important in the current global conditions where rebellions, hostilities, belligerency, terrorism, revolutions, piracy and civil wars are rampant. Worse still where the participants range from governments and other organised groups as well non-state entities such ISIS and Al Qaeda affiliated groups worldwide. What is clearly, however, is that wars, warlike operations, hostilities, and civil war do not include strikes, civil commotions, labour unrests and insurrections which are free of armed groups and/or armed actions.

9.12 Meaning of Strikes, Civil Commotions, Insurrections, ETC

These risks are covered by the Strikes, riots and civil commotion (SRCC) and property cover. An insurance clause referring to loss or damage directly caused by strikers, locked-out workmen, persons' participation in labour disturbances, and riots of various kinds. The ordinary marine insurance policy does not cover this risk.

9.12.1 Meaning of "Strikes"

Although there may be a difference between the legal and insurance definitions of strikes, insurance takes its definition of strikes from the common law definition. This is discernible from case law. *Williams Brothers (Hull) Ltd. v. Naamlooze Vennootschap WH*,[30] for instance, resolved that at common law strike refers to a general concerted withdrawal of labour by employees in consequence of an alleged grievance.'[31] In the case *Tramp Shipping Corporation v Greenwich Marine Incorporated (The New Horizon)*, Lord Denning MR described strikes as: '…a con-

[26] *Spinney's (1948) Ltd v Royal Insurance Co Ltd* [1980] 1 Lloyds Rep 406 at 429 (per Mustill).

[27] Jones, F.H. The Law of Accident and Contingency Insurance", Pitman.

[28] Ibid at 101.

[29] *Spinneys' (1948) Ltd v Royal Insurance Company*, supra.

[30] *Williams Brothers (Hull) Ltd. v. Naamlooze Vennootschap W. H.* (1915) 21 Com. Cas. 253.

[31] Ibid at p. 257.

certed stoppage of work by men done with a view to improving their wages or conditions or giving vent to a grievance or making a protest about something or other or supporting or sympathising with other workmen in such endeavour. It is distinct from a stoppage which is brought about by an external event such as a bomb scare or by apprehension of danger'.[32]

In his judgment, Justice Mustill in *Spinney's (1948) Ltd v Royal Insurance Co Ltd* then goes on to ask the following questions:

(1) Can it be said that the conflict was between opposing 'sides?
(2) What were the objectives of the 'sides', and how did they set about pursuing them? and
(3) What was the scale of the conflict, and of its effect on public order and on the life of the inhabitants?[33]

Strikes lock-out workmen, or participants in labour disturbances, riots, or civil commotions; and terrorists or persons acting from political motives are now covered by the:

(a) Institute Strikes Clauses (Cargo);
(b) Institute War and Strikes Clauses (Hulls—Time);
(c) Institute War and Strikes Clauses (Hulls—Voyage);
(d) Institute War and Strikes Clauses (Freight—Time); and
(e) Institute War and Strikes Clauses (Freight—Voyage).

9.12.2 Meaning of "Riots"

For insurance purposes, the definition of riots is taken from that of the common law, in which "riot" is defined to include insurrection and rebellion. Riot is a violent public disorder specifically, a tumultuous disturbance of the public peace by three or more persons assembled together and acting with a common intent; a public violence, tumult, or disorder; a random or disorderly profusion. According to Justice Phillimore J in *Field v Receiver of the Metropolitan Police*,[34] at common law, riot is said to be constituted by five separate elements:

---

[32] [1975] I.C.R. 261, at p. 266.

[33] [1980] 1 Lloyd's Rep. 406, at pp. 429, 430.

[34] *Field v Metropolitan Police Receiver* [1907] 2 K.B. 853 "From these passages we deduce that there are five necessary elements of a riot—(1.) number of persons, three at least; (2.) common purpose; (3.) execution or inception of the common purpose; (4.) an intent to help one another by force if necessary against any person who may oppose them in the execution of their common purpose; (5.) force or violence not merely used in demolishing, but displayed in such a manner as to alarm at least one person of reasonable firmness and courage." At p. 860 per Phillimore J.

(a) there must be at least[35] twelve persons;
(b) all with a common purpose;
(c) where there has been an inception or execution of that common purpose;
(d) with an intent on the part of the number of persons "to help one another by force, if necessary, against any person who may oppose them in the execution of their common purpose"; and
(e) using "force or violence not merely used" in and about the common purpose, "but displayed in such a manner as to alarm at least one person of reasonable firmness and courage".[36]

Riots include insurrections.

9.12.3 Meaning of "Insurrection"

Riots seem to include "insurrection", a rising of the people in open resistance against established authority to supplanting it.[37] Insurrection seems to fall between war and warlike operations as well as civil war. In his famous judgment, in *The Spinney's* case, on this issue, Justice Mustill was quite prepared to quote a dictionary on this issue. He said: The dictionary defines insurrections in a similar manner [to "rebellion"], but also suggests that the notion of an incipient or limited rebellion. I believe that this reflects the distinction between two exceptions as they are used in the present clause, subject to the rider that a lesser degree of organisation may also mark off an insurrection from a rebellion. But with each exception there must be action against the government with a view to supplanting it.[38] It is possible that there was no legal definition of insurrection, hence Justice Mustil's fall back to the literary and natural meaning of the term in an English dictionary. In *National Oil Co of Zimbabwe v Sturge*[39] Justice Seville described insurrection as an uprising with "a lesser degree of organisation and size than a rebellion" while in *Grell-Taurel Ltd v Caribbean Home Insurance Ltd*[40] violence leading to the kidnapping of the

---

[35] This definition originated in Field V Receiver of the Metropolitan Police (see note below), when the number was fixed at three but was increased to twelve by the *Public Order Act 1986*. The Field definition was approved in *Munday v Metropolitan Police District Receiver* (1949) 1 All ER 337 585; *Municipal Council of Sydney v Campbell* [1925] AC 338 731; *Munster v Lamb* ((1883), L. R. 11 Q. B. D. 588) in which the plaintiff's property was invaded by crowds turned away from a football ground.

[36] *Field v Metropolitan Police Receiver* [1907] 2 K.B. 853 at p.860 (per Phillimore J).

[37] *Lindsay and Pirie v General Accident, Fire and Life Assurance Corpn.* [1914] App D 574.

[38] *Spinney's (1948) Ltd v Royal Insurance Co Ltd* [1980] 1 Lloyds Rep 406 at pp. 436, 437 (per Mustill J).

[39] *National oil co of zimbabwe (private) ltd and others v. nicholas collwyn sturge*. [1991] 2 Lloyd's Rep. 281. Queen's bench division (commercial court).

[40] *Grell-Taurel Ltd v Caribbean Home Insurance Ltd* [2002] Lloyds Rep IR 655[Court of Appeal Trinidad and Tobago].

Trinidadian Prime Minister was adjudged insurrection. Similar position was taken in the Fijian case of *Tappoo Holdings Ltd v Stuchbery.*[41]

9.12.4 Meaning of Rebellion

It would also appear that riot; insurrection and rebellion go together and are a half-way between insurrection and armed resistance and therefore leading to civil war. Rebellion includes but is not necessarily limited to insurrection, rebellion, revolution, usurped power, or action taken by governmental authority in hindering or defending against any of these. In *Spinney's* case, with regard to rebellion, Justice Mustil adopted the same natural meaning approach with insurrection thus: "I adopt the definition in the Oxford English Dictionary (Murray)… 'organised resistance to the ruler or government'. To this I would add that the purpose of the resistance must be to supplant rulers or at least to deprive them of authority over part of their territory".[42]

9.12.5 Meaning of "Civil Commotion"

We then get on to civil commotion and other lesser violent risks. Civil commotion seems to fall just short of rebellion, insurrection and riots. Insurance takes its definition from that of the Common Law. At common law, this term refers to an insurrection of the people for a general purpose though not amounting to a rebellion.[43] The words indicate a stage between a "riot" and a "civil war"[44] above. Lord Buckley in *London and Manchester Plate Glass Co v Heath*[45] thought that "the element of turbulence or tumult is essential to establish civil commotion".[46] However, he immediately qualified his statement by cautioning that an organised conspiracy to commit criminal acts, where there is no tumult or general disturbance until after the acts, does not constitute civil commotion.[47] In *Spinney's (1948) Ltd v Royal Insurance Co Ltd,*[48] Justice Mustill seemed to bear Lord Buckley's qualifications of the definition when he said: "I find nothing in the authorities compelling the authorities the court to hold that a civil commotion must involve a revolt against the government,

---

[41] *Tappoo Holdings Ltd v Stuchbery* [2008] Lloyds Rep IR 34(Supreme Court of Fiji).

[42] Ibid at 436 per Mustill, J.

[43] *Langdale v Mason* (1780)2 Park's Marine Insurances, 8th Edn 965 at pp. 967, 968 (per Lord Mansfield CJ).

[44] *Bolivia Republic v Indemnity Mutual Marine Assurance Co Ltd* [1900]1 KB 785 at p. 801 (per Farwell U).

[45] *London and Manchester Plate Glass Co v Heath* [1913] 3 KB 411.

[46] Ibid at 417, CA (per Buckley, LJ)).

[47] Ibid at 418 (per Buckley, LJ).

[48] *Spinney's (1948) Ltd v Royal Insurance Co Ltd* [1980] 1 Lloyds Rep 406.

although the disturbances must have sufficient cohesion to prevent them from being the work of a mindless mob".[49]

Given that they carry a particular legal meaning, cover against the risk, or range of risks, encompassed by each term must be provided if such cover is requested and procurable. Conversely, cover against risks other than these, even if similar in nature, need not be provided, even if requested and readily procurable, although as a practical matter, a seller who refused to oblige his customers in this respect is likely to find himself without any. Nevertheless, the parties need to be aware of the precise legal scope of their insurance obligations under the contract. There is another twist, whether civil commotion includes civil commotion assuming the proportions of or amounting to a popular uprising.

9.12.6 Extent of "Civil Commotion"

Finally, civil commotions. However, does civil commotion include common assuming the proportions of or amounting to a popular rising? At common law, the term is defined as risks, which are excluded normally under the standard fire policy and other property insurances along with riot and similar perils. Lord Ferwell in the leading case of *Bolivia v Indemnity Mutual Marine Assurance Company Ltd*[50] thought that the words civil commotion indicates a stage between a riot and civil war[51] It refers to people getting out of hand and creating disturbances, which could be described as severe and prolonged. Civil commotion denotes an intermediate state between a riot and civil war. In *London and Manchester Plate Glass Co v Heath*,[52] it determined that, "The element of turbulence or tumult is essential".[53]

Riot and civil commotion can be insured as an additional war peril. Strict limits are not laid down by the insurer for the supply of particulars of a claim on civil commotion and related perils. These limits follow those specified for riots and insurrection. However, there is a difference between civil commotion and popular uprising or civil commotion 'amounting to a popular uprising'.

9.12.7 Civil Commotion and Popular Uprising

Once again, we turn to Spinney's case for guidance on this aspect. For some reason, in his judgment in the *Case* Justice Mustil seems to make a distinction between 'civil commotion' per se and 'civil commotion assuming the proportion of or amounting to popular uprising'. In his judgment in the case, Justice Mustil maintained that the phrases "assuming the proportions or amounting to a popular rising"

---

[49] *Spinney 's (1948) Ltd v Royal Insurance Co Ltd* [1980] 1 Lloyds Rep 406 at 438 (per Mustill J).

[50] *Bolivia v Indemnity Mutual Marine Assurance Company Ltd* [1909]1KB 785.

[51] Ibid at 801 CA.

[52] *London and Manchester Plate Glass Co v Heath* (1913) 3KB 411.

[53] Ibid.

have no recognised technical meaning. Often, they must mean the same as "insurrection." Where there is a distinction, it probably lies in the greater spontaneity and looser organisation of a popular rising.

However, he would still be inclined to consider that there must be some unanimity of purpose among those participating, and that the purpose must involve the displacement of the government. He doubted whether a violent attack by one section of the population on the other on grounds e.g., of religion or race would be described as a rising. In his view the term "proportions" is sometimes used to mean shape or configuration and did not think it has this sense here in the present case and "dimensions." He concluded, rightly so that, one had to identify the dimensions of a popular rising. This cannot be done precisely. All one can say is that it must involve a really substantial proportion of the populace, although obviously not all the population need participate, and that there should be tumult and violence on a large scale:[54]

It would appear from these judicial pronouncements that the latter is nearer in meaning to insurrection. Although they might have the effect in terms of losses and damages, the above-described risks seem to be different both in character and nature than arrest, restraints and capture and seizure below.

9.12.8 Revolutions

Revolutions are related to rebellions and insurrections (above), the difference between them being that revolutions are successful rebellions and/or insurrections. Revolutions are violent actions which change governments or existing orders. Justice Saville considered revolution in *National Oil Co of Zimbabwe v Sturge*[55] to include rebellion. He opined that 'Rebellion' and 'insurrection' have somewhat similar meanings to each other, since each means and organised and violent internal uprising in a country with, as the main purpose, the object of trying to overthrow or supplant the government of that country, though insurrection denotes a lesser degree of organisation and size than a 'rebellion'. He accordingly advised that underwriters accept that if they cannot establish insurrection then they must necessarily fail on rebellion".[56] The Santa Maria and Bolivian Republic[57] are relevant authorities here (More Texts To come).

[54] *Spinney 's (1948) Ltd v Royal Insurance Co Ltd* [1980] 1 Lloyds Rep 406 at 438.

[55] *National Oil Co of Zimbabwe v Sturge* [1991] 2 Lloyds Rep 281.

[56] Ibid at 282.

[57] *Bolivia Republic v Indemnity Mutual Marine Indemnity Assurance Company Ltd* [1908-10] All ER Rep.

9.12.9 Arrests, Restraints, Detainments

The distinction, if any, between arrests and restraints on the one hand and capture and seizure on the other seems to be rather flimsy, although they are all constitute independent war-related risks. A factor further complicated by the fact that they all have roots in murky maritime customs and usages and therefore rather antiquated concepts when monarchs were the norm. Hence the use of 'princes' and 'peoples' (see also para.9.12.9 below (Arrests and Detention below Cases)).

9.12.9.1 Capture and Seizure

Capture and seizure are an actual taking over the vessels and cargo by an enemy as a prize in time of war with the intent to deprive the owner of all property in the vessel including the cargo. *Andersen v Marten*,[58] where the ship was wrecked and became a total loss between the time of capture and condemnation, suggests that the loss is categorised and claimable as an actual total loss. Pursuant to Lord Loreburn L.C. the real question in the case was whether there was a total loss by capture, seizure, or detention, or the consequences of hostilities. He was affirmative that in this case a total loss by capture on February 26, notwithstanding the deployment of other words, such as seizure, and so forth. His Lordship was very clear in his mind that was the day on which the *Romulus* was seized lawfully, as appears by the subsequent condemnation. This is because there was on that day a total loss which, as things were then seen, might afterwards be reduced if in the end the vessel was released.[59]

However, Keller *v Le Mesurier*[60] and *Brandon v Curling*[61] both implied that a policy effected before the commencement of hostilities which insures against capture does not cover loss by British capture. It would therefore, appear that for the risk to attach the capture has to be by foreign rulers or authorities. *Kacianoff v China Trading Insurance Co Ltd*[62] and *Becker v Gray*[63] suggest that abandonment of the adventure for fear of capture does not constitute capture. However, according to *Sanday & Co v British and Foreign Marine Insurance Co Ltd*[64] abandonment of the voyage because continuation would be illegal following declaration of war was covered as a constructive total loss. This contrasts with the leading authorities of *Kuwait Airways Coprn v Kuwait Insurance Co SAK*,[65] and *Bayview Motors Ltd v Mitsui*

---

[58] *Andersen v Marten* [1908] AC 334, HL.

[59] At p. 338.

[60] *Keller v Le Mesurier* (1806) 4 East 396.

[61] *Brandon v Curling* (1806) 4 East 410.

[62] *Kacianoff v China Trading Insurance Co Ltd* [1914] 3 KB 1121 CA.

[63] *Becker v Gray* [1918] AC 101 HL.

[64] *Sanday & Co v British and Foreign Marine Insurance Co Ltd* [1915] 2 KB 781 affirmed on appeal [1916] 1AC 650 HL.

[65] *Kuwait Airways Coprn v Kuwait Insurance Co SAK* [1999] 1 All ER (Comm.)481.

Marine and Fire Insurance Co Ltd[66] which suggest capture and seizure includes capture by revenue and sanitary authorities of a foreign state.

On the other hand, Lord Mansfield CJ in *Goss v Withers*[67] added included deprivation of possession, in the equation to determine whether the seizure was lawful or unlawful and whether by enemies or pirates.[68] Surprisingly, Lord Alvanely in *Touteng v Hubbard*[69] suggested that in unusual circumstances arrest by UK of a UK ship or detention in port by a government-imposed embargo is also constitutes detention within the meaning of the policy.[70] Lord FitzGerald, in *Cory v Burr,*[71] was prepared to widen the nest in his description of "seizure" He thought "seizure' seems to be a larger than 'capture' and goes beyond it, and may reasonably be interpreted to embrace every act of taking forcible possession either by a lawful authority or by overpowering force.[72]

9.12.9.2 Arrests and Detainments

9.12.9.2.1 Definition of

The full name of this risk is 'arrests, restraints and detainments of princesses and peoples'. It is a peril excepted by the Institute Cargo Clauses A-C but insurable against under a marine insurance cargo and hull policy. Furthermore, in Rule 10 of Rules for the Construction of Policy,[73] the term 'arrests, etc. of kings, princes and policy' refers to a political or executive act and does not include a loss caused by riot or ordinary judicial process. However, Justice Byles in *Russell v Niemann*[74] conceived that "Restraint of princes", comprehends every case of interruption by lawful authorities,[75] while *Nesbitt v Lushington*[76] held that the term 'people' means the supreme power of a country and the detention of a ship by a mob is a not a loss by arrests, restraints and detainment of people.[77]

---

[66] *Bayview Motors Ltd v Mitsui Marine and Fire Insurance Co Ltd* [2002] 2 All ER (Comm.) 1095.

[67] *Goss v Withers* (1758)2 Burr 638.

[68] Ibid at 694.

[69] *Touteng v Hubbard* (1802) 3 Bos & P291.

[70] Ibid at 302.

[71] *Cory v Burr* (1883) 8 App.Cas.393.

[72] Ibid at 405.

[73] Rule 10 of the *Rules for the Construction of the Policy*, First Schedule of the Marine Insurance Act 1906.

[74] *Russell v Niemann* (1864)17 CBNS 163.

[75] Ibid at 163.

[76] *Nesbitt v Lushington* (1792) 4 Term 783.

[77] Ibid at.

A number of old authorities such as *Sunport Shipping Ltd v Tryg Baltica International (UK) Ltd* (formerly Balatica Insurance Co Ltd)[78] and *Handelsbanken ASA v Dandridge,*[79] suggest that the phrase refers to political or executive acts and exclude loss by riot or ordinary judicial process. In support of this position *Atlantic Maritime Co v Gibbons*[80] also points to the fact that the use of actual of actual force was not necessary for restraint and that simple prohibition by a government or municipal authorities is sufficient although Justice Bailhach in *Russian Bank for Foreign Trade v Excess Insurance Co Ltd*[81] qualified that notion by holding that ultra vires action by government department without a threat of force did not. Accordingly, the main distinction between capture and arrest is that the former is the forceful taking of the subject matter of insured subject matter during a war with a view of taking it as a prize, whereas the latter is only a temporary detention with a view to ultimate release or repaying its value.[82] That debate notwithstanding, the current Somali piracy (see below) introduced a new element into capture, seizure and detention resulting into total loss, where detention with a view to a ransom has been adjudged to lead to constructive total loss.

9.12.9.2.2 Examples of Restraints of Peoples

Restraint of peoples seems to cover a range of risks. To give a rough idea, loss of by arrests, restraints and detainments has been held to have occurred where:

(a) In *Rodoconachi v Elliott*[83] where goods detained in a city in a state of siege so that nothing could be brought out or out;
(b) In *Robinson Gold Mining Co v Alliance Insurance Co*[84] where goods and vessels were detained in a blockaded port;
(c) In *Miller v Law and Accident Insurance,*[85] where the import of cattle from certain infected countries was prohibited;
(d) In *Auberty v Gray,*[86] where there was an embargo on goods and vessels leaving a port;
(e) In *Societe Belge des Bretons SA v London and Lancashire Insurance Co Ltd,*[87] where property was confiscated in the Spanish Civil War by a committee com-

[78] *Sunport Shipping Ltd v Tryg Baltica International (UK) Ltd (formerly Balatica Insurance Co Ltd)* [2003]1 All ER (comm.)586.

[79] *Handelsbanken ASA v Dandridge* [2002] 2 All ER (Comm.) 39.

[80] *Atlantic Maritime Co v Gibbons* [1954] 1 QB 88 CA.

[81] *Russian Bank for Foreign Trade v Excess Insurance Co Ltd* [1918] 2 KB 123.

[82] Marshall on Marine Insurance (4th ed 394.

[83] *Rodoconachi v Elliott* (1874) LR 9CP 518.

[84] *Robinson Gold Mining Co v Alliance Insurance Co* [1902] 2 KB 489.

[85] *Miller v Law and Accident Insurance* [1903] 1 KB 712.

[86] *Auberty v Gray* (1862) 3B & S 169.

[87] *Societe Belge des Bretons SA v London and Lancashire Insurance Co Ltd* (1938) 60 Ll. L Rep 225.

posed of the Popular Executive Committee, which was the *de facto* and the *de jure* Government of Valencia at the time;

(f) In *Rickards v Forestal Land, Timber and Rlys Co Ltd*,[88] where all shipping under the control of the German Government was ordered to take refuge in the neutral ports or to return to Germany on the outbreak of the Second World War; and
(g) In *Panamanian Oriental Steamship Coprn v Wright*,[89] where a vessel was confiscated by an extraordinary tribunal outside the ordinary judicial system of Vietnam.

9.12.10 Piracy

One can hardly discuss modern export insurance without mentioning piracy. Loss caused by pirates is a marine peril. It is defined/described in s.3 of the MIA 1906 and therefore insurable under a marine insurance contract. Despite the Somali experiences, pirates are still defined as marauders without any allegiance to any recognised flag who, for their own gain, plunder ships, goods and other moveable at sea. This includes passengers who mutiny and rioters who attack from the shore.[90] This apparently business and commercial definition of pirates seems much wider than that in Clauses 99-105 of UNCLOS. However, it still would not have covered political activists disguised as passengers in the *Santa Maria* 1961 and the *Achille Lauro* 1985 hijack incidents.

The term pirates are synonymous with rovers. In the leading case of Bolivia *Republic v Indemnity Mutual Marine Assurance Company Ltd*,[91] Lord Vaughan defined pirates as persons plundering indiscriminately for their own ends and not persons who are simply operating against the property of a particular State for a public end, the end of establishing a government although that act may be illegal, although that act may be criminal and although they not be acting on behalf of a society which is politically organised.[92] Consequently, although considered war risks, strictly speaking actions of revolutionaries organising and carrying out armed expeditions against governments are not pirates within the meaning of that term. A failed attempted piracy still constitutes piracy. It will be recalled Piracy *Jure Gentum*[93] had decided rightly so that persons could still be pirates under International Law even if the attempted piracy act is frustrated.

---

[88] *Rickards v Forestal Land, Timber and Rlys Co Ltd* [1941] 3All ER 62.

[89] *Panamanian Oriental Steamship Coprn v Wright* [1970] 2 Lloyds Rep 365.

[90] Rule 8 of the *Rules for the Construction of the Policy,* First Schedule of the Marine Insurance Act 1906.

[91] *Bolivia Republic v Indemnity Mutual Marine Indemnity Assurance Company Ltd* [1908-10] All ER Rep.

[92] Ibid at 264 per Vaughan William LJ.

[93] *Piracy Jure Gentium* [1934] AC 586 PC.

It will be recalled that Rule 8 of the *Rules of Construction of Policy*[94] defines pirates to include passengers who mutiny and rioters who attack the ship from ashore. Now regarded as the internationally acceptable definition of the offence and risk, Clauses 101–103 of, *The United Nations on the Law of the Sea*, 1982 [UNCLOS], which codified customary international law, defines piracy thus:

"**Clause 101: Definition of Piracy**
Piracy consists of any of the following acts:

(a) any illegal acts of violence or detention, or any act of depredation, committed for private ends by the crew or the passengers of a private ship or a private aircraft, and directed:

  (i) on the high seas, against another ship or aircraft, or against persons or property on board such ship or aircraft;
  (ii) against a ship, aircraft, persons or property in a place outside the jurisdiction of any State;

(b) any act of voluntary participation in the operation of a ship or of an aircraft with knowledge of facts making it a pirate ship or aircraft;

(c) any act of inciting or of intentionally facilitating an act described in subparagraph (a) or (b).

Clause 102: Piracy by a Warship, Government Ship or Government Aircraft Whose Crew Has Mutinied
The acts of piracy, as defined in clause 101, committed by a warship, government ship or government aircraft whose crew has mutinied and taken control of the ship or aircraft are assimilated to acts committed by a private ship or aircraft.

Clause 103: Definition of a Pirate Ship or Aircraft
A ship or aircraft is considered a pirate ship or aircraft if it is intended by the persons in dominant control to be used for the purpose of committing one of the acts referred to in clause 101. The same applies if the ship or aircraft has been used to commit any such act, so long as it remains under the control of the persons guilty of that act".

As indicated above, the current Somali piracy has brought piracy to the fore, although once more the essential characteristics remains use of violence resulting into detention and depredation. The requirement for the offence in the high seas is no consolation to a shipowner or cargo owner deprived of their property due to sea robbery outside the high seas. (See also Ademuni-Odeke: "Somali Piracy: Effect on

[94] Schedule to the Marine Insurance Act 1906.

Oceanborne Commerce and Regional Security and Challenges to International Law and World Order", *Australia and New Zealand Maritime Law Journal, Vol. 25* (2011), pp. 134–160). In *Athens Maritime Enterprises Corpn v Hellenic Mutual War Risks Association (Bermuda) Ltd, (The Andreas Lemos),*[95] Justice Staughton thought that there was no need to limit piracy to acts outside the territorial sea.[96] He was quite prepared to accept that all is needed is for the vessel to be at sea where the attack could be described as a maritime offence.[97] On the other hand, he concedes that theft at sea without force or threat of force would not constitute piracy,[98] neither do actions of clandestine thieves who use violence to escape after committing theft.[99] Piracy cover can be cancelled by the Cargo Piracy Notice of Cancellation Clause (JC2008/024) of the Joint Cargo Committee Clauses.

9.12.11 Are Thieves and Rovers Pirates?

Following Justice Staughton's opinions above, the apparent inclusion of thieves and rovers in the definition of and classes of war risks in the Institute Clauses and other literature is rather baffling. Thieves and rovers are also sometimes included among pirates. S.3 of MIA1906 includes 'thieves' and 'rovers' in the definition of maritime (risks) perils.

3 Marine Adventure and Maritime Perils Defined.

(1) Subject to the provisions of this Act, every lawful marine adventure may be the subject of a contract of marine insurance.
(2) In particular there is a marine adventure where:

  (a) Any ship goods or other movables are exposed to maritime perils. Such property is in this Act referred to as "insurable property";
  (b) The earning or acquisition of any freight, passage money, commission, profit, or other pecuniary benefit, or the security for any advances, loan, or disbursements, is endangered by the exposure of insurable property to maritime perils;
  (c) Any liability to a third party may be incurred by the owner of, or other person interested in or responsible for, insurable property, by reason of maritime perils.

"Maritime perils" means the perils consequent on, or incidental to, the navigation of the sea, that is to say, perils of the seas, fire, war perils, pirates, rovers, thieves, captures, seizures, restraints, and detainments of princes and peoples, jettisons,

[95] *Athens Maritime Enterprises Corpn v Hellenic Mutual War Risks Association (Bermuda) Ltd, (The Andreas Lemos),* [1983] 1 All ER 590.

[96] Ibid at 598.

[97] Ibid.

[98] Ibid at 599.

[99] Ibid at 599–600.

barratry, and any other perils, either of the like kind or which may be designated by the policy.[100]

Thus, although excluded from normal marine policies, it was demonstrated above that "captures, seizures, restraints, and detainments of princes and peoples" are included in the definition of maritime perils. Rule 9 of the *Rules of Construction of Policy*[101] defines thieves in a marine policy to exclude clandestine theft or theft committed by the ship's company, whether crew or passengers. Therefore, the term does not cover clandestine theft or heft committed by any of the ship's crew or passengers. However, robbery accompanied by violence and committed by strangers and not by the crew is loss by thieves.[102] In addition to clandestine theft and theft committed by any of the ship's crew or passengers, this definition also excludes pilferage which is not limited to the taking of a whole package or all of the property insured. That notwithstanding, "Theft and Pilferage (Insured Value) Clause", which specifically includes the risk in a policy for being normal commercial rather that war risks. Justice Donaldson defined pilferage better in *Nishina Trading Co Ltd v Chiyoda Fire and Marine Insurance Co. Ltd*[103] as referring probably to the taking of a small part of the goods rather than of the whole.[104] It should perhaps also be added that there is lack or absence of the element of violence too in the loss by pilferage compared to theft by rovers and pirates.

9.12.12 Armed Robbery Against Ships

A new type of maritime offence which is separate but developed from piracy is armed robbery against ships. It was introduced to cover the gap in Clause 101 of UNCLOS where the offence would not qualify as a ship because is committed in territorial waters rather than the high seas. It is defined in *IMO Resolution A.1025(26) (Annex, par. 2.2 on IMO Code of Practice for the Invrestigation of the Crimes of Piracy and Armed Robbery Against Ships*) 2019 as any illegal act of violence or detention or any act of depredation, or threat thereof, other than an act of piracy, committed for private ends and directed against a ship or against persons or property on board such a ship, within a State's internal waters, archipelagic waters and territorial sea. (See also Ademuni-Odeke: "You are Free to Commit Piracy and Armed Robbery Against Ships But Please Do Not Do It In This Place: Geographical Scope of Piracy and Armed Robbery Against Ships Under UNCLOS and Related International Instruments", *Journal of International Maritime Law*, Vol. 50. No 4 (October 2019), pp. 407–449).

[100] See also Rule 7 of the *Rules for the Construction of the Policy* (Perils of the Sea).

[101] Ibid.

[102] *Haford v Maynard* (1875) 1 Parks's Marine Insurance (8th edn) 36.

[103] *Nishina Trading Co Ltd v Chiyoda Fire and Marine Insurance Co. Ltd* [1968]2 Lloyds Rep 47.

[104] Ibid, at 55.

It should be distinguished from the general use of robbery at sea which refers to someone who robs at sea or plunders the land from the sea without having a commission from any sovereign nation such as buccaneer, pirate and sea rover. What is the difference between piracy and armed robbery at sea?

Piracy has universal jurisdiction while the armed robbery at sea is subject to the state jurisdiction where the crime occurred. The difference between these two actions is piracy occurs on the high seas or outside the jurisdiction of any country while armed robbery at sea occurs within the jurisdiction of a country.

It is different from hijack, where attackers have illegally boarded and taken control of a ship against the crew's will. That notwithstanding armed robbery against ships is now insurable under the general heading of piracy.

9.13 Insurance of Terrorism and Terrorist Offences

9.13.1 Terrorism and Maritime Terrorist Acts

Terrorism is a violent, criminal act committed by individuals and/or groups who are inspired by, or associated with, designated foreign terrorist organizations or nations (state-sponsored). However, this section is concerned with maritime terrorism generally and piracy in particular, being the main and most serious threats to shipping and therefore cargo insurance. Maritime terrorism is any violent act with a political purpose against ships, cargo and passengers, ports and port facilities, and critical maritime infrastructure. Examples include hijackings, hostage takings, kidnappings, mass shootings, car bombings, and, frequently, suicide bombings. These are discussed below. Piracy and maritime terrorism are closely related activities involving 'armed violence at sea which is not a lawful act of war. But a distinction exists between the two acts with piracy being conducted for private ends while terrorism has political motives. It is for those reasons that IMO's SUA[105] and the amended SOLAS conventions have them in maritime terrorism and a threat to maritime security.

9.13.2 Exclusion from Institute Cargo Clauses

In their terrorism exclusion Institute Cargo Clauses, A, B and C define terrorism as:

> 7.3 caused by any act of terrorism being an act of any person acting on behalf of, or in connection with, any organisation which carries out activities directed towards the overthrowing or influencing, by force or violence, of any government whether or not legally constituted

[105] *The Convention for the Suppression of Unlawful Acts against the Safety of Maritime Navigation* or SUA Act (SUA Convention) 1988 as amended is a multilateral treaty by which states agree to prohibit and punish behaviour which may threaten the safety of maritime navigation.

9.13.3 Additional Exclusion Policy

Because of those exclusions the parties have to between them to take out an additional policy to cover this risk. Terrorism insurance provides coverage to individuals and businesses for potential losses due to acts of terrorism. It has developed since the Northern Ireland bombings in the UK, the 9/11 incident in the US and the Somali Antipiracy operations in the Indian Ocean. The latter led to state supported terrorism insurance schemes to supplement coverage under the insurance market mainly by the Lloyds of London Insurance. In the Lloyds of London market, coverage includes:

9.13.3.1 Insurance Against Physical Damage Caused by Terrorism

This is property insurance: see Property and Fire Insurance for guidance on risk location.

9.13.3.2 Terrorism General Liability and Terrorism Employers' Liability Insurance

These are liability insurance: see General Liability Insurance for guidance on risk location.

9.13.3.3 Global Contracts

A global contract is an insurance contract insuring risks located in more than one country. See the guidance referred to above for details.

9.13.3.4 Premium Apportionment

Premium apportionment, normally through an apportionment clause, prescribes the method for determining an insurer's portion of liability for loss where a property is covered by more than one insurance policy. Insurance proceeds are distributed according to this provision in proportion to the total coverage. A global contract may give rise to regulatory and tax exposures in different jurisdictions. Compliance with these requirements requires the overall premium to be apportioned between the countries in which risks are located.

9.13.4 Terrorism Exclusion Clause Notice

Terrorism cover can be cancelled by the Termination of Terrorism Transit Clause (Terrorism) 2009 (JC2009/056) of the Joint Cargo Committee Clauses through the Terrorism Exclusion Clause Notice.

9.13.5 Government Terrorism Insurance Schemes

The UK and other leading economies[106] offer terrorism insurance schemes. In the UK the issue of a certificate by HM Treasury in the UK is required for an act to be recognised as an "act of terrorism" for the purpose of the Pool Re scheme where the act of terrorism is defined as: "'Acts of Terrorism', means acts of persons acting on behalf of, or in connection with, any organisation which carries out activities directed towards the overthrowing or influencing, by force or violence, of Her Majesty's Government in the United Kingdom or any government de jury or de facto and". The definition is taken from s.2 (2) of the Reinsurance (Acts of Terrorism) Act, 1993, under which the scheme is established. The Re Pool Scheme is based on the Reinsurance Company Limited, also known as Pool Re, was set up in 1993 by the insurance industry in cooperation with the UK Government in the wake of the IRA bombing of the Baltic Exchange in 1992. Under the Act the government will from a fund under:

(i) any reinsurance agreement entered into under certain agreements, or;
(ii) any agreement entered into pursuant to any such agreement (s1 (1) amended by SI1997/2781), where the government undertakes liability for reinsurance against:
   - loss of or damage to property in the UK resulting from or consequential on terrorist acts; and
   - any loss which is consequential on such loss or damage

Terrorism risk insurance is also provided by insured and reinsured by the UK government the *Marine Insurance (War Risks) Act* 1952 discussed in Chap. 10 below.

9.13.6 Terrorism Coverage by Other Governments

Terrorism coverage is also available in the following major trading nations: Australia, Austria, Finland, France, Germany, Israel, Iraq, Namibia, Netherlands, Russia, South Africa, Spain, Switzerland, Turkey, and the US.

9.13.7 Kidnappings

Kidnapping is closely associated with especially modern piracy in the Somali basin and the West Indian Ocean involving the kidnapping of the crew and hijacking of vessels and their cargo and holding them for ransom. The risk is also prevalent in the oil and gas industry. There is no precise definition of the term, but it generally means the illegal taking and holding captive of one or more covered person(s) or by

[106] Such as Australia, Austria, Belgium, France 5, Germany, Netherlands, South Africa, Spain, and United States of America.

persons who then demand specifically from assets of the Assured or the assets of an insured person a ransom as a condition of the release of such captive(s). Insurers have had to pay large sums following constructive total losses of vessels and their cargo from the piracy. This is now covered by the Kidnap & Ransom Insurance Policies or K&R Insurance, which provide coverage typically for monies paid to kidnappers or extortionists, loss of ransom in transit and other expenses incurred as a result of a kidnapping. Although recently deployed against especially Somali piracy, these policies are not unique to marine risks and cover all aspects where kidnapping is a risk. Kidnap and ransom insurance or K&R insurance is designed to protect individuals and corporations operating in high-risk areas around the world.

9.13.8 Hijackings

Hijacking also came to prominence from the hijacking and holding vessels, their crew and cargo for ransom during the Somali piracy. An experience borrowed from the aviation industry, hijacking means the illegal holding under duress for a period in excess of six hours of an insured vessel and/or a covered person whilst travelling on an aeroplane, vehicle or watercraft. Unless otherwise specified, all insured kidnapping and hijacking losses are covered up to the full policy limit but subject to the overall policy aggregate. These include the payment of ransoms. Payment of ransom of cash and/or marketable goods or services surrendered or to be surrendered by or on behalf of the assured or insured person(s) to meet a kidnap or extortion demand are payable as insured piracy losses in the London but not US market.

On ransom, Justice Steel in *Masefield AG v. Amlin Corporate Member Ltd*[107] followed the approach in *Fender v. St John Mildmay*[108] where Lord Atkin opined rightly so that the doctrine [of public policy] should only be invoked in clear cases in which the harm to the public is substantially incontestable and does not depend upon the idiosyncratic inferences of a few judicial minds.[109] Likewise, in *Kuwait Airways v Kuwait Insurance*,[110] an authority approving a mid-19th century decision dealing with the effect of capture of a merchant vessel by pirates, where the vessel was subsequently recaptured by an English warship and treated as a prize ship in proceedings in the Admiralty Court, Justice Rix discoursed that in case of capture, because the intent is from the first to take dominion over a ship, there is an actual total loss straightaway, even though there later be a recovery.[111] This contention is supported by an earlier decision of *Dean v. Hornby*.[112]

---

[107] *Masefield AG v. Amlin Corporate Member Ltd [2010] EWHC 280 (Comm).*

[108] *Fender v. St John Mildmay* [1938] AC 1.

[109] Ibid at 12.

[110] *Kuwait Airways v Kuwait Insurance* [1996] 1 Lloyd's Rep. 664.

[111] Ibid.

[112] *Dean v. Hornby* (1854) 3 El. & Bl. 179 (a case of piratical seizure)."

9.13.9 Persons Acting from Political, Ideological, Ethnic and Religious Motives

In the twenty-first century, we current live in a dangerous and turbulent world where numerous peoples have taken up arms to oppose their governments or try to secede for political and religious reasons. Political reasons include ideological reasons. Those opposing governments for political reasons have included the freedom or liberation movements such as the MAUMAU (Kenya), PLO (Palestine), ANC (South Africa), FRELIMO (Mozambique), MPLA (Angola), ZANU (Zimbabwe), HUTU Rebels in Yemen, Castro and several separate groups. Some were freedom fighters opposing colonial governments, others were minorities such as POLSARIO (Saharan Republic) opposing foreign occupation. The issue is not the politics or ideology: it is the fact that they are involved in hostilities which would have consequences on export. Yet they were all included in the definition of terrorism as far as marine insurance risk is concerned. For they could inflict.

While those taking up arms for religious and mixed religious and political reasons have included the TALABAN (Afghanistan and Pakistani), AL QAEDA (Afghanistan and worldwide affiliates), and most recently various jihad groups in Syria (e.g., the Al Nasr Front), Al Shabab (Somalia), and Boko Haram in Nigeria. Whatever the categorisation, they are insurable as war risks arising from persons acting from political and religious reasons. These acts are related terrorism. For instance, the Australian definition of terrorism contained in s 5 of the *Terrorism Insurance Act* 2003 is:

> Action done or threat made, with the intention of advancing a political, religious or ideological cause, with the intention of coercing or influencing by intimidation the government of Australia or the Australian States or Territories, or a foreign country, or intimidating the public

while the German definitions of terrorism under the definition of terrorism under EXTREMUS AG provides that:

> Acts committed for political, religious, ethnic or ideological purposes suitable to create fear in the population or any section of the population and thus to influence a government or public body

9.13.10 Derelict Mines Torpedoes Bombs or Other Weapons of War

The insurance experience of derelict mines, torpedoes, bombs and other weapons of war are from the remains of these weapons after World War II (WWII). This risk, excluded by the Institute Cargo Clauses A, B and C, can be reinstated by the Institute War Clauses (Cargo) and Institute Strikes Clauses. There has been no decided authority on the risk. The only known literature coverage of the risk is a publication by Kenneth Goodcare[113] dealing with the American Cargo War Risk Reinsurance Exchange following the experiences of the WWII.

9.13.11 Hostile Use of Any Weapon or Device Employing Atomic or Nuclear Fission and/or Fusion or Other Like Reaction or Radioactive Force or Matter

This is another risk excluded by Institute Cargo Clauses A, B and C but available either by deleting the exclusion clauses in the policy or inclusion through the Institute War Clauses (Cargo) and the Institute Strikes Clauses. The coverage seems to deal more with accidents arising from operations of nuclear generating stations such as Chernobyl (Ukraine) and the 3 Mile Island (USA) than with active use of the weapons themselves. The two incidents, Hiroshima and Nakagasaki, when nuclear weapons were used could hardly be covered by any policy. The prominence of the risk has been elevated by the threat from proliferation of the weapons and the risks of the weapons falling into the hands of terrorist and other non-state entities. This would include threats from the use of nerve gas from the same groups.

9.13.12 Weapons of Mass Destruction (WMD)

This risk is a generic name for war risks which include "hostile use of any weapon or device employing atomic or nuclear fusion and/or fusion or other like reaction or radioactive force or matter" above. Otherwise a weapon of mass destruction (WMD) refers to a wide range of weapons which include, but are not necessarily limited to, a nuclear, radiological, chemical, biological or other weapon that can kill and bring significant harm to a large number of humans or cause great damage to human-made structures (e.g. buildings), natural structures (e.g. mountains), or the biosphere. The scope and application of the term has evolved and been disputed, often signifying more politically than technically. Coined in reference to aerial bombing with chemical explosives, it has come to distinguish large-scale weaponry of other technologies, such as chemical, biological, radiological, or nuclear. This differentiates the term from more technical ones such as chemical, biological, radiological, and nuclear weapons (CBRN). The difference between this risk and the one above is the absence of chemical and other gas-based weapons.

---

[113] Kenneth Goodcare, *Goodbye to the Memorandum*, 1988, *Witherby & Co Ltd.*

9.14 Further Food for Thoughts

9.14.1 Very Wide Ranging

The threats to cargo and vessel are greater and newer challenges than before. Equally the availability of coverage is so wide ranging that an ordinary insured might not know the full extent or have access to all the information, unless they employ brokers and other cargo insurance specialists.

9.14.2 Parties Would Have to be Very Well Informed

For above reasons, parties would have to be very well informed or employ specialists to advise on extent and availability of insurance.

9.14.3 More and More Government Involvements

All in all, there seems to be more government involvements under separate categories that it is beginning to cause problems. For instance, cover is available under three or different sources (UKEF, 1952 Act) P&I, private sector and private ECs.

9.14.4 Unfair to the Private Sector Who Have to Compete

With the government involvement in cargo, war and credit insurance it seems unfair to the private insurance sector who also pay taxes to finance the state support to compete with state sectors using their tax payers' monies.

9.14.5 Recent Upsurge in the Piracy Insurance Is Distorting the Market

The term "ransom payment" means the transmission of any money or other property or asset, including virtual currency, or any portion thereof, which has at any time been delivered as ransom in connection with a ransomware attack. Kidnaps and ransom demands are not new. Historically the greatest ransom paid was that paid for Atahualpa, the last emperor of the Incas, to the Spanish conquistador Francisco Pizarro in 1532-3 at Cajamarca, Peru, which constituted a hall full of gold and silver, worth in modern money some $1.5 billion (£1 billion). However, it has created a controversial ransom payment in piracy insurance.

The role of ransom payers is causing concern especially in piracy and marine cargo insurance. The FBI does not recommend paying a ransomware demand. This is because it doesn't guarantee you will get your systems back online or your data back and it incentivizes threat actors to continue to target companies. And your organization may even become known as an easy mark. In addition to the insurance solution, there is need for collaboration in the fight against it and international organized crimes. The UK and the US governments do not pay ransoms for hostages or terrorists, while some countries—including Colombia and Italy—have made the payment of ransoms illegal.

9.14.6 The Issue of Exclusions and Reinstatement of the Cover Is Rather Confusing

For contractual parties not conversant with the principles and rules on cargo insurance, the issue of cargo clauses A, B, C levels of cover, exclusions and "all risk" policies can be confusing. In particular the texts show what is covered negatively and only by the process of elimination. Not many would know what to add in order to reinstate full or near full coverage. Add to that reference to the minimum cover and the additional 10% to the contract price in CIF and CIP contracts and one ends up with confusion upon confusion. It would be better if parties were offered another institute cargo clause—"Institute All Risks Cargo Cause). It would provide the 4th option and highest benchmark with which to compare and an informed choice.

9.15 Concluding Remarks

War risk insurance is a type of insurance which covers damage due to acts of war, including invasion, insurrection, rebellion and hijacking. Some policies also cover damage due to weapons of mass destruction. It is most commonly used in the shipping and aviation industries. War risk insurance generally has two components: War Risk Liability, which covers people and items inside the craft and is calculated based on the indemnity amount; and War Risk Hull, which covers the craft itself and is calculated based on the value of the craft. The premium varies based on the expected stability of the countries to which the vessel will travel. War risk insurance is available from the public as well as private market. Private war risk insurance policies for aircraft were temporarily cancelled following the September 11, 2001 attacks and later reinstated with substantially lower indemnities.[4]

In the wake of this cancellation, the US federal government set up a terror insurance program to cover commercial airlines. The International Air Transport Association (IATA) has argued that airlines operating in states which do not provide war risk insurance are at a competitive disadvantage in this area. A detailed study of the Insurance of War Risks and Terrorism, including related perils such as Strikes, Riots, Civil Commotion, and Military or Usurped Power is available from the Insurance Institute of London (Research Study Group Report 258). Although there is more emphasis on CIF insurance, there is no difference in the insurance of CIF from FOB. Neither is insurance of FOB and related contracts different from the general insurance of export risks. Where there was specific application to the FOB and CIF we have indicated. The same applies to war risks.

9.16 Further Readings

Books

- Halsbury's Laws of England (5th edn 2008) Vol.93 (Shipping and Maritime Law), para.35
- Halsbury's Laws of England (5th edn 2008) Vol.94 (Shipping and Maritime Law), para.1249
- Halsbury's Laws of England (5th edn 2011) Vol.60 (Shipping and Maritime Law), para. 793–801
- Dwight Jaffee and Thomas Russell, Public Insurance and Private Markets, 2010, pp. 86–114, Washington, D.C.: AEI Press; distributed by Rowman and Littlefield, Lanham, Md.

Reports

- Insurance Institute of London: *Research Study Group Report* 258.
- Insurance Institute of London (Research Study Group Report 258), October 2007
- See also under Reports in other Chapters of this book

Clauses

- Ademuni-Odeke: "Somali Piracy-Effects on Oceanborne Commerce and Regional Security and Challenges to International Law and World Order", *Australia and New Zealand Maritime Law Journal*, Vol 25(2011) pp 134–160
- Ademuni-Odeke: "Jurisdiction over Foreign Pirates in Domestic Courts and Third States Under International Law", *Journal of International Maritime Law*, Vol.17(2011) pp.121–146
- Ademuni-Odeke: "An Examination of the Basis for Criminal Jurisdiction Over Pirates in International Law", *Tulane Journal of International and Comparative Law*, Vol. 22 (2014) pp.305–340
- Ademuni-Odeke: " Jurisdiction by Agreements Over Foreign Pirates in Domestic Courts: In Re Mohamud Mohamed Dashi & 8 Others", *University of San Francisco Maritime Law Journal* Vol.24 No.1, pp.36–64
- Ademuni-Odeke: "You are Free to Commit Piracy and Armed Robbery Against Ships But Please Do not Do it in This Place: Geographical Scope of Piracy and Armed Robbery Against Ships under UNCLOS and Related International Instruments", *Journal of Maritime Law and Commerce*, Vol.50 No.4 (October 2019), pp.407–449

- Ademuni-Odeke: " The Evolution, Nature and Application of 'Privater Ends' in Piracy Definition", *ASCOMARE YEAR BOOK ON THE LAW OF THE SEA*, Vol 1 Law of the Sea Interpretation and Definitions" 2021, pp.165–197
- Ademuni-Odeke: "Challenges of Apprehending and Prosecuting Somali Pirate Leaders and Financial Backers: The Big Mouth Case", *Journal of International Maritime Law*, Vol 29 (2023), pp.165–184
- Koichi Otani: "Effect and Scope of the Governing Clause in Marine Cargo Policy" *Waseda Business & Economic Studies*, 2007 No. 43
- Satoshi NAKAIDE: "Marine Insurance Law in Japan- A Structure Based on a Combination of Civil Law and English Marine Policy Wordings"
- Edwin Mills: "Terrorism and US real Estate", *Journal of Urban Economics* 51 (2002) 198–204.
- David Barker: "Terrorism insurance subsidies and social welfare", *Journal of Urban Economics* 54 (2003) 328–338
- "Hostilities", Meaning in F. C. and S. Clause *Harvard Law Review* Vol. 32, No. 7 (May, 1919), pp. 859–860

Internet Publication Sources

- National Business Aviation Association (NBAA) *Insurance Coverage for War Risks, Hijacking and Other Related Perils, June 2002* (nbaa.org)
- Thomann, Christian, ed. (2004). "Definitions of terrorism". *War, terrorism and insurance in Europe after September 11, 2001.* Verlag Versicherungswirtsch. pp. 36–41.
- *"Expiring terrorism insurance program alarms Md. industries"*. Baltimore Sun.
- *U.S. Treasury - Office of Domestic Finance - Terrorism Risk Insurance Program*
- *"The Terrorism Risk Insurance Act: Time to End the Corporate Welfare"*, Cato Institute.

Other Export-Import Insurance Avenues and Wider Considerations

10

Abstract

This second chapter of PART IV covers other avenues and considerations that the parties need to take into consideration while deciding their insurance options. After the Introductory paragraph, other factors covered involved include, but are not necessarily limited to the: Need for additional cover for overlooked losses and damages; Sellers' Post Contractual Insurance Obligations; Seller's Pre-Contractual Insurance Considerations; Seller's Own Interest Policy; Buyer's Pre-Contractual Insurance Considerations; need for Avoidance of self-insurance scenarios; Choice of Institute Cargo Clauses; Insurance of CISG Contracts; [Uniqueness of] Institute Common Law Contracts; Alternative/Additional sources of cover from Export Credit Insurance; The Official Export Credit Agencies; Advantages and Disadvantages of Export Credit Insurance; Other State Supported Insurance Policies; Other Private Sector Equivalent Insurance; Consequential Loss Insurance; Miscellaneous Export Risks Insurance; Policy Options; State Restrictions of Export Trade Insurance; Other Incoterms Considerations; Further Aspects of Overlooked Insurance; Additional Contingency Insurance Absent in Incoterms; Sellers' Additional Contingency and Own Insurance; Buyers' Additional Contingency and Own Insurance; Alternative Additional Insurance Consideration; Harmonization of Insurance with International Trade Practices; Comparisons with Commodity Trade Policies; Insurance in selected Major Civil Law and Other Jurisdictions; External Considerations Affecting Insurance Obligations; State Intervention and other Restrictive Practices; WTO and Other Public Aspects of International Trade; "Further Food for Thoughts"; Concluding Remarks; References Used; and Further Readings.

P. Ademuni-Odeke, *Insurance of International Sales' Contracts under Incoterms*, Law for Professionals, https://doi.org/10.1007/978-3-031-75136-3_10

10.1 Introduction

This chapter marks a major departure from the hitherto treatment in existing literature on insurance of international generally, and of FOB-CIF and other Incoterms in particular. For the first time it examines other insurance aspects that the FOB, CIF and other Incoterm contractual parties, although not under contractual duty to, nevertheless need to take into consideration. In doing so the chapter reflects on practical, compared to theoretical considerations, required of parties' treatments that are normally absent in most existing literature. For those reasons the chapter seeks to demonstrate that there is more to insurance than what is apparent in the contract. Thus, the chapter not only covers all such possible risks and issues not covered by all the other chapters, including coverage of such risks by governments and export credit agencies outside the private sector, but also attempts to clarify certain conflicting and confusing concepts.

Although, some of these topics also exist periodically in a limited way in some existing literature, the chapter expands and brings these practical considerations together under one roof and for the first time. Thus, for instance, in addition to the usual marine and commercial risks parties are advised to pay attention to own additional interests, wider sources and external considerations. In addition to the above list, these include, but are not necessarily restricted to:

1. Additional insurance.	9. Buyers' interests' insurances
2. Contingency insurance	10. State regulations of insurance
3. Consequential insurance	11. State assistance for export trade
4. Business interruptions	12. Institute cargo clauses
5. Export credit insurance	13. Institute commodity clauses
6. Sellers' interests' insurance	14. Miscellaneous insurances
7. Pre-shipment insurance	15. Pre-mature passage of risks
8. Post-shipment insurance	16. State War Risks Insurance

These considerations are not conclusive neither are they unique to FOB, CIF and other Incoterms. Rather they common to both FOB and CIF and, indeed all insurances including export. The point here is that parties have to consider all possible risks and liabilities not covered by traditional insurance avenues but which can prove catastrophic if mishap happens. This is what is known as a catch all situation. The considerations are covered in details below.

10.2 Need for Additional Cover for Overlooked Losses and Damages

10.2.1 Toping Up for Minimum Cover

Once more the buyer is reminded that even where the seller has to provide for insurance such as CIF, CIP and FOB with additional duties, those contractual requirements are only minimum and exclude war, contingency, pre-shipment, post-shipment, sellers interest, buyers' interests, needs of specialist trades, publicly provided policies and certain institute clauses excepted risks, to mention but a few. Some of these are covered below.

10.2.2 Reinstatement of Excepted Cover

The insured may wish to review the need for additional insurance to cover all excepted perils contained in the Institute Cargo Clauses. These are mainly war, etc. Other exceptions are made by the contract, common law and other trade usages.

10.2.3 Reassessment of Included Cover

Further to the excepted perils the parties may also wish to review need for additional cover far and above the included cover. Depending on the shipment the included covers might be inadequate.

10.2.4 Needs of the Specialist Trades

Despite everything else there is always the considerations that the customs and usages of a particular may require additional or specialist cover. Examples of these are container and commodity trade insurances such as GAFTA contracts and policies.

10.3 Need for Additional Contingency Insurance

In addition to the normal export insurance, merchants should seriously consider the need for additional insurance to cover contingencies for any gaps they might have overlooked. Due to continued uncertainty as to insurance obligations and adequacy of cover, described above, merchants are advised in practice to have an additional or contingency cover. In commercial practice, it is possible to obtain a special cover for the benefit of the seller who might otherwise be relying on the consignee's insurance in addition to the seller's interest insurance, especially where the retention of title clause is used. Take for example a seller who is selling "FOB" or "C&F" (now Incoterms and a buyer who has stated in his order, "I will insure". Within an established and long-term business relationship, this may well be satisfactory. However, the situation can arise when, even though the seller discharged his obligations under the contract of sale, the buyer refuses to pay for loss of or damage to the goods. A typical example of this situation arises when the buyer refuses to accept goods, knowing that fire has damaged the carrying vessel. Equally, it is known for buyers to refuse acceptance of a sight draft when the ship has sunk on the voyage.

10.4 Sellers' Pre- and Post-Contractual Insurance Considerations

10.4.1 Export Contingency Insurance

To cover themselves for unforeseen eventualities merchants, need either an ordinary or an export contingency insurance. Export contingency insurance is secondary marine insurance cover used when an exporter ships goods under terms (such as free on board or FOB) where the insurance for the cargo is importer's responsibility. This policy comes into effect when the importer either did not arrange insurance or it is insufficient to cover the possible losses. Export contingency cover affected for the benefit of the seller will protect the buyer in such circumstances.[1] There must, of course, be loss or damage to the consignment by a risk insured against, while an essential condition of contingency insurance is that its existence is not revealed to the buyer.[2] This type of insurance cover can be obtained, in many instances, at rates lower than for a full cargo policy.[3] (Say more on contingency insurance including sourcing the Internet)).

10.4.2 Premature Passage of Risks

When goods are sold, they remain at the seller's risk until the property in the goods is transferred to the buyer. Once the property is passed, the goods are at the buyer's risk even if the delivery has not been made. Why is passing of risk important? Consequently, where property is substantially damaged after exchange the risk remains with the seller and the buyer has the right to end the Contract. As a result of this it is of utmost importance that seller maintains their insurance cover over the property until settlement. The need for contingency insurance manifests itself in many aspects. First, is the premature passage of property and risk due to buyer's failure to nominate a vessel (or to do so on time) or the non-arrival of the vessel at the port of loading or appropriation in ascertained goods. Premature passage of risks should normally trigger need for pre-shipment insurance. This type of risk has been adequately dealt with under both Common Law and Incoterms above.

---

[1] *Port Rose v Phoenix Insurance* (1986) 136 NLJ 333, Hogdson J.

[2] Ibid.

[3] .Ibid; see also *Bank Leumic Le Israel BM v British Insurance National Insurance Co* [1988] 1 Lloyds Rep 72, *Seville J; Phoenix General Insurance Co of Greece v Holvanon Insurance Co* [1987] 2 WLR 512 CA.

10.4.3 Pre-Shipment Insurance

10.4.3.1 What It Is

Sometimes known as pre-shipment manufacturers' insurance, and also associated with export credit insurance, this insurance is by and for the seller/exporter's benefit. It attaches from the seller's location and terminates, depending on the contract, latest when goods pass the ship's rail or its equivalent. Anything after that will be covered by post-shipment insurance (below). As an exporter manufacturing non-standard goods for a customer, you will run the risk of the contract being terminated prior to delivery, leaving you with goods of little or no resale value. The termination of a contract may arise through political events such as conflicts, import or export embargoes or by the insolvency of a customer.

Such risks can be insured either as part of a non-payment policy or as a stand-alone policy (for example where payment is secured by a confirmed irrevocable letter of credit) to cover:

(a) Contracts with both private sector and public-sector buyers are eligible and cover;
(b) Pre-shipment policies insure for net loss;
(c) Insured's are required to retain part of the exposure (usually 10%, though the amount can vary); and
(d) The majority of insurers typically require a waiting period of 180 days before a claim is payable.

From the seller's point of view, there is the pre-shipment insurance. Since, as noted, he is liable for loss or damage before the goods cross the ship's rail, the seller has to cover for this specifically or as part of the general business insurance. Although it is a pre-export risk, nevertheless, it is generally regarded as part of the export and the cost thereof which can be legitimately passed on to the buyer. An example, of pre-shipment insurance, is where goods are delivered warehouse to warehouse using a multimodal or combined carriage. The Institute Cargo Clauses (post) now cover this type of risk. In this case, delivery is made long before goods cross the ship's rail.

10.4.3.2 Pre-shipment Policy Clause

Clause 4.14 of Zurich Marine Cargo Policy provides for pre-shipment as follows:

> **4.14 FOB Pre-shipment (imports only – not available for bulk cargo)**
> Notwithstanding the provisions of the contract of sale, where the subject matter insured is purchased, for import, on an FOB, CFR or similar basis, provided such subject matter insured is not bulk cargo, this insurance attaches from the time the subject matter insured is first moved in the warehouse or at the place of storage (at the place named in the contract of insurance) for the purpose of immediate loading into or onto the carrying vehicle or other conveyance for the commencement of transit. In the event of payment under this policy, we are entitled to subrogation of your rights of recourse against the sellers. You must not disclose the existence of this clause to the seller or any other interested part

However, as the text provides, this applies only to FOB contracts, covers imports only and is not available for bulk cargo shipments.

10.4.4 Post-Shipment Insurance

Like pre-shipment, post-shipment insurance is associated with export credit financing and insurance. It is part of contingency insurance. Post-shipment risks can include insolvency or non-payment by the buyer or non-payment of a letter of credit. Coverage for pre- and post-shipment risks can be combined in one policy. Private Buyer coverage does not generally include contract repudiation. Post-shipment insurance covers:

(a) Non-cancellable limits during the policy period;
(b) Up to 90% coverage;
(c) Tenor of up to seven years; and
(d) Minimum premium of e.g. £15,000 ($20,000).

There can be confusion as to the nature of contingency insurance, as it is sometimes also referred to as post-shipment or seller's interest insurance for all eventualities between shipment and buyer taking delivery and signalling acceptance. Contingency insurance is used in this context to mean both pre-shipment and post shipment insurance including buyer and seller's interest insurance. There is no bar for the seller to take out post-shipment to cover non-payment and the buyer pre-shipment to cover door-to-door, pre-loading and loading operation risks.

10.4.5 Buyer's Insolvency

This includes non-payment by buyer (below) for various reasons. Buyer insolvency is the only ground on which an unpaid seller can stop the goods in transit and is one of three grounds for exercising a lien or withholding delivery of the goods.

10.4.6 State Intervention

As prudent businessmen and women exporters and importers normally kept abreast national and international developments in foreign governments' restrictive or interventional shipping and insurance policies that might affect their shipments and purchases respectively. Like all other international trade contracts, FOB-CIF and other Incoterms are subject to such policies. These are further covered in paragraph 9.16 below.

10.4.7 Failure to Deliver

There are a number of other issues that merchants should be aware of: contingent cover is normally suspended until the happening of the event-the contingency (rejection of the goods, or of the documents, or repudiation of the contract). It then re-attaches retrospectively to cover the voyage itself, and any losses or damage caused by insured risks. It is advisable in such covers to stipulate for the freight charges, since a buyer who rejects the documents may refuse to pay the freight, and the seller may force a lien from the ship-owner before he can obtain any of the goods.

10.4.8 Short Delivery Insurance

Short delivery is when less than the amount contracted goods are delivered. This is however, subject to the contract *de minimis* principle- a legal principle which allows for matters that are small scale or of insufficient importance to be exempted from a rule or requirement. It can be used by the courts as an exclusionary tool to dismiss trivial matters from litigation. Under this rule the buyer would be unreasonable to reject 95% and above delivery. Where the principle is not applicable then, if there is short delivery and damage during delivery, the seller's liability shall in any case be limited to the price of the goods not delivered or damaged. He could be required to repair the goods, replace all or any part of the defective goods; or refund the price of those goods which are defective. He then receives a prorate payment, claiming the difference from his insurer.

10.4.8.1 Wrong Delivery Insurance

Wrong-delivery means the delivery of goods which fail to achieve reasonable conformity with the specification of the goods named in the relevant contract; it includes delivery of goods of a fundamentally different nature to that specified by the contract (for example, a computer was contracted for, but a book was delivered). In that case there is total failure of consideration and the seller will be liable for the price of the goods plus damages, loss of profit and interest.

10.4.8.2 Other Sellers' Interest Insurance

Seller's interest insurance is marine insurance that provides protection if the importer is responsible for insuring against or at least bearing the risk of potential damage or loss. As the exporter in these circumstances, the seller may have no direct control over the level of insurance provided by your trading partner. There are a variety of other aspects, which affects the seller. It must be borne in mind that the seller's interest and/or contingency insurance has special features, which should be noted, namely:

(a) the benefit of the insurance applies to the seller only—it is not assignable since it is to take effect only in the contingency that the buyer defaults in some way on his contract;
(b) it should not be made known to the buyer that such cover is being taken out, as to do so might encourage him to default at the insurer's expense, should the market have moved against him so that he is less keen on obtaining the goods than he was previously;
(c) unless specified clearly to the contrary the cover is only for physical damage or loss and does not cover incidental expenses arising from the failure of the buyer to pay for the goods; and
(d) cover will be obtained most economically if all FOB and CFR shipments are covered, the rate payable, which is difficult to establish for a particular cargo only, will be more easily arrived at if a number of such cargoes are being insured by an open cover against which declaration will be made as cargo is dispatched).

Contingency insurance is always a fall-back position when in doubt. One of the subsets or addition to contingency insurance is the seller's interest policy.

10.4.9 Business Interruption Insurance

10.4.9.1 What It Is

Business interruption insurance (also known as business income insurance) is a type of insurance that covers the loss of income that a business suffers after a disaster.[4] The income loss covered may be due to disaster-related closing of the business facility or due to the rebuilding process after a disaster. It differs from property insurance in that a property insurance policy only covers the physical damage to the business, while the additional coverage allotted by the business interruption policy

[4] *Tektrol Ltd v International Insurance Co of Hanover Ltd* [2005] 1 All ER 132 *Langley J; Eagle Star Insurance Co Ltd* v [2007] 1 BCLC 21 *Pumfrey J, Ch.D; Arbory Group Ltd v West Craven Insurance Services*[2007] *Lloyds IR491Grenfel J; Orient Express Hotels v Assicurazioni General SPA* (UK) [2010] EWHC 1186 (Comm) *Hamblen J;Midland Main Line Ltd v Eagle Star Insurance Co Ltd* [2004] 2 Lloyds Rep 604, Brooke J; Claughton (Edt), *Riley on Business Interruption and Construction Insurance & Claims, 6th Edn, 1984.*

covers the profits that would have been earned. This extra policy provision is applicable to all types of businesses, as it is designed to put a business in the same financial position it would have been in if no loss had occurred.

This type of coverage is not sold as a stand-alone policy, but can be added onto the business' property insurance policy or comprehensive package policy such as a business owner's policy (BOP). Since business interruption is included as part of the business' primary policy, it only pays out if the cause of the loss is covered by the overarching policy. The following are typically covered under a business interruption insurance policy:

10.4.9.2 Covers Loss of Profits

Profits mean and include those that would have been earned, based on prior months' financial statements. This policy covers the diminished profits and continuing fixed expenditures if your company stops or slows down its operations due damages caused by fire or additional coverages. Damages that may occur in a workplace due to fire or other risks are covered by the fire policy.

10.4.9.3 Covers Fixed Costs

Fixed costs include operating expenses and other costs still being incurred by the property (based on historical costs). Fixed-Cost Insurance is a traditional insurance program where the insured is charged a fixed premium rate. The rate is tied to a measure of exposure, such as payroll or sales, but is not loss sensitive.

10.4.9.4 Covers Temporary Relocation

Some policies cover the extra expenses for moving to, and operating from, a temporary location.

10.4.9.5 Covers Commissioning and Training Costs

Business Interuption (BI) cover can protect against loss of income or gross profit that a business might suffer after an unexpected event, such as damage to your property caused by fire or flood or unforeseen circumstances affecting the insured's suppliers. Business Interruption (BI) policy essentially covers the cost of commissioning the replacement machinery and providing training to the operators of the machinery replaced by the insurer following the insured events (Commission and Training Costs). In the wake of a business interruption event, a company will often need to replace machinery and retrain personnel on how to use the new machinery. Business interruption insurance may cover these costs.

10.4.9.6 Covers Extra Expenses

Reimbursement for reasonable expenses (beyond the fixed costs) that allow the business to continue operation while the property is being repaired. In addition, businesses can purchase contingent business interruption coverage, which pays out when a business is unable to operate because of an event (such as a natural disaster) that damages the business premises of one of its suppliers, thus preventing it from engaging in normal trade.

10.4.9.7 Covers COVID19 Loses

In these cases, business interruption cover for COVID-19 may apply if COVID-19 is present at the premises and all policy conditions are met. If you are unsure about what your policy covers your business for, check with the broker you purchased the policy from or your insurer if you purchased it directly. The ABI has provisions for COVID19 loses[5] following Justice Jacobs' judgment in the *At the Premises* test case.[6] The defendant insurers in the 2023 "At the Premises" test case argued in the Financial Conduct Authority (FCA) test case that liability to pay out for Covid-related business interruption losses didn't arise where a policy covered losses triggered by an outbreak of an infectious disease at the business' own premises. The High Court disagreed and ruled that it does. From this ruling, many companies, including export and import ones, affected by Covid-19 now have valid business interruption insurance claims following court rulings. Thus, following this case and other Commercial Court proceedings, more businesses will be entitled to pursue unpaid business interruption (BI) claims for their Covid-19 losses. Prior to the *At the Premises* decision, in 2022, *Corbin & King v AXA Insurance*[7] extended Covid-related business interruption recoverability to businesses with 'non-damage denial of access' (NDDA) clauses. (NDDA clauses provide for business interruption losses that are caused as a result of forced closure by a public authority due to events within the geographical limit.) While in *Stonegate v MS Amlin*,[8] also in 2022, the High Court provided further guidance regarding business interruption losses and insurance claims. That case established more detailed principles to help business owners and insurers calculate any indemnity that may be due.

10.5 Sellers' Own Interest Policy

10.5.1 In Transit Risks Policies

In addition to contingency issues above, the seller's interest policy covers a number of instances. First, it covers the period during which the goods are in transit[9] (transit risks) up to FOB (often this only relates to transit within the port area, because bulk cargoes are generally sold from stocks maintained in the port area).[10] Nevertheless, where there is doubt regarding payment for goods the seller might be wise to effect insurance beyond the point of FOB, even as far as delivery to the final destination. Secondly, it is also important, in the case of FOB sales, that the seller' s policy

[5] See:https://www.abi.org.uk/products-and-issues/topics-and-issues/coronavirus-hub/business-insurance/#:~:text=In%20these%20cases%2C%20business%20interruption,if%20you%20purchased%20it%20directly.

[6] *At the Premises Test Case [2023] EWHC 1481 (Comm).*

[7] *Corbin & King v AXA Insurance* [2022] EWHC 409 (Comm).

[8] [2022] EWHC 2548.

[9] For goods in transit see, *Same v Same* [1968] 2 Lloyds Rep 233 Nield J.

[10] Avandero (UK) National Transit Insurance Co [1994] 2 Lloyds 613Neil J.

clearly shows whether cover ceases at FOB or continues to delivery at the final destination or some other alternative point.[11]

10.5.2 Buyers Rejection Policies

This can be covered under a rejection of goods and/or documents insurance either separately or as an extension clause to the main cargo policy. It is a contingency insurance, covering late, over and under deliveries to which rejection is part, also covers losses resulting from various post-shipment risks such as the buyer's rejection of documents relating to goods especially in the case of CIF and/or rejection of goods for late delivery, over delivery or non-conformity. Rejection insurance cover would cease at the warehouse/cold-storage/port of discharge when goods been delivered. Costs covered would include expenses for re-tendering of documents, the return or disposal of goods at the port of destination, etc. Rejection by the buyer is different from non-payment by the buyer discussed below.

10.5.3 Reservation of Title Clause Policies' Issues

Sellers should be aware that reservation of title clauses have consequences to the sale and therefore insurance implications. This contingency insurance also covers for instance the cost of return or disposal of goods at destination or at an intermediate point where: the buyer has failed to discharge his obligations, where conditions on reservation of title have not been met, or when goods are as yet unascertained in which case the inference is that a partial interest only has been transferred. A sale of goods in which the seller retains title to the goods sold, or any products made from them, or the resulting sale proceeds, until the buyer pays for the goods. The Issue gave rise to the Romalpa Clause from the decision in *Aluminium Industrie Vaassen BV v Romalpa Aluminium Ltd*[12] The purpose of a retention of title clause is to offer an opportunity for the seller of the goods to retain the title in them until the buyer has paid the price in full. The best Retention of Title Clause is the All Monies Clause, also known as an All Sums clause, which allows for a supplier of goods to transfer possession of goods which have not yet been paid for, for example goods supplied on credit, whilst ensuring that he retains legal and beneficial title in the goods until the buyer pays for them.

---

[11] *WJ Lane v Sprat* [1963] 3WLR 950 Roskill J.

[12] *Aluminium Industrie Vaassen BV v Romalpa Aluminium Ltd* [1976] 1 WLR 676, a UK insolvency law case, concerning a quasi-security interest in a company's assets and priority of creditors in a company winding up.

10.5.4 Non-Payment by Buyer Policies

At the end of the day, the seller's ultimate goal is to be paid by the buyer. Contingency insurance also covers the risk of non-payment by the buyer, for whatever reason, where guaranteed systems such as letters of credit were not utilised in the payment for the contract and unfair calling on performance bonds. Stoppage in transit and retention of title clauses were once popular remedies this kind of instance; however, they are not insurance schemes. Other aspects of seller's interest insurance include where the seller has delivered the goods to a wrong place from that stipulated in the contract, wrong or short (including partial) deliveries.

However, contingency and seller's interest insurance are not mutually exclusive and do overlap. In certain circumstances, a seller may have an interest in goods, which will arise only in some contingency. For instance, if he sells goods FOB the seller's interest will cease when the goods cross the ship's rail, and the buyer will insure them from that point on. If all goes well the seller will not be concerned further. However, suppose goods are lost or damaged and to avoid payment due to the foreign the buyer rejects the documents. The seller would find himself in a very difficult position, for the only policy in existence (if the buyer bothered to insure) is in the buyer's name and language and he has no interest in it. It is therefore desirable to insure these contingent risks when good s is sold on FOB or CFR terms.

10.5.5 Benefit of Buyer's Policy!

Can the seller use the buyer's policy as a fall-back position? It has also been suggested that one way to obtain cover would be for the seller to arrange with the buyer to have the benefit of the buyer's general policy (below), and vice versa, should anything happen to cause the buyer to reject the goods. This is, however, not a very satisfactory option to suggest since it may put into the buyer's mind the idea that he can avoid the contract if he wants to. It may also suggest that there is some defect in the goods, which the seller expects to be discovered. In addition, even if it can be arranged, it means that the seller is involved with paper work and bureaucracy. In theory it may be otherwise. What it is also still unclear is whether a foreign insurer at a possible disadvantage in language, distance and ability in enforcing the policy. As will be apparent soon, a better way is to obtain an open cover on all goods up to the point of shipment, and contingent cover on all goods after crossing the ship's rail. An insured buyer denied the benefit of the seller's interest policy should consider the buyer's interest policy for the reasons outlined above and vice versa.

10.5.6 'Not to Inure' Effect on Cargo Policies

Seller's benefit of the buyer policies should not be confused with "not to inure policies" effect on policies. The former enables the seller to benefit from the buyer's insurance whereas the latter forbids the seller/buyer's insurance to benefit the career.

For instance, Clause 15 of the *Institute Marine Cargo Clauses*, 'Benefit of Insurance', provides that: "Not to Inure Clause: This insurance shall not inure to the benefit of the carrier or other bailee". However, the clauses do not express forbid any other persons other than the carrier or bailee from benefiting from the insurance.

10.5.7 Seller's Interest Policy Clause

Clause 24.23 of Zurich on sellers' interest under Zurich Marine Cargo (Australia) policy as follows:

> **24.23 Sellers' interest (exports only)**
> This extension will only apply to subject matter insured that is exported if, under a contract of sale, you do not have a responsibility to arrange insurance up to final destination and you make a provisional declaration of all such exports of subject matter insured within the voyage range of this policy at the commencement of each period of insurance for which sellers interest premium is charged.
>
> **24.23.1 Full cover will apply if title reverts to you because the buyer fails to:**
>
> (a) accept the subject matter insured;
>
> (b) take up the documents of title; or
>
> (c) pay for the subject matter insured, and you exercise a right or lien to interrupt the transit and/or suspend the contract of sale in order to protect your interests.
>
> **24.23.2 Cover will remain in force until either:**
>
> (a) the subject matter insured is accepted by the buyer;
>
> (b) the subject matter insured is sold to an alternative buyer;
>
> (c) the subject matter insured is returned to you; or
>
> (d) 60 days from the arrival of the overseas vessel at the port of discharge, whichever first occurs.
>
> **24.23.3 We will not pay for loss or damage to the subject matter insured:**
>
> (a) unless immediate notice is given to us when a contingency in 4.23.1 (a), 4.23.1 (b) and/or 4.23.1 (c) above occurs;
>
> (b) if the existence of this extension is disclosed to the buyer, its insurers or any other interested party;
>
> (c) if this extension or any interest in the subject matter insured is assigned;

(d) if the loss is recoverable form credit insurers;

(e) arising from government action and/or regulations preventing transfer of currency; or

(f) if you have not declared to us all exports of the subject matter insured within the voyage range of this policy where you do not have a contractual responsibility to arrange or provide insurance up to the final destination.

This extension is not a double insurance. You must use all reasonable and usual care, skill and forethought and take all practical measures which may be required by us to prevent or minimise loss and to enforce the contract of sale.

When a claim is paid under this extension, we are entitled to exercise our right of subrogation as outlined in 6.5 'Rights of subrogation'"[13]

Equivalent policies in other jurisdictions contain similar clauses.

10.6 Buyers' Pre and Post-Contractual Insurance Considerations

10.6.1 Buyers' Benefits from Shippers'-Based Policy

Despite certain exceptions to the general rule and cases such as in CIF and CIP contracts, the seller and buyer as the shipper or consignor is primarily responsible for insuring FOB goods since he is always the "shipper". He should not necessarily rely on the seller even in where the seller should have insured such as in "classic" and "extended" or FOB "with additional duties". In addition, and where in doubt, he should take out a buyer's interest policy. The buyer's interest policy attaches from FOB shipment but some buyers prefer to effect their policies for the whole period of transit. There are reasons for this. First, such policies do not pay claims for accidents that occur before the buyer's insurable interest attaches but do protect the buyer where there is some doubt regarding interpretation of the various FOB terms.

[13] Available from: https://www.zurich.com.au/content/dam/au-documents/business-insurance/marine/marine-cargo/annual-marine-cargo-insurance-policy-inc-institute-clauses.pdf.

10.6.2 Buyers' Pre-Shipment Insurance

Secondly, buyer's interest policy covers mainly post-shipment[14] period although it occasionally also covers pre-shipment[15] period. The best example of this in DES and EXW contracts, where the buyer takes delivery from the buyer's premises long before shipment. He has to specifically request, as there has not been much emphasis and, therefore, market on buyer's interest insurance in FOB as he is primarily responsible for the bulk of insurance in the contract. The buyer's position here would be analogous to that of the seller.

10.6.3 Buyers' Post Shipment Insurance

This insurance would cover all sorts of aspects including some already covered in this book. The buyer's position and insurance responsibilities in this case is the same as under the seller's post shipment above. Whatever the difference in the seller and buyer's interest insurance, it is generally accepted that both insurances are common especially in FRC/DCP or FOB/CFR contracts as additional and/or contingent insurance.

10.6.4 Buyers' Interest Clause

Claims in respect of loss or damage to the goods shall be payable hereunder only if and to the extent that the Seller and/or his Insurer fails to pay for such loss or damage. The Insurer to be subrogated to the Assured's rights against the Seller or any other parties interested in the shipment.

10.7 Avoidance of Self-Insurance Scenarios

There has also been confusion between seller's and buyer' interest insurance and whether they duplicate each other and are deemed unnecessary in view of export credit and institute cargo clauses. Detailed discussions of that topic are beyond the scope of this clause.[16] Nevertheless, the rule of the thumb is that if in doubt, the merchants should effect both to avoid the risk of non-insurance. Besides, subrogation would solve the problem of duplication. The important point to note, however, is that the seller's interest cover is geared towards loss or damage to cargo, sold FOB (irrespective of type) or CFR, which subsequently becomes the property, responsibility or risk of the seller, primarily if the buyer fails to pay for such goods.

[14] Risks incurred after shipment, i.e., goods passing the ship's rail.

[15] Risks before shipment, i.e. before goods cross the ship's rail.

[16] For details of the Institute Cargo Clause, see generally, Gough (1988) (hereinafter "Neville Gough".

As will be apparent shortly, the export credit policy,[17] on the other hand, covers the seller against non-payment by the buyer other than where there is loss or damage to the cargo for which the seller holds, or should hold, a normal commercial policy. It is for that reason that exports credit insurances cover 90% of the risk with the other 10% to be covered by the private market. In addition to the seller and buyer's interest policies, merchants should also avail themselves of the insurance opportunities offered by the Institute Cargo Clauses to cover any gaps.

10.8 Choice of Institute Cargo Clauses

The type of insurance under this category will in turn depend on whether the parties use Institute Cargo Clauses (hereinafter "Cargo Clauses", "the Clauses") as the basis of their contracts. Under the Clauses, the seller's duty and passage of property and risk are the same as at Common Law and INCOTERMS, namely that the seller undertakes to deliver the goods on board the vessel, usually nominated by the buyer, at which point property and risk pass to the buyer. However, unlike the position at Common Law or under INCOTERMS, once the insurance responsibility between the parties is established, it is easier to ascertain where the seller's policy ceases and the buyer's policy starts. It should also be borne in mind that overlaps in insurance policies can occur by design or default—hence over insurance or double insurance. However, as noted earlier, it is better to be double or over insured than non-insured.

Under FOB as well as FRC/DCP/CFR contracts, the seller will normally insure or run uninsured and rely on recovery from the carrier up to depot or till on board in country of shipment leaving the buyer to do the rest. In practice the buyer under FRC/DCP or FOB/CFR contracts will arrange for his policy to commence from the time of leaving the seller's premises "so far as concerned", or some such phrase just as the seller under CIF/CIP contracts will similarly ensure that his policy continues until arrival at the buyer's warehouse. There may or may not be an additional premium charge for this. Certainly, such concession helps to overcome the problem of pinning down where loss or damage has occurred during the warehouse-to-warehouse period, even if it is necessary to have such concession clearly worded to override the legal trading position as outlined at Common Law and under Incoterms above.

FOB merchants trading in goods covered by various Commodity Trade Associations have that as an additional window of insurance opportunities. Merchants that are also members of Commodity Trade Associations are bound by the insurance trade terms and rules of the respective bodies in addition to the Institute Clauses. The position under commodity trade associations above is very dissimilar to those under the Institute Cargo Clauses below.

[17] The effect of ECGD policy on FOB contracts is discussed in details in Notes 105–107 and the texts thereunder.

It should be noted that the cargo clauses covered in this book are of the UK as contained in the ILU. However, major trading nations have their own which are similar or equivalent to the UK. These are accepted for tender in other jurisdictions. It is for those reasons that Clauses A5 of CIP provide for "Clauses (C) of the Institute Cargo Clauses (LMA/IUA) or any similar clauses as appropriate to the means of transport used" while CIF provides for Clauses (C).

10.9 Insurance of CISG Contracts

10.9.1 Incoterms and CISG Insurance Compared

10.9.1.1 General Comparisons[18]

Apart from both dealing with international contracts, CISG and Incoterms are not related and have no connections. One is product of intergovernmental agreement while the other private based. Neither are mandatory and are both only the alternative ways of contracting for sales contracts. There are no direct mentions of insurance but its implications can be glimpsed from Chapter IV Clauses 66–70 on passage of property and risks. The UK is not party to CISG, due to possible conflicts with common law principles, although the US and most other countries are.

On the comparisons between CISG and Incoterms' contracts. Coetzee opines that:

> INCOTERMS® do not replace the CISG's provisions on delivery and the passing of risk in toto, but merely supersede them in so far as they are mutually exclusive. For the rest, they function in tandem. Aspects which are not governed by the INCOTERMS® rules, or inadequately regulated, can be supplemented by the Convention, and vice versa. Collaboration between the two instruments strengthens the unified legal framework for international sales transactions with the view to facilitating international trade.[19]

However, CISG is more comprehensive that Incoterms in many respects although Incoterms is more widely used.

10.9.2 Delivery of Goods

Delivery of goods is tied up with passage of risks and therefore insurance liabilities. Delivery is covered in Clauses 31–34 is almost identical in wording to chapter IV (Clauses 66–70). It would appear that when a party has successfully delivered goods in accordance with Clauses 31–34 then risks will pass to the other and therefore fulfilling Chapter IV. Thus Clauses 31–34 and Chapter IV should be read together.

[18] Siddharth Kanojia: Does English Law Provide the Best Framework For The Sale of Commodities? – A Comparison Between English Law, Incoterms and the CISG https://thelawbrigade.com/wp-content/uploads/2019/06/Siddharth-Kanojia.pdf).

[19] Coetzee (2013), pp. 1–22. The original publication is also available at http://jlc.law.pitt.edu/ojs/index.php/jlc.

However, where one falls short the other can supplement but cannot be used interchangeably. For instance, both have common threads in delivery, passage of property and passage of risks and therefore insurance especially between CISG Clauses 66–70 and Incoterms Clauses A4 (delivery), A3 (passage of risks) and A5/B5 insurance related.

10.9.3 Passage of Property and Title[20]

Unlike Incoterms 2020, CISG has wide coverage of the passage of property in international sales. However, the rules of chapter IV apply whether property passes to the buyer or not. These rules supersede any domestic rules on the passage of property; hence the UK decline to ratify the Convention and the US reservations on its ratifications due to conflicts with the UCP 600 on passage of property.

10.9.4 Passage of Risks[21]

Unlike Incoterms 2020, CISG has a more detailed provisions on the passage of risks in Chapter IV (Clauses 66–70). Under Clause 66, once risk passes to the buyer, the buyer must continue in the performance of his part of the contract unless the loss was caused by the seller. Clause 67 concerns the passing of risks in the contract involves carriage of goods. Clause 68 deals with the passage of risks if goods are sold in transit. Clause 69 deals with passing risks in situations which not fall under Clauses 67 and 68 such as in EXW when delivery is at the place of business. Clause 70 regulates the interaction of the rules governing the passing of the risk with the rules dealing with the buyer's rights where the seller has committed fundamental breach.

These rules differ from Clause A3 of Incoterms 2020 on passage of risks. However, although the CISG describes when the risk passes from the seller to the buyer,[22] but it has been observed that in practice most contracts define the seller's delivery obligations quite precisely by adopting an established shipment term under Incoterms, especially in relation to contracts such as the FOB[23] and the CIF.[24]

10.9.5 Insurance Obligations[25]

Despite its comprehensive coverage of the sales contract itself, CISG does not provide for insurance of the contract. It only makes references to especially CIF

[20] Ibid at.

[21] CISG, Clauses 66–70.

[22] Ibid.

[23] Clause 67 CISG; Schwenzer and Fountoullakis (2006), p. 469.
Ibid, at. pp. 485–489.

[24] CISG on CIF-book.

[25] Ibid at.

Incoterms for this purpose, making Incoterms insurance the default position. It has been observed from the readings of Clause 66 that:

> Even if the risk, as will usually be the case, is covered by insurance, is it necessary to determine which of the two parties bears the risk of loss or damage actually occurs: the party who bears the risk must assert a claim against the insurer, may suffer a depletion of current assets while waiting for settlement, etc[26]

It is also explained regarding Clause 69, for passage of risk in delivery at the seller's premises, that "The rationale behind the rule is that the risk should be borne by the party who has custody over the goods; that party will usually have insurance against loss of or damage to the goods".[27]

Finally, clause 87 provides a tricky scenario of who bears the risks, and therefore should insure goods stored in a warehouse. "Depositing the goods in a warehouse has no effect on the allocation of risks. Whether the first party has to insure the goods will depend on the party's agreement, any practices established, or usages applying between the parties. As a general rule, there is no obligation to insure the goods when storing them in the warehouse".[28]

10.10 Uniquness of Institute Crago Clauses in Commodity Trade Contracts

In addition to the Cargo Clauses' requirements, the merchant should bear in mind that a particular commodity trade organisation might have additional requirements; it is therefore difficult to have fast rules. Examples are:

(a) Institute Commodity Clause (A,[29] B[30] and C[31]) agreed with the Federation of Commodity Associations for the insurance of shipments of cocoa, coffee, cotton, fats and oils not in bulk, hides, skins and leather, metals, oil seeds sugar (raw or refined) and tea;
(b) Institute War Clauses[32] (Commodity Trades);
(c) Institute Strikes Clauses[33] (Commodity Trades);
(d) Institute Fosfa Trade Clauses (A,[34] B,[35] and C[36]);

---

[26] Schwenzer and Fountoullakis (2006), p. 469.
[27] Ibid, at pp. 485–489.
[28] Ibid, at pp. 605–606.
[29] For the texts see Neville Gough, pp. 251–252.
[30] Ibid, pp. 253–254.
[31] Ibid, pp. 255–256.
[32] Ibid, pp. 281–283.
[33] Ibid, pp. 284–285.
[34] Ibid, pp. 292–293.
[35] Ibid, pp. 294–296.
[36] Ibid, pp. 297–299.

(e) Institute War Clause[37] (Fosfa Trades);
(f) Institute Strikes Clause[38] (Fosfa Trades); and
(g) Institute Frozen Foods Clauses.[39]

The merchant's insurance duties and obligations will further depend on which, of the many commodities, he is trading in and whether it is compulsory for him to use a particular association's contract forms and insurance. The Grain and Feed Trade Association (GAFTA), for example, has five FOB Contracts[40] in the UK, of which Clause 19 of No.64 on insurance provides thus:

> Marine and war risk insurance including strikes, riots, civil commotions and mine strikes to be effected by the Buyers with first class Underwriters and/or approved Companies. Buyers shall supply Sellers with confirmation thereof at least five consecutive days prior to be expected readiness of vessel(s). If Buyers fail to provide such confirmation Sellers shall have the right to place such insurance at Buyers' risk and expense

Otherwise, the main GAFTA Insurance Clauses Standard Contract No 72 is specifically dedicated to insurance. Clauses 1–5 of that Contract applies to exports from and imports into the UK trade and Clauses 6 covers the GAFTA insurance for FOB contracts to the other Common Law jurisdictions: Australian, Canadian, South African and the US Acts (relating to carriage of goods by sea).

In this context, it is worth mentioning that whereas the LJA'[41] contract terms of purchase clearly state that the buyer has no risk prior to loading; he can nevertheless buy jute on CIF terms. In such circumstances the usual resolution is that the supplier/seller continues to insure his risk up to CIF onwards (depending on the clauses he gets) and then purchases cover from FOB onwards which he passes onto the buyer. In that case, undiscovered loss or damage at time of loading, if possible, with jute, might prove a problem but in practice, there is none. It was often insisted on by insurers that when insurance on jute or jute products on terms wider than Free from Particular Average (FPA) (as it was) was requested, such cover should attach only at the point of FOB. These are however, UK based. Other trade associations, including those in other Common Law jurisdictions, may well have similar provisions, such as the US Cargo Clauses compared to the UK ones.

Up to this point, the FOB risks considered are commercial. Non-commercial risks are covered by export credits, another channel opened to the FOB merchant.

---

[37] Ibid, pp. 300–302.

[38] Ibid, pp. 303–304.

[39] Ibid, pp. 306–326.

[40] The other 4 numbers consisting of the:

(1) Pulse for Human Consumption, Bulk/Bags (No.23),
(2) General Grain in Bulk (No.64),
(3) United Kingdom and Republic of Ireland Grain (No.79A),
(4) Feeding Fish Meal in Bags/Bulk (No.118); and
(5) General Feeding stuffs in bags or bulk (No.119).

[41] Ibid, pp. 327–330.

10.11 Alternative and Additional Sources from Export Credit Insurance

10.11.1 Publicly-Supported Export Credit Insurance Schemes

The UK government has about four schemes which support export trade. One is a non-insurance scheme, assistance in connection with export trade, provided by the same government body which supports ECI schemes. The other three are direct insurance schemes: export credit insurance, insurance in connection with overseas investment and insurance of piracy and other specific war risks. All the three are effected through UKEF under the Export and Investment Guarantees Act 1991. The US government has similar schemes in: The following are some of the key sources of export assistance provided by the U.S. government:

(a) U.S. Export Assistance Centers;
(b) The International Trade Administration;
(c) U.S. and Foreign Commercial Services;
(d) Advocacy Center;
(e) Trade Information Center;
(f) STAT-USA/Internet; and
(g) Small Business Administration.

10.11.1.1. Assistance in Connection with Export of Goods
1 Assistance in Connection with exports of goods and services.

(1) The Secretary of State may make arrangements under this section in connection with supplies by persons carrying on business in the United Kingdom of goods or services to persons carrying on business outside the United Kingdom.

(1A) Arrangements under subsection (1) may be made in connection with goods or services supplied before the arrangements are made or in connection with goods or services which are to be, or which may be, supplied.[42]

(2) The Secretary of State may make arrangements under this section for the purpose of rendering economic assistance to countries outside the United Kingdom.

(3) The Secretary of State may make arrangements under this section with a view to facilitating—

(a) the performance of obligations created or arising, directly or indirectly, in connection with matters as to which he has exercised his powers under this section or section 2 of this Act, or

(b) the reduction or avoidance of losses arising in connection with any failure to

[42] S. 1(1) (1A) substituted (21.5.2009) for s. 1(1) by Industry and Exports (Financial Support) Act 2009 (c. 5), ss. 2(1), 3(2) (with s. 2(2)).

perform such obligations.

(4) The arrangements that may be made under this section are arrangements for providing financial facilities or assistance for, or for the benefit of, persons carrying on business; and the facilities or assistance may be provided in any form, including guarantees, insurance, grants or loans[43]

These are not insurance policies under but rather actions under UKEF which promote export trade.

10.11.1.1 Insurance in Connection with Overseas Investment

2. Insurance in connection with overseas investment.

(1) The Secretary of State may make arrangements for insuring any person carrying on business in the United Kingdom against risks of losses arising—

(a) in connection with any investment of resources by the insured in enterprises carried on outside the United Kingdom, or

(b) in connection with guarantees given by the insured in respect of any investment of resources by others in such enterprises, being enterprises in which the insured has any interest, being losses resulting directly or indirectly from war, expropriation, restrictions on remittances and other similar events.

(2) The Secretary of State may make arrangements for insuring persons providing such insurance.

(3) References in subsection (1) above to a person carrying on business in the United Kingdom and to the insured include any company controlled directly or indirectly by him[44]

Although merchants can insure against most losses (discussed above) they can still suffer due to loss or damage occurring to commercial risks.[45] However, this kind of loss is not the only risk to which the transactions are subject.[46] There is the additional risk that the buyer may become insolvent or refuse, without valid reason, to pay for the goods.[47] There is also the possibility that, willing though the buyer may be to accept and pay for the goods, his own government may, for various reasons,

---

[43] S.1 Export and Investment Guarantees Act 1991–1991 CHAPTER 67-An Act to make new provision as to the functions exercisable by the Secretary of State through the Export Credits Guarantee Department; and make provision as to the delegation of any such functions and the transfer of property, rights and liabilities attributable to the exercise of any such functions. https://www.legislation.gov.uk/ukpga/1991/67/section/3.

[44] Ibid s.2.

[45] https://www.gov.uk/guidance/overseas-investment-insurance.

[46] R. Walters, "The Future of Export Credit Insurance after Matthews" 190 *Acct* 345.

[47] Ali (1984), p. 28.

prevent him from doing so. These risks, broadly classified as commercial and political risks, cannot usually be covered by an ordinary seller's interest, contingency and other commercial insurance policies discussed above.[48]

For those reasons, and in order to promote international trade since World War I(WWI), in the UK, these policies have been provided, in the national interest, by the *Export Credit Guarantee Department* (ECGD) under the former Department of Trade and Industry (DTI) and by private credit insurers since the reorganisation of the ECGD in 1991.[49]

10.12 The Official Export Credit Agencies

10.12.1 The UK Export Credit Agency

10.12.1.1 The UK Export Finance (UKEF)

The UK Export Finance is the operating name of the ECGD, the UK's export credit agency and a ministerial department of the UK government. It is therefore the UK's export credit agency. It helps UK companies by providing insurance to exporters and guarantees to banks to share the risks of providing export finance. In addition, it can make loans to overseas buyers of goods and services from the UK. UKEF works with banks to offer flexible, innovative, and competitive financing solutions. Merchants can also get trade finance and insurance from the UK government through UK Export Finance. It's finance arm, the UK Trade and Investment (UKTI) helps businesses export and grow into global markets. It also helps overseas companies locate and grow in the UK. Our services are provided in over 100 markets throughout the world. For UKEF Policy (see Annex XIII below).

10.12.1.2 Alternative Source of Cover

This is an alternative source of cover not covered by Incoterm rules. Also covered partly above, this is a public insurance source in contrast to the normal private sectors insurance. It is available to Incoterms and all other parties to the export import process and not unique to those using Incoterms. Export Credit Insurance (ECI) protects an exporter of products and services against the risk of non-payment by a foreign buyer. Simply put, exporters can protect their foreign receivables against a variety of risks that could result in non-payment by foreign buyers. To take advantage of state coverage certain key exports and imports.

---

[48] Bollinger (1955), p. 213.

[49] Now provided by the ECGD under the *Export and Investment Guarantee Act 1991* (Cap 67). This Act has two main functions, to re-enact the previous *Export Guarantees and Investment Act* 1978 and to clarify and update that legislation, in the main by way of increasing the Secretary of State's powers in relation to managing the assets and liabilities\acquired by him, when acting through the ECGD and to facilitate the provision of the Insurance Services business of the ECGD.

10.12.1.3 The Export Ctedit Guarantee Department

The guarantee is in the form of an insurance policy issued to the seller, or to a confirming house through which he is selling but may also take the form of a guarantee given by the ECGD directly to a bank or other institution, which is providing finance to the merchant for the transaction. The ECGD issues both comprehensive and specific policies, although it is the former that would be most suitable to a merchant transacting on FOB terms.[50]

10.12.1.4 The Policy Exceptions

The policy has some exceptions, the details of which are omitted herein, but for the purposes of this clause it can be assumed it covers risks of a political nature, such as the inability of the buyer to pay the price, or to pay on time, because of restrictions on import, such as the refusal of an import licence or restrictions on payment such as those imposed by exchange regulations or moratoria.[51] Also covered is non-payment or non-acceptance caused by war, hostilities or revolution in the buyer's country or war between the buyer's country and the UK.

10.12.1.5 The Amount of Coverage

The amount of the cover will normally be 90% of the FOB contract price but will be less where the buyer rejects the goods or more where the loss is due to certain political causes. Decided under UKEF forerunner, the ECDG, Re *Miller Gobb & Co Ltd*[52] decided that these contracts are contracts of indemnity. While *Lonrho Exports v Export Credit Guarantee*[53] decided that in provide insurance under the legislation the ECDG should exercise due diligence otherwise they would be liable to the insured exporter for negligent advice.

The cover will not, of course, be in any event more than the relevant percentage of the credit limit approved by the ECGD for the particular buyer. The other 10% are secured from private commercial as well as private credit insurance companies. The standard ECGD policy includes pre-shipment risks, such as an anticipatory

---

[50] See "ECGD-functions of" 163 Acct 625.

[51]. This is effected under Part I of the Act which bestows a range of powers upon the Secretary of State allowing him to provide the following:

(a) financial facilities and assistance for the purposes of facilitating the supply abroad of goods and services by UK businesses and of rendering economic assistance to countries outside the UK; and
(b) insurance against the risk of losses in respect of investment overseas made by UK companies in certain circumstances. Section 1 of the Act deals with the general assistance in connection with export of goods and services.

[52] *Re Miller Gibb & Co Ltd* [1957] 2 All ER 266.

[53] *Lonrho Exports v Export Credit Guarantee* [1996] 4 All ER 673].

repudiation of the contract by the buyer or the imposition of an export licence requirement by the UK government.[54]

10.12.2 Entitlement to the Export Credit Agency Subrogation Windfalls

10.12.2.1 Windfall and Subrogation

Windfall is a function of an indemnified insured realising more from the tortfeasor than the insured value. It is an obscure insurance occurrence that is hardly mentioned by most authors.[55] Sometimes referred to as a "surplus" or profit, it is a rare occurrence which results into a challenge against the insurance principle of subrogation which governs marine cargo insurance.[56] With origins in contracts of marine insurance of vessels, it was common in export credit insurance. As indicated earlier (Chap. 2 above), subrogation ensures that the insured only receives the indemnity settlement entitled to and therefore they will not profit from the incident.[57] Accordingly, that where the insured has received more from the tortfeasor than the insured valued, he should surrender it to the insurer. However, it must be noted that in certain marine policies such as *Yorkshire Insurance Co Ltd v Nesbit Shipping Co Ltd* including export credit insurance policies such as *Lucas v Export Credit Guarantee Department* especially those involving export credit guarantees where the amount received by the insured exceeds insurable value, then the principle of subrogation might be "suspended" due to the windfall.

10.12.2.2 Origin in Marine Insurance Contracts

Although not known by that name, windfall had its roots in contracts of marine insurance of vessels. On a goods policy in *Brooks v MacDonald*[58] the carrying vessel was captured by a Brazilian cruiser as blockade runner. The assurer declined the assured's abandonment but eventually compromises to settle the claim by paying 35% of the insured value. Years later, the Brazilian Government under a Convention with Great Britain, makes compensation. In the assurer's suit to recover the compensation as subrogation, it was held that the assurer was not entitled to any part of the compensation so paid. Likewise in the American case of *Burnand v*

[54] Detailed cover is contained in Section 2 of the Act dealing with insurance in connection with overseas investments.

[55] Except this author herein, the only author to delve in insurance windfalls is [John] Birds' Modern Insurance Law, 9th Edn, Sweet & Maxwell, 2010 para.17.4.3.

[56] For a detailed discussion on the phenomenon, see, Ademuni-Odeke (2017), pp. 6–44, www.erevija.org.

[57] Ibid; see also generally, Ademuni-Odeke: "Windfall in marine and export credit insurance policies in Anglo-American and other common law jurisdictions- Additional exception or simply a further limitation and modification of indemnity and subrogation? Part II" *The European Insurance Law Review*, 1/2018, pp. 8–44, April 2018, www.erevija.org.

[58] *Brooks v MacDonald* (1853) 41 R.R.336.

Rodocanachi,[59] a cargo insured under a valued policy was destroyed by a Confederate cruiser during the American Civil War. The cargo was worth more than the valuation. After the war compensation was paid to the cargo owner by the US Government under an act which expressly refused to recognise claims made by or on behalf of the insurers for subrogation rights. It was held that the insurers, who had paid for a total loss, were not entitled to the compensation.

It is arguable that these were older decisions and some like *Simpson v Sampson and Burnand v Rodocanachi* were decided on other factors such policy grounds. Hence explanations of the latter by Lord Bowen LJ in *Castellain v Preston*[60]; and by the appeal court in *Stearns v Village Main Reef Company*[61] the explanations However, the relatively modern decision in *Yorkshire Insurance Co Ltd v Nisbet Shipping Co Ltd*,[62] the insured was allowed to keep all the windfall. In the case, a ship insured for £72,000 became a total loss as a result of a collision with a Canadian Government vessel during WWII. The insurers paid the £72,000 to the assured, and then claimed damages from the Canadian Government under subrogation. The action was successful but meanwhile the Pound Sterling had been devalued in 1949 and the loss when quantified and converted into English currency nearly doubled to £127,000, a difference of £55,000. The assured then paid the £72,000 to the assurers and kept the balance. In the assurer's suit against the assured for the £55,000 surplus, the assured contended that the assurers were not entitled to the windfall since they would not be out of pocket. The court held that the assured's contention was correct because the assurers could not recover under the doctrine of subrogation anything more than they had paid. The decision was recently cited in in the recent decision of *Bee v Jenson*.[63]

10.12.2.3 Adoption by the ECGD/UKEF Contracts of the Marine Insurance Principles

A merchant, (Incoterms or otherwise), who has UKEF cover is in a better position, than one who has not, in obtaining financing for export transactions from banks or other lending bodies. Such a body may require that the merchant assigns to it the benefit of the UKEF guarantee, in which arrangements are made for the UKEF to pay directly to the financing body any money due in respect of a loss or on the particular transaction or transactions. However, although these are contracts of indemnity in which subrogation applies, the courts have ruled unusually that the assured is entitled 100%, rather than sharing 90%–10% ratio to the surplus. That was certainly the case

[59] *Burnand v Rodocanachi* (1882) 7 App. Cas 333.

[60] *Castellain v Preston* (1883) 11 Q.B.D at p. 404.

[61] *Stearns v Village Main Reef Company* (1904)10 Com Cass 89 CA.

[62] *Yorkshire Insurance Co Ltd v Nisbet Shipping Co Ltd* [1962] 2 QB 330.

[63] *Bee v Jenson Com C* 21 Dec 2006 (Times 16-Jan-07 year).

in *Re Miller Gibb*[64] under the former ECGD, where the assured was allowed to keep all the surplus. In *Re Miller Gibb*, the issue arose for discussion in circumstances very similar to that in Yorkshire Insurance. By a policy dated in 1951 the ECGD agreed (through the equivalent of Clause 17 of the latter policies) to indemnify the exporters, Gibb and Co., 90% of any such loss as the company may sustain by operation of law which (in circumstances outside the control of the company or of the buyer) restricted the transfer of payments from the buyer's country to the UK.

This was in respect of goods sold and shipped from the UK to a buyer in, among other countries Brazil. Owing to Brazilian exchange control the buyers were unable to pay the £2,880, 4s 9d for the goods. In 1953, the company claimed 90% from the ECGD. Under the terms of the claim, the company assigned to the ECGD its rights in the debt and interest in the goods forming the subject of the claim, and to pay over to the ECGD forthwith any payments, which the company or its agents might receive in respect of the debt. Following from the company's undertakings under the claim form, they informed the exporter's bankers (the bank) by written instructions to hand the proceeds of the bill of exchange over to the ECGD once they were realised. In 1954, the company was wound up and a liquidator appointed. In 1956, the bank received the contract price of the goods plus interest. The liquidator rejected a claim by the then Board of Trade on behalf of the ECGD to 90% of the sum of £3,111,11s 1d received by the bank. The insured had received a windfall and interest totalling £231,6s 4d and the insurer claimed entitlement to both amounts paid out under the indemnification agreement and also the windfall received by the insured.

Yorkshire Insurance's ruling, that in subrogation, the insurer is only entitled to reimbursement of monies equal to the amount paid out under the policy, was not followed. In this instance, the ECGD succeeded in their claim and the Board of Trade were entitled to receive from Martins Bank not only 90% of the contract price as they were contractually entitled to, but also 90% of the windfall (+ the interest). The distinguishing factor in this case and in Lucas and Yorkshire Insurance was the fact that the insured had expressly assigned his interest in the subject matter to the insurers. Quoting Lord Hoffmann in Banque Financiere,[65] Justice Morrison tried to justify the retention of the surplus due to confusion between the insurer's equitable and contractual rights of subrogation when he said:

> My Lords, the subject of subrogation is bedevilled by problems of terminology and classification which are calculated to cause confusion. For example, it is often said that subrogation may arise either from the express or implied agreement of the parties or by operation of law in a number of different situations: see, for example, Lord Keith of Kinkel in *Orakpo v. Manson Investments Ltd. [1978] A.C. 95, 119*. As a matter of current terminology, this is true. Lord Diplock, for example, was of the view that the doctrine of subrogation in con-

[64] *Re Miller Gibb & Co Ltd* [1957] 2 All ER 266.

[65] Banque Financiere at p. 744.

tracts of insurance operated entirely by virtue of an implied term of the contract of insurance *(Hobbs v. Marlowe [1978] A.C. 16, 39*) and although in *Lord Napier and Ettrick v. Hunter [1993] A.C. 713* your Lordships rejected the exclusivity of this claim for the common law and assigned a larger role to equitable principles, there was no dispute that the doctrine of subrogation in insurance rests upon the common intention of the parties and gives effect to the principle of indemnity embodied in the contract.[66]

On restitutionary remedy and other aspects of subrogation, he continued that:

> Furthermore, your Lordships drew attention to the fact that it is customary for the assured, on payment of the loss, to provide the insurer with a letter of subrogation, being no more nor less than an express assignment of his rights of recovery against any third party. Subrogation in this sense is a contractual arrangement for the transfer of rights against third parties and is founded upon the common intention of the parties. But the term is also used to describe an equitable remedy to reverse or prevent unjust enrichment which is not based upon any agreement or common intention of the party enriched and the party deprived. The fact that contractual subrogation and subrogation to prevent unjust enrichment both involve transfers of rights or something resembling transfers of rights should not be allowed to obscure the fact that one is dealing with radically different institutions. One is part of the law of contract and the other part of the law of restitution. Unless this distinction is borne clearly in mind, there is a danger that the contractual requirement of mutual consent will be imported into the conditions for the grant of the Restitutionary remedy or that the absence of such a requirement will be disguised by references to a presumed intention which is wholly fictitious. There is an obvious parallel with the confusion caused by classifying certain, Restitutionary remedies as quasi-contractual and importing into them features of the law of contract.[67]

In trying to clarify the difficulties of the principles in, rationale for, types of, rights of subrogation and their relation to windfall, his Lordship added that:

> And, if more were needed, this statement of principle by Lord Rodger, then sitting as Lord President in the First Division of the Inner House in the *Caledonian North Sea* case [2000] Scottish Law Times 1123 at 1134, arising out of the Piper Alpha disaster, can be added: "Subrogation works by giving the insurer who indemnifies the assured the right to raise proceedings in his name and, by the very nature of the circumstances in which it comes into play, the proceedings by the insurer must necessarily be to recover sums which have already been paid to the assured or paid on behalf of the assured. The remedy could not exist unless, in insurance as in other cases of indemnity, our law took the view that payments made by the indemnifier fall to be ignored in proceedings raised by him in the name of the assured against a third party. Those payments are ignored in all cases where subrogation applies, whatever may be the basis of the action which is raised in the name of the assured after he has been indemnified by the insurer"[68]

---

[66] Ibid at p.

[67] Ibid at p.

[68] Ibid at p. xx.

Yorkshire Insurance was also cited in *Bailii*,[69] a motor insurance case in which Justice Morison opined that English law does not distinguish a claim for subrogation or contract and that any defence that can be mounted against the insurer can also apply to the insured.

Lucas v ECGD[70] reinforced the position that in these export credit guarantee contracts the assured can retain the surplus. In *Lucas*, just as in *Re Miller Gibb.* Clause 17 of the Standard Policy provided first that the ECGD would indemnify the insured 90% of the loss caused by the delay in payment for the goods sold to Egypt (then part of the United Arab Republic (UAR) with Syria) not the fault of either party. This would be calculated in sterling on the exchange market at the date of export. Secondly, that "all sums recovered by the merchant in respect of the loss to which the guarantee applies shall after the date of loss be divided between the parties at a ratio of 9:1 and in the event of the merchant recovering such monies they held it on trust for the guarantor". The risk insured against occurred and the insured indemnified 90% (£372,071,6s 10d) of the insured value (US$1,155,181) (£413, 411, 12s, 0d).

The Egyptian Government removed the barriers and the buyers paid for the goods, but when the US$ were transmitted into £s they amounted to £443, 032,8s 1d, a windfall of £29,620. The insurers claimed 90% (£398, 729,3s 3d) of the greater sum. The Appeal Court limited the insured's liability to 90% of the lesser sum on true construction of Clause 17. They closely examined the sentence, 'the loss to which this guarantee applies', and held that loss in this context referred to the sum of money the insured did not receive from the buyer at the time he should have received it, i.e. the lesser sum.[71] Lord Morris in the House of Lords reversed the Court of Appeal's decision.[72] He held that, as it followed that Clause 17 ceased to apply once the sum was received in respect of the loss covered by the guarantee, any further sum received was not received in respect of the loss.[73]

10.12.2.4 Criticisms of the Decision and System

There were a number of criticisms of this decision in particular and the system where the insured retains the windfall contrary to subrogation principles. Firstly, that undue emphasis was placed on the interpretation of the phrase, 'loss covered by the guarantee' in the case. Second, the court limited itself to the interpretation of

[69] *Bailii*, [2006] EWHC 3359 (Comm).

[70] *Lucas v ECGD* [1974] 1WLR 909.

[71] Ibid, at 910.

[72] *Re Miller Gibb* [1957] 1 Lloyds Rep 258 CA.

[73] Lords Reed and Viscount Dilhorne concurring. Also concurring, Lord Simon added that, "There is nothing either in the public scheme out of which it arises or in the terms of the agreement itself which suggests in any way a profit sharing scheme", at 889.

s.79 (1) of MIA 1906 and was not prepared to consider effect of unusual circumstances, such as currency devaluation, giving rise to the windfall as argued by the defendant's counsel. Thus, the court treated the sterling value several years later as the same without reference to devaluation and its purchasing power. The supposed justification that a 'pound was a pound', was illogical if not perplexing. Application of policy rather than legal reasons for the decision, would be understandable but none was given in this instance. Yet most Incoterms merchants continue to make use of this cover.

10.12.3 The Official European and Export Credit Agencies in Other Jurisdictions

Although the concept was invented by the UK in 1919 to deal with post WWI reconstructions, the system is not exclusive to her. It has spread and all the major trading nations,[74] including some developing ones[75] now provide this credit insurance. Over

[74] These are namely:

(a) *The Australian Trade Commission -trading as Export Finance and Insurance Corporation in Australia;
(b) Bundesministerium fur Finanzen (Federal Ministry of Finance) in Austria;
(c) Office National du Ducriore (OND) in Belgium;
(d) *Export Development Corporation (EDC) in Canada;
(e) Eksportkrediradet (EKR) (The Export Credit Council) in Denmark;
(f) Export Credit Agency (FINNVERA) of Finland;
(g) Compagne Françoise d 'Assurance pour le Commerce Exterieur (COFACE) in France;
(h) Hermes Kreditverscherungs -Aktiengesellschaft (leading partner in the consortium) in Germany;
(i) Export Credit Insurance Organisation (ECIO) in Greece;
(j) *Insurance Corporation of Ireland plc-(ICI) in Ireland;
(k) Sezione Speciale l 'Assicurazione del Credito all 'Esportazione in Italy;
(l) EXIMBANK in Japan;
(m) Office du Ducriore in Luxembourg;
(n) Nederlandsche Credietverzekering Maatschappij N.V (NCM) in the Netherlands;
(o) *Export Guarantee Office (EXGO) for New Zealand;
(p) Garanti-Instituttet for Eksportkredit in Norway;
(q) Companhia de Seguro de Creditos EP (CESCO) in Portugal;
(r) Compania Espanola de Seguros de Credito a la Exportacion, SA(CESCE) in Spain;
(s) Exportkreditnamnden (EKN) (Swedish Export Credits Guarantee Board) in Sweden;
(t) Geschaftsstelle fur die Exportrisikogarantie(ERG) (Office for the Export Risk Guarantee) in Switzerland; and
(u) *The Export-Import of the United States (EXIMBANK) in the US; and
(v) For other agencies in the industrialised countries see under Europe and the Americas in Note 97 below.

The Export Credit systems of the major Common Law countries are highlighted and marked with asterisks, the remaining agencies are included for general information and for the fact that merchants from Common Law jurisdictions do trade globally.

[75] E.g. **the Export Credit Bank of Turkey** (Turk Eximbank) in Turkey.

84 countries globally operate some for some of export credit agencies or export subsidies.[76] Irrespective of where the export or import originate or are destined, the Incoterms and other export merchants can avail himself of the facility.[77]

10.12.4 The Private Export Credit Agencies

Since their inception and to a large even currently most export credit agencies such as the ECGD (now UKEF) and those in other countries listed above are publicly owned or state operated. However, by definition, an export credit agency or investment insurance agency is a private or quasi-governmental institution that acts as an intermediary between national governments and exporters to issue export insurance solutions, guarantees for financing. Nevertheless, following the privatisation of the short-term side of the UK's ECGD in 1991, a concentration of the export trade credit insurance market took place and three groups now account for over 85% of the global credit insurance market.

These main players focused on Western Europe, but rapidly expanded towards Eastern Europe, Asia and the Americas. These are:

(a) *Euler Hermes*: a product of a merger of the two credit insurance companies of the Allianz Group. Euler Hermes is now the world's number one private export credit insurance provider;
(b) *Coface*: a wholly owned subsidiary of Natixis, the financing, asset management and financial services arm of the BPCE Group. As a result, Coface now has the largest direct presence in the world; and.
(c) *Atradius*: another product of a merger between NCM and Gerling Kreditversicherung. It was later renamed Atradius after it was demerged from the Gerling insurance group.

However, these private providers are no comparisons in volume of coverage with the state supported agencies such e.g., the American and the Japanese EXIMBANK and the UK's official UKEF.

[76] For a complete list of export credit agencies in almost all countries see: https://www.cc-solutions.net/WorldECAs.

[77] For export credit insurance policies in other jurisdictions and countries see, ***Morgan Grenfell & Co Ltd v SACE*** [2001] EWCA1932, Clarke LJ CA, a case involving SACE, the Italian equivalent of the UK's Export Credit Guarantee Department (ECGD); and Goudsmit, "Export Credit Insurance in the Netherlands" (1983) 1 *ICLR* 87.

10.13 Advantages and Disadvantages of Export Credit Insurance

10.13.1 Aadvantages

Despite its role since 1919 in the UK and later in other countries, the ECIs have had their advantages and drawbacks. Among the perceived advantages are:

10.13.1.1 Security of Cash Flow

First, is the supposed improved cash flow beneficially to especially smaller enterprises. This is because selling on credit is an inherently risky business. Unless you demand payment upfront, your customer could fail to pay you for the goods or services you provide. For those reasons a trade credit insurance policy helps secure your cash flow by protecting you against non-payment. This could typically be as a result of cash flow difficulties experienced by your customer, or even certain political events.

10.13.1.2 Improved Access to Finance

Second, is the supposed improved access to finance. Your trade export credit insurance policy can be helpful when looking to access finance, as many banks and lending institutions look favourably on businesses whose cash flow is secure. Having a trade credit insurance policy could help you build a strong relationship between your business and your banks or lender.

10.13.1.3 Minimise Bad Debt

Third, is the minimisation of bad debt. It is argued that one of the best ways you can minimise the risk of bad debt is to insure your accounts receivable. Trade credit insurance covers you when you customers fail to pay and protects you from the domino effect that can take hold when a business goes under.

10.13.1.4 Improved Customer Relationships

Fourth, is the theoretical case of improved customer relationship. According to this argument, when assessing the creditworthiness of a customer or potential customer, you have the opportunity to get to know them better and to build mutually beneficial relationships. This may include tweaking your credit terms to help make sure both businesses have liquidity.

10.13.1.5 Confidence to Explore New Markets

Fifth, is the hypothetical confidence to explore new markets. Export trade credit insurance is more than a backstop to protect your business from the risk of unpaid invoices. It is also a tool that can enable trade and help your business grow. You can benefit from the market knowledge and insights of our underwriters and test new products, or explore new sectors or geographies while keeping your exposure to a risk to a minimum. Although credit insurance is not a risk transfer, as our underwriters cannot insure any trade, they consider too risky, any refused credit limits will, in itself, help you identify the best areas in which to invest in trade and nurture business growth.

10.13.1.6 Reduction of Financial Risk

The main function of export credit insurance is to reduce the financial risk to the exporter. The risk can come from either commercial source, such as an importer's bankruptcy, slow payment or default on the payment terms in the import/export contract, or from political sources, such as war, political protests or revocation of the importer's license. The insurer assesses the potential for both types of losses in the transaction before underwriting the policy.

10.13.1.7 Access to Working Capital

An exporter that carries export credit insurance can gain access to overseas working capital. The credit insurance policy shows lenders that the company is protected against potential non-payment by a customer and is a better credit risk for a substantial capital loan. Companies that carry export credit insurance can also obtain standby letters of credit, in which a bank can guarantee payment on the exporter's loans should the importer fail to fulfil the import/export contract.

10.13.1.8 Protect Against Certain Risks

The primary benefit of this sort of insurance is that it does protect against certain kinds of risk when doing business abroad. This is especially useful for firms that are new to exporting. This permits firms to establish themselves in the market by mitigating certain risks. In general, firms can now expand into the export market that would not be willing to take the risk otherwise.

10.13.1.9 Enables Competitiveness

Buying a credit insurance policy for exports can also permit a new firm to offer more competitive credit terms for potential buyers. This insurance can also be used as collateral when approaching banks for credit. In general, export credit insurance is a good bet for new businesses in the field.

10.13.2 Disadvantages

10.13.2.1 Overview

It will come as no surprise to learn that especially the private providers in the major traditional trading nations don't believe there are any disadvantages to a trade credit insurance policy. That is not to say they don't recognise there are limitations. For example, there will be occasions where some agencies even in these wealthy countries feel the risk is too great and will be unable to offer insurance for a buyer. However, they don't just take these decisions in isolation. Generally, the key underwriters are experts in their fields and will explain their decision to the prospective insured. If they feel there is a high risk that the seller's prospective buyer will struggle to pay the seller, the seller can choose to act on that information and possibly seek out a safer buyer to sell their goods or services to or approach the official government supported providers. Rather than being a negative, this will save the seller money and hassle in the long run.

10.13.2.2 Exclusions and Limitations

Exporters may find that export credit insurance is not available in all situations. This is because the agencies are not only divided into the private and public sectors but that about 10% of the market is reserved for the private non-agency insurers to allow for competition and the private-public sector balance in the market.in the market. Consequently, the non-agency insurers may not offer policies for specific types of goods or for shipments to specific countries or businesses. Even when insurers do offer export credit insurance, the policy may not cover the entire amount of the shipment. For instance, a company requesting a £1m/US$1.3m export credit insurance policy may only be eligible for a £500,000/US$750,000 policy, less annual and per-loss deductible payments.

10.13.2.3 Default and Bad Faith

Exporters with export credit insurance may take advantage of their private or public policies to get into export contracts that carry both higher rewards and greater risks. These policies leave the exporter vulnerable to default from the importer. The importer may also engage in "bad faith" behaviours, such as delaying payment or claiming that the exporter did not deliver the goods as promised. Export credit insurance carriers will stop underwriting policies to exporters who are found to engage routinely with risky importers.

10.13.2.4 Limitation of Freedom of Action Abroad

Export insurance can limit one's freedom of action abroad. Generally, only certain kinds of clients and a certain percentage of the loss will be covered. The firm offering the policy will likely demand regular accounting of all export accounts from the firm. In addition, any buyer can claim that the price is in "dispute," and insurance will not cover such a disagreement. Firms overseas can claim a dispute in order to delay or eliminate legal action. More seriously, such insurance can lead to risky behaviours for the firm in question. Firms with a good insurance policy can engage customers who are considered a risk, customers otherwise that would be ignored. The possibility of default and bad faith then increases, leading insurance firms to become stricter about what is covered.

10.14 Other State Supported Insurance Policies

10.14.1 UK Government Insurance and Reinsurance of War Risks for Ships, Aircrafts and Cargoes

In addition to the availability of Export Credit Guarantee Facilities for commercial and political risks, a UK exporter and importer should be aware and may wish to avail themselves of the government assistance to the industry under the following 5 headings. Further and likewise insurance being also available from the P&I facilities. The categories and extent of the government insurance and reinsurance of war risks[78] under the enabling Marine Insurance (War Risks) Act 1952 includes the followings headings:

10.14.2 Power to Enter Into Reinsurance Agreements

Reinsurance is also known as insurance for insurers or stop-loss insurance. Reinsurance is the practice whereby insurers transfer portions of their risk portfolios to other parties by some form of agreement to reduce the likelihood of paying a large obligation resulting from an insurance claim.

10.14.3 Power to Enter Into Reinsurance Agreements

The Secretary of State can reinsure war risks against which a ship or aircraft or the cargo carried in a ship or aircraft. However, the reinsurance is only for British registered ships and aircrafts or foreign ships and aircrafts chartered by the British government, companies, citizens or residents conducting business from the UK. Ships and aircrafts from British dependencies and protectorates are considered British ships. Foreign ships and aircrafts include those registered in Ireland, India and the former Federation of Malay.

10.14.4 Liability of Reinsurance on Insolvency of Insurer

The same powers above extend to the Secretary of State extends to reinsurance cover liabilities arising where the original insurer becomes insolvent. This would be equivalent to contingency insurance discussed in Chap. 9 above.

[78] S.10(2) of the Act defines war risks to mean and include risks arising from hostilities, rebellion, revolution and civil war, civil strife consequence on the happening of any of those events, or action taken (whether before or after the outbreak of any hostilities, rebellion, revolution or civil war) for repelling an imagined attack or preventing or hindering the carrying out of any attack, and includes piracy.

10.14.5 Power to Carry on Insurance Business During a War

Where there are no adequate insurance or reinsurance coverage for British ships, aircrafts and cargoes during a war in which the British government is involved, the Secretary of State[79] may assume the role of the insurer and reinsurer against all risks of:

(a) ships and aircraft (whether British or not), or
(b) cargoes carried in ships and aircraft; or
(c) goods consigned for carriage by sea or air while the goods are transit between the premises from which they are consigned and the ship or aircraft, or between the ship or aircraft and their destination.

However, except where exceptional reasons of defence of the realm or efficient prosecution of a war or hostilities in which the British government are involved, these powers extend to the Secretary duty to carry out these three simultaneous insurance and reinsurance functions only for war risks.

10.14.6 Power to Pay Compensation Under Provision for Transitional Compensation for Goods in Transit

The Secretary of State's liabilities may extend to paying compensation incurred by the insured before or after his involvement if there had been no adequate insurance or reinsurance cover under the following circumstances:

> **Secretary of State Act**
> 1. In the case of goods which have been consigned for carriage by sea or air from a place outside the UK, the Isle of Man or the Channel Islands to a place in one of those countries (goods in process of import), that the goods were:
>
> (a) were discharged in that country from the ship or aircraft before the expiration of the period of seven days beginning with such a day as the Secretary of State may declare to be the day from which he will, during the continuance of any war or hostilities in which the government is engaged, carry on the business of insurance of goods in transit;
>
> (b) after the beginning of that day and before the expiration of the appropriate period, lost or damaged in consequence of a war risk, being one which the Secretary of State was on that day prepared to insure under his general power of insuring goods in transit during such war or hostilities;
>
> (c) lost or damaged while in transit between the ship or aircraft and their destination;

[79] The Secretary of State is the sole judge to determine whether the cover provided is reasonable and adequate-*Point of Ayr Colliers Ltd v Lloyd-George* [1943]2 All AER546 CA.

2. in the case of goods which have been consigned for carriage by sea or air from a place in any one of the countries mentioned above to a place outside that country (goods in the process of export), that before the expiration of that period of seven days, after the beginning of the declared day, the goods were lost or damaged in consequence of such a war or risk while in transit between the premises from which they were consigned and the ship or aircraft;

3. Additional requisite conditions, applicable for both goods in the process of import and to goods in the process of export are that:

(a) the goods were not insured were not insured against the war risk in consequence of which they were lost or damaged;

(b) the claimant and his agents exercised all due diligence for securing that no delay occurred while the goods were in transit; and

(c) the property in the goods was vested in the claimant when the loss or damage occurred (insurable interest).

10.14.7 Amount of Transitional Compensation

Under the Act the Secretary of State is mandated to pay:

Secretary of State Act
(a) in the case of lost goods, their insurable value;

(b) in the case of damaged goods which have been delivered at their destination, an amount equal to such proportion of their insurable value as the difference between the gross sound and damaged values at the place of arrival bears to the gross sound value;

(c) in the case of damaged goods which have not been delivered, an amount equal to such proportion of their insurable value as the difference between the gross sound and damaged values at the place from which they were consigned bears to the gross sound value.

10.14.8 Payments in and Out Under the Marine and Aviation (War Risks) Fund Establish Under the Marine and Aviation (War Risks) Act 1952

These are payable under the Marine and Aviation Insurance (War Risks) Fund Account 2011–2012. This fund was established under Section 5 of the Marine and

Aviation Insurance (War … out of monies provided by Parliament, and that any excess over the amount likely claims under the 1952 Act would not fall to the Marine Aviation// Fund!?

Under the Act:

1952 Act

(i) all sums received by the Minister by virtue of the Act, stands to the credit of the war risks (marine) insurance fund established by the Secretary of State; and.

(ii) all sums required for the fulfilment by him of any of his obligations under the contract.

10.14.9 Reinsurance Against Acts of Terrorism

In almost an identical manner to powers provided by the Marine Insurance War Risks) Act for state insurance and reinsurance of ships, aircrafts and cargoes above, the Reinsurance (Acts of Terrorism) Act 1993 empowers the Treasury to reinsure acts of terrorism[80] under:

Reinsurance (Acts of Terrorism) Act 1993

(a) any reinsurance agreement entered into by an insured;

(b) any guarantee entered into pursuant to such agreement against:

(i) loss or damage to property in the UK resulting from or consequential on acts of terrorism; and

(ii) any loss which is consequential on such loss or damage.

These are detailed in paragraph 9.4 above.

10.15 P&I Clubs Policies and Other Private Sector Insurance

10.15.1 Introduction

Another source of export policy is the P&I Clubs. Protection and indemnity insurance, more commonly known as "P&I" insurance, is a form of mutual maritime insurance provided by a P&I Club. Whereas a marine insurance *company* provides

[80] S.2(2) of the Act defines "Acts of Terrorism" to mean acts of persons acting on behalf of or in connection with any [terrorist] organisation which carries out activities directed towards the overthrowing or influencing, by force or violence the UK or any other government de jure or defacto.

"hull and machinery" cover for shipowners, and cargo cover for cargo owners, a P&I Club provides cover for open-ended risks that traditional insurers are reluctant to insure. Typical P&I cover includes: a carrier's third-party risks for damage cause to cargo during carriage; war risks; and risks of environmental damage such as oil spills and pollution. In the UK, both traditional underwriters and P&I clubs are subject to the MIA 1906. P&I is now covered by s.85 of MIA 1906 thus:

> **85 Modification of Act in case of mutual insurance.**
> (1) Where two or more persons mutually agree to insure each other against marine losses there is said to be a mutual insurance.
>
> (2) The provisions of this Act relating to the premium do not apply to mutual insurance, but a guarantee, or such other arrangement as may be agreed upon, may be substituted for the premium.
>
> (3) The provisions of this Act, in so far as they may be modified by the agreement of the parties, may in the case of mutual insurance be modified by the terms of the policies issued by the association, or by the rules and regulations of the association.
>
> (4) Subject to the exceptions mentioned in this section, the provisions of this Act apply to a mutual insurance.

A P&I Club is a mutual insurance association that provides risk pooling, information and representation for its members. Unlike a marine insurance company, which reports to its shareholders, a P&I club reports only to its members. Originally, P&I Club members were typically ship-owners, ship-operators or demise charterers, but more recently freight forwarders and warehouse operators have been able to join.

10.15.2 P&I Cargo Liabilities

A very important part of the cover provided by the Club is that which relates to the liability of the shipowner under his contract of carriage to pay for any loss of or damage to cargo. Unless prior arrangements are made with the Club managers, this cover will be given on the basis that the shipowner's contract with the owner of the cargo is on terms at least as favourable to the shipowner as the provisions of The Hague or Hague-Visby Rules, that is to say the Brussels Convention of 1924 and its Protocol of 1968 and the Hamburg Rules of 1978. The cover extends beyond the sea leg of the carriage and thus will protect the shipowner throughout a combined transport contract from an inland point to another inland point, provided only that the sea leg is performed by an entered ship.

This part of the cover is extended beyond liabilities as such, in that the shipowner may recover from his Club any additional cost incurred by him in discharging or disposing of damaged cargo. Clubs' Rules impose restrictions on the cover in respect of deviation from the contract voyage (for example an unreasonable departure from the agreed itinerary or the shipment on deck of cargo with underdeck bills) and in respect of other departures from the proper carrying practice, such as the delivery of cargo without production to the master of the relevant bills of lading, or the issue of a "clean" bill of lading for cargo which is patently damaged.

10.15.3 Cargo's Proportion of General Average or Salvage Under the P&I

As an extension of their cover for loss of or damage to cargo, the Clubs again go beyond the insurance of liabilities as such by agreeing to pay to the shipowner any contributions to general average, special charges or salvage which the shipowner would have been able to recover from cargo interests had he not disentitled himself from so recovering by committing some breach of his contract of carriage.

10.16 Consequential Loss Insurance

Last, but not least, an FOB merchant who is still unsure, from the list of possibilities discussed above should take out or add consequential loss risks to the policy. This is a type of insurance giving cover in respect of a loss arising from destruction of a subject matter insured under, e.g. a fire policy and not recoverable under that policy on the grounds that it is too remote. A consequential loss FOB loss policy may cover:

13.1. Loss of profit of a business (economic loss);
13.2. standing charges, e.g. rent, rates and taxes, salaries, directors' fees, interest on loans and debentures etc, which all remain payable even though the subject-matter insured has been destroyed;
13.3. Increased cost of working, e.g. the additional expenditure incurred in keeping a business going during the period of reinstatement;
13.4. Increased cost of reinstatement caused by a rise in the price of materials or the cost of labour after the date of a fire; and
13.5. Business interruption insurance. (Use FOB Cases here)

There is an overlap between contingency insurance and consequential loss insurance, a fact that should be borne in mind by the merchant. An FOB merchant's choice, to take either or both covers, will depend on the terms and conditions of his contract. [check under google]

10.17 Miscellaneous Export Risks' Insurance

The above insurance possibilities are by no means conclusive as there are no limits to risks undertaken and tricks used by parties to protect themselves. It is almost impossible to foresee and legislative against all possible risks. A lot will depend on the nature of the contract and the parties' bargains. Other avenues are for example those cited by Sassoon in the opening quotation to this clause, where: "In order to overcome this undesirable situation, the seller therefore frequently inserts a provision in the contract, whereby the buyer undertakes to confirm his insurance before loading commences". Sassoon, in the same quoted text, also quotes incidences whereby: "Occasionally, the buyer agrees to hold the policy at the seller's disposal and to deposit it with him until the price has been paid". Such mechanisms relate to the sellers' and buyer's interest policies and are employed in the event of the seller's retention of title clauses to protect himself against non-payments for various reasons.

10.18 Cargo Policy Options

- **Open Covers**[81]
- **Blanket policies,**[82]
- **Floating policies,**[83]
- **Special cargo policy,**[84]
- **Etc.**

The common documentation in these would be bordereaux.[85] Parties who consider all these aspects should be adequately covered.

---

[81] Also known as, *open insurance policy*, a marine insurance policy covering more than one export shipment. The policyholder reports specific transactions weekly, monthly or quarterly on a declaration form supplied by the underwriter. Premiums are based on the information provided in the declaration forms. Exports not declared when shipped are covered if the insurance value is not exceeded.

[82] This is an insurance insuring several items. *A blanket policy* is written for a total sum up to the ceiling, without regard to the value of individual items covered by the policy. It is a type of open cover.

[83] This is a type of open and (normally) export insurance policy with a maximum pays out unrelated to the specific items insured. The coverage is not revised when the policyholder adds or deletes an item. *Floating policies* can, for example, be used to cover inventory, so long as the insured value remains constant.

[84] This is a cargo policy with a coverage limited to a specific shipment. Special cargo policies are available for infrequent shippers or extremely valuable cargoes. It would therefore suit a one-off or occasional FOB merchant.

[85] Documents used to export individual shipments covered by open insurance policy. An underwriter will frequently issue a blanket policy for shipments by a single policyholder. Open policies are written for large-volume exporters who make regular shipments. Bordereaux record the details of a given shipment.

10.19 State Restrictions of Export Trade Insurance

Export/import merchants need to be aware of restrictive state practices on shipping and insurance. Information on foreign restrictions on the free placement of shipping and cargo insurance would be available from any of the sources of export, shipping and insurance available to the merchant or failing that the local chamber of commerce and/or government departments. In the case of the UK this is the Department of Trade and Industry offices and/or websites. There are many reasons for restrictive practices. The practices can be part of the countries' general economic policies,[86] policies to promote shipping and the insurance industries[87] or fulfilment of the governments' sanctions[88] in aid of some international policy.

Although marine insurance services the international trading community and strives to operate to a free, competitive environment, there has been a growing list of countries attempting to inhibit this freedom of marine cargo insurance. The principal barriers to the free placement of cargo insurance take the form of restrictive insurance legislation or decree, discriminatory taxation or foreign exchange controls. The American Institute of Marine Underwriters (AIMU) publishes periodically for its Members a list, by country, of restrictive marine insurance practices.[89]

10.20 Other Incoterms Insurance Considerations

10.20.1 Incoterms and Commodity Standard Form Insurance

The above considerations may vary in commodities trades. With regard to commodities insurance for instance, Clause 20[90] of *Gafta Standard Contract Terms for Shipment of Feeding Stuffs in Bulk* (Tale Quale-CIF) provides all the insurance requirements, which are based on the common law and similar to Incoterms 2010, the UCP insurance Clause provides that:

> INSURACE -Sellers shall provide insurance on terms not less favourable than those set out hereunder, and as set out in detail in The Grain and Feed Trade Association Form. 72 viz: - then it continues to list: risks covered; war clauses (cargo); strikes, riots and civil commotion clauses (cargo); insurers; insurable value; freight contingency; certificates/policies; total loss; currency of claims; war and strikes risks/premiums; sellers'/buyers' settlements

[86] Also known as trade protectionism. Trade protectionism is a policy that protects domestic industries from unfair foreign competition. The four primary tools used in trade protectionism are tariffs, subsidies, quotas, and currency manipulation.

[87] See Ademuni-Odeke Protectionism and the future of International Shipping, Kluwer International Publishers 1990.

[88] See generally, Matthew Moran and Daniel Salisbury, "Sanctions and the Insurance Industry-Challenges and Opportunities", Centre for Science & Security Studies, Occasional Papers, September 2013 http://www.kcl.ac.uk/sspp/departments/warstudies/research/groups/csss/pubs/insurancereport.pdf.

[89] *For AIMU see* https://www.aimu.org/brochures.html.

[90] *Gafta Contract, Series No.100* (Effective 1st September 2010).

Clause 20 is in turn detailed in *Gafta's Standard General Standard Terms Insurance Clauses No.*72.[91] The insurance terms may however also vary for shipment of feeding stuffs in bulk under Tale Quale-CIF/CIFFO/C&FFO Terms[92] and shipment of vegetable and marine in bulk-CIF Delivered Weights of the Federation of Oils Seeds and Fats Associations Limited (FOSFA) International.[93]

10.21 Further Aspects of Overlooked Insurance

10.21.1 Pre-Mature Transfer of Risks Insurance

Another caution relates to premature transfer of risks. This too is not covered by Incoterms generally or the Insurance Clauses in particular. However, since coverage of risks of loss or damage to goods is the primary function of insurance, parties need to pay particular attention to their passage. Risks can pass after contracting, but before shipment, and/or on delivery-so called premature transfer of risks. In that case an extension to the Incoterms agreed insurance or an additional policy may be necessary. This policy extension would cover scenarios where risks pass anytime, through sellers' or buyers' fault, before delivery at shipment or destination. It also covers incidences where risk, such as late delivery or failure to nominate vessel, passes to the buyer due to his failure to perform a contractual obligation such as contracting with the carrier and insurer or to load.[94] One remedy for this, other than policy extension, is the use of "door to door" or "warehouse to warehouse" or "held covered" policy, prevalent in CIF and CIP contracts. The other rule where such a policy may be necessary is EXW.

Parties should also pay particular attention to pre-shipment risks on which both Incoterms and its insurance clauses are silent.

10.21.2 Pre-Shipment Insurance Risks

In practice risks in all contracts including Incoterms can and do pass pre-shipment: there are, therefore, elements of premature transfer of risks in pre-shipment insurance. Pre-shipment risk insurance covers the exporter's prime costs of an export transaction if production has to be stopped because an insured risk has occurred. Similar to post-shipment, it is part of export contingency insurance (below). It

---

[91] Ibid.

[92] Done under Clauses 181 and 18.2; for a sample copy of the contract see Appendix XIII in, *Sassoon, CIF and FOB Contracts*, Note 3, pp. 722–729 at 725–726.

[93] Clause 5; for a text thereof see, Sassoon, *CIF and FOB Contracts* Note 3, at pp. 730–733 at 730.

[94] For premature transfer of risks in Incoterms, see Jan Ramberg, *ICC Guide to Incoterms 2000*, ICC Pub.No.620 pp.61; for a treatment of the same subject in the earlier Incoterms 1990, see *Guide to Incoterms* 1990, ICC Pub.No.461/90, at p. 35.

focuses on political and foreign customer's del credere risks.[95] The insured amount can also include any cash paid in response to an unjustified call of the advance payment guarantee. This eradicates the need to take out additional contract bond insurance to cover aspects where of loss or damage occurs before or between the seller's premises and shipment and/or delivery.

At the other end of pre-shipment spectrum is post-shipment risks, which too are not covered by Incoterms and the respective Insurance Clauses.

10.21.3 Post-Shipment Insurance Risks Insurance

Like all export contracts, Incoterms shipments are exposed to post-shipment risks. Post-shipment policy protects the seller against the risk of an overseas buyer failing to pay for goods received on credit. Like pre-shipment insurance, it is also part of export contingency insurance (see post). The main source of post-shipment insurance are the private and public export credit agencies. It is intended to protect transactions with repayment terms not exceeding 12 months and mainly includes the supply of consumer goods, raw materials, semi-finished goods and spare parts. It can cover all post-shipment losses or damage despite passage of property to the buyer at the time. The policy is covered by specific export contingency insurance or general contingency insurance. The cost of these risks may be transferable to the buyer or built into the sellers' organization. Borderline costs which might be passed to the buyer are considered below. Either way, existence of both should would be undisclosed from the buyer, being part of sellers personal, non-contractual and additional insurance requirements below.

In addition to pre-mature passage of risks and pre- and post-shipment insurances, both parties need to cover their own additional insurance requirements. A novice merchant could be lured into false safety and overlook the necessity of own additional policy by the NO OBLIGATION to insure phrase in Clause B5.

10.22 Additional and Contingency Insurance Absent in Incoterms

10.22.1 Cover for Non-Contractual Obligations

Just as it provides for only the minimum cover, Incoterms insurance clauses are similarly not concerned with the parties' non-contractual obligations. However, these are essential practical matters which relate to parties' own insurance requirements and additional requirements such as war, strikes, civil commotion and labour disturbances where they are not covered by the available options in Clause A5.

---

[95] A risk covering the probability that a buyer who purchases through a buyer or a guarantor will be unable to fulfil his payment obligations. This is occurring because the agent functions as a surety in the event that the vendee fails to make the required payments.

These requirements, also excepted in clauses 4–7 of most cargo clauses, can be covered either by the CIP insurance clause (Clause A5) or extension policies for CIF and other rules (where applicable). Nevertheless, although their provision become contractual and obligatory once agreed by the parties, these extensions are nonetheless at the buyer's request, risks and expense. Furthermore, outside of Incoterms insurance obligations, the seller should take care of his additional insurance needs to cover such risks as rejection by the buyer, buyer's insolvency, buyer's bank insolvency, state interventions, sanctions, embargoes, force majeure and other restrictive trade practices not covered by post-shipment insurance.

There are two further features to the considerations: those relating to extras anticipated in Clause A5 of the CIF and CIP rules and those resulting from trade restrictions external to the provision. The buyer should, likewise, take care of his corresponding insurance needs. These corresponding needs can be covered by some, most or all covered by additional insurances listed below.

10.23 Sellers' Additional Contingency and Own Insurance

10.23.1 Sellers' Interests Insurance

One aspect of the sellers' own and/or additional requirement not covered by Incoterms-the so-called sellers' interest insurance. This insurance policy permits the seller to arrange for insurance cover (known as Contingency Cover/Seller's Interests Insurance) for goods whose risks may have already been transferred to the buyer. Examples include post-shipment above, seller's Agriculture and Food Export interest and other types of contingency insurance. These, in turn, fall under the export contingency insurance.

10.23.2 Export Contingency Insurance

The second aspect of the seller's additional requirement is the export contingency insurance. This insurance covers policies that do not normally fall naturally into one of the principal classes of export insurance. This protection, therefore, also forms part of the sellers' interest insurance. It is a secondary marine cargo insurance cover used when a seller ships goods under terms such as FOB where the insurance for the cargo is buyer's responsibility. It comes into effect when the importer either did not arrange insurance at all or only insufficient protection against all the possible losses. It is normally provided by export credit insurance and covers all possible contingencies such as political risks not covered by contractual insurance such as buyers and buyers bank insolvencies.

10.23.3 Buyers' Insolvency Risk Insurance

The third aspect not covered is, therefore, buyer's insolvency insurance. As a contingency insurance, the primary function of buyer's insolvency insurance, provided under export trade credit insurance, is to protect sellers against buyers that do not or cannot pay. Also, part of the export contingency policy above, it insures against a buyer that has declared bankruptcy, insolvency or a similar legal status, as well as protecting insured sellers against buyers who delay payments such as under a bankruptcy protection arrangement. he insolvency insurance covers both the buyer and the buyer's bank: buyers' bank insolvency insurance.

10.23.4 Buyers' Bank Insolvency

The fourth aspect, a subset of buyers' insolvency insurance above, buyers' bank insolvency insurance can be either an extension of the buyer's insolvency or a free-standing cover. It is part or continuation of buyers' risks covered under for instance the UK Export Finance (UKEF)[96] s Comprehensive Short-term Guarantees. The Comprehensive Short-Term Guarantee normally covers the whole of the policy-holder's export turnover for a minimum period of a year. In some cases, the UKEF will accept business on a range of markets selected by the policyholder. This normally includes buyer's insolvency, buyer's failure to pay within 6 months after the due date for goods accepted, buyer's failure or refusal to accept goods despatched that comply with the contract. Export Credit systems exist in the EU, OECD and other major trading nations.[97]

10.23.5 Duty to Deliver the Goods

It is the duty of the seller to deliver the goods and the buyer to pay for them and accept them, as per the terms of the contract, SOGA 1979 and the general law on sales in all jurisdictions. The delivery of goods and payment of the price are concurrent conditions as per the law on sales unless the parties agree otherwise. Under A1The seller must provide the goods and the commercial invoice in conformity with the contract of sale and any other evidence of conformity that may be required by the contract. Any document to be provided by the seller may be in paper or electronic form as agreed or, where there is no agreement, as is customary.

[96] This replaced the former Export Credit Guarantee Department (ECGD).

[97] For a list of the Export Credit Agencies in major trading nations see: https://www.oecd.org/mena/competitiveness/ismed-export-credit-agencies.htm (accessed on 20/06/2020).

10.23.6 Duty to Pay: Sellers Remedies

In return to the sellers' duty to deliver the goods and accompanying documents, there is a corresponding buyers' duty to pay under all contractual statutory and non-statutory laws. Under Clause B1 for instance the Incoterms buyer must pay the price of the goods as provided in the contract of sale. Any document to be provided by the buyer may be in paper or electronic form as agreed or where there is no agreement, as is customary. Other than Incoterms is not concerned with the details of the payments for and financing of international sales.

10.23.7 Rights of Unpaid Seller Against Buyer

In normal domestic contracts, the rights of unpaid sellers include:

(a) Suit for Price;
(b) Suit for Damages for Non-Acceptance;
(c) Repudiation of Contract before Due Date; and
(d) Suit for Interest.

However, being predominantly externally oriented, not all the above remedies are available to the unpaid seller. It is for those reasons that most of these contracts are based on letters of credit and other payment guarantee systems.

10.24 Buyers' Additional Contingency and Own Insurance

10.24.1 Buyers Corresponding Interest Insurance

Some of the seller's concerns under Sellers" own and additional insurance above apply to the buyer too. Further risks are covered below.

10.24.2 Sellers' Failure to Deliver

The corresponding sellers' requirements (above) apply at this juncture too. These include seller's total failure to deliver. The contingency policy would cover the buyer who makes losses above cost and profit margin in mitigation by buying replacements expensively in such eventualities. *SGA* 1979 s. 51(1) stated damages for non-delivery, "where the seller wrongfully neglects or refuses to deliver the goods to the buyer, the buyer may maintain an action against the seller for damages for non-delivery". Where the seller fails to deliver, the buyer is entitled to: Damages of Non-Delivery; Suit for Specific Performance; Suit for Breach of Warranty; and Repudiation of Contract.

10.24.3 Sellers' Late Delivery

Late delivery of export goods means their arrival later than contracted for. In that case there are options open to the buyer. If he has an automatic right to reject then he may do so. Depending on the circumstances, he may decide to take delivery and sue for late delivery if the goods are unique or non-available in the market at all or at such short notice. If the buyer doesn't have an automatic right to end the contract, then he will have no choice but take delivery and sue for damages for late delivery and for any loss or damage incurred therein. For those reasons the buyer may wish to cover his loss from the insurers if that risk was covered in the policy or take out an additional or specialist policy to cover such eventualities. Where he recovers his insurers will of course have subrogation rights to sue the carrier or anyone else responsible for the late delivery.

10.24.4 Sellers' Short Deliveries

A delivery of goods that has fewer items than invoiced or a smaller total weight than invoiced. It may also be an attempt by the seller to make an extra profit, in which case the buyer would be well advised to make a claim for short delivery.

A short shipment is when cargo is listed on a shipping list but not included in a shipment, or not. Short shipment can be reported by the recipient if some of the goods disappear in transit, such as by theft or loss, problems due to paperwork not matching up with the actual delivery, and need to be manually corrected.

There may be reasons why a delivery of goods that has fewer items than invoiced or a smaller total weight than invoiced. It may also be an attempt by the seller to make an extra profit, in which case the buyer would be well advised to make a claim for short delivery.

Alternatively, the seller may just make late or short delivery of the contract goods. Parallel to the above, this policy would cover losses incurred therefrom and costs of mitigations losses, as above. On the other hand, the risk of loss may be due to the carrier rather than the seller's fault.

10.24.5 Shippers' Cargo Policy

This facility is available to an Incoterm buyer or assignee who is not the shipper. While a regular cargo policy is issued to sellers and buyers for particular goods and/or merchandise incidental to their export-import business, shipper's cargo interest is a policy designed by cargo policy underwriters taking into account that a freight forwarder will transport an incalculable variety of commodities. In addition to the seller-shipper such as in CIF and CIP rules, an FOB buyer-shipper among the remaining 9 rules as well as consignees, buyers afloat and other transferees in a chain contract can avail themselves of this cover. However, cargo clauses normally restrict third party benefits to this policy under the "Not to Inure Clause".[98]

10.24.6 Damage from Stranding and Loss of Ship

An Incoterm buyer who has paid and is in receipt of the shipping and insurance documents, and to whom risks and property have passed and is, therefore, unable to recover from the seller can sue the carrier in negligence subject to exceptions therein. This is possible under Shipowners Liability Cover (SOLC) or Shipowners Liability Cover to Cargo (SOLCC) policy, in addition to the buyer's general average recovery where applicable, which would include the costs of salvage and transhipment where appropriate. SOLC or SOLCC are is, therefore, a common policy term used to describe the insurance arranged to cover a carrier's liabilities arising from a breach of contract of carriage, where such a breach deprives the carrier of the right to rely on defences or rights of limitation which would otherwise have been (see post).

10.24.7 Purchasers Interest Policy

Also known as the buyer's interest policy, this policy both resembles and differs from the seller's interest policy above-being the exact opposite. This policy operates in almost the same way as the seller's interest insurance above but in reverse. These are not specifically covered by Incoterms insurance provisions but by general cargo insurance principles. An experienced importer would be aware of this while novices should be advised through their brokers, insurers and even their carriers and financiers.

10.24.8 Effect of "Stoppage in Transit" on Policy

Meaning of stoppage in transit in English the legal right of a seller of goods to stop the sale at any time before the buyer receives them, especially in situations where it becomes clear that the buyer cannot pay for the goods: He may still be able to recover the goods by exercising his right of stoppage in transit//Right of Stoppage in Transit. The right of stoppage in transit means that an unpaid seller has the right to stop the goods while they are in transit, regain possession, and retain them till he receives the full price. Goods are deemed to be in course of transit from the time when they are delivered to a carrier or other bailee for the purpose of transmission to the buyer, until the buyer or his agent in that behalf takes delivery of them from such carrier or other bailee.

---

[98] A clause, in a policy, which prohibits the extension of benefit of the insurance to a bailee, or other party who has care of the insured goods.

10.24.9 Effect of Reservation of Title Clauses

Retention of title is a security right by which it is contractually stipulated that ownership does not transfer until the third-party acquirer has paid the agreed upon sum in full. In other words, the buyer will only acquire the good following a payment in full. The purpose of a retention of title clause is to offer an opportunity for the seller of the goods to retain the title in them until the buyer has paid the price in full. Also known as the *Romalpa Clause*,[99] the clause protects the seller if the buyer becomes insolvent, as the seller is able to retake possession of the goods or proceeds of the sale of the goods if they have already been on-sold by the buyer.

10.25 Alternative and Additional Insurance Recourse

10.25.1 Benefits of Shipowners/Carriers' Liability Insurance

The final aspect is for both parties to avail themselves of the shipowner and/or carriers' insurance. This option forms part of the shipper's cargo policy discussed earlier. It provides relief for the seller who is also the shipper and who has not transferred shipping and insurance documents to claim under the carrier's liability insurance. The distinction with the damage from stranding above is that the former applies to consignee-buyer who is not the shipper. This is because, with certain exceptions, carriers are liable for the shipments that they convey under the carrier's liability policy. Otherwise, cover is provided by the SOLC/SOLCC insurance covering carrier's liabilities arising from a breach of contract of carriage, where such a breach deprives the carrier of the right to rely on defences or rights of limitation which would otherwise have been. In the CIF, CIP and Extended FOB rules providing for insurance, sellers or buyer-beneficiary of the policy can sue under this policy for loss or damage both in contract and torts. Incoterm insured sellers and buyers can therefore avail themselves of this insurance facility.

10.25.2 Business Interruption Insurance[100]

Business Interruption Insurance is covered earlier. This is yet another alternative source of cover to Incoterm merchants. Sellers and buyers, whether trading under Incoterms or not, can as business concerns, avail themselves of Business Interruption Insurance. This is insurance coverage replaces income lost in the event that business is halted for some reason, such as a fire or a natural disaster. Losses under the

[99] Deriving its name from the *Romalpa Case: Aluminium Industrie Vaassen BV v Romalpa Aluminium Ltd* [1976] 1 WLR 676 is a UK insolvency law case, concerning a quasi-security interest in a company's assets.

[100] Profits, Fixed Costs, Temporary Relocation, Commission and Training Costs and Extra Expenses.

current COVID-19 (2019-2020) would be the best example. This type of insurance also covers operating expenses, a move to a temporary location, if necessary, payroll, taxes, and loan payments. It is noteworthy that this is a general business rather than purely export-import related insurance policy. However, their costs can be factored into the export-import pricing by either party.

10.25.3 Other State supported Insurances

Other state supported facilities are available to Incoterms merchants too. So, Incoterm sellers and buyers can also avail themselves of other state and other publicly-supported insurance in addition to state and private sector export credit agencies. The former would cover insurance of special war, piracy, terrorism, etc, in addition to and/or above those available in the private sector. In addition to the above contractual and extra-contractual (additional insurance) requirements, to which parties may have some control and/or influence, all exporters and importers regardless of the rule should also be aware of external factors (below) that might affect their insurance obligations but over which they have no controls/and or influence. Incoterms exporters and importers are not immune to this.

10.26 Harmonization with International Trade Practices

10.26.1 Importance of Carriage Contracts on Insurance Clauses

Although all Incoterms rules refer to carriers and Incoterms parties' insurance contracts as alternative source of insurance cover, they are rather sketchy. SOLC/SOLCC benefits being one of those. Unani,[101] for instance, cautions that the rules (including Incoterms 2020) do not deal with those matters in details. Furthermore, he points out that the rules only indicate which party (seller or buyer) organises carriage and/or insurance of the goods. Besides, Incoterm rules do not bind the carrier or his insurer Accordingly, parties may need to make separate contracts for carriage and insurance for five reasons namely:

(a) because the binding effect of the contracts are between only contracting parties;
(b) the carrier is only bound to issue transport documents as required by the contract of carriage it makes with the other party to that contract but is not bound to issue a transport document complying with the Incoterms rules;
(c) the insurer is bound to issue a policy to the level and in the terms agreed with the party purchasing the insurance but not a policy which complies with Incoterm rules;

[101] Prof.Dr.Ahmet Samim Unan, "Incoterms 2020 and Insurance", in Incoterms 2020 Mena Regional Launch Summit, Istanbul, 5 December.

(d) where the contract is to be financed by letters of credit, this could cause problems in relation to the requirements of Art 28 of the UCP 600 on insurance documents to be tendered; and finally
(e) Incoterms do not concern themselves with losses arising from external factors such as sanctions, embargoes and other force majeures (see post).

Both Incoterms and their respective insurance clauses have been affected by insurance practices of commodity trade and respective insurance clauses when using CIF and FOB standard terms. This is more so in GAFTA contracts.

10.26.2 Comparisons with Commodity Trade Insurance Clauses

10.26.2.1 The Feed and Grain Trade Association(GAFTA) Contracts

Examples of GAFTA will be used to demonstrate this practice being the largest of the International Commodity Trade Organisations. GAFTA GAFTA Contracts, such as GAFTA Contract No.72, with the relevant extracts below below, provide insurance coverage for goods for both FOB and CIF related contracts during transit attaching from the point of departure and continuing until delivery with special clauses outlining coverage and exclusions.

10.26.2.2 For Contracts Concluded on CIF/CIFFO[102] Terms

Commodity trade do use modified CIF and FOB contracts with their own standard term insurance clauses. Although these have no relation to the official ICC Incoterms, they are nevertheless compulsory to and binding on parties who are members of the particular Commodity Trade Association. This can be confusing as it creates two tiers: for those trading on the official Incoterms and others on alternative trade terms. That, notwithstanding for the Grain and Feed Trade Association (GAFTA) and the Federation of Oils, Seeds and Fats Associations (FOSFA International) (FOSFA International) members, for instance, the underlying sales' contracts are executed in conjunction, with GAFTA Insurance Terms No.72, Clause 13 of which provides the following terms for sellers and buyers:

[102] CIFFO means Cost Insurance and Freight Free Out (FO). This is a variation of the CIF contract term peculiar to the commodity trade in international shipping term and in ocean freight industry that indicates that the buyer (consignee or recipient) is responsible for the cost of unloading cargo from the vessel at the destination. CF. Cost Insurance and Freight Free in and Out (CIFFIO) another variation where the carrier is NOT responsible for the cost of loading and unloading gods onto/from the vessel.

10.26.2.3 CIF/CIFFO Sellers Insurance Obligations

For Contracts Concluded on CIF/CIFFO[103] terms, sellers shall provide insurance on terms not less favourable than those set out hereunder, and as set out in detail in *GAFTA Insurance Terms No.72*, covering:

GAFTA Insurance Terms No.72

(a) Risks Covered:

Cargo Clauses (WA) payable, with 3% franchise or better terms,[104]

War Clauses (Cargo)[105] and

Strikes, Riots and Civil Commotions Clauses (Cargo)[106] risks;

(b) Underwriters- Should be "first class" [107];

(c) Insurable value is 102% [108];

(d) Includes freight contingency of 102% [109];

(e) Includes sellers serving all policies and/or certificates and/or letters of insurance[110];

(f) Total loss of 102% claimable by the seller, buyer or consignees[111];

(g) Claims to be paid in the currency of the contract[112]; and

(h) War and Strike Risks Premiums in excess of 0.50% to be for account of Buyers.[113]

---

[103] Ibid.

[104] Clause 13.1(a); Section 2 of Form 72; "franchise" appears in Clause 28 UCP 600, not in Clause A5 of CIF-CIP//.

[105] Ibid. Clause 13.1(a); Section 4 of Form 72; these are optional upon buyer's request and expenses in Clause A5 of CIF-CIP.
Clause 13.1(a); Section 5 of Form 72; also, optional as above.

[106] Clause 13.1(a); Section 5 of Form 72; also, optional as above.

[107] Clause 13.1(b); rather than "insurance companies of good repute" as in Clause A5 of CIF-CIP.

[108] Clause 13.1(c); this is comparable to the 110% in Clause A5 of CIF-CIP.

[109] Clause 13.1(d); same as above but not clear of the difference between the "insurable" and "freight contingency".

[110] Clause 13.1(e); although omitting mention of "the policy", this tallies with the expansion of alternatives documents in Clause A5 of CIF-CIP and Clause 28(a) of the UCP 600//.

[111] Clause 13.1(f); cf. paragraph (c) and (d) above.

[112] Clause 13.1(g); the currency requirements tally with those of Clause A5 of CIF-CIP and Clause 28 of the UCP 600.

[113] Clause 13.1(h); implies that strikes risks, where provided, should not exceed 0.5%; see also paragraph (a)/Note 72 above.

10.26.2.4 CIF/CIFFO Buyers Obligations

For buyers for Contracts Concluded on C&F/C&FFO terms, clause 13.2 provides that:

> Buyers shall be responsible for obtaining insurance cover as per Clause 13.1 above and shall, if required by Sellers, provide evidence to Sellers prior to the commencement of loading that they have obtained suitable cover. If Buyers refuse or fail to provide evidence Sellers are entitled (but not obliged) to cover insurance on the same terms at the Buyers' expense.

10.26.2.5 For Contracts Concluded on FOB

10.26.2.5.1 Buyer's Insurance Obligations

GAFTA does not have standard insurance terms for FOB, equivalent to the GAFTA Insurance Terms No.72 for CIF above. For FOB contracts, this is instead effected through, for example under Clause 9 of the Contract for the delivery of goods Central and Eastern Europe in Bulk or Bags Terms,[114] which provides that:

> Marine and war risk insurance including strikes, riots, civil commotions and mine risks to be effected by Buyers with first class underwriters and/or approved companies. Buyers shall supply Sellers with confirmation thereof at least 5 consecutive days prior to expected readiness of vessel(s). If Buyers fail to provide such confirmation, Sellers shall have the right to place such insurance at Buyers' risk and expense (emphasis provided)

First, reference to "first class" underwriters are in contrast to the use of: "insurance companies of good repute" in Clause A5 of both CIF and CIP official Incoterms rules. Secondly, the former can be confusing as it might suggest different levels of marine cargo underwriters. For those reasons, use of the latter is preferable as it reflects the underwriters' historical ability to honour undertakings rather than its class in the insurance pecking order.

10.26.2.5.2 Seller's Insurance Obligations

There is no equivalent provision for FOB sellers as they have no insurance obligations either at common law or official ICC Incoterms or commodity trade contracts. The educated advice would use the sellers' interest insurance and other facilities discussed in paragraph 10 above.

Finally, although insurance Clauses A5/B5 in CIF and CIP rules refer to provision of insurance policy and/or evidence, they do not detail the tender process. Instead, it is covered under another ICC publication.

---

[114] Contract No.49, Clause 9, Effective 1st April 2012.

10.26.3 The Federation of Oils, Seeds and Fats Associations (FOSFA) Contracts

10.26.3.1 General

The Federation of Oils, Seeds and Fats Associations Ltd (FOSFA) is a professional international contract issuing and arbitral body concerned exclusively with the world trade in oilseeds, oils and fats with 1180 members in 87 countries. After GAFTA, FOSFA is the second largest food commodity trade association. FOSFA has a long list of contracts for all the major producing countries and regions. They all include the CIF and FOB options and all use the Institute Cargo Clauses

10.26.3.2 FOSFA CIF Contract

The FOSFA CIF Contract is No.13 (CONTRACT FOR SESAMESEED IN BAGS) Revised and Effective from 1st February 2015.

10.26.3.2.1 Insurance Clauses

Contract No.13 contains clause 6 governing insurance and providing that:

> **6. Insurance and War Risks Insurance:**
> *(a) Insurance:
>
> Insurance in accordance with the Institute/FOSFA Trades Clauses (B) and the Institute War and Strikes Clauses (FOSFA Trades) to be effected with,
>
> at Sellers' option, first class underwriters and/or companies who are domiciled in the UK or for the purpose of any legal proceedings accept a British
>
> domicile and provide an address for service of process in London but for whose solvency the Sellers shall not be responsible. Claims to be payable
>
> in the currency of the contract. Policies and/or Certificates and/or Letters of Insurance required under this contract shall be for not less than 5% over
>
> the invoice amount including freight. Buyers shall accept insurance including Exclusion Clauses on the FOSFA Insurance Exclusion Clause List.
>
> War risks insurance:
>
> War risks insurance shall be effected on the terms and conditions in force and approved at the time of shipment by the Institute of London Underwriters (Institute War Clauses [FOSFA Trades]). Any expense for covering war risks insurance in excess of ½ % shall be for account of Buyers. The rate of insurance shall not exceed the rate ruling in London at the time of shipment or date of ship's sailing whichever may be adopted by underwriters. Notice of extra expense to be borne by Buyers shall be given by Sellers at the time of declaration under this contract or not later than 3 business days after the rate has been agreed with underwriters whichever is the later. Failure to give such notice shall invalidate the Sellers' claim unless in the opinion of arbitrators the delay is justifiable.

*(b) Insurance shall be effected with companies and/or underwriters of good repute (but for whose solvency the Sellers shall not be responsible) at the price of this contract plus 5% in accordance with the Institute/FOSFA Trades Clauses (B)/(C). Claims to be payable in the currency of the contract. The Sellers shall also insure the goods against *war, *strikes, *riots and *civil commotions risks in accordance with the Institute War and Strikes Clauses (FOSFA Trades). The Buyers may request the Sellers to pass on the name of the underwriters and the conditions of the insurance policy/ies or certificate/s. Any excess of the rate of ½ % for war and strikes insurance shall be for Buyers' account. The rate of insurance not to exceed the rate in force on the date of the Bill of Lading or the date of departure of the ship, whichever may be adopted by underwriters. Any excess of the rate shall be advised to Buyers at time of declaration, or not later than 3 business days after the rate has been agreed with the underwriters, whichever may be the later, and to be paid upon presentation of the documents.

Unless specifically agreed otherwise, clause (a) shall apply.

10.26.3.3 FOSFA FOB Contract

10.26.3.3.1 Insurance Clause

As would be expected the insurance clause (Clause 17 of Contract No.4) is short and simple and provides that;

> 17. INSURANCE: Buyers to cover insurance with first class underwriters on customary conditions. Current Institute Strikes, Riots and Civil Commotions Clauses shall be deemed to form part of this insurance. War risks insurance to be covered by Buyers. Insurance to be confirmed to Sellers prior to expected readiness of ship.

This because, like in all FOB contracts, it is not the sellers' obligations to provide insurance for the buyer. So, the buyer provides own insurance especially they wish to resale the goods either afloat or on arrival.

The current FOSFA FOB Contract is Contract No.4 (CONTRACT FOR SESAMESEED IN BAGS) Revised and Effective from 1st January 2015.

Other than the CIF and FOB contracts, FOSFA is not known to offer contracts on any of the remaining 9 Incoterms rules.

10.27 Comparison with Other Commodity Trade Contracts

Other trade associations have similar contracts to GAFTA and FOSFA in having both CIF and FOB contracts and identical insurance cargo clauses. Of the rest, the lading 4 are;

10.27.1 The Gas Trade

The Gas Trade Standard Term Contract comes in two parts and a User Guide namely:

(i) A Gas Supply Agreement in which the parties specify the variable terms of trade;
(ii) A schedule of the standard, non-variable terms of trade; and
(iii) Gas Contract User Guide.

10.27.2 Oil Trade

10.27.2.1 The Sales Contracts

An example of the Oil Trade Contracts is the General TERMS and Conditions of Sale of Crude Oil and Oil Products EDITION JANUARY 2007used mainly by:

(i) Shell Nederland Raffinaderij B.V,
(ii) Shell Deutschland Oil GmbH; and
(iii) Shell Trading Rotterdam B.V).

10.27.2.2 References to Incoterms

The general contract is arranged as follows:

- II General Terms and Conditions for Sale Special Provisions for FOB/FCA sales
- III General Terms and Conditions for Sale Special Provisions for CFR/CPT, CIF/CIP sales
- IV General Terms and Conditions for Sale Special Provisions for DDU, DDP, DAF, DES sales

Reference to Incoterms is made Definitions (Clause 2) as follows:

Clause 2

2.19 "Incoterms 2000" means Incoterms 2000 as published by the International Chamber of Commerce, as amended from time to time.

2.20 "FCA", "FOB", "CFR", "CIF", "CPT", "CIP", "DAF", "DES", "DDU", "DDP", shall have the meaning in accordance with Incoterms 2000, except as modified by these General Terms and Conditions. If there is any conflict between Incoterms 2000 and these General Terms and Conditions, these General Terms and Conditions shall prevail.

2.21 "Delivered" means the group D terms DDU and DDP of Incoterms 2000, except as modified by these General Terms and Conditions. If there is any conflict between Incoterms and these General Terms and Conditions, these Conditions shall prevail

Reference to "Incoterms 2000" should now refer to "Incoterms 2020". Of those contracts only the "DES", ''DAF" and "DES" no longer exist since Incoterms 2010.

10.27.2.3 Insurance Clauses

Only Part (III (2)), Special Provisions for CFR/CPT, CIF/CIP sales, contain insurance provisions, namely that:

> **2. Insurance**
> 2.1 In case of a CIF or CIP sale, Seller shall procure insurance of the oil by an insurance company of first class international standing for the benefit of Buyer, for 110 percent of the CIF/CIP value of the oil, which shall cover the period from the time when the risk passes to Buyer until delivery of the oil at destination and shall be covered by the same terms and conditions as a standard Lloyd's Marine Insurance Policy MAR with Institute Cargo Clauses (A), Institute War Clauses (Cargo) and Institute Strikes Clauses (Cargo) attached.
>
> 2.2 Claims for leakage and/or shortage shall be subject to a deductible of one half percent which figure shall be deemed to include ordinary loss.
>
> 2.3 Seller will provide to Buyer the insurance policy or if not available in time a copy thereof before discharge of the barge. In case this policy is not available before discharge any demurrage incurred as a result, thereof will be for account of Seller.

Once again, as in all other Incoterms rules, the seller provides insurance only in the CIF and CIP contracts. The buyer takes care of insurance needs in all the remaining 9 Incoterms rules.

10.27.3 Coal Trade

Using the Coal Trade Master Contract.

10.27.4 The Metals Trade

There are numerous metal trade standard term contracts but the leading 3 are:

(i) The Gold and Silver Trade

Using the:

- Gold and Silver Futures Contracts, and the
- London Metal Exchange (LME) Contracts

(ii) The Tin Trade

Using the Tin Futures Contract

(iii) The Copper Trade

Using the Copper Futures Contract.

Apart from few differences to accommodate particular trade customs, they all use either CIF or FOB contracts with insurance terms based on those of the cargo clauses.

10.28 External Considerations Affececting Insurance Obligations

10.28.1 Effect of Trade Barriers On the Parties' Insurance Obligations

10.28.1.1 Trade Restrictions and Practices

Parties should be aware of trade two aspects of external factors: protectionism and trade restrictions on their policy. Although they may have the same effect, they are nevertheless different. Trade protectionism is the result of governments acting to save certain sectors of their economies from foreign competition. Protectionist policies have also been directed by developed countries against each other, but this is usually carefully negotiated to avoid retaliation.

Trade restrictions, on the other hand, are typically undertaken in an effort to protect companies and workers in the home economy from competition by foreign firms. Whereas a protectionist policy is one in which a country restricts the importation of goods and services produced in foreign countries. Because of the strong link with foreign trade, marine cargo insurance and shipping tend to be the favourite targets for these.

Intended for saving and/or earnings of foreign currency, the development of indigenous industry and provision of employment related practices range from directives on insuring with national insurance companies to the manipulations of CIF and FOB contract shipments; use of cargo preferences, cargo reservations and flag discriminations; cabotage policies and maritime subsidies.

10.28.2 Incoterms and Trade Barriers

Thus, in additions to "What Incoterms Do and Do not Do", are above external trade policy considerations which can affect parties' choices of which Incoterm rule to use. Sassoon details how, for instance, governments have manipulated the differences between the CIF and FOB contracts to achieve national trade and economic objectives. Export-Import merchants including those applying Incoterms, therefore, need to be aware of those state restrictive practices on exports, shipping and cargo insurance. They are not covered by either Incoterms or the respective insurance clauses. Information on foreign restrictions on the free placement of shipping and cargo insurance would be available from any of the export, shipping and insurance sources available to the parties and, failing that then from local chambers of commerce and relevant government departments.

10.28.3 Manipulations of FOB and CIF for Protectionism

In the case of the UK, this is the Department of Trade and Industry offices or websites. There are many reasons for such restrictive practices. Incoterm merchants should, therefore, be aware that in many countries buyers and sellers may be compelled to take out insurance in their own country—either to minimise expenditures in foreign currencies and to support the domestic insurance industry. In those cases, a buyer may be ordered to contract for imports on FOB and related terms instead of letting the seller arrange for insurance on CIF, CIP and CPT terms. Conversely, a seller in these countries may be obliged to sell their goods on CIF and CIP terms for the same reasons. The practices can be part of the countries' general economic policies, policies to promote shipping and the insurance industries or fulfilment of the governments' sanctions in aid of some international policy. They form part of the broad state or government interventions and shipping trade restrictive practices in marine insurance and maritime transport.

10.29 State Intervention and Other Restrictive Policies

To emphasize, trade policy considerations include state interventions and restrictive trade practices also sometimes known as protectionism. As noted by Sassoon above limitations such as state regulation of or restriction might include not just the interplay between CIF-CIP and FOB rules but also the shipping cargo insurance market itself. Although marine insurance services international trading community and strives to operate to a free, competitive environment, there has been a growing list of countries attempting to inhibit this freedom of cargo insurance. The principal barriers to free placement of cargo insurance take the form of restrictive insurance legislation or decree, discriminatory taxation or foreign exchange controls. The International Unions of Marine Underwriters (IUMU), the American Institute of Marine Underwriters (AIMU) and the American trade Commission, publish periodically for its Members' a list, by country, of such restrictive marine insurance practices.[115]

[115] Marine Insurance Restrictions (in the U.S. and in Foreign Countries) Restrictive Laws / Regulations (In United States and in Foreign Countries)- https://aimu.org/marineinsurancerestrictions.html (accessed 21/01/2022).

The ICC has been aware of these[116] restrictive practices affecting Incoterms insurance in earlier revision of the rules over 40 decades ago where it both advocated awareness thereof and advised that, directly or indirectly, government authorities may guide or even instruct parties in their country to sell on CIF rules and to buy on FOB or FCA rules' terms. There are several reasons for the said state practices.

First, because trade terms constitute an important tool for directing the flow of goods to national shipping lines or other carriers. They can also be used to promote the domestic insurance market. Secondly, it is possible to save foreign currency. A seller who has undertaken to pay for carriage and insurance will increase these costs in his price for the goods and thereby obtain more foreign currency. On the other hand, a buyer who has assumed these costs will pay less for the goods, and may sometimes be able to pay for transportation and insurance services in domestic currency. For those reasons Incoterms 2020 cautions with regard to CIF/CIP insurance that "The seller must also contract for insurance cover against the, buyer's risk of loss of or damage to the goods from the point of delivery to at least the point of destination. This may cause difficulty where the destination country requires insurance cover to be purchased locally: in this case the parties should consider selling and buying under CPT".[117]

10.30 Effect of Sanctions, Embragoes and Force Majeures on Insurance Obligations

10.30.1 Effects of Sanctions on the Policy

Users of Incoterms contracts generally and of CIF and CIP insurance clauses in particular should also be aware of the likely effect of external factors such as sanctions, embargoes and other force majeures on the underlying export sales' contract. Unlike protectionism and restrictive practices, international sanctions are political and economic decisions that are part of diplomatic efforts by countries, multilateral or regional organizations against states or organizations either to protect national security interests, or to protect international law, and defend against threats to international peace.

Unlike protectionism, restrictive practices and sanctions, an embargo is a tool of economic warfare that may be employed for a variety of political purposes, including demonstrating resolve, sending a political signal, retaliating for another country's actions, compelling a country to change its behaviour, deterring it from engaging in undesired activities, and weakening its economy. Trade embargoes forbid trade with another country. The embargo is the harshest type of trade barrier and is usually enacted for political purposes to hurt a country economically.

The differences between these state interventions, not withstanding, their cumulative effects can have catastrophic consequences on sellers' and buyers' contractual

---

[116] Explanatory Notes for Users, Incoterms 2020, para 4 (Insurance) pp. 51–53 at.52.

[117] Ibid.

obligations generally and insurance liabilities in particular. This might affect not only the insurance clause itself but also the fact that where the underlying sales' contract is terminated, for any or all of the above reasons, then the task falls on insurance to indemnify the affected parties.[118] Thus, a reputable insured should seek advice from their brokers, insurers, carriers, government departments, local chamber of commerce, freight forwarders or financiers who should normally be up-to-date with economic intelligence on these issues.

Few insurers do, but not most do not, provide cover for additional premium. So, both parties should be aware of the presence of a sanctions regulation clause (below) in the policy excluding liability for loss or damage resulting from the risk.

10.30.2 Example of a Sanctions' Regulation Clause

Clause 7.10 of Zurich Marine Cargo Policy (Australia) provides that:

> **7.10 Sanctions Regulation**
> Notwithstanding any other terms or conditions under this policy, Zurich shall not be deemed to provide coverage and will not make any payments nor provide any service or benefit to any insured or any other party to the extent that such cover, payment, service, benefit and/or any business or activity of the insured would violate any applicable trade or economic sanctions, law or regulation[119]

Clause 7 (C) (ADDITIONAL CONDITIONS) of the American Cargo Clauses provides that:

> **7(C) Economic & Trade Sanctions**
> Whenever coverage provided by this policy would be in violation of any U.S. economic or trade sanctions such as, but not limited to, those sanctions administered and enforced by the U.S. Treasury Department's Office of Foreign Assets Control ("OFAC"), such coverage shall be null and void.

10.31 WTO Law and Other Public Sector Aspects of International Sales Trade

In addition to the above both incoterms and the insurance clauses there do not deal with other public related aspects of international commercial contracts, or their consequences, such as the effects on the contacts of:

[118] See "Sanctions Programs and Country Information" https://home.treasury.gov/policy-issues/financial-sanctions/sanctions-programs-and-country-information (accessed 27/01/2021); see also Note 92, op ct.

[119] Available at: https://www.zurich.co.uk/business/business-insurance/specialty-lines/marine/marine-cargo.

(a) the imposition of tariffs;
(b) export-import licenses;
(c) export or import prohibitions;
(d) intellectual property rights; and
(e) sanitary and phytosanitary matters.

Yet the buyers' failure to obtain or contravene any of these duties and/or restrictions could have catastrophic effect their liabilities and insurance obligations. Most export-import contracts including Incoterms might factor in commercial related aspects of export-import licences and export-import prohibitions but few, if any, will touch on the mainly public aspects of tariffs, intellectual property rights and sanitary and phytosanitary matters. The former being the subject of private international law while the former are the concerns of the WTO: therefore, reasons why Incoterms do not touch them.

10.32 Further Food for Thoughts

10.32.1 General Comments

Food for thought issues from Chaps. 2, 5 and 8 regarding insurance apply here. See also issues relating to provide an acceptable insurance document in Chap. 11.

10.32.2 Who Determines Which Contracts Need and Do Not Need Insurance?

A number of factors determine contracts needing or not needing insurance. First, are the general terms and conditions of the sales agreement between the parties. Second, is the actual insurance provision within that contract. Third are the terms and nature of the particular Incoterms contract, e.g., FOB will be the buyer unless otherwise provided while CIF will always be the seller. Fourth, are the membership of either or both parties of a organization, e.g., GAFTA will require use of their standard insurance contract. Fifth, are the external factors in the parties countries, e.g., restrictive shipping and insurance practices requiring interchangeable use of FOB/CIF for revenue purposes. Finally is the need for contingency insurance where applicable.

10.32.3 How Come Not All Incoterms Require Insurance? Wouldn't It Be Easier?

Instead of the strict rules that only CIF and CIP require insurance, which might not reflect external factors affecting insurance including contingency insurance raised above, it would be easier for all parties if all contracts stipulated.

10.32.4 Is It Necessary to Have CIF and CIP, Providing Both Insurance But with Very Little Other Differences Between Them?

From the discussions in Chaps. 8 and 9 above, on the insurance of CIF and CIP, it might be confusing for the un initiated to determine their insurance needs as the subtle insurance differences between the two is understandable only to the experts.

10.32.5 Creation of a New Incoterm: CNI

In the alternative to the above, perhaps the creation of an entirely new Incoterms. It has been suggested that the new Incoterm would be denominated as CNI (Cost and Insurance) and would cover a gap between FCA and CFR/CIF.[120] Unlike FCA, which would include the cost of international insurance on account of the seller-exporter, and as opposed to CFR/CIF that would not include freight. As in the other Incoterms in "C," this new Incoterm would be an "arrival Incoterm," i.e., the risk of transport would be transmitted from the seller to the buyer at the port of departure.

10.32.6 Balance Between Contractual and *Minimum*

Despite provisions in the respective contracts regarding parties' insurance obligations parties need to be aware that it is only the minimum. Even that is subject to agreements to the contrary and/or customary requirements such as in commodity trades.

10.32.7 Primary Duty Owed to Yourself

Furthermore, that where they do not owe a duty to the other party, they do so to themselves. Thus, there is a whole range that parties need to consider such as own insurance interest and contingency insurances.

10.32.8 Insurance Being the Default or Last Hope

All avenues need to be considered. It is therefore better to be double or over-insured than under-insured or not insured at all.

120 OLEGARIO LLAMAZARES- https://www.globalnegotiator.com/en/practical-guide-incoterms.

10.32.9 Best Advice to Both Parties

Experienced exporters and importers and importers might know this, but not the novice. For the rest, the network of export-import network, state information and competition for business ensures that they cannot escape the safety net. The best advice is if not sure please ask your broker or providers of your services such as the bank, freight forwarders, carriers, etc.

10.33 Concluding Remarks

This chapter has demonstrated that there is much to be done by the insured seller or buyer than what the contract might initially provide. This is common practice in the industry as the risks involved go far beyond those provided in the contract. This may be news to academics and other non-professionals but is not news to seasoned insurers, insureds and the EXIMPORT industry.

10.34 Further Readings

Books

- Sassoon, David: FOB and CIF Insurance, Sweet and Maxwell, Chapter 4
- Schmithoff, Clive, Insurance of International Trade, Chapters
- Jason, Chuah: Law of international trade: cross border commercial transactions. 4th revised edition 2009, Sweet & Maxwell Ltd, Chapter xx
- Carr, Indira: International Trade, Chapter
- Dunt, John: Cargo Insurance, Chapter

Clauses

- Siddharth Kanojia: Does English Law Provide the Best Framework For The Sale of Commodities? – A Comparison Between English Law, Incoterms and the CISG https://thelawbrigade.com/wp-content/uploads/2019/06/Siddharth-Kanojia.pdf (accessed 23/05/2021)
- Coetzee, J. 2013. "The Interplay Between Incoterms® and the CISG". Journal of Law and Commerce, 32(1):1-22. doi: https://doi.org/10.5195/jlc.2013.39. The original publication is also available at http://jlc.law.pitt.edu/ojs/index.php/jlc
- Quora: What is the relationship between CISG contracts and the Incoterms? https://www.quora.com/What-is-the-relationship-between-CISG-contracts-and-the-Incoterms
- Robert Kerwin. "Overview on Incoterms/CISG and Why They Are Important to International Business" https://iamers.org/2012/07/overview-on-incotermscisg-and-why-they-are-important-to-international-business/
- William P Johnson: "Analysis of Incoterms as Usage under Article 9 of the CISG 35 U. Pa. J. Int'l L. 379 (2013-2014)

- Juana Coetezee: “The Interplay between Incoterms and the CISG” 32 J.L. & Com. 1 (2013-2014)
- Carsten Fink, Aaditya Mattoo, Ileana Cristina Neagu “Trade in International Maritime Services: How Much Does Policy Matter?” *The World Bank Economic Review*, Volume 16, Issue 1, June 2002, Pages 81–108, https://doi.org/10.1093/wber/16.1.81 Published: 01 June 2002
- Ã–zlem Yalaz & Sedat Arslan “Evaluation of Turkish insurance sector in terms of competition”, *International Journal of Innovative Research in Education* (IJIRE) March,*2015,* Vol 2, No 1
- K.A. Votre “Trade in Services: Proposals for the Liberalization of International Trade in Insurance” *Bridgeport L. Rev., 1992* – HeinOnline
- JB Ricker Jr “Restrictive Legislation: Its Effect on the US Marine Insurance Industry” *J. Mar. L. & Com.,* 1974 – HeinOnline
- DE Taylor: “Problems Underwriters Encounter When Insuring Cargo”, Tul. L. Rev., 1970 – HeinOnline
- GJ Petersson: “Insurance and cartels through wars and depressions: Swedish Marine insurance and reinsurance between the World Wars” - 2011 - diva-portal.org
- -Falegan, Johri Ibitoye State intervention and control of insurance business in Nigeria
- (Unpublished Doctoral thesis, The City University,1991. https://openaccess.city.ac.uk/id/eprint/18318/
- “Insurance market mechanisms and government interventions” Journal of Banking & Finance. January 2008;
- Paul A. Raschky & Erwann Michel-Kerjan, “The Effects of Government Intervention on the Market for Corporate Terrorism Insurance” *European Journal of Political Economy Volume 27, Supplement 1, December 2011, Pages S122-S132*
- American Institute of Marine Underwriters: Marine Insurance Restrictions (in the U.S. and in Foreign Countries) RESTRICTIVE LAWS /REGULATIONS (IN UNITED STATES AND IN FOREIGN COUNTRIES)
- Kellie Griffith. A LIST OF COUNTRIES WITH RESTRICTIVES MEASURES IN THE FIELD OF MARINE INSURANCE INTERNATIONAL TRADE, December10,2016https://silo.tips/download/a-list-of-countries-with-restrictives-measures-in-the-field-of-marine-insurance

References

Ademuni-Odeke (2017) Windfall in marine and export credit insurance policies in Anglo-American and other common law jurisdictions- additional exception or simply a further limitation and modification of indemnity and subrogation? Part I. Eur Insur Law Rev 4:6–44

Ali A (1984) Export credit financing in the United Kingdom. ICLR 2:28

Bollinger R (1955) Export credit cover for construction projects abroad. ICLR 2:213

Coetzee J (2013) The interplay between incoterms® and the CISG. J Law Commer 32(1):1–22. https://doi.org/10.5195/jlc.2013.39

Gough N (1988) Institute cargo clause and trade related clauses, a detailed analysis and commentary. Lloyds of London Press

Schwenzer I, Fountoullakis C (2006) International sales law. Routldge-Cavendish, p 469

11 Tender of Insurance Documents at Common Law and Under UCP for Incoterms and Sales Financed by Credit

Abstract

As one of the 3 principal documents in international sales, the insurance policy covers the risks involved. Thus, it is central to the tender of documents especially where the sales are financed by a letter of credit or other advances. Apart from the documents stipulated in the contract, other customary documents may be tendered. Thus, in addition to the Introductory paragraph, other sub-headings discussed include: Tender of CIP Policy; Tender of Insurance Documents under Statute; Tender of Insurance Documents at Common Law; Tender of Insurance Documents under Incoterms; Tender of Insurance Documents under the UCP 600; Collection Under Uniform Rules for Collections; Cosequences of Failure to tender Insurance Document; Further Food for Thoughts; Concluding Remarks; References Used; and Further Readings.

11.1 Introduction

11.1.1 General Obligations to Tender

Earlier chapters discussed types and role of the policy, other insurance and transport documents. This chapter brings deals with the tender of documents under common law, statute, Incoterms and the UCP. It focuses on the tender of the policy, certificate, the cover-note, letter of insurance, declarations under open policy and the slip in export documentation. It also lists and discusses those documents in their order of importance, demonstrates importance of the policy plays in the tender of documents in payments and makes references to the MIA1906 and other statutory provisions and guidelines on tender. The chapter includes references and provides requirements for tender such as insurable interest and assignment of the policy.

P. Ademuni-Odeke, *Insurance of International Sales' Contracts under Incoterms*, Law for Professionals, https://doi.org/10.1007/978-3-031-75136-3_11

Other statutes covered are the *SGAs*, 1893, 1979, 1992 and 1995. Difference, if any, between common law and other tenders are noted.

Incoterms are generally silent on the detailed aspects of tender. Otherwise, tender under common law is in practice no different from the process under Incoterms and UCP. Although Incoterms are a set of rules which describe the rights and obligations of the parties, they provide basic guidelines and mention tender only in passing but do not deal with detailed rules as to tender. However, they seem to be synchronised with the UCP. The main focus of tender of documents is therefore the UCP. This inevitably involves discussions of the UCP 500, UCP 600 and the ICC Uniform Rules for Collections-1995 Revision (URC) under which it is done, and the letters of credit, the instrument which controls it. However, the chapter is concerned only with the tender of the insurance documents and not the complex and detailed UCP and URC rules of tender such the doctrine of strict compliance, autonomy of credits and the fraud exception rules under letters of credit.

11.1.2 Tender Under Incoterms and Letters of Credit

It is not a full-blown discussion on the law relating to the UCP and letters of credit, but is rather limited to Clause 28 of UCP 600 dealing with insurance. The reader is referred to major and specialist work in the bibliography at the end of the chapter dealing with those two subjects. The chapter notes that in recognition of the changing environment in international trade law and practice, from UCP 500 onwards has in practice emphasis has now shifted from reference to tender of 'insurance policy' to 'insurance documents' just as they have from tender of the 'bill of lading' to tender of 'transport documents. In so doing it is difficult to omit discussions on the ICC as the main organisation that covers both the UCP and letters of credit. The chapter inevitably continues with discussions, from Chap. 1 ante, on the development of the ICC and its relationship to Incoterms and the UCP. This is necessary for background and, therefore, fuller appreciation of the entire tender process.

The chapter does not dwell on the detailed process of tender of documents in international trade. The actual manner, time and roles of the tenderor and tendoree are practical matters governed where applicable either by the parties' agreement on the sales, insurance or letter of credit contracts. Where the contract is silent, tender may be made or governed by customs of the particular trade. In theory the seller should tender insurance and related documents to the buyer once he has fulfilled his contractual obligations. In practice the tender is made by the seller, beneficiary or sellers' agent or assignee to the buyer's paying bank under the letters of credit. Either way, the tenderor attaches the insurance policy/document or certificate to the: bill of lading/transport document; commercial invoice; other certificates; export/import licences and other contractual documents and presents them to the buyer's bank for payment.

11.1.3 Letter of Credit Institute Clause

To utilise letters of credit it is necessary to attach the Letter of Credit Institute Clause which provides that:

> **Letter of Credit Institute Clause**
> It is agreed that certificates and/or policies (including S.G. Policy form which is indicated "Policy Body") may be issued hereunder to enable the Assured to comply with the insurance requirements of any Letter of Credit and/or Sales Contract, such agreement being conditional on the following wording being incorporated in such certificate and/or policy.
>
> "The following insurance conditions referred to in the Letter of Credit and/or Sales Contract are noted"
>
> The following should be considered to be inserted into the policy after any special conditions required by Letter of Credit and/or Sales Contract wording:
>
> "But in no event is the cover herein extended wider than the terms of Institute Cargo Clauses (A), (1/1/09)"
>
> It is also agreed that regardless of the conditions on which any certificates and/or policies may be issued pursuant to the foregoing, the Assured shall continue to enjoy the full protection of this contract

11.1.4 Tender Under Commodity Trade Contracts

Attention is drawn to similar aspects from FOB and CIF commodity contracts as well as contractual issues. For example, Form 72 *Gafta Contract Series No. 100* (Effective 1st September 2010) provides that:

> ***Form 72 Gafta Contract Series No. 100***
> (e) Certificates/Policies - Sellers shall give all policies and/or certificates and/or letters of insurance provided for in this contract, (duly stamped if applicable) for original and increased value (if any) for the value stipulated in (c) above. In the event of a certificate of insurance being supplied, it is agreed that Sellers shall exchange such certificate for a policy if required and such certificate shall state on its face that it is so exchangeable. If required by Buyers, letter(s) of insurance shall be guaranteed by a recognised bank or by any other guarantor who is acceptable to Buyers.

And Clause 5 and 6 of the Sample GAFTA insurance clause in a CIF contract provides that:

Tender of Documents

5. The Seller shall ship the goods in the ship and despatch the documents relating to the said goods namely the contract of affreightment, insurance policy, invoice, bills of lading etc. to Its Bankers at the port of arrival.

6. The said documents duly endorsed in favour of the Buyer will be handed over to the Buyer's Bankers against encashment of the Letter of Credit and the Buyer will receive the same from Its Bankers to enable the Buyer to get the goods cleared at the port of arrival. Such delivery of documents will be deemed to be delivery of the goods to the Buyer and thereafter the goods will be at the risk of the Buyer.[1]

It is significant that the equivalent FOB Gafta and Sample FOB contracts also contains the insurance or documents tender clauses. It is noticeable that unlike the up-to-date UCP 600 and URC, the insurance clauses in the FOB and CIF Commodity Contracts still use 'insurance policy' rather than 'insurance documents'

Like all the others, the chapter provides ample further readings.

11.2 Tender of CIF/CIP Policy/Insurance Documents

11.2.1 Importance and Tender of CIF Documents

Due to importance of documents in CIF, their tender to the buyer is also of crucial importance. That tender includes insurance policy or and any of the alternative or substitute documents. The detailed rules of tender were dealt with in the previous (Chap. 6). To fulfil his obligations in tender the seller must meet those requirements. That includes insurance policy and/or documents.[2] The Australian case of *Piecesse v Tasmanian Orchadists & Producer's Co-op Assocn. Ltd.*,[3] involving the shipment of Scandinavian paper CIF Hobart, demonstrated that insurance policy forms part of the tender and should not be omitted. However, it is also authority that tender of the policy is not always necessary as there are some CIF cases which are exceptions. This was a CIF contract which provided for delivery of the goods, 'nett cash against bills of lading or delivery orders.

Although the insurance policy was omitted from tender, it was, nevertheless held by Justice XX that it was not necessary in order to constitute a tender of delivery entitling the party making the same to payment, to tender the policies of insurance. The tender would have been vitiated by the delay due to deviation. This decision must be regarded with caution as it applied to the limited circumstances (delay among them) of a particular case. That caution is born in another Australian case of

[1] See Annex III to this s book for the extracts of the GAFTA Contracts.

[2] [See Failure to Tender (below), Tender under UCP-this chapter below].

[3] *Piecesse v Tasmanian Orchadists & Producer's Co-op Assocn Ltd.* (1919) Tas LR 67(Aus).

Lascelles & Co v Willis & Co Ltd,[4] (shipment from New York CIF Sidney), where *Piecesse* was distinguished. The rationale for the difference in approach was due to the deviation in breach of the contract (seller's fault-treated as serious) in the latter compared to a delay which was not of the seller's fault (not regarded as serious) in the former. However, it was immaterial in *Piecesse* that the document in question was a certificate instead of a policy, the whole policy would have been vitiated by the deviation anyway.

11.2.2 Tender of Policy to Buyer Central to the CIF Contract

It has been maintained consistently in the book that role and tender of the policy and its effects is central to the CIF contract. It is for those reasons that in *The Julia* Lord Porter did not accept tender of a delivery order and omission of the policy. His Lordship emphasized the rationale for this when, in his seminal decision thought that:

> The object and the result of a c.i.f. contract is to enable sellers and buyers to deal with cargoes or parcels afloat and to transfer them freely from hand to hand by giving constructive possession of the goods which are being dealt with. Undoubtedly, the practice of shipping and insuring produce in bulk is to make the process more difficult, but a ship's delivery order and a certificate of insurance transferred to or held for a buyer still leaves it possible for some, though less satisfactory, dealing with the goods while at sea to take place. The practice adopted between buyers and sellers in the present case renders such dealing well-nigh impossible. The purchaser gets neither property nor possession until the goods is delivered to him at Antwerp, and the certificate of insurance, if it ensures to his benefit at all, except on the journey from ship to warehouse, has never been held for or delivered to him.[5]

In addition to *The Julia*, and the two Australian decisions on the necessity for and consequences of the omission of the insurance from the tender, it will be remembered that *Hickox v Adams*,[6] was another authority that partly dealing with omissions. In a contract to sell and deliver wheat from New York to Bristol, tender of documents was rejected by the buyers for, inter alia, the misstatement on the bill of lading and policy and the omission of the policy in the tender. Asking himself whether the English buyers were entitled to reject the bill of lading without the policy of insurance in the case, Lord Mellish[7] was affirmative in his answer.

11.2.3 Tender Must Be Within a Reasonable Time

The time for tender will normally be contained in the contractual terms and conditions. Failure to tender within that period is breach of tender and merits rejection of

---

[4] *Lascelles & Co v Willis & Co Ltd* (1921) 21 SRNSW 773; 38 NSWWN238 (Aus.

[5] [1948-49] Ll.L Rep 270 at 283.

[6] *Hickox v Adams* (1876) 34 LT404; 3 Asp MLC 142 CA.

[7] For details see paras. 7-023 to 7-025 , ante For details see paras. 7-023 to 7-025, ante.

the documents. Where the contract is either ambiguous or silent as to time of tender, case law suggests that the tender should be as soon as possible or within a reasonable time. There is no English authority but the Australian Piecesse held that as a general rule tender must be within a reasonable time. This is backed up by Canadian,[8] Indian, Irish,[9] Northern Ireland,[10] South African[11] and Scottish[12] authorities. [Case provides that Tender must be within reasonable time]

11.2.4 What Is Reasonable Time for Tender

What constitutes a 'reasonable time' within which to tender documents will be a matter of fact to be gathered from the circumstances of each case. Again, there seems to be no English cases. Once more what is reasonable time was the subject of the Australian decision in *Lyon v Creati*[13] *and the Canadian case of Dauphin Consumers Co-op Ltd v Puchalski Bros.*[14] Agreeing with that the South African case of *Adler v De Wal*[15] added that the reasonableness of time cannot depend upon circumstances unknown to the buyer, and which were undisclosed to him by the seller. However, the reasonable time will consider extension of time where time was not fixed[16] and in written contracts which do not provide for time of tender.[17]

11.2.5 Tender Under Incoterms and UCP 600 for Letters of Credit

Whatever is discussed in this paragraph and chapter is subject to the detailed rules relating to the tender of documents for the purposes of CIF and letters of credit under the UCP. Detailed rules as to tender of documents are beyond the scope of this chapter. The common denominator however is that they should be tendered as per contract, where the contract is silent as to the time of tender then they it should be as soon as is reasonably possible. The contracts will also detail when, how, by whom and to whom the documents are tendered. To be complete the insurance policy or certificate, should accompany the invoice, bill of lading, bill of exchange or other

[8] *Luxfer Prism Co Ltd v McLeod* (1908) 8WLR 627; Sask LR 75 and *Heintzman & Co v Rundle* (1912) 4DLR 688; 20 WLR 202; Sask LR 121.

[9] *Juggunath v Beck* (1870) 2 NW 60.

[10] *Ross Bros Ltd v Shaw* [1917] 2IR 367 (such a reasonable time may be explained or controlled by custom or usage).

[11] *Graf & Co v Bassa* (1925) 46 NLR(SA).

[12] *Federal Tobacco Works v Barron & Co* [1904] TS 483.

[13] *British Motor Body Co Ltd v Thomas Shaw (Dundee) Ltd* [1914] SC 922.

[14] *Lyon v Creati* (1892) 18 VLR 629.

[15] **[1984] 2 WWR 673.**

[16] *Adler v De Wal* (1887) 8NLR 87.

[17] *Curran v O'Leary* (1907) 5EDL 80(Can).

drafts or other transport documents, packing list, Phytosanitary and various other certificates.[18]

11.2.6 Waiver of Requirement to Tender

The issue of whether the requirement for tender of the policy and other documents can be waived came up indirectly in *Tamvaco v Lucas*.[19] In the fourth, final, of his long judgment, the Chief Justice Cockburn decided that there may be time when, although the buyers are within their rights to reject, it may be in their interest to waive those rights. "There seems to be another view of this case which is also unfavourable to the defendants. Assuming that, upon a contract of this sort, the shipping documents must be substantially sufficient, yet, as this is a term in the contract introduced for the benefit of the buyer, it certainly is one that may be waived by him. In the present case, it does not appear that the buyer ever repudiated this contract, or denied his liability to be bound by its terms, on the ground that these documents or any of them were insufficient. Long before the shipping documents arrived in this country the buyer repudiated his liability, on the ground that the defendants had exceeded their authority as agents. And, again, when the shipping documents arrived, and it was sought to make the buyers fulfil the terms of the contract, the defendants never for a moment set up the insufficiency of these shipping documents; but they sought to force the contract on the buyers for whom they had acted, as one which the buyers were bound to complete.

Now, as has been pointed out by more than one of my learned brothers in the course of the argument, if, at the time these shipping documents were originally tendered, there had been any objection taken on the score of the insufficiency of this policy, there would have been no difficulty (for this was long before the arrival of the cargo) in making good the defect by means of supplementary insurance. I think, therefore, there has been a waiver on the part of the buyers, the principals in the contract, and also a waiver on the part of the defendants, who, as agents, were liable on this del credere contract. There was an absolute and entire waiver of any objection which might by possibility have been taken to the insufficiency of the policy. On every ground, therefore, and in every point of view in which I can look at the case, I cannot but think that the defendants have failed to make out, on this technical objection, any ground why the verdict should be disturbed".[20] However, that waiver should probably be read within the confines and context of this case rather than as providing a precedent for general waiver in tender of the policy and accompanying documents in the CIF contract.

---

[18] *More v Canadian Fairbank Co* (1913) 14 DLR 49; 41 NBR 485; 13 EDL 517(Can).

[19] The types of insurance documents tenderable at common law, under incoterms and the UCP are covered in this chapter below.

[20] *Tamvaco v Lucas* (1861) 121 E.R. 683 on appeal. Ibid, at 690.

11.3 Tender of Insurance Documents

11.3.1 Tender Under Statute

11.3.1.1 The Marine Policy for the [FOB and CIF] Contracts

The policy in use in FOB, CIF and other international trade contracts is the marine policy whose particulars are contained in ss.22–24 of the MIA 1906. The Act provides exhaustive and clear guidelines as to the nature and contents of the policy: its embodiment, details of the parties to it and detailed requirements as to signature it, thus:

> **The Policy**
> 22 Contract must be embodied in policy.
>
> Subject to the provisions of any statute, a contract of marine insurance is inadmissible in evidence unless it is embodied in a marine policy in accordance with this Act. The policy may be executed and issued either at the time when the contract is concluded, or afterwards.[21]
>
> 23 What policy must specify.
>
> A marine policy must specify
>
> (1) The name of the assured, or of some person who effects the insurance on his behalf:
>
> (2) — (5).[22]
>
> 24 Signature of insurer
>
> (1) A marine policy must be signed by or on behalf of the insurer, provided that in the case of a corporation the corporate seal may be sufficient, but nothing in this section shall be construed as requiring the subscription of a corporation to be under seal.
>
> (2) Where a policy is subscribed by or on behalf of two or more insurers, each subscription, unless the contrary be expressed, constitutes a distinct contract with the assured.

---

[21] C1S. 22 excluded by Marine and Aviation Insurance (War Risks) Act 1952 (c. 57), s. 7(1) and Finance Act 1959 (c. 58), s. 30(6)(7).

[22] S. 23(2)–(5) repealed as to instruments made or executed after 1.8.1959 by Finance Act 1959 (c. 58), Sch. 8 Pt. II.

We know that in export practice other documents other than the policy can be tendered for payment and in evidence in courts. This is due to existence and use other more practical documents and insurance schemes in lieu of the policy as described in this chapter. Life and other types of insurance may well still insist on tender of policy in evidence.

11.3.1.2 Assignment and Transfer of the Policy Under Statute

These are now contained in the Lloyds Mar and Companies Mar Policy as covered in Chap. 1 above. For this purpose, the parties would be the seller or their agents in CIF, CIP and certain FOB variations and the buyer or their agents in all the rest of the export contracts. At common law both the bill of lading and the policy were not transferable even where the seller had disposed of his interests in the property insured. This bill of lading position in the Bill of Lading Act 1855 was changed by the various sales of goods[23] and carriage of goods by sea[24] legislations, which among other things modified the passage of property and title in sale of goods in bulk. Traditionally the policy is not a negotiable instrument that could be transferred by simply handing over or endorsement and handing over. However, put together with the other export documents, it acquires quasi-negotiable instrument characteristics by international trade customs and usages. While the policy was changed, inter alia, by ss. 50 and 51 of the MIA1906 thus:

Assignment of Policy
50 **When and how policy is assignable**

(1) A marine policy is assignable unless it contains terms expressly prohibiting assignment. It may be assigned either before or after loss.

(2) Where a marine policy has been assigned so as to pass the beneficial interest in such policy, the assignee of the policy is entitled to sue thereon in his own name; and the defendant is entitled to make any defence arising out of the contract which he would have been entitled to make if the action had been brought in the name of the person by or on behalf of whom the policy was effected.

(3) A marine policy may be assigned by indorsement thereon or in other customary manner.

---

[23] Sale of Goods Act 1893, Sale of Goods Act 1979, Supply of Goods and Services Act 1982, Supply and Sale of Goods Act 1994, and Sale of Goods (Amendment) Act 1995.

[24] Carriage of Goods by Sea 1925, Carriage of Goods by Sea 1971 and Carriage of Goods Sea 1992.

> 51 **Assured who has no interest cannot assign**
>
> Where the assured has parted with or lost his interest in the subject-matter insured, and has not, before or at the time of so doing, expressly or impliedly agreed to assign the policy, any subsequent assignment of the policy is inoperative:
>
> Provided that nothing in this section affects the assignment of a policy after loss.

In international trade transfer is permitted by customs and usages of merchants by simple indorsement of the documents to the buyer on payment. Such a custom in international trade was in fact noted by Ivamy, that "In practice, policies on goods do not contain clauses prohibiting assignment, for, if they did, international trade would be hampered"[25] in fact is thinks that the signing, transfer and tender of the policy have now also been further clarified by both the UCP 500 and UCP 600 discussed below.

However, ss. 50 and 51 seem to contradict s.15 of the Act. Despite the above the section provides that:

> **15 Assignment of interest.**
> Where the assured assigns or otherwise parts with his interest in the subject-matter insured, he does not thereby transfer to the assignee his rights under the contract of insurance, unless there be an express or implied agreement with the assignee to that effect.
>
> But the provisions of this section do not affect a transmission of interest by operation of law.

In *William Pickersgill & Sons Ltd v London and Provincial Marine and General Insurance Co Ltd,*[26] Justice Hamilton[27] held that under s 50(2) of the *Marine Insurance Act 1906*, even an innocent assignee of the policy cannot claim on the policy on which the assignor failed to disclose material facts before assignment. However, in the American case of *Reliable Maritime Boiler Repair Inc. v Frank B Hall Inc., et al,*[28] the lessee payee was stopped from subsequently revoking payment order authorisation instructions to the prejudice of the unpaid repairer who ha effected repairs in reliance upon assignment of the insurance proceeds.

Two years earlier than *William Pickersgill and Sons Ltd v London and Provincial Marine and General Insurance Co Ltd* above, the same judge had in *Baker v Adam*[29] decided that although s 50*(3)* of the MIA 1906 provides that, "A marine policy may be assigned by indorsement thereon or in other customary manner", [mere] delivery

---

[25] Ivamy (1993), p. 73 (Note).

[26] *William Pickersgill & Sons Ltd v London and Provincial Marine and General Insurance Co Ltd* (1912) 107 LT305.

[27] Ibid at 307.

[28] *Reliable Maritime Boiler Repair Inc. v Frank B Hall Inc.*, et al (1971) AMC 1941.

[29] *Baker v Adam* (1910) 102 LT248.

does not constitute a sufficient assignment, and it must be accompanied by indorsement[30] Except that the last line seems to accept operation of the law. It would therefore appear that the section is intended to retain the operation of the common law as much as possible where applicable. That seems to be the only plausible explanation of the apparent contradiction. However, assignment under FOB and CIF contracts would be covered by the exception under 'express or implied agreement with the assignee'.

11.4 Tender of Insurance Documents at Common Law

11.4.1 Under General Provisions

Although there are apparent differences in the nature, characteristics and performance between the various contracts at common law, the documentation is the same and apart from emphasis, the tender of especially the transportation documents and the insurance policy is the same. Thus, apart from a few areas of differences, the law relating to tender of documents generally and insurance documents in particular under CIF would apply to FOB contracts. This applies to FOB-related contracts listed and discussed in Chaps. 4 **and 5).** Thus, from the foregone, the first and ideal insurance document is the policy itself. It therefore follows that from the foregone, we can surmise that unless there is provision in the contract or, probably, a custom of the particular trade (e.g. acceptance of certificates) in *Diamond Alkali Export Corpn v Bourgeois*[31] and (e.g. tender of certificates) *Malmberg v HJ Evans & Co*[32]

---

[30] Ibid at 249.

[31] See *Diamond Alkali Export Corpn v Bourgeois* [1921] 3 KB 443, per Justice McCardie at 457, 458. "It may well be that this decision is disturbing to business men. It is my duty, however, to state my view of the law without regard to mere questions of convenience. I desire to add four remarks: (1.) That there is no finding or evidence before me of any course of dealing between the parties. (2.) That there is no finding or evidence before me of any custom or general usage which modifies the long and clearly established legal rights of a buyer under a c.i.f. contract. If any such custom or usage be asserted then the point can be dealt with in some future action in the Commercial Court. Whether such an assertion can be proved may well be a question of doubt in view of the matters appearing in the *Manbre Saccharine Case* [1919] 1 K. B. 198. 206: see, too, *Wilson v. Holgate & Co.'s Case* [1920] 2 K. B. 1, 8, where Bailhache J. said: 'I am not satisfied that since Ireland v. Livingston L. R. 5 H. L. 395 was decided any custom has arisen which obviates the necessity for a tender by the seller of a policy of insurance if the buyer requires it.' (3.) It may well be that legislation is needed to enlarge the operation of the Bills of Lading Act, 1855, and the Marine Insurance Act, 1906. (4.) It may be well also that the greater part of the difficulties indicated in this judgment can be easily, promptly and effectively met by the insertion of appropriate clauses in c.i.f contracts.

For the reasons given I find in favour of the buyers with the results stated in the award."

[32] *Malmberg v HJ Evans & Co* (1924) 30 Com Cas 107 at 116; [1924] Vol. 20 Ll. L. Rep. 40, at p. 43: Lord Justice Atkin: "We have not to give any decision upon the question whether this document [Swedish insurance policy/certificate] would be a good tender under a contract c.i.f. drawn in these terms, because there is an admission that it would not be a good tender unless the terms of the written contract are varied, by the course of business between the parties, so as to amount either

to the contrary and *Burstall & Co v Grimsdale*,[33] nothing short of an actual insurance policy is a good tender under especially a CIF contract as in *Manbre Saccharine Co Ltd v Corn Products Co Ltd*[34] and *The Julia.*[35]

For example, neither the broker's covernote, nor certificate of insurance, or other document which does not include all the terms of the usual contract of insurance, is good tender under the ordinary CIF contract as in *Wilson, Holgate & Co Ltd v Belgian Grain and Produce Co Ltd.*[36] If, as is often the case, the shipper makes use of a floating policy[37] of insurance or an *open cover*[38] instead of a policy to insure the particular goods, it is doubtful whether, in the absence of provision in the contract or, probably, custom in the particular trade, the tender under such a policy or *open cover*[39] of a certificate containing all the terms of the usual contract of insurance would be an effective mode of implementing the contract of sale. In *Wilson, Holgate & Co Ltd v Belgian Grain and Produce Co Ltd*,[40] Justice Bailhache regarded tender

---

to a variation of the contract or in some other way estopping the buyers from taking advantage of the alleged breach. Therefore, I say nothing more about it except to say this: that I am inclined to think that in a lot of dealings, such as c.i.f. contracts, cash against documents, the conditions have now been understood by authoritative decisions defining the terms of the contract, and defining the documents which have to be delivered under that contract. I doubt myself whether it is open to the parties to say that a course of business between themselves existed prior to the contract which would have the effect of varying the terms which otherwise would be by law attributed to those words. I say no more about it than that, nor do I wish, therefore, to consider the question whether or not a document in the form in which this document issued by the Swedish Company is, would be a policy of insurance within the meaning of that term as laid down by the decisions which are appropriate to c.i.f. contracts."

[33] See *Burstall & Co v Grimsdale* (1906) 11 Com Cas 280 (where a certificate of insurance was held to be sufficient). See also *The Julia* [1949] AC 293 at 309, [1949] 3 All ER 269 at 274–275, HL, per Lord Porter; John Martin of *London Ltd v AE Taylor & Co Ltd* [1953] 2 Lloyd's Rep 589. If a certificate of insurance is accepted by the buyer, there is an implied warranty by the seller that the policy will be issued: *Harper & Co Ltd v Mackechnie & Co* [1925] 2 KB 423.

[34] *Manbre Saccharine Co Ltd v Corn Products Co Ltd* [1919] 1 KB 198, per Justice McCardie at pp. 204, 205: "Under an ordinary c.i.f. contract the vendor is obviously bound to tender a proper policy of insurance together with the other documents required... The policy must be tendered even if the goods have safely arrived at the time of tender."; *Wilson, Holgate & Co Ltd v Belgian Grain and Produce Co Ltd* [1920] 2 KB 1; *Diamond Alkali Export Corpn v Bourgeois* [1921] 3 KB 443; *Donald H Scott & Co v Barclays Bank Ltd* [1923] 2 KB 1, CA. See also *Malmberg v HJ Evans & Co* (1924) 30 Com Cas 107 at 113, CA (propriety of tendering a policy incorporating conditions or rules in some other document).

[35] *The Julia* [1949] AC 293 at 309, [1949] 3 All ER 269 at 274–275, HL, per Lord Porter.

[36] *Wilson, Holgate & Co Ltd v Belgian Grain and Produce Co Ltd* [1920] 2 KB 1 (broker's note); *Diamond Alkali Export Corpn v Bourgeois* [1921] 3 KB 443 (certificate of insurance); *Promos SA v European Grain and Shipping Ltd* [1979] 1 Lloyd's Rep 375 (brokers' cover note). See also the cases cited in note 59.

[37] As to floating policies see Halsbury's *Laws*, Vol. 60, Note 7, paras. 245, 282–283; John Dunt, Note 8, pp. 213–215.

[38] As to open cover policies, including floating policy by ship or ships see s 29 of the *UK Marine Insurance Act 1906*; *Note* 7, pp. 121–123 and 143; John Dunt, Note 8, pp. 213–214.

[39] Ibid.

[40] See the references to 'American certificates' in *Wilson, Holgate & Co Ltd v Belgian Grain and Produce Co Ltd* [1920] 2 KB 1; and *Donald H Scott & Co Ltd v Barclays Bank Ltd* [1923] 2 KB 1 at 11, CA, per Bankes LJ.

of an American insurance certificate as equivalent to a marine policy,[41] as did Lord Bankes in *Donald H Scott & Co Ltd v Barclays Bank Ltd.*[42]

However, it would seem to be essential, as was the case in the above authorities, that the certificate should be one on which contains all the essential terms and conditions of the contract and in which liability can be legally established against the insurer in case of a loss within the insurance. This is despite the requirement above that under English law a contract of marine insurance is inadmissible in evidence unless embodied in a marine policy.[43] That notwithstanding, being a marine policy, a CIF policy must be assignable by indorsement or in other customary manner.[44] What should not be lost of in mind is Lord Porter's reminder in *The Julia*[45] of the essential aspect of the CIF policy which is for the seller to put the buyer in a position where he should claim directly and in his own name from the insurers in the event of loss or damage.[46]

11.4.2 Whether Tender of Certificate of Insurance Acceptable in CIF Policy?

Certificates of insurance are second in league to the actual marine policy. In the absence of the policy, for whatever reasons, can the seller substitute tender of the certificate instead? A certificate of insurance is a document stating that in accordance with an authorisation granted to the person signing the certificate, the insurers are liable to the insured subject to the terms and conditions stated therein. An insured, whether exporter or not will need one of these in addition to or in lieu of the policy. Justice Bailhache's ruling in *Wilson, Holgate & Co Ltd v Belgium Grain & Produce Co Ltd*[47] is authority for two positions on this. First, that under a CIF contract for the sale of goods, the sellers, in the absence of any custom or special stipulation to the contrary, do not perform their obligation of tendering to the buyer along with the other shipping documents a policy of insurance by tendering instead of a proper policy either a broker's cover note[48] or a certificate of insurance.

---

[41] Ibid at p. 7: "It must be borne in mind that, in dealing with certificates of insurance, I am not referring to American certificates of insurance which stand on a different footing and are equivalent to policies, being accepted in this country as policies."

[42] *Donald H Scott & Co Ltd v Barclays Bank Ltd* [1923] 2 KB 1 per Bankes LJ at 11, CA: "It is to be observed that in *Wilson & Co. v. Belgian Grain, Co.* [1920] 2 K. B. 7 Bailhache J. used words, which were not necessary to the decision, but to which the learned judge's experience gives weight; the spoke of 'American certificates of insurance which stand on a different footing and are equivalent to policies, being accepted in this country as policies.' I do not know what form of certificate the learned judge had in mind; it may have been one containing all the terms necessary to constitute a valid policy of insurance according to English law. However that may be, his words must not be taken to include American certificates of insurance in whatever form they may be expressed."
Ibid at p. 7.

[43] See the *Marine Insurance Act 1906* s 22; and Halsbury's *Laws*, Vol. 60 (2011), Note 7, para. 243.

[44] See the *Marine Insurance Act 1906* s 50(3); *Halsbury's Laws*, Vol. 91, Note 7, para. 377.

[45] *The Julia* [1949] AC 293 at 309, [1949] 3 All ER 269.

[46] Ibid at pp. 274–275, HL, per Lord Porter which remain one of the principles of the CIF contract.

[47] *Wilson, Holgate & Co Ltd v Belgium Grain & Produce Co Ltd* [1920] 2 KB 1.

[48] But see UCP 600, Clause 28(c) (below).

Secondly, that where the parties to a CIF contract for the sale of goods, which have been duly shipped, enter into a stipulation that the seller, instead of tendering with the order shipping documents a policy of insurance, may tender a certificate of insurance with a broker's undertaking to hold the policy for the buyer's account, the seller does not perform their obligation under the stipulation by tendering a certificate of insurance without a broker's undertaking. *Wilson & Holgate* is still good common law authority and was considered, as to the second point, in *Diamond Alkali and Scott (Donald H and Scott v Barclays Bank.*[49] However, tender of a certificate is or requires a warrant of liability on the part of the beneficiary/seller and/or their agents to validate it. Schmitthoff makes a distinction between law, theory and practice on the document.[50]

Otherwise, as will be apparent below, a certificate of insurance is acceptable tender in both INCOTERMS and UCP 500[51] but not in UCP 600.[52] Is there a contradiction or conflict between the two? In addition to the statutory requirements of the policy, particular commodity trades might also specify the insurance documents required for tender. For instance, of GAFTA[53] details requirements for certificates thus:

> 20 (e) Certificates/Policies - Sellers shall give all policies and/or certificates and/or letters of insurance provided for in this contract, (duly stamped if applicable) for original and increased value (if any) for the value stipulated in (c) above. In the event of a certificate of insurance being supplied, it is agreed that Sellers shall exchange such certificate for a policy if required and such certificate shall state on its face that it is so exchangeable. If required by Buyers, letter(s) of insurance shall be guaranteed by a recognised bank or by any other guarantor who is acceptable to Buyers (emphasis added).

As is apparent (post), a broker's covernote is not normally an acceptable tender.[54]

11.4.3 Necessity for "Warranty of Validity" of Certificate in CIF Policy

Due to the problems intimated above, at common law there is necessity for warranty of validity of insurance certificate in CIF policy. In *Harper (AC) & Co v Mackechine & Co,*[55] Justice Roche's ruling[56] determined the liability of vendor under a CIF con-

---

[49] *Scott v Barclays Bank* [1921] 2KB 1.

[50] See Schmitthoff, Note 5, para. 19—011 at pp. 413–414; For an extensive treatment of the subject see Sassoon, *CIF and FOB Contracts*, Note 3 at pp. 168–172.

[51] UCP 500, Note 20, Art 34(a).

[52] UCP 600 Clause 28(a), Note 20; also See comparison of the texts in UCP 500 and UCP 600 in Byrne's "The Comparison of the UCP 600 & UCP 500", *I I L & B L& Practice*, pp. 212–218, 2007.

[53] Clause 20(e) "20 (e) Certificates/Policies.

[54] UCP 600, Note 20, Clause 28(c); John Dunt, Note 8, pp. 214–215.

[55] *Harper (AC) & Co v Mackechine & Co* [1925] 2 KB 423.

[56] Ibid, at p. 428: "It is well established that the Court cannot imply more than is necessary to give business efficacy to a contract. But I think it is necessary to such efficacy to imply the terms which the plaintiffs here suggest. I hold that the defendants in handing over the certificate warranted by

tract, when a certificate of insurance is tendered by the seller and accepted by the buyer in fulfilment of the contract and in lieu of a policy of insurance. The case determined that there is an implied warranty by the seller that the assertions in the certificate are true, and that the seller will produce or procure the production of the policy referred to in the certificate. The seller in such a case is liable for a breach of this warranty as a collateral contract, even if insurance brokers do in fact sign the certificate and the brokers fail to effect an insurance, which will continue valid throughout the transit of the goods. What is unclear, however, is whether the tender of a lesser regarded insurance document, the letter of insurance. Otherwise, previously, certificates of insurance were not valid tender.[57] It remains unclear whether this cure and/or addresses the issue of divergence on this issue between the common law and UCP 600 raised earlier. Neither is of any help when using letters of insurance which is a document inferior to both certificates and covernotes.

11.5 Tender of Documents Under Incoterms

11.5.1 The General Incoterms Approach

Incoterms provides the rules as the rights and obligations of the parties. As is apparent in Chap. 7 above, only the CIF and CIP, and to a certain extent the old C&F or the new CFR, provide for insurance of the contract by the seller in Clauses A5 and B5 respectively. In all the rest of the incoterms the buyer provides his own insurance although the parties may have to negotiate to vary the terms of insurance therein such as in FOB with additional duties. However, Incoterms do not provide any rules or guidelines as to tender of the insurance documents. However, they work in unison with the UCP 500 and UCP 600 discussed below, the detailed rules therein might shade light as what should happen to Incoterms.

11.5.2 Delivery of Transport Document Under Incoterms 2020

Incoterms provides for tender of general transport documents as well as specific insurance documents. In the former case Clause A6 provides that the seller must provide the buyer at the seller's cost with the usual proof that the goods have been delivered in accordance with Clause A2. The seller must provide assistance to the

implication that the assertions contained in it were true, that the plaintiffs were not merely to rely on the brokers, but that the defendants undertook to produce or to procure the production of the policy referred to in the certificate. In the case of a c.i.f. contract where there is a chain of sellers, there is a contract between the broker and the original seller, and each successive seller, if he chooses to accept the certificate and to pass it on to a buyer, undertakes to make good what the certificate asserts. The ultimate remedy, if there is any irregularity shifts back until it reaches the original seller and the brokers themselves. If it were not so the position would be impossible."

[57] See again *Diamond Alkali Export Corp v Fl. Bourgeois* [1921] 3KB 443 and *Phoenix Insurance Co of Hartford v De Monchy* (1929) 45 TLR 543.

buyer, at the buyer's request, risk and cost, in obtaining a transport document. Where the buyer has instructed the carrier to issue to the seller a transport document under Clause B6, the seller must provide any such document to the buyer. Clause B6 provides that the buyer must accept the proof that the goods have been delivered in accordance with Clause A2.

If the parties have so agreed, the buyer must instruct the carrier to issue to the seller, at the buyer's cost and risk, a transport document stating that the goods have been loaded (such as a bill of lading with an onboard notation).

This is in addition to providing invoices (commercial, consular), export/import licenses, certificates and other shipping documents as well as tenders of all the documents for resale of goods bought afloat.

11.5.3 Tender of Insurance Documents Under Incoterms 2020

The seller must provide the buyer with the insurance policy or certificate or any other evidence of insurance cover. Although it specifically provides for the policy or certificate it is open to other evidence which is open ended. However, this is limited or clarified by the UCP 600 below for Incoterms financed and or paid by letters of credit. Furthermore, it uses outmoded phrases such as the policy rather than the modern insurance documents. Although Clause CIP/CIP Clause A5 refers to a provision of insurance documents, it is silent on tender. This is instead covered by UCP 600. Incoterms 2020 has continued the progressive developments, since Incoterms 1980, of accommodating changes in international trade practices by allowing for wider use and tender of "insurance documents" including electronic ones[58] instead of just the "insurance policy" prior to it. This has also included taking cognizance of other related ICC functions such as finance and transportation.[59] In this respect, the *ICC* Banking Practise has made changes to tender of insurance documents from the narrow insurance policy just as the ICC Transport Practices made alterations from tender of the narrow "bill of lading" to the more accommodating "transport documents"[60]

11.5.4 Tender of Underwriter's Cover-notes

The underwriter's covernote is third in line to the policy and certificate among the insurance documents. The role of covernotes in export policies had always been contentious. Covernotes are issued either by the insurers or brokers. This paragraph

[58] For Incoterms Rules and Documentary Credits and Electronic Documents, see, Ramberg, J: ICC Guide to Incoterms 2010, ICC Pub. No. 720E, pp. 36–41.

[59] See, (m) Ramberg, 'Synchronization of Contracts of Sale, Carriage, Insurance and Financing in International Trade' in Sarcevic (ed.) International Contracts and Conflicts of Laws (A Collection of Essays) (1990) p. 86 at 87.

[60] The same approach of transformation from Bills of Lading to Transport Documents is covered in Clauses 19–27 of the UCP 600.

deals with the former and the subsequent one deals with the latter. We have seen above that to cure a problem, where the status of the certificate is in doubt, the seller might be required to warrant the validity of the certificate in CIF contracts. It is not clear that is applicable to the insurers and broker's covernotes. In *Julien Praet et Cie SA v HG Poland Ltd*[61] Justice Pearson explored most aspects of the underwriter's covernote. He said:

> Traditionally, the underwriter of a syndicate sits in his box in the underwriting room at Lloyd's, and the Lloyd's broker who has prepared the proposed policy presents a slip giving details of the proposed risk to the underwriter, and the underwriter, if he finds the risk acceptable, insures it by initialling the slip. The policy is then prepared and issued. The Lloyd's broker is the agent of the assured. The underwriter deals only with the Lloyd's broker and not with any outside broker, nor with the assured. This procedure, if it had to be maintained in its full rigour without relaxation or modification, would impede foreign insurance business .....[and would and would make motor insurance business impossible][62]

On motor insurance, where the role of the covernote is best demonstrates, observed that the typical motorist is an impatient person in the sense that, having bout a car, he wishes to take delivery and drive off in it at once, and he would be willing to wait for the traditional steps to be taken at Lloyd's before he could obtain cover. Therefore, even in the United Kingdom, there has to be the familiar system of the covernote, which is issued at once on receipt of a proposal and covers the assured and puts the underwriters on risk for the period while the proposal is being considered and until a policy is either granted or refused.[63] On the external effect of a covernote, which would include tender for export/import, where applicable, he noted that that there are hundreds of motor distributors and other people in the UK who are authorised to issue covernotes on behalf of Mr Poland's syndicate when proposals for 'HP' policies are made.

He warned that great care should be taken, however, to comply with the requirements of Lloyd's because the authority to issued covernotes is applied for and granted through a Lloyd's broker, and the proposals are sent to him and presented by him to the underwriter, and he receives the policy from the underwriter and sends it to the assured as his agent. His Lordship justified his observations that the underwriter looks to the Lloyd's broker the premium, and has his accounts with the Lloyd's broker; the main insurance is duly granted at Lloyd's, and the preliminary covernote, which is inevitably granted outside Lloyd's by a person acting as an agent for the underwriter, is regarded as merely as incidental or ancillary matter.[64] So, the underwriters covernote is in theory issued by the underwriter but in practice by the broker or agent on their behalf. Were the loss to occur before issuance of the policy by the underwriter, then they should be tenderable.

[61] *Julien Praet et Cie SA v HG Poland Ltd* [1960] 1 Lloyd's Rep 420.

[62] Ibid at 428.

[63] Ibid.

[64] Ibid.

11.5.5 Tender of the "Brokers' Covernote

The underwriter's covernote issued by the underwriter or agent on their behalf is different from the broker's covernote, which is issued by the broker. The latter does not bind the underwriter and would therefore carry lesser weight than the former. In *Promos SA v European Grain & Shipping Ltd*,[65] Justice Parker determined the role of broker's cover notes[66] as a basic document in CIF contracts. However, the case does not distinguish between an ordinary (insurer's) cover note and the broker's cover note.[67] The former is legal document whereas the latter is issued by the broker either on his own behalf or on behalf of the insurer. In *Promos*, a contract for the sale of grain provided for payment to be made in exchange for certain shipping documents, including an insurance certificate, the sellers were required to insure the goods against certain specified risks whilst they were in transit between warehouses. In February 1974, the contract was varied by an agreement, which provided for the goods to be delivered from a warehouse during April 1974, the sellers were also required to provide free insurance for a period after presentation of the appropriate documents.

On 26 April 1974, the sellers tendered an insurance certificate, which did not apply to goods stored in a warehouse or cover the risks specified in the original insurance clause. The buyers rejected the insurance certificate. The sellers then obtained insurance covering the goods in store against all specified risks but the cover note delivered to the buyers on 1 May 1974 was also rejected. The buyers contended that the documents tendered were not in accordance with the contract. The GAFTA Board of Appeal found in favour of the sellers, but stated their award in the form of a special case. Justice Parker had no problem finding; first, that although the insurance clause in the original contract did not apply to goods in store, the provisions requiring insurance against specified risks remained in force notwithstanding the variation of the contract:

> The second question is: if the matter is to be approached via a marine policy, what are the usual terms which would have to be imported to cover the non-marine risk in store? There is a specific finding that the usual risks or the risks usually covered under in-store insurance

---

[65] *Promos SA v European Grain & Shipping Ltd* [1979] 1 Lloyd's Rep 375, at p. 388: "I take the cover note first. This is no more than a certificate that a contract of insurance on unspecified terms has been effected for the sellers. It may or may not have been on terms which cover other people than the sellers; it may or may not have included appropriate or usual conditions; it may or may not have been one which was transferable by endorsement or anything of that sort. It is no more than a statement by some brokers that an insurance has been effected... a cover note is not the same as a certificate of insurance as appears from the documents before me in the trade, and just as the buyer under c.i.f. contract is entitled to have the document for which he calls and not something like it, so under this contract the buyers were entitled to have, in my judgment, a certificate of insurance and not something like it.

[66] A broker's cover note is a document issued an insurance broker confirming that the insurance has been effected in certain terms. It does not bind the insurer [*Broit v Cohen & Sons (NSW) Ltd* (1926) 27)]. The issue of a note does not make the broker an insurer.

[67] The Insurance Company's covernote is probably more easily acceptable than a broker's one.

> do include strikes, civil commotions and riots. Therefore, even if cl. 17 did not remain, as I have held effective in its specification of risks, I would be of the opinion that it was in any event the sellers' duty to cover such risks on the basis that they were the usual risks to be covered in an in-store policy.[68]

Therefore, the sellers' insurance certificate tendered on 29 April was inadequate, as those risks were not covered.

Secondly, the court also found that the insurance certificate was also inadequate because it covered the goods from warehouse to warehouse only whereas the contract as varied applied to goods stored in a warehouse. Accordingly, the sellers were not entitled to rely on the cover note delivered on 1 May since it did not constitute an insurance certificate. Thus, the buyers were entitled to reject the entire documents tender: certificate and covernote. It should be noted that neither the insurance certificate nor the cover note complied with the contract since no provision was made for the insurance for a period after presentation of the shipping documents. Although the decision in the case rested on its peculiar circumstances, Sassoon seems to agree with this position.[69] However, a broker's cover note may be valid tender in both Incoterms 2010[70] and UCP 500[71] but not in UCP 600.[72] Schmitthoff, on the other hand, does not seem to make a distinction between them.[73]

11.5.6 Whether Tender of Letter of Insurance Acceptable in CIF Policy

In export policies letters of insurance are sometimes used instead of covernotes, certificates or policies. Letters of insurance are used where neither certificate nor policy is issued such as in open covers, blanket policies and floating policies where the importer may require a simple certification or some other form of assurance from the insurer that the exporter is insured. There is no legal or insurance definition of the letters of insurance, as it is used only in practice. Since *Manbre Saccharine Co v Corn Products Co Ltd,*[74] Justice McCardie's ruling[75] has been and remains the author-

---

[68] At p. 388.

[69] Sassoon, *CIF and FOB Contracts*, Note 3, at pp. 1730174.

[70] Incoterms 2010 CIF Clause A3 (b), Notes 20/67, at pp. 110 is silent on the type of document to be tendered.

[71] UCP 500, Note 20, Clause 34(c), is also silent on the documents to be tendered.

[72] UCP 600, Note 20, Clause 28(c), but was acceptable under UCP 500 Clause 34 (c) if specifically authorised by the Credit.

[73] Schimitthoff, *The Law and Practice of International Trade*, Note 5, para. 19-011 at pp. 413–414.

[74] *Manbre Saccharine Co v Corn Products Co Ltd* [1919] 1KB 198 at 216; [1918-19] All ER Rep 980.

[75] Ibid, at p. 205 "In the present case the defendants tendered no policy of insurance at all. They merely made the following statement in their letter of March 14, 1917: 'We hereby hold you covered by insurance for the amount of 4,3221. in accordance with the terms of policy of insurance in our possession re shipment ex s.s. Algonquin.'… It was suggested on behalf of the plaintiffs that

ity for the proposition. Among other many authorities, the case once more, stands for authority first, that under a CIF contract the vendor is bound to the purchaser for a proper policy of insurance together with the other shipping documents, and that that obligation is not performed by the vendor guaranteeing to hold the purchaser covered by insurance in accordance with the terms of the policy of insurance in the vendor's possession (a letter of insurance). Secondly, the case is also further authority for the principle that the purchaser under a CIF contract is entitled to demand a policy of insurance, which covers, and covers only, the goods mentioned in the bills of lading and invoices.[76] The rationale for the principle is understandable. This is to stop the seller from substituting other policies for the contract goods.

This throws into confusion the difference between practice and theory. In practice, letters of insurance issued under blanket policies[77] such as open covers[78] are acceptable as valid tenders. These are cheaper and more efficient ways of conducting business as they cut back tender of a broker's cover note[79] in lieu of the policy/certificate/letter.[80] Tender of insurance documents might not be a requirement under certain circumstances in other common law jurisdictions.[81] However, a letter of insurance is not valid tender either under INCOTERMS 2020 or UCP 600 unless it falls under a 'declaration under an open cover'.[82]

---

the letter amounted either to an equitable assignment of the insurance moneys to the extent of 4,322l. or to a declaration of trust to such amount in respect of these moneys. Even if this suggestion be well founded yet there is a wide difference between an actual policy of insurance transferable to the defendants as contemplated by s. 50, sub. s. 3, of the Marine Insurance Act, 1906 (6 Edw. 7, c. 41), and such a letter as that of the defendants here. The plaintiffs, I hold, were clearly entitled to a policy and not to a mere assertion by the defendants that a policy existed and that the defendants would hold the plaintiffs covered."

[76] Although not directly relevant to the issue in point, the case also authority for the fact that a vendor under a CIF contract for the sale of goods, who has shipped the appropriate goods under a proper contract of carriage and obtained the proper documents, can effectively tender those documents to the purchaser notwithstanding that he knows at the time of such tender of the loss of goods- the presumption being that they will be covered by a valid policy.

[77] Blanket policies, Open Covers and Floating Policies are policies which in a single sum insured, covers a number of separate items of property without subdivision of the amount. The approach is not unique to CIF or exports and indeed started in fire insurance and motor insurance for large risks and also in fidelity guarantee insurance to cover the whole staff without mention of the name or position, the premium being computed on the number of employees in specific categories insurance.

[78] Ibid; Open covers have almost same meaning and function as blanket policies above and floating policies below. It is borrowed from unvalued policy in s 27(1) of the *Marine Insurance Act 1906*.it is the business language equivalent of a floating policy. When there are regular shipments of goods it is usual to arrange an open cover to avoid the necessity of separate policies for each sending. The two most common methods are the *floating policy* and the *open cover.*

[79] See Note 184–191 post.

[80] See Schmitthoff, Note 5, at para. 19-011 at pp. 413–414 at 414; and the sub-paragraph (f) below and authorities cited therein.

[81] For Australian practice, see *Piesse v Tasmanian Ochardists & Producers Co-op Assocn Ltd* (1919) 15Tas LR67 where omission of the policy did not affect tender in the CIF contract; and *Lascelles& Co Ltd* (1921) 21 SRNSW 773; 38 NSWWN 238 where tender of a certificate instead of a policy was acceptable even where there was deviation.

[82] It is not mentioned in UCP 600, Note 20, Clause 28(a).

11.5.7 Whether a "Declaration of Insurance" Valid Tender Under Open Cover/Blanket/Floating Policies?

11.5.7.1 Declaration Under Open Cover

Also called open cover, open cover is a marine cargo insurance that provides blanket cover against loss or damage to all goods transported by a specific carrier, or by a specific shipper, during a stated period. An open policy is one in which the amount of the interest of the insured is not fixed by the policy, and is to be ascertained in case of loss. Under its terms, the insured is required to periodically provide the insurer with the description, quantity, and value of goods shipped during that period. This type of insurance policy intended to cover an indefinite number of future individual shipments. The insurance contract remains in force until cancelled. Under the open policy, individual successive shipments are periodically reported or declared to the insurer and reported shipments are automatically covered on or after the policy's inception date. Open policies can provide efficiency and savings for all parties concerned, especially when the insured conducts a significant volume of highly similar transactions/like letters of insurance, where open covers, blanket policies and floating policies[83] such as in *Johnson & Co Ltd v Bryant*[84] are issued, the insured simply makes a declaration of export or import against the policies.

It is, however, doubtful whether a letter of insurance ranks above a declaration under an open cover and/or blanket policies in the hierarchy of insurance documents. Nevertheless, since open covers[85] and blanket policies are both known to common law and export insurance practice, it would follow that such tenders are valid. That was so in *Macleod Ross & Co Ltd v Compagnie d'Assurances Generals Helvetia of St. Gall.*[86] It will be remembered that an open cover policy is a form of long-term cargo contract effected on the original contract without any limit in the aggregate and requires that policies be issued off the cover on each. According to *Phoenix Insurance Co of Hartford v Monchy*,[87] under the open cover the underwriter agrees to cover all shipments commencing transit within a specified period or if "always open", from a specified attaching date.

11.5.7.2 Declaration Under a Blanket Policy

A blanket policy,[88] on the other hand is a policy, which, in a single sum insured, covers a number of separate shipments without subdivision of the amount. The approach is used in large risks to cover the whole shipments without mention of

---

[83] Floating policies have same meaning as open covers and/or blanket policies, See *Marine Insurance Act* 1906 s.29(1); *Halsbury's Laws*, Note 7, paras. 282–283 and texts thereunder; *Johnson & Co Ltd v Bryant* (1896) 12 TLR368; Schmitthoff, *The Law and Practice of International Trade*, Note 5, pp. 407–410.

[84] *Johnson & Co Ltd v Bryant* (1896) 12 TLR368.

[85] Schmitthoff, Note 5 at pp. 410–412; See also *Macleod Ross & Co Ltd v Compagnie d'Assurances Generals Helvetia of St. Gall* [1952] W.N.56 and

[86] (Macleod Ross & Co Ltd v Compagnie d'Assurances Generals Helvetia of St.Gall [1952] W.N.56).

[87] Ibid; see also *Phoenix Insurance Co of Hartford v Monchy* (1929) 45 TLR.

[88] Schmitthoff, Note 5, at p. 412.

specific categories and for large declaration of shipments. Both policies resemble floating policies,[89] which defines the insurance in general terms with the actual shipment to be defined by subsequent declarations and which runs until the insured sum is exhausted by the declarations and the declarations made in a chronological order unless the policy provides otherwise/. The policy is taken to cover losses within the particular time and place. The policy is taken for a certain amount and premium is paid on the whole of it in the beginning of the policy and is re-adjusted at the end of the policy according to the actual amount at risk. If the actual coverage of risk is less than the total amount of insurance, the premium related to the excess amount is returned to the insured. On the other hand, if the amounts of shipments are greater than the insured sum, additional premium is charged over the excess protection.

11.5.7.3 Declaration Under a Floating Policy

Although not frequent in modern use, of the three the floating policy is the only one provided for in the MIA1906.[90] The type of floating policy contained in the Act relates to ships rather than goods although the former affects the latter.

> **29 Floating policy by ship or ships.**
> (1) A floating policy is a policy which describes the insurance in general terms, and leaves the name of the ship or ships and other particulars to be defined by subsequent declaration.
>
> (2) The subsequent declaration or declarations may be made by indorsement on the policy, or in other customary manner.
>
> (3) Unless the policy otherwise provides, the declarations must be made in the order of dispatch or shipment. They must, in the case of goods, comprise all consignments within the terms of the policy, and the value of the goods or other property must be honestly stated, but an omission or erroneous declaration may be rectified even after loss or arrival, provided the omission or declaration was made in good faith.
>
> (4) Unless the policy otherwise provides, where a declaration of value is not made until after notice of loss or arrival, the policy must be treated as an unvalued policy as regards the subject-matter of that declaration.

In any case the hull policy is now adopted for goods as well.

Floating policies are available at both Lloyds[91] and non-Lloyds markets. The policy is a good mechanism to cover "held covered" clauses in export policies.[92] In

---

[89] Ibid, at pp. 407–410; See also *Arnould's Law of Marine Insurance* (17th edn, 2008, with 2010 supplement), para. 9-04 for legal of declarations.

[90] *Marine Insurance Act 1906* Section 29.

[91] For the operation of the floating policy at Lloyds see Dover (1975), p. 133.

[92] And with it the need for the insured to give notice to the insurer in event of possible loss: *Thames and Mersey Insurance Co Ltd v HLT & Co* [1917] 2KB 48.

Union Society of Canton Ltd v Wills & Co,[93] a floating policy on goods, it was held that: "the declaration of interests must be made to insurer's agents "as soon as possible".[94] (Author to sort out the page numbers 21 or 28 in the case and for treatment of the floating policy under s.29 (1).) The full consequences of the declaration under a floating policy was given by their Lordships, delivered by Lord Parmoor in the case:[95]

> The policy is an open or floating policy under which the liability of the insurers in the first instance attaches before the sailing of the vessel, and therefore at a time before the declaration of interest is due to be made. It was referred to as "a warehouse to warehouse policy," but in any case, it is clear that the declaration of interest is not a condition precedent in the sense that a non-compliance therewith vitiates the whole policy ab initio. If, for instance, the merchandise insured had been destroyed by fire in port before the sailing of the vessel, the promise to make a declaration after the sailing of the vessel would not avoid the policy, and the insurers would be liable, if in other respects the conditions of the policy had been complied with. A condition, however, is not the less a warranty because it is a condition subsequent, and unless such a subsequent condition is complied with at the time when its performance is due under the contract, the insurer is discharged from liability as from the date of the breach. Their Lordships have already referred to s. 39, sub-s. 3, of the Commonwealth Marine Insurance Act, No. 11, 1909, which affirms the common law principle that this discharge is without prejudice to any liability incurred by the insurer before that date.[96]

and Justice Moor-Bick in *Glencore International AG v Alpina Insurance* Co (No. 2):[97]

> One comes back, therefore, to the construction to be placed on the declarations by which cover was requested for these cargoes. In my view an important factor to be taken into account when answering this question is the fact that condition 1.18 forms part of an open cover and is of a facultative/obligatory nature. The essential purpose of a contract of this kind is to ensure that cover is continuously available in respect of goods bought and sold in the course of trading and is available when, and for as long as, it may be required. The nature of commodity trading is such that it will often be difficult to tell how long goods placed in store are likely to remain there, so it is likely to be of advantage to the insured to be able to obtain cover for an indefinite rather than a fixed period and no doubt insurers are aware of that….
>
> I am satisfied that a request for cover in the form of a declaration to which no specific time limit was attached is to be construed as a request for continuous cover until the goods ceased to be on risk or Alpina [the insurer] was notified that cover was no longer required.[98]

11.5.7.4 Whether a Slip Can Be Tendered

In hierarchical terms the slip is normally the lowest of the insurance documents. The evidential nature of the slip is now contained in s.89 of the MIA,1906 thus:

---

[93] *Union Society of Canton Ltd v Wills & Co* [1916] 1 AC 21.

[94] Ibid at 28!!??

[95] *Union Insurance Society of canton Ltd v George Willis & Co* [1916] 1 AC 281.

[96] Ibid at 287.

[97] *Glencore International AG v Alpina Insurance Co* (No. 2) [2004] 1 Lloyd's Rep 567.

[98] Ibid at 569.

89 Slip as evidence

Where there is a duly stamped policy, reference may be made, as heretofore, to the slip or covering note, in any legal proceeding.

Like certificate of insurance it is a document containing the essential features of the proposed insurance and submitted by the broker to the underwriters for their consideration and initialling. In *Ionides v Pacific Fire and Marine Insurance*[99] Lord Blackburn held that:

As a slip is clearly a contract for marine insurance, and is equally clearly not a policy, it is, by virtue of these enactments (the stamp laws) not valid, that is, not enforceable at law or equity; but it may be given in evidence whatever it is, though not valid, material

In *Grover and Grover Ltd v Mathews,*[100] Justice Hamilton ruled that such an initialling constitutes an acceptance of the proposed insurance.[101] And in *Cory v Patton*[102] it was held the slip was evidence for purposes of correcting an error in the name of the ship: also, that the insured's duty to disclose material facts ceases on the slip being initialled and that if the insurer seeks to avoid the avoid the policy on the grounds of non-disclosure of a material fact, the date on the slip would be material to show whether, when the fact came to the knowledge of the assured, the contract had or had not been concluded.[103] Since the contract is concluding on initialling, it would that were the loss to occur after that but before the issuance of the certificate and/or actual policy then the seller may tender the slip.

One reads this from Justice Mathew's opined in *Thompson v Adams*[104] that once the slip has been initialled the underwriter binds himself to sign the policy in accordance with it.[105] He concluded that in those circumstances the signing of the policy is a mere formality and may take place even after loss, and the underwriter cannot refuse to sign the policy on the ground that the broker failed to tender it within a reasonable time after the initialling of the slip.[106] However, the slip cannot be used to contradict the terms of the policy (*British and Foreign Marine Insurance Co Ltd v Sturge (1897 2 Com Cas 244*), unless there is a clear case of common mistake. It may then be used for the purpose of rectifying the policy *Empress Assurance Coprn v Bowring (1905)* 11Com Cas 107 at 114 per Kennedy J. However, a slip is different from a 'slip policy' which should be tenderable like any other ordinary policy.

11.5.7.5 Whether a ppi. Policy May Be Tendered

The policy is issued to avoid the complication of the principle of insurable interest. These are called 'Policy Proof of Interest' and are honoured by the insurer even in

[99] *Ionides v Pacific Fire and Marine Insurance* (1872) LR 7QB517.

[100] *Grover and Grover Ltd v Mathews* (1910) 15 Com Cas249.

[101] Ibid at 256.

[102] *Cory v Patton* (1874) LR 9 QB 577 Ex Ch.

[103] For the assured's duty of disclosure, see s 18(1) of the *Marine Insurance Act* 1906 and for conclusion of the contract see s.21.

[104] *Thompson v Adams* (1889) 23 QBD 361.

[105] Ibid, at 364–365.

[106] Ibid.

absence of insurable interest. This policy is based on mutual understanding, so, it is called honoured policies. This is also called wagering policies because insurable interest is not required; consequently, it cannot be legally enforceable. The policy is known as a gaming and wagering policy. It is an offence to deal in such policies under s1 of the Marine Insurance (Gambling Policies) Act 1905. Furthermore, the policy is forbidden and is null and void under s1 of the Life Assurance Act 1774. It is now contained in s.4 of the MIA 1906 which provides that:

4. Avoidance of wagering or gaming contracts
(1) Every contract of marine insurance by way of gaming or wagering is void.

(2) A contract of marine insurance is deemed to be a gaming or wagering contract—

(a) Where the assured has not an insurable interest as defined by this Act, and the contract is entered into with no expectation of acquiring such an interest; or

(b) Where the policy is made "interest or no interest," or "without further proof of interest than the policy itself," or "without benefit of salvage to the insurer," or subject to any other like term:

Provided that, where there is no possibility of salvage, a policy may be effected without benefit of salvage to the insurer.

Thomas Cheshire & Co v Vaughan Bros & Co,[107] Lord Scrutton opined that a policy containing a ppi clause would be void even though the assured has in fact, an insurable interest;[108] Justice Lawrence in *Re London County Commercial Reinsurance Office Ltd*[109] went even further suggesting that a policy containing a detachable ppi clause, is void even though at the time of claim under it the clause may have been detached by the assured.[110] As such is not surprising that Justice McCardie in *John Edwards & Co v Motor Union Insurance Co Ltd*[111] ruled that there is no right of subrogation under a ppi policy.[112] For those reasons it is unlikely that this type of policy can be tendered to a third party such as buyer and/or buyer's bank. An insurer without rights of subrogation would not pay out under such policy either.

---

[107] *Thomas Cheshire & Co v Vaughan Bros & Co* (1920) 123 LT 487.

[108] Ibid at 493.

[109] Re *London County Commercial Reinsurance Office Ltd* (1922) 127 LT20.

[110] Ibid at 26.

[111] *John Edwards & Co v Motor Union Insurance Co Ltd* (1923) 128 LT 276.

[112] Ibid at 278.

11.6 Tender of Insurance and Other Documents Under UCP 600

11.6.1 The UCP Background

The drafting of the UCP started in 1927 and took two years to 1929. The first Revision was produced in 1933.[113] This was followed by the second Revision in 18 years later in 1951.[114] Those two contained Commercial in their title. The third Revision came 11 years later in 1962[115] and the fourth Revision 12 years later in 1974.[116] The 1974 was the turning point as the numbering takes the 100s numbers. The much more modern fifth Revision 19 years later in 1993[117] and sixth and latest Revision 14 years later in 2007[118] were almost identical and both included electronic supplementary versions.

Thus, the UCP 500 (UCP 500) and UCP 600 (UCP 600) were universally and modern recognised set of rules regulating the operation of letters of credit, and the rights and duties of the parties inter se. The UCP, first published in 1933, is also produced by the International Chamber of Commerce (ICC), and like INCOTERMS, has been regularly updated to take into account changes in international business practices. Until 1 July 2007 the 1993 revision, UCP 500, which came into effect on 1 January 1994, was the applicable. It contained a number of provisions, which deal with matters relating to insurance documents. Since CIF and CIP are the only trade terms where the procurement of insurance cover forms an integral part of the sales contract, and where insurance documents therefore necessarily form part of the shipping documents, these provisions effectively relate only to contracts concluded on these terms.

11.6.2 Relationship with Incoterms

INCOTERMS state that “lacking agreement, minimum cover of the Institute Cargo Clauses be provided”. This is essentially “named perils” coverage which is rarely adequate for the needs of the buyer. Insurance must also be in negotiable form enabling losses to be payable to the buyer or other party having an insurable interest in the shipment at the time of loss. Proof, or evidence, of insurance is required which is usually accomplished by issuance of a Special Cargo Policy or Certificate

---

[113] Uniform Customs and Practice for Documentary Commercial Credits, ICC Publications No. 82.

[114] Uniform Customs and Practice for Documentary Commercial Credits, ICC Publications No. 151.

[115] Uniform Customs and Practice for Documentary Credits, ICC Publications No. 400.

[116] Uniform Customs and Practices for Documentary Credits, ICC Publications No. 500 and Supplement eUCP 500.

[117] Uniform Customs and Practice for Documentary Credits, ICC Publications No 600 and Supplement eUCP 600.

[118] Supplements eUCP 500 and eUCP600.

of Insurance by the seller or his insurer. Insurance should cover the shipment from the place of origin to the final destination of the buyer.

Incoterms and the UCP are, of course, separate documents: the former relate to the sales contract, and deals with the buyer's and seller's obligations to each other; the latter relates to the tender of documents for payments under a letter of credit contract. The UCP relevant provisions with which we are concerned, i.e. those relating to insurance documents, deal with the seller's obligations to the paying bank. However, most letters of credit are ordinarily governed by the UCP, and parties who stipulate that their sales contract shall be governed by Incoterms will generally stipulate that the tender of documents for credit contracts be governed by the UCP.

Thus, where payment is to be made under a letter of credit, both sets of requirements will apply. Where this is the case, the seller will effectively owe two sets of obligations to two separate persons relating to the same matter. Thus, it is pertinent to look at both sets of obligations to see whether they clash, or whether it is possible to fulfil them both in the same manner. Although the UCP 500 has been replaced by the UCP 600, parties are free to use either, hence the coverage of the former below. Although UCP 600 might supersede UCP 500 in some jurisdictions and merchants, this chapter will discuss both. Like Incoterms, parties are free to use earlier or older UCPs.

11.6.3 Tender Under CIF Contracts Financed by Banks

One potential area of conflict between the requirements of CIF terms and insurance coverage is when insurance actually ceases. By definition CIF refers to the port of destination. CIF also obligates the seller to provide insurance covering the buyer's risk of loss or damage which in almost all cases extends until the goods are delivered to his place of destination. Banks are usually involved in the financing of CIF shipments. If a Letter of Credit stipulates CIF port of destination and the insurance certificate stipulates another place, the bank may reject the certificate. Conversely, if the certificate shows the port of destination as the final place of insurance in order to comply with the Letter of Credit, the buyer will have no insurance for transit beyond the port of destination. Therefore, it is important for the actual place of insured destination to be shown clearly in the sales contract, invoice, letter of credit instructions and the certificate. A suggestion would be: Name of Buyer's Warehouse, Street Address, City, State/Province, Country, or other appropriately identified location.

11.6.4 Tender Documents for Letters of Credit

As indicate, the UCP clarifies some of the Incoterms' ambiguities by focusing on insurance documents instead of the policy, the same way it does for transport documents in Clause 19-27 rather than just bills of lading. The insurance documents and risks coverage, for export-import trade are contained in Clause 28 of UCP 600 as follows:

Clause 28 of UCP 600

(a) The change of usage from "insurance policy" to "insurance documents", which allowed for the introduction and tender of substitutes (except for insurance covernotes) to the policy and other documents;[119]

(b) Arising from (a) above, the widening of tender to include substitute documents such as insurance certificates or a declaration under an open cover in lieu of the insurance policy;[120]

(c) However, maintenance of the pre-eminence of the insurance policy itself but keeping its tender in lieu of the above substitutes;[121]

(d) Reconciling the duration of the risk cover with Incoterms, common law and international trade practice;[122]

(e) Synchronising Clause A3/B3 CIF and CIP rules, common law and now international requirement that the insurance premium be in the same currency as both the sales contract and credit contract;[123]

(f) Retaining the minimum requirement and indication of the percentage thereof, of the coverage in CIF and CIP Incoterms, common law and international practice;[124]

---

[119] (28(a)) "An insurance document, such as an insurance policy, an insurance certificate or a declaration under an open cover, must appear to be issued and signed by an insurance company, an underwriter or their agents or their proxies".

[120] (28(d)) "An insurance policy is acceptable in lieu of an insurance certificate or a declaration under an open cover".

[121] Ibid.

[122] (28(e)) "The insurance document must indicate that risks are covered at least between the place of taking in charge or shipment and the place of discharge or final destination as stated in the credit".

[123] (28(f)(i)) "When the CIF or CIP value cannot be determined from the documents, the amount of insurance coverage must be calculated on the basis of the amount for which honour or negotiation is requested or the gross value of the goods as shown on the invoice, whichever is greater".

[124] (28(f)(ii)) "A requirement in the credit for insurance coverage to be for a percentage of the value of the goods, of the invoice value or similar is deemed to be the minimum amount of coverage required. If there is no indication in the credit of the insurance coverage required, the amount of insurance coverage must be at least 110% of the CIF or CIP value of the goods".

(g) Harmonising the same requirements and provisions regarding the insured value of CIF and CIP rules to be 110%

(h) Clarifying, however, that where CIF and CIP rules' insurable value cannot be determined then the gross value should be shown instead;[125]

(i) Stupefying the type of cover provided including any additional risks covered;[126]

(j) Clarifying the issue of the nature and extent of the "all risks" policy and exclusions to it;[127] including exclusion clauses therein;[128] and

(k) Allowing for the normal insurance market practice of tendered of policy and related documents to be subject to "franchise" or "excess" (deductible)

This provision (Art 28 of UCP 600) reproduces the essentials of insurance clauses of CIF and CIP and synchronises with similar provisions of cargo clauses. The CIF[129] and FOB[130] insurance clauses are also now standard terms in GAFTA[131] and commodity trade contracts and adopted by other international sales contracts.

Under Clauses 4 and 5 of the CIF Sample Contract for Sale of Goods, Tender of Documents requirements are provided as follows:

---

[125] Ibid.

[126] Ibid.

[127] (28(g)) "A credit should state the type of insurance required and, if any, the additional risks to be covered. An insurance document will be accepted without regard to any risks that are not covered if the credit uses imprecise terms such as "usual risks" or "customary risks".

[128] 28(h)) "When a credit requires insurance against "all risks" and an insurance document is presented containing any "all risks" notation or clause, whether or not bearing the heading "all risks", the insurance document will be accepted without regard to any risks stated to be excluded"

[129] (28(i)), "An insurance document may contain reference to any exclusion clause".

[130] 28(j), "An insurance document may indicate that the cover is subject to a franchise or excess (deductible).".

[131] GAFTA INSURANCE TERMS No. No. 72, Effective 1st April 2012. See, also clause 13 (Insurance) of GAFTA CONTRACT No. 38, FOB TERMS, Effective 1st September 2018; and the more elaborate Clause 13(Insurance) of the GRAIN AND FEED TRADE ASSOCIATION, CONTRACT FOR THE SHIPMENT OF GOODS FROM CENTRAL AND EASTERN EUROPE IN BULK PARCELS OR CARGOES TALE QUALE – CIF/CIFFO/C&F/C&FFO TERMS, Contract No. 48, Effective 1st September 2010.

CIF Sample Contract for Sale of Goods, Tender of Documents

4/5. The Seller shall ship the goods in the ship and despatch the documents relating to the said goods namely the contract of affreightment, insurance policy, invoice. bills of lading etc. to Its Bankers at the port of arrival.

5/6. The said documents duly endorsed in favour of the Buyer will be handed over to the Buyer's Bankers against encashment of the Letter of Credit and the Buyer will receive the same from Its Bankers to enable the Buyer to get the goods cleared at the port of arrival. Such delivery of documents will be deemed to be delivery of the goods to the Buyer and thereafter the goods will be at the risk of the Buyer.[132]

11.6.5 Sellers's Obligations

11.6.5.1 Insurance Documents Deemed Issued and Signed by the Insurer

With regard to the insurance documents and coverage, Clause 28(a) of the new UCP 600 provides that an insurance document, such as an insurance policy, an insurance certificate or a declaration under an open cover, must appear to be issued and signed by an insurance company, an underwriter or their agents or their proxies.[133] This sub-clause outlines the type of documents that are covered, e.g., an insurance policy, insurance certificate or declaration under an open cover. An insurance document may not be signed by a proxy for or on behalf of an insurance company or underwriter. Similar language has been used to that in the transport provisions[134] to describe how an agent or proxy is to declare the capacity in which it is signing if an insurance document is signed by an agent or proxy, it must indicate whether it has signed for or no behalf of the insurance company or underwriter. Clause continues that: "Any signature by an agent or proxy must indicate whether the agent or proxy has signed for or on behalf of the insurance company or underwriter.[135]

11.6.5.2 Documents Issued in More Than One Original

This is covered in Clause 28(b) stating that when the insurance document indicates that it has been issued in more than one original, all originals must be presented.[136] The sub-clause requires that in this event, all of the original must be presented even if the documentary credit makes reference to a single original. An insurance document stated to be issued "in duplicate" does not necessarily infer that tow originals had been created. In this event, the document marked "duplicate" will be considered to be a copy and need not be presented unless the insurance document itself includes

[132] Ref: for text see Annex IX to this book.

[133] Art 28(a).

[134] Clauses 19–25.

[135] ibid.

[136] Art. 28(b) See "Brokers Cover note" above.

reference to the fact that either the "original" or "duplicate" may be presented in the event of claim. In such an event, the insurance document marked "original" and "duplicate" must be presented.

11.6.5.3 Tender of Cover Notes in Lieu of Policy

This is covered in Clause 28(c) which stating that cover notes will not be accepted.[137] This sub-clause expands the principle in clause 34 of the UCP 500 above to state that a cover note issued by any party (not just the broker) is not acceptable. Presentation of an insurance policy is acceptable when the credit requires an insurance certificate or a declaration under an open cover. The UCP 500 position is unchanged in the wording of sub-clause (d) below.

11.6.5.4 Tender of Policy in Lieu of Certificate or Declaration Under Open Cover

This is covered in Clause 28(d), which provides that an insurance policy is acceptable in lieu of an insurance certificate or a declaration under an open cover.[138] However, presentation an insurance certificate or a declaration under an open cover is not acceptable if the credit requires and insurance policy. It is understood that whilst an insurance certificate or declaration under an open cover provides proof of insurance, in the case of a claim, if there is any discrepancy of insurance coverage between the policy and the certificate or declaration under an open cover, the insurance coverage in the policy will prevail. It is understood that some ICC National Committees suggested that the date of an insurance document, which is later than the date of shipment, should be acceptable, since the Institute Cargo Clause cover the "Transit Clause" as indicated in the policy. The insurance attaches from the time the goods the goods leave the warehouse or place of storage at the place named therein for the commencement of the transit. However, the principle of examining a presentation to determine, based on the documents alone, whether or not the documents appear on their face to constitute a complying presentation, applies.

11.6.5.5 The Date of the Insurance Document

This is covered in Clause 28(e) which provides that the date of the insurance document must be no later than the date of shipment, unless it appears from the insurance document that the cover is effective from a date not later than the date of shipment.[139] Under sub-clause (e), a document examiner is not expected to check details of the specific Institute Cargo Clause to ascertain the effective date of cover. If the insurance document shows that the cover is effective from the date not later than the date of shipment, as determined by the appropriate transport clause[140] it is acceptable even if the date of the insurance document is later than the date of shipment. An

[137] Art 28(c).

[138] Art 28 (d).

[139] Art 28(e).

[140] Clauses 19–25).

insurance document that is dated later than the date of shipment or evidences cover effective from the date later than the date of shipment is no acceptable.

11.6.5.6 Amount and Currency of Cover

This is covered in Clause 28(f) (i) which provides that the insurance document must indicate the amount of insurance coverage and be in the same currency as the credit.[141] Sub-clause (f) requires that the insurance document indicate the amount of insurance coverage. The amount of insurance coverage must be in the same currency as in the credit. It must be at least 110% of the CIF value or CIP value, if there is no indication in the documentary of the amount of insurance coverage. If the CIF or CIP value is not determinable from the presentation, the amount of insurance coverage must be calculated on whichever is greater of (a) the amount for which honour or negotiation is requested; or (b) the gross value of the goods as shown in the invoice. When accredit requires, for example, an insurance coverage for a percentage of the invoice value, that percentage amount is deemed to be a requirement for a minimum percentage of the invoice value. An insurance document presented showing the amount of insurance coverage exceeding this minimum requirement is acceptable. There is no limit to the maximum especially as, in this event, the beneficiary is not disadvantaged.

11.6.5.7 Stipulation on Minimum Amount of Coverage

This is covered in Clause 28(f) (ii) which provides that a requirement in the credit for insurance coverage to be for a percentage of the value of the goods, of the invoice value or similar is deemed to be the minimum amount of coverage required.[142] If there is no indication in the credit of the insurance coverage required, the amount of insurance coverage must be at least 110% of the CIF or CIP value of the goods.[143] When the CIF or CIP value cannot be determined from the documents, the amount of insurance coverage must be calculated on the basis of the amount for which honour or negotiation is requested or the gross value of the goods as shown on the invoice, whichever is greater".[144]

11.6.5.8 Duration of Cover

Duration of cover is dealt with in Clause 28(f) (iii) which provides that the insurance document must indicate that risks are covered at least between the place of taking in charge or shipment and the place of discharge or final destination as stated in the credit.[145] Finally, sub-clause (f) requires that the insurance document cover at least the risks between the place of taking in charge or shipment and the place of discharge or final destination as stated in the documentary credit. For example, if a documentary credit requiring insurance document calls for a dispatch to be effected

[141] Art 28(f)(i).

[142] Art 28(f)(ii).

[143] ibid.

[144] ibid.

[145] Art 28(f)(iii).

from London Heathrow Airport to Singapore Changi Airport, an insurance document presented showing that the insurance coverage commenced from Liverpool, through to London Heathrow Airport, and until the goods arrived at Singapore Changi Airport, will be acceptable.

11.6.5.9 Type and Extent of Cover

Type of cover and any mention additional, usual and customary risks are covered by Clause 28(g), which provides that a credit should state the type of insurance required and, if any, the additional risks to be covered. An insurance document will be accepted without regard to any risks that are not covered if the credit uses imprecise terms such as "usual risks" or "customary risks".[146] Sub-clause (g) requires that a documentary credit specify the type of insurance coverage required, and the additional risks to be covered, if any, when an insurance document is to be presented. The main clauses in use are:

(a) Institute Cargo Clause "A", which provide cover on comprehensive basis "All Risks";
(b) Institute Cargo Clauses "B", which provide cover only against specified risks;
(c) Institute Cargo Clauses "C", which provide cover for fewer specified risks; and
(d) Institute Cargo Clauses (Air) (excluding sending by post), which provide cover for shipment by air on "All Risks".

It is important to note that only Institute Cargo Clauses (Air) will provide cover for air shipment. It is not correct to call for an insurance document covering Institute Cargo Clauses "A", if shipment is to be effected by air. There are other classes specially designed to cover certain commodities (for example, frozen food, timber, sugar, etc), and these should be clearly called in the documentary credit. Any imprecise terms such as "usual risks", or "customary risks", must not be used. If they are used in a documentary credit, a bank will accept an insurance document as presented without regard to any risks that are not covered.

11.6.5.10 Meaning of an "*All Risks*" Notation in the Policy

This is covered by Clause 28(h), which provides that: "When a credit requires insurance against "all risks" and an insurance document is presented containing any "all risks" notation or clause, whether or not bearing the heading "all risks", the insurance document will be accepted without regard to any risks stated to be excluded".[147] Sub-clause 28(h) continues the themes in sub-clause 28(g). Accordingly, a documentary credit should not call for an insurance coverage against "all risks", as there are various types of "all risks" coverage in different markets. Thus, sub-clause 28(h) implies that the documentary credit should be more specific in its requirement for insurance against "all risks", an insurance document containing any "all risks"

[146] Art 28(g).

[147] Art 28(h). See the "All risks policy" in note—supra.

notation or clause will be accepted without regard to any risks stated to be excluded, even if it does not bear the heading "all risks" in the document.

11.6.5.11 Notation on Exclusions in the Policy

This is covered in Clause 28 (i) which provides that an insurance document may contain reference to any exclusion clause.[148] An insurance document containing reference to any exclusion clause is acceptable. Thus, the drafters due to the numerous exclusion clauses currently appearing on insurance documents included the rule in this sub-clause 28(i). These relate mainly to acts of terrorism. The insurance industry, when approached by the Drafting Committee, indicated that such clauses were considered industry standard exclusions. During the drafting process, the Drafting Committee created a list of the clauses that were being seen at that time with a view to incorporating them in sub-clause 28(i). However, because of this list could change (deletions or additions) and because of the inability to amend the list once the UCP 600 was published other than via ICC opinions approved by the ICC Banking Commission, a decision was made to cater for any possible exclusion clauses.

11.6.5.12 Provisions as to Franchise and Deductibles

11.6.5.12.1 Document Subject to Franchise Acceptable

Clause 28(j) provides that an insurance document may indicate that the cover is subject to a franchise or excess (deductible).[149] The UCP does not define a franchise but case law does. For insurance purposes, a franchise is a clause in the policy stating that no claim is payable unless the amount involved exceeds a stated amount. Once the claim exceeds that amount the entire claim is payable. The franchise eliminates small claims but unlike an excess, which can also be used to eliminate small claims, does not reduce the cost of all claims by the amount of the excess. The franchise concept originated in marine insurance.[150] Finally, sub-clause 28(j) adopts a position that an insurance document indicating that the cover is subject to a franchise or excess (deductible) is acceptable, remains unchanged from that appearing in UCP sub-clause 35(c). Neither the sub-clause nor the Neither UCP 500 nor UCP 600 defines these three terms.

11.6.5.12.2 Notation on Excess

For guidance, however, excess (including excess clause) refers to a specified sum in the policy, which the insured must bear before insurers pay their liability. I the event

---

[148] Art 28(i).

[149] Art 28 (j).

[150] Commercial franchising in the US began in the Colonies, in Philadelphia, when on Sept. 13, 1731, Benjamin Franklin and Thomas Whitmarsh entered into an agreement "for the carrying on of the Business of Printing in Charlestown in South Carolina."; for the concept itself see para. 11.6.4.12.5(Franchise) below.

See generally, *Beacon Insurance Co Ltd. v Lansdale* [1939] 4 All ER 204 at 207; 83 Sol Jo 908; 65 Ll. L Rep 57, CA.

of liability exceeding the limit of indemnity specified in the insurers pay the limit specified providing the insured has borne the limit of his policy excess. The clause was interpreted, in relation to motor insurance, by Lord Justice Slesser in *Beacon Insurance Co Ltd. v Lansdale*[151] upholding the judgment of Justice Dumas and distinguishing Justice Green MR' ruling in *Groom v Croker.*[152]

11.6.5.12.3 Excess Clause

Excess is normally included by way of an excess clause, specifying that the insured must be liable up to a specified sum if a loss occurs, e.g., the first £500/US$750. Only after this limit has been reached are the insurers liable and then only for the sum by which that limit is exceeded. Where there is an excess clause in the FOB/CIF export policy and the insurers make a bona fide settlement of the claim for the damages brought against the insured by a third party, they are entitled to recover the sum stated in the excess clause from the importer or exporter.[153] In a practise now discontinued this use to refer to a Memorandum in the policy of marine insurance construed as a "franchise clause" and not an "excess clause"

11.6.5.12.4 Excess Policy

To protect his excess in an export policy the party or parties might take out another policy known as an excess policy. This is a policy in respect of a subject matter which is also insured under another policy, stating that the insurer is under no liability until the assured has been paid in full under that other policy.

11.6.5.12.5 Franchise

Franchise (or franchise clause) on the other hand is a clause stating that no claim is payable unless the amount involved exceeds a stated amount. Once the claim exceeds that amount the whole the entire claim is payable. The franchise eliminates small claims but unlike and excess, which can also be used to eliminate small claims, does not reduce the cost of all claims by the amount of the excess. Both clauses have their origins in marine insurance where the memorandum is construed as franchise and not excess.

11.6.5.12.6 Franchise Clause

This is a clause stating that any loss which occurs must be borne by the insured provided that it does not exceed a specified percentage. When the loss exceeds that percentage, he is entitled to recover the whole of the loss and not merely the excess. In the olden days of the SG Policy, this used to refer to a Memorandum in a marine insurance policy construed as "franchise clause", not an "excess clause"

---

[151] See generally, *Beacon Insurance Co Ltd. v Lansdale* [1939] 4 All ER 204 at 207; 83 Sol Jo 908; 65 Ll. L Rep 57, CA.

[152] [1938] 2 All ER 394 at 400; 108 LJKB 296; 158 LT 477; 54 TLR 861; 82 Sol Jo 374; 60 Ll. L393, CA-considered on this point in *Lee v Thompson* [1989] 40 EG 89; *TSB Bank PLC v Robert Irving & Burns* (a firm) (*Colonia Baltic Insurance Ltd, third party*) [2000] 2 All ER 826.

[153] See for instance, *Beacon Insurance Co Ltd v Langdale* [1939] 4 All ER 204.

11.6.5.12.7 Deductible

Deductible, on the other hand is the portion of an insured loss borne by the policyholder. The amount or percentage is specified in the policy. Normally application of a deductible reduces the insurer's limit of indemnity by the amount specified. Unlike deductible, excess sits below any sum insured and does not erode it. The two terms are not therefore interchangeable and should be used with care although they might have common intentions and results. For instance, deductible is often used when a substantial amount is involved and they enable the insured to secure large premium deductions. Furthermore, the deductible can be on an individual loss or event basis or on an aggregate basis for all claims in the period of insurance. Whereas excess s is normally for quite small ums e.g., for accidental damage. Excess may also be voluntary to secure neither premium reduction nor compulsory as an underwriting measure or simply to eliminate small claims.

11.6.5.12.8 Deductible Clause

Deductible sometimes means just a form of excess clause used in marine insurance policies. A typical deductible clause would provide that:

> No claim arising from a peril insured against shall be payable under this insurance unless the aggregate of all such claims arising out of each separate accident or occurrence (including claims under the Running Down and Suing and Labour Clauses) exceeds. in which case this sum shall be deducted. Nevertheless
>
> The expenses of sighting the bottom after the stranding, if reasonably incurred specifically for that purpose, shall be paid even if no damage be found. This paragraph shall not apply to a claim for a total or constructive total loss of the vessel

11.6.6 Buyers' UCP Obligations

As would be expected the buyer has no insurance obligations under either UCP 500[154] or UCP 600[155] except to pay for the documents, which, includes insurance documents.

11.7 Collection of Insurance and Other Documents Under Uniform Rules

Like the UCP 600, the ICC Uniform Rules for Collections 1995 Revision (URC) is a set of rules are a practical set of rules to aid bankers, buyers, and sellers in the collections process. Although intended primarily to assist bankers in the process of collecting debts or owed money or assets but is applicable for collection of insurance documents as part of trade documents. The URCs were established or proposed by the worldwide organization that serves to promote and facilitate business

[154] UCP 500 Clause 34.

[155] UCP 600 Clause 28.

interests and trade between nations. a "Collection" means the handling by banks of documents as defined in sub-Clause 2(a), in accordance with instructions received, in order to: obtain payment and/or acceptance, or deliver documents against payment and/or against acceptance, or 3 deliver documents on other terms and conditions.

The definition of documents under Clause 2(b) is wide enough to include insurance documents. Under the provision "Documents" means financial documents and/or commercial documents: include, commercial, transport documents, documents of title or other similar documents, or any other documents whatsoever, not being financial documents.

11.8 Consequences of Failire to Tender

11.8.1 Failure to Insure

Discussed above. Difference between failure to insure and failure to tender [see more].

11.8.2 Failure to Tender: Generally

Since insurance is a contractual obligation, the CIF seller is liable for damages and loss of goods that are shipped uninsured. This is a cardinal principle in CIF insurance. It will be remembered *Orient Co Ltd v Brekke and Howlid*,[156] involving shipment from Bordeaux CIF Hull (England) but without effecting insurance, it was held that the seller remains liable even if the contract goods arrive safely to their destination. In contractual terms, this is regarded as a fundamental breach of the contract for which the injured party can reject the documents, reject goods (since he has two rights), terminate the contract and sue for damages for breach of the contract. However, failure to insure might affect even just a portion rather than the whole transit. Thus, in *LindonTricotagefabrik v White and Meacham*,[157] where goods were stolen following a mis-delivery during transhipment, the sellers were found to be in breach for failure to insure an inland portion of the transportation. The American law tallies with English and other common law jurisdictions on this point but without suggestions as to consequences of failure to insure.

11.8.3 Failure to Tender: English Law

It is not enough that the policy is taken out by the seller. The seller must actually tender the policy or its substitute to the buyers in accordance with the contract. In

[156] *Orient Co Ltd v Brekke and Howlid* [1913] 531.

[157] *Lindon Tricotagefabrik v White and Meacham*[1975]1Lloyd's Rep 384 CA.

support of the above authorities, *Burstall v Grimsdale*,[158] involving sale of American meal CIF London containing liberty to deviate, also suggests tender of CIF documents without the insurance documents is not valid tender. This position was followed in Orient Co. Ltd v *Brekke and Howlid*[159] (above). Likewise, in *Denbigh, Cowan &Co v Atcherley Co*,[160] involving shipment of Java tapioca CIF Liverpool, 'cash against delivery order', the court held that the buyers were entitled to reject tender of documents which contained a delivery order but without a policy. The appeal court rejected the seller's contention that the policy was not necessary in a contract, which they regarded as an arrival contract. The American Supreme Court too adopted the same position in *Harper v Hochstim*[161] as pertaining in the US. There are possible three causes of action in this respect: breach of the sales contract, breach of the insurance contract and breach of the letter of credit contract. It will be remembered similar circumstances involving tender delivery order instead of policy, occurred in The Julia. Although normally part of the same sales transaction package, these three are regarded as 3 independent and/or autonomous contracts, each giving rise to separate causes of actions and damages.

11.8.4 Failure to Tender: American Law

The American position on this is generally the same as under English. However, the *Commentary to the Ohio State Revised Code* explains the background, rationale and some of the consequences for the failure.

> The seller's failure to tender a proper insurance document is waived if the buyer refuses to make payment on other and untenable grounds at a time when proper insurance could have been obtained and tendered by the seller if timely objection had been made. Even a failure to insure on shipment may be cured by seasonable tender of a policy retroactive in effect; e.g., one insuring the goods "lost or not lost". The provisions of this Clause [Chapter] on cure of improper tender and on waiver of buyer's objections by silence are applicable to insurance tenders under a C.I.F. term. Where there is no waiver by the buyer as described above, however, the fact that the goods arrive safely does not cure the seller's breach of his obligations to insure them and tender to the buyer a proper insurance document (*emphasis supplied*).

It will be remembered that Justice Compton made reference to waiver of tender in *Tamvaco* but that was for a different reason rather than for the buyer's failure to tender as in the American approach.

---

[158] *Commentary to Ohio State Revised Code*, para. 9.

[159] *Burstall v Grimsdale* (1906) 11 Com.Cas.280.

[160] *Denbigh, Cowan & Co v Atcherley Co* [1921] 90 LJKB 836.

[161] *Harper v Hochstim* 27 Fed R102102 (1921) (US).

11.9 Further Food for Thoughts

11.9.1 Insurance Policy

This is probably academic. The document traditionally required is the insurance policy. But in practice it is a bulky document and most export policies need just the insurance certificate, letter of insurance and/or declaration under open covers or blanket policy. Letters of insurance and declarations are very rare documents. The UCP does not allow for covernotes from insurance or broker, but it is not clear what else in practice is tenderable.

11.9.2 From "Insurance Policy" to "Insurance Documents"

As indicated the above, the traditional document is the policy. However, modern requirements like the UCP Clause 28(x) uses insurance documents instead of the policy, thereby leaving it open for alternative and practical documents such as the certificate, etc. However, insurance documents include: insurance documents themselves and insurance policy documents. The first, Insurance Documents, means and includes all slips, cover notes, contracts, policies themselves, certificates of entry or other insurance documents evidencing or constituting the insurances from time to time in effect. In Canada Insurance Documents means certified documents issued by an insurance company licensed to operate by the Government of Canada or the Province of Ontario certifying that the bidder is insured in accordance with the City of Windsor's insurance requirements as contained in the Bid documents. The second, insurance policy document, (PDS) is another important legal document that usually forms part of the insurance contract. It includes a description of the features, benefits, cost and risks associated with the policy. That said under the UCP 600, insurance document is limited to those documents listed in the UCP.

11.9.3 Insurance in Clause A5/B5 of Incoterms 2020

Among other requirements Clause A5 of CIF and CIP contracts provide that the seller must provide the buyer with the insurance policy or certificate or "any other evidence of insurance cover". This leaves it open to provide and tender any insurance documents including but not limited to the policy, certificate of insurance, Insurance Documents means collectively all slips, cover notes, contracts, policies, certificates of entry or other insurance documents evidencing or constituting the Insurances and, in the singular means any of them. It would include such items such Proof of insurance and Proof of insurance coverage.

The first, is the Proof of Insurance (POI), is any type of documentation that a person can provide to another individual proving that the person has valid insurance with an insurance company. The most common form of a POI is a paper card provided by the insurance company listing policy information and effective dates. This would be possible in other types of insurance but note marine cargo policy.

The second is Proof of Insurance Coverage (POIC). For this the insured may also use a proof of coverage letter from his insurance company that has details about his policy. Another document would be an Insurance ID cards which together with the proof of coverage letters, is normally included when the policy is sent to the insured. Again, this might not be appropriate in marine cargo insurance involving large sums and sometimes payable overseas.

Third, further Proof of Coverage, evidence might could be electronic form of the insured's ID card as proof of insurance. Other evidence in this category includes but are necessarily limited to:

(i) Form 1095 information forms;
(ii) Insurance cards;
(iii) Explanation of benefits;
(iv) Statements from your insurer;
(v) Payroll statements reflecting health insurance deductions; and
(vi) Records of advance payments of the premium tax credit.

However, such proofs relate more to insured individuals such as in life, property, medical and related insurances and not company insured such the export or import company. It is unlikely that is what Clause A5 of CIF/CIF insurance had in mind in "any other evidence of insurance"

11.9.4 Apparent Conflict Between Incoterms and UCP 600

Although partly covered in Chap. 8 above, this is revisited here. There is both a similarity and conflict between provision of policy and insurance documents in Incoterms 2020 and UCP. The similarities are that although they define mention the documents, they both nevertheless leave it open for other instruments. Incoterms Clause A5 provides for the policy, certificate or any other evidence of insurance cover. Whereas the UCP (28(a) provides for "An insurance document, such as an insurance policy, an insurance certificate or a declaration under an open cover", also leaving it for ejusdem generis interpretation allowing generic documents. The former is less liberal (restricting to policy and certificate) whereas although including one more document (declaration), it is nevertheless both more liberal and probably forward looking for future documents in using "such as". Furthermore, it explains and details characteristics that the insurance document should meet. It refers to the minimum requirements and the 110% insurable values of CIF and CIP contracts. This is understandable.

At the same time, however, the UCP does not accept tender of covernotes. Again, understandable as it deals specifically with tender under letters of credit whereas Incoterms Clause A5 concerns the wider/general tender. That said it would have been helpful if the two important instruments were to harmonise this aspect of export trade practice. Incoterms drafted after Incoterms 2010 had the benefit of hindsight after the UCP drafted in the early 1970s coming into force in 1976.

11.9.5 Conflict Between Theory and Practice

From the above, is there is an apparent difference between theory and practice in terms of prescribed documents on the one hand and tenderable documents on the other? It must also be borne in mind that the complexity of international trade would rule out certain prescribed documents. It is in the same way as the presumptions that a contract needn't be in write although in practice they should for evidential and fraud avoidance purposes.

11.9.6 Conflicts of the *Minimum* with the *110%* Cover

This is also partly covered in Chap. 8 above. There are inconsistencies in the minimum cover and requirement of not less than 110% cover for CIF and CIP contracts. Again, these are only guidelines. Secondly, they apply only to the CIF and CIP contracts, not all others. Those contracts in which the seller does not provide insurance, but do so e.g., Extended FOB, is silent on these. In that case parties are free to provide the levels acceptable and/or affordable to them. Furthermore, in commodity contracts such as GAFTA Contract No 72, the figure quoted are as low as 102%.

11.9.7 Failure to Align Incoterms with Letters of Credit

Where payment is with a letter of credit or a documentary collection, failure to align the Incoterms rule with the security requirements or the requirements of the banks. It is essential that documents called for in a documentary letter of credit are completed correctly and in accordance with the terms of the credit. Mistakes can might lead to: the bank's rejection of the documents; cause extra work for which for which an additional charge may be payable; or delay in receiving payment. In relation to insurance, the followings are faults and problems that commonly occur:

(a) amount of cover is insufficient;
(b) does not include risks mentioned in the credit;
(c) is not issued in the currency of the credit;
(d) is not indorsed by the insured and/or signed by the insurer;
(e) certificate or policy bears a date later than the date of shipment/dispatch, except where warehouse to warehouse is indicated;

(f) incorrect description of the goods;
(g) alterations are not authenticated;
(h) is not in a transferable form when required;
(i) carrying vessel's name not recorded; and
(j) does not cover shipment when bills of lading indicate it will take place

It is reiterated that when a policy is called for under a credit, a certificate is not acceptable, however, a policy is acceptable when a certificate is called for. Brokers' cover notes are not acceptable unless specifically permitted in the credit.

11.10 Concluding Remarks

The whole purpose of international trade is that the buyer gets paid for his shipments. Payment is normally the last stage of the international sales process. Requirements of conditions for that payment is meant to safeguard the buyer against fraud. First, and foremost, is that the seller should tender documents stipulated in the contract. That is so regardless of whether payment is by bank-to-bank transfer, by letters of credit or other means. The seller performs this final part of the contract by tendering to the buyer the following leading documents:

(a) the bill of lading or transport documents;
(b) insurance policy or insurance documents;
(c) and invoice, together with any other documents required by the contract, such as
(d) export/import licenses;
(e) certificates of:
    (i) quality
    (ii) origin
    (iii) (iii)pre-shipment
    (iv) quantity; and
    (v) phytotropic,
    (vi) etc.

Documents are also proof that the seller has performed his part of the bargain such as provision and delivery of the contract goods, shipments and insuring the shipments.

The bill of leading helps to pass title to the goods while the invoice provides details of the shipment and their costs. One of the most functions is the protection of goods against risks of loss or damage to the goods. The insurance policy protects the buyer, and sometimes the seller, against most risks of loss or damage to the goods during transit. The policy is particular important in the CIF and related Incoterms where the role of insurance sometimes renders the contract a sale of documents rather than of goods. This is because the policy provides the comfort that if all else fails, then the buyer can always claim from the insurer. The contract will stipulate the type of insurance document to be tendered. Further guidance is provided by the MIA 1906, the Incoterms 2010, the UCP and the common law. That withstanding the actual policy is the default document.

11.11 Further Readings

Books

- Jones, "UCP 600-Eight Years on", 10(3) S. & T.I May (2015) pp. 4–7
- Ramberg, 'Synchronization of Contracts of Sale, Carriage, Insurance and Financing in International Trade' in Sarcevic (ed.) International Contracts and Conflicts of Laws (A Collection of Essays) (1990) 86 at 87.
- Debattista. "The new UCP 600 - changes to the tender of the Sellers's shipping documents under letters of credit", J.B.L. 2007, June, pp. 329–354. (accessed on 04/02/2022)
- Ellinger: "Documentary Credits and fraudulent documents", in Kee and Chan (eds), Current Problems of International Trading Finance, 2nd Edn., National University of Singapore
- Gao: The Fraud Rule in Letters of Credit: A comparative Study 2002 Kluwer.
- ICC Incoterms 1990 ICC Document No.460
- ICC Guide to Incoterms 1990 ICC Document No.461/90
- ICC Incoterms 2000 ICC Document No. 560
- ICC Guide to Incoterms 2000 ICC Document No.620
- ICC Incoterms 2010. Incoterms® 2010 By the International Chamber of Commerce (ICC) ICC Pub. No. 715E.
- Prof. Ramberg, Jan: ICC Guide to Incoterms 2010 ICC Guide to Incoterms® 2010 ICC Pub. No. 720E,
- ICC: Commentary on UCP 600, ICC Banking Commission, ICC Document No.680
- Byrne, James E: The Comparison of UCP 600 & UCP 500, Institute of International Banking Law & Practice, 2007, MD, US
- Collyer Gare: Frequently asked questions on UCP 600, Vol I to IV
- GLOBAL NEGOTIATOR (Business Publications)-INCOTERMS 2020, Obligations, Costs and Risks, Global Marketing Strategies SL, London, 2021Go
- ICC: Uniform Rules for Collection (URC), ICC Document No.522
- Jan Ramberg: International Commercial Transactions, ICC Pub. No. 711E.
- ICC Guide to Export/Import Global Standards for International Trade by Prof. Guillermo C. Jimenez ICC Pub. No. 686E.
- Drafting and Negotiating International Commercial Contracts by Prof. Fabio Bortolotti ICC Pub. No. 743E,
- ICC: ICC Guide on Transport and the Incoterms 2010 Rules ICC Pub. No. 775E,

- Jin Saibo: The Law of Letters of Credit in China Commentary and Materials on the Chinese Supreme People's Court's Judicial Interpretations of Letters of Credit, ICC Pub. No. 736E.
- ICC: INCOTERMS® 2010 Q&A Questions & Expert ICC Guidance on Incoterms 2010, ICC Pub. No. 744E.
- Incoterms 2010 Wallchart Size: 30cm x 63cm ICC Pub. No. 716E, (per pack of ten posters)
- Incoterms 2010 Deskpad Size: 58cm x 38cm ICC Pub. No. 767E, (per pack of five)
- The Incoterms 2010 Pocket Guide Size: 7.5cm x 11cm ICC Pub. No. 721E, €15 (per pack of five)
- The Incoterms 2010 Flip Book Size: 11cm x 12cm ICC Pub. No. 722E, €39 (per pack of five)
- ICC: ICC Uniform Customs and Practice for Documentary Credits — UCP 600 ICC Pub. No. 600E, (e-edition).
- ICC: ICC Uniform Rules for Bank Payment Obligations ICC Pub. No. 750E, €25
- ICC: The ICC Guide to the Uniform Rules for Bank Payment Obligations by David J. Hennah

Clauses

- Arora: "The dilemma of the issuing bank: to accept or reject documents under a letter of credit" [1984] *LMCLQ* 81
- Bennett: "Documentary credits: a reasonable time for what?" [1997] *LMCLQ*169
- ----------: "Strict compliance under UCP 500", [1997] *LMCLQ* 7
- ----------: "Original sins under the UCP [2001] *LMCLQ* 88
- Buckley: "Potential pitfalls with letters of credit", [1996] *70ALJ* 217
- Chatterjee: "Letters of credit transactions and discrepant documents: an analysis of the judicial guidelines developed by English courts", [1996] *JIBL* 510
- Dolan: "Strict Compliance with letters of credit: striking a balance", [1985] *Banking LJ* 18
- Kozolochyk: "Strict Compliance the reasonable document checker", [1990] 56 Brooklyn LR 48
- Ulph, "UCP 600: Documentary Credits in the Twenty-first Century" J.B.L. 2007, June, pp. 355–377

Reports

- ICC, Commercial Crime Bureau, Special Report: Prime Banking Instrument Frauds, 1994

Website

- Andrzej Blajer, "UCP 600: Article by Article Analysis", ***http://www.renanconsulting.com/introduction-early-and-contemporary-history-of-letter-of-credit-rules/***

- Taylor, The Complete UCP Uniform Customs and Practice for Documentary Credits Texts, Rules and History 1920-2007, ***http://store.iccwbo.org/Content/uploaded/pdf/ICC-The-Complete-UCP-Uniform-Customs-and-Practice-for-Documentary-Credits-Texts-Rules-and-History-1920-2007.pdf***

References

Dover VA (1975) Handbook of Marine Insurance, 8th edn, p 133
Ivamy HER (1993) Chalmers Marine Insurance Act 1906, 10th edn. Butterworths, p 73

Part V

Dispute Settlement, Claims and Concluding Remarks

Conflicts of Law

12

Abstract

This chapter deals with conflicts of law in international sales contracts generally, and export insurance in particular. Following the customary Introduction, the chapter covers, *inter alia*: The Doctrine of the Proper Law of the Contract; Applicable Law of the Contract; Choice of Law under English Law; Choice of Law under the EU (Rome Convention); Jurisdiction generally; Jurisdiction through the EU (Brussels Convention); Jurisdiction outside the EU; Enforcement of Insurance contract disputes in the EU; Enforcement Process; Conciliation and Derecognition and Enforcement of Insurance Judgments; Consequences of Brexit on international sales contracts generally and on export insurance ones in particular; Further Food for Thoughts; Concluding Remarks; References Used; and Further Readings.

12.1 Introduction

This chapter is devoted to the law applicable to international sales contracts generally and to the respective insurance contracts in particular. Included are:

1. The doctrine of the proper of the contract 2. The law applicable rules 3. The choice under English law 4. The Choice of Law under *SGA* 1979 5. The Choice of Law under the Marine Insurance Act 1906 6. Choice of Law under the Institute Cargo Clauses 7. The Choice under EU Law	8. Jurisdiction Principles 9. Arbitrations 10. Conciliations 11. Recognition of Foreign Judgements 12. Enforcement of Foreign Judgments 13. Other Conflicts of Laws Issues.

P. Ademuni-Odeke, *Insurance of International Sales' Contracts under Incoterms*, Law for Professionals, https://doi.org/10.1007/978-3-031-75136-3_12

Discussions include the process both in the UK, EU and externally. The chapter is restricted to dispute settlement in insurance contracts only. Any other connections to the wider aspects of the subject are only as far as they touch on insurance as a commercial transaction within the law of international trade generally and FOB and CIF in particular. Other factors which might affect the law applicable to the FOB and CIF insurance contracts are the principles of English law, the underlying sales contract, the letter of credit payments contract, the trade category (e.g., commodities), the requirements of the Marine Insurance Act, the European law applicable and jurisdiction rules and other factors.

12.2 The Doctrine of the Proper Law of the Contract

As international contracts, FOB and CIF insurance contracts are subject to the doctrine of the proper law of the contract. The doctrine is the main system of law applied to decide the validity of most aspects to the contract including its formation, validity, interpretation, and performance. This does not deny the power of the parties to agree that different aspects of the contract shall be governed by different systems of law. But, in the absence of such express terms, the court will not divide the proper law unless there are unusually compelling circumstances. And note the general rule of the lex fori which applies the provisions of the proper law as it is when the contract is to be performed and not as it was when the contract was made.

The parties' intention as to which law is to govern the contract. The claimed advantage of this approach is that it satisfies more abstract considerations of justice if the parties are bound by the law they have chosen. But it raises the question of whether the test is to be subjective, i.e. the law actually intended by the parties, or objective, i.e. the law will impute the intention which reasonable men in their position would probably have had. It cannot safely be assumed that the parties did actually consider which of the several possible laws might be applied when they were negotiating the contract. Hence, although the courts would prefer the subjective approach because this gives effect the parties' own wishes, the objective test has gained in importance. So, the proper law test today is three-stage:

1. it is the law intended by the parties when the contract was made which is usually evidenced by an express choice of law clause; or
2. it is implied by the court because either the parties incorporated actual legal terminology or provisions specific to one legal system, or because the contract would only be valid under one of the potentially relevant systems; or
3. if there is no express or implied choice, it is the law which has the closest and most real connection to the bargain made by the parties.

It is only fair to admit that the task of imputing an intention to the parties in the third situation presents the courts with another opportunity for uncertainty and arbitrariness, but this overall approach is nevertheless felt to be the lesser of the available evils.

12.3 Parties' Choice on Which Law Governs the Contract

Like all other parties to an international sales contract, parties to an Incoterms contract have the possibility of three choices. This especially as Incoterms does not deal with the law applicable to the contract. However, these choices depend on whether they use the liberal Incoterms or one of the restrictive Standard Terms Commodity Trade Contracts such as GAFTA or FROFSA discussed above.

12.3.1 To Keep the Law of the Exporting Country

That would be very often the wish of the seller who would prefer to apply his own law considering that it is the one that he knows well. However, it is not always the best solution. As a matter of fact, some laws, such as the French and Belgian laws, protect much more the buyer than say English common law.

12.3.2 To Keep the Law of the Importing Country

This law can be more interesting for the exporter since it is less constraining; however, it is important to know it and master it well because it could be very dangerous to be subject to regulations that are totally or partially unknown.

12.3.3 To Keep the Law of a Third Country

This choice allows neutralizing the legal nationalism. It is often used in commercial interests for compromising or for convenient reasons (in the case where the court of competent jurisdiction belongs to this third country).

12.3.4 Advantages of the Neutral Law

Swiss law is often recommended because it favours much more the exporter and, most of all, it has the benefit of belonging to a neutral state, which is an advantage for the parties who are conducting commercial trade.[1]

---

[1] Santander Trade Markets, Analysis on Incoterms, https://santandertrade.com/en/portal/analyse-markets/incoterms; ***See also,*** Fountoulakis (2006).

12.4 Legal Doctrine on Applicable Law of the Contract

12.4.1 Express Law of the Contract

The law governing the contract is discernible from either express or implied law of the contract. The former is when the parties have expressed a clear intention in a choice-of-law clause, there is a rebuttable presumption that this is the proper law because it reflects the parties' freedom of contract and it produces certainty of outcome. It can only be rebutted when the choice is not bona fide, it produces illegality, or it breaches public policy. For example, the parties may have selected the particular law to evade the operation of otherwise mandatory provisions of the law which has the closest connection with the contract. The parties are not free to put themselves above the law and, in such cases, it will be for the parties to prove that there is a valid reason for selecting that law other than evasion.

A typical sample law and choice of law clause reads:

> This contract shall be governed by and construed in accordance with English law and all disputes arising out of or in connection with this contract shall be referred to the High Courts of Justice in London.

12.4.2 Implied Law of the Contract

Implied law of the contract is presumed from where the parties have not expressed provided for the law but have instead implied from various circumstances. When the parties have not used express words, their intention may be inferred from the terms and nature of the contract, and from the general circumstances of the case. For example, a term granting the courts of a particular state exclusive jurisdiction over the contract would imply that the *lex fori* is to be the proper law. This is normally included in the Forum Selection Clause, which in a contract (including cargo insurance contracts) with a conflict of laws element allows the parties to agree that any disputes relating to that contract will be resolved in a specific forum. They usually operate in conjunction with a choice of law clause which determines the proper law of the relevant contract.

12.4.3 Where No Law Provided

Where the parties have provided neither express nor implied law, then the courts have a choice whether to render the contract null and void or to try to rescue it through a number of the rules listed below. In other words, in default, the court has to impute an intention by asking, as just and reasonable persons, which law the parties ought to, or would, have intended to nominate if they had thought about it when they were making the contract.

12.4.4 "Closest and Most Real Connection"

In arriving at its decision in the above scenario, the court uses a list of connecting factors, i.e., facts which have an unambiguous geographical connection, and whichever law scores the most hits on a league table created from the list will be considered the proper law. The current list of factors includes the following:

(a) the habitual residence/domicile/nationality of the parties;
(b) the parties' main places of business and of incorporation;
(c) the place nominated for any arbitration proceedings in the event of a dispute (the lex loci arbitri);
(d) the language in which the contract documents are written;
(e) the format of the documents, e.g., if a form is only found in one relevant country, this suggests that the parties intended the law of that country to be the proper law;
(f) the currency in which any payment is to be made;
(g) the flag of any ship involved;
(h) the place where the contract is made (which may not be obvious where negotiations were concluded by letter, fax or e-mail);
(i) the place(s) where performance is to occur;
(j) any pattern of dealing established in previous transactions involving the same parties; and
(k) where any insurance companies or relevant third parties are located.

12.5 Choice Under English Common Law

Until Brexit, English now closely followed EU on choice of law jurisprudence. Under English law then, the *Contracts (Applicable Law) Act* 1990 formally incorporated the:

(a) *Convention on the Law Applicable to Contractual Obligations* the "Rome Convention") opened for signature in Rome on June 19, 1980, and signed by the United Kingdom on December 7, 1981;
(b) *Convention on the Accession of the Hellenic Republic to the Rome Convention* (the "Luxembourg Convention") signed by the United Kingdom in Luxembourg on April 10, 1984; and
(c) *First Protocol on the Interpretation of the Rome Convention by the European Court* (the "Brussels Protocol") signed by the United Kingdom in Brussels on December 19, 1988.

It remains to be seen whether any aspect of these will be maintained after Brexit.

Otherwise, English courts will also apply other laws which provide expressly or impliedly that English law shall govern the contract even if it had no immediate connection to the English jurisdiction. This was certainly the case in *Amin Rasheed Shipping Corporation v Kuwait National Insurance Corporation*[2].

12.6 Choice of Law Under the Sale of Goods Act 1979

Further guidance should be gathered from s.56 (Conflict of laws), which provides that:

> **s. 56 (Conflict of Laws)**
> (1) Where the proper law of a contract for the sale of goods would, apart from a term that it should be the law of some other country or a term to the like effect, be the law of any part of the United Kingdom, or where any such contract contains a term which purports to substitute, or has the effect of substituting, provisions of the law of some other country for all or any of the provisions of sections 12 to 15 and 55 above, those sections shall, notwithstanding that term but subject to subsection (2) below, apply to the contract.
>
> (2) *Nothing in subsection (1) above prevents the parties to a contract for the international sale of goods from negativing or varying any right, duty or liability which would otherwise arise by implication of law under sections 12 to 15 above.*
>
> (3) *In subsection (2) above "contract for the international sale of goods" means a contract of sale of goods made by parties whose places of business (or, if they have none, habitual residences) are in the territories of different States (the Channel Islands and the Isle of Man being treated for this purpose as different States from the United Kingdom) and in the case of which one of the following conditions is satisfied: —*
>
> (a) the contract involves the sale of goods which are at the time of the conclusion of the contract in the course of carriage or will be carried from the territory of one State to the territory of another; or
>
> (b) the acts constituting the offer and acceptance have been effected in the territories of different States; or
>
> (c) delivery of the goods is to be made in the territory of a State other than that within whose territory the acts constituting the offer and the acceptance have been effected.

Subsections (2) and (3) thereof are self-explanatory.

---

[2] AMIN RASHEED SHIPPING CORPORATION v. KUWAIT INSURANCE CO. (THE "AL WAHAB") [1982] 1 Lloyd's Rep. 638.

12.7 Choice of Law Under Marine Insurance Act 1906

There is no Applicable Law provision in the MIA 1906. However, it is common knowledge that it is English law.

12.8 Choice of Law Under the UK Institute Cargo Clauses

Clause 19 of all the ICC A-C (LAW AND PRACTICE) provide that:

> 19. This insurance is subject to English law and practice.

12.9 Choice of Law in Other Institute Cargo Clauses

12.9.1 American Institute Cargo Clauses 2004 Free of Particular Average-American Conditions

Clause 9 (K) (Choice of Law) of the American Institute Cargo Clauses of American Institute of Marine Underwriters (AIMU) Cargo Clauses (FPAAC) January 1, 2004 provides that:

> **Clause 9**
> It is agreed that this policy and its endorsement(s) is a contract of marine insurance protecting against marine risks and has been applied for, priced and underwritten as such, and the law applicable to any interpretation of this policy and the rights and obligations of the Company and the Assured hereunder shall be US federal maritime common law or, in the absence of US federal maritime common law, the law of the state of New York, irrespective of any principles of choice of law

This is more detailed and more comprehensive than the English cargo clauses.

12.10 Under EU the Rome Convention

Until Brexit UK Courts (and those of other then signatory states) applied the *Rome Convention on the Law Applicable to Contractual Obligations* (Rome Convention). This 1980 Convention was the product of work of the European Union aimed at establishing uniform rules in this area. The Convention came into force following its seventh ratification by a contracting state and makes provision as to the law applicable to contractual obligations in the case of a choice of laws of different countries. The Rome Convention was enacted into English law by *The Contracts (Applicable Law) Act* 1990. However, the Rome Convention is the only Community private international law instrument that remains in international treaty form.

The Regulation applies to insurance contracts covering a "large risk" whether or not the risk covered is situated in a Member State, and to all other insurance contracts covering risks situated inside Member States (see Clause 7.1). Clause 7 does not apply to reinsurance contracts, but these would appear to be covered by the general provisions of the Regulation since they are not excluded in Clause 1. However, Clause 1(3) and 1(4) provide that:

Clause 1(3) and 1(4)
3. The rules of this Convention do not apply to contracts of insurance which cover risks situated in the territories of the Member States of the European Economic Community. In order to determine whether a risk is situated in these territories the court shall apply its internal law

4. The preceding paragraph does not apply to contracts of re-insurance.

2 The following shall be excluded from the scope of this Regulation:

(j) insurance contracts arising out of operations carried out by organisations other than undertakings referred to in Clause 2 of Directive 2002/83/EC of the European Parliament and of the Council of 5 November 2002 concerning life assurance the object of which is to provide benefits for employed or self-employed persons belonging to an undertaking or group of undertakings, or to a trade or group of trades, in the event of death or survival or of discontinuance or curtailment of activity, or of sickness related to work or accidents at work.

Rome I 2008
(20) Where the contract is manifestly more closely connected with a country other than that indicated in Clause 4(1) or (2), an escape clause should provide that the law of that other country is to apply. In order to determine that country, account should be taken, inter alia, of whether the contract in question has a very close relationship with another contract or contracts

(21) In the absence of choice, where the applicable law cannot be determined either on the basis of the fact that the contract can be categorised as one of the specified types or as being the law of the country of habitual residence of the party required to affect the characteristic performance of the contract, the contract should be governed by the law of the country with which it is most closely connected. In order to determine that country, account should be taken, inter alia, of whether the contract in question has a very close relationship with another country or contracts

(32) Owing to the particular nature of contracts of carriage and insurance contracts, specific provisions should ensure an adequate level of protection of passengers and policy holders. Therefore, Clause 6 should not apply in the context of those particular contracts.

(33) Where an insurance contract not covering a large risk covers more than one risk, at least one of which is situated in a Member State and at least one of which is situated in a third country, the special rules on insurance contracts in this Regulation should apply only to the risk or risks situated in the relevant Member State or Member States

Remains to be seen what will happen now that the UK has left the European Union.

12.11 Jurisdictions Generally

12.11.1 Principles of Jurisdiction

Jurisdiction means the competence of a court to hear and decide a case. A juristic act is an action intending to, and capable of having, a legal effect, such as the creation, termination or modification of a legal right. In Europe, the Brussels Convention sets a common system for the countries of the EU, disciplining the jurisdiction of the courts of a member state with respect to the national courts of other member states.

12.11.2 Jurisdiction in International Commercial Contracts

In a typical legal dispute arising from an international trade transaction, it is foreseeable that an issue in the realm of private international law might arise. The main questions are:

(a) which country's courts should have jurisdiction to try the dispute;
(b) which country's laws should be applied to resolve the dispute; and
(c) whether any foreign judgement obtained abroad might be enforceable in the home country/ UK

12.11.3 Jurisdiction and Conflict of Laws

Jurisdiction is linked with the Conflict of laws. Conflict of laws is a set of rules aiming to provide national Courts with the instruments to decide a case containing foreign elements. It is concerned with civil and commercial law rather than criminal or administrative matters and includes the la applicable and jurisdiction. These laws can be divided into three areas:

(a) the jurisdiction of a Court, its competence to hear and decide a case;
(b) the law governing a relationship, the rules applicable for deciding a case; and
(c) the recognition and enforcement of judgements rendered by foreign courts.

Conflict of law issues arise whenever the situation out of which a dispute has arisen has contacts with more than one legal jurisdiction, where more than one set of laws appears to be of relevance. The conflict of laws must choose between the competing sets.

12.11.4 Jurisdiction Under English Insurance Law

The jurisdiction of English courts over personal actions involving a foreign element varies according to whether or not the defendant is a member of the EU. If so, the Civil Jurisdiction and Judgements Act will apply. If not the jurisdictional rules of the common law (to be found in the White Book) will operate. (More Text to Come)

12.12 Jurisdictions Under the EU Brussels Convention

12.12.1 Summary of the Brussels Rules

These are governed by the *Council Regulation* (EC) No 44/2001 of 22 December 2000 on jurisdiction and the recognition and enforcement of judgments in civil and commercial matters .The regulation lays down rules governing the jurisdiction of courts in civil and commercial matters. A judgment given in a European Union (EU) country is to be recognised without special proceedings, unless the recognition is contested. A declaration that a foreign judgment is enforceable is to be issued following purely formal checks of the documents supplied. The regulation lists grounds for non-enforcement; however, courts are not to raise these of their own motion. The regulation does not cover revenue, customs or administrative matters. Neither does it apply to:

12.12.2 EU Rules of Jurisdiction

The basic principle is that jurisdiction is to be exercised by the EU country in which the defendant is domiciled, regardless of his/her nationality. Domicile is determined in accordance with the domestic law of the EU country where the matter is brought before a court. If a party is not domiciled in the EU country of the court considering the matter, the court is to apply the law of another EU country to determine whether the party is domiciled in said state. In the case of legal persons or firms, domicile is determined by the country where they have their statutory seat, central administration or principal place of business. In the case of trusts, domicile is defined by the court that is considering the case by applying its own rules of private international law.

12.12.3 Suing the Defendant in Another EU Country

Where both parties are members of the EU, they can choose which country's law applies to the contract and which state's courts will have jurisdiction over disputes. If these terms are not agreed prior to a dispute, then defendants can be sued in the courts of the state where they are 'domiciled' (where the individual resides or the state where the company is based) irrespective of their nationality. Apart from the basic principle on jurisdiction, in certain circumstances a defendant may be sued in the courts of another EU country. The regulation lists areas of jurisdiction where this is so: special or exclusive jurisdiction, as well as jurisdiction on matters relating to insurance, consumer contracts and individual contracts of employment.

12.12.4 Jurisdiction on Consumer Contracts

The regulation also lays down rules on jurisdiction in matters relating to contracts concluded by consumers. "Consumers" are defined as persons who conclude a contract with a professional for a purpose outside of their own trade or profession. All contracts concluded with a person who pursues commercial or professional activities in the EU are covered, with the exception of contracts of transport, other than those providing for a combination of travel and accommodation for an inclusive price. The consumer is protected in the way described here if the contract concluded on the sale of goods is financed on instalment credit terms or through a loan repayable by instalments or any other form of credit. In order for the consumer to enjoy this protection in other cases, the contract must have been concluded with a person who pursues commercial or professional activities in the EU country in which the consumer is domiciled or directs such activities to that country. A consumer may bring proceedings either in the courts of the EU country in which the defendant is domiciled or in the courts for the place where the consumer (the plaintiff) is domiciled. Proceedings may be brought against a consumer by the other party to the contract only in the courts of the EU country in which the consumer is domiciled.

12.12.5 Jurisdiction in Insurance Contracts

This is now governed by the new Regulation. In the Regulation jurisdiction on insurance is covered in the same chapter (Chapter II) dealing with Insurance, consumer and employment contracts.[3] In matters relating to insurance,[4] an insurer may be sued in the courts of the EU country where she is domiciled or of the EU country where the plaintiff is domiciled if the actions are brought by the policy holder, the insured or a beneficiary. In respect of liability insurance or insurance of immovable property, the insurer may, in addition, be sued in the courts for the place where the harmful event occurred.[5]

---

[3] For a coverage of these see Carr, Indira, International Trade, 2018, pp. 536–547.

[4] Ibid pp. 537–539.

[5] See also, generally, Ademuni-Odeke (1996), pp. 7–14.

12.13 Jurisdiction Outside the EU

Jurisdictional disputes outside of the EU are regulated by international conventions regarding legal issues such as choice of law. Should these fall short of solving the dispute with a particular state it may be worth checking whether the UK has entered into an agreement, setting out the basis on which jurisdiction is determined by the two countries, with the foreign jurisdiction. Also consider the appropriate legal position under UK law regarding the type of dispute, or goods/ services involved.

12.14 Enforcement of Insurance Claims

12.14.1 Introduction

One inevitable fact in insurance business is that insurers will sometimes and for various reasons be required to contest or defend certain claims made by their insured. The traditional dispute resolution mechanism employed by insurers was litigation. Another well-known though less widely used mechanism was arbitration. However, new alternative dispute resolution (ADR) mechanisms like mediation are now part of the variety of dispute resolution options available to insurers. To determine the best option in any given situation two critical matters must be considered and they are:

(a) cost; and
(b) time.

Other considerations are:

(c) procedure;
(d) enforceability; and
(e) publicity.

12.14.2 Litigation

Litigation would be the logical first option. This is an affordable option because apart from the cost of filing processes (fees are usually small) in court the Government and not the parties bear the cost of the judicial umpire. However, each party must still bear the cost of their legal representation. The major disadvantage is that parties have limited control over the time required for the conduct of the proceedings and therefore huge delays are commonplace. One advantage of litigation (apart from low cost) over all other dispute resolution options is the coercive power of the judicial umpire and the ability to enforce the judgment or orders of the court. The venue and content of court proceedings are open to the public (a constitutional requirement) with attendant media publicity which may adversely affect the image of the insurer. The conduct of litigation is formal and complex rules of procedure and evidence are applicable causing several legal objections which delay the proceedings. As a matter of fact, most, if not all, maritime disputes, in the London market at least, is resolved through the maritime arbitration. For those reasons it becomes the fall-back option after exhaustion of arbitration and other ADR options.

12.15 Arbitration Process

Apart from being the preferred industry option, arbitration has several advantages over litigation. The venue and content of the proceedings are not open to the public and there is no risk of adverse publicity. The time frame for the conduct of proceedings is usually agreed between the parties and the arbitrator and therefore delays are largely eliminated. The procedure is less formal and complex rules of procedure and evidence are not applicable greatly reducing legal objections which delay the proceedings. The disadvantage of arbitration is that parties bear the cost of the Arbitrator and this is usually high. There is a fixed scale of fees which is determined by the nature of the claim or the duration of the proceedings. In addition, each party must still bear the cost of legal representation at the arbitration. Furthermore, in the practice of arbitration the loser alone may bear the cost of the Arbitrator. The prohibitive cost of arbitration remains the major reason why despite all the advantages it is still not the most favoured option. One disadvantage of arbitration as a dispute resolution option is the absence of coercive power by the arbitrator and their inability to make orders to enforce the arbitral award. Parties are forced to approach the court to enforce the award and conversely parties may also approach the courts to challenge and set aside the award.

12.16 Conciliation and ADR

This option has several advantages over litigation. The venue and content of the proceedings are not open to the public and there is no risk of adverse publicity. The time frame for the conduct of proceedings is usually agreed between the parties and the arbitrator and therefore delays are largely eliminated. The procedure is less formal and complex rules of procedure and evidence are not applicable greatly reducing legal objections which delay the proceedings. The disadvantage of arbitration is that parties bear the cost of the Arbitrator and this is usually high. There is a fixed scale of fees which is determined by the nature of the claim or the duration of the proceedings. In addition, each party must still bear the cost of legal representation at the arbitration. Furthermore, in the practice of arbitration the loser alone may bear the cost of the Arbitrator. The prohibitive cost of arbitration remains the major reason why despite all the advantages it is still not the most favoured option. One disadvantage of arbitration as a dispute resolution option is the absence of coercive power by the arbitrator and their inability to make orders to enforce the arbitral award. Parties are forced to approach the court to enforce the award and conversely parties may also approach the courts to challenge and set aside the award.

12.17 Recognition and Enforcement of Insurance Judgments

12.17.1 Principle of Recognition

The judgments of one State's courts have no force by themselves in another State. This is often unsatisfactory. Parties are interested in transnational legal certainty and in avoiding repeated litigation and conflicting decisions; the general public has an interest in avoiding resources spent on re-litigation and in international decisional harmonies; and States have a common interest in promoting inter-State transactions. However, States have valid reasons to deny foreign judgments the same force they grant their own judgments since the foreign procedure may be viewed as deficient, or the outcome of the foreign litigation may be viewed as objectionable. The field of recognition and enforcement of foreign judgments mediates between these competing considerations. Recognition and enforcement of foreign judgments is one of the three parts of conflict of laws, besides jurisdiction.

12.17.2 Principle of Enforcement

In law, the enforcement of foreign judgments is the recognition and enforcement in one jurisdiction of judgments rendered in another ("foreign") jurisdiction. Foreign judgments may be recognized based on bilateral or multilateral treaties or understandings, or unilaterally without an express international agreement. The "recognition" of a foreign judgment occurs when the court of one country or jurisdiction accepts a judicial decision made by the courts of another "foreign" country or jurisdiction, and issues a judgment in substantially identical terms without rehearing the substance of the original lawsuit.

12.17.3 Enforcement Under English Law

Judgments and court orders from outside the EU may be recognised under English law through a long and windy. However, this is restricted to the Laws of England and Wales. Although closely resembling those of England and Wales, Scotland and Northern Ireland having their own systems. This is despite the Marine Insurance Act being a federal legislation applicable to the whole of the UK

12.17.4 List the Process

However, once recognised the judgment can be enforced. If you have obtained a judgment or court order outside England and Wales, you may wish to enforce it in England or Wales because your debtor has assets there or is located there. Methods of enforcing a judgment depend largely on the country or state of its origin and the nature of the judgment or order, among other things.

English law splits countries into one or more of four categories which, in descending order of ease and convenience, are:

(a) countries to which the European Enforcement Order (EEO) Regulation applies;
(b) countries which have signed the Brussels Regulation or the Lugarno Convention;
(c) countries with which the UK has bilateral enforcement conventions in place; and
(d) countries for which none of the above apply - notably the USA, Japan and China.

A foreign judgment can only be enforced if it is for a definite sum of money. The England and Wales court will not enforce judgments for taxes or penalties, such as fines - this means that USA-style punitive damages will not be recoverable.

12.17.5 Enforcement in the EU

A judgment given in an EU country is to be recognised in the other EU countries without any special procedure being required. "Judgment" means any judgment given by a court or tribunal of an EU country, whatever the judgment may be called, including a decree, order, decision or writ of execution. Under no circumstances may a foreign judgment be reviewed as to its substance.

A judgment will not be recognised if:

(a) such recognition is manifestly contrary to public policy in the EU country in which recognition is sought;
(b) the defendant was not served with the document that instituted the proceedings in sufficient time and in such a way as to enable the defendant to arrange for his/her defence;
(c) it is irreconcilable with a judgment given in a dispute between the same parties in the EU country in which recognition is sought; and
(d) it is irreconcilable with an earlier judgment given in another EU or non-EU country involving the same cause of action and the same parties.

A court in which recognition is sought of a judgment given in another EU country may stay the proceedings, if an ordinary appeal against the judgment has been lodged. A judgment is to be enforced in another EU country when, on the application of any interested party, it has been declared enforceable there. The parties may appeal against a decision on an application for a declaration of enforceability.

Section 3
Jurisdiction in matters relating to insurance

Clause 8

In matters relating to insurance, jurisdiction shall be determined by this Section, without prejudice to Clause 4 and point 5 of Clause 5.

Clause 9

1. An insurer domiciled in a Member State may be sued:

(a) in the courts of the Member State where he is domiciled, or

(b) in another Member State, in the case of actions brought by the policyholder, the insured or a beneficiary, in the courts for the place where the plaintiff is domiciled,

(c) if he is a co-insurer, in the courts of a Member State in which proceedings are brought against the leading insurer.

2. An insurer who is not domiciled in a Member State but has a branch, agency or other establishment in one of the Member States shall, in disputes arising out of the operations of the branch, agency or establishment, be deemed to be domiciled in that Member State.

Clause 10

In respect of liability insurance or insurance of immovable property, the insurer may in addition be sued in the courts for the place where the harmful event occurred. The same applies if movable and immovable property is covered by the same insurance policy and both are adversely affected by the same contingency.

Clause 11

1. In respect of liability insurance, the insurer may also, if the law of the court permits it, be joined in proceedings which the injured party has brought against the insured.

2. Clauses 8, 9 and 10 shall apply to actions brought by the injured party directly against the insurer, where such direct actions are permitted.

3. If the law governing such direct actions provides that the policyholder or the insured may be joined as a party to the action, the same court shall have jurisdiction over them.

Clause 12

1. Without prejudice to Clause 11(3), an insurer may bring proceedings only in the courts of the Member State in which the defendant is domiciled, irrespective of whether he is the policyholder, the insured or a beneficiary.

2. The provisions of this Section shall not affect the right to bring a counter-claim in the court in which, in accordance with this Section, the original claim is pending.

Clause 13

The provisions of this Section may be departed from only by an agreement:

1. which is entered into after the dispute has arisen, or

2. which allows the policyholder, the insured or a beneficiary to bring proceedings in courts other than those indicated in this Section, or

3. which is concluded between a policyholder and an insurer, both of whom are at the time of conclusion of the contract domiciled or habitually resident in the same Member State, and which has the effect of conferring jurisdiction on the courts of that State even if the harmful event were to occur abroad, provided that such an agreement is not contrary to the law of that State, or

4. which is concluded with a policyholder who is not domiciled in a Member State, except in so far as the insurance is compulsory or relates to immovable property in a Member State, or

5. which relates to a contract of insurance in so far as it covers one or more of the risks set out in Clause 14.

Clause 14

The following are the risks referred to in Clause 13(5):

1. any loss of or damage to:

(a) seagoing ships, installations situated offshore or on the high seas, or aircraft, arising from perils which relate to their use for commercial purposes;

(b) goods in transit other than passengers' baggage where the transit consists of or includes carriage by such ships or aircraft;

2. any liability, other than for bodily injury to passengers or loss of or damage to their baggage:

(a) arising out of the use or operation of ships, installations or aircraft as referred to in point 1(a) in so far as, in respect of the latter, the law of the Member State in which such aircraft are registered does not prohibit agreements on jurisdiction regarding insurance of such risks;

(b) for loss or damage caused by goods in transit as described in point 1(b);

3. any financial loss connected with the use or operation of ships, installations or aircraft as referred to in point 1(a), in particular loss of freight or charter-hire;

4. any risk or interest connected with any of those referred to in points 1 to 3;

5. notwithstanding points 1 to 4, all "large risks" as defined in Council Directive 73/239/EEC (7), as amended by Council Directives 88/357/EEC (8) and 90/618/EEC (9), as they may be amended.

12.17.6 Enforcement Outside the EU

Enforcement outside the EU will be governed by the New York Convention on the Recognition and Enforcement of Foreign Arbitral Awards, depending on the ratification of the convention by plaintiff and defendant's respective countries.[6] The *Convention on the Recognition and Enforcement of Foreign Arbitral Awards*, also known as the New York Arbitration Convention or simply the New York Convention, is one of the key instruments in international arbitration. The New York Convention applies to the recognition and enforcement of foreign arbitral awards and the referral by a court to arbitration. The Convention on the Recognition and Enforcement of Foreign Arbitral Awards, also known as the New York Convention, was adopted by a United Nations diplomatic conference on 10 June 1958 and entered into force on 7 June 1959.

12.18 Consequences of Brexit

12.18.1 Introduction

On 29 March 2017, the UK government served two-years notice under Clause 50 of The Treaty on European Union to terminate the UK's membership of the EU. This means that the UK exit (or 'Brexit') will take effect on 29 March 2019. In the meantime, the UK and EU are negotiating the terms of a UK/EU Withdrawal Agreement (including a declaration on the outline terms of their future trading relationship). If a Withdrawal Agreement is successfully concluded, this will include a transitional

[6] See generally, Mengis (1987).

arrangement for the continued application of EU law in and to the UK, until the end of 2020. Some of the immediate challenges for businesses will arise from the impact of Brexit on the free movement of goods, services and workers and a number of areas covered by the single market, including the protection of IP rights. Forward planning is, therefore, key. Regardless of which model it adopts, the UK will no longer be required to apply some (if not all) EU legislation.

The UK has implemented certain EU laws (generally, EU directives) via primary legislation that will continue to be part of English law, unless these are amended or repealed. Other EU laws (generally, EU regulations) have direct applicability in the UK without the need for implementation, which means that these laws would fall away once the UK withdraws from the EU, unless they are transposed into UK law. Finally, thousands of statutory instruments have been made pursuant to the *European Communities Act 1972*. If this act is repealed upon the UK's withdrawal from the EU, then, unless transposed into UK law, these statutory instruments will cease to apply as well. Therefore, the UK will have to perform a complex exercise to determine which EU laws and EU-derived laws it wishes to retain, amend or repeal, driven in part by the nature of any agreement reached with the EU during exit negotiations.

12.18.2 Insurance Contract Law Principles

Insurance contract law in England was not governed by EU law, but has been shaped by UK derived law, such as the MIA1906, the Insurance Act 2015 (which came into force 12 August 2016) and the *Consumer Insurance (Disclosure and Representations) Act* 2012, so no changes to these regimes would be expected after of Brexit. Brexit changes the nature of the formal relationship between the U.K. and the EU and throws London's place as a global financial centre into question. It creates new trade restrictions between the U.K. and the rest of Europe and limits the ability of British citizens to move as freely around the EU. Following the end of the Brexit transition period (31 December 2020), EEA-authorised insurers and insurance intermediaries can no longer rely on passporting rights to carry out regulated insurance activities in the UK.

12.18.3 Governing Law and Jurisdiction

If Brexit happens, underwriters and brokers will have to take care over the choice of governing law and jurisdiction clauses they use in policy wordings, particularly the jurisdiction aspect. Currently, the Rome I and Rome II Regulations apply to the governing law rules in English law for contractual and non-contractual obligations respectively. In the event of Brexit, if England reverted to the position before the Regulations came into force, the position on contractual obligations would remain the same because the UK is a signatory to the Rome Convention. The regime for non-contractual obligations would not give the parties an express right to choose the law governing their relationship (under the *Private International law (Miscellaneous Provisions) Act 1995*), but the courts of other EU member states would continue to apply the rules set out in Rome I and II, so a choice of English law would be upheld.

More radical is the effect on jurisdiction rules. Currently in English law, under the Recast Brussels Regulation, the general rule is that the courts where the defendant is domiciled have jurisdiction, except where the parties have agreed otherwise and subject to certain other special jurisdiction provisions, such as for torts. However, there is an insurance exception to the general rule which only affects the insurer/insured relationship (not insurer to insurer or reinsured to reinsurer) which means that the insured has the option of bringing proceedings in his own domicile, and the insurer is restricted to suing the insured in the insured's country of domicile. The ability to circumvent the rules by a jurisdiction agreement is very limited as the rules are there to protect the customer who is seen to be in a weaker position. In the event of Brexit where the Recast Brussels Regulation would no longer apply the English Court would likely uphold express clauses between the parties' conferring jurisdiction on the English courts. However, the question of how other EU member states would view such clauses, which would be a matter for the laws of those member states, could give rise to considerable uncertainty. It may be prudent for insurers to follow the provisions in the Recast Brussels Regulation anyway (and write them into the policy) in order to be seen to be treating customers fairly under FCA principles.

12.18.4 Recognition and Enforcement of Judgments

The Recast Brussels Regulation provides a simplified mechanism for the recognition and enforcement of judgments of courts in EU member states. Judgments may be recognised and enforced in other member states without the need to follow special procedures, such as obtaining a declaration of enforceability in the courts of the member state in which enforcement is sought, which would involve taking local legal advice. In the event of Brexit this mechanism would no longer apply to English judgments, making the enforcement procedure more complex, uncertain, lengthy and costly. If England became known as a country from which it was difficult to enforce judgments, it might influence the preference of choice of court, or encourage an alternative choice of dispute resolution such as arbitration. If the UK were to leave the EU, in certain ongoing litigation it might be appropriate for insurers to seek early judgment to ensure use of the recognition and enforcement mechanism in the Recast Brussel Regulation, or to settle a case to avoid potential issues.

12.18.5 Other Insurance Related Issues

Other aspects of Brexit on insurance law would be:

(a) Regulatory aspects of Insurance regime;

(b) Regulatory impacts on policy wordings;
(c) Other insurance regulation;
(d) Underwriting Issues;
(e) Risk Management;
(f) Policy wordings and claims issues;
(g) Parallel proceedings;
(h) Service proceedings; and
(i) Passporting arrangements.

12.19 Food for Further Thoughts

The single main food for thoughts here is Life outside the EU for UK and European insurers and insureds. The inevitable question is what will happen now that the UK has exited the EU and EU jurisdiction. Throughout UK's 47-year membership of the EU, EU law had expanded into further areas of UK national laws and now covers areas such as: social policies, agriculture, environmental, employment, public health, immigration and asylum, consumer protection, energy, transport, security, justice and culture and tourism.[7] In contracts, including insurance, these were governed by the Rome and Brussels Conventions.

12.20 Concluding Remarks

Except for a few exceptions the principal of the law governing international contracts applies to FOB and CIF insurance contracts. They may apply in particular circumstances or as part of the wider sales contract, or payments contracts, or carriage contract or the institute cargo clauses guidelines. There are rules governing the three jurisdictions in the UK, the EU disputes and disputes with parties from outside the EU. The subject is more important in international trade by its very nature of internationality. The jurisdiction in which an insurance case is heard is often critical to the outcome, as the court will apply its own choice of law rules to the contract and those rules may point to an applicable law whose content is quite different from that of English law.

The jurisdiction in which an insurance case is heard is often critical to the outcome, as the court will apply its own choice of law rules to the contract and those rules may point to an applicable law whose content is quite different from that of English law. The area of insurance presents a unique problem in the law of conflict of laws, since by its nature, insurance blends contract principles with those of tort. Choice of law questions often arise in such cases, because the place of the contract and the place of the accident often are not the same- Choice of law deals with the

[7] Womble Bond Dickinson (UK) LLP: "Legal implications of Brexit for the London insurance sector" https://www.lexology.com/library/detail.aspx?g=15b31906-dd16-4348-97e2-d7180a95cac4 *(accessed on 12/02/2022).*

body of law under which the policy will be construed and interpreted in the event of dispute between the Insured and the Insurer over the coverage granted by the Insurer. Choice of jurisdiction deals with the venue or court system where such litigation will take place.

From the examples above, it is appatent that from the legal perspective Brexit would cause inevitable delay and cost caused by uncertainty and the need to put alternative agreements in place which could take some time. This would affect regulatory, claims and underwriting areas.

12.21 Further Readings

Major Publications

- Carr, Indira: International Trade Law, 5th Edn
- Schimthoff, Clive: International Trade, 12th Edn, Chapters
- Sassoon, David: CIF and FOB Contracts, Chapters
- Chua, Jason H: International Trade, 4th Edn, Chapters
- Dunt, John: Insurance of International Trade
- Collins et al [Eds]: Dicey, Morris and Collins on the Conflict of Laws, 15th Edn, 2012, Sweet & Maxwell
- Hill and Chong: International Commercial Disputes, 4th Edn 2010, Hart Publishing
- Stone: EU Private International Law, 2nd 2010, Edward Edgar
- Blackaby, et al: Hunter on International Arbitration, 2009 OUP
- Lew, et al: Comparative International Commercial Arbitration, 2003, Kluwer Law International
- Merkin: Arbitration Law, 2004 Informa
- Mustil and Boyd: The Law and Practice of Commercial Arbitration in England, LexisNexis, 3rd Edn 2014
- Saunders: Quo Vadis Arbitration? Sixty Years of Arbitration Practice, a Comparative Study, 1999, Kluwer Law International
- Sarcevic: Essays on International Arbitration, 1989, Graham & Trotam
- Stone: EU Private International Law, 3rd edn 2014 Edward Elgar
- Alexander (ed): Global Trends in Mediation, 2008, Kluwer Law International
- Katsch et al: Online Dispute Resolution: Resolving Conflicts in Outerspace,2001, Jossy Bass
- Mota, et al: Civil and Commercial Mediation in Europe, 2012, BISAC Law
- McDuff (ed): Essays on Mediation, Dealing with Disputes in 21st Century 2016, Wolters Kluwer
- Hendrikse & J.G.J. Rinkes (eds.), Insurance and Europe, Zutphen: Uitgeverij Paris 2007
- Xandra, Kramer: "Conflict of Laws on Insurance Contracts in Europe The Rome I proposal – Towards Uniform Conflict Rules for Insurance Contracts?" in M.L. Hendrikse & J.G.J. Rinkes (eds.), Insurance and Europe, Zutphen: Uitgeverij Paris 2007, pp. 85–102

Clauses

- Brooker & Lavers: "Issues in the development of ADR for commercial and construction disputes" [2000] 19 CJQ 353
- ----------------------: "Commercial and Construction ADR: Lawyers attitudes and experience", [2001] 20 CJQ 327
- ----------------------: "Commercial Lawyers' attitudes and experience with mediation 2002(4) Web JCLI
- http://webjcli.ncl..ac.uk/2002/issue4/brooker4.html
- Deason: "Predictable mediation and confidentiality in the US federal system" [2002] 17 *Ohio State Journal on Dispute Resolution*, 239
- Genn: "Court-based ADR initiatives for non-family civil disputes: The Commercial Court and the Court of Appeal" 2002, Lord Chancellor's Department Research Series No.1/02
- McAdoo & Welsh, "Does ADR really have a place in the lawyer's philosophical map?" [1999] 18 *Hamlin Journal of Public Law and Policy*, 376
- McAdoo & Nino: "The EU Directive on Mediation in Civil and Commercial Matters and the principle of effective judicial protection" 2012 XIX (2), Lex ET Scientia, Juridical Series 105
- Mengis: Conflict of Laws Symposium: Conflict of Laws in Louisiana-Insurance, *Louisiana Law Review* Volume 47, Number 5 May 1987; https://digitalcommons.law.lsu.edu/lalrev/vol47/iss5/14
- Mota, et al, [eds] Civil and Commercial Mediation in Europe, 2012, BISAC Law
- Renfrew, "The American Experience with dispute resolution in all its forms", 16 CJQ 145
- Rosenberg: "Keeping the lid on confidentiality: the mediation privilege and the conflict of law", [1994] 10 *Ohio State Journal on Dispute Resolution* 157
- Teitz: "Providing Legal Services for the middle class in cyberspace: the promise and challenge of online dispute resolution", [2001] 70 *Fordham LR* 985
- Thornburg: "Going private: technology, due process, and internet dispute resolution", [2000] 34 *University of California Davis LR* 151
- "choice of law clause", Webster's New World Law Dictionary (Hoboken, New Jersey: Wiley Publishing, Inc.), 2006
- Lea Brilmayer and Jack Goldsmith, *Conflicts of Law: Cases and Materials, Fifth Edition* (2002), pp. 280–303
- Tetley, William QC: International Conflict of Laws: Common, Civil and Maritime, Blais International Shipping Publications, Montreal, 1994
- M.L. Hendrikse & J.G.J. Rinkes (eds.), Insurance and Europe, Zutphen: Uitgeverij Paris 2007
- Xandra Kramer: "Conflict of Laws on Insurance Contracts in Europe The Rome I proposal – Towards -Uniform Conflict Rules for Insurance Contracts?", in M.L. Hendrikse & J.G.J. Rinkes (eds.), Insurance and Europe, Zutphen: Uitgeverij Paris 2007, pp. 85–102

Internet Sources

- Brooker & Lavers: "Commercial Lawyers attitudes and experience with mediation" 2002[4] *WebJCLI,* http://webjcli.ncl.ac.uk/2002/issue4/brooker4.html

References

Ademuni-Odeke (1996) The EC conflicts of laws' regime for insurance contracts. Tolley's Prof Neg 12(1):7–14

Fountoulakis C (2006) The parties' choice of 'neutral law' in international sales contracts. Eur J Law Reform VII(3/4):303–329. https://core.ac.uk/download/pdf/18238341.pdf

Mengis MW (1987) "Conflict of laws: insurance" report of the symposium on conflicts of law in Louisiana. La Law Rev 47

Claims and Settlement 13

Abstract

This final formal chapter deals with Claims and Settlement in insurance contracts and their effect on export insurance. This is an essential aspect of insurance law and practice. After the Introductory paragraph, the chapter goes on to treat: Claims Options; The Claims Process; Claims Procedures; Claimable Losses and Damages; Types of Losses; Hurdles to Successful Claims; Settlement of Claims; Recoveries and Policy Adjustment; Remedies of the Contract; Further Food for Thoughts; Concluding Claims; Claims Recoveries; and Further Readings.

13.1 Introduction

In most cases contractual performance runs smoothly without problems. However, in the minority of cases involving loss and/or damage to the goods or occurrence of other insured risks, the party at loss has to make an insurance claim from either the tort-feasor or the insurer. An insurance claim is a formal application to the insurers by the insured or his agent or other beneficiaries for payment of the sum due under the policy following a loss or damage to the insured subject matter. Following a loss or damage to the subject matter or interest insured the insured, his assignee or agent or broker or other representative should make a claim to the assurer directly or through the assurer's agents, depending on the terms and conditions of the policy.

As a general rule of thumb, the insured must first report the accident of loss or damage to his insurer as soon as is reasonably possible, preferably within 24 h, especially if the insured wants the claim settled as soon as possible. Most insurers have their own rules anywhere from a day to a few weeks. the fulfilment by an insurer of its obligation to receive, investigate and act on a claim filed by an insured. These, included the methods for communicating the loss and claims, will normally be included in a contractual clause.

P. Ademuni-Odeke, *Insurance of International Sales' Contracts under Incoterms*, Law for Professionals, https://doi.org/10.1007/978-3-031-75136-3_13

In practice most insurers will have agents at major stations far from home base, to handle and/or assist the insured with the claims. This marks the export-import insurance process different from other insurance businesses. At the end of this process, the insurance company may reimburse the money to the healthcare provider in whole or in part. When you make a claim on an insurance policy, you are formally notifying the insurance company that you have suffered a loss or damage that you believe is covered by the policy and you are requesting action. The insurer will review your claim and see if the event or circumstances are risks covered by the policy.

Claims will depend on the terms and conditions of the policy and the type of loss. The claim will be subject to what is covered and what is excluded, limitations and what excuses the insurer has under the policy, etc. In addition to the terms and conditions of the policy, claims will be further governed by the law applicable, the jurisdiction and the type of transportation

13.2 Claims Under the Transport Conventions

13.2.1 Introduction

And, therefore, the relevant provisions of the transport Convention governing that contract where a claim is against the carrier. It will also depend on the size and location of the insurer—Lloyds and other larger and established insurers will normally have overseas agents where the assignee can make claims while claims against a credit insurance such as UKEFL would have to be made through the London Headquarters.

The policy, other trade customs and usages and the applicable cargo clauses will indicate which party can claim, the claims procedures and processes. Most claims are settled amicably and quickly, few go to litigation as both insurers and insureds are mindful of their reputations and effect of publicity on their business (more to come).

13.2.2 Under the Air (Warsaw) Convention 1929 as Amended

Air cargo insurance is governed by the Warsaw Convention—an international agreement setting limits of liability for freight, baggage, and bodily injury (BI) on international flights. Under Chapter III (Clauses 17–30) the air carrier is liable for loss and damages for carriage under its responsibility. Combined Transport Carriage is contained in Chapter IV (Clause 31) of the convention. Additionally, the agreement puts the responsibility on the air carrier to prove that it did not cause the loss to avoid reimbursement to the claimant. The limitation on liability for cargo and checked baggage is 250 francs per kilogram. For unchecked baggage the limit is 5000 francs per passenger. The sums in francs refer to French francs each equivalent to 65 milligrams of gold. This would cover the FCA which replaced FOB(A), FOB(T) and FOB(R) and carriage under multimodal contracts.

13.2.3 Under the Rail Transport Convention COTIF (CIM Rules) 1980

The Rail Transport Convention is coached differently from the others. The main convention being COTIF, with two Annexes: Appendix A (Rules for Carriage of Passengers-CIV) and Appendix B (Rules for Carriage of Goods-CIM). This part of the book is concerned with especially international transport—in accordance with the Convention on the Agreement for the International Carriage of Goods by Rail (COTIF Convention). Title IV (Clauses 35–51) of the CIM Rules concern the carrier's liability. Parties should pay attention to Clauses 40 (Compensation). Title V (Clauses 52–58) deals with the Assertion of Rights by the shipper, often the seller or simply a consignor acting on its behalf. For insurance purposes, these rights would be assigned to the consignee-often the buyer and his subsequent assigns(sub-buyers). The insurance covers liability for damage incurred in the goods taken over for the purpose of road freight transport. The sum insured is set by the insured and should correspond to the value of the transported cargo. Claims are contained in Clause 53; persons entitle to claim Clause 54 and persons against who claims be brought (the rail carrier) (Clause 55) The Incoterms involved would include the FCA.

13.2.4 Under the Road Transport Convention- (CMR) 1956

The insurance covers liability for damage incurred in the goods taken over for the purpose of road freight transport-International transport—in accordance with the *Convention on the Agreement for the International Carriage of Goods by Road* (CMR Convention). The carriers' liability is contained in Chapter IV (Clauses 17–29) of the convention, while Claims and Actions are found in Chapter V (Clauses 30–33). The sum insured is set by the insured and should correspond to the value of the transported cargo. This would include the FCA.

13.2.5 Under the Maritime Transport Conventions

Neither the carrier nor the ship shall be liable for loss or damage arising or resulting from unseaworthiness unless caused by want of due diligence on the part of the carrier to make the ship seaworthy, and to secure that the ship is properly manned, equipped and supplied, and to make the holds, refrigerating and cool. What are the liabilities of a carrier by sea? The typical obligations of a carrier by sea to a shipper of cargo are: to provide a seaworthy ship to issue a bill of lading.to "properly and carefully load, handle, stow, carry, keep, care for, and discharge the goods carried", to proceed with "reasonable despatch". This covers Incoterms for carriage by sea and inland waterways (FOB, FAS, CFR and CIF).

13.2.5.1 Under the Hague Rules 1924

The duties and liabilities of the carrier is contained in Art III (2), providing that the carrier shall properly and carefully load, handle, stow, carry, keep, care for and discharge the goods delivered. The standard imposed is equivalent to that of 'reasonable care' and the goods must be carried in accordance with a sound system. However, shippers—who may be sellers or simply consignor agents should be aware of the exceptions under Clause 4 that neither the carrier nor the ship shall be liable for loss or damage arising or resulting from unseaworthiness unless caused by want of due diligence on the part of the carrier to make the ship seaworthy and to secure that the ship is properly manned, equipped and supplied, and to make the holds, refrigerating and cooling. Furthermore, that the carrier might agree to surrender their Clause III rights under Clause 5 or that both the carrier and shipper could agree to modify the rights, obligations and liabilities by Clauses 6–7.

13.2.5.2 Under the Hague Visby Rules 1967

The Hague Visby Rules follows the patterns of the Hague Rules except for the numbering of clauses. The duties and liabilities of carrier are contained in Clause III, the exceptions in Clause IV, liability of servants in Clause IVbis, and surrender of rights by the carrier and agreements by both parties to vary the terms and conditions of carriage in Clauses V–VII respectively. Thus, under the Hague-Visby Rules the carrier is exonerated from liability (a) in respect of loss of or damage to the goods arising or resulting from unseaworthiness unless caused by the breach by the carrier of his due diligence obligation and, (b) as well as for loss of or damage to the goods arising from fault of the master.

13.2.5.3 Under the Hamburg Rules 1978

Generally, the carrier is liable for loss resulting from loss of or damage to the goods, as well as from delay in delivery, if the occurrence which caused the loss, damage or delay took place while the goods were in his charge as defined in clause 4, unless the carrier proves that he, his servants or agents took all measures. Under Part II (Clauses 4–11) of the Hamburg Rules the carrier is liable for loss, damage, or delay in delivery of goods, if the loss occurred while the goods were under the carrier's charge, unless the carrier proves that he, his servant or agents took all measures that would reasonably be required to avoid the occurrence and its consequences. Under Part III (Clauses 12–14) of the convention the shipper—who may be the seller or simply a consignee—is has some liabilities which may affect the its or the consignor's (buyer and other assignees) rights and therefore insurance obligations. In that case parties should be aware of the insurance claims' actions and procedures under Clauses 19–22 of the convention.

13.2.5.4 Under the Multimodal Transport Convention 1980

The position under the multimodal transport convention is slightly complicated in that it can potentially involve principles of all other transport conventions, depending the nature and number of contracts involved. Liability of the MTO is in Part III (Clauses 14–21), Liability of the Consignor (most likely the Seller) is in Part IV (Clauses 22–23) and Claims and Actions in Part V (Clauses 24–27) of the Convention. Otherwise, generally, the shipper bears strict liability in two situations: damage caused by the dangerous goods in the carrier having not been informed of their dangerous character, or the goods are not properly marked or labelled (Art. 32) and inaccurate information provided for the compilation of transport documents (Art). What are the challenges of multimodal transport that might have a bearing on insurance? Especially with different modes of transport involved, shippers need to have security that in reality means being prepared for supply chain disruptions and having different intermodal and multimodal solutions as alternatives. Challenge: safety concerns, disrupted service, and inflated shipping costs. This would include Incoterms for all modes of transportation.

13.2.5.5 Under the Rotterdam Rules 2008

This is the latest of the maritime conventions but is not yet in force. Otherwise the *UN Convention on Contracts for the International Carriage of Goods Wholly or Partly by Sea*, known as the Rotterdam Rules, adopted in December 2008, provides mandatory standards of liability for loss or damage arising from the international carriage of goods by sea and is intended to provide a modern successor to. Under Chapter 5 (Clauses 17–23) the carrier is liable for loss of or damage to the goods, as well as for delay in delivery, if the claimant proves that the loss, carrier's liability, limitation of liability and time for suit. Chapter 13 (Clauses 62–65) provide for time for suits and, therefore, possible insurance claims. For suits and insurance claims purposes, parties need to take note Clause 22 relating to the calculation of compensation. In such case the provisions of that instrument will apply—(Clause 26).

Otherwise, there is a pattern that runs through all the maritime transport conventions. For instance, under the Hamburg Rules and the Rotterdam Rules the carrier is always liable for loss, damage or delay caused by fault of the carrier, his servants or agents, unlike Hague-Visby Rules. On the other hand, the time-bar under the Hamburg Rules is two years rather than one under Hague-Visby Rules.

13.3 Claims' Options

13.3.1 Introduction: What Are Claims?

The claim can be made to the carrier or other third party liable for or damage, or directly to the insurer, whichever is applicable. The law sometimes makes it hard by using loss and damage or damage leading to loss to mean the same thing. The policy will provide detailed instructions on when, by who and how claims are to be made under the policy. There seems to be a difference between theory and practice in this respect. Due to the nature of international trade, the differences in time zones and trade customs and cultures, most insurance companies make it easier for their customers to enable claims even through overseas offices or agents. Most Claims to Lloyds Members should also be made through Lloyds Agents overseas.

13.3.2 Requirement (s) for a Claim

As almost invariably required by the condition of the policy, the insured must:

(a) give notice of the loss;[1]
(b) furnish particulars of the loss;[2]
(c) furnish proof of loss;[3] and
(d) make no fraudulent claim.[4]

This is in addition to fulfilling the requirements for abandonment and notice thereof below. The claim may be made in Claim Form, where provided, orally but preferably in writing. It can be made in person or through a broker of agent within the UK or the insurance representative overseas.

13.3.3 Who Can Claim?

13.3.3.1 Shipper

Who claims will depend on whether the loss occurs before or after the transfer of the insurance documents to the buyer/beneficiary. Before the transfer a shipper who is also the seller and consignor can claim. Furthermore, a shipper who consigns goods to himself and is, therefore, also a consignee can claim. That shipment dispenses with the need to transfer the insurance documents. The difference between a shipper and a consignee is that the consignee is the receiver of the shipment and is usually the owner of the goods. This may be an individual or a company [needn't be exporter/seller].

13.3.3.2 Seller/Exporter

A seller of goods in his capacity as the shipper can claim in his own name, where the loss has occurred before the shipment and/or transfer of risks, titles and insurance documents.

[1] *Re Solvency Mutual Guarantee Society, Hawthorne's Case* (1862) 31 LJ Ch 625.

[2] *London Guarantee Co v Fearnley* (1880) 5 App Cas 911, HL; *Worsely v Wood* (1796) 6 Term Rep 710 at 718 (per Lord Kenyon); *Gamble v Accident Assurance Co* (1869) 4 IR CL 204 at 214 (per Lord Pigot CB).

[3] *Braunstein v Accidental Death Insurance Co* (1861) 1 B& S 782 at 754 (per Wightman J) IR 4 CL 204.

[4] *Britton v Royal Insurance Co* (1866) 4 F & F 905, *Worsely v Wood.*

13.3.3.3 Consignor

A consignor of goods of rejected goods that are damaged or lost after rejection can claim from the insurers. The consignor could be the shipper or seller of the goods. [whether buyer or not]

13.3.3.4 Consignee/Buyer

A consignee of the goods would have a prior right to claim by virtue of the transfer of the documents, policy and goods to them. In a contract of carriage, the consignee is the entity who is financially responsible (the buyer) for the receipt of a shipment. Generally, but not always, the consignee is the same as the receiver.

13.3.3.5 Assignee

An assignee (by agreement or custom) of the policy can claim. An assignee can be the consignee, named person, lender/mortgagee. [subsequent buyer or debtee]

13.3.3.6 "Named Person"

A person named in the insurance policy and/or bill of lading or by the party with insurable interest in the goods can claim. [such as agent or buyer]

13.3.3.7 The Lender/Mortgagee

A bank or other lender that has advanced the purchase funds for goods that are lost or damaged on transit can join the consignee or claim in its own name as a mortgagee.

13.3.3.8 Freight Forwarder

A freight forwarder can sue either as a shipper or agent of the consignor or consignee (see also agent below).

13.3.3.9 Agent

An agent (insurance or forwarding) of the consignor or consignee, as the case may be, can claim on the principal's behalf.

13.3.3.10 Broker

Like the agent, a broker can effect claims on behalf of his assured client.

13.3.4 Claiming in Person

Under Incoterms or other terms of sale, the seller takes out insurance for the benefit of the buyer. For other insurance claims (excluding the seller making a claim for the buyer), you should follow the guidelines below. In the event of damage or loss to goods in transit, the consignee (or buyer) should follow these guidelines:

13.3.4.1 Steps Necessary for a Claim

(a) carry out a thorough inspection of all the goods and note damaged or missing items;

(b) take any steps necessary to minimise or prevent further damage;
(c) make a note of any expenses incurred in carrying out the above for the insurer to reimburse;
(d) keep as evidence the shipping container, packing materials, damaged merchandise and shipping documents;
(e) contact the insurer (or broker if appropriate) so that a survey of damage can be arranged; and
(f) Etc.

13.3.4.2 Information Necessary for a Claim

Some policies provide more others less detailed information necessary for a successful and speedy claim. However, the common factor among all policies is that the consignor, consignee or their respective agents should first file a letter of claim against the freight forwarder or carrier—this should include:

(a) its company name and (if applicable) voyage or flight number;
(b) sea waybill or bill of lading or air waybill number (if applicable);
(c) date of arrival at destination;
(d) description of cargo;
(e) container numbers;
(f) the amount being claimed; and
(g) any other relevant information and/or documents.

Failing that they should inform the insurer who together will guide and even join them on the claim.

13.3.4.3 Documents Necessary for a Claim

The same situation as described above applies to documents necessary for a claim. Once again, the general practice is that at the same time, the consignor, consignee or their agents should send full details of the claim to the insurer (through the seller, if they are using the Incoterms—CIF or CIP—this should include at the very least:

(a) a commercial invoice;
(b) consular invoice (if any);
(c) pre-shipment inspection (psi) certificates (if any);
(d) insurance policy details and certificate number;
(e) bill of lading or air waybill number (as applicable);
(f) standard terms and conditions of the carrier/forwarder;
(g) any correspondence with the carrier/freight forwarder concerning loss or damage;
(h) survey report; and
(i) any other relevant document(s) and/or information.

Once more this list is not exhaustive for the reasons given above. A particular contract or insurer might require less or more than the above list.

13.3.4.4 Further Information (if any) Necessary for a Claim

In addition to the above documents, further information required might include the followings:

(a) Copy of all B/L's—ocean, air, inland and/or charterparty—covering the entire shipment along with paid freight bills;
(b) Shipper's commercial invoice covering the entire shipment;
(c) Copy of the packing list(s);
(d) For U.S. Imports, the Duty Consumption Entry Report (customs forms);
(e) All delivery receipts, showing exceptions or not, as well as any bad order slips and carrier;
(f) inspection reports;
(g) For non-deliveries, written confirmation from the transportation carrier that they cannot make delivery;
(h) Copy of the claimant's letters to the transportation carriers placing them on notice, plus any replies received;
(i) Statement of claim;
(j) Copies of all relevant correspondence;
(k) Original certificate of insurance is applicable;
(l) Photos, if available; and
(m) any other relevant document and/or information.

13.4 The Claims Process

13.4.1 The Actual Claims Process

Submission of the actual claim should include, at the minimum, the followings:

(a) A claim form duly completed;
(b) A letter of claim (Demand Letter) lodged with the Carrier or Shipper's agent;
(c) Details on extent of loss or damage or an estimate of repair or replacement cost;
(d) Original Cover Note issued;
(e) Correspondences exchanged with Third Parties;
(f) Police Abstract report, where applicable;
(g) Bill of lading;
(h) Delivery Note/Road Consignment Note;
(i) Commercial Invoice;
(j) Packing List; and
(k) Port Documents, if any.

A loss adjuster will be appointed to adjust the loss and may request to be provided with a copy of the contract between yourselves and the Third Parties. A similar procedure should be followed by the seller if, under the terms of sale, they carried the risk at the time of loss or damage. In international trade policies the claimant is spoilt for choice; he can claim in person, or through an agent or through the process of arbitration.

13.4.2 Claiming Through an Agent

As indicated above although in theory the insured or beneficiary is the party to file a claim, in practice this is normally done through an agent. Were this to be the case and a problem arises as between the principal, the agent and a third party, then the full principles of the law of agency will apply. Despite that, the best way to claim is to use one's agent who will have full knowledge of the policy and the expertise to do so. It works both ways as larger insurers like Lloyds also use agents in many parts of the world to handle and process claims. This has the advantage of avoiding the time differences, customs and practices of various jurisdictions.

13.4.3 Denial of a Claim

In most cases the insurer will accept and pay (settle) the claim. In few incidents they may not and when that happens it can be for all or any of the following reasons:

(a) The incident took place outside of the policy period;
(b) The type of incident or damage isn't covered under the policy;
(c) The claim was filed outside of the time required by the policy (for example, some policies require you to file a claim within 24 h);
(d) The insured having an outstanding payment on his insurance premium; and
(e) Ant other reasonable excuses.

The insurance company will normally full report of the reasons for the decline and suggest the way forward, for instance by requiring more documentary proofs. Occasionally, and in very exceptional circumstances, the insurer might agree to pay without admitting liability (ex-gratis). In the event of a deadlock, the insured can explore claims through arbitration, mediation or litigation.

13.4.4 Through Litigation

Although litigation is a possible way of resolving an insurance dispute, the insured should be aware that this should be the last resort, only where and other ADR systems discussed below have been exhausted or where an important of law and injustice is involved. Insureds should only consider going through litigation with the insurer if he has accepted that there will be no future business relationship between them, in a relationship based largely on the utmost good faith. Apart from expenses in money and time, litigation, relationships can be severe, and this could harm future income.

13.4.5 Through Arbitration

The most common forms of ADR are arbitration, mediation, the rent-a-judge program, summary jury trial, and mini-trial, although techniques can be combined to form hybrids suited to a particular dispute or legal jurisdiction. Less formal than a courtroom trial, arbitration is a legal proceeding where you and the insurance company present information about your claim to a neutral referee, known as an arbitrator. Arbitration can be a good choice for resolving settlement disputes because it can save you time and money. Arbitration is important in shipping, insurance and export trade disputes. Some aspects of it such as commodity trade are based entirely on arbitral proceedings for their dispute settlement. Even within the arbitration process, the insured has a further two choices—through the arbitration per se or through an insurance mediation directive. If insurers refuse to pay a claim when a covered cargo loss occurs, the insured can pursue claims against both them and/or the carrier/forwarder. If the insured pursues litigation on two fronts, costs incurred in the action against the carrier/forwarder are recoverable if the other action is successful. This is because the costs are seen as a direct result of the insurance company's breach of contract.

13.4.6 Through Insurance Mediation Directive (IMD)

Mediation is sometimes preferred to even arbitration as an alternative dispute resolution method. One such example is the IMD under the Financial Services Authority (FSA). The FSA regulates the conduct of any company or individual who provides insurance brokerage services, through the IMD. An exemption from the IMD for freight forwarders or storage firms means that those conducting insurance mediation no longer need to be registered with the FSA//Insurance mediation is a form of Alternative Dispute Resolution (ADR) in which a neutral, third-party mediator, who is chosen by the parties in conflict, works with both parties to arrive at a mutually beneficial conclusion to the conflict.

13.5 The Claims Procedures

13.5.1 Need for Notice of Abandonment

There are a number of tasks to be undertaken by the claimant to effect a claim. These are principally namely to give notice of abandonment. The policy will provide details on when, how, by who and to whom this is to be done. However, the default guideline is the statutory provision in s.62 and 63[5] of the MIA1906, both of which provide as follows:

[5] For notice of abandonment see Blame *Steamship V Ministry of Transport* [1951] 2KB 965.

62 Notice of abandonment

(1) Subject to the provisions of this section, where the assured elects to abandon the subject-matter insured to the insurer, he must give notice of abandonment. If he fails to do so the loss can only be treated as a partial loss.

(2) Notice of abandonment may be given in writing, or by word of mouth, or partly in writing and partly by word of mouth, and may be given in any terms which indicate the intention of the assured to abandon his insured interest in the subject-matter insured unconditionally to the insurer.

(3) Notice of abandonment must be given with reasonable diligence after the receipt of reliable information of the loss, but where the information is of a doubtful character the assured is entitled to a reasonable time to make inquiry.

(4) Where notice of abandonment is properly given, the rights of the assured are not prejudiced by the fact that the insurer refuses to accept the abandonment.

(5) The acceptance of an abandonment may be either express or implied from the conduct of the insurer. The mere silence of the insurer after notice is not an acceptance.

(6) Where notice of abandonment is accepted the abandonment is irrevocable. The acceptance of the notice conclusively admits liability for the loss and the sufficiency of the notice.

(7) Notice of abandonment is unnecessary where, at the time when the assured receives information of the loss, there would be no possibility of benefit to the insurer if notice were given to him.

(8) Notice of abandonment may be waived by the insurer.

(9) Where an insurer has re-insured his risk, no notice of abandonment need be given by him.

Notice of abandonment is only required for constructive total loss, not actual total loss. There is normally a gap or lacuna between the giving of the notice of abandonment and the insurer's reaction to it. In fact, the insurers tend not to react immediately. Reasons for this include the insurer's need to establish the information and at the same time trying to do something to preserve the subject matter or attempting to reduce a partial loss from becoming a total loss. However, there is no cause for alarm on the part of the insured once he has given the notice. He should only establish he has followed the procedure correctly and thereby given an effective and valid notice. This is where there is an advantage to employ agents, brokers or other professionals-need to eliminate costly errors.

13.5.2 Effect of Notice of Abandonment

Everything going to plan the act provides for the effect of abandonment in s.63 thereof, thus:

> **63 Effect of abandonment.**
> (1) Where there is a valid abandonment, the insurer is entitled to take over the interest of the assured in whatever may remain of the subject-matter insured, and all proprietary rights incidental thereto.
>
> (2) Upon the abandonment of a ship, the insurer thereof is entitled to any freight in course of being earned, and which is earned by her subsequent to the casualty causing the loss, less the expenses of earning it incurred after the casualty; and, where the ship is carrying the owner's goods, the insurer is entitled to a reasonable remuneration for the carriage of them subsequent to the casualty causing the loss.

Once more abandonment, designated for loss of ships in marine insurance and vehicle damages in motor insurance, has been extended to marine and cargo insurance.

13.5.3 Duty of Assured on to Minimise Losses

One of the undertakings the insured would have made under the contract is to minimise the loss where damage has occurred. This is alternatively known as the duty to act as if uninsured and is contained in the duty of assured clause in the Institute Cargo Clauses. One such clause, clause 16, reads as follows:

> **16. - Duty of Assured Clause**
> 16 It is the duty of the Assured and their servants and agents in respect of loss recoverable hereunder
>
> 16.1 to take such measures as may be reasonable for the purpose of averting or minimising such loss, and
>
> 16.2 to ensure that all rights against carriers, bailees or other third parties are properly preserved and exercised and the Underwriters will, in addition to any loss recoverable hereunder, reimburse the Assured for any charges properly and reasonably incurred in pursuance of these duties.

13.6 Claimable Losses and Damages

As discussed above, not all losses are claimable. Thus, the following factors and insurance principles, outlined in Chaps. 1 and 2 above, will kick in when the insured makes a claim for loss or damage to the insured cargo.

13.6.1 Requirement for Insurable Interest in Claims

It was mentioned above for an insured to take out a policy on the subject-matter he must have an insurable interest under ss 60 of the Act. Otherwise, he will be wagering (betting) which is an offence under the *Insurance (Gambling Policies) Act* 1959, the *Gambling Act 1854* and the *Gambling Act 2005*. This requirement is also now enshrined in the Insurable Interest Clause in the Institute Clauses. One such Clause 11 provides:

> **11.-Insurable Interest Clause**
> 11.1 In order to recover under this insurance the Assured must have an insurable interest in the subject-matter insured at the time of the loss.
>
> 11.2 Subject to 11.1 above, the Assured shall be entitled to recover for insured loss occurring during the period covered by this insurance, notwithstanding that the loss occurred before the contract of insurance was concluded, unless the Assured were aware of the loss and the Underwriters were not.

13.7 Types of Losses and Damages

13.7.1 Included and Excluded Losses

> **55 Included and excluded losses**
> (1) Subject to the provisions of this Act, and unless the policy otherwise provides, the insurer is liable for any loss proximately caused by a peril insured against, but, subject as aforesaid, he is not liable for any loss which is not proximately caused by a peril insured against.
>
> (2) In particular—
>
> (a) The insurer is not liable for any loss attributable to the wilful misconduct of the assured, but, unless the policy otherwise provides, he is liable for any loss proximately caused by a peril insured against, even though the loss would not have happened but for the misconduct or negligence of the master or crew;
>
> (b) Unless the policy otherwise provides, the insurer on ship or goods is not liable for any loss proximately caused by delay, although the delay be caused by a peril insured against;
>
> (c) Unless the policy otherwise provides, the insurer is not liable for ordinary wear and tear, ordinary leakage and breakage, inherent vice or nature of the subject-matter insured, or for any loss proximately caused by rats or vermin, or for any injury to machinery not proximately caused by maritime perils.

13.7.2 Partial l Loss

Partial loss was covered in Chap. 2. It is covered in s.56 of the MIA 1906 providing that:

56 Partial and total loss
(1) A loss may be either total or partial. Any loss other than a total loss, as hereinafter defined, is a partial loss.

(2) A total loss may be either an actual total loss, or a constructive total loss.

(3) Unless a different intention appears from the terms of the policy, an insurance against total loss includes a constructive, as well as an actual, total loss.

(4) Where the assured brings an action for a total loss and the evidence proves only a partial loss, he may, unless the policy otherwise provides, recover for a partial loss.

(5) Where goods reach their destination in specie, but by reason of obliteration of marks, or otherwise, they are incapable of identification, the loss, if any, is partial, and not total.

13.7.3 Total Loss

13.7.3.1 Actual Total Loss (ss)

Actual total loss was covered in Chap. 2 and is contained in s.57 of the MIA 1906 providing that:

57 Actual total loss
(1) Where the subject-matter insured is destroyed, or so damaged as to cease to be a thing of the kind insured, or where the assured is irretrievably deprived thereof, there is an actual total loss.

(2) In the case of an actual total loss no notice of abandonment need be given.

The wordings of this text are self-explanatory-the guiding principles being the subject matter, either "ceasing to be a thing of the kind insured", or the insured being "irretrievably deprived" of its use.

13.7.3.2 Measure of Total Loss

This is now covered in s.68 of MIA 1906 thus:

13.7.3.3 Partial Loss of Ship

It will be recalled from Sect. 13.7.2 above that a partial loss refers to damage to an insured property that is not total, meaning that it does not prevent the property from performing its function nor does the damage exceed the coverage limit of the insurance policy.

> **69 Partial loss of ship**
>
> Where a ship is damaged, but is not totally lost, the measure of indemnity, subject to any express provision in the policy, is as follows: —
>
> (1) Where the ship has been repaired, the assured is entitled to the reasonable cost of the repairs, less the customary deductions, but not exceeding the sum insured in respect of any one casualty:
>
> (2) Where the ship has been only partially repaired, the assured is entitled to the reasonable cost of such repairs, computed as above, and also to be indemnified for the reasonable depreciation, if any, arising from the unrepaired damage, provided that the aggregate amount shall not exceed the cost of repairing the whole damage, computed as above:
>
> (3) Where the ship has not been repaired, and has not been sold in her damaged state during the risk, the assured is entitled to be indemnified for the reasonable depreciation arising from the unrepaired damage, but not exceeding the reasonable cost of repairing such damage, computed as above.

The same principle applies to cargo insurance. The extent of loss and damage of an insured cargo owner involved in a partial loss of the vessel will be determined by a loss adjuster.

13.7.3.4 Partial Loss of Freight

This is relevant to all export policies involving shipment and, therefore, payment of freight by either party to the sales contract.

> **70 Partial loss of freight**
>
> Subject to any express provision in the policy, where there is a partial loss of freight, the measure of indemnity is such proportion of the sum fixed by the policy in the case of a valued policy, or of the insurable value in the case of an unvalued policy, as the proportion of freight lost by the ass71 Partial loss of goods, merchandise, &c.
>
> Where there is a partial loss of goods, merchandise, or other moveables, the measure of indemnity, subject to any express provision in the policy, is as follows: —

(1) Where part of the goods, merchandise or other moveable's insured by a valued policy is totally lost, the measure of indemnity is such proportion of the sum fixed by the policy as the insurable value of the part lost bears to the insurable value of the whole, ascertained as in the case of an unvalued policy:

(2) Where part of the goods, merchandise, or other moveable's insured by an unvalued policy is totally lost, the measure of indemnity is the insurable value of the part lost, ascertained as in case of total loss:

(3) Where the whole or any part of the goods or merchandise insured has been delivered damaged at its destination, the measure of indemnity is such proportion of the sum fixed by the policy in the case of a valued policy, or of the insurable value in the case of an unvalued policy, as the difference between the gross sound and damaged values at the place of arrival bears to the gross sound value:

(4) "Gross value" means the wholesale price, or, if there be no such price, the estimated value, with, in either case, freight, landing charges, and duty paid beforehand; provided that, in the case of goods or merchandise customarily sold in bond, the bonded price is deemed to be the gross value. "Gross proceeds" means the actual price obtained at a sale where all charges on sale are paid by the sellers, insured bears to the whole freight at the risk of the assured under the policy.

13.7.4 Constructive Total Loss Under the Act

As noted above, a constructive total loss is when the cost for repair of an item (e.g., boat, or cargo) is more than the current value of that item. It also refers to the insurance claim that is settled for the full value of the associated coverage

60 Constructive total loss defined
(1) Subject to any express provision in the policy, there is a constructive total loss where the subject-matter insured is reasonably abandoned on account of its actual total loss appearing to be unavoidable, or because it could not be preserved from actual total loss without an expenditure which would exceed its value when the expenditure had been incurred.

(2) In particular, there is a constructive total loss—

(i) Where the assured is deprived of the possession of his ship or goods by a peril insured against, and (a) it is unlikely that he can recover the ship or goods, as the case may be, or (b) the cost of recovering the ship or goods, as the case may be, would exceed their value when recovered; or

(ii) In the case of damage to a ship, where she is so damaged by a peril insured against that the cost of repairing the damage would exceed the value of the ship when repaired.

In estimating the cost of repairs, no deduction is to be made in respect of general average contributions to those repairs payable by other interests, but account is to be taken of the expense of future salvage operations and of any future general average contributions to which the ship would be liable if repaired; or

(iii) In the case of damage to goods, where the cost of repairing the damage and forwarding the goods to their destination would exceed their value on arrival.

61 Effect of constructive total loss.
Where there is a constructive total loss, the assured may either treat the loss as a partial loss, or abandon the subject-matter insured to the insurer and treat the loss as if it were an actual total loss.

13.7.5 Constructive Total Loss Under the Institute Clauses

Constructive total loss is allowable under Clause 13 of the cargo clauses.

13. - Constructive Total Loss Clause
13 No claim for Constructive Total Loss shall be recoverable hereunder unless the subject-matter insured is reasonably abandoned either on account of its actual total loss appearing to be unavoidable or because the cost of recovering, reconditioning and forwarding the subject-matter to the destination to which it is insured would exceed its value on arrival.

This is reproduced from s.60 of MIA 1906 above, where an assured cargo owner can claim for a constructive total loss if the costs of repairing the damage (inclusive of salvage charges and other expenses) would be more than the value of the cargo when repaired.

13.7.6 Other Claimable Losses

13.7.6.1 Salvage Charges Under MIA 1906

Salvage charges are amounts paid to protect the vessel and/or cargo against additional loss. This could be as simple as adding a barrier to a broken window or as complicated as a salvage company protecting the vessel if grounded. Cargo and most marine insurance policies provide salvage charges as part of the normal goods' insurance policies. The basis is s.65 of MIA 1906, providing that:

65 Salvage charges

(1) Subject to any express provision in the policy, salvage charges incurred in preventing a loss by perils insured against may be recovered as a loss by those perils.

(2) "Salvage charges" means the charges recoverable under maritime law by a salvor independently of contract. They do not include the expenses of services in the nature of salvage rendered by the assured or his agents, or any person employed for hire by them, for the purpose of averting a peril insured against. Such expenses, where properly incurred, may be recovered as particular charges or as a general average loss, according to the circumstances under which they were incurred.

They form part of the cargo clauses

13.7.6.2 Subject to Particular Average

Marine insurance provision under which damages or expenses incurred by a shipper (whose cargo is exposed to a danger) are borne by that shipper only. Such damages or expenses occur by direct harm to the ship and/or cargo, or in a course of action to prevent initial or additional harm to them. Particular average, like general-average is independent of the insurance cover bought for the cargo. Instead, it arises out of the contract between the cargo-owner and the ship-owner. Now largely replaced by the relevant institute cargo clause. See also free of particular average. It is a loss at sea, as through accident or negligence, that is borne solely by the owner of the lost cargo or property, not all other owners as in general average.

It is divided into several concepts such:

13.7.6.3 Particular Average Loss

This is a partial loss or damage caused to any particular cargo or property where the damage is suffered by a particular interest. The damage or loss should be of a particular subject matter in which case the damage suffered cannot be partially shifted to others and the loss would be borne by the persons directly affected by the damage to the said cargo. Remember that it is a partial loss hence not the entire cargo or property would be damaged but a part of it. The damage could either be to the cargo or the ship. A particular average loss with regards a cargo may either be depreciation in value of the cargo or a total loss of a part of it. For instance, when part of a cargo is destroyed by say sea water or about 4 out of 10 of a number of cargoes are destroyed.

This is now contained in s.64 (1) of the MIA1906, which stipulates that:

64 Particular average loss

(1) A particular average loss is a partial loss of the subject-matter insured, caused by a peril insured against, and which is not a general average loss.

With regards the ship (hull or machinery), the damage must be caused to just a part of the ship and not a loss of the entire ship. For instance, damage to the propellers of a ship would be considered a particular average loss and the insured would be indemnified to tune of the damage caused. Indemnity may however depend on certain clauses in the insurance contract example "New for Old" in which case new equipment would be acquired to replace the old one.

It is related to or is alternatively known as:

13.7.6.4 Partial Loss

A partial loss refers to damage to an insured property that is not total, meaning that it does not prevent the property from performing its function nor does the damage exceed the coverage limit of the insurance policy. Partial loss is damage to or loss of a ship or its cargo affecting only the shipowner or one cargo owner.

13.7.6.5 Particular Average Warranties

In the contract the insured provides a particular average warranty. These are contained in s. 76(1) of MIA 1906.

13.7.6.6 Particular Charges

Particular charges are expenses incurred by or on behalf of an insured for the purpose of preserving the subject-matter insured from a peril insured against, but do not include a general average loss or salvage charges. Particular charges or particular losses are charges other than general average charges or losses.

They are covered in s. 64(2) of MIA 1906

> (2) Expenses incurred by or on behalf of the assured for the safety or preservation of the subject-matter insured, other than general average and salvage charges, are called particular charges. Particular charges are not included in particular average.

A particular charge 's an expense incurred by the assured, his agents or assigns to prevent or minimise a loss of the subject matter insured from an insured peril.

13.7.7 Subject to General Average

13.7.7.1 General Average

General average loss on the other hand refers to a loss that directly affects two or more interest in a common marine adventure unlike particular average loss which affects a particular interest only. This loss involves an extraordinary sacrifice reasonably made during a peril for the sole purpose of preserving other properties in a common marine adventure. This sacrifice could include throwing of some cargo over board (jettison), using cargo as fuel, cutting away of spare or sails etc. The act must however be extraordinary, beyond the normal routine work of the ship crew and master and the peril or danger that warrants such a sacrifice must also be more than the ordinary perils of the sea. The sacrifice in itself should be aimed at preserving the whole marine adventure and should be made for the common safety of all other interests. The sacrifice could also be in the form of an extraordinary expenditure (general average expenditure) which includes money expended for the general safety of ship, cargo and crew with certain expenditures like charges for repairs, expenses incurred in lightening and reloading a vessel etc. A general average loss would require contributions from all the other interest (cargo owners) involved in the marine adventure to make good the sacrifices or expenses. This is known as general average contribution.

13.7.7.2 General Average Act

There is a general average act when, and only when, any extraordinary sacrifice or expenditure is intentionally and reasonably made or incurred for the common safety, for the purpose of preserving from the peril, the property involved in a common maritime adventure. General Average is a principle of maritime law where in the event of emergency, if cargo is jettisoned or expenses incurred, the loss is shared proportionately by all parties with a financial interest in the voyage.

13.7.7.3 General Average Clause

As noted earlier general average is a principle of maritime law where in the event of emergency, if cargo is jettisoned or expenses incurred, the loss is shared proportionately by all parties with a financial interest in the voyage The cargo policy covers the insured for a general average. This is effected through a General Average Clause (see Sect. 13.7.8 below). A clause in ocean marine insurance that requires ship and freight interests other than the insured to respond to losses suffered by the insured interest when those losses result from voluntary, necessary, and successful sacrifice of the insureds? freight because of shipping peril. General average is a global maritime industry loss mitigation convention whereby ship owners and cargo interests proportionately contribute to fully reimburse those in the venture who sustained loss or damage in preventing the total loss of a vessel, crew and its cargo (see Sect. 13.7.8 below).

13.7.7.4 General Average Contribution

An insured may be required to make a general average contribution. General average contribution is defined to be a contribution by all the parties in a sea adventure to make good the loss sustained by one of their number on account of sacrifices voluntarily made of part of the ship or cargo to save the residue and the lives of those on board from an impending peril, or for. General average is a global maritime industry loss mitigation convention whereby ship owners and cargo interests proportionately contribute to fully reimburse those in the venture who sustained loss or damage in preventing the total loss of a vessel, crew and its cargo.

13.7.7.5 General Average Expenditure

The term General Average Expenditure denotes an extraordinary expenditure incurred by the ship owner intentionally and reasonably to preserve from peril the property involved in a common maritime adventure. A principle of maritime law where in the event of emergency, if cargo is jettisoned or expenses incurred, the loss is shared proportionately by all parties with a financial interest in the voyage. General average is a global maritime industry loss mitigation convention whereby ship owners and cargo interests proportionately contribute to fully reimburse those in the venture who sustained loss or damage in preventing the total loss of a vessel, crew and its cargo.

13.7.7.6 General Average Loss

General average is a global maritime industry loss mitigation convention whereby ship owners and cargo interests proportionately contribute to fully reimburse those in the venture who sustained loss or damage in preventing the total loss of a vessel, crew and its cargo. A principle of maritime law where in the event of emergency, if cargo is jettisoned or expenses incurred, the loss is shared proportionately by all parties with a financial interest in the voyage.

13.7.7.7 General Average Sacrifice

The law of general average is a principle of maritime law whereby all stakeholders in a sea venture proportionally share any losses resulting from a voluntary sacrifice of part of the ship or cargo to save the whole in an emergency. A principle of maritime law where in the event of emergency, if cargo is jettisoned or expenses incurred, the loss is shared proportionately by all parties with a financial interest in the voyage. General average is a global maritime industry loss mitigation convention whereby ship owners and cargo interests proportionately contribute to fully reimburse those in the venture who sustained loss or damage in preventing the total loss of a vessel, crew and its cargo. General average is now covered in s.66 of the MIA1906, thus:

> **66 General average loss**
>
> (1) A general average loss is a loss caused by or directly consequential on a general average act. It includes a general average expenditure as well as a general average sacrifice.
>
> (2) There is a general average act where any extraordinary sacrifice or expenditure is voluntarily and reasonably made or incurred in time of peril for the purpose of preserving the property imperilled in the common adventure.
>
> (3) Where there is a general average loss, the party on whom it falls is entitled, subject to the conditions imposed by maritime law, to a rateable contribution from the other parties interested, and such contribution is called a general average contribution.
>
> (4) Subject to any express provision in the policy, where the assured has incurred a general average expenditure, he may recover from the insurer in respect of the proportion of the loss which falls upon him; and, in the case of a general average sacrifice, he may recover from the insurer in respect of the whole loss without having enforced his right of contribution from the other parties liable to contribute.

(5) Subject to any express provision in the policy, where the assured has paid, or is liable to pay, a general average contribution in respect of the subject insured, he may recover therefor from the insurer.

(6) In the absence of express stipulation, the insurer is not liable for any general average loss or contribution where the loss was not incurred for the purpose of avoiding, or in connexion with the avoidance of, a peril insured against.

(7) Where ship, freight, and cargo, or any two of those interests, are owned by the same assured, the liability of the insurer in respect of general average losses or contributions is to be determined as if those subjects were owned by different persons.

13.7.8 General Average Clause

Incoterms insurance policies are subject to general average during the process of claims and recovery. The law of general average is a legal principle of maritime law according to which all parties in a sea venture proportionally share any losses resulting from a voluntary sacrifice of part of the ship or cargo to save the whole in an emergency. It is a legal principle of maritime law according to which all parties in a sea venture proportionally share any losses resulting from a voluntary sacrifice of part of the ship or cargo to save the whole in an emergency. It arises from the principle that in the exigencies of hazards faced at sea, crew members often have precious little time in which to determine precisely whose cargo they are jettisoning. Thus, to avoid quarrelling that could waste valuable time, there arose the equitable practice whereby all the merchants whose cargo landed safely would be called on to contribute a portion, based upon a share or percentage, to the merchant or merchants whose goods had been tossed overboard to avert imminent peril.

General Average is normally included in the policy through the General Average Clause. The general average clause in ocean marine insurance obligates the insurers of various interests to share the cost of losses incurred voluntarily to save the voyage from complete destruction. A General Average Clause is normally couched in cargo clauses as follows:

> This insurance covers general average and salvage charges, adjusted or determined according to the contract of affreightment and/or the governing law and practice, incurred to avoid or in connection with the avoidance of loss from any cause except those excluded in Clauses 4, 5, 6 and 7 or elsewhere in this insurance.

13.7.9 Conditions for General Average Applications

In order for General Average to be properly declared:

(a) there must be an event which is beyond the shipowner's control, which imperils the entire adventure;
(b) there must be a voluntary sacrifice; and
(c) there must be something saved.

The voluntary sacrifice might be the jettison of certain cargo, the use of tugs, or salvors, or damage to the ship, be it, voluntary grounding, knowingly working the engines that will result in damages. "General Average" requires all parties concerned in the maritime venture (Hull/Cargo/Freight/Bunkers) to contribute to make good the voluntary sacrifice. They share the expense in proportion to the "value at risk" in the adventure. "Particular Average" is the term applied to partial loss be it hull or cargo.

13.7.10 York Antwerp Rules

The international rules governing general average are the York Antwerp Rules as emended since 1929. They are a set of maritime rules that were established in 1890 and have been amended several times since their inception, this set of maritime rules outlines the rights and obligations of both ship and cargo owners in the case that cargo must be jettisoned in order to save a ship. The law specifies that all parties involved in a sea venture must proportionately share in any losses that result from sacrifices made to the cargo to save the remainder. They are covered by the general average clause and principles covering general average contributions. A cargo owner who has made a general average sacrifice loss is entitled to general average contribution from the other participants. Both general average sacrifice and contributions risks are covered by the MIA1906 and the Institute Cargo Clauses.

13.7.11 Forwarding Charges

Forwarding charges is the outlining of the costs of the physical movement of goods between countries (transnational logistics) and, in many cases, the costs of the legal processes of such a movement (customs duties) by clearing and forwarding agents who render such services to exporters and importers. In the Institute Clauses, they are normally included by a Forwarding Charges Clause reading as follows:

> **12. - Forwarding Charges Clause**
> 12 Where, as a result of the operation of a risk covered by this insurance, the insured transit is terminated at a port or place other than that to which the subject-matter is covered under this insurance, the Underwriters will reimburse the Assured for any extra charges properly and reasonably incurred in unloading storing and forwarding the subject-matter to the destination to which it is insured

hereunder. This Clause 12, which does not apply to general average or salvage charges, shall be subject to the exclusions contained in Clauses 4, 5, 6 and 7 above, and shall not include charges arising from the fault negligence insolvency or financial default of the Assured or their servants.

13.7.12 Increased Value Charges

Increased Value Insurance or Hull Interest Insurance, is a property insurance which insures the full value, or mortgage value, of a vessel and/or the additional costs of replacing a vessel it is a total loss. An Increased Value Clause in Clause 14 of the Institute Cargo Clauses normally reads as follows:

14. - Increased Value Clause
14.1 If any Increased Value insurance is affected by the Assured on the cargo insured herein the agreed value of the cargo shall be deemed to be increased to the total amount insured under this insurance and all Increased Value insurances covering the loss, and liability under this insurance shall be in such proportion as the sum insured herein bears to such total amount insured. In the event of claim the Assured shall provide the Underwriters with evidence of the amounts insured under all other insurances.

14.2 Where this insurance is on Increased Value the following clause shall apply: The agreed value of the cargo shall be deemed to be equal to the total amount insured under the primary insurance and all Increased Value insurances covering the loss and effected on the cargo by the Assured, and liability under this insurance shall be in such proportion as the sum insured herein bears to such total amount insured. In the event of claim the Assured shall provide the Underwriters with evidence of the amounts insured under all other insurance

13.7.13 Sue and Labour Charges

The sue and labour clause requires the ship owner to make every attempt to reduce or save the exposed interests from loss. Under the terms of the clause, the insurer pays for any necessary costs incurred in carrying out the requirements of the sue and labour clause. These are known as sue and labour losses or expenses. Thus, if a ship is stranded, under the sue and labour clause the hull owner would be required to hire salvors to attempt to save//. Sue and Labour Clause Definition: A standard clause in a maritime insurance policy which allows the insured to recover from the insurer any reasonable expenses incurred by the insured in order to minimize or avert a loss to the insured property, for which loss the insurer would have been liable under the policy.

13.7.14 Other Charges

These would be charges incidental to and related loss and damage. They include, but are not necessarily limited to the cost of unloading and forwarding charges in the event of stranding or delay or lawful change of voyage.

13.8 Hurdles to Successful Claims

13.8.1 Requirement for Insurable Interest

For a successful claim the FOB and CIF merchant must have interest at loss but not necessarily at inception[6]

Institute Marine Cargo Clauses A reinforces the insurable interest requirement thus:

> **11. - Insurable Interest Clause**
> 11.1 In order to recover under this insurance the Assured must have an insurable interest in the subject-matter insured at the time of the loss.
>
> 11.2 Subject to 11.1 above, the Assured shall be entitled to recover for insured loss occurring during the period covered by this insurance, notwithstanding that the loss occurred before the contract of insurance was concluded, unless the Assured were aware of the loss and the Underwriters were not.

As noted in Chaps. 1 and 2 above, Insurable interest is a type of investment that protects anything subject to a financial loss. A person or entity has an insurable interest in an item, event or action when the damage or loss of the object would cause a financial loss or other hardships.

13.8.2 Loss Subject to Indemnity

An indemnity is a primary obligation; it does not depend on having to prove a breach of a contractual obligation. This offers a number of advantages over bringing a damages' claim for a breach of contract: An indemnity will typically be triggered by losses being incurred, without the need to prove any "fault".

[6] See *H. Cousins & Co v D & S Carriers* [1971] 2 WLR 85 CA.

13.8.3 Institute Clauses Guidelines

16 Measure of insurable value
Subject to any express provision or valuation in the policy, the insurable value of the subject-matter insured must be ascertained as follows:

(1) In insurance on ship, the insurable value is the value, at the commencement of the risk, of the ship, including her outfit, provisions and stores for the officers and crew, money advanced for seamen's wages, and other disbursements (if any) incurred to make the ship fit for the voyage or adventure contemplated by the policy, plus the charges of insurance upon the whole: The insurable value, in the case of a steamship, includes also the machinery, boilers, and coals and engine stores if owned by the assured, and, in the case of a ship engaged in a special trade, the ordinary fittings requisite for that trade:

(2) In insurance on freight, whether paid in advance or otherwise, the insurable value is the gross amount of the freight at the risk of the assured, plus the charges of insurance:

(3) In insurance on goods or merchandise, the insurable value is the prime cost of the property insured, plus the expenses of and incidental to shipping and the charges of insurance upon the whole:

(4) In insurance on any other subject-matter, the insurable value is the amount at the risk of the assured when the policy attaches, plus the charges of insurance]

The sum which the assured can recover in respect of a loss on a policy by which he is insured, in the case of an unvalued policy to the full extent of the insurable value, or, in the case of a valued policy to the full extent of the value fixed by the policy is called the measure of indemnity, covered in ss67–78 of MIA 1906 and repeated in cargo clauses.

13.8.4 Unassignable Rights. (s50)

Where the assured has parted with or lost his interest in the subject-matter insured and has not, before or at time of so doing, expressly or impliedly agreed to assign the policy, any subsequent assignment of the policy is inoperative

An assured who has no more insurable interests can assign. Section 17 of MIA 1906 states that:

Where the asserted assigns or otherwise parts with his interest in the subject-matter insured, he does not thereby transfer to the assignee his rights under the contracts of insurance

This is reinforced by s.51 of MIA 1906 provides that:

51 Assured who has no interest cannot assign
Where the assured has parted with or lost his interest in the subject-matter insured, and has not, before or at the time of so doing, expressly or impliedly agreed to assign the policy, any subsequent assignment of the policy is inoperative:

Provided that nothing in this section affects the assignment of a policy after loss.

As to when and how the policy is assignable s.50 of MIA 1906 provides that:

(1) A marine policy is assignable unless it contains terms expressly prohibiting assignment. It may be assigned either before or after loss.
(2) Where a marine policy has been assigned so as to pass the beneficial interest in such policy, the assignee of the policy is entitled to sue thereon in his own name; and the defendant is entitled to make any defence arising out of the contract which he would have been entitled to make if the action had been brought in the name of the person by or on behalf of whom the policy was effected.
(3) A marine policy may be assigned by indorsement thereon or in other customary manner.

Whereas in ordinary insurance contracts the assignment may be done contractually, in export policies, including FOB and CIF, they are achieved as a matter of export trade customs. In the latter the intention is at the outset to transfer the policy to the buyer once he has paid for the goods. In such contracts assignment is done by the simple process of tendering the export documents (including the policy) with or without endorsements[7]]

13.8.5 Insured's Duty to Act as Though Uninsured

Arranging insurance for their cargo doesn't mean that sellers should neglect their normal duty of care regarding its transportation. They should act to minimise the chance of a pay out by:

(a) ensuring goods are packed safely and securely—you'll only be insured against risk, not certain disaster, which poor packaging makes more likely;
(b) maintaining the upkeep of vehicles used for transportation;
(c) having a robust selection policy for drivers of these vehicles and for contractors involved in loading and storage; and
(d) making sure the buyer of the goods provides information on any loss or damage to goods within a short period of time.

[7] For the manner in which courts have interpreted policies generally and FOB and CIF policies in particular **see Chap. 4 above.**

13.8.6 Insurer's Rights on Payment

13.8.6.1 Subrogation

As indicated above all cargo insurances FOB, CIF and other Incoterms insurance contracts are subject to subrogation[8] with minor changes such as windfall (surplus)[9]

> **78 Right of subrogation**
>
> (1) Where the insurer pays for a total loss, either of the whole, or in the case of goods of any apportionable part, of the subject-matter insured, he thereupon becomes entitled to take over the interest of the assured in whatever may remain of the subject-matter so paid for, and he is thereby subrogated to all the rights and remedies of the assured in and in respect of that subject-matter as from the time of the casualty causing the loss.
>
> (2) Subject to the foregoing provisions, where the insurer pays for a partial loss, he acquires no title to the subject-matter insured, or such part of it as may remain, but he is thereupon subrogated to all rights and remedies of the assured in and in respect of the subject-matter insured as from the time of the casualty causing the loss, in so far as the assured has been indemnified, according to this Act, by such payment for the loss.

Subrogation is a term describing a right held by most insurance carriers to legally pursue a third party that caused an insurance loss to the insured. This is done in order to recover the amount of the claim paid by the insurance carrier to the insured for the loss.

13.8.6.2 Under Insurance

As in over or double insurance, an exporter can under insure but will not recover more than the insured value. Underinsurance refers to an insufficient insurance policy. Although a good insurance policy won't prevent any of life's calamities, it should make the financial consequences easier to bear. Underinsurance, however, can leave the enrollee liable for a large financial expense if a serious event occurs. He is supposed to be self-insured or co-insured for the uninsured portion.

> **81 Effect of under insurance**
>
> Where the assured is insured for an amount less than the insurable value or, in the case of a valued policy, for an amount less than the policy valuation, he is deemed to be his own insurer in respect of the uninsured balance.

When a contract party or anyone else self-insures, they basically set aside extra funds to pay for any accidents or bills yourself. That would mean they do not have

---

[8] See *The Yasin* [1979] 2 Lloyds Report 45 Lloyd J; see also John Birds Contractual Subrogation in Insurance [1979] JBL 124 and the Clause in [1975] JBL 114.

[9] See *Lucas v ECGD* [1974] 2 All ER 885 HL.

insurance to cover emergency needs. Instead, they can plan to pay for everything out of their own pockets. Putting it simply, this means that if, in the case of house insurance, their home burns down, they will have to pay out of their own pockets to rebuild it. The same principle applies to cargo and all property insurance.

13.8.6.3 Double Insurance

As in over insurance below, an export holder can insure but will not get more double or more than the insured value. Double insurance occurs when a business has insurance cover in respect of the same risk and subject matter from more than one insurer. Double insurance is not of itself a problem, but it can lead to insurers arguing about whether they need to pay out at all causing unwanted delay in the processing of claims.

> **32 Double insurance**
>
> (1) Where two or more policies are effected by or on behalf of the assured on the same adventure and interest or any part thereof, and the sums insured exceed the indemnity allowed by this Act, the assured is said to be over-insured by double insurance.
>
> (2) Where the assured is over-insured by double insurance
>
> (a) The assured, unless the policy otherwise provides, may claim payment from the insurers in such order as he may think fit, provided that he is not entitled to receive any sum in excess of the indemnity allowed by this Act;
>
> (b) Where the policy under which the assured claims is a valued policy, the assured must give credit as against the valuation for any sum received by him under any other policy without regard to the actual value of the subject-matter insured;
>
> (c) Where the policy under which the assured claims is an unvalued policy, he must give credit, as against the full insurable value, for any sum received by him under any other policy:
>
> (d) Where the assured receives any sum in excess of the indemnity allowed by this Act, he is deemed to hold such sum in trust for the insurers, according to their right of contribution among themselves.

13.8.6.4 Over Insurance

Like all insurance policies, an export policy holder can over insure or double insure a particular risk but will not get more than the indemnity except in certain exceptional circumstances. Over insurance can be defined as the situation where an insured has bought so much coverage that it exceeds the actual cash value (or the replacement cost) of the risk or property insured. The over insurance especially by double insurance and their consequences are covered by s.80 of the MIA 1906 thus:

> **80. Right of contribution**
> (1) Where the assured is over-insured by double insurance, each insurer is bound, as between himself and the other insurers, to contribute rateably to the loss in proportion to the amount for which he is liable under his contract.
>
> (2) If any insurer pays more than his proportion of the loss, he is entitled to maintain an action for contribution against the other insurers, and is entitled to the like remedies as a surety who has paid more than his proportion of the debt.

13.8.6.5 Contribution

Unwanted consequences of over insurance and double insurance is avoided by the doctrine of contribution under s80(2) of the MIA 1906. The insurer's rights to contribution by virtue of indemnity and subrogation arises from the doctrine of over or double insurance under s.80(2) above. The principle holding those two or more insurers each liable for a covered loss should participate in the payment of that loss. Having paid its share of a loss, an insurer may be entitled to equitable contribution—a legal right to recover part of the payment from another insurer whose policy was also applicable. Many insurance policies stipulate the formula under which contribution among multiple insurers will take place. Two standard methods are Contribution by limits and Contribution by equal shares.

13.8.7 Subject to Excess and Deductibles

13.8.7.1 Excess

Incoterms contract insurance policies are subject to excess. Some export policies include either an excess or franchise clause.[10] Insurance excess is a pre-agreed amount of money that the insured needs to pay to his insurance provider in the event of a claim, such as a car accident or a flood at home. In many cases, the insured will be asked to pay the excess immediately so that the claim process can begin. In that case the excess represents a predetermined amount that is deducted from a claim and is used to discourage irresponsible, malicious and small claims.[11] In other words, excess has the same meaning as a franchise (below), i.e., a percentage of the value of a loss, below which no payment is made but above which total compensa-

[10] See Top and Drop in, *Teal Assurance Co Ltd v WR Berkley* [2012] 1 All ER 969, Longmore LJ; *Denby v English and Scottish Marine Insurance* [1998] CLC870, Hobhouse LJ; for insured cargo financed by letters of credit, see para 11.6 above (tender UCP 600).

[11] See the Scottish case of *Teal Assurance Co Ltd v W.R. Berkley Insurance [Eur] Ltd* 2013 4 All ER 643, Lord Neuberger Pres. SC; *North African Insurance Co Ltd v Bishopsgate Insurance Co Ltd* [1998] 1 Lloyds Rep 459, Walker J.

tion is paid.[12] The principle applies to reinsurance as well.[13] It is also included in the UCP (see Chap. 11 above on tender)

13.8.7.2 Excess and Franchise Clauses

Some policies include either an excess or franchise clause.[14] The Excess clause sets out the amount that you must pay before the Insurer makes a payment. There are two main purposes behind the setting of the level of excess. To give you an interest in avoiding claims. To avoid paying small claims. It is not often the case that that excess represents a predetermined amount that is deducted from a claim and is used to discourage irresponsible, malicious and small claims.[15] An excess may or may not be applied. An excess amount payable is usually expressed as the first amount falling due, up to a ceiling, in the event of a loss. It may be expressed in either monetary or percentage terms. As indicate above, an excess is typically used to discourage moral hazard and to remove small claims, which are disproportionately expensive to handle.

13.8.8 Franchises

Incoterms contract policies are subject to franchises insurance. A minimum amount of loss that must be incurred before insurance coverage applies. Franchise means a percentage of the value of a loss, below which no payment is made but above which total compensation is paid.[16] The principle applies to reinsurance as well.[17] A franchise deductible differs from an ordinary deductible in that, once it is met, the entire amount of the loss is paid, subject to the policy limit. Franchise deductibles can be stated either as a £ sterling amount or as a percentage of the policy limit. A minimum amount of loss that must be incurred before insurance coverage applies. Franchises are either a franchise deductible or ordinary deductibles. A franchise deductible differs from an ordinary deductible in that, once it is met, the entire

[12] For a slightly earlier case see *Equitas Ltd v R & D Reinsurance* [2010] 2 All ER 855; *Professional Indemnity and Standard Life Assurance v Oak Dedicated Ltd* [2008] 2 All ER 916, *Tomlinson J; Brown (Re) v Gjo Insurance Ltd* [1995] Lloyds IR201, Walker J.

[13] *English and American Insurance Co Ltd v AXA Re SA* [2007] 1 CLC 1 Gloster J; *Chester and Orion Insurance Co v General Fire Casualty Co* [1975] 1 Lloyds Rep 677 US Supp. Ct.

[14] See Top and Drop in, *Teal Assurance Co Ltd v WR Berkley* [2012] 1 All ER 969, Longmore LJ; *Denby v Englsih and Scottish Marine Insurance* [1998] CLC870, Hobhouse LJ.

[15] See the Scottish case of *Teal Assurance Co Ltd v W.R. Berkley Insurance [Eur] Ltd* 2013 4 All ER 643, Lord Neuberger Pres. SC; *North African Insurance Co Ltd v Bishopsgate Insurance Co Ltd* [1998] 1 Lloyds Rep 459, Walker J.

[16] For a slightly earlier case see *Equitas Ltd v R & D Reinsurance* [2010] 2 All ER 855; *Professional Indemnity and Standard Life Assurance v Oak Dedicated Ltd* [2008] 2 All ER 916, *Tomlinson J; Brown (Re) v Gjo Insurance Ltd* [1995] Lloyds IR201, Walker J.

[17] *English and American Insurance Co Ltd v AXA Re SA* [2007] 1 CLC 1 Gloster J; *Chester and Orion Insurance Co v General Fire Casualty Co* [1975] 1 Lloyds Rep 677 US Supp. Ct.

amount of the loss is paid, subject to the policy limit. It is also included in UCP (see Chap. 11 on tender)

13.8.9 Deductibles

13.8.9.1 General

Incoterms insurance contracts policies are subject to deductibles. In the insurance policy, the deductible is an amount the insurer will deduct from the loss before paying up to its policy limits: the amount that the insured agrees to pay out of own pocket before the insurer opens a pop-up and steps in and pay the remaining balance of a claim. Most property insurance policies contain a per-occurrence deductible provision that stipulates that the deductible amount specified in the policy declarations will be subtracted from each covered loss in determining the amount of the insured's loss recovery. Usually, the amount of the deductible is not subtracted from policy limits.

13.8.10 Excluded Risks in Claims

13.8.10.1 Statutory General Exclusions

An insurance contract and claims therein are subject to exclusions. An exclusion is a policy provision that eliminates coverage for some type of risk. Exclusions narrow the scope of coverage provided by the insuring agreement. Insurers utilize exclusions to carve away coverage for risks they are unwilling to insure. Cargo and general marine insurance excluded losses are governing by MIA 1906. Section 55 specifically states that there are particular exclusions for which the insurer is not liable. Clause (b) provides that, "Unless the policy otherwise provides, the insurer on ship or goods is not liable for any loss proximately caused by delay, although the delay be caused by a peril insured against." Detailed excluded losses and in s 55 of MIA 1916 are as follows:

> **55 Included and excluded losses**
> (1) Subject to the provisions of this Act, and unless the policy otherwise provides, the insurer is liable for any loss proximately caused by a peril insured against, but, subject as aforesaid, he is not liable for any loss which is not proximately caused by a peril insured against.
>
> (2) In particular—
>
> (a) The insurer is not liable for any loss attributable to the wilful misconduct of the assured, but, unless the policy otherwise provides, he is liable for any loss proximately caused by a peril insured against, even though the loss would not have happened but for the misconduct or negligence of the master or crew;

(b) Unless the policy otherwise provides, the insurer on ship or goods is not liable for any loss proximately caused by delay, although the delay be caused by a peril insured against;

(c) Unless the policy otherwise provides, the insurer is not liable for ordinary wear and tear, ordinary leakage and breakage, inherent vice or nature of the subject-matter insured, or for any loss proximately caused by rats or vermin, or for any injury to machinery not proximately caused by maritime perils.

An exclusion is a policy provision that eliminates coverage for some type of risk. Exclusions narrow the scope of coverage provided by the insuring agreement. In many insurance policies, the insuring agreement is very broad. Insurers utilize exclusions to carve away coverage for risks they are unwilling to insure. These are all reproduced in Cargo Clauses.

13.8.10.2 Institute General Exclusion Clause

4. - General Exclusion Clause

4 In no case shall this insurance cover

4.1 loss damage or expense attributable to wilful misconduct of the Assured

4.2 ordinary leakage, ordinary loss in weight or volume, or ordinary wear and tear of the subject-matter insured

4.3 loss damage or expense caused by insufficiency or unsuitability of packing or preparation of the subject-matter insured (for the purpose of this Clause 4.3 "packing" shall be deemed to include stowage in a container or liftvan but only when such stowage is carried out prior to attachment of this insurance or by the Assured or their servants)

4.4 loss damage or expense caused by inherent vice or nature of the subject-matter insured

4.5 loss damage or expense proximately caused by delay, even though the delay be caused by a risk insured against (except expenses payable under Clause 2 above)

4.6 loss damage or expense arising from insolvency or financial default of the owner's managers charterers or operators of the vessel

4.7 loss damage or expense arising from the use of any weapon of war employing atomic or nuclear fission and/or fusion or other like reaction or radioactive force or matter.

13.8.10.3 Institute Unseaworthiness and Unfitness Exclusion Clause

5. - Unseaworthiness and Unfitness Exclusion Clause

5.1 In no case shall this insurance cover loss damage or expense arising from unseaworthiness of vessel or craft, unfitness of vessel craft conveyance container or liftvan for the safe carriage of the subject-matter insured, where the Assured or their servants are privy to such unseaworthiness or unfitness, at the time the subject-matter insured is loaded therein.

5.2 The Underwriters waive any breach of the implied warranties of seaworthiness of the ship and fitness of the ship to carry the subject-matter insured to destination, unless the Assured or their servants are privy to such unseaworthiness or unfitness.

13.8.10.4 Institute War Exclusion Clause

6. - War Exclusion Clause

6 In no case shall this insurance cover loss damage or expense caused by

6.1 war civil war revolution rebellion insurrection, or civil strife arising therefrom, or any hostile act by or against a belligerent power

6.2 capture seizure arrest restraint or detainment (piracy excepted), and the consequences thereof or any attempt thereat

6.3 derelict mines torpedoes bombs or other derelict weapons of war.

13.8.10.5 Institute Strikes Exclusion Clause

7. - Strikes Exclusion Clause

7 In no case shall this insurance cover loss damage or expense

7.1 caused by strikers, locked-out workmen, or persons taking part in labour disturbances, riots or civil commotions

7.2 resulting from strikes, lock-outs, labour disturbances, riots or civil commotions

7.3 caused by any terrorist or any person acting from a political motive.

13.9 Recoveries and Policy Adjustments

13.9.1 Role of Adjusters

Adjusters inspect property damage or personal injury claims to determine how much the insurance company should pay for the loss. They might inspect a home, a business, or an automobile. Adjusters interview the claimant and witnesses, inspect the property, and do additional research, such as look at police reports There are three types of insurance claims adjusters: company adjusters, independent adjusters, and public adjusters. Adjuster who works for insurance companies as full-time employees.

A claims adjuster investigates insurance claims to determine the extent of insuring a company's liability. Claims adjusters may handle property claims involving damage to structures, and/or liability claims involving personal injuries or third-person property damage.

13.9.2 Determination of Damage

How do adjusters determine damage? For car insurance claims, for instance, the adjuster will go over the car with a fine tooth comb. They'll also take a lot of pictures from several angles. When damage is identified they'll look closely to see if it was likely caused in this particular accident or if it was pre-existing. The practice is not different in other property insurance claims. This practice may be different in marine insurance generally and cargo insurance in particular.

Before a claim is settled, in the latter, it will be subject to a rigorous check by a policy claims adjuster. This is a complicated practical process involving lots of calculations, details of which are beyond the scope of this book. Relevant facts and adjuster's notes sufficient detail needs to be shown so that all the relevant facts are at the underwriter's disposal. What is stated will obviously depend on the circumstances of the loss, but the summary is likely to include some or all of the following, as relevant:

(a) Specific details of the carriage throughout the insured transit (e.g. by road from the shipper's premises at named place, by vessel from named port to named port, by barge to named final inland destination, etc);
(b) Relevant dates in connection with the transit (e.g., when voyage commenced, when vessel sailed, etc);
(c) Any other relevant dates in connection with the loss;
(d) When and where the loss happened;
(e) The circumstances in which the loss happened;
(f) The extent of the loss;
(g) What steps were taken to deal with and/or minimise the loss;
(h) Whether the carriers or any other third parties have been held liable;
(i) Why the adjuster considers the claim to be covered by the policy; and
(j) Any other details or issues the adjuster considers relevant to the claim.[18]

[18] Lloyds Agencies: *Cago Claims and Recoveries, Module 3 p. 76.*

13.10 Amicable Settlement of Claims

13.10.1 Settlements of Accepted Claims

The four major types of claims settlements are:

(a) Payment of money;
(b) Replacement of the item covered.
(c) Reinstatement: and
(d) Paying for repairs.

However, Insurance companies are businesses. Settling a claim often means paying out more than they want to. Their goal is paying as little as possible and limiting their liability in the event of an accident. For this reason, insurers may refuse to settle because they want to try to lessen how much they pay, if anything.

Once an insurance company has admitted liability and agreed to process the claim, they tend to move quickly. Some claimants receive their compensation in a few days. More commonly, the claimant will receive their compensation payment within 2 and 4 weeks. If an insurer settles a claim, it pays money to a policyholder for the occurrence of a loss or risk against which they were insured. Insurance companies use the premiums they receive not only to settle claims but also to generate additional income and profit by investing their funds in financial securities. Settlement does not mean that the claimed amount is credited in the account. But yes! It surely means that amount will be deposited in the next coming step. Settle only means that PF officer has approved and dispatched your claim.

In my case claim status was shown settled on in that state, insurance companies are required to accept or deny the claim within 40 days after receiving proof of the claim. If the claim is accepted, payment must be made within 30 days from the date settlement was reached. When it comes down to whether or not a motor insurance company can settle a claim without your consent, the short answer in most cases is yes. In most states, insurance companies are provided with the right to be able to settle claims as they see fit. claims adjuster is a representative of the insurance company. Depending on the nature of the claim, the insured claimant may receive a check directly, or the insurance company may pay vendors on your behalf. The total amount you receive will be based on the amount of coverage in your policy and the specific details of your claim. The insurance company will reimburse the insured for those costs.

13.11 Settlement of Disputed Claims

13.11.1 Settlement Through Loss Adjusters and Brokers

When there is a dispute, a claim can be pursued through a loss adjustor. An adjuster coordinates an appraisal, gathers the facts and reports the details of a claim to the insurer. The adjuster recommends whether a claim is covered under the policy. A claim could also be pursued an insurance broker or agent. They also negotiate with the policyholder on behalf of the insurance company. Throughout the claims process, the insurance broker can handle everything for the client. But too often the insured finds that their broker, while an expert on the coverages, is not as skilled in the area of claims. In fact, some brokers never even become involved in any way in the claims process. However, because of the nature of international trade, largest reputable insurers would have overseas offices or agents who handle claims so as not to inconvenient policy holders.

13.11.2 Settlement Through the Financial Conduct Authority

An unpaid or dissatisfied insured claimant can pursue claims with the Financial Ombudsman Services (FOS)[19] through the Financial Conduct Authority (FCA). The Financial Ombudsman Service is an ombudsman in the United Kingdom. It was established in 2000, and given statutory powers in 2001 by the Financial Services and Markets Act 2000, to help settle. The FCA is a financial regulatory body in the United Kingdom, but operates independently of the UK Government, and is financed by charging fees to members of the financial services industry. These are contained in Chapter 8 of Chapter 8 Claims handling—FCA Handbook[20] according to which an insurer must:

(1) handle claims promptly and fairly;
(2) provide reasonable guidance to help a policyholder make a claim and appropriate information on its progress;
(3) not unreasonably reject a claim (including by terminating or avoiding a policy); and
(4) settle claims promptly once settlement terms are agreed

Deals with cases where:

(a) where rejection of consumer's claim is unreasonable: contracts before 1 August 2017-for matters before the Insurance Act 2015; and
(b) where rejection of consumer's claim is unreasonable: contracts on or after 1 August 2017-for matters after the coming into force of the Insurance Act 2015.

13.11.3 Settlement Through Litigation

Litigation or court process is the act of last resort in insurance claims. It is bad for both parties. It is expensive and delays the claimants' schedules from normal business. For the insurance company, it gives a bad reputation. Claims handling service

[19] ***https://www.financial-ombudsman.org.uk/consumers/complaints-can-help/insurance***.

[20] ***https://www.handbook.fca.org.uk/handbook/ICOBS/8.pdf***.

is the basis on which an insurance company is ultimately judged by clients and the key issue affecting the reputation of the insurer. The payment of legitimate claims represents the delivery of the promise at the heart of the insurance contract. However, if all else fails the insured can sue his insurance company if they refuse to pay, violate or fail the terms of the insurance policy. Common violations include not paying claims in a timely fashion, not paying properly filed claims, or making bad faith claims.

Following the UK *Enterprise Act 2016* a new section 13A was inserted into the 2015 Insurance Act, which introduced a new implied term into all insurance and reinsurance contracts entered into on or after 4 May 2017.[21] Business and consumer insurance policyholders may now pursue their insurers in the courts if they do not settle claims within a reasonable amount of time. This will require insurers to pay claims within a 'reasonable time' unless they have reasonable grounds for disputing it. This is rear and both parties tend to avoid except in cases of suspected fraud, unique loses or complicated cases. (Otherwise, see Chap. 12 ante)

13.12 Further Food for Thoughts

13.12.1 Likely Questions

(a) What happens if and when the insurer declines payments of the claim?
(b) Or pays less than the loss;
(c) Please always read your policy;
(d) Acquaint yourself with the deductibles, excesses and exceptions to the policy;
(e) Follow instructions;
(f) Act quickly to avoid disappointments; and
(g) Problems caused by BREXIT.

13.12.2 Other Food for Thoughts

See under Food for Thoughts in other chapters.

13.13 Concluding Remarks

Claims processes are normally relatively easy and simple to follow. It can be done in person, if in doubt the insured should claim through an agent, a loss adjuster or their lawyers of freight forwarders. In the majority of cases the insurer will accept the claim and settle. Larger established insurers have overseas offices or agencies

[21] See generally, "Right to damages for 'unreasonably' late insurance claims settlement now in force", https://www.out-law.com/en/articles/2017/may/right-to-damages-for-unreasonably-late-insurance-claims-settlement-now-in-force/.

from where overseas claims can be processed and paid. In a few cases, they may refuse, for the reasons given above, at least in the first instance. They will however provide a full report detailing reasons for the decline including suggestions as to the way forward, such as requiring more documentary proofs. In the event of a deadlock, the dispute settlement clause in the policy will kick in; in most cases these will be arbitration, mediations and, as a last resort, litigations. Before that UK policyholders should avail themselves of services of the Financial Ombudsman Services (FOS) through the Financial Conduct Authority (FCA). Only when that remedy has been exhausted should they proceed.

Both parties are aware of the disadvantages of litigation to their business and reputations. It may at first appear large but the export-import business is a small world where everybody knows each other. An insurer with a poor claims and settlement reputation could lose business. Equally an insured with repetitive and frivolous claims could be blacklisted. Trading on open covers, blanket and open policies creates a cliental bond and trust which makes it easier to accept and process claims and settlements.

13.14 Further Readings

Major Publications

- Lloyds of London Insurance: Cargo Claims and Recoveries, Module 3, 2013, Lloyds of London Insurance
- Brown R.H. & Novitt, J.J: Marine Insurance, Vol. 2-Principles, 4th edn, 1985, Witherby & Co Ltd
- ----------------: Marine Insurance, Vol. 2-Cargo Practice, 4th edn, 1985, Witherby & Co Ltd
- Goodacre, Kenneth J: Collected Papers on Marine Claims Vol. 1, 1992, Witherby & Co Ltd
- --------------------------: Collected Papers on Marine Claims Vol. 2, 1992, Witherby & Co Ltd
- Richard Cornah & Julian Cooke: "Lowndes & Rudolf: The Law of General Average and the York-Antwerp Rules" (13th Edition), 2007.
- Rose, Francis D. (2005). General Average: Law & Practice, 2nd Edn.
- Tetley, William, QC: Marine Cargo Claims, 2nd edn, Butterworths, Toronto, 1978
- Lloyds Agency: Cargo Claims and Recoveries, 2020

14 Concluding Remarks

This book originally set out to examine the incidents of the FOB and CIF insurance under Anglo-American and Other Common Law jurisdictions. However, it transpired that obligation laid out in Incoterms with regard to the procuring of insurance FOB, CIF and CIP contracts were not very different from those at common law or indeed all universal international sales contracts. Furthermore, international sales and contracts law and practice being universal, there is not much difference between the common law and civil law jurisdictions. Hence the change of the title to its current.

Indeed, the provisions of the current Clauses A5/B5 of the FOB and CIF/CIP are derived from the common law principles covered in Chaps. 4 and 6 of this book. Thus, although no attempt was made to compare the obligations with those that exist under the common law FOB and CIF terms, it is self-evident that the basic outline of the duty remains the same as under the common law term. Furthermore, although they are common law-based insurance of exports/imports, just as the practice of international trade is now universal. Insurance has been, is and will always be a dominant factor in commerce generally and international commerce in particular.

Nevertheless, the fact that parties' contract on Incoterms CIF or CIP rather than FOB simplicities is significant, for it means that their rights and obligations must be determined by examining the current edition of Incoterms,[1] rather than dated common law cases. It should be noted that only a few cases concerning Incoterms have come before the English courts, and few involve a discussion of Incoterms itself, so it is hard to predict the court's approach to the matter. However, the clear manner in which Incoterms is presented, and a full understanding by both sellers and buyers of their Incoterms duties should ensure that the matter never reaches the unfortunate stage of having to be interpreted by a court of law.

[1] I.e. the edition current at the time they contracted. In the event that the edition is revised after the parties have contracted, but before performance of the contract, the former edition governs.

P. Ademuni-Odeke, *Insurance of International Sales' Contracts under Incoterms*, Law for Professionals, https://doi.org/10.1007/978-3-031-75136-3_14

As far as the obligation to procure insurance in Incoterms CIF and CIP contracts is concerned, it is clearly laid out in the Incoterms provision, and corresponds closely with the UCP 600 requirement pertaining to the tender of insurance documents (Chap. 11). Both the current Incoterms 2020 and the UCP 600 are recent editions to the ICC family of documents and their (combined) usage by businessmen is a clear indication of the progress that the international business community is making in regard to the formalisation and standardisation of the terms upon which they trade: a trend which reduces the likelihood of misunderstandings and subsequent disputes.

Parties are free to draw up own contracts, use a standard form such as Lloyds Form or Incoterms or sales contract guidelines or commodity trade contracts. In contracts to the FOB and related contracts not requiring sellers to insurer, seller's insurance obligations in the CIF/CIF contracts at first seems obvious. Whatever the source or form utilised, the CIF/CIP seller must insure the goods. That is also the positions under the English, American and other common law jurisdictions. This despite the fact that America is the only common law jurisdiction that has also codified its laws, the American UCC has largely preserved its CIF common law tradition as inherited from English common law. Neither has it deviated from Incoterms. Australian, Canadian, New Zealand and other common law jurisdictions follow English law such that authorities between them are fully applicable or quasi-applicable precedent.

The civil and other non-common law jurisdictions seem to follow common law arrangements. Indeed, insurance being the only discipline without an international convention, the UK MIA 1906 is the defacto global enactment on marine insurance generally and cargo insurance in particular. However, this book set out to, and has demonstrated, that in practice the parties' detailed insurance obligations, in either contract categories, are not as easy as provided. Sales contractual terms, common law guidance and Incoterms provisions on the FOB family and the CIF/CIP insurance obligations provide only the basic outline of the extent of Incoterms parties' insurance duties. For those reasons, parties need to pay particular attention to details in their specific additional needs including differences between theory and practice, the port and trade usages and of unique jurisdictional customs.

It is apparent that the duties of either party to insure the FOB and related exports, without sellers' obligations to insure, may not be as simple or as clear-cut as they first appear. This point was emphasised by Sassoon's observations cited at the beginning of Chap. 4 of this book. This book has demonstrated that the full extent of these duties will depend on the nature of the particular contract and the surrounding circumstances. For instance, a one-off contract, which costs considerably less, will not need more than the minimum insurance by the buyer. At the other extreme, a substantial contract that consists of several shipments, payments by letters of credit, bank finance, and export credit guarantees will involve wider risks and, therefore, careful consideration of coverage alternatives is necessary.

Other relevant factors in evaluating the risks and the respective insurance requirements are the availability or unavailability of adequate shipping and insurance facilities at both ends of the contract. This does not pose much of a problem if both parties are from industrialised countries where shipping and insurance facilities are adequately available. The situation may well be different where one party is from a developing nation and the other is from an industrialised country or planned-economy/state-trading nation. In that case, the parties should be aware of the commercial, economic and political environment that currently exists in both countries, including state interventions and other restrictive policies mentioned in Chaps. 8 and 10 above.

A reasonable export/import merchant must, therefore, keep abreast of these policies and obtain the best commercial intelligence available. Of course, whether one or both parties belong to a trade association (e.g., Grain or Sugar Traders) that imposes duties on its members to insure on standard terms or opt for Institute Cargo Clause is another determinant of the complexity of insurance issues. Still, the factors outlined above regarding the determination of the nature and extent of the parties' insurance obligations are neither exhaustive nor conclusive.

Additionally, there are always differences between academic authors and commentaries on the one hand and the more practical approach to this subject on the other. Accordingly, a prudent seller or buyer will have to consider all the possible factors involved both in pre- and post-shipment risks. When in doubt, such a merchant should consult his insurance agent or freight forwarder, but should also bear in mind that reliance on the use of agents alone may not always be prudent. Thus, the legal position provided under common law jurisdictions should be regarded as a general rule that is subject to exceptions. Equally, the book has demonstrated FOB insurance is a general proposition which is in turn subject to whether the FOB is "classic," "simple," and "extended" contract classifications. Furthermore, Incoterms provide sufficient insurance guidelines for those who choose to use it.

What insurance the buyer or seller obtains will depend not only on his immediate contract obligations but also on the nature of the wider risks he perceives, as well as his desire to protect himself, and his ability to do so. Accordingly, an occasional merchant has different needs from the regular and large enterprise. That notwithstanding, as was apparent in Chap. 7 of this book, apart from minor exceptions, there is not much difference between the law and practice on the subject in the Anglo-American and other common law jurisdictions with regard to FOB and Contracts. Equally, the Incoterms insurance provisions are not that much different from those applied in other common law jurisdictions. The flexibility of the FOB and related contracts and the consequent uncertainty involved makes it rather difficult for a merchant to determine when and how to insure.

This is in marked contrast to the CIF/CIP contracts where each party's duties, both at common law and under Incoterms, are clearly stated. Although initially different from the CIF/CIP in insurance and freight requirements, the modern FOB and related contracts are no longer significantly different in their insurance requirements. With the exception of a few areas, the FOB and related contracts' insurance obligations, taken in a wider and global context, are in practice almost the same as those of the CIF/CIP. Therefore, the traditional assumption that FOB-related insurance positions are simple and that the duty to insure is strictly the sellers' preserve should be regarded with some caution. Those positions and duties are based on shipment rather than each party's overall export-import insurance requirements.

The sum total of all these factors is, therefore, that the parties' CIF/CIP insurance obligations may not be as clear-cut and as easy as provided for in the sales contract, Incoterms, statutes and literature. Although information on the history and link between common law and Incoterms is scanty, the CIF is largely a creature of English commercial common law customs and mercantile usages. Its insurance and other characteristics also arose from common law environment. Following the need harmonise international trade law norms the said common law norms were later codified by Incoterms. This is because English common law did not only predate Incoterms by about 100 years, but also that English and other common law jurists and delegates to Incoterms drafting conferences probably heavily influenced its developments, drafting, direction and philosophy. Furthermore, English common law, both judicial and statutory, has provided the only authoritative judicial interpretation of insurance implications of CIF/CIP Incoterms and hereby filled the gaps left therein. Hence one of the theses of this book that the lacunae in the CIF/CIP contractual provisions and Incoterms has been filled by common law judicial decisions.

The UK and London's leading global position in insurance, trade, finance, law, arbitration and shipping has farther aided English common law dominance of the law and practice of the subject. The apparent near global adherence to MIA 1906, adaptation of Lloyds Marine Insurance Policy, London Institute Cargo Clauses and sometimes-even English law have all had global influence on CIF/CIP in particular and international business transactions generally. Hence, the reasonable assumption that Incoterms has, in turn, all but codified common law on the subject, especially in relation to CIF and CIP insurance. Thus, based on Incoterms' wide global application and common law dominance thereof, civil law and other non-common law jurisdictions seem to follow English common law and practice.

English common law CIF practice has in turn been influenced and complemented by commodity trade standard terms, Institute Cargo Clauses, the UCP and Incoterms. For the above reasons and addition to the sales contract, common law guidelines and Incoterms provisions, practice in this area of the law is so complex that prudent parties are advised to protect themselves by, for instance, taking out contingency or other type of additional insurances to cover unforeseen and unusual risks. The CIF/CIP policy is normally in the buyer's name and for the buyer's benefit. Hence, the need for separate CIF 'sellers' interest' policy following transfer of the policy to the buyer, agents and subsequent buyers.

From the buyer's viewpoint, the contractual policy covers only the minimum risks. Hence the need for separate additional CIF/CIP 'buyers' interest' insurances. In both cases, and depending on the nature and level of risks involved, this might include buyers availing themselves of state insurance facilities, where necessary and applicable. One such avenue is from state insurance such as the UK ECGD (now UKEF) policies. Other major trading nations and jurisdictions have equivalent export credit guarantee agencies as well as cargo clauses. Using this facility might result in the CIF/CIP parties being over-insured or double-insured. However, when it comes to CIF/CIP and the general export trade insurance, wisdom dictates that it is better to be over insured or double insured than under-insured.

Apart from the near resemblance between 'Extended FOB' and CIF/CIP insurance, there seems to be a narrowing of the differences in insurance matters between the common law and Incoterms on the one hand and CIF/CIP and FOB and related contracts on the other regarding sellers' notice to the buyer. Both parties now have to provide notice to the other: the seller as a matter of contractual obligations; the buyer as a matter of practical necessity; and both to cover possible individual breaches of a contractual obligation. Further narrowing is also evident in the use of letters of credit as the preferred payments' system and selling and buying afloat. As a recommendation, it would be preferable to standardise law and practice in insurance of international business transactions between the common law, Incoterms, UCP, the CISG and the relevant transport conventions.

Incoterms insurance clauses is only part of the wider insurance considerations in international sales. They may be specialized templates but are exposed to the same risks and, therefore, subject to the same export-import insurance regime. These are treated in details elsewhere.[2] That notwithstanding Incoterms and its insurance clauses have influenced other aspects of international commercial law. Accordingly, even the Commodity Trade [e.g., Clove GAFTA-FOB/GAFTA-CIF] and FOSFA contracts (to mention but a few) simply provide that the Incoterms or Commodity Trade Insurance Clause, themselves based on Cargo Clauses, shall apply. Together with Cargo Clauses they now form the basis of the commodity trade terms and insurance provisions. Equally, CIF and CIP insurance clauses together with the cargo clauses have also become the standard bearers of insurance clauses in international trade law and practice.

However, despite their apparent merits, Incoterms similarly do not deal with many issues of both the underlying sales contract, external factors affecting insurance obligations and the parties' comprehensive insurance needs. Yet, these factors have direct bearings on the parties' contractual liabilities and insurance obligations since they can arise from contravention of any of the 10 Incoterm Clauses. Incoterms may be specialist contracts but parties thereto are not immune from the interface between insurance and wider aspects of international trade as demonstrated herein. These may be common knowledge to seasoned merchants but could also have lethal consequences to novices' assumption of their inclusiveness.

For those reasons, it has made efforts to harmonise with related fields. These have included the widening of the insurance market to include contributions of the LMA and IUA, IUMI and the broadening of the scope of insurance documents for tender under UCP 600 for letters of credit. Hence, besides keeping abreast other international trade practices, Incoterms has also kept up-to-date with financial requirements. In particular it has involved harmonizing with the UCP 600 to and passage from references to "insurance policy" to "insurance documents". In so doing it has allowed the tender of alternative documents such as the certificate of

[2] See, Ademuni-Odeke: "Insurance of CIF Contracts I" pp. 31–33; "Insurance of CIF Contracts II", pp. 27–34.

insurance, declarations under open cover, and letters of insurance (but not a cover-note) under Clause 28 of the UCP 600.

Other developments have included additions of the requirement for notices and/or information between the parties which had been the preserve of common law FOB. Starting with notices related to shipment and/or delivery of the goods, it was extended to information for insurance purposes. This is intended to cover any gaps resulting from the many shortcomings in Incoterms and insurance clauses liberal provision of only the minimum cover. It was also a realisation that parties need to liaise beyond simply contracting. Realising the practical difficulties that might be involved That way Incoterms wanted to provide lee-ways for rather than making it a contractual undertaking. Indeed, it would be expecting what is a basically a template, guide or code to go into these details.

In relation to the CIF on the one hand and the "Free" Incoterms (FOB, FCA, FAS, etc.) the notice, information and other requirements have moved CIF nearer Common Law FOB. This is one of the indicatives of progressive development of not only the insurance clause, now contained in Clauses A5 and B5 of CIF, CIP and all other Incoterms, but also of the whole Incoterms family since their inception in Incoterms 1936. Those developments have been more pronounced in the last 40 years since Incoterms 1980. Incoterms 2020 and its insurance clauses have not only come along way but have also greatly improved from their rudimentary Incoterms 1953 edition. The current form they have tried to harmonise and standardize international sales practices and bridged the gap between itself and the common law. However, on insurance, it is still confusing. It would been helpful if they standardised all insurance obligations, made them explicit and drew users' attention to the 90% or so insurance aspects it does not cover.

All said, exports and imports (EXIMPORTS) are an essential aspect of nations economic well-being and prosperity. It is a unique and privileged industry. It is those reasons that cargo insurance it is probably the only aspect of insurance where both the state and the private sector provide coverage. It was not accidental that the UK first initiated the ECGD for regeneration of exports, reconstruction of the war torn economies and economic development, following the ravages of WWI. Recently global developments in piracy, terrorism generally and maritime terrorism in particular have cargo insurance in the limelight.

Although not very perfect but insurance ranks as one of the human race's inventions. The fact that for payments of a fraction of the subject matter the merchant gets fully indemnified is mind boggling. The alternative would be bankruptcy, economic ruins and deterrence to economic development. Thus, although not compulsory, no merchant in their right mind can trade without insurance. Indeed, such a merchant would not access credit to finance his adventures. An institution that started somewhere in China, can be traced to Hammurabi, was enhanced by the Roman Empire and refined by the English common law has come to be the pillar of finance capital. It will remain until the unlikely invention of a better alternative.

Part VI

Important Legal Documents

15 Key Legal Documents

15.1 Tableted CIF Incoterms 2020 Obligations

A. SELLER'S OBLIGATIONS	B. BUYER'S OBLIGATIONS
A1 General obligations The seller must provide the good and the commercial invoice inconformity with the contract of sale and any other evidence of conformity that may be required by the contract. Any document to be provided by the seller may be in paper or electronic form as agreed or, where there is no agreement, as is customary.	**B1 General Obligations** The buyer must pay the price of the goods as provided in the contract of sale. Any document to be provided by the buyer may be in paper or electronic form as agreed or, where there is no agreement, as is customary.
A2 Delivery The seller must deliver the goods either by placing them on board the vessel or by procuring the goods so delivered. In either case, the seller must deliver the goods on the agreed date or within the agreed period and in the manner customary at the port.	**B2 Taking delivery** The buyer must take delivery of the goods when they have been delivered under A2 and receive them from the carrier at the named port of destination.
A3 Transfer of risks The seller bears all risks of loss of or damage to the goods until they have been delivered in accordance with A2, with the exception of loss or damage in the circumstance described in B3.	**B3 Transfer of risk** The buyer bears all risks of loss of or damage to the goods from the time they have been delivered under A2. If the buyer fails to give notice in accordance with B10, then it bears all risks of loss of or damage to the goods from the agreed date or the end of the agreed period for shipment, provided that the goods have been clearly identified as contract goods

P. Ademuni-Odeke, *Insurance of International Sales' Contracts under Incoterms*, Law for Professionals, https://doi.org/10.1007/978-3-031-75136-3_15

A. SELLER'S OBLIGATIONS	B. BUYER'S OBLIGATIONS
A4 Carriage The seller must contract or procure a contract for the carriage of the goods from the agreed point of delivery, if any, at the place of delivery to the named port of destination or, if agreed, any point at that port. The contract of carriage must be made on usual terms at the seller's cost and provide for carriage by the usual route in a vessel of the type normally used for the transport of the type of goods sold. The seller must comply with any transport-related security requirements for transport to the destination.	**B4 Carriage** The buyer has no obligation to the seller to make a contract of carriage.
A5 Insurance Unless otherwise agreed or customary in the particular trade, the seller must obtain, at its own cost, cargo insurance complying with the cover provided by Clauses (C) of the Institute Cargo Clauses (LMA/IUA) or any similar clauses. The insurance shall be contracted with underwriters or an insurance company of good repute and entitle the buyer, or any other person having an insurable interest in the goods, to claim directly from the insurer. When required by the buyer, the seller must, subject to the buyer providing any necessary information requested by the seller, provide at the buyer's cost any additional cover, if procurable, such as cover complying with the Institute War Clauses and/or Institute Strikes Clauses (LMA/IUA) or any similar clauses (unless such cover is already included with the cargo insurance described in the preceding paragraph). The insurance shall cover, at a minimum, the price provided in the contract plus 10% (i.e., 110%) and shall be in the currency of the contract. The insurance shall cover the goods from the point of delivery set out in A2 to at least the named port of destination. The seller must provide the buyer with the insurance policy or certificate or any other evidence of insurance cover. Moreover, the seller must provide the buyer, at the buyer's request, risk and cost, with information that the buyer needs to procure any additional insurance.	**B5 Insurance** The buyer has no obligation to the seller to make a contract of insurance. However, the buyer must provide the seller, upon request, with any information necessary for the seller to procure any additional insurance requested by the buyer under A5

A. SELLER'S OBLIGATIONS	B. BUYER'S OBLIGATIONS
A6 Delivery/transport document The seller must, at its own cost, provide the buyer with the usual transport document for the agreed port of destination. This transport document must cover the contract goods, be dated within the period agreed for shipment, enable the buyer to claim the goods from the carrier at the port of destination and, unless otherwise agreed, enable the buyer to sell the goods in transit by the transfer of the document to a subsequent buyer or by notification to the carrier When such a transport document is issued in negotiable form and in several originals, a full set of originals must be presented to the buyer	**B6 Delivery/transport document** The buyer must accept the transport document provided under A6 if it is in conformity with the contract.
A7 Export/import clearance a) Export clearance Where applicable, the seller must carry out and pay for all export clearance formalities required by the country of export, such as: • export licence; • security clearance for export; • pre-shipment inspection; and • any other official authorisation b) Assistance with import clearance Where applicable, the seller must assist the buyer, at the buyer's request, risk and cost, in obtaining any documents and/or information related to all transit/import clearance formalities, including security requirements and pre-shipment inspection, needed by any country of transit or the country of import.	**B7 Export/import clearance** a) Assistance with export clearance Where applicable, the buyer must assist the seller at the seller's request, risk and cost in obtaining any documents and/or information related to all export clearance formalities, including security requirements and pre-shipment inspection, needed by the country of export. b) Import clearance Where applicable, the buyer must carry out and pay for all formalities required by any country of transit and the country of import, such as: • import licence and any licence required for transit; • security clearance for import and any transit; • pre-shipment inspection; and • any other official authorisation
A8 Checking/packaging/marking The seller must pay the costs of those checking operations (such as checking quality, measuring, weighing, counting) that are necessary for the purpose of delivering the goods in accordance with A2. The seller must, at its own cost, package the goods, unless it is usual for the particular trade to transport the type of goods sold unpackaged. The seller must package and mark the goods in the manner appropriate for their transport, unless the parties have agreed on specific packaging or marking requirements.	**B8 Checking/packaging/marking** The buyer has no obligation to the seller.

A. SELLER'S OBLIGATIONS	B. BUYER'S OBLIGATIONS
A9 Allocation of costs The seller must pay: a) all costs relating to the goods until they have been delivered in accordance with A2, other than those payable by the buyer under B9; b) the freight and all other costs resulting from A4, including the costs of loading the goods on board and transport-related security costs; c) any charges for unloading at the agreed port of discharge that were for the seller's account under the contract of carriage; d) the costs of transit that were for the seller's account under the contract of carriage;	**B9 Allocation of costs** The buyer must pay: a) all costs relating to the goods from the time they have been delivered under A2, other than those payable by the seller under A9; b) the costs of transit, unless such costs were for the seller's account under the contract of carriage; c) unloading costs including lighterage and wharfage charges, unless such costs and charges were for the seller's account under the contract of carriage; d) the costs of any additional insurance procured at the buyer's request under A5 and B5; e) the seller for all costs and charges related to providing assistance in obtaining documents and information in accordance with A5 and A7(b); f) where applicable, duties, taxes and any other costs related to transit or import clearance under B7(b); and g) any additional costs incurred if it fails to give notice in accordance with B10, from the agreed date or the end of the agreed period for shipment, provided that the goods have been clearly identified as contract goods
A10 Notices The seller must notify the buyer that the goods have been delivered in accordance with A2. The seller must give the buyer any notice required to enable the buyer to receive the goods.	**B10 Notices** The buyer must, whenever it is agreed that the buyer is entitled to determine the time for shipping the goods and/or the point of receiving the goods within the named port of destination, give the seller sufficient notice

15.2 Table of FOB Incoterms 2020 Obligations

A. SELLERS OBLIGATIONS	B. BUYERS OBLIGATIONS
A1 General obligations The seller must provide the goods and the commercial invoice inconformity with the contract of sale and any other evidence of conformity that may be required by the contract. Any document to be provided by the seller may be in paper or electronic form as agreed or, where there is no agreement, as is customary	**B1 General obligations** The buyer must pay the price of the goods as provided in the contract of sale. Any document to be provided by the buyer may be in paper or electronic form as agreed or, where there is no agreement, as is customary.
A2 Delivery The seller must deliver the goods either by placing them on board the vessel nominated by the buyer at the loading point, if any, indicated by the buyer at the named port of shipment or by procuring the goods so delivered. The seller must deliver the goods 1. on the agreed date or 2. at the time within the agreed period notified by the buyer under B10or, 3. if no such time is notified then at the end of the agreed period, and 4. in the manner customary at the port. If no specific loading point has been indicated by the buyer, the seller may select the point within the named port of shipment that best suits its purpose.	**B2 Taking delivery** The buyer must take delivery of the goods when they have been delivered under A2.
A3 Transfer of risks The seller bears all risks of loss of or damage to the goods until they have been delivered in accordance with A2, with the exception of loss or damage in the circumstances described in B3.	**B3 Transfer of risks** The buyer bears all risks of loss of or damage to the goods from the time they have been delivered under A2. If: a) the buyer fails to give notice in accordance with B10; or b) the vessel nominated by the buyer fails to arrive on time to enable the seller to comply with A2, fails to take the goods, or closes for cargo earlier than the time notified in accordance with B10; then the buyer bears all risks of loss of or damage to the goods: (i) from the agreed date, or in the absence of an agreed date, (ii) from the date selected by the buyer under B10, or, if no such date has been notified (iii) from the end of any agreed period for delivery, provided that the goods have been clearly identified as the contract goods.

A. SELLERS OBLIGATIONS	B. BUYERS OBLIGATIONS
A4 Carriage The seller has no obligation to the buyer to make a contract of carriage. However, the seller must provide the buyer, at the buyer's request, risk and cost, with any information in the possession of the seller, including transport-related security requirements, that the buyer needs for arranging carriage. If agreed, the seller must contract for carriage on the usual terms at the buyer's risk and cost. The seller must comply with any transport-related security requirements up to delivery	**B4 Carriage** The buyer must contract at its own cost for the carriage of the goods from the named port of shipment, except when the contract of carriage is made by the seller as provided for in A4.
A5 Insurance The seller has no obligation to the buyer to make a contract of insurance. However, the seller must provide the buyer, at the buyer's request, risk and cost, with information in the possession of the seller that the buyer needs for obtaining insurance.	**B5 Insurance** The buyer has no obligation to the seller to make a contract of insurance.
A6 Delivery/transport document The seller must provide the buyer, at the seller's cost, with the usual proof that the goods have been delivered in accordance with A2. Unless such proof is a transport document, the seller must provide assistance to the buyer, at the buyer's request, risk and cost, in obtaining a transport document.	**B6 Delivery/transport document** The buyer must accept the proof of delivery provided under A6
A7 Export/import clearance a) Export clearance Where applicable, the seller must carry out and pay for all export clearance formalities required by the country of export, such as: • export licence; • security clearance for export; • pre-shipment inspection; and • any other official authorisation b) Assistance with import clearance Where applicable, the seller must assist the buyer, at the buyer's request, risk and cost, in obtaining any documents and/or information related to all transit/ import clearance formalities, including security requirements and pre-shipment inspection, needed by any country of transit or the country of import.	**B7 Export/import clearance**

A. SELLERS OBLIGATIONS	B. BUYERS OBLIGATIONS
A8 Checking/packaging/marking The seller must pay the costs of those checking operations (such as checking quality, measuring, weighing, counting) that are necessary for the purpose of delivering the goods in accordance with A2. The seller must, at its own cost, package the goods, unless it is usual for the particular trade to transport the type of goods sold unpackaged. The seller must package and mark the goods in the manner appropriate for their transport, unless the parties have agreed on specific packaging or marking requirements	**B8 Checking/packaging/marking** The buyer has no obligation to the seller.
A9 Allocation of costs The seller must pay: a) all costs relating to the goods until they have been delivered in accordance with A2, other than those payable by the buyer under B9; b) proof to the buyer under A6 that the goods have been delivered; c) where applicable, duties, taxes and any other costs related to export clearance under A7(a); and d) the buyer for all costs and charges related to providing assistance in obtaining documents and information in accordance with B7(a)	**B9 Allocation of costs** The buyer must pay: a) all costs relating to the goods from the time they have been delivered under A2, other than those payable by the seller under A9; b) the seller for all costs and charges related to providing assistance in obtaining documents and information in accordance with A4, A5, A6 and A7(b); c) where applicable, duties, taxes and any other costs related to transit or import clearance under B7(b); and d) any additional costs incurred, either because: (i) the buyer has failed to give notice under B10, or (ii) the vessel nominated by the buyer under B10 fails to arrive on time, fails to take the goods, or closes for cargo earlier than the time notified in accordance with B10, provided that the goods have been clearly identified as the contract goods.
A10 Notices The seller must notify the buyer that the goods have been delivered in accordance with A2. The seller must give the buyer any notice required to enable the buyer to receive the goods.	**B10 Notices** The buyer must, whenever it is agreed that the buyer is entitled to determine the time for shipping the goods and/or the point of receiving the goods within the named port of destination, give the seller sufficient notice

15.3 GAFTA [FOB] Insurance Contract No. 72 (Effective 1st April 2012)

THE GRAIN AND FEED TRADE ASSOCIATION INSURANCE TERMS

Insurance cover shall be provided in the proportions and manner agreed pursuant to the sale contract, including whenever incorporated by reference the clause(s) set out in the following sections.

SECTION 1—CARGO CLAUSES (ALL RISKS)

1. This insurance attaches from the time the subject matter leaves the warehouse or place of storage at the place named in the policy for the commencement of the transit, continues during the ordinary course of transit and terminates either on delivery

(a) to the Consignees' or other final warehouse or place of storage at the destination named in the policy,

(b) to any other warehouse or place of storage, whether prior to or at the destination named in the policy, which the Assured elects to use either

(i) for storage other than in the ordinary course of transit

or

(ii) for allocation or distribution,

or (c) on the expiry of 60 days after completion of discharge overside of the subject matter hereby insured from the oversea vessel at the final port of discharge, whichever shall first occur.

If, after discharge overside from the oversea vessel at the final port of discharge, but prior to termination of this insurance, the subject matter is to be forwarded to a destination other than that to which they are insured hereunder, this insurance whilst remaining subject to termination as provided for above, shall not extend beyond the commencement of transit to such other destination.

This insurance shall remain in force (subject to termination as provided for above and to the provisions of Clause 2 below) during delay beyond the control of the Assured, any deviation, forced discharge, reshipment or transhipment and during any variation of the adventure arising from the exercise of a liberty granted to shipowners or charterers under the contract of carriage.

Transit Clause (incorporating Warehouse to Warehouse Clause)

2. If owing to circumstances beyond the control of the Assured either the contract of carriage is terminated at a port or place other than the destination named therein or the adventure is otherwise terminated before delivery of the subject matter as provided for in Clause 1 above, then, subject to prompt notice being

given to insurers/underwriters and to an additional premium if required, this insurance shall remain in force until either

(i) the subject matter is sold and delivered at such port or place, or, unless otherwise specially agreed, until the expiry of 60 days after completion of discharge overside of the subject matter hereby insured from the oversea vessel at such port or place, whichever shall first occur,

or (ii) if the subject matter is forwarded within the said period of 60 days (or any agreed extension thereof) to the destination named in the policy or to any other destination, until terminated in accordance with the provisions of Clause 1 above.

Termination of Adventure Clause

3. Including transit by craft raft or lighter to or from the oversea vessel. Each craft raft or lighter to be deemed a separate insurance. The Assured is not to be prejudiced by any agreement exempting lightermen from liability.

Craft and C. Clause

4. Held covered at a premium to be arranged in case of change of voyage or of any omission or error in the description of the subject matter insured, carrying vessel or voyage.

Change of Voyage Clause

5. This insurance is against all risks of loss of or damage to the subject matter insured but shall in no case be deemed to extend to cover loss damage or expense proximately caused by delay or inherent vice or nature of the subject matter insured. Claims recoverable here under shall be payable irrespective of percentage.

All Risk Clause

6. No claim for Constructive Total Loss shall be recoverable hereunder unless the subject matter is reasonably abandoned either on account of their actual total loss appearing to be unavoidable or because the cost of recovering, reconditioning and forwarding the subject matter to the destination to which they are insured would exceed their value on arrival.

Constructive Total Loss Clause

7. General Average and Salvage Charges payable according to Foreign Statement or to York-Antwerp Rules if in accordance with the contract of carriage.

G.A. Clause

8. The seaworthiness of any carrying vessel as between the Assured and insurers/underwriters is hereby admitted.

In the event of loss the Assured's right of recovery hereunder shall not be prejudiced by the fact that the loss may have been attributable to the wrongful act or misconduct of the shipowners or their servants, committed without the privity of the Assured.

Seaworthiness Admitted Clause

9. It is the duty of the Assured and their Agents, in all cases, to take such measures as may be reasonable for the purpose of averting or minimising a loss and to ensure that all rights against carriers, bailees or other third parties are properly preserved and exercised. Should expenses be incurred thereby insurers/underwriters will reimburse the Assured for such expenditure provided the loss or damage falls within the provisions of this insurance.

Bailee Clause

10. This insurance shall not inure to the benefit of the carrier or other bailee.

Not to Inure Clause

11. This insurance is extended to indemnify the Assured against such proportion of liability under the contract of carriage "Both to Blame Collision" Clause as is in respect of a loss recoverable hereunder.72/2

In the event of any claim by shipowners under the said Clause, the Assured agree to notify the insurers/underwriters who shall have the right, at their own cost and expense, to defend the Assured against such claim.

"Both to Blame Collision" Clause

12. Warranted free of capture, seizure, arrest, restraint or detainment, and the consequences thereof or any attempt thereat; also from the consequences of hostilities or warlike operations, whether there be a declaration of war or not; but this warranty shall not exclude collision, contact with any fixed or floating object (other than a mine or torpedo), stranding, heavy weather or fire unless caused directly (and independently of the nature of the voyage or service which the vessel concerned or, in the case of collision, any other vessel involved therein, is performing) by a hostile act by or against a belligerent power; and for the purpose of this warranty "power" includes any authority maintaining naval, military or air forces in association with a power.

Further warranted free from the consequences of civil war, revolution, rebellion, insurrection, or civil strife arising therefrom, or piracy.

F.C. and S. Clause

Should Clause No. 12 be deleted, or the relevant War Clauses as set out in Section 4 are specifically included then the same shall be deemed to form part of this insurance.

13. Warranted free of loss or damage

(a) caused by strikers, locked-out workmen, or persons taking part in labour disturbances, riots or civil commotions;

(b) resulting from strikes, lock-outs, labour disturbances, riots or civil commotions. F.S.R and C.C. Clause

Should Clause No. 13 be deleted, or the relevant Strikes, Riots and Civil Commotions Clauses as set out in Section 5 be specifically included then the same shall be deemed to form part of this insurance.

14. In the event of any additional insurance being placed by the Assured for the time being on the subject matter herein insured, the value stated in this policy shall, in the event of loss or claim, be deemed to be increased to the total amount insured at the time of loss or accident.

Where the insurance is on "Increased Value" the following Clause shall apply: -

£................ being increased value of the subject matter to be deemed to be part of the total amount insured on the subject matter valued at such total amount.

Where the original policies effected on the subject matter, also cover Advance Freight then the word "subject matter" in this policy shall be deemed also to include "Advance Freight".

In the event of any additional insurance being placed by the Assured for the time being on the subject matter herein insured, the value of the subject matter shall, in the event of loss or claim, be deemed to be increased to the total amount insured at the time of loss or accident. Increased Value Clause

15. It is a condition of this insurance that the Assured shall act with reasonable despatch in all circumstances within their control.

Reasonable Despatch Clause

16. Where the benefit of this insurance has been passed to a party hereunder in good faith who has bought or agreed to buy or acquired an insurable interest in the subject matter insured, the insurers/underwriters shall not reject a claim or invalidate this insurance on grounds of breach of obligation of good faith, or non-disclosure or misrepresentation and/or breach of any statutory obligation by any third party or by any other previous assured or on grounds of breach of warranty (whether express or implied) unless the party claiming hereunder is privy to the said breach, non-disclosure, misrepresentation or breach of warranty.

"No Policy Defence Admitted" Clause

NOTE: It is necessary for the Assured when they become aware of an event under which it is "held covered" under this insurance to give prompt notice to insurers/underwriters and the right to such cover is dependent upon compliance with this obligation.

SECTION 2—CARGO CLAUSES (W.A.)

1. This insurance attaches from the time the subject matter leaves the warehouse or place of storage at the place named in the policy for the commencement of the

transit, continues during the ordinary course of transit and terminates either on delivery

(a) to the Consignee's other final warehouse or place of storage at the destination named in the policy,

(b) to any other warehouse or place of storage, whether prior to or at the destination named in the policy, which the Assured elects to use either

(i) for storage other than in the ordinary course of transit

or

(ii) for allocation or distribution, or (c) on the expiry of 60 days after completion of discharge overside of the subject matter hereby insured from the oversea vessel at the final port of discharge, whichever shall first occur.

If, after discharge overside from the oversea vessel at the final port of discharge, but prior to termination of this insurance, the subject matter is to be forwarded to a destination other than that to which they are insured hereunder, this insurance whilst remaining subject to termination as provided for above, shall not extend beyond the commencement of transit to such other destination.

This insurance shall remain in force (subject to termination as provided for above and to the provisions of Clause 2 below) during delay beyond the control of the Assured, any deviation, forced discharge, reshipment or transhipment and during any variation of the adventure arising from the exercise of a liberty granted to shipowners or charterers under the contract of carriage, but shall in no case be deemed to extend to cover loss damage or expense proximately caused by delay or inherent vice or nature of the subject matter insured.

Transit Clause (incorporating Warehouse to Warehouse Clause)

2. If owing to circumstances beyond the control of the Assured either the contract of carriage is terminated at a port or place other than the destination named therein or the adventure is otherwise terminated before delivery of the subject matter as provided for in Clause 1 above, then, subject to prompt notice being given to insurers/underwriters and to an additional premium if required, this insurance shall remain in force until either

(i) the subject matter is sold and delivered at such port or place, or, unless otherwise specially agreed, until the expiry of 60 days after completion of discharge overside of the subject matter hereby insured from the oversea vessel at such port or place, whichever shall first occur, or

(ii) if the subject matter is forwarded within the said period of 60 days (or any agreed extension thereof) to the destination named in the policy or to any other destination, until terminated in accordance with the provisions of Clause 1 above.72/3

3. Including transit by craft raft or lighter to or from the oversea vessel. Each craft raft or lighter to be deemed a separate insurance. The Assured is not to be prejudiced by any agreement exempting lightermen from liability.

Craft and C. Clause

4. Held covered at a premium to be arranged in case of change of voyage or of any omission or error in the description of the subject matter insured, carrying vessel or voyage.

Change of Voyage Clause

5. Warranted free from average under the percentage specified in the policy, unless general average, or the oversea vessel or craft be stranded, sunk or burnt, but notwithstanding this warranty the insurers/underwriters are to pay the insured value of any bag or package forming part of the subject matter insured which may be totally lost in loading, transhipment or discharge, also for any loss of or damage to the subject matter insured which may reasonably be attributed to fire, explosion, collision or contact of the vessel and/or craft and/or conveyance with any external substance (ice included) other than water, or to discharge of the subject matter at a port of distress. This Clause shall operate during the whole period covered by the policy.

Average Clause

6. No claim for Constructive Total Loss shall be recoverable hereunder unless the subject matter is reasonably abandoned either on account of their actual total loss appearing to be unavoidable or because the cost of recovering, reconditioning and forwarding the subject matter to the destination to which they are insured would exceed their value on arrival. Constructive

Total Loss Clause

7. General Average and Salvage Charges payable according to Foreign Statement or to York-Antwerp Rules if in accordance with the contract of carriage.

G.A. Clause

8. The seaworthiness of any carrying vessel as between the Assured and insurers/ underwriters is hereby admitted.

In the event of loss, the Assured's right of recovery hereunder shall not be prejudiced by the fact that the loss may have been attributable to the wrongful act or misconduct of the shipowners or their servants, committed without the privity of the Assured.

Seaworthiness Admitted Clause

9. It is the duty of the Assured and their Agents, in all cases, to take such measures as may be reasonable for the purpose of averting or minimising a loss and to ensure that all rights against carriers, bailees or other third parties are properly

preserved and exercised. Should expenses be incurred thereby insurers/underwriters will reimburse the Assured for such expenditure provided the loss or damage falls within the provisions of this insurance.

Bailee Clause

10. This insurance shall not inure to the benefit of the carrier or other bailee.

Not to Inure Clause

11. This insurance is extended to indemnify the Assured against such proportion of liability under the contract of carriage "Both to

Blame Collision" Clause as is in respect of a loss recoverable hereunder.

In the event of any claim by shipowners under the said Clause, the Assured agree to notify the insurers/underwriters who shall have the right, at their own cost and expense, to defend the Assured against such claim.

"Both to Blame Collision" Clause

12. Warranted free of capture, seizure, arrest, restraint or detainment, and the consequences thereof or any attempt thereat; also from the consequences of hostilities or warlike operations, whether there be a declaration of war or not; but this warranty shall not exclude collision, contact with any fixed or floating object (other than a mine or torpedo), stranding, heavy weather or fire unless caused directly (and independently of the nature of the voyage or service which the vessel concerned or, in the case of collision, any other vessel involved therein, is performing) by a hostile act by or against a belligerent power; and for the purpose of this warranty "power" includes any authority maintaining naval, military or air forces in association with a power.

Further warranted free from the consequences of civil war, revolution, rebellion, insurrection, or civil strife arising therefrom, or piracy.

F.C. and S. Clause

Should Clause No. 12 be deleted, or the relevant War Clauses as set out in Section 4 are specifically included then the same shall be deemed to form part of this insurance.

13. Warranted free of loss or damage

(a) caused by strikers, locked-out workmen, or persons taking part in labour disturbances, riots or civil commotions;

(b) resulting from strikes, lock-outs, labour disturbances, riots or civil commotions.

F.S.R and C.C. Clause

Should Clause No. 13 be deleted, or the relevant Strikes, Riots and Civil Commotions Clauses as set out in Section 5 be specifically included then the same shall be deemed to form part of this insurance.

14. In the event of any additional insurance being placed by the Assured for the time being on the subject matter herein insured, the value stated in this policy shall, in the event of loss or claim, be deemed to be increased to the total amount insured at the time of loss or accident.

Where the insurance is on "Increased Value" the following Clause shall apply: -

£.............. being increased value of the subject matter to be deemed to be part of the total amount insured on the subject matter valued at such total amount.

Where the original policies effected on the subject matter, also cover Advance Freight then the word "subject matter" in this policy shall be deemed also to include "Advance Freight".

In the event of any additional insurance being placed by the Assured for the time being on the subject matter herein insured, the value of the subject matter shall, in the event of loss or claim, be deemed to be increased to the total amount insured at the time of loss or accident.

Increased Value Clause

15. It is a condition of this insurance that the Assured shall act with reasonable despatch in all circumstances within their control.

Reasonable Despatch Clause

16. Where the benefit of this insurance has been passed to a party hereunder in good faith who has bought or agreed to buy or acquired an insurable interest in the subject matter insured, the insurers/underwriters shall not reject a claim or invalidate this insurance on grounds of breach of obligation of good faith, or non-disclosure or misrepresentation and/or breach of any statutory obligation by any third party or by any other previous assured or on grounds of breach of warranty (whether express or implied) unless the party claiming hereunder is privy to the said breach, non-disclosure, misrepresentation or breach of warranty.

No Policy Defence Admitted" Clause

NOTE: It is necessary for the Assured when they become aware of an event under which it is "held covered" under this insurance to give prompt notice to insurers/underwriters and the right to such cover is dependent upon compliance with this obligation.72/4

SECTION 3—CARGO CLAUSES (F.P.A.)

1. This insurance attaches from the time the subject matter leaves the warehouse at the place named in the policy for the commencement of the transit and continues until the subject matter is delivered to the Consignee's or other final warehouse at the destination named in the policy.

Transit Clause

2. Subject to the provisions of Clause 3 hereunder this insurance shall remain in force during

(i) deviation, delay, beyond the control of the assured, forced discharge, re-shipment and transhipment

(ii) any other variation of the adventure arising from the exercise of a liberty granted to shipowners or charterers under the contract of carriage, but shall in no case be deemed to extend to cover loss damage or expense proximately caused by delay or inherent vice or nature of the subject matter insured.

Extended Cover Clause

3. If owing to circumstances beyond the control of the Assured either the contract of carriage is terminated at a port or place other than the destination named therein or the adventure is otherwise terminated before delivery of the subject matter into Consignees' or other final warehouse at the destination named in the policy, then, provided notice is given immediately after receipt of advices and subject to an additional premium if required, this insurance shall remain in force

(i) until the subject matter is sold and delivered at such port or place or

(ii) if the subject matter is forwarded to the destination named in the policy or to any other destination, until the subject matter has arrived at Consignees' or other final warehouse at such destination.

Termination of Adventure Clause

4. Including transit by craft, raft and/or lighter to and from the oversea vessel. Each craft, raft or lighter to be deemed a separate insurance. The Assured is not to be prejudiced by any agreement exempting lightermen from liability.

Craft and C. Clause

5. Held covered at a premium to be arranged in case of change of voyage or of any omission or error in the description of the subject matter insured, carrying vessel or voyage.

Change of Voyage Clause

6. Warranted free from particular average unless the vessel and/or craft be stranded, sunk, burnt, or in collision with another ship or vessel but notwithstanding this warranty the insurers/underwriters are to pay for loss of or damage to the subject matter hereby insured which may reasonably be attributed to fire, explosion or contact (other than collision with another ship or vessel) of the oversea vessel and/or craft and/or conveyance with any substance, ice included, other than water, or owing to discharge of the subject matter at a port of distress. Insurers/underwriters shall pay partial loss occurring during transhipment and to pay the insured value of any bag or package forming part of the total subject matter insured which may be totally lost in loading or discharge, and the insured value of any portion of the subject matter condemned at a port of distress owing to perils insured against. Insurers/underwriters shall also pay special charges for landing warehousing and forwarding if incurred at an intermediate port of call or

refuge, for which insurers/underwriters would be liable hereunder with the Cargo Clauses (W.A.), (as set out in GAFTA Form 72), attached.

This Clause shall operate during the whole period covered by the policy

F.P.A. Clause

7. No claim for Constructive Total Loss shall be recoverable hereunder unless the subject matter is reasonably abandoned either on account of their actual total loss appearing to be unavoidable or because the cost of recovering, reconditioning and forwarding the subject matter to the destination to which they are insured would exceed their value on arrival. Constructive

Total Loss Clause

8. General Average and Salvage Charges payable according to Foreign Statement or to York-Antwerp Rules if in accordance with the contract of carriage.

G.A. Clause

9. The seaworthiness of any carrying vessel as between the Assured and the insurers/underwriters is hereby admitted. In the event of loss, the Assured's right of recovery hereunder shall not be prejudiced by the fact that the loss may have been attributable to the wrongful act or misconduct of the shipowners or their servants, committed without the privity of the Assured.

Seaworthiness Admitted Clause

10. It is the duty of the Assured and their Agents, in all cases, to take such measures as may be reasonable for the purpose of averting or minimising a loss and to ensure that all rights against carriers, bailees or other third parties are properly preserved and exercised. Should expenses be incurred thereby, insurers/underwriters will reimburse the Assured for such expenditure provided the loss or damage reasonably falls within the provisions of this insurance.

Bailee Clause

11. This insurance shall not inure to the benefit of the carrier or other bailee.

Not to Inure Clause

12. This insurance is extended to indemnify the Assured against such proportion of liability under the contract of carriage "Both to Blame Collision" Clause as is in respect of a loss recoverable hereunder.

In the event of any claim by shipowners under the said Clause the Assured agree to notify the insurers/underwriters who shall have the right, at their own cost and expense, to defend the Assured against such claim.

"Both to Blame Collision" Clause

13. Warranted free of capture, seizure, arrest, restraint or detainment, and the consequences thereof or any attempt thereat; also from the consequences of

hostilities or warlike operations, whether there be a declaration of war or not; but this warranty shall not exclude collision, contact with any fixed or floating object (other than a mine or torpedo), stranding, heavy weather or fire unless caused directly (and independently of the nature of the voyage or service which the vessel concerned or, in the case of collision, any other vessel involved therein, is performing) by a hostile act by or against a belligerent power; and for the purpose of this warranty "power" includes any authority maintaining naval, military or air forces in association with a power.

Further warranted free from the consequences of civil war, revolution, rebellion, insurrection, or civil strife arising therefrom, or piracy.

F.C. and S. Clause

Should Clause No. 12 be deleted, or the relevant War Clauses as set out in Section 4 are specifically included then the same shall be deemed to form part of this insurance.

14. Warranted free of loss or damage

(a) caused by strikers, locked-out workmen, or persons taking part in labour disturbances, riots or civil commotions;

(b) resulting from strikes, lock-outs, labour disturbances, riots or civil commotions.

F.S.R and C.C. Clause

Should Clause No. 13 be deleted, or the relevant Strikes, Riots and Civil Commotions Clauses as set out in Section 5 be specifically included then the same shall be deemed to form part of this insurance.72/5

15. In the event of any additional insurance being placed by the Assured for the time being on the subject matter herein insured, the value stated in this policy shall in the event of loss or claim, be deemed to be increased to the total amount insured at the time of loss or accident.

Where the insurance is on "Increased Value" the following Clause shall apply: -

£.................. being increased value of the subject matter to be deemed to be part of the total amount insured on the subject matter valued at such total amount.

Where the original policies effected on the subject matter also cover Advance Freight then the word "subject matter" in this policy shall be deemed also to include "Advance Freight".

In the event of any additional insurance being placed by the Assured for the time being on the subject matter herein insured, the value of the subject matter shall, in the event of loss or claim, be deemed to be increased to the total amount insured at the time of loss or accident.

Increased Value Clause

16. It is a condition of this insurance that the Assured shall act with reasonable despatch in all circumstances within their control.

Reasonable Despatch Clause

17. Where the benefit of this insurance has been passed to a party hereunder in good faith who has bought or agreed to buy or acquired an insurable interest in the subject matter insured, the insurers/underwriters shall not reject a claim or invalidate this insurance on grounds of breach of obligation of good faith, or non-disclosure or misrepresentation and/or breach of any statutory obligation by any third party or by any other previous assured or on grounds of breach of warranty (whether express or implied) unless the party claiming hereunder is privy to the said breach, non-disclosure, misrepresentation or breach of warranty.

"No Policy Defence Admitted" Clause

NOTE: It is necessary for the Assured when they become aware of an event under which it is "held covered" under this insurance to give prompt notice to insurers/underwriters and the right to such cover is dependent upon compliance with this obligation.

SECTION 4—WAR CLAUSES (CARGO)

1. This insurance covers the risks otherwise excluded under the standard F.C. and S. Clauses above, except as provided in Clause 3 below, loss of or damage to the subject matter insured caused by

1.1. war civil war revolution insurrection, or civil strife arising therefrom, or any hostile act by or against a belligerent power

1.2. capture seize arrest restraint or detainment, arising from risks covered under 1.1 above, and the consequences thereof or any attempt thereat

1.3. derelict mines torpedoes bombs or other derelict weapons of war.

2. This insurance covers general average and salvage charges, adjusted or determined according to the contract of carriage and/or the governing law and practice, incurred to avoid or in connection with the avoidance of loss from a risk covered under these clauses.

3. This insurance excludes

3.1. any claim based upon loss of, or frustration of, the insured voyage or adventure caused by arrests, restraints or detainments of Kings, Princes, Peoples, Usurpers or persons attempting to usurp power.

3.2. loss, damage or expense arising from any hostile use of any weapon of war employing atomic or nuclear fission and/or fusion or other like reaction or radio-active force or matter

3.3. loss or damage proximately caused by delay inherent vice or loss of market, or any claim for expenses arising from delay except such expenses as would be recoverable in principle under English law and practice under York-Antwerp Rules.

4. Claims recoverable shall be payable irrespective of percentage.

5. This insurance, except for the risks of mines and derelict torpedoes, floating or submerged, referred to in Clause 6 below

5.1. attaches from the time the subject matter insured or part thereof is loaded on the board the oversea vessel and continue, subject to 5.3 and 5.4 below, until such time as the subject matter insured or part thereof is discharged from the oversea vessel at the final port or place of discharge, or on expiry of 15 days counting from midnight of the day of arrival of the oversea vessel at the final port or place of discharge, whichever shall first occur.

5.2. nevertheless, subject to prompt notice to the insurers/underwriters and to an additional premium, such insurance reattaches when, without having discharged the subject matter at the final port or place of discharge, the oversea vessel sails therefrom, and terminates, subject to 5.3 and 5.4 below, either as the subject matter or part thereof is thereafter discharged from the oversea vessel at the final (or substituted) port or place of discharge, or on expiry of 15 days counting from midnight of the day of re-arrival of the oversea vessel at the final port or place of discharge or arrival of the oversea vessel at a substituted port or place of discharge, whichever shall first occur.

5.3. If during the insured voyage the oversea vessel arrives at an intermediate port or place to discharge the subject matter for on-carriage by another oversea vessel, such insurance terminates on expiry of 15 days counting from midnight of the day of arrival of the first oversea vessel at the intermediate port or place, but reattaches as the subject matter or part thereof is loaded on the second on-carrying oversea vessel. During the period of 15 days such insurance remains in force after discharge only whilst the subject matter or part thereof is at such intermediate port or place of discharge. If the insurance reattaches, it thereafter terminates in accordance with 5.1.

5.4. If the voyage in the contract of carriage is terminated at a port or place other than the destination agreed therein, such port or place shall be deemed the final port of discharge and such insurance terminates in accordance with 5.1. If the subject matter is subsequently reshipped to the original or any other destination, then, provided notice is given to the insurers/underwriters before the commencement of such further transit and subject to an additional premium, if any, such insurance reattaches.

(i) in the case of the subject matter having been discharged, as the subject matter or part thereof is loaded on the on- carrying oversea vessel for the voyage

(ii) in the case of the subject matter not having been discharged, when the oversea vessel sails from such deemed final port of discharge; thereafter such insurance terminates in accordance with 5.2.

(For the purpose of Clause 5 "arrival" shall be deemed to mean that the oversea vessel is anchored moored or otherwise secured at a berth or place within the Harbour Authority area. If such a berth or place is not available, arrival is deemed to have occurred when the oversea vessel first anchors, moors or otherwise secures either at or off the intended port or place of discharge).

6. The insurance against the risks of mines and derelict torpedoes, floating or submerged,72/6

6.1. attaches as the subject matter or part thereof is first loaded on any carrying vessel or craft after such subject matter leaves the warehouse or place of storage at the place named in the insurance for the commencement of the transit and

6.2. terminates either

6.2.1. as the subject matter or part thereof is discharged finally from any carrying vessel or craft prior to delivery to the warehouse or place of storage at the destination named in the insurance, or at a substituted destination in the event of a change of voyage agreed to by the insurers/underwriters, or

6.2.2. when, before the subject matter is discharged finally from any carrying vessel or craft prior to delivery to the warehouse or place of storage at the destination named in the insurance, or at a substituted destination in the event of a change of voyage agreed to by the insurers/underwriters the voyage or transit in the contract of carriage is terminated at a port or place other than the destination agreed therein, nevertheless subject to prompt notice to the insurers/underwriters and to an additional premium being agreed if required, such insurance reattaches, and thereafter terminates either

(i) as the subject matter or part thereof is discharged from any carrying vessel or craft prior to sale and delivery at such port or place, or

(ii) unless otherwise specifically agreed by the insurers/underwriters, on the expiry of 60 days whilst afloat after completion of discharge overside of the subject matter from an oversea vessel at such port or place, whichever shall first occur. If the subject matter is forwarded within the 60 days (or any agreed extension thereof) to the destination named in the insurance or to any other destination, then, subject to prompt notice to the insurers/underwriters and to an additional premium being agreed if required, such insurance remains in force until terminated as the subject matter or part thereof is finally discharged from any such vessel or craft prior to delivery to the warehouse or place of storage at the destination named in the insurance, or at a substituted destination in the event of a change of voyage agreed to by the insurers/underwriters.

(For the purpose of Clause 5 and Clause 6 "oversea vessel" shall be deemed to mean the vessel carrying the subject matter from one port or place to another where such voyage involves a sea passage by that vessel.)

7. Anything contained in this contract which is inconsistent with Clauses 3.1,

3.2, 5 or 6 shall, to the extent of such inconsistency, be null and void.

8. Subject to prompt notice to the insurers/underwriters and to an additional premium being agreed, the subject matter is held covered within the provisions of these clauses in the case of

(i) change of or deviation from the voyage

(ii) variation of the adventure by reason of the exercise of any liberty granted to the shipowner or charterer under the contract of carriage.

9. It is a condition of this insurance that the Assured shall act with reasonable despatch in all circumstances within their control.

NOTE: It is necessary for the Assured when they become aware of an event under which it is "held covered" under this insurance to give prompt notice to insurers/underwriters and the right to such cover is dependent upon compliance with this obligation.

SECTION 5—STRIKES, RIOTS AND CIVIL COMMOTIONS CLAUSES

1. This policy covers loss of or damage to the subject matter hereby insured caused by

(a) strikers, locked-out workmen, or persons taking part in labour disturbances, riots or civil commotions;

(b) persons acting maliciously.

2. Warranted free of

(i) loss or damage proximately caused by

(a) delay, inherent vice or nature of the subject matter hereby insured;

(b) the absence, shortage or withholding of labour of any description whatsoever during any strike, lock-out, labour disturbance, riot or civil commotion;

(ii) any claim for expenses arising from delay except such expenses as would be recoverable in principle in English law and practice under York-Antwerp Rules;

(iii) loss or damage caused by hostilities war-like operations, civil war, or by revolution, rebellion, insurrection or civil strife arising therefrom.

3. This insurance attaches from the time the subject matter leaves the warehouse at the place named in the policy for the commencement of the transit and continues until the subject matter is delivered to the Consignees' or other final warehouse at the destination named in the policy.

4. Subject to the provisions of Clause 5 hereunder this insurance shall remain in force during

(i) deviation, delay beyond the control of the Assured, forced discharge, re-shipment and transhipment

(ii) any other variation of the adventure arising from the exercise of a liberty granted to shipowners or charterers under the contract of carriage.

5. If owing to circumstances beyond the control of the Assured either the contract of carriage is terminated at a port or place other than the destination named therein or the adventure is otherwise terminated before delivery of the subject matter into Consignees' or other final warehouse at the destination named in the policy, then, provided notice is given immediately after receipt of advices and subject to an additional premium if required, this insurance shall remain in force

(i) until the subject matter is sold and delivered at such port or place

or (ii) if the subject matter is forwarded to the destination named in the policy or to any other destination, until the subject matter has arrived at Consignees' or other final warehouse at such destination.

6. General Average and Salvage Charges payable (subject to the terms of these clauses) according to Foreign Statement or York-

Antwerp Rules if in accordance with the contract of carriage.

7. Claims for loss or damage within the terms of these clauses shall be payable without reference to conditions of average.

8. Held covered at a premium to be arranged in case of change of voyage or of any omission or error in the description of the subject matter insured, carrying vessel or voyage.

9. It is a condition of this insurance that the Assured shall act with reasonable despatch in all circumstances within their control.72/7

NOTE: It is necessary for the Assured, when they become aware of an event under which it is "held covered" under this insurance to give prompt notice to insurers/underwriters, and the right to such cover is dependent upon compliance with this obligation.

SECTION 6—AUSTRALIAN, CANADIAN, SOUTH AFRICAN AND UNITED STATES OF AMERICA ACTS

(Relating to Carriage of Goods by Sea)

The assured is held covered against "loss or damage arising or resulting from act, neglect or default of the master, mariner, pilot or the servants of the carrier in the navigation or in the management of the ship" for which the "carrier" or "ship" is relieved of responsibility under:

Clause 4 of the Commonwealth of Australia Sea Carriage of Goods Act, 1924, or

Clause IV Section 2 of the Rules appended to the Water Carriage of Goods Act, 1936, of Canada, or

Chapter 8 Section 309 (2) of the Union of South Africa Merchant Shipping Act, No. 57, of 1951, or

Section 3 of the Act of Congress of the United States, approved 13th February, 1893, or

Section 4; sub-Section 2 of the Carriage of Goods by Sea Act, 1936, of the United States of America

but nothing in this clause contained shall limit or affect any rights which insurers/underwriters may have by subrogation or otherwise, against the owners of the said vessel.

Claims arising under this clause are not subject to the F.P.A. warranty.

NOTE: It is necessary for the Assured, when they become aware of an event under which it is "held covered" under this insurance to give prompt notice to insurers/underwriters, and the right to such cover is dependent upon compliance with this obligation.

SECTION 7—SPONTANEOUS COMBUSTION

Notwithstanding anything to the contrary this insurance covers loss of or damage to the subject matter insured caused by heating, sweating or spontaneous combustion.

NOTE: It is necessary for the Assured, when they become aware of an event under which it is "held covered" under this insurance to give prompt notice to insurers/underwriters, and the right to such cover is dependent upon compliance with this obligation.

SECTION 8 - Irrespective of which conditions and clauses have been agreed the Institute Radioactive Contamination, Chemical, Biological, Bio-Chemical, Electromagnetic Weapons Exclusion Clause (CL 370) and the Institute Cyber Attack Exclusion Clause (CL 380) shall apply in any case.

15.4 CIF GAFTA Contract No. 81 Insurance Clause (Effective 1st January 2020)

19. INSURANCE
19.1 For Contracts Concluded on CIF/CIFFO terms Sellers shall provide insurance on terms not less favourable than those set out hereunder, and as set out in detail in GAFTA Insurance Terms No. 72 viz.: - Cargo Clauses (W.A.), with average payable, with 3% franchise or better terms - - Section 2 of Form 72 War Clauses (Cargo) - Section 4 of Form 72 Strikes, Riots and Civil Commotions Clauses (Cargo) - Section 5 of Form 72

19.2 For Contracts Concluded on C & F/C&FFO terms Buyers shall be responsible for obtaining insurance cover as per Clause 19.1 above and shall, if required by Sellers, provide evidence to Seller's prior to the commencement of loading that they have obtained suitable cover. If Buyers refuse or fail to provide evidence Sellers are entitled (but not obliged) to cover insurance on the same terms at the Buyers' expense.

15.5 Institute Cargo Clauses A

RISKS COVERED
Risks

1. This insurance covers all risks of loss of or damage to the subject-matter insured except as excluded by the provisions of Clauses 4, 5, 6 and 7 below.

General Average

2. This insurance covers general average and salvage charges, adjusted or determined according to the contract of carriage and/or the governing law and practice, incurred to avoid or in connection with the avoidance of loss from any cause except those excluded in Clauses 4, 5, 6 and 7 below.

"Both to Blame Collision Clause"

3. This insurance indemnifies the Assured, in respect of any risk insured herein, against liability incurred under any Both to Blame Collision Clause in the contract of carriage. In the event of any claim by carriers under the said Clause, the Assured agree to notify the Insurers who shall have the right, at their own cost and expense, to defend the Assured against such claim.

EXCLUSIONS

4. In no case shall this insurance cover

4.1 loss damage or expense attributable to wilful misconduct of the Assured

4.2 ordinary leakage, ordinary loss in weight or volume, or ordinary wear and tear of the subject-matter insured

4.3 loss damage or expense caused by insufficiency or unsuitability of packing or preparation of the subject matter insured to withstand the ordinary incidents of the insured transit where such packing or preparation is carried out by the Assured or their employees or prior to the attachment of this insurance (for the purpose of these Clauses "packing" shall be deemed to include stowage in a container and "employees" shall not include independent contractors)

4.4 loss damage or expense caused by inherent vice or nature of the subject-matter insured

4.5 loss damage or expense caused by delay, even though the delay be caused by a risk insured against (except expenses payable under Clause 2 above)

4.6 loss damage or expense caused by insolvency or financial default of the owner's managers charterers or operators of the vessel where, at the time of loading of the subject-matter insured on board the vessel, the Assured are aware, or in the ordinary course of business should be aware, that such insolvency or financial default could prevent the normal prosecution of the voyage

This exclusion shall not apply where the contract of insurance has been assigned to the party claiming hereunder who has bought or agreed to buy the subject-matter insured in good faith under a binding contract

4.7 loss damage or expense directly or indirectly caused by or arising from the use of any weapon or device employing atomic or nuclear fission and/or fusion or other like reaction or radioactive force or matter.

5. 5.1 In no case shall this insurance cover loss damage or expense arising from

5.1.1 unseaworthiness of vessel or craft or unfitness of vessel or craft for the safe carriage of the subject-matter insured, where the Assured are privy to such unseaworthiness or unfitness, at the time the subject-matter insured is loaded therein

5.1.2 unfitness of container or conveyance for the safe carriage of the subject-matter insured, where loading therein or thereon is carried outprior to attachment of this insurance or by the Assured or their employees and they are privy to such unfitness at the time of loading.

5.2 Exclusion 5.1.1 above shall not apply where the contract of insurance has been assigned to the party claiming hereunder who has bought or agreed to buy the subject-matter insured in good faith under a binding contract.

5.3 The Insurers waive any breach of the implied warranties of seaworthiness of the ship and fitness of the ship to carry the subject-matter insured to destination.

6. In no case shall this insurance cover loss damage or expense caused by

6.1 war civil war revolution rebellion insurrection, or civil strife arising therefrom, or any hostile act by or against a belligerent power

6.2 capture seizure arrest restraint or detainment (piracy excepted), and the consequences thereof or any attempt thereat

6.3 derelict mines torpedoes, bombs or other derelict weapons of war.

7. In no case shall this insurance cover loss damage or expense

7.1 caused by strikers, locked-out workmen, or persons taking part in labour disturbances, riots or civil commotions

7.2 resulting from strikes, lock-outs, labour disturbances, riots or civil commotions

7.3 caused by any act of terrorism being an act of any person acting on behalf of, or in connection with, any organisation which carries out activities directed towards the overthrowing or influencing, by force or violence, of any government whether or not legally constituted

7.4 caused by any person acting from a political, ideological or religious motive.

DURATION
Transit Clause

8. 8.1 Subject to Clause 11 below, this insurance attaches from the time the subject-matter insured is first moved in the warehouse or at the place of storage (at the place named in the contract of insurance) for the purpose of the immediate loading into or onto the carrying vehicle or other conveyance for the commencement of transit, continues during the ordinary course of transit and terminates either

8.1.1 on completion of unloading from the carrying vehicle or other conveyance in or at the final warehouse or place of storage at the destination named in the contract of insurance,

8.1.2 on completion of unloading from the carrying vehicle or other conveyance in or at any other ware house or place of storage, whether prior to or at the destination named in the contract of insurance, which the Assured or their employees elect to use either for storage other than in the ordinary course of transit or for allocation or distribution, or

8.1.3 when the Assured or their employees elect to use any carrying vehicle or other conveyance or any container for storage other than in the ordinary course of transit or

8.1.4 on the expiry of 60 days after completion of discharge overside of the subject-matter insured from the oversea vessel at the final port of discharge, whichever shall first occur.

8.2 If, after discharge overside from the oversea vessel at the final port of discharge, but prior to termination of this insurance, the subject-matter insured is to be forwarded to a destination other than that to which it is insured, this insurance, whilst remaining subject to termination as provided in Clauses

8.1.1 to 8.1.4, shall not extend beyond the time the subject-matter insured is first moved for the purpose of the commencement of transit to such other destination.

8.3 This insurance shall remain in force (subject to termination as provided for in Clauses 8.1.1 to 8.1.4above and to the provisions of Clause 9 below) during delay beyond the control of the Assured, any deviation, forced discharge, reshipment or transhipment and during any variation of the adventure arising from the exercise of a liberty granted to carriers under the contract of carriage.

Termination of Contract of Carriage

9. If owing to circumstances beyond the control of the Assured either the contract of carriage is terminated at a port or place other than the destination named therein or the transit is otherwise terminated before unloading of the subject-matter insured as provided for in Clause 8 above, then this insurance shall also insurance shall remain in force, subject to an additional premium if required by the Insurers, either

9.1 until the subject-matter insured is sold and delivered at such port or place, or, unless otherwise specially agreed, until the expiry of 60 days after arrival of the subject-matter insured at such port or place, whichever shall first occur,

or

9.2 if the subject-matter insured is forwarded within the said period of 60 days (or any agreed extension thereof) to the destination named in the contract of insurance or to any other destination, until terminated in accordance with the provisions of Clause 8 above.

Change of Voyage

10. 10.1 Where, after attachment of this insurance, the destination is changed by the Assured, this must be notified promptly to Insurers for rates and terms to be agreed. Should a loss occur prior to such agreement being obtained cover may be provided but only if cover would have been available at a reasonable commercial market rate on reasonable market terms.

10.2 Where the subject-matter insured commences the transit contemplated by this insurance (in accordance with Clause 8.1), but, without the knowledge of the Assured or their employees the ship sails for another destination, this insurance will nevertheless be deemed to have attached at commencement of such transit.

CLAIMS
Insurable Interest

11. 11.1 In order to recover under this insurance the Assured must have an insurable interest in the subject matter insured at the time of the loss.

11.2 Subject to Clause 11.1 above, the Assured shall be entitled to recover for insured loss occurring during the period covered by this insurance, notwithstanding that the loss occurred before the contract of insurance was concluded, unless the Assured were aware of the loss and the Insurers were not.

Forwarding Charges

12. Where, as a result of the operation of a risk covered by this insurance, the insured transit is terminated at a port or place other than that to which the subject-matter insured is covered under this insurance, the Insurers will reimburse the Assured for any extra charges properly and reasonably incurred in unloading, storing and forwarding the subject-matter insured to the destination to which it is insured.

This Clause 12, which does not apply to general average or salvage charges, shall be subject to the exclusions contained in Clauses 4, 5, 6 and 7 above, and shall not include charges arising from the fault negligence insolvency or financial default of the Assured or their employees.

Constructive Total Loss

13. No claim for Constructive Total Loss shall be recoverable hereunder unless the subject-matter insured is reasonably abandoned either on account of its actual total loss appearing to be unavoidable or because the cost of recovering, reconditioning and forwarding the subject-matter insured to the destination to which it is insured would exceed its value on arrival.

Increased Value

14. 14.1 If any Increased Value insurance is effected by the Assured on the subject-matter insured under this insurance the agreed value of the subject-matter insured shall be deemed to be increased to the total amount insured under this insurance and all Increased Value insurances covering the loss, and liability under this insurance shall be in such proportion as the sum insured under this insurance bears to such total amount insured.

In the event of claim the Assured shall provide the Insurers with evidence of the amounts insured under all other insurances.

14.2 Where this insurance is on Increased Value the following clause shall apply:

The agreed value of the subject-matter insured shall be deemed to be equal to the total amount insured under primary insurance and all Increased Value insurances covering the loss and effected on the subject-matter insured by the Assured, and liability under this insurance shall be in such proportion as the sum insured under this insurance bears to such total amount insured.

In the event of claim the Assured shall provide the Insurers with evidence of the amounts insured under all other insurances.

BENEFIT OF INSURANCE

15. This insurance

15.1 covers the Assured which includes the person claiming indemnity either as the person by or on whose behalf the contract of insurance was effected or as an assignee,

15.2 shall not extend to or otherwise benefit the carrier or other bailee.

MINIMISING LOSSES

Duty of Assured

16. It is the duty of the Assured and their employees and agents in respect of loss recoverable hereunder

16.1 to take such measures as may be reasonable for the purpose of averting or minimising such loss, and

16.2 to ensure that all rights against carriers, bailees or other third parties are properly preserved and

Exercised and the Insurers will, in addition to any loss recoverable hereunder, reimburse the Assured for any charges properly and reasonably incurred in pursuance of these duties.

Waiver

17. Measures taken by the Assured or the Insurers with the object of saving, protecting or recovering the subject matter insured shall not be considered as a waiver or acceptance of abandonment or otherwise prejudice the rights of either party.

AVOIDANCE OF DELAY
18. It is a condition of this insurance that the Assured shall act with reasonable despatch in all circumstances within their control.

LAW AND PRACTICE

19. This insurance is subject to English law and practice.

NOTE: - Where a continuation of cover is requested under Clause 9, or a change of destination is notified under Clause 10, there is an obligation to give prompt notice to the Insurers and the right to such cover is dependent upon compliance with this obligation.

CL382

01/01/2000

15.6 Institute Cargo Clauses B

RISKS COVERED
Risks

1. This insurance covers, except as excluded by the provisions of Clauses 4, 5, 6 and 7 below,

1.1 loss of or damage to the subject-matter insured reasonably attributable to

1.1.1 fire or explosion

1.1.2 vessel or craft being stranded grounded sunk or capsized

1.1.3 overturning or derailment of land conveyance

1.1.4 collision or contact of vessel craft or conveyance with any external object other than water

1.1.5 discharge of cargo at a port of distress

1.1.6 earthquake volcanic eruption or lightning,

1.2 loss of or damage to the subject-matter insured caused by

1.2.1 general average sacrifice

1.2.2 jettison or washing overboard

1.2.3 entry of sea lake or river water into vessel craft hold conveyance container or place of storage,

1.3 total loss of any package lost overboard or dropped whilst loading on to, or unloading from, vessel or craft.

General Average

2. This insurance covers general average and salvage charges, adjusted or determined according to the contract of carriage and/or the governing law and practice, incurred to avoid or in connection with the avoidance of loss from any cause except those excluded in Clauses 4, 5, 6 and 7 below.

"Both to Blame Collision Clause"

3. This insurance indemnifies the Assured, in respect of any risk insured herein, against liability incurred under any Both to Blame Collision Clause in the contract of carriage. In the event of any claim by carriers under the said Clause, the Assured agree to notify the Insurers who shall have the right, at their own cost and expense, to defend the Assured against such claim.

EXCLUSIONS

4. In no case shall this insurance cover

4.1 loss damage or expense attributable to wilful misconduct of the Assured

4.2 ordinary leakage, ordinary loss in weight or volume, or ordinary wear and tear of the subject-matter insured

4.3 loss damage or expense caused by insufficiency or unsuitability of packing or preparation of the subject matter insured to withstand the ordinary incidents of the insured transit where such packing or preparation is carried out by the Assured or their employees or prior to the attachment of this insurance (for the purpose of these Clauses "packing" shall be deemed to include stowage in a container and "employees" shall not include independent contractors)

4.4 loss damage or expense caused by inherent vice or nature of the subject-matter insured

4.5 loss damage or expense caused by delay, even though the delay be caused by a risk insured against (except expenses payable under Clause 2 above)

4.6 loss damage or expense caused by insolvency or financial default of the owner's managers charterers or operators of the vessel where, at the time of loading of the subject-matter insured on board the vessel, the Assured are aware, or in the ordinary course of business should be aware, that such insolvency or financial default could prevent the normal prosecution of the voyage

This exclusion shall not apply where the contract of insurance has been assigned to the party claiming hereunder who has bought or agreed to buy the subject-matter insured in good faith under a binding contract

4.7 deliberate damage to or deliberate destruction of the subject-matter insured or any part thereof by the wrongful act of any person or persons

4.8 loss damage or expense directly or indirectly caused by or arising from the use of any weapon or device employing atomic or nuclear fission and/or fusion or other like reaction or radioactive force or matter.

5. 5.1 In no case shall this insurance cover loss damage or expense arising from

5.1.1 unseaworthiness of vessel or craft or unfitness of vessel or craft for the safe carriage of the subject-matter insured, where the Assured are privy to such unseaworthiness or unfitness, at the time the subject-matter insured is loaded therein

5.1.2 unfitness of container or conveyance for the safe carriage of the subject-matter insured, where loading therein or thereon is carried out prior to attachment of this insurance or by the Assured or their employees and they are privy to such unfitness at the time of loading.

5.2 Exclusion 5.1.1 above shall not apply where the contract of insurance has been assigned to the party claiming hereunder who has bought or agreed to buy the subject-matter insured in good faith under a binding contract.

5.3 The Insurers waive any breach of the implied warranties of seaworthiness of the ship and fitness of the ship to carry the subject-matter insured to destination.

6. In no case shall this insurance cover loss damage or expense caused by

6.1 war civil war revolution rebellion insurrection, or civil strife arising therefrom, or any hostile act by or against a belligerent power

6.2 capture seizure arrest restraint or detainment, and the consequences thereof or any attempt thereat

6.3 derelict mines torpedoes bombs or other derelict weapons of war.

7. In no case shall this insurance cover loss damage or expense

7.1 caused by strikers, locked-out workmen, or persons taking part in labour disturbances, riots or civil commotions

7.2 resulting from strikes, lock-outs, labour disturbances, riots or civil commotions

7.3 caused by any act of terrorism being an act of any person acting on behalf of, or in connection with, any organisation which carries out activities directed towards the overthrowing or influencing, by force or violence, of any government whether or not legally constituted

7.4 caused by any person acting from a political, ideological or religious motive.

DURATION
Transit Clause

8. 8.1 Subject to Clause 11 below, this insurance attaches from the time the subject-matter insured is first moved in the warehouse or at the place of storage (at the place named in the contract of insurance) for the purpose of the immediate loading into or onto the carrying vehicle or other conveyance for the commencement of transit, continues during the ordinary course of transit and terminates either

8.1.1 on completion of unloading from the carrying vehicle or other conveyance in or at the final warehouse or place of storage at the destination named in the contract of insurance,

8.1.2 on completion of unloading from the carrying vehicle or other conveyance in or at any other warehouse or place of storage, whether prior to or at the destination named in the contract of insurance, which the Assured or their employees elect to use either for storage other than in the ordinary course of transit or for allocation or distribution, or

8.1.3 when the Assured or their employees elect to use any carrying vehicle or other conveyance or any container for storage other than in the ordinary course of transit or

8.1.4 on the expiry of 60 days after completion of discharge overside of the subject-matter insured from the oversea vessel at the final port of discharge, whichever shall first occur.

8.2 If, after discharge overside from the oversea vessel at the final port of discharge, but prior to termination of this insurance, the subject-matter insured is to be forwarded to a destination other than that to which it is insured, this insurance, whilst remaining subject to termination as provided in Clauses 8.1.1 to 8.1.4, shall not extend beyond the time the subject-matter insured is first moved for the purpose of the commencement of transit to such other destination.

8.3 This insurance shall remain in force (subject to termination as provided for in Clauses 8.1.1 to 8.1.4 above and to the provisions of Clause 9 below) during delay beyond the control of the Assured, any deviation, forced discharge, reshipment or transhipment and during any variation of the adventure arising from the exercise of a liberty granted to carriers under the contract of carriage.

Termination of Contract of Carriage

9. If owing to circumstances beyond the control of the Assured either the contract of carriage is terminated at a port or place other than the destination named therein or the transit is otherwise terminated before unloading of the subject-matter insured as provided for in Clause 8 above, then this insurance shall also terminate unless prompt notice is given to the Insurers and continuation of cover is requested when this insurance shall remain in force, subject to an additional premium if required by the Insurers, either

9.1 until the subject-matter insured is sold and delivered at such port or place, or, unless otherwise specially agreed, until the expiry of 60 days after arrival of the subject-matter insured at such port or place, whichever shall first occur, or

9.2 if the subject-matter insured is forwarded within the said period of 60 days (or any agreed extension thereof) to the destination named in the contract of insurance or to any other destination, until terminated in accordance with the provisions of Clause 8 above.

Change of Voyage

10. 10.1 Where, after attachment of this insurance, the destination is changed by the Assured, this must be notified promptly to Insurers for rates and terms to be agreed. Should a loss occur prior to such agreement being obtained cover may be provided but only if cover would have been available at a reasonable commercial market rate on reasonable market terms.

10.2 Where the subject-matter insured commences the transit contemplated by this insurance (in accordance with Clause 8.1), but, without the knowledge of the Assured or their employees the ship sails for another destination, this insurance will nevertheless be deemed to have attached at commencement of such transit.

CLAIMS
Insurable Interest

11. 11.1 In order to recover under this insurance the Assured must have an insurable interest in the subject matter insured at the time of the loss.

11.2 Subject to Clause 11.1 above, the Assured shall be entitled to recover for insured loss occurring during the period covered by this insurance, notwithstanding that the loss occurred before the contract of insurance was concluded, unless the Assured were aware of the loss and the Insurers were not.

Forwarding Charges

12. Where, as a result of the operation of a risk covered by this insurance, the insured transit is terminated at a port or place other than that to which the subject-matter insured is covered under this insurance, the Insurers will reimburse the Assured for any extra charges properly and reasonably incurred in unloading storing and forwarding the subject-matter insured to the destination to which it is insured.

This Clause 12, which does not apply to general average or salvage charges, shall be subject to the exclusions contained in Clauses 4, 5, 6 and 7 above, and shall not include charges arising from the fault negligence insolvency or financial default of the Assured or their employees.

Constructive Total Loss

13. No claim for Constructive Total Loss shall be recoverable hereunder unless the subject-matter insured is reasonably abandoned either on account of its actual total loss appearing to be unavoidable or because the cost of recovering, reconditioning and forwarding the subject-matter insured to the destination to which it is insured would exceed its value on arrival.

Increased Value

14. 14.1 If any Increased Value insurance is effected by the Assured on the subject-matter insured under this insurance the agreed value of the subject-matter insured shall be deemed to be increased to the total amount insured under this insurance and all Increased Value insurances covering the loss, and liability under this insurance shall be in such proportion as the sum insured under this insurance bears to such total amount insured.

In the event of claim the Assured shall provide the Insurers with evidence of the amounts insured under all other insurances.

14.2 Where this insurance is on Increased Value the following clause shall apply:

The agreed value of the subject-matter insured shall be deemed to be equal to the total amount insured under the primary insurance and all Increased Value insurances covering the loss and effected on the subject-matter insured by the Assured, and liability under this insurance shall be in such proportion as the sum insured under this insurance bears to such total amount insured.

In the event of claim the Assured shall provide the Insurers with evidence of the amounts insured under all other insurances.

BENEFIT OF INSURANCE
15. This insurance

15.1 covers the Assured which includes the person claiming indemnity either as the person by or on whose behalf the contract of insurance was effected or as an assignee,

15.2 shall not extend to or otherwise benefit the carrier or other bailee.

MINIMISING LOSSES
Duty of Assured

16. It is the duty of the Assured and their employees and agents in respect of loss recoverable hereunder

16.1 to take such measures as may be reasonable for the purpose of averting or minimising such loss, and

16.2 to ensure that all rights against carriers, bailees or other third parties are properly preserved and exercised and the Insurers will, in addition to any loss recoverable hereunder, reimburse the Assured for any charges properly and reasonably incurred in pursuance of these duties.

Waiver

17. Measures taken by the Assured or the Insurers with the object of saving, protecting or recovering the subject matter insured shall not be considered as a waiver or acceptance of abandonment or otherwise prejudice the rights of either party.

AVOIDANCE OF DELAY
18. It is a condition of this insurance that the Assured shall act with reasonable despatch in all circumstances within their control.

LAW AND PRACTICE
19. This insurance is subject to English law and practice.

NOTE: - Where a continuation of cover is requested under Clause 9, or a change of destination is notified under Clause 10, there is an obligation to give prompt notice to the Insurers and the right to such cover is dependent upon compliance with this obligation.

CL383

01/01/2009

15.7 Institute Cargo Clauses C

RISKS COVERED
Risks

1. This insurance covers, except as excluded by the provisions of Clauses 4, 5, 6 and 7 below,

1.1 loss of or damage to the subject-matter insured reasonably attributable to

1.1.1 fire or explosion

1.1.2 vessel or craft being stranded grounded sunk or capsized

1.1.3 overturning or derailment of land conveyance

1.1.4 collision or contact of vessel craft or conveyance with any external object other than water

1.1.5 discharge of cargo at a port of distress,

1.2 loss of or damage to the subject-matter insured caused by

1.2.1 general average sacrifice

1.2.2 jettison.

General Average

2. This insurance covers general average and salvage charges, adjusted or determined according to the contract of carriage and/or the governing law and practice, incurred to avoid or in connection with the avoidance of loss from any cause except those excluded in Clauses 4, 5, 6 and 7 below.

"Both to Blame Collision Clause"

3. This insurance indemnifies the Assured, in respect of any risk insured herein, against liability incurred under any Both to Blame Collision Clause in the contract of carriage. In the event of any claim by carriers under the said Clause, the Assured agree to notify the Insurers who shall have the right, at their own cost and expense, to defend the Assured against such claim.

EXCLUSIONS
4. In no case shall this insurance cover

4.1 loss damage or expense attributable to wilful misconduct of the Assured

4.2 ordinary leakage, ordinary loss in weight or volume, or ordinary wear and tear of the subject-matter insured

4.3 loss damage or expense caused by insufficiency or unsuitability of packing or preparation of the subject matter insured to withstand the ordinary incidents of the insured transit where such packing or preparation is carried out by the

Assured or their employees or prior to the attachment of this insurance (for the purpose of these Clauses “packing” shall be deemed to include stowage in a container and “employees” shall not include independent contractors)

4.4 loss damage or expense caused by inherent vice or nature of the subject-matter insured

4.5 loss damage or expense caused by delay, even though the delay be caused by a risk insured against (except expenses payable under Clause 2 above)

4.6 loss damage or expense caused by insolvency or financial default of the owner’s managers charterers or operators of the vessel where, at the time of loading of the subject-matter insured on board the vessel, the Assured are aware, or in the ordinary course of business should be aware, that such insolvency or financial default could prevent the normal prosecution of the voyage

This exclusion shall not apply where the contract of insurance has been assigned to the party claiming hereunder who has bought or agreed to buy the subject-matter insured in good faith under a binding contract

4.7 deliberate damage to or deliberate destruction of the subject-matter insured or any part thereof by the wrongful act of any person or persons

4.8 loss damage or expense directly or indirectly caused by or arising from the use of any weapon or device employing atomic or nuclear fission and/or fusion or other like reaction or radioactive force or matter.

5. 5.1 In no case shall this insurance cover loss damage or expense arising from

5.1.1 unseaworthiness of vessel or craft or unfitness of vessel or craft for the safe carriage of the subject-matter insured, where the Assured are privy to such unseaworthiness or unfitness, at the time the subject-matter insured is loaded therein

5.1.2 unfitness of container or conveyance for the safe carriage of the subject-matter insured, where loading therein or thereon is carried out prior to attachment of this insurance or by the Assured or their employees and they are privy to such unfitness at the time of loading.

5.2 Exclusion 5.1.1 above shall not apply where the contract of insurance has been assigned to the party claiming hereunder who has bought or agreed to buy the subject-matter insured in good faith under a binding contract.

5.3 The Insurers waive any breach of the implied warranties of seaworthiness of the ship and fitness of the ship to carry the subject-matter insured to destination.

6. In no case shall this insurance cover loss damage or expense caused by

6.1 war civil war revolution rebellion insurrection, or civil strife arising therefrom, or any hostile act by or against a belligerent power

6.2 capture seizure arrest restraint or detainment, and the consequences thereof or any attempt thereat

6.3 derelict mines torpedoes bombs or other derelict weapons of war.

7. In no case shall this insurance cover loss damage or expense

7.1 caused by strikers, locked-out workmen, or persons taking part in labour disturbances, riots or civil commotions

7.2 resulting from strikes, lock-outs, labour disturbances, riots or civil commotions

7.3 caused by any act of terrorism being an act of any person acting on behalf of, or in connection with, any organisation which carries out activities directed towards the overthrowing or influencing, by force or violence, of any government whether or not legally constituted

7.4 caused by any person acting from a political, ideological or religious motive.

DURATION
Transit Clause

8. 8.1 Subject to Clause 11 below, this insurance attaches from the time the subject-matter insured is first moved in the warehouse or at the place of storage (at the place named in the contract of insurance) for the purpose of the immediate loading into or onto the carrying vehicle or other conveyance for the commencement of transit, continues during the ordinary course of transit and terminates either

8.1.1 on completion of unloading from the carrying vehicle or other conveyance in or at the final warehouse or place of storage at the destination named in the contract of insurance,

8.1.2 on completion of unloading from the carrying vehicle or other conveyance in or at any other warehouse or place of storage, whether prior to or at the destination named in the contract of insurance, which the Assured or their employees elect to use either for storage other than in the ordinary course of transit or for allocation or distribution, or

8.1.3 when the Assured or their employees elect to use any carrying vehicle or other conveyance or any container for storage other than in the ordinary course of transit or

8.1.4 on the expiry of 60 days after completion of discharge overside of the subject-matter insured from the oversea vessel at the final port of discharge, whichever shall first occur.

8.2 If, after discharge overside from the oversea vessel at the final port of discharge, but prior to termination of this insurance, the subject-matter insured is to be forwarded to a destination other than that to which it is, this insurance, whilst remaining subject to termination as provided in Clauses

8.1.1 to 8.1.4, shall not extend beyond the time the subject-matter insured is first moved for the purpose of the commencement of transit to such other destination.

8.3 This insurance shall remain in force (subject to termination as provided for in Clauses 8.1.1 to 8.1.4above and to the provisions of Clause 9 below) during delay beyond the control of the Assured, any deviation, forced discharge, reshipment or transhipment and during any variation of the adventure arising from the exercise of a liberty granted to carriers under the contract of carriage.

Termination of Contract of Carriage

9. If owing to circumstances beyond the control of the Assured either the contract of carriage is terminated at a port or place other than the destination named therein or the transit is otherwise terminated before unloading of the subject-matter insured as provided for in Clause 8 above, then this insurance shall also terminate unless prompt notice is given to the Insurers and continuation of cover is requested when this insurance shall remain in force, subject to an additional premium if required by the Insurers, either

9.1 until the subject-matter insured is sold and delivered at such port or place, or, unless otherwise especially agreed, until the expiry of 60 days after arrival of the subject-matter insured at such port or place, whichever shall first occur, or

9.2 if the subject-matter insured is forwarded within the said period of 60 days (or any agreed extension thereof) to the destination named in the contract of insurance or to any other destination, until terminated in accordance with the provisions of Clause 8 above.

Change of Voyage

10. 10.1 Where, after attachment of this insurance, the destination is changed by the Assured, this must be notified promptly to Insurers for rates and terms to be agreed. Should a loss occur prior to such agreement being obtained cover may be provided but only if cover would have been available at a reasonable commercial market rate on reasonable market terms.

10.2 Where the subject-matter insured commences the transit contemplated by this insurance (in accordance with Clause 8.1), but, without the knowledge of the Assured or their employees the ship sails for another destination, this insurance will nevertheless be deemed to have attached at commencement of such transit.

CLAIMS
Insurable Interest

11. 11.1 In order to recover under this insurance the Assured must have an insurable interest in the subject matter insured at the time of the loss.

11.2 Subject to Clause 11.1 above, the Assured shall be entitled to recover for insured loss occurring during the period covered by this insurance, notwithstanding that the loss occurred before the contract of insurance was concluded, unless the Assured were aware of the loss and the Insurers were not.

Forwarding Charges

12. Where, as a result of the operation of a risk covered by this insurance, the insured transit is terminated at a port or place other than that to which the subject-matter insured is covered under this insurance, the Insurers will reimburse the Assured for any extra charges properly and reasonably incurred in unloading storing and forwarding the subject-matter insured to the destination to which it is insured.

This Clause 12, which does not apply to general average or salvage charges, shall be subject to the exclusions contained in Clauses 4, 5, 6 and 7 above, and shall not include charges arising from the fault negligence insolvency or financial default of the Assured or their employees.

Constructive Total Loss

13. No claim for Constructive Total Loss shall be recoverable hereunder unless the subject-matter insured is reasonably abandoned either on account of its actual total loss appearing to be unavoidable or because the cost of recovering, reconditioning and forwarding the subject-matter insured to the destination to which it is insured would exceed its value on arrival.

Increased Value

14. 14.1 If any Increased Value insurance is effected by the Assured on the subject-matter insured under this insurance the agreed value of the subject-matter insured shall be deemed to be increased to the total amount insured under this insurance and all Increased Value insurances covering the loss, and liability under this insurance shall be in such proportion as the sum insured under this insurance bears to such total amount insured.

In the event of claim the Assured shall provide the Insurers with evidence of the amounts insured under all other insurances.

14.2 Where this insurance is on Increased Value the following clause shall apply:

The agreed value of the subject-matter insured shall be deemed to be equal to the total amount insured under the primary insurance and all Increased Value insurances covering the loss and effected on the subject-matter insured by the Assured, and liability under this insurance shall be in such proportion as the sum insured under this insurance bears to such total amount insured.

In the event of claim the Assured shall provide the Insurers with evidence of the amounts insured under all other insurances.

BENEFIT OF INSURANCE
15. This insurance

15.1 covers the Assured which includes the person claiming indemnity either as the person by or on whose behalf the contract of insurance was effected or as an assignee,

15.2 shall not extend to or otherwise benefit the carrier or other bailee.

MINIMISING LOSSES
Duty of Assured

16. It is the duty of the Assured and their employees and agents in respect of loss recoverable hereunder

16.1 to take such measures as may be reasonable for the purpose of averting or minimising such loss, and

16.2 to ensure that all rights against carriers, bailees or other third parties are properly preserved and

Exercised and the Insurers will, in addition to any loss recoverable hereunder, reimburse the Assured for any charges properly and reasonably incurred in pursuance of these duties.

Waiver

17. Measures taken by the Assured or the Insurers with the object of saving, protecting or recovering the subject matter insured shall not be considered as a waiver or acceptance of abandonment or otherwise prejudice the rights of either party.

AVOIDANCE OF DELAY
18. It is a condition of this insurance that the Assured shall act with reasonable despatch in all circumstances within their control.

LAW AND PRACTICE
19. This insurance is subject to English law and practice.

NOTE: - Where a continuation of cover is requested under Clause 9, or a change of destination is notified under Clause 10, there is an obligation to give prompt notice to the Insurers and the right to such cover is dependent upon compliance with this obligation.

(IUA).

CL384

01/10/2009

15.8 UCP 600

UCP 600 - Clause 1
Application of UCP

The Uniform Customs and Practice for Documentary Credits, 2007 Revision, ICC Publication no. 600 ("UCP") are rules that apply to any documentary credit ("credit") (including, to the extent to which they may be applicable, any standby letter of credit) when the text of the credit expressly indicates that it is subject to these rules. They are binding on all parties thereto unless expressly modified or excluded by the credit.

UCP 600 - Clause 2
Definitions

For the purpose of these rules:

Advising bank means the bank that advises the credit at the request of the issuing bank. Applicant means the party on whose request the credit is issued.

Banking day means a day on which a bank is regularly open at the place at which an act subject to these rules is to be performed.

Beneficiary means the party in whose favour a credit is issued.

Complying presentation means a presentation that is in accordance with the terms and conditions of the credit, the applicable provisions of these rules and international standard banking practice.

Confirmation means a definite undertaking of the confirming bank, in addition to that of the issuing bank, to honour or negotiate a complying presentation.

Confirming bank means the bank that adds its confirmation to a credit upon the issuing bank's authorization or request.

Credit means any arrangement, however named or described, that is irrevocable and thereby constitutes a definite undertaking of the issuing bank to honour a complying presentation.

Honour means:

a. to pay at sight if the credit is available by sight payment.

b. to incur a deferred payment undertaking and pay at maturity if the credit is available by deferred payment.

c. to accept a bill of exchange ("draft") drawn by the beneficiary and pay at maturity if the credit is available by acceptance.

Issuing bank means the bank that issues a credit at the request of an applicant or on its own behalf.

Negotiation means the purchase by the nominated bank of drafts (drawn on a bank other than the nominated bank) and/or documents under a complying presentation, by advancing or agreeing to advance funds to the beneficiary on or before the banking day on which reimbursement is due to the nominated bank.

Nominated Bank means the bank with which the credit is available or any bank in the case of a credit available with any bank.

Presentation means either the delivery of documents under a credit to the issuing bank or nominated bank or the documents so delivered.

Presenter means a beneficiary, bank or other party that makes a presentation.

UCP 600 - Clause 3
Interpretations

For the purpose of these rules:

Where applicable, words in the singular include the plural and, in the plural, include the singular. A credit is irrevocable even if there is no indication to that effect.

A document may be signed by handwriting, facsimile signature, perforated signature, stamp, symbol or any other mechanical or electronic method of authentication.

A requirement for a document to be legalized, visaed, certified or similar will be satisfied by any signature, mark, stamp or label on the document which appears to satisfy that requirement.

Branches of a bank in different countries are considered to be separate banks.

Terms such as "first class", "well known", "qualified", "independent", "official", "competent" or "local" used to describe the issuer of a document allow any issuer except the beneficiary to issue that document.

Unless required to be used in a document, words such as "prompt", "immediately" or "as soon as possible" will be disregarded.

The expression "on or about" or similar will be interpreted as a stipulation that an event is to occur during a period of five calendar days before until five calendar days after the specified date, both start and end dates included.

The words "to", "until", "till", "from" and "between" when used to determine a period of shipment include the date or dates mentioned, and the words "before" and "after" exclude the date mentioned.

The words "from" and "after" when used to determine a maturity date exclude the date mentioned.

The terms "first half" and "second half" of a month shall be construed respectively as the 1st to the 15th and the 16th to the last day of the month, all dates inclusive.

The terms "beginning", "middle" and "end" of a month shall be construed respectively as the 1st to the 10th, the 11th to the 20th and the 21st to the last day of the month, all dates inclusive.

UCP 600 - Clause 4
Credits v. Contracts

a. A credit by its nature is a separate transaction from the sale or other contract on which it may be based. Banks are in no way concerned with or bound by such contract, even if any reference whatsoever to it is included in the credit. Consequently, the undertaking of a bank to honour, to negotiate or to fulfil any other obligation under the credit is not subject to claims or defences by the applicant resulting from its relationships with the issuing bank or the beneficiary.

A beneficiary can in no case avail itself of the contractual relationships existing between banks or between the applicant and the issuing bank.

b. An issuing bank should discourage any attempt by the applicant to include, as an integral part of the credit, copies of the underlying contract, proforma invoice and the like.

UCP 600 - Clause 5
Documents v. Goods, Services or Performance

Banks deal with documents and not with goods, services or performance to which the documents may relate.

UCP 600 - Clause 6
Availability, Expiry Date and Place for Presentation

a. A credit must state the bank with which it is available or whether it is available with any bank. A credit available with a nominated bank is also available with the issuing bank.

b. A credit must state whether it is available by sight payment, deferred payment, acceptance or negotiation.

c. A credit must not be issued available by a draft drawn on the applicant.

d.

i. A credit must state an expiry date for presentation. An expiry date stated for honour or negotiation will be deemed to be an expiry date for presentation.

ii. The place of the bank with which the credit is available is the place for presentation. The place for presentation under a credit available with any bank is that of any bank. A place for presentation other than that of the issuing bank is in addition to the place of the issuing bank.

e. Except as provided in sub-clause 29 (a), a presentation by or on behalf of the beneficiary must be made on or before the expiry date.

UCP 600 - Clause 7
Issuing Bank Undertaking

a. Provided that the stipulated documents are presented to the nominated bank or to the issuing bank and that they constitute a complying presentation, the issuing bank must honour if the credit is available by:

i. sight payment, deferred payment or acceptance with the issuing bank;

ii. sight payment with a nominated bank and that nominated bank does not pay;

iii. deferred payment with a nominated bank and that nominated bank does not incur its deferred payment undertaking or, having incurred its deferred payment undertaking, does not pay at maturity;

iv. acceptance with a nominated bank and that nominated bank does not accept a draft drawn on it or, having accepted a draft drawn on it, does not pay at maturity;

v. negotiation with a nominated bank and that nominated bank does not negotiate.
b. An issuing bank is irrevocably bound to honour as of the time it issues the credit.

c. An issuing bank undertakes to reimburse a nominated bank that has honoured or negotiated a complying presentation and forwarded the documents to the issuing bank. Reimbursement for the amount of a complying presentation under a credit available by acceptance or deferred payment is due at maturity, whether or not the nominated bank prepaid or purchased before maturity. An issuing bank's undertaking to reimburse a nominated bank is independent of the issuing bank's undertaking to the beneficiary.

UCP 600 - Clause 8
Confirming Bank Undertaking

a. Provided that the stipulated documents are presented to the confirming bank or to any other nominated bank and that they constitute a complying presentation, the confirming bank must:

i. honour, if the credit is available by

a. sight payment, deferred payment or acceptance with the confirming bank;

b. sight payment with another nominated bank and that nominated bank does not pay;

c. deferred payment with another nominated bank and that nominated bank does not incur its deferred payment undertaking or, having incurred its deferred payment undertaking, does not pay at maturity;

d. acceptance with another nominated bank and that nominated bank does not accept a draft drawn on it or, having accepted a draft drawn on it, does not pay at maturity;

e. negotiation with another nominated bank and that nominated bank does not negotiate.

ii. negotiate, without recourse, if the credit is available by negotiation with the confirming bank.

a.

b. A confirming bank is irrevocably bound to honour or negotiate as of the time it adds its confirmation to the credit.

c. A confirming bank undertakes to reimburse another nominated bank that has honoured or negotiated a complying presentation and forwarded the documents to the confirming bank. Reimbursement for the amount of a complying presentation under a credit available by acceptance or deferred payment is due at maturity, whether or not another nominated bank prepaid or purchased before maturity. A confirming bank's undertaking to reimburse another nominated bank is independent of the confirming bank's undertaking to the beneficiary.

d. If a bank is authorized or requested by the issuing bank to confirm a credit but is not prepared to do so, it must inform the issuing bank without delay and may advise the credit without confirmation.

UCP 600 - Clause 9
Advising of Credits and Amendments

a. A credit and any amendment may be advised to a beneficiary through an advising bank. An advising bank that is not a confirming bank advises the credit and any amendment without any undertaking to honour or negotiate.

b. By advising the credit or amendment, the advising bank signifies that it has satisfied itself as to the apparent authenticity of the credit or amendment and that the advice accurately reflects the terms and conditions of the credit or amendment received.

c. An advising bank may utilize the services of another bank ("second advising bank") to advise the credit and any amendment to the beneficiary. By advising the credit or amendment, the second advising bank signifies that it has satisfied itself as to the apparent authenticity of the advice it has received and that the advice accurately reflects the terms and conditions of the credit or amendment received.

d. A bank utilizing the services of an advising bank or second advising bank to advise a credit must use the same bank to advise any amendment thereto.

e. If a bank is requested to advise a credit or amendment but elects not to do so, it must so inform, without delay, the bank from which the credit, amendment or advice has been received.

f. If a bank is requested to advise a credit or amendment but cannot satisfy itself as to the apparent authenticity of the credit, the amendment or the advice, it must so inform, without delay, the bank from which the instructions appear to have been received. If the advising bank or second advising bank elects nonetheless to advise the credit or amendment, it must inform the beneficiary or second advising bank that it has not been able to satisfy itself as to the apparent authenticity of the credit, the amendment or the advice.

UCP 600 - Clause 10
Amendments

a. Except as otherwise provided by clause 38, a credit can neither be amended nor cancelled without the agreement of the issuing bank, the confirming bank, if any, and the beneficiary.

b. An issuing bank is irrevocably bound by an amendment as of the time it issues the amendment. A confirming bank may extend its confirmation to an amendment and will be irrevocably bound as of the time it advises the amendment. A confirming bank may, however, choose to advise an amendment without extending its confirmation and, if so, it must inform the issuing bank without delay and inform the beneficiary in its advice.

c. The terms and conditions of the original credit (or a credit incorporating previously accepted amendments) will remain in force for the beneficiary until the beneficiary communicates its acceptance of the amendment to the bank that advised such amendment. The beneficiary should give notification of acceptance or rejection of an amendment. If the beneficiary fails to give such notification, a presentation that complies with the credit and to any not yet accepted amendment will be deemed to be notification of acceptance by the beneficiary of such amendment. As of that moment the credit will be amended.

d. A bank that advises an amendment should inform the bank from which it received the amendment of any notification of acceptance or rejection.

e. Partial acceptance of an amendment is not allowed and will be deemed to be notification of rejection of the amendment.

f. A provision in an amendment to the effect that the amendment shall enter into force unless rejected by the beneficiary within a certain time shall be disregarded.

UCP 600 - Clause 11
Teletransmitted and Pre-Advised Credits and Amendments

a. An authenticated teletransmission of a credit or amendment will be deemed to be the operative credit or amendment, and any subsequent mail confirmation shall be disregarded.

If a teletransmission states "full details to follow" (or words of similar effect), or states that the mail confirmation is to be the operative credit or amendment, then the teletransmission will not be deemed to be the operative credit or amendment. The issuing bank must then issue the operative credit or amendment without delay in terms not inconsistent with the teletransmission.

b. A preliminary advice of the issuance of a credit or amendment ("pre-advice") shall only be sent if the issuing bank is prepared to issue the operative credit or amendment. An issuing bank that sends a pre advice is irrevocably committed to issue the operative credit or amendment, without delay, in terms not inconsistent with the pre-advice.

UCP 600 - Clause 12
Nomination

a. Unless a nominated bank is the confirming bank, an authorization to honour or negotiate does not impose any obligation on that nominated bank to honour or negotiate, except when expressly agreed to by that nominated bank and so communicated to the beneficiary.

b. By nominating a bank to accept a draft or incur a deferred payment undertaking, an issuing bank authorizes that nominated bank to prepay or purchase a draft accepted or a deferred payment undertaking incurred by that nominated bank.

c. Receipt or examination and forwarding of documents by a nominated bank that is not a confirming bank does not make that nominated bank liable to honour or negotiate, nor does it constitute honour or negotiation.

UCP 600 - Clause 13
Bank-to-Bank Reimbursement Arrangements

a. If a credit states that reimbursement is to be obtained by a nominated bank ("claiming bank") claiming on another party ("reimbursing bank"), the credit must state if the reimbursement is subject to the ICC rules for bank-to-bank reimbursements in effect on the date of issuance of the credit.

b. If a credit does not state that reimbursement is subject to the ICC rules for bank-to-bank reimbursements, the following apply:

i. An issuing bank must provide a reimbursing bank with a reimbursement authorization that conforms with the availability stated in the credit. The reimbursement authorization should not be subject to an expiry date.

i.e. claiming bank shall not be required to supply a reimbursing bank with a certificate of compliance with the terms and conditions of the credit.

liana issuing bank will be responsible for any loss of interest, together with any expenses incurred, if reimbursement is not provided on first demand by a reimbursing bank in accordance with the terms and conditions of the credit.

via reimbursing bank's charges are for the account of the issuing bank. However, if the charges are for the account of the beneficiary, it is the responsibility of an issuing bank to so indicate in the credit and in the reimbursement authorization. If a reimbursing bank's charges are for the account of the beneficiary, they shall be deducted from the amount due to a claiming bank when reimbursement is made. If no reimbursement is made, the reimbursing bank's charges remain the obligation of the issuing bank.

c. An issuing bank is not relieved of any of its obligations to provide reimbursement if reimbursement is not made by a reimbursing bank on first demand.

UCP 600 - Clause 14
Standard for Examination of Documents

a. A nominated bank acting on its nomination, a confirming bank, if any, and the issuing bank must examine a presentation to determine, on the basis of the documents alone, whether or not the documents appear on their face to constitute a complying presentation.

b. A nominated bank acting on its nomination, a confirming bank, if any, and the issuing bank shall each have a maximum of five banking days following the day of presentation to determine if a presentation is complying. This period is not curtailed or otherwise affected by the occurrence on or after the date of presentation of any expiry date or last day for presentation.

c. A presentation including one or more original transport documents subject to clauses 19, 20, 21, 22, 23, 24 or 25 must be made by or on behalf of the beneficiary not later than 21 calendar days after the date of shipment as described in these rules, but in any event not later than the expiry date of the credit.

d. Data in a document, when read in context with the credit, the document itself and international standard banking practice, need not be identical to, but must not conflict with, data in that document, any other stipulated document or the credit.

e. In documents other than the commercial invoice, the description of the goods, services or performance, if stated, may be in general terms not conflicting with their description in the credit.

f. If a credit requires presentation of a document other than a transport document, insurance document or commercial invoice, without stipulating by whom the document is to be issued or its data content, banks will accept the document as presented if its content appears to fulfil the function of the required document and otherwise complies with sub-clause 14 (d).

g. A document presented but not required by the credit will be disregarded and may be returned to the presenter.

h. If a credit contains a condition without stipulating the document to indicate compliance with the condition, banks will deem such condition as not stated and will disregard it.

i. A document may be dated prior to the issuance date of the credit, but must not be dated later than its date of presentation.

j. When the addresses of the beneficiary and the applicant appear in any stipulated document, they need not be the same as those stated in the credit or in any other stipulated document, but must be within the same country as the respective addresses mentioned in the credit. Contact details (telefax, telephone, email and the like) stated as part of the beneficiary's and the applicant's address will be disregarded. However, when the address and contact details of the applicant appear as part of the consignee or notify party details on a transport document subject to clauses 19, 20, 21, 22, 23, 24 or 25, they must be as stated in the credit.

k. The shipper or consignor of the goods indicated on any document need not be the beneficiary of the credit.

l. A transport document may be issued by any party other than a carrier, owner, master or charterer provided that the transport document meets the requirements of clauses 19, 20, 21, 22, 23 or 24 of these rules.

UCP 600 - Clause 15
Complying Presentation

a. When an issuing bank determines that a presentation is complying, it must honour.

b. When a confirming bank determines that a presentation is complying, it must honour or negotiate and forward the documents to the issuing bank.

c. When a nominated bank determines that a presentation is complying and honours or negotiates, it must forward the documents to the confirming bank or issuing bank.

UCP 600 - Clause 16
Discrepant Documents, Waiver and Notice

a. When a nominated bank acting on its nomination, a confirming bank, if any, or the issuing bank determines that a presentation does not comply, it may refuse to honour or negotiate.

b. When an issuing bank determines that a presentation does not comply, it may in its sole judgement approach the applicant for a waiver of the discrepancies. This does not, however, extend the period mentioned in sub-clause 14 (b).

c. When a nominated bank acting on its nomination, a confirming bank, if any, or the issuing bank decides to refuse to honour or negotiate, it must give a single notice to that effect to the presenter.

The notice must state:

i. that the bank is refusing to honour or negotiate; and

ii. each discrepancy in respect of which the bank refuses to honour or negotiate; and iii.

a) that the bank is holding the documents pending further instructions from the presenter; or

b) that the issuing bank is holding the documents until it receives a waiver from the applicant and agrees to accept it, or receives further instructions from the presenter prior to agreeing to accept a waiver; or

c) that the bank is returning the documents; or

d) that the bank is acting in accordance with instructions previously received from the presenter.

d. The notice required in sub-clause 16 (c) must be given by telecommunication or, if that is not possible, by other expeditious means no later than the close of the fifth banking day following the day of presentation.

e. A nominated bank acting on its nomination, a confirming bank, if any, or the issuing bank may, after providing notice required by sub-clause 16 (c) (iii) (a) or (b), return the documents to the presenter at any time.

f. If an issuing bank or a confirming bank fails to act in accordance with the provisions of this clause, it shall be precluded from claiming that the documents do not constitute a complying presentation.

g. When an issuing bank refuses to honour or a confirming bank refuse to honour or negotiate and has given notice to that effect in accordance with this clause, it shall then be entitled to claim a refund, with interest, of any reimbursement made.

UCP 600 - Clause 17
Original Documents and Copies

a. At least one original of each document stipulated in the credit must be presented.

b. A bank shall treat as an original any document bearing an apparently original signature, mark, stamp, or label of the issuer of the document, unless the document itself indicates that it is not an original.

c. Unless a document indicates otherwise, a bank will also accept a document as original if it:

i. appears to be written, typed, perforated or stamped by the document issuer's hand; or

ii. appears to be on the document issuer's original stationery; or

iii. states that it is original, unless the statement appears not to apply to the document presented.

d. If a credit requires presentation of copies of documents, presentation of either originals or copies is permitted.

e. If a credit requires presentation of multiple documents by using terms such as "in duplicate", "in two-fold" or "in two copies", this will be satisfied by the presentation of at least one original and the remaining number in copies, except when the document itself indicates otherwise.

UCP 600 - Clause 18
Commercial Invoice

a. A commercial invoice:

i. must appear to have been issued by the beneficiary (except as provided in clause 38);

ii. must be made out in the name of the applicant (except as provided in sub-clause 38 (g));

iii. must be made out in the same currency as the credit; and

iv. need not be signed.

b. A nominated bank acting on its nomination, a confirming bank, if any, or the issuing bank may accept a commercial invoice issued for an amount in excess of the amount permitted by the credit, and its decision will be binding upon all parties, provided the bank in question has not honoured or negotiated for an amount in excess of that permitted by the credit.

c. The description of the goods, services or performance in a commercial invoice must correspond with that appearing in the credit.

UCP 600 - Clause 19
Transport Document Covering At least Two Different Modes of Transport

a. A transport document covering at least two different modes of transport (multimodal or combined transport document), however named, must appear to:

i. indicate the name of the carrier and be signed by:

- the carrier or a named agent for or on behalf of the carrier, or

- the master or a named agent for or on behalf of the master.

Any signature by the carrier, master or agent must be identified as that of the carrier, master or agent.

Any signature by an agent must indicate whether the agent has signed for or on behalf of the carrier or for or on behalf of the master.

ii. indicate that the goods have been dispatched, taken in charge or shipped on board at the place stated in the credit, by:

- pre-printed wording, or

- a stamp or notation indicating the date on which the goods have been dispatched, taken in charge or shipped on board.

The date of issuance of the transport document will be deemed to be the date of dispatch, taking in charge or shipped on board, and the date of shipment. However, if the transport document indicates, by stamp or notation, a date of dispatch, taking in charge or shipped on board, this date will be deemed to be the date of shipment.

iii. indicate the place of dispatch, taking in charge or shipment and the place of final destination stated in the credit, even if:

a. the transport document states, in addition, a different place of dispatch, taking in charge or shipment or place of final destination,

or

b. the transport document contains the indication "intended" or similar qualification in relation to the vessel, port of loading or port of discharge.

iv. be the sole original transport document or, if issued in more than one original, be the full set as indicated on the transport document.

v. contain terms and conditions of carriage or make reference to another source containing the terms and conditions of carriage (short form or blank back transport document). Contents of terms and conditions of carriage will not be examined.

vi. contain no indication that it is subject to a charter party.

b. For the purpose of this clause, transhipment means unloading from one means of conveyance and reloading to another means of conveyance (whether or not in different modes of transport) during the carriage from the place of dispatch, taking in charge or shipment to the place of final destination stated in the credit.

c.

i. A transport document may indicate that the goods will or may be transhipped provided that the entire carriage is covered by one and the same transport document.

ii. A transport document indicating that transhipment will or may take place is acceptable, even if the credit prohibits transhipment.

UCP 600 - Clause 20
Bill of Lading

a.A bill of lading, however named, must appear to:

i. indicate the name of the carrier and be signed by:

- the carrier or a named agent for or on behalf of the carrier, or

- the master or a named agent for or on behalf of the master.

Any signature by the carrier, master or agent must be identified as that of the carrier, master or agent.

Any signature by an agent must indicate whether the agent has signed for or on behalf of the carrier or for or on behalf of the master.

ii. indicate that the goods have been shipped on board a named vessel at the port of loading stated in the credit by:

- pre-printed wording, or

- an on board notation indicating the date on which the goods have been shipped on board.

The date of issuance of the bill of lading will be deemed to be the date of shipment unless the bill of lading contains an on board notation indicating the date of shipment, in which case the date stated in the on board notation will be deemed to be the date of shipment.

If the bill of lading contains the indication "intended vessel" or similar qualification in relation to the name of the vessel, an on board notation indicating the date of shipment and the name of the actual vessel is required.

iii. indicate shipment from the port of loading to the port of discharge stated in the credit.

If the bill of lading does not indicate the port of loading stated in the credit as the port of loading, or if it contains the indication "intended" or similar qualification in relation to the port of loading, an on board notation indicating the port of loading as stated in the credit, the date of shipment and the name of the vessel is required. This provision applies even when loading on board or shipment on a named vessel is indicated by pre-printed wording on the bill of lading.

iv. be the sole original bill of lading or, if issued in more than one original, be the full set as indicated on the bill of lading.

v. contain terms and conditions of carriage or make reference to another source containing the terms and conditions of carriage (short form or blank back bill of lading). Contents of terms and conditions of carriage will not be examined.

vi. contain no indication that it is subject to a charter party.

b. For the purpose of this clause, transhipment means unloading from one vessel and reloading to another vessel during the carriage from the port of loading to the port of discharge stated in the credit.

c.

i. A bill of lading may indicate that the goods will or may be transhipped provided that the entire carriage is covered by one and the same bill of lading.

ii. A bill of lading indicating that transhipment will or may take place is acceptable, even if the credit prohibits transhipment, if the goods have been shipped in a container, trailer or LASH barge as evidenced by the bill of lading.

d. Clauses in a bill of lading stating that the carrier reserves the right to tranship will be disregarded.

UCP 600 - Clause 21
Non-Negotiable Sea Waybill

a. A non-negotiable sea waybill, however named, must appear to:

i. indicate the name of the carrier and be signed by:

- the carrier or a named agent for or on behalf of the carrier, or

- the master or a named agent for or on behalf of the master.

Any signature by the carrier, master or agent must be identified as that of the carrier, master or agent.

Any signature by an agent must indicate whether the agent has signed for or on behalf of the carrier or for or on behalf of the master.

ii. indicate that the goods have been shipped on board a named vessel at the port of loading stated in the credit by:

- pre-printed wording, or

- an on-board notation indicating the date on which the goods have been shipped on board.

The date of issuance of the non-negotiable sea waybill will be deemed to be the date of shipment unless the non-negotiable sea waybill contains an on-board notation indicating the date of shipment, in which case the date stated in the on board notation will be deemed to be the date of shipment.

If the non-negotiable sea waybill contains the indication "intended vessel" or similar qualification in relation to the name of the vessel, an on-board notation indicating the date of shipment and the name of the actual vessel is required.

iii. indicate shipment from the port of loading to the port of discharge stated in the credit.

If the non-negotiable sea waybill does not indicate the port of loading stated in the credit as the port of loading, or if it contains the indication "intended" or similar qualification in relation to the port of loading, an on-board notation indicating the port of loading as stated in the credit, the date of shipment and the name of the vessel is required. This provision applies even when loading on board or shipment on a named vessel is indicated by pre-printed wording on the non-negotiable sea waybill.

iv. be the sole original non-negotiable sea waybill or, if issued in more than one original, be the full set as indicated on the non-negotiable sea waybill.

v. contain terms and conditions of carriage or make reference to another source containing the terms and conditions of carriage (short form or blank back non-negotiable sea waybill). Contents of terms and conditions of carriage will not be examined.

vi. contain no indication that it is subject to a charter party.

b. For the purpose of this clause, transhipment means unloading from one vessel and reloading to another vessel during the carriage from the port of loading to the port of discharge stated in the credit.

c.

i. A non-negotiable sea waybill may indicate that the goods will or may be transhipped provided that the entire carriage is covered by one and the same non-negotiable sea waybill.

ii. A non-negotiable sea waybill indicating that transhipment will or may take place is acceptable, even if the credit prohibits transhipment, if the goods have been shipped in a container, trailer or LASH barge as evidenced by the non-negotiable sea waybill.

d. Clauses in a non-negotiable sea waybill stating that the carrier reserves the right to tranship will be disregarded.

UCP 600 - Clause 22
Charter Party Bill of Lading

a. A bill of lading, however named, containing an indication that it is subject to a charter party (charter party bill of lading), must appear to:

i. be signed by:

- the master or a named agent for or on behalf of the master, or

- the owner or a named agent for or on behalf of the owner, or

- the charterer or a named agent for or on behalf of the charterer.

Any signature by the master, owner, charterer or agent must be identified as that of the master, owner, charterer or agent.

Any signature by an agent must indicate whether the agent has signed for or on behalf of the master, owner or charterer.

An agent signing for or on behalf of the owner or charterer must indicate the name of the owner or charterer.

ii. indicate that the goods have been shipped on board a named vessel at the port of loading stated in the credit by:

- pre-printed wording, or

- an on-board notation indicating the date on which the goods have been shipped on board.

The date of issuance of the charter party bill of lading will be deemed to be the date of shipment unless the charter party bill of lading contains an on-board notation indicating the date of shipment, in which case the date stated in the on board notation will be deemed to be the date of shipment.

iii. indicate shipment from the port of loading to the port of discharge stated in the credit. The port of discharge may also be shown as a range of ports or a geographical area, as stated in the credit.

iv. be the sole original charter party bill of lading or, if issued in more than one original, be the full set as indicated on the charter party bill of lading.

b. A bank will not examine charter party contracts, even if they are required to be presented by the terms of the credit.

UCP 600 - Clause 23
Air Transport Document

a. An air transport document, however named, must appear to:

i. indicate the name of the carrier and be signed by:

- the carrier, or

- a named agent for or on behalf of the carrier.

Any signature by the carrier or agent must be identified as that of the carrier or agent. Any signature by an agent must indicate that the agent has signed for or on behalf of the carrier.

ii. indicate that the goods have been accepted for carriage.

iii. indicate the date of issuance. This date will be deemed to be the date of shipment unless the air transport document contains a specific notation of the actual date of shipment, in which case the date stated in the notation will be deemed to be the date of shipment.

Any other information appearing on the air transport document relative to the flight number and date will not be considered in determining the date of shipment.

iv. indicate the airport of departure and the airport of destination stated in the credit.

v. be the original for consignor or shipper, even if the credit stipulates a full set of originals.

vi. contain terms and conditions of carriage or make reference to another source containing the terms and conditions of carriage. Contents of terms and conditions of carriage will not be examined.

b. For the purpose of this clause, transhipment means unloading from one aircraft and reloading to another aircraft during the carriage from the airport of departure to the airport of destination stated in the credit.

c.

i. An air transport document may indicate that the goods will or may be transhipped, provided that the entire carriage is covered by one and the same air transport document.

ii. An air transport document indicating that transhipment will or may take place is acceptable, even if the credit prohibits transhipment.

UCP 600 - Clause 24
Road, Rail or Inland Waterway Transport Documents

a. A road, rail or inland waterway transport document, however named, must appear to:

i. indicate the name of the carrier and:

- be signed by the carrier or a named agent for or on behalf of the carrier, or

- indicate receipt of the goods by signature, stamp or notation by the carrier or a named agent for or on behalf of the carrier.

Any signature, stamp or notation of receipt of the goods by the carrier or agent must be identified as that of the carrier or agent.

Any signature, stamp or notation of receipt of the goods by the agent must indicate that the agent has signed or acted for or on behalf of the carrier.

If a rail transport document does not identify the carrier, any signature or stamp of the railway company will be accepted as evidence of the document being signed by the carrier.

ii. indicate the date of shipment or the date the goods have been received for shipment, dispatch or carriage at the place stated in the credit. Unless the transport document contains a dated reception stamp, an indication of the date of receipt or a date of shipment, the date of issuance of the transport document will be deemed to be the date of shipment.

iii. indicate the place of shipment and the place of destination stated in the credit.

b.

i. A road transport document must appear to be the original for consignor or shipper or bear no marking indicating for whom the document has been prepared.

ii. A rail transport document marked "duplicate" will be accepted as an original.

iii. A rail or inland waterway transport document will be accepted as an original whether marked as an original or not.

c. In the absence of an indication on the transport document as to the number of originals issued, the number presented will be deemed to constitute a full set.

d. For the purpose of this clause, transhipment means unloading from one means of conveyance and reloading to another means of conveyance, within the same mode of transport, during the carriage from the place of shipment, dispatch or carriage to the place of destination stated in the credit.

e.

i. A road, rail or inland waterway transport document may indicate that the goods will or may be transhipped provided that the entire carriage is covered by one and the same transport document.

ii. A road, rail or inland waterway transport document indicating that transhipment will or may take place is acceptable, even if the credit prohibits transhipment.

UCP 600 - Clause 25
Courier Receipt, Post Receipt or Certificate of Posting

a. A courier receipt, however named, evidencing receipt of goods for transport, must appear to:

i. indicates the name of the courier service and be stamped or signed by the named courier service at the place from which the credit states the goods are to be shipped; and

ii. indicate a date of pick-up or of receipt or wording to this effect. This date will be deemed to be the date of shipment.

b. A requirement that courier charges are to be paid or prepaid may be satisfied by a transport document issued by a courier service evidencing that courier charges are for the account of a party other than the consignee.

c. A post receipt or certificate of posting, however named, evidencing receipt of goods for transport, must appear to be stamped or signed and dated at the place from which the credit states the goods are to be shipped. This date will be deemed to be the date of shipment.

UCP 600 - Clause 26
"On Deck", "Shipper's Load and Count", "Said by Shipper to Contain" and Charges Additional to Freight

a. A transport document must not indicate that the goods are or will be loaded on deck. A clause on a transport document stating that the goods may be loaded on deck is acceptable.

b. A transport document bearing a clause such as "shipper's load and count" and "said by shipper to contain" is acceptable.

c. A transport document may bear a reference, by stamp or otherwise, to charges additional to the freight.

UCP 600 - Clause 27
Clean Transport Document

A bank will only accept a clean transport document. A clean transport document is one bearing no clause or notation expressly declaring a defective condition of the goods or their packaging. The word "clean" need not appear on a transport document, even if a credit has a requirement for that transport document to be "clean on board".

UCP 600 - Clause 28
Insurance Document and Coverage

a. An insurance document, such as an insurance policy, an insurance certificate or a declaration under an open cover, must appear to be issued and signed by an insurance company, an underwriter or their agents or their proxies.

Any signature by an agent or proxy must indicate whether the agent or proxy has signed for or on behalf of the insurance company or underwriter.

b. When the insurance document indicates that it has been issued in more than one original, all originals must be presented.

c. Cover notes will not be accepted.

d. An insurance policy is acceptable in lieu of an insurance certificate or a declaration under an open cover.

e. The date of the insurance document must be no later than the date of shipment, unless it appears from the insurance document that the cover is effective from a date not later than the date of shipment.

f.

i. The insurance document must indicate the amount of insurance coverage and be in the same currency as the credit.

ii. A requirement in the credit for insurance coverage to be for a percentage of the value of the goods, of the invoice value or similar is deemed to be the minimum amount of coverage required.

If there is no indication in the credit of the insurance coverage required, the amount of insurance coverage must be at least 110% of the CIF or CIP value of the goods.

When the CIF or CIP value cannot be determined from the documents, the amount of insurance coverage must be calculated on the basis of the amount for which honour or negotiation is requested or the gross value of the goods as shown on the invoice, whichever is greater.

iii. The insurance document must indicate that risks are covered at least between the place of taking in charge or shipment and the place of discharge or final destination as stated in the credit.

g. A credit should state the type of insurance required and, if any, the additional risks to be covered. An insurance document will be accepted without regard to any risks that are not covered if the credit uses imprecise terms such as "usual risks" or "customary risks".

h. When a credit requires insurance against "all risks" and an insurance document is presented containing any "all risks" notation or clause, whether or not bearing the heading "all risks", the insurance document will be accepted without regard to any risks stated to be excluded.

i. An insurance document may contain reference to any exclusion clause.

j. An insurance document may indicate that the cover is subject to a franchise or excess (deductible).

UCP 600 - Clause 29
Extension of Expiry Date or Last Day of Presentation

a. If the expiry date of a credit or the last day for presentation falls on a day when the bank to which presentation is to be made is closed for reasons other than those referred to in clause 36, the expiry date or the last day for presentation, as the case may be, will be extended to the first following banking day.

b. If presentation is made on the first following banking day, a nominated bank must provide the issuing bank or confirming bank with a statement on its covering schedule that the presentation was made within the time limits extended in accordance with sub-clause 29 (a).

c. The latest date for shipment will not be extended as a result of sub-clause 29 (a).

UCP 600 - Clause 30
Tolerance in Credit Amount, Quantity and Unit Prices

a. The words "about" or "approximately" used in connection with the amount of the credit or the quantity or the unit price stated in the credit are to be construed as allowing a tolerance not to exceed 10% more or 10% less than the amount, the quantity or the unit price to which they refer.

b. A tolerance not to exceed 5% more or 5% less than the quantity of the goods is allowed, provided the credit does not state the quantity in terms of a stipulated number of packing units or individual items and the total amount of the drawings does not exceed the amount of the credit.

c. Even when partial shipments are not allowed, a tolerance not to exceed 5% less than the amount of the credit is allowed, provided that the quantity of the goods, if stated in the credit, is shipped in full and a unit price, if stated in the credit, is not reduced or that sub-clause 30 (b) is not applicable. This tolerance does not apply when the credit stipulates a specific tolerance or uses the expressions referred to in sub-clause 30 (a).

UCP 600 - Clause 31
Partial Drawings or Shipments

a. Partial drawings or shipments are allowed.

b. A presentation consisting of more than one set of transport documents evidencing shipment commencing on the same means of conveyance and for the same journey, provided they indicate the same destination, will not be regarded as covering a partial shipment, even if they indicate different dates of shipment or different ports of loading, places of taking in charge or dispatch. If the presentation consists of more than one set of transport documents, the latest date of shipment as evidenced on any of the sets of transport documents will be regarded as the date of shipment.

A presentation consisting of one or more sets of transport documents evidencing shipment on more than one means of conveyance within the same mode of transport will be regarded as covering a partial shipment, even if the means of conveyance leave on the same day for the same destination.

c. A presentation consisting of more than one courier receipt, post receipt or certificate of posting will not be regarded as a partial shipment if the courier receipts, post receipts or certificates of posting appear to have been stamped or signed by the same courier or postal service at the same place and date and for the same destination.

UCP 600 - Clause 32
Instalment Drawings or Shipments

If a drawing or shipment by instalments within given periods is stipulated in the credit and any instalment is not drawn or shipped within the period allowed for that instalment, the credit ceases to be available for that and any subsequent instalment.

UCP 600 - Clause 33
Hours of Presentation

A bank has no obligation to accept a presentation outside of its banking hours.

UCP 600 - Clause 34
Disclaimer on Effectiveness of Documents

A bank assumes no liability or responsibility for the form, sufficiency, accuracy, genuineness, falsification or legal effect of any document, or for the general or particular conditions stipulated in a document or superimposed thereon; nor does it assume any liability or responsibility for the description, quantity, weight, quality, condition, packing, delivery, value or existence of the goods, services or other performance represented by any document, or for the good faith or acts or omissions, solvency, performance or standing of the consignor, the carrier, the forwarder, the consignee or the insurer of the goods or any other person.

UCP 600 - Clause 35
Disclaimer on Transmission and Translation

A bank assumes no liability or responsibility for the consequences arising out of delay, loss in transit, mutilation or other errors arising in the transmission of any messages or delivery of letters or documents, when such messages, letters or documents are transmitted or sent according to the requirements stated in the credit, or when the bank may have taken the initiative in the choice of the delivery service in the absence of such instructions in the credit.

If a nominated bank determines that a presentation is complying and forwards the documents to the issuing bank or confirming bank, whether or not the nominated bank has honoured or negotiated, an issuing bank or confirming bank must honour or negotiate, or reimburse that nominated bank, even when the documents have been lost in transit between the nominated bank and the issuing bank or confirming bank, or between the confirming bank and the issuing bank.

A bank assumes no liability or responsibility for errors in translation or interpretation of technical terms and may transmit credit terms without translating them.

UCP 600 - Clause 36
Force Majeure

A bank assumes no liability or responsibility for the consequences arising out of the interruption of its business by Acts of God, riots, civil commotions, insurrections, wars, acts of terrorism, or by any strikes or lockouts or any other causes beyond its control.

A bank will not, upon resumption of its business, honour or negotiate under a credit that expired during such interruption of its business.

UCP 600 - Clause 37
Disclaimer for Acts of an Instructed Party

a. A bank utilizing the services of another bank for the purpose of giving effect to the instructions of the applicant does so for the account and at the risk of the applicant.

b. An issuing bank or advising bank assumes no liability or responsibility should the instructions it transmits to another bank not be carried out, even if it has taken the initiative in the choice of that other bank.

c. A bank instructing another bank to perform services is liable for any commissions, fees, costs or expenses (“charges”) incurred by that bank in connection with its instructions.

If a credit states that charges are for the account of the beneficiary and charges cannot be collected or deducted from proceeds, the issuing bank remains liable for payment of charges.

A credit or amendment should not stipulate that the advising to a beneficiary is conditional upon the receipt by the advising bank or second advising bank of its charges.

d. The applicant shall be bound by and liable to indemnify a bank against all obligations and responsibilities imposed by foreign laws and usages.

UCP 600 - Clause 38
Transferable Credits

a. A bank is under no obligation to transfer a credit except to the extent and in the manner expressly consented to by that bank.

b. For the purpose of this clause:

Transferable credit means a credit that specifically states it is "transferable". A transferable credit may be made available in whole or in part to another beneficiary ("second beneficiary") at the request of the beneficiary ("first beneficiary").

Transferring bank means a nominated bank that transfers the credit or, in a credit available with any bank, a bank that is specifically authorized by the issuing bank to transfer and that transfers the credit. An issuing bank may be a transferring bank.

Transferred credit means a credit that has been made available by the transferring bank to a second beneficiary.

c. Unless otherwise agreed at the time of transfer, all charges (such as commissions, fees, costs or expenses) incurred in respect of a transfer must be paid by the first beneficiary.

d. A credit may be transferred in part to more than one second beneficiary provided partial drawings or shipments are allowed.

A transferred credit cannot be transferred at the request of a second beneficiary to any subsequent beneficiary. The first beneficiary is not considered to be a subsequent beneficiary.

e. Any request for transfer must indicate if and under what conditions amendments may be advised to the second beneficiary. The transferred credit must clearly indicate those conditions.

f. If a credit is transferred to more than one second beneficiary, rejection of an amendment by one or more second beneficiary does not invalidate the acceptance by any other second beneficiary, with respect to which the transferred credit will be amended accordingly. For any second beneficiary that rejected the amendment, the transferred credit will remain unamended.

g. The transferred credit must accurately reflect the terms and conditions of the credit, including confirmation, if any, with the exception of:

- the amount of the credit,

- any unit price stated therein,

- the expiry date,

- the period for presentation, or

- the latest shipment date or given period for shipment,

any or all of which may be reduced or curtailed.

The percentage for which insurance cover must be affected may be increased to provide the amount of cover stipulated in the credit or these clauses.

The name of the first beneficiary may be substituted for that of the applicant in the credit.

If the name of the applicant is specifically required by the credit to appear in any document other than the invoice, such requirement must be reflected in the transferred credit.

h. The first beneficiary has the right to substitute its own invoice and draft, if any, for those of a second beneficiary for an amount not in excess of that stipulated in the credit, and upon such substitution the first beneficiary can draw under the credit for the difference, if any, between its invoice and the invoice of a second beneficiary.

i. If the first beneficiary is to present its own invoice and draft, if any, but fails to do so on first demand, or if the invoices presented by the first beneficiary create discrepancies that did not exist in the presentation made by the second beneficiary and the first beneficiary fails to correct them on first demand, the transferring bank has the right to present the documents as received from the second beneficiary to the issuing bank, without further responsibility to the first beneficiary.

j. The first beneficiary may, in its request for transfer, indicate that honour or negotiation is to be effected to a second beneficiary at the place to which the credit has been transferred, up to and including the expiry date of the credit. This is without prejudice to the right of the first beneficiary in accordance with sub-clause 38 (h).

k. Presentation of documents by or on behalf of a second beneficiary must be made to the transferring bank.

UCP 600 - Clause 39
Assignment of Proceeds

The fact that a credit is not stated to be transferable shall not affect the right of the beneficiary to assign any proceeds to which it may be or may become entitled under the credit, in accordance with the provisions of applicable law. This clause relates only to the assignment of proceeds and not to the assignment of the right to perform under the credit.

15.9 UKE EXPORT FINANCE [UKEF] [ECGD] Finance Sample Policy

Export Insurance Policy Number BG\EXIP\ [Country]\[Number]
issued by The Secretary of State acting through the Export Credits Guarantee Department (operating as UK Export Finance) ("UKEF")

SCHEDULE

Insured: [-], a company or organisation incorporated and existing under the laws of England and Wales.

Company Number: [-].

Registered Address: [-].

Insured's Address

for Communications: Post (if different from above):

Email:

Attention:

Premium: [-].

Insured Percentage: [95%]

Maximum Liability: [-] (or its equivalent in any other currency)

Buyer: [-]

Start Date: [-]

End Date: [-]

Terms of Payment: [-]

Contract: The contract between the Insured and the Buyer under which the Insured agrees to supply to the Buyer [describe goods and services to be supplied or works to be performed].

Goods: [-]

Services: [-]

Permitted Variations: [None]

Letter of Credit: [None]

Surety: [None]

Security: [None]

Loss Payee: [None]

Loss Payee Account: [None]

Proposal: The proposal dated [-] which was submitted to UKEF by the Insured in order to request UKEF to enter into this Policy.

UKEF's address for

Communications: Post: UK Export Finance 1 Horse Guards Road London

SW1A 2HQ

Email: exipunderwriting@ukexportfinance.gov.uk

Attention: Business Group

Broker:

Broker's Address:

Commission Rate:

For and on behalf of the Secretary of State acting through the

Export Credits Guarantee Department (operating as UK Export Finance)

Signature: ....

Name: ....

Position: ....

Date: ....

For and on behalf of

[-]

Signature: ....

Name: ....

Position: ....

Date: ....

CONTENTS

7 NOTIFICATION, MITIGATION AND CONSULTATION

8 SUBROGATION

9 REIMBURSEMENT OF EXPENSES

10 ALLOCATION OF RECOVERIES

11 ANTI-CORRUPTION PROVISIONS

12 SET-OFF

13 RECORDS

14 GENERAL

15 NOTICES

16 THIRD PARTY RIGHTS

17 GOVERNING LAW AND JURISDICTION

EXPORT INSURANCE POLICY No. BG\EXIP\ [Country]\[Number] issued by The Secretary of State acting through the Export Credits Guarantee Department (operating as UK Export Finance) ("UKEF").

IT IS AGREED as follows: -

1 **DEFINITIONS AND INTERPRETATION**

1.1 In this Policy:

"Arbitration Award" means an award against the Buyer pursuant to an agreement for arbitration contained or incorporated in the Contract;

"Business Day" means any day other than a Saturday, Sunday or public holiday in England and Wales;

"Buyer" means the party specified as such in the Schedule; "Clause" means a clause of this Policy;

"Communication" means each claim, notice or other communication which may be served or made pursuant to this Policy;

"Contract" means the contract between the Insured and the Buyer specified in the Schedule;

"Contract Suite" means the Contract itself and all agreements, financial instruments (including, without limitation, any letter of credit or bill of exchange), undertakings, consents, authorisations or other documents relating to the Contract or issued in connection with any payments made or to be made under it;

"Due Date" means the date on which the Buyer is required to make payment to the Insured pursuant to the Contract;

"Endorsement" means a written amendment to this Policy in the format prescribed by UKEF;

"End Date" means the date specified as such in the Schedule or such later date as UKEF may from time to time notify to the Insured;

"Goods" means goods which the Insured has agreed to supply to the Buyer under the Contract;

"Insured" means the company or organisation specified in the Schedule; "Insured Percentage" means the percentage described as such in the Schedule;

"Interest" means any sum paid or payable to the Insured in respect of interest pursuant to the Contract, any Security, any Judgment or any Arbitration Award or otherwise in connection with the Contract;

"Judgment" means a final and non-appealable judgment of a court specified in the Contract as having exclusive jurisdiction to determine a claim for payment of a

Sum Due or breach of the Contract by the Buyer or any other court which may be approved for this purpose in writing by UKEF;

"Letter of Credit" means such irrevocable and unconditional letter of credit required for the purpose of making any payments under the Contract or as is described in the Schedule;

"Loss Payee" means any person described as such in the Schedule;

"Loss Payee Account" means the bank account specified as such in the Schedule;

"Maximum Liability" means the amount specified as such in the Schedule;

"Other Contract" means any contract between the Insured and the Buyer other than the Contract;

"Permitted Variation" means any variation specified as such in the Schedule; "Premium" bears the meaning attributed to it in the Schedule;

"Proposal" means the proposal referred to in the Schedule together with any further information received by UKEF from the Insured before entering into this Policy;

"Purchase Price" means the full amount payable by the Buyer pursuant to the Contract excluding any value added tax;

"Recovery" and "Recoveries" means any sum recovered from any source which mitigates the loss sustained by the Insured and any Interest;

"Relevant Event" means any act, omission, event or circumstance which indicates that the Buyer may not pay, or may be unable to pay, any Sum Due;

"Relevant Rights" means (in relation to a loss sustained by the Insured that has led to any payment by UKEF under this Policy) all rights, remedies, claims, guarantees and securities available to the Insured to mitigate such loss, including any rights against a guarantor or a surety;

"Schedule" means the schedule to this Policy;

"Security" means such security (if any) for the Contract as is referred to in the Schedule;

"Services" means services which the Insured has agreed to supply to the Buyer under the Contract;

"Start Date" means the latest date of signature of this Policy or the date on which UKEF receives the premium in full, whichever is the later;

"Sum Due" means an amount which has become payable by the terms of the Contract in respect of the supply of any of the Goods and/or Services (exclusive of any Interest) or which would have become payable but for the effect of any moratorium or prohibition on payment;

"Surety" means any party described as such in the Schedule;

"Terms of Payment" means the terms extended by the Insured to the Buyer for payment as specified in the Schedule; and

"United Kingdom" means the United Kingdom of Great Britain and Northern Ireland together with the Channel Islands and the Isle of Man.

1.2 The headings in this Policy are solely for reference and shall not in any way affect the meaning or interpretation of this Policy.

2 **COVER**

2.1 If the Insured sustains a loss as a result of:

(a) the failure of the Buyer to pay any Sum Due for a period of [six] months after the Due Date; or

(b) any act or omission of the Buyer in breach of any other obligation under the Contract which terminates, or results in the termination of, the Insured's obligation to supply any Goods and/or Services; or

(c) any:

(i) act, decision or legislative or administrative measure of the government or courts of any country (including the non-renewal or cancellation of an export or import licence but excluding a refusal or failure to grant a United Kingdom export licence or other United Kingdom authorisation required as at the date of the Contract for its performance); or

(ii) war, civil war, revolution, or insurrection

which, in either case, renders illegal or impossible the performance of any obligation under the Contract,

UKEF will, subject to Clause 2.3 and 2.4 and the other provisions of this Policy, pay to the Insured the Insured Percentage of the amount determined in accordance with Clause 3.

2.2 The period of [six] months in Clause 2.1(a) shall be reduced so as to expire on the date of any intervening court order falling within Clause 2.1(c), or the provision of evidence satisfactory to UKEF of the insolvency of the Buyer, which prevents the Buyer from paying the Sum Due.

2.3 As regards Clause 2.1(a), where a dispute exists between the Buyer and the Insured concerning or affecting the Buyer's obligation to pay the sum in question (including one involving any set-off or cross-claim), UKEF shall (unless and to the extent that it may otherwise agree in writing) have no liability unless and in so far as the Insured has obtained (at its own expense and risk) an Arbitration Award or Judgment determining that the Buyer is obliged to pay the sum and is not justified in refusing or failing to do so.

2.4 As regards Clause 2.1(b), UKEF shall (unless and to the extent that it may otherwise agree in writing) have no liability unless and in so far as the Insured has obtained (at its own expense and risk) an Arbitration Award or Judgment determining that the act or omission in question occurred and constituted a breach of an obligation under the Contract.

3 **AMOUNT OF INDEMNIFIABLE LOSS**

3.1 In respect of any loss sustained by the Insured as a direct result of any failure referred to in Clause 2.1(a) UKEF will, subject to Clause 3.6, pay the Insured Percentage of the amount of any Sum Due remaining unpaid by the Buyer, a Surety or any third person.

3.2 In respect of any loss sustained by the Insured as a direct result of any act or omission referred to in Clause 2.1(b) or any event or other matter referred to in Clause 2.1(c), UKEF will, subject to Clause 3.6, pay the Insured Percentage of:

(a) any costs which the Insured has incurred wholly and necessarily for the purpose of supplying any Goods and/or Services which, in consequence, it has not supplied, such amount not to be in excess of the amount which would have been payable by the Buyer under the Contract in respect of those Goods and/or Services, less:

(b) any advance payment paid or accrued payable which is attributable to such Goods and/or Services (other than that which the Insured returns to the Buyer under the terms of the Contract, as a result of the non-renewal or cancellation of any United Kingdom export licence or other authorisation required for the supply to the Buyer of the Goods and/or Services), and

(c) the value of any Goods and/or Services available for resale and any other benefit which the Insured may have received by not supplying such Goods and/or Services.

3.3 Upon receipt of any amount from the Buyer which is not appropriated to a specific debt the Insured will apply such amount in the following order of priority in or towards satisfaction of the following:

(a) any Sum Due which forms the subject of a claim under this Policy;

(b) any other Sum Due under the Contract;

(c) any other amount payable, but not then due, under the Contract;

and the Sum Due remaining unpaid shall be calculated on the basis that such application has been made, whether or not that is the case.

3.4 Regardless of any act or legislation of any country other than the United Kingdom, any payment in a currency other than that specified by the Contract shall not be considered as payment for the purposes of this Policy unless, and to the extent that, it is accepted by the Insured.

3.5 For the avoidance of doubt, UKEF shall be under no obligation to make any payment whose purpose is or whose effect would be to reimburse or indemnify the Insured in respect of any legal costs expended on or incurred or occasioned by obtaining or attempting to obtain any Arbitration Award or Judgment referred to in Clause 2.3 or 2.4.

3.6 The aggregate amount payable by UKEF under this Policy shall in no circumstances exceed the Maximum Liability.

4 **THE CONTRACT AND PERIOD OF COVER**

4.1 Cover under this Policy takes effect on the Start Date if and only if as at that date:

(a) the Insured is unaware of the occurrence or likely occurrence of any of the causes of loss referred to in Clause 2.1 in relation to the Contract or any Other Contract;

(b) no amount which had fallen due for payment under the Contract or any Other Contract has remained unpaid for more than 30 days;

(c) none of the Goods have been dispatched and in the case of Services, no invoice has been rendered;

(d) no amount payable by the Buyer pursuant to the Contract has fallen due;

(e) none of the events or circumstances set out in Clause 2.1 has occurred in relation to any Other Contract;

(f) all necessary consents and approvals to the creation and performance of the Contract have been obtained;

(g) any Security specified in the Schedule has been established in favour of the Insured; and

(h) any Letter of Credit has been opened in favour of, and (where required by the Contract) confirmed to, the Insured.

4.2 UKEF shall have no liability under this Policy for any loss arising from any default or breach by the Buyer or any other event occurring after the End Date.

5 **CLAIMS**

5.1 Any claim under this Policy shall be made in such form as may be required by UKEF by no later than 12 months after the End Date, after which time UKEF shall have no further liability in any circumstances.

5.2 The burden of proving the occurrence of a loss insured under this Policy shall be on the Insured.

5.3 If the Insured makes a fraudulent claim under this Policy, UKEF:

(a) is not liable to pay the claim;

(b) may recover from the Insured any sums paid by UKEF to the Insured in respect of the claim; and

(c) may by notice to the Insured treat this Policy as having been terminated with effect from the time of the fraudulent act.

5.4 If UKEF exercises its right under Clause 5.3(c) above, UKEF:

(a) shall not be liable to the Insured in respect of any loss arising from any default, breach or other event occurring after the time of the fraudulent act; and

(b) need not return any of the Premium paid.

5.5 If the Schedule specifies a Loss Payee, the Insured irrevocably and unconditionally:

(a) directs UKEF to pay to the Loss Payee Account each amount which may from time to time be payable by UKEF to the Insured pursuant to this Policy; and

(b) agrees that payment of any such amount by UKEF to the Loss Payee Account shall discharge UKEF from its obligation under this Policy to pay that amount.

6 **CONDITIONS OF COVER**

6.1 Unless and to the extent that UKEF otherwise expressly agrees in writing, if, at any stage, the Insured:

(a) departs from the terms of the Contract or agrees to or acquiesces in any variation of them or any departure from them by the Buyer in relation to

(i) the identity of the buyer, (ii) the Buyer's country, (iii) the destination of the goods, (iv) the Terms of Payment, (v) the Purchase Price, (vi) a reduction in the proportion of UK content to below 20%, or (vii) the identity of any agent, unless that variation or departure would be a Permitted Variation;

(b) materially departs from the terms of the Contract or agrees to or acquiesces in any variation of them or any departure from them by the Buyer in relation to the nature of the Goods and/or Services;

(c) assigns, mortgages, charges, pledges or otherwise disposes of this Policy or any rights arising under it or the benefit of it;

(d) uses the name of Her Majesty's Government or UKEF or the insurance provided under this Policy directly in connection with the raising of funds from the capital markets (which expression shall not include the Insured's own treasury department); or

(e) fails promptly to provide UKEF with any information, in writing, that UKEF may request from time to time regarding the progress and performance of the Contract,

then UKEF shall have no liability under this Policy.

6.2 If, at any stage, without UKEF's express approval in writing, the Insured:

(a) materially departs from the terms of the Contract or agrees to or acquiesces in any material variation of them or any material departure from them by the Buyer in a way that falls outside Clause 6.1(a) or 6.1(b) above, unless that variation or departure would be a Permitted Variation;

(b) materially fails to comply with the terms of any component of the Contract Suite (to include a failure to make a compliant presentation of documents under any Letter of Credit);

(c) waives or releases, or fails to take all necessary actions to preserve the legal enforceability of, its rights under any component of the Contract Suite;

(d) fails to take all necessary actions to preserve the legal enforceability of any security for the performance of the Buyer's obligations, or does something which prejudices its rights against any surety for payment; or

(e) assigns, mortgages, charges or pledges or otherwise disposes of all or part of the Contract Suite or any of its rights or interests thereunder, including its right to recover in respect of loss,

then UKEF shall not be liable under this Policy in respect of a loss unless the Insured can show that the act or omission in question could not have increased the risk of that loss taking place.

7 NOTIFICATION, MITIGATION AND CONSULTATION

7.1 This Clause 7 applies if the Insured becomes aware of a Relevant Event or the Buyer fails to pay any Sum Due under the Contract.

7.2 The Insured shall notify UKEF of any Relevant Event within 15 days of becoming aware of it, and (at the same time or as soon as is practicable thereafter) provide all available information relating to that Relevant Event in writing to UKEF.

7.3 The Insured shall notify UKEF immediately if the Buyer has failed to pay any part of the Sum Due under the Contract 30 days after its Due Date.

7.4 The Insured shall:

(a) promptly take all practicable steps to prevent or minimise any loss covered by this Policy (and preserve its rights to take such steps in the future) including (i) enforcing security for the performance of the Buyer's obligations and (ii) any steps which may be required by UKEF; and

(b) not enter into any compromise of any relevant claim against any person without the written consent of UKEF.

7.5 If the Insured fails to comply with any of Clauses 7.2-7.4 above then UKEF shall have no liability under this Policy in respect of a loss unless the Insured can show that such failure to comply could not have increased the risk of that loss taking place.

7.6 The Insured shall upon request assign to UKEF such rights as it has under the Contract, and to any Goods and/or Services and any documents and securities relating to the Contract. If the Insured fails to do so then UKEF shall have no liability under this Policy.

8 **SUBROGATION**

8.1 Upon payment of any amount due to the Insured under this Policy, UKEF is subrogated to all Relevant Rights, whether or not the exercise of such rights might, in addition, involve claims, rights or remedies concerning obligations other than those whose non-performance has created a loss under this Policy. These rights of subrogation shall be in addition and without prejudice to all rights and benefits to which UKEF is entitled under the general law of subrogation.

8.2 At all times after payment of any amount due to the Insured under this Policy, the Insured shall:

(a) execute and deliver all instruments and papers and do whatever else is necessary to enable UKEF to exercise the Relevant Rights;

(b) exercise or enforce or refrain from exercising or enforcing all Relevant Rights solely in accordance with the directions of UKEF and take all steps for this purpose as UKEF may require;

(c) on request assign and transfer all Relevant Rights to UKEF, and execute and deliver to UKEF all such documents as UKEF may require for this purpose; and

(d) authorise and permit UKEF, in the name of the Insured, to settle or compromise any claim which the Insured may have against the Buyer, the Surety or any other party in connection with the Contract or institute and conduct legal or arbitral proceedings in respect of any such claim.

9 **REIMBURSEMENT OF EXPENSES**

9.1 UKEF shall reimburse the Insured Percentage of all expenses agreed in writing in advance by UKEF which the Insured reasonably incurs when taking steps required by UKEF pursuant to Clause 8.2(b).

9.2 Save as expressly provided in Clause 9.1, UKEF shall have no liability to reimburse the Insured in respect of any expenditure which the Insured may incur.

9.3 UKEF may at its discretion reimburse up to the Insured Percentage of any expenses not agreed in advance by UKEF that the Insured incurred in acting to minimise any loss.

10 **ALLOCATION OF RECOVERIES**

10.1 If at any time the Insured receives a Recovery, it shall hold that Recovery on trust for UKEF and, as soon as practicable after receiving that Recovery, notify UKEF of that receipt and pay that Recovery to UKEF.

10.2 UKEF shall retain the Insured Percentage of each Recovery received by it and shall pay the remainder to the Insured.

11 **ANTI-CORRUPTION PROVISIONS**

11.1 In this Clause 11 the following terms have the following meanings in relation to the Contract:

"Consortium Party" means any company, person or other legal entity (other than the Insured) which is a party to any written joint venture, consortium or other similar arrangement (other than a sub-contract) to which the Insured is also a party and which joint venture, consortium or other arrangement has been, or will be, entered into in connection with the performance of the Contract;

"Corrupt Activity" means any bribery or corrupt activity (including without limitation the offering of payment, reward or other advantage to any public official or other person), that:

1) constitutes an offence under the Prevention of Corruption Acts 1889 to 1916 or the Bribery Act 2010 (as from time to time amended or re- enacted) or any offence relating to bribery or corruption under the law of any jurisdiction outside the United Kingdom; or

2) renders the Contract or any Related Agreement illegal, void, voidable or unenforceable under its governing law; and

"Related Agreement" means:

1) any agreement or undertaking, other than any agreement or undertaking for the supply of Goods and/or Services to the Insured or any Consortium Party, which relates to the Contract and to which the Insured or any Consortium Party is a party; and/or

2) any consent or authorisation, required by the Insured or any Consortium Party for the obtaining or performance of the Contract and of which the Insured or any Consortium Party is the direct recipient or beneficiary.

11.2 The Insured represents and warrants that it has not:

a) engaged in, authorised or consented to any Corrupt Activity in

relation to the Contract or any Related Agreement;

b) failed to report to the relevant authorities any Corrupt Activity in relation to the Contract or any Related Agreement of which it has become aware.

11.3 The Insured warrants and undertakes that:

a) it will not:

i) engage in, authorise or consent to any Corrupt Activity in relation to the Contract or any Related Agreement; or

ii) fail to report to the relevant authorities any such Corrupt Activity in relation to the Contract or any Related Agreement of which it becomes aware;

b) if the Insured becomes aware that any person (including any Consortium Party or any of its employees) has engaged in any Corrupt Activity in relation to the Contract or any Related Agreement, the Insured shall promptly notify UKEF accordingly and supply UKEF with full details of the Corrupt Activity in question save where such notification would, or might reasonably be considered to, constitute the offence of "tipping off" under s.333A of the Proceeds of Crime Act 2002; and

c) the Insured shall:

i) if it has not done so already, require every person (including any of its employees) acting on its behalf and involved in obtaining or in performing the Contract or any Related Agreement not to engage in any Corrupt Activity in relation to the Contract or any Related Agreement;

ii) monitor compliance with that requirement; and

iii) take appropriate action against anyone found to have engaged in any such Corrupt Activity.

11.4 Subject to the provisions of Clause 11.5, if at any time, whether during or after the term of this Policy, the Insured:

a) is found by a court of competent jurisdiction (after all available rights of appeal have been exhausted or expired) to have engaged in, authorised or consented to Corrupt Activity;

b) admits to having engaged in, authorised or consented to any such Corrupt Activity other than where that admission is made under duress;

c) fails to report to the relevant authorities any Corrupt Activity of which it becomes aware; or

d) becomes subject to any administrative sanction (for example, a deferred prosecution agreement or civil forfeiture order) or any other administrative measure in the United Kingdom for contravening any laws of the United Kingdom which prohibit bribery, including bribery of foreign public officials, in relation to the Contract or any Related Agreement,

then UKEF shall be discharged from any liability under this Policy and may cancel this Policy with effect from its commencement and in either event (i) UKEF shall be entitled to retain all premium which it may have received and

(ii) the Insured shall on demand repay to UKEF all sums which UKEF may have paid to the Insured under this Policy.

11.5 Clause 11.4 shall not apply, and none of the matters represented and warranted in Clause 11.2 shall be deemed to be untrue or incorrect, or any of the undertakings and warranties on the part of the Insured in Clause 11.3 deemed breached, if the Corrupt Activity concerned has occurred solely by virtue of changes to any laws or regulations of any jurisdiction other than the United Kingdom that have retrospective effect.

12 **SET-OFF**

12.1 UKEF may at its option set off any amounts due to or from the Insured under this Policy or any other contracts.

13 **RECORDS**

13.1 In this Clause 13 the following terms have the following meanings:

"Administration Records" means any records (other than those covered by legal privilege) preserved in any medium or form (and including records stored electronically) which relate to the performance of the Contract;

"Confidential Information" means (1) the Records, (2) the contents of the Records and (3) all written or oral explanations provided in respect of the Records pursuant to Clause 13.2 (c);

"Contract Records" means records, for the period up to the date of award of the Contract, preserved in any medium or form (including records stored electronically) which relate specifically to the Insured's obtaining of the Contract or the employment of, and payments to, or for the benefit of, any agent;

"Information Legislation" means the Freedom of Information Act 2000 and the Environmental Information Regulations 2004 as, in each case, amended or re-enacted from time to time and any other legislation from time to time governing the disclosure of information held by public bodies in response to requests from individuals or organisations; and

"Records" means the Administration Records and the Contract Records.

13.2 The Insured shall:

(a) permit any person authorised by UKEF (and, if other than an official of UKEF, approved by the Insured, such approval not to be unreasonably

withheld or delayed by the Insured) to visit, during business hours, any of the Insured's premises in the United Kingdom where Records are kept for the sole purpose of inspecting, auditing and taking copies of any Administration Records provided that UKEF gives to the Insured at least five Business Days' notice of that visit;

(b) permit any person authorised by UKEF (and, if other than an official of UKEF, approved by the Insured, such approval not to be unreasonably withheld or delayed) to visit, during business hours, any of the Insured's premises in the United Kingdom where Contract Records are kept in order to inspect any Contract Records to the extent necessary to verify the accuracy of any statements made, and any information given, by the Insured provided that UKEF gives to the Insured at least five Business Days' notice of that visit; and

(c) in relation to sub-Clauses 13.2 (a) and 13.2 (b), furnish such oral or written explanation within its knowledge of any Records as UKEF's authorised representative (or, as the case may be, UKEF's personnel) may reasonably require and permit them to take any copies of any of the Records which they may reasonably require upon condition that UKEF will, on request, pay to the Insured the cost of supplying any copies of the Records.

13.3 Any Confidential Information acquired by UKEF pursuant to Clause 13.2 will be held by UKEF in confidence on the terms set out in section 13 of the Proposal.

13.4 Wherever practicable, UKEF will give notice to the Insured of any application made under the Information Legislation for the disclosure of Confidential Information. Nothing in this Clause shall imply that the Insured considers any Confidential Information to be disclosable under the Information Legislation.

13.5 To the extent permitted by its obligations at law and its responsibilities as a government department, UKEF will destroy Confidential Information, or, if so requested, return it to the Insured, when UKEF considers that it has served the purpose for which it was obtained.

13.6 Nothing in this Clause 13 obliges the Insured or UKEF to act unlawfully or in breach of any requirement of any regulatory or investigatory body or in breach of any duty of confidence.

13.7 The Insured shall not unreasonably delay or withhold its consent to the disclosure by UKEF of any information which is otherwise confidential by virtue of the provisions of the Proposal.

14 **GENERAL**

14.1 Any amendment to this Policy is valid only if evidenced by an Endorsement.

14.2 This Policy (including the Schedules and any Endorsement agreed from time to time) is the entire agreement between the Insured and UKEF.

14.3 UKEF is deemed not to have excused, waived or accepted any failure by the Insured to comply with any term of this Policy unless it has expressly recorded this in writing.

15 **NOTICES**

15.1 Each Communication:

(a) shall be in writing;

(b) may be given in person, by post or by e-mail;

(c) shall be sent to its intended recipient at its address for Communications as given in the Schedule (or to such other address as the intended recipient shall have most recently notified to the sender as being the intended recipient's address for Communications); and

(d) shall be marked for the attention of such employee or department of the intended recipient as is specified in the Schedule (or such other person or department as the intended recipient shall have most recently notified to the sender as being that to which Communications should be addressed).

15.2 Subject to Clause 15.3, any Communication will be deemed to have been received by its intended recipient:

(a) if delivered in person, at the time of delivery;

(b) if sent by first class letter post, three Business Days after being deposited in the post in a correctly addressed envelope; or

(c) if sent by email when received in a legible form.

15.3 A Communication which, pursuant to Clause 15.2, is deemed to have been received on a day which is not a Business Day or after 17:00hrs in the place of receipt will be deemed to have been received on the next Business Day in that place.

16 **THIRD PARTY RIGHTS**

For the avoidance of doubt, UKEF and the Insured do not intend that any of the terms of this Policy should be enforceable by virtue of the Contracts (Rights of Third Parties) Act 1999 by any person other than UKEF or the Insured.

17 **GOVERNING LAW AND JURISDICTION**

17.1 This Policy and any non-contractual rights and obligations arising in connection with it are governed by, and shall be construed in accordance with, the laws of England and Wales.

17.2 Save as provided in Clause 17.4, the courts of England and Wales shall have exclusive jurisdiction to hear and determine all disputes, actions, claims and proceedings of whatever nature arising out of, or in connection with, this Policy or the transaction contained in it, and for such purpose the Insured submits to the exclusive jurisdiction of, and waives any objections to proceedings being brought against it in, those courts.

17.3 All legal process relating to proceedings before the courts of England and Wales shall be sufficiently served upon the Insured if addressed to the Insured and delivered by post or by hand to its address as stated at the head of this Policy.

17.4 UKEF shall be at liberty to take proceedings against the Insured in whichever jurisdiction UKEF

15.10 Lloyds MAR Policy

Lloyd's
Marine Policy

We, The Underwriters, hereby agree, in consideration of the payment to us by or on behalf of the Assured of the premium specified in the Schedule, to insure against loss damage liability or expense in the proportions and manner hereinafter provided. Each Underwriting Member of a Syndicate whose definitive number and proportion is set out in the following Table shall be liable only for his own share of his respective Syndicate's proportion.

This insurance shall be subject to the exclusive jurisdiction of the English Courts, except as may be expressly provided herein to the contrary. In Witness whereof the General Manager of Lloyd's Policy Signing Office has subscribed his Name on behalf of each of Us.

MAR 91 LPO62A (1/11/91)

FOR CARGO INSURANCES ONLY

In the event of loss or damage which may result in a claim under this insurance, immediate notice must be given to the Lloyd's Agent at the port or place where the loss or damage is discovered in order that he may examine the goods and issue a survey report.

15.11 Marine Insurance Act 1906

Changes to legislation: *There are currently no known outstanding effects for the Marine Insurance Act 1906. (See end of Document for details)*

1906 CHAPTER 41 6 Edw 7

An Act to codify the Law relating to Marine Insurance. [21st December 1906]

Modifications etc. (not altering text)

C1 This Act is not necessarily in the form in which it has effect in Northern Ireland

C2 Act extended by S.I. 1972/971, art. 4, **Sch. 15**

Marine Insurance

1 **Marine insurance defined.**

A contract of marine insurance is a contract whereby the insurer undertakes to indemnify the assured, in manner and to the extent thereby agreed, against marine losses, that is to say, the losses incident to marine adventure.

2 **Mixed sea and land risks.**

(1) A contract of marine insurance may, by its express terms, or by usage of trade, be extended so as to protect the assured against losses on inland waters or on any land risk which may be incidental to any sea voyage.

(2) Where a ship in course of building, or the launch of a ship, or any adventure analogous to a marine adventure, is covered by a policy in the form of a marine policy, the provisions of this Act, in so far as applicable, shall apply thereto; but, except as by this section provided, nothing in this Act shall alter or affect any rule of law applicable to any contract of insurance other than a contract of marine insurance as by this Act defined.

3 **Marine adventure and maritime perils defined.**

(1) Subject to the provisions of this Act, every lawful marine adventure may be the subject of a contract of marine insurance.

  (a) In particular there is a marine adventure where any ship goods or other moveables are exposed to maritime perils. Such property is in this Act referred to as "insurable property";

  (b) The earning or acquisition of any freight, passage money, commission, profit, or other pecuniary benefit, or the security for any advances, loan, or disbursements, is endangered by the exposure of insurable property to maritime perils;

(c) Any liability to a third party may be incurred by the owner of, or other person interested in or responsible for, insurable property, by reason of maritime perils.

"Maritime perils" means the perils consequent on, or incidental to, the navigation of the sea, that is to say, perils of the seas, fire, war perils, pirates, rovers, thieves, captures, seisures, restraints, and detainments of princes and peoples, jettisons, barratry, and any other perils, either of the like kind or which may be designated by the policy.

Insurable Interest

4 Avoidance of wagering or gaming contracts.

(1) Every contract of marine insurance by way of gaming or wagering is void.
(2) A contract of marine insurance is deemed to be a gaming or wagering contract—
   (a) Where the assured has not an insurable interest as defined by this Act, and the contract is entered into with no expectation of acquiring such an interest; or
   (b) Where the policy is made "interest or no interest," or "without further proof of interest than the policy itself," or "without benefit of salvage to the insurer," or subject to any other like term:

   Provided that, where there is no possibility of salvage, a policy may be effected without benefit of salvage to the insurer.

5 Insurable interest defined.

(1) Subject to the provisions of this Act, every person has an insurable interest who is interested in a marine adventure.
(2) In particular a person is interested in a marine adventure where he stands in any legal or equitable relation to the adventure or to any insurable property at risk therein, in consequence of which he may benefit by the safety or due arrival of insurable property, or may be prejudiced by its loss, or by damage thereto, or by the detention thereof, or may incur liability in respect thereof.

6 When interest must attach.

(1) The assured must be interested in the subject-matter insured at the time of the loss though he need not be interested when the insurance is effected:

Provided that where the subject-matter is insured "lost or not lost," the assured may recover although he may not have acquired his interest until after the loss, unless at the time of effecting the contract of insurance the assured was aware of the loss, and the insurer was not.

(2) Where the assured has no interest at the time of the loss, he cannot acquire interest by any act or election after he is aware of the loss.

7 **Defeasible or contingent interest.**

(1) A defeasible interest is insurable, as also is a contingent interest.
(2) In particular, where the buyer of goods has insured them, he has an insurable interest, notwithstanding that he might, at his election, have rejected the goods, or have treated them as at the seller's risk, by reason of the latter's delay in making delivery or otherwise.

8 **Partial interest.**

A partial interest of any nature is insurable.

9 **Re-insurance.**

(1) The insurer under a contract of marine insurance has an insurable interest in his risk, and may re-insure in respect of it.
(2) Unless the policy otherwise provides, the original assured has no right or interest in respect of such re-insurance.

10 **Bottomry.**

The lender of money on bottomry or respondentia has an insurable interest in respect of the loan.

11 **Master's and seamen's wages.**

The master or any member of the crew of a ship has an insurable interest in respect of his wages.

12 **Advance freight.**

In the case of advance freight, the person advancing the freight has an insurable interest, in so far as such freight is not repayable in case of loss.

13 **Charges of insurance.**

The assured has an insurable interest in the charges of any insurance which he may effect.

14 **Quantum of interest.**

(1) Where the subject-matter insured is mortgaged, the mortgagor has an insurable interest in the full value thereof, and the mortgagee has an insurable interest in respect of any sum due or to become due under the mortgage.

(2) A mortgagee, consignee, or other person having an interest in the subject-matter insured may insure on behalf and for the benefit of other persons interested as well as for his own benefit.
(3) The owner of insurable property has an insurable interest in respect of the full value thereof, notwithstanding that some third person may have agreed, or be liable, to indemnify him in case of loss.

15 **Assignment of interest.**

Where the assured assigns or otherwise parts with his interest in the subject-matter insured, he does not thereby transfer to the assignee his rights under the contract of insurance, unless there be an express or implied agreement with the assignee to that effect.

But the provisions of this section do not affect a transmission of interest by operation of law.

INSURABLE VALUE

16 **Measure of insurable value.**

Subject to any express provision or valuation in the policy, the insurable value of the subject-matter insured must be ascertained as follows: —

(1) In insurance on ship, the insurable value is the value, at the commencement of the risk, of the ship, including her outfit, provisions and stores for the officers and crew, money advanced for seamen's wages, and other disbursements (if any) incurred to make the ship fit for the voyage or adventure contemplated by the policy, plus the charges of insurance upon the whole: The insurable value, in the case of a steamship, includes also the machinery, boilers, and coals and engine stores if owned by the assured, and, in the case of a ship engaged in a special trade, the ordinary fittings requisite for that trade:
(2) In insurance on freight, whether paid in advance or otherwise, the insurable value is the gross amount of the freight at the risk of the assured, plus the charges of insurance:
(3) In insurance on goods or merchandise, the insurable value is the prime cost of the property insured, plus the expenses of and incidental to shipping and the charges of insurance upon the whole:

(4) In insurance on any other subject-matter, the insurable value is the amount at the risk of the assured when the policy attaches, plus the charges of insurance.

Disclosure and Representations
17 **Insurance is uberrimæ fidei.**

A contract of marine insurance is a contract based upon the utmost good faith[F1]....

Textual Amendments
F1 Words in s. 17 omitted (12.8.2016) by virtue of Insurance Act 2015 (c. 4), **ss. 14(3)(a)**, 23(2) (with ss. 14(3)(b), 22(1))

[F2]18 **Disclosure by assured.**

Modifications etc. (not altering text)
C3 S. 17 modified (6.4.2013) by Consumer Insurance (Disclosure and Representations) Act 2012 (c. 6), **ss. 2(5)(b)**, 12(2) (with s. 12(4)(5)); S.I. 2013/450, art. 2

Textual Amendments
F2 S. 18 omitted (12.8.2016) by virtue of Insurance Act 2015 (c. 4), **ss. 21(2)**, 23(2) (with ss. 21(3), 22(1))

[F3]19 **Disclosure by agent effecting insurance.**
[F4]20 **Representations pending negotiation of contract.**

Textual Amendments
F3 S. 19 omitted (12.8.2016) by virtue of Insurance Act 2015 (c. 4), **ss. 21(2)**, 23(2) (with ss. 21(3), 22(1))

Textual Amendments
F4 S. 20 omitted (12.8.2016) by virtue of Insurance Act 2015 (c. 4), **ss. 21(2)**, 23(2) (with ss. 21(3), 22(1))

Textual Amendments
F5 Words repealed as to instruments made or executed after 1.8.1959 by Finance Act 1959 (c. 58), **Sch. 8 Pt. II**

21 When contract is deemed to be concluded.

A contract of marine insurance is deemed to be concluded when the proposal of the assured is accepted by the insurer, whether the policy be then issued or not; and, for the purpose of showing when the proposal was accepted, reference may be made to the slip or covering note or other customary memorandum of the contract . . . **F5**

The Policy

22 **Contract must be embodied in policy.**

Subject to the provisions of any statute, a contract of marine insurance is inadmissible in evidence unless it is embodied in a marine policy in accordance with this Act. The policy may be executed and issued either at the time when the contract is concluded, or afterwards.

Modifications etc. (not altering text)

C4 S. 22 excluded by Marine and Aviation Insurance (War Risks) Act 1952 (c. 57), **s. 7(1)** and Finance Act 1959 (c. 58), **s. 30(6)(7)**

23 What policy must specify.

A marine policy must specify—

(1) The name of the assured, or of some person who effects the insurance on his behalf:

(2) **F6**

Textual Amendments

F6 S. 23(2)–(5) repealed as to instruments made or executed after 1.8.1959 by Finance Act 1959 (c. 58), **Sch. 8 Pt. II**

24 Signature of insurer.

(1) A marine policy must be signed by or on behalf of the insurer, provided that in the case of a corporation the corporate seal may be sufficient, but nothing in this section shall be construed as requiring the subscription of a corporation to be under seal.

(2) Where a policy is subscribed by or on behalf of two or more insurers, each subscription, unless the contrary be expressed, constitutes a distinct contract with the assured.

25 **Voyage and time policies.**

(1) Where the contract is to insure the subject-matter "at and from," or from one place to another or others, the policy is called a "voyage policy," and where the contract is to insure the subject-matter for a definite period of time the policy is called a "time policy." A contract for both voyage and time may be included in the same policy.
(2) F7

Textual Amendments
F7 S. 25(2) repealed as to instruments made or executed after 1.8.1959 by Finance Act 1959 (c. 58), **Sch. 8 Pt. II**

26 Designation of subject-matter.

(1) The subject-matter insured must be designated in a marine policy with reasonable certainty.
(2) The nature and extent of the interest of the assured in the subject-matter insured need not be specified in the policy.
(3) Where the policy designates the subject-matter insured in general terms, it shall be construed to apply to the interest intended by the assured to be covered.
(4) In the application of this section regard shall be had to any usage regulating the designation of the subject-matter insured.

27 **Valued policy.**

(1) A policy may be either valued or unvalued.
(2) A valued policy is a policy which specifies the agreed value of the subject-matter insured.
(3) Subject to the provisions of this Act, and in the absence of fraud, the value fixed by the policy is, as between the insurer and assured, conclusive of the insurable value of the subject intended to be insured, whether the loss be total or partial.
(4) Unless the policy otherwise provides, the value fixed by the policy is not conclusive for the purpose of determining whether there has been a constructive total loss.

28 **Unvalued policy.**

An unvalued policy is a policy which does not specify the value of the subject-matter insured, but, subject to the limit of the sum insured, leaves the insurable value to be subsequently ascertained, in the manner herein-before specified.

29 **Floating policy by ship or ships.**

(1) A floating policy is a policy which describes the insurance in general terms, and leaves the name of the ship or ships and other particulars to be defined by subsequent declaration.

(2) The subsequent declaration or declarations may be made by indorsement on the policy, or in other customary manner.
(3) Unless the policy otherwise provides, the declarations must be made in the order of dispatch or shipment. They must, in the case of goods, comprise all consignments within the terms of the policy, and the value of the goods or other property must be honestly stated, but an omission or erroneous declaration may be rectified even after loss or arrival, provided the omission or declaration was made in good faith.
(4) Unless the policy otherwise provides, where a declaration of value is not made until after notice of loss or arrival, the policy must be treated as an unvalued policy as regards the subject-matter of that declaration.

30 **Construction of terms in policy.**

(1) A policy may be in the form in the First Schedule to this Act.
(2) Subject to the provisions of this Act, and unless the context of the policy otherwise requires, the terms and expressions mentioned in the First Schedule to this Act shall be construed as having the scope and meaning in that schedule assigned to them.

31 **Premium to be arranged.**

(1) Where an insurance is effected at a premium to be arranged, and no arrangement is made, a reasonable premium is payable.
(2) Where an insurance is effected on the terms that an additional premium is to be arranged in a given event, and that event happens but no arrangement is made, then a reasonable additional premium is payable.

Double Insurance

32 **Double insurance.**

(1) Where two or more policies are effected by or on behalf of the assured on the same adventure and interest or any part thereof, and the sums insured exceed the indemnity allowed by this Act, the assured is said to be over-insured by double insurance.
(2) Where the assured is over-insured by double insurance—
    (a) The assured, unless the policy otherwise provides, may claim payment from the insurers in such order as he may think fit, provided that he is not entitled to receive any sum in excess of the indemnity allowed by this Act;
    (b) Where the policy under which the assured claims is a valued policy, the assured must give credit as against the valuation for any sum received by him under any other policy without regard to the actual value of the subject-matter insured;
    (c) Where the policy under which the assured claims is an unvalued policy he must give credit, as against the full insurable value, for any sum received by him under any other policy:

(d) Where the assured receives any sum in excess of the indemnity allowed by this Act, he is deemed to hold such sum in trust for the insurers, according to their right of contribution among themselves.

Warranties, &c.

33 **Nature of warranty.**

(1) A warranty, in the following sections relating to warranties, means a promissory warranty, that is to say, a warranty by which the assured undertakes that some particular thing shall or shall not be done, or that some condition shall be fulfilled, or whereby he affirms or negatives the existence of a particular state of facts.
(2) A warranty may be express or implied.
(3) A warranty, as above defined, is a condition which must be exactly complied with, whether it be material to the risk or not. **F8**...

F9 34 **When breach of warranty excused.**

Textual Amendments

F8 Words in s. 33(3) omitted (12.8.2016) by virtue of Insurance Act 2015 (c. 4), **ss. 10(7)(a)**, 23(2) (with s. 22(2))

Textual Amendments

F9 S. 34 omitted (12.8.2016) by virtue of Insurance Act 2015 (c. 4), **ss. 10(7)(b)**, 23(2) (with s. 22(2))

35 Express warranties.

(1) An express warranty may be in any form of words from which the intention to warrant is to be inferred.
(2) An express warranty must be included in, or written upon, the policy, or must be contained in some document incorporated by reference into the policy.
(3) An express warranty does not exclude an implied warranty, unless it be inconsistent therewith.

36 **Warranty of neutrality.**

(1) Where insurable property, whether ship or goods, is expressly warranted neutral, there is an implied condition that the property shall have a neutral character at the commencement of the risk, and that, so far as the assured can control the matter, its neutral character shall be preserved during the risk.
(2) Where a ship is expressly warranted "neutral" there is also an implied condition that, so far as the assured can control the matter, she shall be properly documented, that is to say, that she shall carry the necessary papers to establish her neutrality, and that she shall not falsify or suppress her papers, or use simulated papers. If any loss occurs through breach of this condition, the insurer may avoid the contract.

37 **No implied warranty of nationality.**

There is no implied warranty as to the nationality of a ship, or that her nationality shall not be changed during the risk.

38 **Warranty of good safety.**

Where the subject-matter insured is warranted "well" or "in good safety" on a particular day, it is sufficient if it be safe at any time during that day.

39 **Warranty of seaworthiness of ship.**

(1) In a voyage policy there is an implied warranty that at the commencement of the voyage the ship shall be seaworthy for the purpose of the particular adventure insured.
(2) Where the policy attaches while the ship is in port, there is also an implied warranty that she shall, at the commencement of the risk, be reasonably fit to encounter the ordinary perils of the port.
(3) Where the policy relates to a voyage which is performed in different stages, during which the ship requires different kinds of or further preparation or equipment, there is an implied warranty that at the commencement of each stage the ship is seaworthy in respect of such preparation or equipment for the purposes of that stage.
(4) A ship is deemed to be seaworthy when she is reasonably fit in all respects to encounter the ordinary perils of the seas of the adventure insured.
(5) In a time policy there is no implied warranty that the ship shall be seaworthy at any stage of the adventure, but where, with the privity of the assured, the ship is sent to sea in an unseaworthy state, the insurer is not liable for any loss attributable to unseaworthiness.

40 **No implied warranty that goods are seaworthy.**

(1) In a policy on goods or other moveables there is no implied warranty that the goods or moveables are seaworthy.
(2) In a voyage policy on goods or other moveables there is an implied warranty that at the commencement of the voyage the ship is not only seaworthy as a ship, but also that she is reasonably fit to carry the goods or other moveables to the destination contemplated by the policy.

41 **Warranty of legality.**

There is an implied warranty that the adventure insured is a lawful one, and that, so far as the assured can control the matter, the adventure shall be carried out in a lawful manner.

The Voyage

42 **Implied condition as to commencement of risk.**

(1) Where the subject-matter is insured by a voyage policy "at and from" or "from" a particular place, it is not necessary that the ship should be at that place when the contract is concluded, but there is an implied condition that the adventure

shall be commenced within a reasonable time, and that if the adventure be not so commenced the insurer may avoid the contract.

(2) The implied condition may be negatived by showing that the delay was caused by circumstances known to the insurer before the contract was concluded, or by showing that he waived the condition.

43 **Alteration of port of departure.**

Where the place of departure is specified by the policy, and the ship instead of sailing from that place sails from any other place, the risk does not attach.

44 **Sailing for different destination.**

Where the destination is specified in the policy, and the ship, instead of sailing for that destination, sails for any other destination, the risk does not attach.

45 **Change of voyage.**

(1) Where, after the commencement of the risk, the destination of the ship is voluntarily changed from the destination contemplated by the policy, there is said to be a change of voyage.

(2) Unless the policy otherwise provides, where there is a change of voyage, the insurer is discharged from liability as from the time of change, that is to say, as from the time when the determination to change it is manifested; and it is immaterial that the ship may not in fact have left the course of voyage contemplated by the policy when the loss occurs.

46 **Deviation.**

(1) Where a ship, without lawful excuse, deviates from the voyage contemplated by the policy, the insurer is discharged from liability as from the time of deviation, and it is immaterial that the ship may have regained her route before any loss occurs.

(2) There is a deviation from the voyage contemplated by the policy—

  (a) Where the course of the voyage is specifically designated by the policy, and that course is departed from; or

  (b) Where the course of the voyage is not specifically designated by the policy, but the usual and customary course is departed from.

(3) The intention to deviate is immaterial; there must be a deviation in fact to discharge the insurer from his liability under the contract.

47 **Several ports of discharge.**

(1) Where several ports of discharge are specified by the policy, the ship may proceed to all or any of them, but, in the absence of any usage or sufficient cause to the contrary, she must proceed to them, or such of them as she goes to, in the order designated by the policy. If she does not there is a deviation.

(2) Where the policy is to "ports of discharge," within a given area, which are not named, the ship must, in the absence of any usage or sufficient cause to the

contrary, proceed to them, or such of them as she goes to, in their geographical order. If she does not there is a deviation.

48 **Delay in voyage.**

In the case of a voyage policy, the adventure insured must be prosecuted throughout its course with reasonable dispatch, and, if without lawful excuse it is not so prosecuted, the insurer is discharged from liability as from the time when the delay became unreasonable.

49 **Excuses for deviation or delay.**

(1) Deviation or delay in prosecuting the voyage contemplated by the policy is excused—
  (a) Where authorised by any special term in the policy; or
  (b) Where caused by circumstances beyond the control of the master and his employer; or
  (c) Where reasonably necessary in order to comply with an express or implied warranty; or
  (d) Where reasonably necessary for the safety of the ship or subject-matter insured; or
  (e) For the purpose of saving human life, or aiding a ship in distress where human life may be in danger; or
  (f) Where reasonably necessary for the purpose of obtaining medical or surgical aid for any person on board the ship; or
  (g) Where caused by the barratrous conduct of the master or crew, if barratry be one of the perils insured against.

(2) When the cause excusing the deviation or delay ceases to operate, the ship must resume her course, and prosecute her voyage, with reasonable dispatch.

Assignment of Policy

50 **When and how policy is assignable.**

(1) A marine policy is assignable unless it contains terms expressly prohibiting assignment. It may be assigned either before or after loss.

(2) Where a marine policy has been assigned so as to pass the beneficial interest in such policy, the assignee of the policy is entitled to sue thereon in his own name; and the defendant is entitled to make any defence arising out of the contract which he would have been entitled to make if the action had been brought in the name of the person by or on behalf of whom the policy was effected.

(3) A marine policy may be assigned by indorsement thereon or in other customary manner.

51 **Assured who has no interest cannot assign.**

Where the assured has parted with or lost his interest in the subject-matter insured, and has not, before or at the time of so doing, expressly or impliedly agreed to assign the policy, any subsequent assignment of the policy is inoperative:

Provided that nothing in this section affects the assignment of a policy after loss.

The Premium

52 **When premium payable.**

Unless otherwise agreed, the duty of the assured or his agent to pay the premium, and the duty of the insurer to issue the policy to the assured or his agent, are concurrent conditions, and the insurer is not bound to issue the policy until payment or tender of the premium.

53 **Policy effected through broker.**

(1) Unless otherwise agreed, where a marine policy is effected on behalf of the assured by a broker, the broker is directly responsible to the insurer for the premium, and the insurer is directly responsible to the assured for the amount which may be payable in respect of losses, or in respect of returnable premium.
(2) Unless otherwise agreed, the broker has, as against the assured, a lien upon the policy for the amount of the premium and his charges in respect of effecting the policy; and, where he has dealt with the person who employs him as a principal, he has also a lien on the policy in respect of any balance on any insurance account which may be due to him from such person, unless when the debt was incurred he had reason to believe that such person was only an agent.

54 **Effect of receipt on policy.**

Where a marine policy effected on behalf of the assured by a broker acknowledges the receipt of the premium, such acknowledgement is, in the absence of fraud, conclusive as between the insurer and the assured, but not as between the insurer and broker.

Loss and Abandonment

55 **Included and excluded losses.**

(1) Subject to the provisions of this Act, and unless the policy otherwise provides, the insurer is liable for any loss proximately caused by a peril insured against, but, subject as aforesaid, he is not liable for any loss which is not proximately caused by a peril insured against.
(2) In particular—
    (a) The insurer is not liable for any loss attributable to the wilful misconduct of the assured, but, unless the policy otherwise provides, he is liable for any loss proximately caused by a peril insured against, even though the loss

would not have happened but for the misconduct or negligence of the master or crew;

(b) Unless the policy otherwise provides, the insurer on ship or goods is not liable for any loss proximately caused by delay, although the delay be caused by a peril insured against;

(c) Unless the policy otherwise provides, the insurer is not liable for ordinary wear and tear, ordinary leakage and breakage, inherent vice or nature of the subject-matter insured, or for any loss proximately caused by rats or vermin, or for any injury to machinery not proximately caused by maritime perils.

56 **Partial and total loss.**

(1) A loss may be either total or partial. Any loss other than a total loss, as hereinafter defined, is a partial loss.
(2) A total loss may be either an actual total loss, or a constructive total loss.
(3) Unless a different intention appears from the terms of the policy, an insurance against total loss includes a constructive, as well as an actual, total loss.
(4) Where the assured brings an action for a total loss and the evidence proves only a partial loss, he may, unless the policy otherwise provides, recover for a partial loss.
(5) Where goods reach their destination in specie, but by reason of obliteration of marks, or otherwise, they are incapable of identification, the loss, if any, is partial, and not total.

57 **Actual total loss.**

(1) Where the subject-matter insured is destroyed, or so damaged as to cease to be a thing of the kind insured, or where the assured is irretrievably deprived thereof, there is an actual total loss.
(2) In the case of an actual total loss no notice of abandonment need be given.

58 **Missing ship.**

Where the ship concerned in the adventure is missing, and after the lapse of a reasonable time no news of her has been received, an actual total loss may be presumed.

59 **Effect of transhipment, &c.**

Where, by a peril insured against, the voyage is interrupted at an intermediate port or place, under such circumstances as, apart from any special stipulation in the contract of affreightment, to justify the master in landing and reshipping the goods or other moveables, or in transhipping them, and sending them on to their destination, the liability of the insurer continues, notwithstanding the landing or transhipment.

60 **Constructive total loss defined.**

(1) Subject to any express provision in the policy, there is a constructive total loss where the subject-matter insured is reasonably abandoned on account of its actual total loss appearing to be unavoidable, or because it could not be pre-

served from actual total loss without an expenditure which would exceed its value when the expenditure had been incurred.

(2) In particular, there is a constructive total loss—
   (i) Where the assured is deprived of the possession of his ship or goods by a peril insured against, and (a) it is unlikely that he can recover the ship or goods, as the case may be, or (b) the cost of recovering the ship or goods, as the case may be, would exceed their value when recovered; or
   (ii) In the case of damage to a ship, where she is so damaged by a peril insured against that the cost of repairing the damage would exceed the value of the ship when repaired.
   In estimating the cost of repairs, no deduction is to be made in respect of general average contributions to those repairs payable by other interests, but account is to be taken of the expense of future salvage operations and of any future general average contributions to which the ship would be liable if repaired; or
   (iii) In the case of damage to goods, where the cost of repairing the damage and forwarding the goods to their destination would exceed their value on arrival.

61 **Effect of constructive total loss.**

Where there is a constructive total loss the assured may either treat the loss as a partial loss, or abandon the subject-matter insured to the insurer and treat the loss as if it were an actual total loss.

62 **Notice of abandonment.**

(1) Subject to the provisions of this section, where the assured elects to abandon the subject-matter insured to the insurer, he must give notice of abandonment. If he fails to do so the loss can only be treated as a partial loss.
(2) Notice of abandonment may be given in writing, or by word of mouth, or partly in writing and partly by word of mouth, and may be given in any terms which indicate the intention of the assured to abandon his insured interest in the subject-matter insured unconditionally to the insurer.
(3) Notice of abandonment must be given with reasonable diligence after the receipt of reliable information of the loss, but where the information is of a doubtful character the assured is entitled to a reasonable time to make inquiry.
(4) Where notice of abandonment is properly given, the rights of the assured are not prejudiced by the fact that the insurer refuses to accept the abandonment.
(5) The acceptance of an abandonment may be either express or implied from the conduct of the insurer. The mere silence of the insurer after notice is not an acceptance.
(6) Where notice of abandonment is accepted the abandonment is irrevocable. The acceptance of the notice conclusively admits liability for the loss and the sufficiency of the notice.

(7) Notice of abandonment is unnecessary where, at the time when the assured receives information of the loss, there would be no possibility of benefit to the insurer if notice were given to him.
(8) Notice of abandonment may be waived by the insurer.
(9) Where an insurer has re-insured his risk, no notice of abandonment need be given by him.

63 **Effect of abandonment.**

(1) Where there is a valid abandonment, the insurer is entitled to take over the interest of the assured in whatever may remain of the subject-matter insured, and all proprietary rights incidental thereto.
(2) Upon the abandonment of a ship, the insurer thereof is entitled to any freight in course of being earned, and which is earned by her subsequent to the casualty causing the loss, less the expenses of earning it incurred after the casualty; and, where the ship is carrying the owner's goods, the insurer is entitled to a reasonable remuneration for the carriage of them subsequent to the casualty causing the loss.

Partial Losses (including Salvage and General Average and Particular Charges)

64 **Particular average loss.**

(1) A particular average loss is a partial loss of the subject-matter insured, caused by a peril insured against, and which is not a general average loss.
(2) Expenses incurred by or on behalf of the assured for the safety or preservation of the subject-matter insured, other than general average and salvage charges, are called particular charges. Particular charges are not included in particular average.

65 **Salvage charges.**

(1) Subject to any express provision in the policy, salvage charges incurred in preventing a loss by perils insured against may be recovered as a loss by those perils.
(2) "Salvage charges" means the charges recoverable under maritime law by a salvor independently of contract. They do not include the expenses of services in the nature of salvage rendered by the assured or his agents, or any person employed for hire by them, for the purpose of averting a peril insured against. Such expenses, where properly incurred, may be recovered as particular charges or as a general average loss, according to the circumstances under which they were incurred.

66 **General average loss.**

(1) A general average loss is a loss caused by or directly consequential on a general average act. It includes a general average expenditure as well as a general average sacrifice.

(2) There is a general average act where any extraordinary sacrifice or expenditure is voluntarily and reasonably made or incurred in time of peril for the purpose of preserving the property imperilled in the common adventure.
(3) Where there is a general average loss, the party on whom it falls is entitled, subject to the conditions imposed by maritime law, to a rateable contribution from the other parties interested, and such contribution is called a general average contribution.
(4) Subject to any express provision in the policy, where the assured has incurred a general average expenditure, he may recover from the insurer in respect of the proportion of the loss which falls upon him; and, in the case of a general average sacrifice, he may recover from the insurer in respect of the whole loss without having enforced his right of contribution from the other parties liable to contribute.
(5) Subject to any express provision in the policy, where the assured has paid, or is liable to pay, a general average contribution in respect of the subject insured, he may recover therefor from the insurer.
(6) In the absence of express stipulation, the insurer is not liable for any general average loss or contribution where the loss was not incurred for the purpose of avoiding, or in connexion with the avoidance of, a peril insured against.
(7) Where ship, freight, and cargo, or any two of those interests, are owned by the same assured, the liability of the insurer in respect of general average losses or contributions is to be determined as if those subjects were owned by different persons.

Measure of Indemnity
67 **Extent of liability of insurer for loss.**

(1) The sum which the assured can recover in respect of a loss on a policy by which he is insured, in the case of an unvalued policy to the full extent of the insurable value, or, in the case of a valued policy to the full extent of the value fixed by the policy is called the measure of indemnity.
(2) Where there is a loss recoverable under the policy, the insurer, or each insurer if there be more than one, is liable for such proportion of the measure of indemnity as the amount of his subscription bears to the value fixed by the policy in the case of a valued policy, or to the insurable value in the case of an unvalued policy.

68 **Total loss.**

Subject to the provisions of this Act and to any express provision in the policy, where there is a total loss of the subject-matter insured,—

(1) If the policy be a valued policy, the measure of indemnity is the sum fixed by the policy:
(2) If the policy be an unvalued policy, the measure of indemnity is the insurable value of the subject-matter insured.

69 **Partial loss of ship.**

Where a ship is damaged, but is not totally lost, the measure of indemnity, subject to any express provision in the policy, is as follows:—

(1) Where the ship has been repaired, the assured is entitled to the reasonable cost of the repairs, less the customary deductions, but not exceeding the sum insured in respect of any one casualty:

(2) Where the ship has been only partially repaired, the assured is entitled to the reasonable cost of such repairs, computed as above, and also to be indemnified for the reasonable depreciation, if any, arising from the unrepaired damage, provided that the aggregate amount shall not exceed the cost of repairing the whole damage, computed as above:

(3) Where the ship has not been repaired, and has not been sold in her damaged state during the risk, the assured is entitled to be indemnified for the reasonable depreciation arising from the unrepaired damage, but not exceeding the reasonable cost of repairing such damage, computed as above.

70 **Partial loss of freight.**

Subject to any express provision in the policy, where there is a partial loss of freight, the measure of indemnity is such proportion of the sum fixed by the policy in the case of a valued policy, or of the insurable value in the case of an unvalued policy, as the proportion of freight lost by the assured bears to the whole freight at the risk of the assured under the policy.

71 **Partial loss of goods, merchandise, &c.**

Where there is a partial loss of goods, merchandise, or other moveables, the measure of indemnity, subject to any express provision in the policy, is as follows: —

(1) Where part of the goods, merchandise or other moveables insured by a valued policy is totally lost, the measure of indemnity is such proportion of the sum fixed by the policy as the insurable value of the part lost bears to the insurable value of the whole, ascertained as in the case of an unvalued policy:

(2) Where part of the goods, merchandise, or other moveables insured by an unvalued policy is totally lost, the measure of indemnity is the insurable value of the part lost, ascertained as in case of total loss:

(3) Where the whole or any part of the goods or merchandise insured has been delivered damaged at its destination, the measure of indemnity is such proportion of the sum fixed by the policy in the case of a valued policy, or of the insurable value in the case of an unvalued policy, as the difference between the gross sound and damaged values at the place of arrival bears to the gross sound value:

(4) "Gross value" means the wholesale price, or, if there be no such price, the estimated value, with, in either case, freight, landing charges, and duty paid beforehand; provided that, in the case of goods or merchandise customarily sold in bond, the bonded price is deemed to be the gross value. "Gross proceeds" means the actual price obtained at a sale where all charges on sale are paid by the sellers.

72 **Apportionment of valuation.**

(1) Where different species of property are insured under a single valuation, the valuation must be apportioned over the different species in proportion to their respective insurable values, as in the case of an unvalued policy. The insured value of any part of a species is such proportion of the total insured value of the same as the insurable value of the part bears to the insurable value of the whole, ascertained in both cases as provided by this Act.
(2) Where a valuation has to be apportioned, and particulars of the prime cost of each separate species, quality, or description of goods cannot be ascertained, the division of the valuation may be made over the net arrived sound values of the different species, qualities, or descriptions of goods.

73 **General average contributions and salvage charges.**

(1) Subject to any express provision in the policy, where the assured has paid, or is liable for, any general average contribution, the measure of indemnity is the full amount of such contribution, if the subject-matter liable to contribution is insured for its full contributory value; but, if such subject-matter be not insured for its full contributory value, or if only part of it be insured, the indemnity payable by the insurer must be reduced in proportion to the under insurance, and where there has been a particular average loss which constitutes a deduction from the contributory value, and for which the insurer is liable, that amount must be deducted from the insured value in order to ascertain what the insurer is liable to contribute.
(2) Where the insurer is liable for salvage charges the extent of his liability must be determined on the like principle.

74 **Liabilities to third parties.**

Where thc assured has effected an insurance in express terms against any liability to a third party, the measure of indemnity, subject to any express provision in the policy, is the amount paid or payable by him to such third party in respect of such liability.

75 **General provisions as to measure of indemnity.**

(1) Where there has been a loss in respect of any subject-matter not expressly provided for in the foregoing provisions of this Act, the measure of indemnity shall be ascertained, as nearly as may be, in accordance with those provisions, in so far as applicable to the particular case.
(2) Nothing in the provisions of this Act relating to the measure of indemnity shall affect the rules relating to double insurance, or prohibit the insurer from disproving interest wholly or in part, or from showing that at the time of the loss the whole or any part of the subject-matter insured was not at risk under the policy.

76 **Particular average warranties.**

(1) Where the subject-matter insured is warranted free from particular average, the assured cannot recover for a loss of part, other than a loss incurred by a general average sacrifice, unless the contract contained in the policy be apportionable; but, if the contract be apportionable, the assured may recover for a total loss of any apportionable part.
(2) Where the subject-matter insured is warranted free from particular average, either wholly or under a certain percentage, the insurer is nevertheless liable for salvage charges, and for particular charges and other expenses properly incurred pursuant to the provisions of the suing and labouring clause in order to avert a loss insured against.
(3) Unless the policy otherwise provides, where the subject-matter insured is warranted free from particular average under a specified percentage, a general average loss cannot be added to a particular average loss to make up the specified percentage.
(4) For the purpose of ascertaining whether the specified percentage has been reached, regard shall be had only to the actual loss suffered by the subject-matter insured. Particular charges and the expenses of and incidental to ascertaining and proving the loss must be excluded.

77 **Successive losses.**

(1) Unless the policy otherwise provides, and subject to the provisions of this Act, the insurer is liable for successive losses, even though the total amount of such losses may exceed the sum insured.
(2) Where, under the same policy, a partial loss, which has not been repaired or otherwise made good, is followed by a total loss, the assured can only recover in respect of the total loss:

Provided that nothing in this section shall affect the liability of the insurer under the suing and labouring clause.

78 **Suing and labouring clause.**

(1) Where the policy contains a suing and labouring clause, the engagement thereby entered into is deemed to be supplementary to the contract of insurance, and the assured may recover from the insurer any expenses properly incurred pursuant to the clause, notwithstanding that the insurer may have paid for a total loss, or that the subject-matter may have been warranted free from particular average, either wholly or under a certain percentage.
(2) General average losses and contributions and salvage charges, as defined by this Act, are not recoverable under the suing and labouring clause.
(3) Expenses incurred for the purpose of averting or diminishing any loss not covered by the policy are not recoverable under the suing and labouring clause.
(4) It is the duty of the assured and his agents, in all cases, to take such measures as may be reasonable for the purpose of averting or minimising a loss.

Rights of Insurer on Payment
79 **Right of subrogation.**

(1) Where the insurer pays for a total loss, either of the whole, or in the case of goods of any apportionable part, of the subject-matter insured, he thereupon becomes entitled to take over the interest of the assured in whatever may remain of the subject-matter so paid for, and he is thereby subrogated to all the rights and remedies of the assured in and in respect of that subject-matter as from the time of the casualty causing the loss.
(2) Subject to the foregoing provisions, where the insurer pays for a partial loss, he acquires no title to the subject-matter insured, or such part of it as may remain, but he is thereupon subrogated to all rights and remedies of the assured in and in respect of the subject-matter insured as from the time of the casualty causing the loss, in so far as the assured has been indemnified, according to this Act, by such payment for the loss.

80 **Right of contribution.**

(1) Where the assured is over-insured by double insurance, each insurer is bound, as between himself and the other insurers, to contribute rateably to the loss in proportion to the amount for which he is liable under his contract.
(2) If any insurer pays more than his proportion of the loss, he is entitled to maintain an action for contribution against the other insurers, and is entitled to the like remedies as a surety who has paid more than his proportion of the debt.

81 **Effect of under insurance.**

Where the assured is insured for an amount less than the insurable value or, in the case of a valued policy, for an amount less than the policy valuation, he is deemed to be his own insurer in respect of the uninsured balance.

Return of Premium
82 **Enforcement of return.**

Where the premium or a proportionate part thereof is, by this Act, declared to be returnable, —

(a) If already paid, it may be recovered by the assured from the insurer; and
(b) If unpaid, it may be retained by the assured or his agent.

83 **Return by agreement.**

Where the policy contains a stipulation for the return of the premium, or a proportionate part thereof, on the happening of a certain event, and that event happens, the premium, or, as the case may be, the proportionate part thereof, is thereupon returnable to the assured.

84 **Return for failure of consideration.**

(1) Where the consideration for the payment of the premium totally fails, and there has been no fraud or illegality on the part of the assured or his agents, the premium is thereupon returnable to the assured.

(2) Where the consideration for the payment of the premium is apportionable and there is a total failure of any apportionable part of the consideration, a proportionate part of the premium is, under the like conditions, thereupon returnable to the assured.

(3) In particular—

(a) Where the policy is void, or is avoided by the insurer as from the commencement of the risk, the premium is returnable, provided that there has been no fraud or illegality on the part of the assured; but if the risk is not apportionable, and has once attached, the premium is not returnable:

(b) Where the subject-matter insured, or part thereof, has never been imperilled, the premium, or, as the case may be, a proportionate part thereof, is returnable:

Provided that where the subject-matter has been insured "lost or not lost" and has arrived in safety at the time when the contract is concluded, the premium is not returnable unless, at such time, the insurer knew of the safe arrival.

(c) Where the assured has no insurable interest throughout the currency of the risk, the premium is returnable, provided that this rule does not apply to a policy effected by way of gaming or wagering;

(d) Where the assured has a defeasible interest which is terminated during the currency of the risk, the premium is not returnable;

(e) Where the assured has over-insured under an unvalued policy, a proportionate part of the premium is returnable;

(f) Subject to the foregoing provisions, where the assured has over-insured by double insurance, a proportionate part of the several premiums is returnable:

Provided that, if the policies are effected at different times, and any earlier policy has at any time borne the entire risk, or if a claim has been paid on the policy in respect of the full sum insured thereby, no premium is returnable in respect of that policy, and when the double insurance is effected knowingly by the assured no premium is returnable.

Modifications etc. (not altering text)

C5 S. 84 modified (6.4.2013) by Consumer Insurance (Disclosure and Representations) Act 2012 (c. 6), s. 12(2), **Sch. 1 para. 17** (with s. 12(4)(5)); S.I. 2013/450, art. 2

C6 S. 84 modified (12.8.2016) by Insurance Act 2015 (c. 4), s. 23(2), **Sch. 1 para. 12** (with s. 22(2))

Mutual Insurance

85 **Modification of Act in case of mutual insurance.**

(1) Where two or more persons mutually agree to insure each other against marine losses there is said to be a mutual insurance.

(2) The provisions of this Act relating to the premium do not apply to mutual insurance, but a guarantee, or such other arrangement as may be agreed upon, may be substituted for the premium.
(3) The provisions of this Act, in so far as they may be modified by the agreement of the parties, may in the case of mutual insurance be modified by the terms of the policies issued by the association, or by the rules and regulations of the association.
(4) Subject to the exceptions mentioned in this section, the provisions of this Act apply to a mutual insurance.

Supplemental

86 **Ratification by assured.**

Where a contract of marine insurance is in good faith effected by one person on behalf of another, the person on whose behalf it is effected may ratify the contract even after he is aware of a loss.

87 **Implied obligations varied by agreement or usage.**

(1) Where any right, duty, or liability would arise under a contract of marine insurance by implication of law, it may be negatived or varied by express agreement, or by usage, if the usage be such as to bind both parties to the contract.
(2) The provisions of this section extend to any right, duty, or liability declared by this Act which may be lawfully modified by agreement.

88 **Reasonable time, &c. a question of fact.**

Where by this Act any reference is made to reasonable time, reasonable premium, or reasonable diligence, the question what is reasonable is a question of fact.

89 **Slip as evidence.**

Where there is a duly stamped policy, reference may be made, as heretofore, to the slip or covering note, in any legal proceeding.

90 **Interpretation of terms.**

In this Act, unless the context or subject-matter otherwise requires, — “Action” includes counter-claim and set off:

“Freight” includes the profit derivable by a shipowner from the employment of his ship to carry his own goods or moveables, as well as freight payable by a third party, but does not include passage money:

“Moveables” means any moveable tangible property, other than the ship, and includes money, valuable securities, and other documents:

“Policy” means a marine policy.

91 **Savings.**

(1) Nothing in this Act, or in any repeal effected thereby, shall affect—

(a) The provisions of the [M1]Stamp Act 1891, or any enactment for the time being in force relating to the revenue;
(b) The provisions of the [M2]Companies Act 1862, or any enactment amending or substituted for the same;
(c) The provisions of any statute not expressly repealed by this Act.

(2) The rules of the common law including the law merchant, save in so far as they are inconsistent with the express provisions of this Act, shall continue to apply to contracts of marine insurance.

92, 93. [F10]

Marginal Citations
M1 1891 c. 39.
M2 1862 c. 89.

94 **Short title.**

Textual Amendments
F10 Ss. 92, 93, Sch. 2 repealed by Statute Law Revision Act 1927 (c. 42)

This Act may be cited as the Marine Insurance Act 1906.

Changes to legislation: There are currently no known outstanding effects for the Marine Insurance Act 1906. (See end of Document for details)

Rules for Construction of Policy

The following are the rules referred to by this Act for the construction of a policyintheaboveorotherlikeform,wherethecontextdoesnototherwiserequire:—

Lost or not lost.

1 Where the subject-matter is insured "lost or not lost," and the loss has occurred before the contract is concluded, the risk attaches unless, at such time the assured was aware of the loss, and the insurer was not.

From.

2 Where the subject-matter is insured "from" a particular place, the risk does not attach until the ship starts on the voyage insured.

At and from.

3 (a) Where a ship is insured "at and from" a particular place, and she is at that place in good safety when the contract is concluded, the risk attaches immediately.

(b) If she be not at that place when the contract is concluded, the risk attaches as soon as she arrives there in good safety, and, unless the policy otherwise provides, it is immaterial that she is covered by another policy for a specified time after arrival.

(c) Where chartered freight is insured "at and from" a particular place, and the ship is at that place in good safety when the contract is concluded the risk attaches immediately. If she be not there when the contract is concluded, the risk attaches as soon as she arrives there in good safety.

(d) Where freight, other than chartered freight, is payable without special conditions and is insured "at and from" a particular place, the risk attaches pro rata as the goods or merchandise are shipped; provided that if there be cargo in readiness which belongs to the shipowner, or which some other person has contracted with him to ship, the risk attaches as soon as the ship is ready to receive such cargo.

From the loading thereof.

4 Where goods or other moveables are insured "from the loading thereof," the risk does not attach until such goods or moveables are actually on board, and the insurer is not liable for them while in transit from the shore to the ship.

Safely landed.

5 Where the risk on goods or other moveables continues until they are "safely landed," they must be landed in the customary manner and within a reasonable time after arrival at the port of discharge, and if they are not so landed the risk ceases.

Touch and stay.

6 In the absence of any further licence or usage, the liberty to touch and stay "at any port or place whatsoever" does not authorise the ship to depart from the course of her voyage from the port of departure to the port of destination.

Perils of the seas.

7 The term "perils of the seas" refers only to fortuitous accidents or casualties of the seas. It does not include the ordinary action of the winds and waves.

Pirates.

8 The term "pirates" includes passengers who mutiny and rioters who attack the ship from the shore.

Thieves.

Modifications etc. (not altering text)

C7 Sch. 1 rules 8, 10 amended by Public Order Act 1986 (c. 64, SIF 39:2), **s. 10(2)**

9 The term "thieves" does not cover clandestine theft or a theft committed by any one of the ship's company, whether crew or passengers.

Restraint of princes.

10 The term "arrests, &c., of kings, princes, and people" refers to political or executive acts, and does not include a loss caused by riot or by ordinary judicial process.

Barratry.

Modifications etc. (not altering text)

C8 Sch. 1 rules 8, 10 amended by Public Order Act 1986 (c. 64, SIF 39:2), **s. 10(2)**

11 The term "barratry" includes every wrongful act wilfully committed by the master or crew to the prejudice of the owner, or, as the case may be, the charterer.

All other perils.

12 The term "all other perils" includes only perils similar in kind to the perils specifically mentioned in the policy.

Average unless general.

13 The term "average unless general" means a partial loss of the subject-matter insured other than a general average loss, and does not include "particular charges."

Stranded.

14 Where the ship has stranded, the insurer is liable for the excepted losses, although the loss is not attributable to the stranding, provided that when the stranding takes place the risk has attached and, if the policy be on goods, that the damaged goods are on board.

Ship.

15 The term "ship" includes the hull, materials and outfit, stores and provisions for the officers and crew, and, in the case of vessels engaged in a special trade, the ordinary fittings requisite for the trade, and also, in the case of a steamship, the machinery, boilers, and coals and engine stores, if owned by the assured.

Freight.

16 The term "freight" includes the profit derivable by a shipowner from the employment of his ship to carry his own goods or moveables, as well as freight payable by a third party, but does not include passage money.

Goods.

17 The term "goods" means goods in the nature of merchandise, and does not include personal effects or provisions and stores for use on board.

In the absence of any usage to the contrary, deck cargo and living animals must be insured specifically, and not under the general denomination of goods.